D0857092

ANNEXE DE LA BIBLIOTHÈQUE
u Ottawa
LIBRARY ANNEX

ANNEXE DE LA BIBLIOTHÈQUE
u Ottawa
LIBRARY ANNEX

THE BODY POLITIC

IAN GILMOUR

HUTCHINSON OF LONDON

HUTCHINSON & CO (*Publishers*) LTD
178-202 *Great Portland Street, London, W*.1

London Melbourne Sydney
Auckland Bombay Toronto
Johannesburg New York

First published 1969

© Ian Gilmour, 1969

*Set in Monotype Garamond and printed in
Great Britain on antique wove paper by Fisher, Knight
and Co. Ltd., St. Albans, Herts, and bound by
Wm. Brendon and Son Ltd, Tiptree, Essex*

09 095820 9

JN
234
1969
.G 54

To Caroline

Governments can do so little and prevent so little nowadays. Power has passed from the hands of statesmen, but I should be very much puzzled to say into whose hands it has passed. It is all pure drifting.

LORD SALISBURY in 1895

A Constitution can be built, constitutions enough *à la Sieyès*; but the frightful difficulty is, that of getting men to come and live in them!

THOMAS CARLYLE

The French Revolution

CONTENTS

PREFACE

The following pages attempt to describe the British political system as it is, not as it is widely assumed to be. The thesis, if there is one, evolved during research and writing; it was not preconceived from the start. The book produced the thesis, not the thesis the book.

The dangerous might of the executive, the impotence and irrelevance of Parliament—these and other fashionable orthodoxies dissolved under scrutiny. A number of things appeared to me to be wrong with British government, but the chief faults were not those I had expected to find. Moreover, even at a time when Britain has not been notably successful, this country has seemed far luckier in its system of government than is usually allowed. We may be bankrupt, but we are far better off than practically everybody else. There is little political fear. The pavements of London have not yet been turned into barricades by students, nor do mayors manipulate political parties or policemen club the young. The advantages of living in a free and relatively peaceful country may be taken for granted; but they are nonetheless real.

Nevertheless this is not a defence of the British Constitution. Like all political institutions those of Britain are in need of change, and as well as criticisms some suggestions for reform are put forward in this book. But I have not attempted to produce a blue-print for the future. For the political process is not like the industrial. Probably in no other sphere is the gap between thought and action so wide, and to draw up *a priori* schemes is all too often to adopt what Reinhold Niebuhr has called 'the strategy of fleeing from difficult problems by taking refuge in impossible solutions'.

Nor have I aimed for completeness. I have felt free to omit such important points as, for example, the impartiality of the Speaker of the House of Commons and to give more space to more controversial subjects.

Of the many people who have helped me, I am indebted most of all to Mr. Robert Blake, Mr. John Grigg, Mr. Nicholas Henderson and Mr. Ludovic Kennedy. Their kindness in giving up their time to making detailed criticisms of the manuscript led to its considerable improvement. I am also very grateful to Mr. Peter Benenson, Mr. George Hutchinson, Mr. Robin McEwen, Mr. Anthony Lincoln, Q.C., Mr. Peter Walker, M.P., and Mr. Denis Walters, M.P., who at various stages read parts or all of the manuscript and made many useful suggestions. Naturally, however, the errors and opinions are mine and mine alone.

Mrs. Joan Baylis has typed and retyped numerous drafts, and I owe her my warmest thanks for performing an arduous task with such remarkable willingness and good temper. I must also express my gratitude to the Librarian of the House of Commons and his staff for being unfailingly helpful.

Finally, I should like to thank Mr. Iain Hamilton, with whom the book was first mooted, and Mr. Robert Lusty and Mr. Harold Harris of Hutchinson for summoning up reserves of patience and encouragement.

IAN GILMOUR

Thwaite House,
Aldborough,
Norfolk

INTRODUCTION

WHERE HAS ALL THE POWER GONE?

There are two objects in forming systems of government—safety for the people, and energy in the administration. . . . If the latter object be neglected, the people's security will be as certainly sacrificed as by disregarding the former.

ALEXANDER HAMILTON[1]

The first condition then required in order to a sound constitution of the Body Politic is a due proportion of the free and permeative life and energy of the Nation to the organised powers brought within containing channels. . . . What the exact proportion . . . of the two kinds of force should be it is impossible to predetermine. But the existence of a disproportion is sure to be detected sooner or later by the effects.

SAMUEL TAYLOR COLERIDGE[2]

The mainspring of representative government is not in machinery, however perfected; it is the light that it sheds on the acts of the rulers; it is the publicity which attaches to all their sayings and doings.

M. OSTROGORSKI[3]

'What,' Lloyd George asked the Labour leaders when he was forming his War Coalition, 'is a government for except to dictate? If it does not dictate, then it is not a government . . .'[4] Just over a year later he told Lord Riddell: 'It is no use being Prime Minister unless you can do what you want to do. It is useless for me to say I can, because I can't,'[5] In these two remarks Lloyd George travelled from the form to the reality of government in Britain.

The essence of the constitution, thought L. S. Amery[6], 'is strong and stable government.' And in appearance, indeed, a British government is more powerful than almost any free government in the world. In reality it is stable but not strong. Once elected, British governments usually survive until the next election. This stability is not to be despised; most countries do not possess it. Yet stability is not strength. A stable government is merely one that does not fall. A strong government is one that acts, and is capable of taking

I

quick, difficult and unpopular decisions. British governments in the twentieth century have usually been stable, but time and again they have shown themselves incapable of taking vital decisions until events forced them to do so.

There are in Britain virtually no institutions able to say 'no' to the executive. The Monarchy is above politics; the Second Chamber has been paralysed; the House of Commons passes the government's legislation; the law has been made subservient to the executive; local government has been subjected to Whitehall control; the press and television are hamstrung by government secrecy. Yet the negative principle in British government usually wins. British government says 'No' to itself. It is a paper tiger.

Churchill once called Baldwin a 'power-miser'.[7] That was unfair. Most British Prime Ministers since 1918—except of course Churchill himself during the war—have seemed to hoard power rather than use it. Conceivably they were all power misers. Maybe the system naturally produces weak or moderate leaders. Possibly, as Carlyle said of Loménie de Brienne, 'it took such talent and industry to *gain* the place, that to *qualify* for it hardly any talent or industry was left disposable.'[8] Whatever the reason, at a time when constitutional developments are said to have exalted the position of the Prime Minister, and books have been written extolling his almost unlimited power and favourably comparing it with that of American Presidents and even dictators, British Prime Ministers and governments have shown themselves reluctant or unable to use the great power they are alleged to possess.

British history since 1918 contains many examples of governments failing to act, or acting when it was too late: The Tory failure to reform and strengthen the economy in the 1920s; foreign and defence policy in the 1930s; the Attlee government's refusal to join the discussions on the European Coal and Steel Community; Britain's refusal to join Europe in the fifties; the failure of successive governments to bring local government into the twentieth century; failure to reform the Trade Unions; and, going slightly further back, the drift towards civil war over Home Rule for Ireland. These incidents or evasions do not suggest the presence of great power in the British government.

The existence of a problem can easily be denied. Arguably what happened or did not happen was inevitable; or even if it was avoidable, neither politicians nor the political process were an important factor; or the incidents and omissions mentioned were the inescapable cost of a free society; or they were not mistakes but were triumphs of statesmanship and of the empirical approach to politics. If, however, despite its theoretic strength, the weakness in practice of British government is admitted to pose a problem, there are many possible explanations: the character of the Conservative party and its long tenure of power since 1918; a Socialist party having become the second major party in the country; the nature of the party system; the strength of pressure groups; the slaughter of the country's future leaders in the First World War; rigid party orthodoxy normally being a requirement for political success; an out of date Civil Service; the British genius for compromise having been taken to extremes; war weariness; a sluggish, wayward, and uninformed public opinion; a fault in political theory; the type of man who becomes Prime Minister in the twentieth century; the gruelling nature of the Whitehall obstacle race; or the conflict between industry and labour.

Some of these factors or allegations were contributory causes of at least some of the British failures during the last fifty years. It seems likely, however, that an additional cause is flaws in the political system, which lead to leakages of power or to power failures.

The present tendency is to downgrade the importance of political institutions and to concentrate instead upon sociology, class, interest groups, or the 'political culture'. De Tocqueville, in a much quoted apophthegm, said that since the British constitution 'may undergo perpetual changes, it does not in reality exist'.[9] Tom Paine[10] and others have thought the same. At the opposite extreme, Croker laid down that 'Westminster Abbey is part of the British constitution'.[11] If everything is part of the constitution, then in a sense nothing is. Either view is fully tenable depending upon the meaning that is given to the word 'constitution'. But in its implications Croker's remark is more in accord with British reality than de Tocqueville's. Britain is not governed merely by a series of organisations and a set of legal rules.

Institutions form only part of the governmental process; that process consists also of a series of interlocking relationships, a set of habits and traditions, a confusion of true and untrue and obsolete ideas, and an amalgam of constitutional conventions, myths and fictions. The process depends as much upon the ideas and traditions and interests of the men and women taking part in it and upon the atmosphere in which they work, as it does upon the nature and disposition of the political institutions. All the same, those institutions in their turn help to shape the conduct and ideas of those who govern the country. Disciplined parties provide clear proof that the influence is not all one way.

Ideas, habits and traditions are more effective than legal enactments. That early behaviourist, Disraeli, scoffed at France's worship of the phrase 'the Sovereignty of the People'. 'The people,' he wrote, 'shouted in its honour, all was satisfactorily settled, and thirty-two millions were again to be governed by a phrase.'[12] His gibe rightly pointed to the constitutional importance of phrases, ideas and myths. Whatever their meaning and whatever their truth, phrases or incantations like 'ministerial responsibility', 'parliamentary sovereignty', or 'the rule of law' have considerable constitutional importance. After the demythologisers have done their work, the idea or the phrase may still hold sway. To demythologise does not necessarily end a practice or even destroy a doctrine; it may result in even stronger attachment to the myth.

The British tradition of liberty is more valuable than any formal promulgation of freedom's virtue and necessity. Custom is as important an ingredient in the behaviour of the governors as in that of the governed. The existence of an impartial and incorruptible Civil Service is more reassuring and valuable than any number of pious constitutional provisions and protestations. Article 125 of the Russian constitution guarantees freedom of speech and freedom of assembly. The South African constitution begins with the announcement that 'the people of the Union acknowledge the sovereignty and guidance of Almighty God'. To the Bantus or the Cape Coloureds the introduction of Divine guidance has not proved an unmixed blessing.

The early mortality of most written constitutions with their entrenched safeguards for all the good things of life is well known. France has already had two constitutions since 1939 and fourteen since 1789. Germany had a new one after each war. In Europe only Sweden and Norway, Holland, Belgium and Switzerland have constitutions dating from before 1914.

Even when fixed constitutions and their safeguards have not been blown away by events, their contribution to liberty has not always been obvious. The success and survival of the American constitution are plain. Yet the history of the 14th Amendment and of the negro is notorious. The Supreme Court has often acted as a bulwark of liberty against executive or congressional encroachments and also on occasion as a barrier to the mildest reforms. But neither the prestige of the Court nor the authority of the constitution was sufficient to protect trade union leaders and other unpopular figures after the First War, or, for that matter some career diplomats and screen writers in the early 1950s.

Institutions are as fallible as those who man them. They are made to act according to the interests of their dominant members and usually serve some quite other purpose than what was intended.* They cannot be treated as entities reliably restraining each other. Institutions do not mark their opposite numbers like football players. As John Adams put it, 'Passion, interest, and power . . . can be resisted only by passion, interest and power.'[14] Social forces are more important than institutional arrangements, though institutional arrangements influence social forces.

The lack of any legal distinction between basic constitutional laws and the most trivial legislative enactments, and the absence of legal or institutional curbs on parliamentary sovereignty do not threaten British liberty. More unexpectedly, the lack of institutional curbs on the executive has not made British government strong. Admittedly, modifications have continually been made to help government, and few to help control it. No institutions were created to take the place of an unshorn House of Lords or the 'proprietary factions'. Sometimes accidents happen. The registration clauses in the great Reform Bill, by encouraging the growth of party, helped the parliamentary opposition to compete effectively with those in power.[15] That was unintended and unusual. Governments do not intentionally set up new obstacles to take the place of those that have disappeared.

Naturally, therefore, the constitution suits, or rather is thought to suit, those who work it. Similarly in Spanish bullfights the bulls over the years have become smaller, but the picador's pic has remained the same size. Though it is now too big for the bull nothing is done because the bull fighters and promoters, not the bulls, make the decisions or refuse to make them.

In Britain the executive makes the rules, and it has apparently

---

* The Afghans, who were not members of the League of Nations, attended the Disarmament Conference in 1932. Their objective was not to make earnest speeches in favour of disarmament. They were short of arms and thought a Disarmament Conference might be a good place to pick them up cheaply.[13]

defeated the legislature and the judiciary, and swept away the separation of powers. With the making of decisions ostensibly concentrated in its hands, a seemingly obedient parliamentary majority at its back, the support of devoted adherents in the country, powerful departments of state, a developed cabinet system, and no independent institutions to obstruct it, the British executive looks exquisitely adapted for tough and decisive government. In fact, in extending its constitutional power, the executive has weakened its political power. The pic has become too big for the picador, not for the bulls. The separation of powers is intended to curb government; in Britain the apparent unity of powers has curbed it more effectively. The various governmental agencies oppose and restrain each other and do so in secret. The separation of powers has gone underground.

Moreover the growth of government has been balanced by the growth of private organisations and interest groups. Though constitutionally supreme, the executive still has to gain the consent of other institutions, bodies and pressure groups. There is concentration of responsibility, but dispersal of power. Government cannot command, or operate like an army. When asked about inter-service co-operation, Lord Montgomery replied: 'Co-operation, my dear chap, no problem there. I tell them what to do and they do it.'[16] But in civilian life there is a problem. The government is more like a merchant than a general, making bargains rather than giving orders. It has to farm out powers, like its predecessors had to farm out taxes. There are private as well as public citadels of power. The government cannot make all the decisions itself, nor, if it could, would it be able to impose them.

So the constitutional victories of the executive have been pyrrhic. They have been won at heavy cost in political power. All free governments depend upon public opinion, and the constitutional supremacy of the executive by cutting down public conflict and facilitating the imposition of secrecy has deprived it of adequate means of influencing public opinion. Despite or because of the executive's constitutional victories, therefore, the two party system and disciplined parties, general elections, the House of Commons, the Civil Service all provide as much restraint as impulse to action.

'The Constitution of this country,' Canning told his Liverpool constituents in 1818, 'is a monarchy, controlled by two assemblies:

the one hereditary, and independent alike of the Crown and the people; the other elected by and for the people, but elected for the purpose of controlling and not of administering the government'.[17] Despite all the changes of the last 150 years, Canning's description remains true in its denial of the Commons' right or power to administer the government, and in its assertion that 'the Constitution of this country is a monarchy'. Names here are not important; they are all in some degree misleading. The Monarch no longer wields his power in person. But the government is monarchical, and the executive operates in a monarchical manner. Parliament does not govern, and at least since the days of the Commonwealth never has governed. The King in Parliament governs. The government is formed from the ranks of parliamentarians, and in a real sense is parliamentary. But Parliament does not administer the government. Parliament may control the government, or it may merely think that it controls the government. That is all. The legislative formula of a statute, still much what it was in the reign of Henry VII, expresses so far as Parliament as a whole is concerned the true position. 'Be it enacted by the Queen's most excellent Majesty, by and with the advice and consent of the Lords spiritual and Temporal, and Commons, in the present Parliament assembled, and by the authority of the same as follows. . . .' As Amery put it,[18] government in Britain is 'of the people, for the people with, but not by, the people'.*

The means which a constitution provides or fails to provide for changing the government supplies more reliable guidance to the nature of a country's politics than any classification by form of government. In free states the government is usually changed by Parliament or by the electorate. The French Third and Fourth Republics were clear examples of the first or parliamentary kind of democracy: the electorate fixed the broad limits but governments were formed and changed by shifts and manoeuvres in the assembly, not by the votes cast at general elections. There could be half a dozen different governments between elections. The electorate did not choose the government.† A plain example of the second or electoral kind of democracy is Britain, where the government is normally changed by the vote of the electorate and not by parliamentary plots and coalitions.

* Professor Beer has rather oddly described this as the Tory view of the constitution. The Attlee and Wilson governments have shown that it is also the Labour view.[19]

† M. Mollet became Prime Minister after the French general election in 1956. 1.2 er cent of the French electorate wished this to happen.[20]

Since 1867 the government of Britain has only four times been changed by a defeat in the House of Commons: in 1885, in 1886, in 1895, and in 1924*. The government was also changed by a vote in the House in 1940; a Conservative revolt led to the substitution of Mr. Churchill for Mr. Chamberlain and the formation of the great wartime coalition, even though Mr. Chamberlain had a majority of eighty in the division. In late 1924, a general election which led to a change of government was precipitated by a defeat in the House of Commons. Otherwise changes of government were caused, except for the formation and break-up of war coalitions and in the exceptional circumstances of 1931, by general elections. 'The people' are now generally responsible for changes of government.

This does not mean that power lies with 'the people'. Indeed the question 'where does power lie?' is something of a hangover from the Austinian theory of sovereignty—the theory that somewhere there is always a sovereign, that there can be no law without a sovereign. No doubt this was true of Henry VIII, as it was of Stalin, but since then in Britain at least sovereignty has always been fragmented. The idea of sovereignty is a nineteenth century formulation of a seventeenth century idea relating to sixteenth and seventeenth century conditions and has very little application to the present day. Nowadays it is impossible to give a simple answer to the question 'where does power lie?' or even to the question 'what is power?' Power lies in different places at different times and in different degrees according to the circumstances and the personalities involved. The term parliamentary sovereignty is useful in that it signifies that there is no legal superior to what is enacted by the King or Queen in Parliament. It is not a signpost to where power is to be found.

The electorate is not sovereign. For one thing, the electorate is an abstraction; for another, as Carlyle pointed out, government 'is a thing that *governs*'.[21] And plainly the electorate does not and could not govern. It can, moreover, only choose between two highly organised hierarchies, which usually bear a close resemblance to each other, and it can change only the upper part of the iceberg. The rest, and far larger part, of the government continues on its way whatever the result of the general election.

Still, the electorate or an election changes the visible government,

---

* In January 1924 because no party had a majority, Baldwin waited to be defeated in the House before resigning, but he had already been defeated in the election at the end of the previous year.

and general elections are the dominant event in the British political process. The need to win an election determined the nature of the parties and the party system, and the parties and the party system have largely determined the development of other governmental institutions.

The monarchical executive is thus confronted by, and occasionally defeated at, general elections without parliament being able to act as an electoral buffer state, changing the government and precipitating elections, as it did in the mid-nineteenth century. There is nothing necessarily incongruous in such a marriage of opposites. All free government is oligarchic, and the Greeks would probably have regarded Britain as an excellent example of an oligarchy. In theory such a combination should work well. After all, plebiscitary democracy has been successful in non-free states. And in many ways electoral democracy has worked well in Britain.*

There has been no failure of consent. At least since the seventeenth century Britain has been successful in securing consent. In 1838 Cobden complained that people were 'mystified into the notion that they are not political bondmen, by that juggle of the *English Constitution*', which he stigmatised as 'a thing of monopolies and churchcraft and sinecures, armorial hocus-pocus, primogeniture and pageantry'.[22] Similar complaints are made today. But the monarchy, the House of Commons, fair elections, the party system, an impartial Civil Service, the political tradition, still provide an unrivalled organisation of political consent. While Churchill could 'doubt whether any of the dictators had as much power throughout his nation as the British War Cabinet',[23] Mussolini was lamenting that he was 'the most disobeyed man in history'.[24]

In his address at Westminster Hall, General de Gaulle asked: 'At the worst moments, whoever contested the legitimacy or the authority of the state? Today, at Westminster, allow me to testify to what is due to Britain in this respect as in others.'[25] In Britain legitimacy does not have to be sought; the system is impregnated with it.

'Every constitution,' said Bagehot,[26] 'must first gain authority and then use authority.' It is in the second task that the executive has fallen down. It has made scant attempt to adapt itself to modern conditions. It has acted as though general elections and universal

---

* The expression 'electoral democracy' is used because 'plebiscitary democracy' carries authoritarian overtones. 'Electoral democracy' does not imply that parliament is not still important, only that it no longer changes the government.

suffrage were an alien if dominant intruder, an evil that had to be lived with but could not be exorcised. Habits in harmony with a limited electorate and the slow moving days of Britain's supremacy were unlikely to be suitable for the totally different conditions of electoral democracy. Yet the workings of the British executive have become less, not more, appropriate to universal suffrage than they were in the nineteenth century. One hundred years ago the executive was much less secretive than it has since become. In the past parliament was able to bring interest and light to the activities of government. The press similarly was able to disclose much. The Civil Service had not yet fully retired to the cloister, leaving ministers its only contact to the outside world. The contrast between closed and open politics was much less pronounced. Yet it scarcely seems to have occurred to the executive that changes were needed. At any rate they were not made; hence the basic contradiction between a closed and secret government attempting to govern a free people, who are able to overthrow it. The monarchical executive and electoral democracy co-exist; they have not been joined together.

Smoothness and Conflict

The British Government's apparent coherence and smoothness have excited much envy and admiration. James Forrestal, America's first Secretary of Defence, thought that the United States needed 'to create something similar to the British system for co-ordinated and focussed government action'.[27] From one point of view British government is highly efficient. Departmental co-ordination is excellent, everybody gets briefed in time, spheres of action are usually delineated, chaos is rare. It is difficult to imagine a British delegation arriving like the American delegation to the London Conference of 1933: unbriefed and without proper instructions.[28] British delegations always get instructions even if they may be like those sent to Balfour in Geneva after he had complained of his previous ones. 'Anyway,' they ended, 'we agree with what you want to do whatever it may be'.[29]

Often the British system is only smooth from the outside. The Prime Minister's need to say something palatable to the 1922 Committee[30] or to square the Miners' Union on the eve of a Labour party conference may have an effect similar to a Congressional refusal to go along with the President.

Sometimes British policy making lacks coherence even from the outside. On March 15 1939 the policy of appeasement was still in being. Hitler's march to Prague was regrettable but understandable. Chamberlain told the Commons that the end of Czechoslovakia 'may or may not have been inevitable'.[31] The guarantee given to her at Munich six months before was blithely glossed over. The country must still work for an accommodation with Herr Hitler. This policy was plainly unpopular; even hardened stomachs felt queasy. It was accordingly reversed. Two days later Neville Henderson was recalled from Berlin, and the same evening Chamberlain made, for him, a tough speech at Birmingham.

In any case the smoothness of the British process, such as it is, is only beneficent within narrow limits. As President Kennedy once said: 'When things are . . . beautifully co-ordinated . . . it must be that not much is going on'.[32]

'The essence of democratic method,' declared the Council of Ten at the instance of Lloyd George, 'is not that the deliberation of a Government should be conducted in public, but that its conclusions should be subject to the consideration of a popular Chamber and to free, open discussion in the press.'[33] This is unexceptionable in theory; in practice the deliberation of a government is profoundly influenced by the anticipated reactions of parliament and the public. If the deliberations wholly precede the popular discussion, or if they do not seek to influence it, the conclusions will usually be timorous, and tailored to suit an uninstructed, unrealistic and unco-operative public opinion. At best the decision will be delayed.

Mr. Macmillan's government finally decided to try to join the Common Market in July 1961. Only after the decision had been taken did the public debate begin.[34] As a result the negotiations proceeded so cautiously that they were not completed before the referendum on Algeria had so strengthened General de Gaulle that he felt able to veto the British application, the state of British public opinion being one of the excuses the French used for their action.

A British government has seldom either the wish or the means to mobilise public opinion. It wants to win votes and the best way of winning the next election is to follow Walpole's motto of *Quieta Non Movere*, and to rely upon the resulting mood of contented torpor together with governmental prestige to produce a vote against change. Any government has to disturb some dogs during its term of office, but seldom the big ones. Unless they are inescapable or uncontroversial large schemes of reform are hastily scotched.

As Mr. Richard Rovere has pointed out, the only thing creative politicians normally create is trouble.

When the government does have a motive for mobilising public opinion, it scarcely has the means of doing so. Ministers may descend upon all parts of the country at week-ends, and make a series of speeches. But their utterances rarely catch the ear of the public, only of party zealots. The Prime Minister, or other ministers, may address the country on television. Mr. Macmillan's broadcast on the Common Market in the autumn of 1962 successfully if belatedly rallied the Conservative party behind the government's attempt to enter the community. But that talk was unusual in its effect and in its circumstances. Normally, exhortation, harangues, man to man talks, fireside chats, calls to action, appeals to the Dunkirk spirit, all the paraphernalia of the soap-box and the pulpit, leave the voter sceptical and unmoved. While the means of communicating with the voter are better and more varied than ever before, little comes through. A vital connection is missing.

To instruct public opinion, to keep it almost level with events, and to prepare it for unpalatable decisions, government has to be made interesting. Otherwise the public pays no attention and, because public opinion is not yet ready, the government in its turn fails to take decisions or takes them too late. Occasionally government can be made interesting by a personality, such as Churchill. Normally politicians, despite all the frantic press build-up they receive, do not manage to make either government or themselves interesting. Shaw said of a parliamentary committee that 'Disraeli would have made this job something between a coronation and an arctic expedition.'[35] Political showmanship rarely reaches that standard. After all the publicity for Mr. George Brown's National Plan, Research Services Limited discovered four days after its publication that more than half the men in the country and seven out of ten of the women had not heard of it.[36]

Virtually the only way of making government interesting to the public is by public controversy. Most people are greatly interested only in their own concerns, and can only be brought to take an active interest in public affairs by the spectacle of a good public row and the pleasure of taking sides. Thus conflict is a more likely producer of strong and far sighted government than smoothness. There is no substitute for a quarrel, and this the executive refuses to supply. So from a wider point of view British government is not efficient.

Parliament made British government interesting to the political nation for much of the nineteenth century. Parliamentary quarrels and conflicts compelled attention because their outcome was uncertain. In the twentieth century parliament is often boring. A tightly organised party system has made it predictable.

Between the general elections of 1964 and 1966, Labour's tiny majority in the House of Commons lent interest to British government. In theory, at least, Mr. Wilson might have been defeated at almost any time. This cliff-hanging serial secured widespread public interest in parliament and the government. And Labour duly benefited on March 31 1966.

Of course, there still is public conflict in the British process, but it no longer occurs at the crucial points. The parties fight each other energetically and magnify their differences. But much of their warfare is formalised and taken for granted. And the theory that parties are always locked in mortal combat with each other leads to a general feeling that internally they should be united. Internal party differences and disunity within the party become treason in the face of the enemy; real controversy within the parties is stifled in deference to the sometimes idle controversy between them.

Conflict within a government department is shielded from the public and parliament by the dogma of ministerial responsibility. Similarly, conflict within the Cabinet is hidden by the doctrine of Cabinet responsibility. Conflict between departments at a lower level is concealed because of the belief that there is only one government and it must not disagree with itself in public. The parties have largely removed useful public conflict from the British political process. The instruments of popular government have served to shield government from the public gaze and have emasculated that other great weapon of democracy, the press. They have made the political process smooth, unitary and closed. Division in government produces news and public interest; unity produces public relations officers and public indifference.

What was done in the nineteenth century by the legislature could in the twentieth century be done only with the co-operation of the executive. Like the government today, the House of Commons used to believe in the importance of its own theoretical unanimity. Before Elizabeth's reign divisions were rare, and until near the end of the sixteenth century, when a bill had been passed after a division, the whole House, both the bill's supporters and its opponents, used to go out and carry the bill in again in order to emphasise that it had gained the consent of the whole community.[37] Swords were drawn in the Commons over printing the Grand Remonstrance 'because even the pretence of unanimity was being abandoned'.[38] As late as the eighteenth century Speaker Onslow deplored the taking of divisions in the House of Commons.[39]

Only if the executive went through a similar evolution, rather more quickly, could British government become interesting again. Parliamentary debate and the party battle are no longer enough. Only if the executive abandoned the dogma of its unity and infallibility, and the public administration were made genuinely public, could parliament fulfil the functions the House of Commons performed in the nineteenth century; and only by such conflict and debate could the executive make itself genuinely strong.

Britain led the way in a free and open legislative debate; she has lagged behind in creating a free and open executive. The true comparison with parliament's refusal in the eighteenth century to allow its debates to be reported is not the Commons' attempt to interfere with broadcast discussions or its refusal to be televised but the determination of the executive to maintain the occultness of its proceedings and to shield them from public view.

Exceptionally then, there is too much agreement and compromise in British government. The absence of conflict causes weakness. The essence of the British political system is that it is more important to travel peacefully than to arrive. British institutions ensure peaceful travel; they are less reliable in ensuring arrival at a destination. A remark made by a Permanent Secretary about the Civil Service is true of the whole political process: 'We may spend so much time in being sure of keeping in step that we hardly advance at all . . . in other words, things that ought to happen do not happen while we are making sure that nobody will be upset if they do happen.'[40] Of course in a free country decisions have to be generally acceptable. Hence the gaining of consent is more important than the quality of decisions. Decisions are useless if people do not act upon them, whereas the failure to take decisions merely results in their being taken by events. 'Life will decide', as Lenin used to say,[41] and 'too little too late' is at least preferable to anarchy and violence. The British system enables minor adjustments to be made with the minimum of friction.

Yet caution and compromise do not necessarily produce social peace or good government. There are dangers in always allowing 'the lamest man' to 'govern the army's march',[42] Problems are left unsolved and grow more intractable, evils are perpetuated, weeds blossom. Diplomatic problems are often insoluble; it is therefore futile and dangerous to try to solve them. But problems of internal politics are not usually improved by waiting. Even such a conservative lawyer as Dicey pointed to the dangers of delay. 'It keeps alive irritation which constantly robs improvement itself of almost the whole of its legitimate benefit.'[43]

More public conflict in the governmental system would not in the long run produce more social conflict. There is a clear distinction between the two things. It is the job of politicians to reconcile conflicts and to diminish social dissension. Palmerston once sharply reminded Gladstone that 'The function of a government is to calm rather than to excite agitation.'[44] But it is not the job of politicians to abolish or conceal all public conflict in the governmental system. More governmental conflict would produce more public awareness and a more active consensus, not the consensus of stagnation. The point at which a consensus is reached is not a constant. More tension in government would also produce more governmental action. As Churchill said when arguing the case for a Ministry of Supply, 'You would get a new energy from the very friction that would result.'[45] Nor would stronger government lead to increased social dissension. The nearest this country has come to civil war was over Ulster when the Asquith government drifted through weakness and indecision, yet its two strongest men, Lloyd George and Churchill, had from the first advocated the exclusion of Ulster from Home Rule.

To lament the lack of public discussion and quarrels in the political system is not therefore to plead for violence, class war, crusading ideologies, or the end of tolerance. Conflict binds people together as well as dividing them. And to lance a wound is less painful and harmful than to let it fester. Public conflict in the political process, by interesting the governed and stimulating the executive, would enable governments to deal with problems at an earlier stage before the damage had been done. What is needed is more conflict without more extremism.

Still less is it a plea for bureaucratic tyranny or a concentration of power in 10 Downing Street. Strong government is no more likely to develop into petty tyranny or harm the interests of individuals than weak government—indeed less so. No accretion or concentration of state power is needed. The advocacy of stronger government is merely a plea that decisions should be taken in time, and that governments should occasionally see what is going to happen.

Since governmental conflict always exists, it can only be concealed by secrecy. Clandestine government leads to government at the mercy of events and of untutored public opinion. A Ministry of Labour document of 1936 said there could be no adequate manpower policy without a general recognition 'of the issue before the country, popular support of the government, and a government strong enough and decisive enough to make use of this popular support'.[46] None of these requirements was present. As the prospects of war with Germany grew, the preparations for controlling labour in that war might have been expected to become stricter and more far-reaching. Not at all. Because of the state of public opinion the opposite happened. 'As the Second World War grew more imminent, so did the proposals for labour control grow more attenuated.'[47] Even more extraordinary, 'In November 1939 the War Cabinet, fearing public discontent, had even considered relaxing the controls so recently imposed.'[48] There could hardly be a more convincing demonstration of the weakness of British governmental institutions, or a heavier condemnation of private government.

For fear of splitting the party, alienating the voters, and losing the next election, the government waits for public opinion to crystallise, but the secrecy under which it works usually prevents public opinion from crystallising until the tyranny of events has been established and no alternative remains. Governmental secrecy is the opiate, the tranquilliser, of the British people; and then the government turns round and complains that the people are drugged and sluggish. 'One of the weaknesses of a democracy,' said Baldwin, 'is that until it is right up against it it will never face the truth.'[49] It seldom gets the chance. Government secrecy is also the opiate of the government. By itself, secret government knows no deadlines. Papers and files can circulate without end. Meetings can multiply indefinitely. Minutes are timeless. Only publicity can provide a deadline.

'Many of the failures of British statesmanship,' wrote Duff Cooper,[50] 'have been due to the reluctance of Ministers to deal with a problem so long as postponement was possible. Too often have we been forced in the end to accept an unsatisfactory and even a humiliating solution because we have refused at the beginning to agree to a far better one.' This is not the result of British politicians being particularly prone to procrastination. Politicians of any country seldom act in great affairs unless they have to do so. But they are more likely to be driven to action if they are working in conditions of publicity. Furthermore politicians prefer talking about a policy to actually having one. Here again secrecy helps to conceal policy's absence.

Under the British system the pressure of publicity arrives at the last possible moment. This is particularly true of foreign policy. Britain is notoriously reluctant to tell other nations how she will act in certain circumstances. Her usual answer to enquiries is that the question is hypothetical, an attitude that had disastrous results in 1914,* and again in the thirties.[52] This is partly due to British empiricism, but a deeper reason is surely that the system is conducive to not having a policy until the last moment. A British government is unable to say what it will do because it does not know. And it will not know until it has seen the state of British opinion at the time. In the meantime, it can do little to influence that opinion. And it does little. The executive and the public remain separate. The 'monarchical executive' does not mix with his people. He is usually frightened to tell them unpalatable facts in case they transfer their patronage to the opposition. And when he tries to talk to them, they are normally too bored to listen.

Secrecy thus produces the contrary result of what is intended: fear, not leadership, of public opinion. Admittedly, both secrecy and fear of public opinion are found to greater or lesser degree in all free states (and also in most dictatorships). Respect for public opinion is an indispensable attribute of a free society. Moreover, a relatively open political system does not infallibly lead to good government. The United States has political problems of its own. But the excessive secrecy of British government aggravates the natural weakness of a democracy towards its own public opinion. And in Britain the method of government is not geared to the means of changing the government.

British government is not free of restraints; it is riddled with them. But because they are mostly private and personal, not public and institutional, the resultant conflicts do not give government the power and energy to do difficult and unpopular things. The concentration of constitutional power in the government does not produce political power. Public opinion comes up the backstairs and takes command.

This does not lead to bad government. British government is rarely bad. It is usually competent, grave, conscientious, orderly,

* As late as August 1 1914 France was told that 'she must take her own decision at this moment without reckoning on an assistance which we are not now in a position to promise'.[51]

responsible and well meaning. It is more coherent and consistent than most. It is usually in tune with the popular mood. But it is not far sighted. British government is normally at least one step behind events.

> Things are in the saddle,
> And ride mankind.[53]

wrote Emerson in the nineteenth century. No doubt that is normally true everywhere, especially in democracies, but some governments are better poised than others occasionally to swing into the saddle. British government is a good, diligent, and reliable horse, nearly always obedient to the directions of its rider. It is very seldom a jockey.

The production of paper schemes to reform the British system of government so as to make it fully worthy of the admiration of Mr. Podsnap presents no problem. Nothing is easier than 'constructive criticism' of that kind—or more futile. There is no obvious all-embracing remedy for Britain's institutional ills. If there were, it probably would not be adopted. The constitution is not a formula but a process. Governmental institutions are not pieces of machinery, which a skilled mechanic can mend or replace. A shortcoming in one sphere may be the unavoidable price of excellence in another. In government nothing is unalloyed benefit, and few things are pure detriment. Hence gains in one direction are almost bound to be accompanied by losses in another. Politicians and civil servants have to deal with an existing situation. The pressures and compulsions that surround them cannot be conjured away by a chart or a theorem. Few plans or institutions work as their creators intended; certainly little of the British constitution is the result of conscious intention. The last two hundred years have done nothing to refute Hume's observation about 'the great mixture of accident which commonly concurs with a small ingredient of wisdom and foresight in erecting the complicated fabric of the most perfect government'.[54] We were lucky in the nineteenth century, less so today.

But suspicion of theoretical schemes need not entail a complete avoidance of any proposals for reform. Though the political system largely adapts itself to new conditions, there is no automatic regulator to ensure that the adaption is always the best available. Part of the process may grind on in accordance with the obsolete ideas and needs of another age. Hence the advocacy of piecemeal reform is not an unreasonable approach; and indeed piecemeal reform is what is needed. For despite the current denigration, much of the praise that used to be lavished on the British constitution was justified. Under it the British people have probably lived a life as safe, as free, as happy and as good as any other people in the world. The constitution has lasted from 1689 without a break, a revolution, or a civil war, which is a record of stability and peaceful change unequalled by any other country. But, for all its undoubted and widely envied virtues, the history of this country since 1918 suggests the presence of flaws in the system. In 1900 Salisbury told the House of Lords: 'I do not believe in the perfection of the British Constitution as an instrument of war. As an instrument of peace it has not yet met its match, but for purposes of war there is more to be said . . . I do not think that the British Constitution as at present worked is a good fighting machine.'[55] Since 1918, conditions have been far nearer those of war than those of the peace known by Salisbury. The British governmental process is still geared to a peace that has passed away.

PART ONE

THE STRUGGLE FOR POWER

I

THE PARTY SYSTEM

Here, then, they met,
Two doughty champions; flaming Jacobite
And sullen Hanoverian! You might think
That losses and vexations, less severe
Than those which they had severally sustained,
Would have inclined each to abate his zeal,
For his ungrateful cause; no—I have heard
My revered Father tell me that, 'mid the calm
Of that small town encountering thus, they filled
Daily, its bowling-green with harmless strife;
Plagued with uncharitable thoughts the Church
And vexed the market place. But in the breasts
Of these opponents gradually was wrought,
With little change of general sentiment,
Such leaning towards each other, that their days
By choice were spent in constant fellowship;
And if, at times, they fretted with the yoke,
Those very bickerings made them love it more.

WORDSWORTH[1]

What is called a constitution today is nothing but 'get out so that I can get in'.

METTERNICH[2]

I explained that we had two parties in Britain, and I only belonged to one of them. 'One party is much better,' said Stalin, with deep conviction.

WINSTON S. CHURCHILL[3]

Brought into being by the workings of the British Constitution in the nineteenth century, organised parties and the party system before long dominated what had created them. Here at any rate the child is father of the man. The rise of party determined the position of the Cabinet and the Commons, altered the nature of elections, transformed the relationship between an M.P. and his constituents, and removed the Crown from politics. Party even wrought a

23

change in political morality[4]: perpetual loyalty to party or to government became the sign of a good party man putting party before self, or anyway party before country, not the sign of a placeman or pensioner earning his money. 'My country right or wrong' is no longer a popular doctrine; my party right or wrong is the tacit rule of life of most politicians and voters. 'Reason of party' even more than 'reason of state' is assumed to explain conduct which would otherwise be condemned.

The nature and the number of parties now determine the whole operation of government and parliament. The end of strong disciplined parties or the rise of a third governing party in addition to the other two would recast British politics and British government. The party system is a far more dominating feature of the constitution than the number of legislative chambers, the nature of the executive, or any other 'constitutional' provision.

One of the explorers of the origins of the British parties and the party system started with Henry VIII and Anne Boleyn.* Some have begun with 1640 and the Long Parliament; others, less intrepid, have contented themselves with starting at the Exclusion crisis of 1679–81, when the words Whig and Tory became current. But, as Hume observed,[7] 'To determine the nature of these parties is perhaps one of the most difficult problems that can be met with . . . we have seen the conduct of the two parties during the course of 70 years, in a vast variety of circumstances . . . yet are we at a loss to tell the nature, pretensions, and principles of the different factions.'

Between 1689 and 1832 the parties changed places more than once. 'Except for their name,' Ogden Nash sang of the U.S. Republicans and Democrats, 'they are identically the same.' In eighteenth and early nineteenth century Britain the situation was still more confusing. They were 'exactly the same', but their names altered. The continuity was of power and opposition, not of names and parties.

The absorption of the Grenvilleites by Lord Liverpool in 1821 saw the end of the last 'proprietary faction'. The Reform Bill crippled the electoral power of the Crown. Three years later the King, having dismissed Melbourne and sent for Peel, had to take

* One French historian trying to trace the causes of the French Revolution was driven back to the birth of Christ, and an enthusiastic chronicler of the fortunes of the French Radical party claimed that the first radical was Adam.[5] But Eve, surely, has the better claim. Indeed, Sir Robert Filmer, the theorist of the divine right of kings, considered that Adam, so far from being a radical, was an absolute monarch by creation.[6]

Melbourne back again because the general election, unlike any other election since 1679, returned a majority against the King's government.* The disappearance of the proprietary factions and an end to the King's ability to secure a parliamentary majority for the ministers of his choice were the essential preliminaries to a party system as we know it. 'Sire,' Canning told George IV, 'your father broke the domination of the Whigs. I hope your Majesty will not endure that of the Tories.' 'No, I'll be damned if I do,' replied the Monarch.[8] Yet William's experience in 1835 indicated that George's successors would have to endure the domination of both of them.

The Tory split in 1846 restored some freedom of manoeuvre to the Monarch over the choice of Prime Minister, but the Crown could only manoeuvre within the framework of a House of Commons chosen by the voters. It could no longer influence the composition of that framework. From 1867 onwards its influence in politics was further diminished. The government and usually the Prime Minister were now chosen by the voters. The voters displaced the Crown because, the Irish apart, there were only two parties. Had there been three or more of roughly equal size, the government and the Prime Minister would have been chosen not by the voters but by party and parliamentary manoeuvring, and the Monarchy might have preserved for itself a role at least as active as the President of the Third Republic or even the King of Italy.

'There can be in *Parliament* only two parties,' said Brougham in 1835, 'and I must be either for a government or against it.'[9] Britain's enjoyment of a two-party instead of a group system has been held by some to be due to the shape of the House of Commons, rectangular instead of semi-circular like most chambers on the continent. But in the two party United States the Senate and the House of Representatives deliberate in semi-circular rooms; and the Netherlands, the only country in Europe to have an oblong chamber, has had a party system nearer to that of its semi-circular neighbours than to two-party Britain.

The traditional division of British politics was between Court

* This fiasco did not have the same effect as the similar fiasco under the Third Republic in 1877, which resulted in there not being another dissolution in France until 1955.

and country or between the ins and the outs. In the eighteenth century, of course, a large number of M.P.s were not involved in the factional struggle at all. They were not interested in office, and for those who sat for county constituencies to seek it was often impracticable.* Except in some grave crisis like the American war, the independent country gentleman could usually be relied upon to support the King's government. An eighteenth century parliament could sustain as many administrations as an assembly of the Third Republic. The absence of organised parties, the restricted franchise and electoral corruption made an M.P.'s vote easily transferable; the multiplicity of parties in France and the combinations of parties necessary to form a government similarly put the choice of government out of the control of the electorate and at the whim of the politicians. The flexibility of the eighteenth century system depended upon the electors knowing their place, as outlined to them by Burke at Bristol, and not seeking to interfere with the 'judgment and conscience' of their member.† But before the middle of the nineteenth century the government was ceasing to be the King's (or the Queen's) government in the same sense. With the Queen out of the struggle it was impracticable for a country gentleman to be merely a general supporter of the Crown. He was driven to take sides, though still preserving some of his traditional independence. Hence the instability of British governments between the first two Reform Bills.

'When I first entered Parliament,' Sidney Herbert said of the 1830s, 'the House of Commons was divided into camps. A leader guarded both; a leader whom no man questioned and whom every man on his side followed.'[10] And in Trollope's *Ralph the Heir*, written in the 1860s, one of the Members for Percycross 'always followed the Conservative leader, and the other the Liberal leader into the respective lobbies of the House of Commons'.[11] The politician and the novelist both exaggerated. There was in the thirties and sixties a basic two party theme. But there were group variations, and the variations frequently overbore the theme.

The groups were neither regional nor very extreme. While elections were often decided on local issues, those in whose hands the political life of the nation still largely lay were not regional-

* The re-election that had to be undergone by those taking office under the Crown would have been too expensive in many counties.

† The electors of Bristol did not know their place. They declined to support Burke at the next election after his famous speech.

minded. Their interests were the same as those of the rest of their class and they looked towards London. There was in the country nothing resembling the French provinces' suspicion of Paris bred by that capital's revolutionary fervour. Through his election for County Clare, O'Connell forced Wellington and Peel to bring in catholic emancipation, but the 'Irish' landlords were able to prevent the formation of an Irish party until the Ballot Act of 1872 destroyed their power and opened the way for Parnell.

Revolutionary parliamentary groups were also absent. The Radicals were leaderless and divided among themselves; most of the post Reform intake had either been defeated or had graduated into supporters of Melbourne by 1841. Had the Radicals ever been able to form a coherent party with any chance of achieving a majority they would probably have frightened the Tories and Whigs into joining each other. Their weakness made it safe for the Tories and the Whigs to remain separate.

Harold Laski believed that from 1688 until the rise of Labour, Britain was governed by what was in reality one party, since both the alleged parties belonged to the same class. He was right about the class. In 1869 Salisbury lamented in the House of Lords that 'we belong too much to one class'[12]; the same was true of the Commons even after the second Reform Bill, Burt and Macdonald being the first working men to penetrate to Westminster seven years later. Yet the continuing, if non-Marxist, division between Whig and Tory preserved the two party system. Had they been thrown together, a cluster of groups on the continental pattern would almost certainly have followed.

A two party system usually originates from the growth of one party, which prompts the groups that oppose it to coalesce into one formation. Though it fell apart more than once, the first such party in England was the Tory party, formed by the fears and tensions caused by the French Revolution, the Napoleonic wars and their aftermath. The first party is likely to be a conservative party; it is easier for the forces of order to combine than the forces of reform, and it is usually the right which has something to defend. But not after a revolution. At least in the early stages of the Third Republic it was the left which had something to conserve: the Republic. The left was therefore conservative. But not until Combes and the 'Délégation des Gauches' was the left even approximately united and it never succeeded in forming itself into one party. A united party of the right could not be formed under the Third

Republic, because the right was split into Bourbon, Orleanist and Bonapartist factions, and because the Church was estranged. The Church's refusal to recognise the state of Italy—'Neither electors nor elected' was the Catholic slogan and edict—and the opposition of some of the upper classes to the *Risorgimento* prevented the formation of a conservative party in Italy. As a result France and Italy were saddled with a group system.

With no change of dynasty in Britain since 1714, the opposition was always loyal; unlike France, there were no far right adherents of previous or other regimes; nor was there a very extreme left. The distance from right to left in the English Parliament was much shorter than in the French Assembly which was elected by manhood suffrage. The gradual extension of the franchise was quick enough to avoid violence by those excluded (except the women) yet slow enough to keep the political nation sufficiently united to be split only into two or two and a half. At the same time the governing parties were not scared into union.

By the Second Reform Bill, therefore, the two party theme dominated though there were still group variations. Because of the two party theme, elections were an election of governments, as Disraeli recognised by resigning in 1868 before Parliament met. The need to be 'for a government or against it' was extended from M.P.s to the voters. Previously the lack of party organisation in the country had kept elections and parliament in separate compartments. Occasionally an election was plebiscitary—for or against Palmerston in 1857—but after it M.P.s felt quite free to act as they wished. If M.P.s had to be 'either for a Government or against it', they did not have to be always for or against the same government.

1867 soon changed all that. Disraeli's Reform Bill so enlarged the electorate that the trusty old method of getting votes and winning elections, bribery, was no longer either economic or efficient. Mass party organisation was now essential. The change from parliamentary democracy and bribery to electoral democracy and party organisation was not immediate. Corruption of the old sort was common at least until the passing of the Corrupt Practices Act in 1883, but it was obsolescent from 1867 onwards, and the debasement in the coinage of bribery, from individual payments to party promises, was fairly rapid. In the past, Dean Inge later complained, governments had used their own money to bribe voters, afterwards they used the Dean's.

Similarly the party organisations took time to grow. It was not until the 1885 election that local party associations began to acquire a virtual monopoly over the nomination of candidates. The Speaker thought in 1872 that 'of the two leading men 'in the House,' Gladstone and Disraeli, neither has a strong hold on his followers'.[13] Nevertheless, they were followers, in plain contrast to France. There the Republicans refused to behave as one party with Gambetta as their leader. And the reason given by Jules Ferry, 'To remain united, truly united, united without any humbug, the real way is to remain distinct,'[14] pleased Gambetta as little as it would have pleased Disraeli or Gladstone. Still, a two party system is scarcely possible when one of them is at best a reluctant acceptor of the regime, as were the Republicans' opponents.

At all events, in England the two party system in giving the electors the power to choose the government withdrew it from M.P.s. Arising out of the pattern of parliamentary politics, the two party system then riveted that pattern onto parliament. Like most of the British constitution this was not intentional; it was the outcome of national continuity.

The events of 1884, 1885 and 1886 went far to see that the continuity was maintained. The Liberal party had been the dominant force in British politics since the first Reform Bill; after 1885 it only once won a majority in the House of Commons. The Liberal schism produced a period of Conservative dominance—what John Morley[15] called a 'curious . . . reversal'—and the issue on which the party fractured, Ireland, gave the Conservatives an issue, a war cry, and an emotion, when the future direction of the Tory party was in serious doubt. The Liberal split was not altogether helpful to the Tories. The accretion of the Liberal Right wing with their business mentality made it no easier for the Conservatives to introduce adequate social reform. At the same time, the crossing of the floor by Chamberlain and the radicals restricted the ability of the Liberals to appeal to working class voters. Hence neither party was in a position to prevent the emergence of the Labour party.

But if 1886 opened the way for the third party, 1884 and 1885 made likely the continuance of a two party system. The House of Lords, acting on advice Disraeli had given four years before, insisted upon redistribution as its price for accepting Gladstone's Reform Bill—a price which it erroneously assumed Gladstone would be unable to pay. With a few exceptions the country was divided up into single member constituencies and the division was made on an arithmetical basis of the number of voters in the area instead of on the traditional basis of the representation of communities. Gladstone would have liked to preserve the rights of the ancient boroughs; Salisbury, the Conservative leader, had no such conservative prejudices. He preferred electoral districts with single members in both the boroughs and the counties. Gladstone expressed himself astonished at Salisbury's radicalism; and the Queen did not believe that the 'too Radical nature' of the Conservative proposals could be intended.[16] The bill was indeed radical, but it helped the Conservative party.

Up to 1884 the notion had persisted that the House of Commons, as its name suggests, was composed of the representatives of communities. That notion was now succeeded by the radical idea that representatives should as far as possible be elected by aggregates of individuals in exactly equal constituencies, a suggestion which Disraeli had strongly opposed in 1867. The Conservative interest in virtually abolishing the ancient system of two member constituencies was obvious: the Liberal expedient of keeping the party together by putting up a Whig or a right winger together with a Radical or a left winger was ruled out. The Conservative interest in abandoning the idea of representation of the ancient boroughs was less obvious but no less real: without redistribution traditionally Conservative rural strongholds would have been invaded by hordes of urban voters; with it the ratio of Conservative M.P.s to Conservative voters would be increased. In this conflict between traditional Conservative principles and the interests of the Conservative party, the party won. 'Damn your principles, stick to your party', has a collective as well as an individual application.

The Electoral System
The electoral system established in 1884–5 favours united parties and a two party system. The simple majority vote favours two main parties. Under it, third or fourth parties, unless they are regional, have to win an exorbitant number of votes to gain even a few seats. Any number of seconds and thirds do not add up to a first. And since elections are choices of governments more than choices of M.P.s, voters are reluctant to throw away their votes on a minority party.

Single member constituencies make difficult any electoral arrangement within the parties, as was made between the Whigs and the Radicals before 1885. They also make electoral arrangements between parties difficult though not impossible. In 1886 the Conservatives and the Liberal Unionists made an arrangement on the basis of 'what we have we hold', the Conservative leadership in a remarkable display of discipline managing to persuade all except six of its local associations not to run a candidate against the sitting Liberal Unionist member. This arrangement would not have lasted long, had it not soon become apparent that the Liberal Unionists were becoming an adjunct of the Tory party.

The secret election pact between Herbert Gladstone and Ramsay Macdonald in 1903 was facilitated by the survival of a few of the two member seats. At the election in 1906, out of twenty-four double-member constituencies ten returned 1 Liberal and 1 Labour member; out of the other 600 or so seats Labour returned only 19 members.

Single member constituencies also tend against a multiplicity of parties and in favour of party unity. Admittedly they did not do so in France or in Italy, where if they did not add to the disunity and fragmentation of parties they did not diminish it. Gambetta complained of France seeing herself in a 'broken mirror'.[17] But in both France and Italy there was a second ballot, which encourages the formation of splinter parties. In a two ballot system, even more than with double member seats, Labour and Liberals would have found it easy to combine electorally, as Radicals and Socialists often did under the Third Republic.

The mode of elections greatly influences the party system, but does not determine it. Single member districts and the simple majority vote do not necessarily produce two parties. Nor, although Proportional Representation has nowhere produced two parties, does it necessarily produce a multi party system. Belgium had three parties before its introduction, and with some minor and occasional exceptions has had three parties since. And the party system in its turn strongly influences the electoral system. Parties alter the electoral rules to suit themselves. Between 1870 and 1958 France changed her electoral laws eleven times. The advent of Socialism led nearly the whole of Western Europe to adopt Proportional Representation.

In England, no such change was made. This was largely luck. The reluctance of the working class to take to socialism helped to blind many Liberals to the strength of the threat presented by Labour. A Royal Commission on electoral systems in 1910 reported unanimously in favour of the alternative vote but no heed was paid to it.

The Speaker's Conference in 1917 advocated Proportional Representation, but on a free vote the proposal was defeated in the Commons by eight votes despite the advocacy of F. E. Smith. The alternative vote was then substituted for P.R. The Lords countered by restoring P.R., and both were dropped. But a majority of the House of Commons had voted for one device or the other.[18] In 1924 the Labour government unsuccessfully recommended that the party should support a bill to introduce P.R. And in 1931 the Commons passed a bill bringing in the alternative vote; the Lords restricted the application of the bill to constituencies in boroughs with a population of more than 200,000. The end of the Labour government killed this attempt to resurrect the Liberal party.

A longer and less one-sided struggle between the Liberals and Labour would very likely have produced a change in the electoral system to procure the survival of three main parties and alter fundamentally the British process of government. In the event, the Liberal party declined too quickly to be able effectively to bargain its parliamentary support in exchange for electoral reform. As late as 1950 Mr. Churchill expressed himself in favour of a measure of electoral reform, and in 1965 when the Government had a majority of three, the Labour Chief Whip put out a rather mouldy piece of bait to the Liberals. Yet the simple majority system survived. It was a close thing.

The danger is not yet quite passed. Were the Liberals ever to stage a serious revival, then whichever of the other two parties was the weaker might be tempted to offer electoral 'reform' as a reward or incentive for Liberal or third party support. Alternatively if one of the main parties declined spectacularly fast, its conversion to the democratic virtues of Proportional Representation or the alternative vote would be sudden. In such circumstances, however, the Liberals would undergo an equally sudden counter-conversion to a belief in the present system. Mr. Jimmy Durante used to say that you should be nice to people on the way up because you met the same people on the way down. Having neglected that wise precaution the fading main party would be lucky to be tossed any electoral crumbs by the resurgent Liberals.

The British are often said to have a deep-seated preference for the two party system, a preference which they exhibit at practically every general election. Almost certainly, however, the British people have no preference for any particular party system. The system is largely self-perpetuating. It encourages people not to waste their ballot by voting for a party with no chance of forming a government. Only if there are at the same time three fairly strong non-regional parties, which the system makes unlikely, is it in danger of being altered. That people vote for the two main parties is not proof that they prefer a two party system, merely that they do not like wasting their vote. The two party system, which may be defined as one in which almost invariably there are at least three parties only two of which have any chance of forming a government, is the result neither of the wishes of the British people nor of the foresight of British statesmen. Like Tristram Shandy, it was begotten in a fit of absence of mind.

'England does not love coalitions,' said Disraeli shortly after he had failed to form one with first Palmerston then Bright. In fact the English people have often exhibited considerable liking for coalitions; but coalitions happen to be uncongenial to the country's party, electoral and cabinet systems. Cabinet government, as known in England, works properly only if one party has a majority in the House of Commons. Co-operation between parties in the cabinet and in the Commons is difficult, when all know that it is to be succeeded by cut-throat competition in an election. Except in the gravest national emergencies, coalitions could be produced only by a change in the mode of election and the creation of a cluster of parties—a heavy price to pay for an undesirable result.

The two party system produces in Britain a ruling executive and a dependent parliament. The government is chosen at an election, and a parliament is thrown in at the same time. The party leaders influence the voters, the parliamentary rank and file do not. Once the electors have chosen a government, it is not for M.P.s to thwart the voters by changing the government between elections. British M.P.s owe their election entirely to their possession of the right party clothes and to their express or implied willingness to follow their leader. The members of the winning party are elected to support a government, not to change it.

The two party system is intensely conservative and the major element of stability in the country. The electoral system which produces it is itself conservative. M. Duverger has summed up the effects of the various electoral systems.[19] Proportional Representation is much the least conservative of the three; in normal times it goes on producing election results which hardly vary for years on end, but it is highly susceptible to new and extreme currents of opinion, and it does not mitigate their force by compelling them to mingle with other currents. Probably the rise of fascism in Italy was helped by Proportional Representation;* the rise of Hitler was certainly helped by it. Under the Fourth Republic the Poujadists, new to national elections, polled 2½ million votes in 1955.

The simple-majority two-ballot system, which was in force in France for most of the Third Republic and in Italy until shortly before the advent of Mussolini, encourages moderation because to be successful on the second ballot groups have to enter into alliances with each other. On the other hand it allows new extremist groups to have their unrestricted and uncompromising say, if they do not mind going down to electoral disaster. And when, as in the first elections of the Fifth Republic in 1958, the parties have difficulty in combining, moderation is not the outcome. On that occasion at least, the system gave birth to an assembly much more 'unrepresentative' than the British single ballot system is accustomed to produce.

The single majority vote is sensitive in the sense that a small change of opinion may lead to a change of government, but because it tends to produce a two party system it is the most stable and conservative of the three. Under it, new groups and parties have no chance of doing well in a general election. There was a certain amount of 'Poujadist' sentiment in England in 1956; but had there been an election in that year Poujadism would not have achieved representation in Parliament. Startling new attitudes, to have any serious effect, must capture one or both of the existing parties, a difficult and lengthy undertaking. The alternative to capturing one of the main parties is to wait for twenty to thirty years, the time needed for a new party to gain power.

The party system supplies a ready-made scapegoat. The party in power atones for the sins of the government, of the bureacracy, and for the frustrations of the modern world. The system has a similarly soothing effect upon its more active participants. When there are many parties, the rank and file are generally more opposition-minded than their leaders, unless, as in nineteenth century America, the system produces jobs for the rank and file as well as for the leaders. In a two party system the leaders are necessarily government-minded; and the followers, because of the conspicuous

* Giolitti, who was opposed to P.R., made the extraordinary mistake of including the fascists on his list.

difference between winning and losing, are also anxious to win. The parties are therefore more government orientated than in a multi party system.

More important, the energies of the parties are concentrated upon opposing each other. The one in power wants to stay there, the one in opposition wants to displace it. They are both too busy running the system to spend much time in thinking of changing it. In his letters on the Spirit of Patriotism, Bolingbroke complained of the fundamentally conservative nature of the system. 'Whilst the minister was not hard pushed,' he wrote, 'nor the prospect of succeeding him near, they appeared to have but one end, the reformation of government . . . But, when his destruction seemed to approach, the *object* of his *succession* interposed to the sight of many, and the *reformation* of the *government* was no longer their point of view. They divided the skin, at least in their thoughts, before they had taken the beast . . . '[20]

The two party system is almost bound to produce a majority* and a government which can govern. In a multi party system a government may be driven to governing by decree, as Brüning was under the Weimar Republic, because no majority exists; alternatively there may be no government at all. In the two years from the fall of M. Mollet's government to the collapse of the Fourth Republic, France was without a government for eighty-six days. There had to be an 'intermezzo' in Holland from 1926 to 1929 because parliament could not produce a working majority.[21] The absence of a stable majority helped to discredit the parliamentary system in many countries less fortunate than Holland.

Not only does the two party system produce a majority, it helps to gain the consent of the minority. The existence of two major parties presupposes a fair degree of unity in a country; the system itself greatly increases that unity. The parties, while appearing to divide the country, are in reality almost its most potent unifiers. Michels observed of socialist parties that 'the masses are far more subject to their leaders than to their governments'.[22] The same is true of all parties, and in a two party system this obedience to party is as a rule a useful aid to obedience to government. The parties fill

* A majority in the House of Commons but not in the country. Only twice in this century, in 1931 and in 1935, has a party or coalition won a majority of the votes cast.

a small part of the gap created in society by the disappearance of post-feudalism and the decline of the churches. They do something to lessen the isolation of the individual which has followed the weakening of hierarchical social bonds. They are a form of tribalism and fulfil its functions. By enabling the party leaders to make a direct appeal to all voters and so lessening the need for party activity by the rank and file, television will probably diminish the tribal role of the parties, at the same time perhaps replacing it with a tribalism of its own. But its usurpation will not be complete.

Only one in four of the electors subscribes to a political party on purpose,* and one in a hundred works for them unpaid. Yet the feeling of being involved and of belonging is an important element in binding the country together. If the voter's party wins the election, he believes that the government is to some extent 'his' government however he may rail against it.† And if his party loses, he still has a comfortable feeling of being one of 10,000,000 or so similar unfortunates, and hopes for better luck next time. With a cluster of parties the voter is less able to feel that the shifting combinations which form succeeding governments are 'his' government, whether he voted for one of its component parts or not. The crucial manoeuvres are being performed by 'them' and are beyond his control.

Nature of the Parties

Burke's famous definition,[23] 'Party is a body of men united for promoting by their joint endeavours the national interest upon some particular principle in which they are all agreed' is obviously not applicable to modern parties in a two party system. It perhaps more nearly describes the present day pressure group, which is usually agreed 'upon some particular principle', though 'the national interest' is not always the primary object of its promotion. Parties do seek to promote the national interest; otherwise Burke's definition might be amended to read 'party is a body of men united in their opposition to other parties.' Any greater degree of unity in a party seeking nearly 50 per cent of the votes cast at an election is rare, and even that amount is sometimes unattainable. Parties have gone up in the social scale. Much of Burke's most dithyrambic tribute to the state could now be applied to them: '. . . a partnership in all science, a partnership in all art, a partnership in every virtue and

* See also page 414.

† Many people who did not back the winning side also soon gain this feeling. They begin to believe that they did in fact vote for the government.

all perfection. As the ends of such a partnership cannot be obtained in many generations, it becomes a partnership not only between those who are living, but between those who are living, those who are dead, and those who are to be born.'[24]

The nature of these partnerships is, or should be, determined by there being only two of them that have a chance of achieving a majority in the House of Commons. Their energies should be directed towards securing a majority of votes at the next election and forming a government. Graham laid down as long ago as 1839 that 'the possession of power ... is the sole object of political warfare.'[25] In 1960, Mr. Crossman suggested that it should not be the 'main object' of politicians to gain power. That kind of behaviour, he thought, was all right for Tories but not for Socialists.[26] But politicians whose main concern is to preserve the consistency and purity of their own or their supporters' beliefs are out of place in the British system. Such an attitude may be justified in some continental parties which have no chance of obtaining a majority but not in Britain. Political leaders who behave as if the party system were other than it is doom themselves to frustration and the party system to distortion. In the event, Labour disregarded Mr. Crossman's plea and skilfully exploited the party system to gain power.

The object being to gain more votes than its opponents, the party must be above all broad and comprehensive, like the Church of England in aspiration. It must be subject to strong central control; otherwise the party zealots will be able to narrow its base and exclude dissenters. It must be national; no region will be able to give to it a majority in the House of Commons. It must be ideologically blurred; half the country will not be able to agree on any strict formulations of theory and doctrine. At the same time it must have strong emotional appeal if it is to bind together the loyalty of a vast agglomeration of people and win the voluntary aid of an army of party workers. Tradition produces much of the needed fund of loyalty. Symbols and war cries are also necessary. Preferably these should not be sullied by too close contact with current politics.

The ideal cry was described by Taper in *Coningsby*.[27] 'I am all for a religious cry,' he said. 'It means nothing and, if successful, does not interfere when we are in.' 'Waving the bloody shirt,' the dwelling of the U.S. Republican party upon the victory won and the blood shed in the Civil War successfully kept the party together in the 'seventies and 'eighties. It hardly impinged upon any political issue except in the South, though the shirt became rather tattered and more difficult to recognise as time went by. Anti-slavery was a bad war cry because it was at the core of the political struggle. It enabled the Republicans to win the election of 1860, but it split the country and finally the Democratic party and brought on the Civil War. Despite being rather too central to the struggle, Gambetta's 'clericalism, there is the enemy' worked well for a time. Later the Radicals under Combes took it too seriously and, egged on by the Socialists who foresaw the result, went so far as actually to separate church and state, thereby depriving themselves of a slogan and an issue. The glories of the Risorgimento worked well enough for the various liberal groups in Italy. The preservation of the union with Ireland did the Conservatives good service, when Ireland was only a significant issue. When it became a crucial one, it nearly caused civil war. Imperialism was much less dangerous because much vaguer, but it caused some inconveniences when the time came to dismantle the empire. Patriotism and nationalism are almost ideal, though even they lead to some embarrassment over the Common Market. Free Trade was a useful old soldier for the Liberal party, but the Liberals found it difficult to make him fade away long after it was clear that he had died. Labour had done best with such primeval figures as the Tolpuddle martyrs and Ben Tillett and the Docker's tanner, and with emphasis upon the great Labour movement. Socialism has been much less valuable; it has been of no interest to many, and has tended to divide the party while uniting its opponents.

The left has been inclined to think that the evocation of patriotism and the use of symbols and war cries, other than its own, have been capitalist devices to distract the proletariat from the real business of politics: the waging of the class struggle and the building of Socialism. It has now learned its lesson. In his two television broadcasts in the 1966 election, Mr. Wilson mentioned 'government' 39 times, 'Britain' 42 times and Labour not at all.[28]

Limited Patronage

Emotions are all the more important because, apart from parliament, the parties have no supply of jobs with which to promote loyalty and obedience. In the nineteenth century they threw away a vast area of possible patronage by establishing the competitive Civil Service. What Disraeli called the advancement 'of the permanent at the expense of the parliamentary officials'[29] was carried out under their noses. 'Such reform,' Disraeli thought, 'is not our métier, as the Emperor Joseph said to the first French Republicans.'[30] It soon became our métier to a remarkable degree. And the English parties achieved an almost unrivalled discipline and unity despite an exceptional scarcity of the means by which such a condition of party health is usually achieved: jobs.

So long as the franchise was closely restricted, neither parliament nor the parties, such as they were, could claim to represent the whole nation, or to embody public opinion. They had no democratic cloak to give respectability and to conceal their depredations. And since the distribution of jobs to friends, relatives, dependants, and supporters seldom gains the sympathetic understanding of those who are excluded, patronage was one of the fields in which caution and restraint were wise. Hence the decline from fifty peerages a year created by the younger Pitt to the three a year created by Peel. This austerity in the recruitment of legislators was paralleled in the recruitment of bureaucrats. From 1782 onwards the number of sinecures such as that of Grand Falconer of England and the Remembrancer of First Fruits was diminished; the Select committee of 1834 thundered that 'Anything in the nature of a sinecure office . . . is alike indefensible in principle, pernicious as a means of influence and grievous as an undue addition to the general burden of the nation,'[31] and while the recruitment of working government officials continued to be by patronage, it was mitigated in most spheres by some rudimentary tests of fitness. In England, therefore, parties were prevented from engrossing the whole field of the public service within their sway by their own primitive nature and by their fear of public opinion.

There were no such restraints on their presumption in America. Manhood suffrage was largely achieved by 1830 and the parties could claim to represent the whole country. There was no aristocracy either to take the jobs for itself or to inculcate the belief that government was something the people should obey and not try to run. On the contrary the government had avowedly been set up by 'we the people of the United States'. Besides, jobs were the sinews of war. Elections and the parties fed upon each other. 'Democracy' enjoined that posts had to be filled by election, and frequent and wide-ranging elections made the organisation of the parties ever more elaborate. The organisation of mass parties capable of soliciting the suffrage of the entire country and presenting candidates for innumerable offices entailed political professionalism and the single ticket. Elections became a major industry and jobs became the currency of politics.

In England the economy of politics was in a more primitive stage. With mass parties impossible without a mass electorate, and elections confined to infrequent contests for membership of parliament, gold was still the political currency.

By the time mass parties had appeared in England and the law seriously hindered bribery, it was too late for the parties to be able to develop as they had developed in America. Public opinion had grown used to the idea of the Civil Service being non-political, an idea which the Labour movement accepted without question. The Civil Service has been carefully removed to the non-partisan cloister by its dissolute protector, the aristocracy,* before the mass parties or their successors were of an age and a strength to enjoy it.

The parties were able to make people work for them without the hope of employment. There was less to do than in America and the incentive to do it was greater. The great political questions of Church and State, education, and the franchise, had not already been solved, and these questions are capable of engaging the emotions in a way that the more straightforward economic 'stuff of politics' in the United States was not. Also, in many parts of the country, the upper classes thought it their right and duty, if not to run their party at the local level, at least to be nominated by it. They did not want either jobs or pay. Party funds were less necessary than they were in the United States, and most candidates provided their own election expenses.

It is timing, then, which explains the small place that patronage has played in all but the highest reaches of British party politics. Had manhood suffrage been achieved in England over half a century earlier, non-commissioned officers would have shown the same public spirit as their leaders in wishing to serve in the employ-ment of the state. As it is, paid jobs go only to the party elites: Members of Parliament and peers. For the rest, party produces posts of prestige and service. The way to local influence is guarded by the party organisations. Office in local government, on hospital or school boards, on the bench, and other positions of local dignity, is most likely to be achieved through party. But almost all such positions demand unpaid though not unhonoured service. Most of the great extensions of government patronage in the nationalised industries and elsewhere are beyond the reach of local activists. Virtually the only paid posts that are available except at the top are not in government but in the party. Both parties have a growing

---

* The far from dissolute Mr. Gladstone was its principal agent in raising the Civil Service from its fallen state to a condition of unassailable purity.

bureaucracy, but in both paid officials are still a relatively small proportion of the total working army.

Leaders in Control

Nevertheless the party leaderships have maintained control. They have been helped by the atomisation of local parties. Constituencies are mere geographical expressions instead of being recognisable and historic communities. The English electoral 'grid' system, combined with the relative unimportance of British local government, has powerfully contributed to the nationalisation of British politics and to the elimination of regional variations and local strongholds of political power. Unlike in America, where elections for governor and senator necessitate the organisation of the parties upon a state wide basis and where the importance of the Mayor or local government produces a strong organisation in the big cities, no feudal boss whom the central organisation has to treat almost as an equal has arisen in England, at least since the heyday of the late Lord Derby. While the maintenance of two great parties has been facilitated by the extreme homogeneity of England, the electoral system has itself greatly increased that homogeneity by flattening the electoral landscape into one vast plain dominated by the Palace of Westminster and the twin party fortresses in Smith Square.

The power of the party headquarters and the powerlessness of the local associations does not extend to the choice of candidate. The fragmentation of the national parties outside London, so favourable in all other respects to the party headquarters, here works against them. There are too many fragments for the party headquarters to keep an eye on the whole time. In their local activities, of which the choice of candidates is one, the local parties have considerable freedom of action. Still if the party headquarters do not have the power to nominate candidates, this is not a serious inconvenience. Nearly all candidates are selected from a list of people who are more or less agreeable to party headquarters, and the right of veto is retained, though seldom used.

Any centrifugal bias arising from single member seats and local selection of candidates is adequately counteracted by the centripetal force of the conventions of the House of Commons and the demands of electoral democracy. Indeed the danger is the opposite one. As a skilful party manager admitted, 'the party machines are powerful forces and it is no part of their business to encourage a spirit of independence among their members'.[32]

In a multi party system parties can be more or less responsible to their supporters, leaving the coalition as a whole to look after the voters. In a two party system this is impossible. The party that forms the government was supported by less than half the country. The government is the government of the whole country. It cannot therefore be solely responsible to those who elected it or to those who worked for its election. It has to look to its opponents as well as its supporters. Its job is government not representation. Besides the conventions of cabinet government demand that the country be ruled by its leaders in parliament, not by a party caucus or by party militants outside parliament.

Active party workers moreover are not even representative of those who voted for the party. They nearly always hold opinions much further from the centre than those of their party leaders. But they are not the extremist cranks and fanatics they are often assumed to be. This is truer of the Conservatives than of Labour.[33] But there are not even many Labour extremists. The Newcastle study indicated that the left wing *bloc* of Labour supporters and the right wing *bloc* of Conservative supporters were both small.[34] There is a veering towards the wings and necessarily an intensity of party opinion among the party activists, which makes them unrepresentative of ordinary voters, but there is not much extremism.

A party controlled by its activists would have little chance of winning in a two party system; it would be too inflexible. To win, a party must be able to absorb new forces and new people, without neglecting or alienating the old. As a French Radical deputy put it, 'the main task of a great party is the same as that of a good stomach: not to reject but to assimilate'.[35] Certainly the French Radical party had an admirable digestive system. British parties, too, have strong stomachs partly because they are controlled by their heads, and partly because like the Radicals they have to stay in the centre to gain power.

The word party, like parliament, covers a large number of activities. British parties are not single simple entities. Party as a form of elective machinery is different if not separate from party as a method of running the government. For the machinery to take charge of its minders would be blank defiance of the division of labour. The parliamentary leaders generally have a surer judgment of what is needed than a somewhat random selection of their followers in the country. Like Branting, the Swedish Social Democrat, most people would oppose that 'primitive democracy which originates in the belief that from the beginning the masses understood everything better than those who have insight and knowledge'.[36] Others would reject the possibility of intra-party democracy: where there are no competing teams of leaders presenting alternatives, the decisions of the masses owe nothing to 'primitive democracy' and a lot to sophisticated methods of manipulating opinion and choice.

Intra-party democracy does not and cannot exist, yet all parties practise guided democracy. The proportion of guidance and democracy varies, but neither is ever wholly absent. Though the leaders ultimately determine policy, they cannot ignore the opinions or feelings of their followers in the country. Trotsky's prophetic vision of Bolshevism that the party would be 'replaced by the organisation of the party, the organisation by the Central Committee, and finally the Central Committee by the dictator',[37] is not yet true of English parties even in its preliminary stage. The parties are not controlled by their members, but the leadership is far from having freedom of action. The voluntary unpaid character of British parties give the rank and file considerable influence. Political leaders depend upon their troops to get them elected; rows between the leadership and the party workers damage the party's electoral prospects. Salisbury's son thought that 'in home affairs he paid very much attention to opinion especially that of his own party.'[38] The same has been true of all party leaders. If they do not pay attention to opinion, they split the party or lose their job. Bonar Law was forced to give way over food taxes in 1913, Gaitskill over Clause 4 in 1960, and such retreats in private or public are common. Party loyalty is powerful, but even armies sometimes mutiny.

While avoiding or minimising disaffection among their active supporters, party leaders have to remember that many of those who voted for them gave only grudging support and are ready to withdraw it. These people must not be alienated. The majority of the country who voted for other parties must also not be forgotten. They must not be driven beyond endurance. Moderation is the only way to keep a majority.

Drawn Together
The parties' search for votes draws them together. Marxists thought the Tories and the Liberals were so similar because they both came from the same class and were really only one party. In fact the experience of other countries and of Britain since the displacement

of the Liberals by the Labour party has shown that there is a general tendency in a two party system for the parties to be close together or to move towards each other. There is even such a tendency in a multi party system, though it is much less pronounced and is more liable to be counteracted by the emergence of a new party. The Whigs and the Tories, like the Edinburgh and Quarterly reviews, reminded Hazlitt 'of opposition coaches, that raise a great dust or spatter one another with mud, but both travel the same road and arrive at the same destination'. The opposition, he wrote, 'have pressed so long against the ministry without effect, that . . . they have been moulded into their image and superscription, spelt backwards, or they differ as concave and convex . . . or like man and wife, they two have become one flesh. . . .'[39]

The parties are 'concave and convex' only very partly because, as the French proverb has it, *'Chacun prend à l'adversaire, qu'il le veuille on non.'* The essential cause is that both have to adjust themselves to the wishes and needs of the same people, and there is a limit to the extent these people can be deceived. If the voters want butter for their breakfast, it is no use a party offering them 'marmalade instead.'[40] If it wants to win an election it must offer butter, as Disraeli well knew. When it became plain that protection was electoral suicide, he said 'Protection is not only dead but damned,'[41] and buried it.

Economic or military disaster, excessive ideological commitment, political dishonesty, incompetence, and unscrupulousness, may make the differences between the parties seem wide for a time. But provided the opposition is loyal to the regime and accepts the parliamentary conventions, there are only two occasions when the parties are likely to be more than temporarily far apart: when one of them is new and when one of them has been out of power for a long time. A new party has to begin by displacing one of the two parties in possession of the system. When it has done so, the survivor of the two old parties cannot fail to recognise that there is much popular support for the newcomer. It is influenced by meeting its opponents' members in Parliament and trims its sails accordingly. The Conservative party confronted by the Labour party moved towards it between the wars. 'I am opposed to Socialism,' Baldwin said in the 'twenties, 'but I have always endeavoured to make the party face left in its anti-Socialism.'[42] Baldwin's successor, Neville Chamberlain, combined extreme and reciprocated antipathy to the Labour party with espousal of many of its aims and objectives.

'Hoare and I,' he once wrote, 'are the only Socialists in the government.'[43] Meanwhile a similar process is going on in the new party. Parliamentary contact with its opponents mellows it a little and makes things seem more complicated than they did at home. Single-mindedness is reduced on both sides. David Kirkwood, one of the wild men of the Clyde, who entered Parliament in 1922, recorded that he found it 'full of wonder. I had to shake myself occasionally as I found myself moving about and talking with men whose names were household words. More strange was it to find them all so simple and unaffected and friendly.'[44]

No wonder party militants have been inclined to think of parliaments and representative assemblies as little better than the modern manifestation of Sodom and Gomorrah! But the blandishments and the *douceur de vivre* of the *ancien régime* are of only minor importance in pulling any major new party towards the centre. Kirkwood was especially susceptible. Most of the Clydesiders remained unimpressed. The primary factor is the logic of the party's situation. So long as the new party remains a minority it can do little but feel its influence trickling into the benches opposite—a dispiriting form of proselytism. Better far to proselytise the voter and win a majority by loosening orthodoxy.

Parties and politicians tend to start on the extremities and finish in the centre. Under the Third Republic it was a commonplace that politicians began on the left and ended in the centre or even on the right. Millerand, Briand, Laval and many others executed this manoeuvre. In the party 'city state' conditions of French politics, politicians could behave like *condottieri* and change their party at will. In the party 'nation state' conditions of England it is virtually impossible to be such a soldier of fortune. Joseph Chamberlain's entry into both parties on the left and emergence on their right was a unique progression. Normally the progression has to be within the party. Attlee and Cripps considerably modified their views between the twenties and thirties and their arrival in office. By 1968 many of Mr. Harold Wilson's opinions bore little relation to those he expressed in the early 1950s. Similarly in the Fourth Republic, which was more rigid than the Third, M. Guy Mollet moved from the extreme non-co-operative Marxist left of the Socialist party to its extreme governmental right.

Whole parties executed this movement as well as individuals. In the loose group or party system of the pre-fascist Italian monarchy, Radicals soon became virtually indistinguishable from other

Liberals. Indeed the process of '*trasformismo*' made all the various groups and parties seem alike. In the Third Republic, the Radicals began on the Left and moved into the centre. Their route was later followed by the French Socialist party.

There is then nothing unusual in the British Labour party's drift from the left, or in the Conservative party's drift from the right, to the centre. Such movements are the natural result of the parliamentary and electoral process. It is all very well for the keen party member outside parliament to insist upon the party not abandoning its principles, which were handed down as revealed truth many years ago and in the furtherance of which he spends much of his spare time. But a parliamentarian has to seek the votes of a great many people who have never heard of these principles and would disapprove of them if they had.* Rigidity of principle is much less attractive to him. The average parliamentarian thinks power is worth a doctrinal muddle.

With the exception of the Communists and the Irish nationalists, all parliamentary parties have been less strictly orthodox in their doctrine and their principles than the mass of the party workers outside the parliament. The Irish nationalists were forbidden to accept hospitality from M.P.s of other parties, and before election had to pledge that if 'it be determined by resolution . . . supported by a majority of the Irish party that I have not fulfilled the above pledges, I hereby undertake to resign my seat'.[46] Yet they did not remain united for long. The Communists have been able to retain the doctrinal purity of their parliamentary representatives by remaining totally aloof from normal parliamentary politics and regarding parliament as something not to be worked but to be sabotaged. The French Communist party lays down that the Communist deputy 'is responsible not to the anonymous mass of electors, but to the Communist party'.[47]† Even so the French Communist leaders have felt it necessary to demand from each deputy an undated document of resignation, which they can publish in the event of deviation or disobedience. M. Poujade was not able to procure discipline among his following on Suez despite the use of such expedients as housing them in one hotel and threatening to hang anybody who rebelled.[48]

* This ignorance extends even to members of the party. In Newcastle-under-Lyme two months after the Labour Party Conference of 1960, 54 per cent of Labour members had not heard of Clause 4 of the party's constitution.[45]

† The British Communist party holds a similar doctrine but rarely has a Member of Parliament to impose it on.

The main parties in England have not needed such aids. Enough M.P.s have realised that because a party is always a minority it has to compromise to win the centre. That is the only route to power. In a multi party system, the centre may be a centre party as the Radicals became under the Third Republic and the U.D.S.R. was in the Fourth. Elected in some parts of the country by the Right who were afraid of the Socialists and in other parts by the Left who were afraid of the Clericals, the Radicals occupied a similarly central position in the Chamber, often achieving the perfect parliamentary double of being at the same time both in power and in opposition.*

Under a two party system the existence of the centre is less blatant but no less real. The uncommitted have to be won by one of them, and the party which repels them least usually wins. It is the job of the party leaders, therefore, to keep their parties moderate; and the means they use is strict party discipline in parliament and central control in the country. Party votes in the House of Commons both conceal and preserve the consensus that exists; they register disagreement, while confining the real differences between the parties within narrow limits. The two front benches play the part of the French Radical party. The Communists and other totalitarian parties use strict party discipline in parliament to keep their deputies or M.P.s extreme; British parties use it to keep them moderate. With two exceptions British parties have hugged the centre since 1868. From 1909 to 1914 Balfour lost his hold on the Conservative party, the right wing gained control and under severe provocation from the Liberal government nearly involved the country in civil war. In the thirties the vanished prospect of electoral victory drove the Labour party to the left instead of to the centre. As a rule, however, the parties have managed to stay close to the middle way.

This 'centrism' of the leaders mirrors the feelings and the centrism of the voters. Most people, Hume thought, 'associate themselves they know not why; from example, from passion, from idleness'.[49] They join or support one party and not the other, because of their parents or because of the people who influenced them when their political attitudes were formed, because of their social environment, because of chance circumstances or because of individual choice. In consequence there are people of every sort in both parties. Indeed

---

* A similar problem often confronts the British Parliamentary Liberal party, some of whom are largely dependent upon support from the Right, others on support from the Left. They however, achieve a different double from the French Radicals: usually they are neither in power nor in opposition.

in each party there are always some who would be more at home with their party's opponents.*

Politics is a fringe activity or interest for the great majority. Voters see many good points in both parties and often vote for one when more in agreement with the other. Others see little difference between them. There is a good deal of political agreement among the supporters of all parties and little total hostility. Voters like the parties are internally divided.

No wonder, then, that the differences between the parties are seldom clear and distinct. Macaulay thought the two parties could be compared to the front and hind legs of a horse—one always a little ahead of the other. This was an outcome of the Whig interpretation of history, which saw British development as a progressive unfolding of Liberal truths by the good Whigs despite the obscurantist machinations of the bad Tories culminating in God's greatest work: the Whig-Liberal party and Mid-Victorian England. But the idea of some primordial division between progressives and conservatives is delusive. Individuals and parties are conservative and progressive in varying degrees, depending on the issue and the time.

The Tory Ashley took the lead in trying to improve the conditions of factory workers, and was opposed by many leading Liberals. Disraeli's 1867 Reform Act enfranchised six times more people than Gladstone's Reform Bill had proposed the year before. Some of Disraeli's social legislation in the seventies was far in advance of Gladstone's. And the man who had proclaimed the mystical union between the Conservative party and the land did nothing to help agriculture when the agricultural depression hit Britain in the seventies. The Liberals were anxious to solve the land question but not the industrial question. Palmerston's government of 1859 to 1866 was the most 'conservative' England has had since the earlier days of Lord Liverpool's long administration

Political personalities fit no more easily into Macaulay's conception. Of the leading politicians between 1827 and 1859 Russell, Wellington and Grey were almost the only ones to remain in the

* When the Liberal, Lord Aberdare, was asked to subscribe £2,500 for the general election of 1900, he replied: 'I . . . am not sure that for many reasons I should not be happier on the other side of the House. However the differences are to me so small, and consistency and tradition so much that I remain where I am, but am not inclined to pay more than £1,000 for so doing.'[50]

same party throughout their career. Peel, Palmerston, Stanley, Melbourne, Disraeli, Gladstone all left, changed or were separated from their party. Disraeli began life as a Radical, and had he won his election under that label he might have become the Liberal leader. Gladstone began life as a Conservative, and had Disraeli remained a Radical, Gladstone would probably have stayed a Conservative and become the leader of the party. The two most archetypal John Bullish imperialistic figures in nineteenth century Britain were the former Tory, Palmerston, who became Liberal Prime Minister, and the renegade Radical, Joseph Chamberlain, who was never a Tory Prime Minister but who became the most powerful man in a Tory cabinet. In his autobiography Balfour wrote that 'in the sixties the line between the moderate Liberal and the moderate Conservative was more than usually blurred'. What seems to have decided him was that 'the family tradition on both sides was Conservative'.[51]

Dr. Johnson and Lord Acton, among others, believed that a conservative-liberal division marks some quasi perennial cleavage in ideas and outlook. But any such classic conflict between authority and freedom, pessimism and optimism, belief in original sin and faith in the perfectibility of man did not coincide with the party lines of battle in Victorian England. In any case there is no classic Conservative-Labour conflict. A Conservative-Labour division does not correspond to any deep seated cleavage in the hearts and minds of men. Labour has been more 'progressive' on social issues. But whether or not favouring entry into the Common Market in 1961 as opposed to five years later is a fair 'litmus paper' to use as a test of progressivism, the Trade Union leaders in the Labour party have often been undeniably conservative. A belief in state control as against individual initiative is an equally inadequate ground for distinguishing 'natural' conservatives and 'natural' socialists. Conservatives have often not been averse from state interference if it suited them.* There was very little that was individualist about British industry under Conservative governments between the wars. 'As long as state action does not involve what is unjust or oppressive,' said Lord Hugh Cecil, 'it cannot be said that the principles of Conservatism are hostile to it.'[53] A feeling for the under-dog is a slightly more plausible line of demarcation, until the threats of Laski and Cripps are recalled. Nor during the Attlee government

---

* Right wing American bankers during the depression objected to federal aid for the unemployed; they did not object to federal aid to banks, 'the millionaires' dole'.[52]

did Mr. Shinwell with his 'tinker's cuss', or Sir Hartley Shawcross with his 'We are the masters now', prompt the thought that at long last the meek had inherited Whitehall.

Radicalism and conservatism also fail to provide a clearly marked frontier. Nearly everybody wants to be radical about some things, and nearly everybody wants to be conservative about some things.* Salisbury was radical over redistribution in 1884. No tory alderman could have been more conservative on local government than Aneurin Bevan. The word radical is a label which is virtually meaningless unless it is followed by information as to the sphere in which radicalism is proposed. Some people may have radical temperaments, others conservative temperaments, but such differences do not determine a man's choice of party or ideas. For some people it is conservative to support Labour. Equally it is radical for some people to join the Conservatives. It all depends on their environment. Nor do differences of temperament determine the stand parties as a whole take up. That is decided by the nature of the issue. Class also does not provide a clear division. The class basis of the parties in parliament and the country is different, but the class lines are hopelessly blurred.

Not even a belief or disbelief in Socialism marks a dividing line. More than most creeds the meaning of Socialism has defied definition. Metternich described himself to Guizot as a 'Conservative Socialist'.[55] That aside, Lord Hugh Cecil[56] pointed out that Conservatism 'is not, considered as a system of political thought, directly antagonistic to either Liberalism or Socialism'.† More important, a belief in Socialism has not been a prominent or even a necessary part of the intellectual make up of all Labour leaders. Jimmy Thomas used to say he was not a Socialist.[58]

Lloyd George similarly said he was not a Liberal. Neville Chamberlain wanted to get 'rid of that odious title of Conservative'.[59] All dispositions and almost all views are found in both parties and are blended by them. As Gladstone said of himself, 'my opinions went one way, my lingering sympathies the other'.[60] The dividing line between the parties does not follow a natural frontier of opinion, and it never has. In consequence, centrism prevails.

* A proposal to provide minority representation in 1867 was vehemently opposed by the Radical Bright. In defence of 'the ancient ways of the constitution', he urged the House not to be deluded by such 'new fangled ideas'.[54]

† 'Socialism is the end of all, the negation of Faith, of Family, of Property, of Monarchy, of Empire.' This Syllabus of Errors was pronounced not by a Tory but by the Liberal Rosebery.[57]

The Party Battle

Yet there are of course ideological and other differences between the parties, and the party battle is not a mock struggle, mere farce and fraud. The parties may be, as Belloc thought, Siamese twins. They are not identical twins. 'The Tories,' said David Hume, 'have been so long obliged to talk in the republican style, that they seem to have made converts of themselves by their hypocrisy, and to have embraced the sentiments, as well as language, of their adversaries.'[61] This is a process which all civilised parties undergo, but even after it they are different from their opponents. The parties represent interests and classes in different proportions and have different pressure groups behind them. Their heads are close together; their stomachs are further apart. The folk-memories of a party, in addition to the presumed economic interests of many of its supporters, give it underlying ideas and feelings that differ from those of its opponents. So there is bound to be some ideological strife between the parties. Yet two-party politics do not lend themselves to a straightforward contest of ideas. Quite apart from the governmental inconvenience such a struggle would involve, it would split the country. Parties are multiple marriages of convenience, not of ideological love. Ideas like symbols are weapons, but an army marches on its stomach.

Stating that there is rarely room for more than one political debate in a generation, Mr. Quintin Hogg pointed out that 'the great debate of our time is Socialism. . . .'[62] The behaviour of the parties over Socialism, in the sense of public ownership, is the best test of centrism in action and the best illustration of how the party system works. The chosen instrument of the Labour Government of 1945–51 in its attempt to bring Socialism to Britain was the public corporation, and all the industries nationalised by the Labour government, coal, electricity, the railways, gas, and iron and steel, were given into the care of such bodies. Nationalisation was vehemently opposed by the Conservatives. But before the war the history of the public corporation was very different. In 1919 the Electricity Commission and the Forestry Commission were set up by the Coalition government. Though both were public corporations, they were slightly different from subsequent manifestations of the species. In 1926 however, the year of the General Strike, Baldwin's Conservative government brought in two nationalisation measures. They set up a public corporation, the Central Electricity Board, to standardise the electrical generating industry and to build up a national grid; and they gave a monopoly of broadcasting to a public corporation, the B.B.C. Both these bodies bore a close resemblance to the public corporations set up after the war by the Labour government. In 1928 the Racecourse Betting Control Board was established by the Baldwin government; and in the same year the Liberal 'Yellow Book' expressed support for the public corporation, Keynes having written two years before that progress lay 'in the growth and the recognition of semi-autonomous bodies within the state. . . .'[63] In 1908 a Liberal government had created the Port of London Authority.

Thus, not only before the Labour party had created one single corporation, but before it had even decided that it favoured such corporations, the Conservative party had started setting them up and the Liberal party had pronounced in their favour. Labour was the last of the three parties to be converted to that peculiar institution. It was not until Mr. Herbert Morrison, as Minister of Transport in the second Labour government, had seen the working of the Central Electricity Board and decided to use it as a model for his London Passenger Transport Board, that the Labour party began to see that this device of the capitalist parties was in fact the true brand of Socialism.

Morrison's nationalisation of London Transport was carried into law, appropriately enough, by the Conservative-dominated Macdonald government in 1933. Coal deposits were nationalised in 1938 and pre-war nationalisation was completed by the Chamberlain government's creation of the British Overseas Airways Corporation in 1939. The acceptance of public corporations by all parties during the pre-war period was paralleled by their rejection or dislike of competition in industry. Despite this consensus the Labour leaders were not anxious to extend nationalisation after the war. The National Executive's main economic resolution at the party conference in December, 1944, did not even mention public ownership, and in moving it Mr. Shinwell said that the executive did not think nationalisation essential for post-war reconstruction. It was only a revolt from the floor that foisted nationalisation upon the Labour leadership and upon the country.[64] In view of what had happened before the war, Mr. Churchill could reasonably say of the nationalisation of the Bank of England that it 'does not, in my opinion, raise any matter of principle'[65]; and Mr. Macmillan had history on his side when on the second reading of the bill nationalising the coal industry he said that 'This is not Socialism; it is state capitalism.'[66]

The Tories denationalised only steel and road transport, and Churchill's announcement that in those industries where national-isation was going to remain 'we have done and are doing our utmost to make a success of it, even though this may somewhat mar the symmetry of party recrimination',[67] was a return to the pre-war and the war-time position. The symmetry was yet further blemished in 1954 when the Conservative government established a public corporation to run the atomic energy programme, and the Labour party completed the baroque confusion of the controversy by opposing the measure. During the fifties and early sixties, there was considerable disillusionment in the country and throughout much of the Labour party both with public ownership as such and with the policy of setting up public corporations. This disillusionment produced a bewildering variety of nationalisation proposals from Labour. Industries were ripe for nationalisation at one election and unripe at the next. Labour wanted to nationalise the command-ing heights of the economy; it was never sure for long which those heights were. As Mr. Crossman admitted, 'their "shopping list" was seldom drawn up on the merits of the case. Usually it was the product of a last minute haggle between contending factions in the Executive.'[68]

Meanwhile the Conservative government allowed the extension of the nationalised sector of the steel industry by permitting Richard Thomas and Baldwin to take over Whiteheads; the reason given was that this operation would make it easier to denationalise Richard Thomas and Baldwins. It was not clear whether the Tories thought yet more nationalisation was going to be necessary in order to produce de-nationalisation. During the fifties and sixties both the Conserva-tive and Labour parties in contrast with their pre-war ideas em-phasised the value and virtues of competition in industry. Having opposed the transfer of atomic energy to a public corporation when they were in opposition, Labour in office proposed similar treatment for the Post Office. More controversially it renationalised steel, extended transport nationalisation, and made generally threatening noises. There was therefore more symmetry in the recrimination after 1964, but on the question on which party lines have for long been most clearly drawn centrism has not broken down.

Likewise, the symmetry was far from perfect in the previous ideogolical struggle: protection versus free trade. There was until the slump a body of Conservative free traders led by Churchill and

C

Derby. On the other side Lloyd George in private expressed agreement with Joe Chamberlain.[69] And Asquith wrote in 1908, 'I have realised from the first that if it could not be proved that social reform (not Socialism) can be financed on Free Trade lines, a return to protection is a moral certainty.'[70] Liberal governments sustained or increased tariffs, and until Ottawa the Conservatives were, except in 1923, chary either of advocating or carrying out protection.

As to the struggle being a fraud, it would be as sensible to say that the wars of the eighteenth century were frauds because they were not total, the antagonists striving merely for limited gains instead of seeking to destroy one another. The War of the Austrian Succession was perfectly real, notwithstanding that French ships continued until 1748 to be insured at Lloyds.* When they were sunk by British ships, their owners duly gained compensation from their British insurers. There is no necessary connection between reality and totality. The similarity between British parties is a sign of health and good sense, not of disease and decadence. The limited party struggle, the fact that as Salisbury put it, 'half the earnestness of a political struggle belongs to the sporting category of feelings',[72] does not appeal to nature's crusaders, who are to be found in all parties and in all countries. But the dissatisfaction of the crusaders with the humdrum party struggle and with their failure to drive the parties apart often says more about their own psychological needs than about the defects of the two party system. It is curious to want the country to be divided into Montagus and Capulets. That is not the sort of conflict the system needs. Admirable as some crusaders are, others of them, like a character in *Babbitt*, 'exult in the opportunity to be vicious in the name of virtue.' There is usually something wrong with a cause if it has to be 'elevated' into a crusade. The whole point of free government is that the political struggle should be in some degree

A Tournament of blows, some hardly dealt,
Though short of mortal combat;[73]

---

* An act was eventually passed in the last year of the war prohibiting such insurance. The Solicitor General Murray, later Lord Mansfield, in opposing the bill said: '. . . To carry on trade for the mutual benefit of both nations is not aiding or assisting the enemy.'[71]

The alternative, after all, to the parties filling the political arena 'with harmless strife', is for them to fill it with hatred and bloodshed. By remaining fairly close together and fairly like each other, they enable the two party system to discharge its two chief functions: binding the country together and providing a peaceful alternation of governments. Those who like Aneurin Bevan in 1945 call for 'the political extinction of the Tory party and twenty-five years of Labour government',[74] are either heady with election fever or misunderstand the whole party system, the British political tradition and much else besides.

Quite apart from it being a necessary condition of freedom, party warfare provides political education. Politics only hold the interest when seen in controversial and personal terms. And what matter if the teachers do not always have complete belief in what they are saying? Many teachers of the classics and other subjects must often have doubts about the intrinsic worth of what they are trying to teach; that does not affect its educational value. Politicians are in any event remarkably adept in securing your own assent to what they say. Much as the result of a boxing match is often difficult to fix, because if one of the boxers hits his opponent harder than he intended the resultant anger produces a genuine contest, so an opponent's denunciation stings a politician into counter-attack. There is nothing like an opponent's dialectic for making a man believe his own.*

Of course the consensus between the parties can be overdone, and the party struggle become a pure stage fight. It was so in Spain in the seventies and eighties of the last century, when a change of government was with justification called the changing of the guard. The party struggle was also a stage fight in Portugal, where the parties agreed under a system called rotativism to alternate in office[76]. In Italy it was occasionally so between the *Risorgimente* and 1914, particularly during the heyday of Giolitti. Giolitti's feat was in some ways similar to that of the French Radical party. He would become Prime Minister when the times looked propitious, and when he saw bad weather ahead he would leave the pilot's seat and slip below deck.† Then after a few years in opposition he would become Prime Minister again. The sheer virtuosity of this per-

* A Kentucky Senator, asked what stand he was going to take in an election, replied: 'I haven't made up my mind, son, but when I do I am going to be damned bitter about it.'[75]

† Had Lloyd George possessed similar foresight or modesty, he would have left 10 Downing Street before 1922, and might have returned later.

formance deserves admiration, and the Italian system of '*trasfor-mismo*' performed many valuable tasks of reconciliation. Yet it devitalised Italian politics and lowered the prestige of Italian liberalism, thereby paving the way for Mussolini. The Italian, Spanish and Portuguese systems had one thing in common: in all of them the government, like an eighteenth century English government, always won an election.* In such a situation politics are orientated towards the court, and become almost exclusively a struggle for place.

In a healthy party system the struggle for place is part of a larger struggle for votes. Politicians trim and tack in their quest for power, but they do so in order to get the wind of votes in their sails. If this wind is lacking or can be broken by government control of the elections or by parliamentary manoeuvring afterwards, the party and parliamentary systems become becalmed in the muddy waters of intrigue, corruption and influence. Only once in England has the two party system verged upon fraud: during Palmerston's last administration when the Tory opposition made a truce with the Prime Minister.[78]

This alliance of the front-benchers, formed not to enable the government to pass different measures but to let sleeping Whigs lie, was only possible because of the restricted franchise.† Under a wide franchise such an alliance is virtually impossible; there is no disfranchised section of the community against which the two parties can combine. When all the sections of the community have votes, the parties must compete for them, not combine against them. The negro has been badly treated in the deep south of the United States largely because of one party rule there. Had there been two parties as there are now beginning to be, they would have sought his vote; one party was able to stop him voting at all. Robert Michels quoted German Socialist papers to show the effects of the election fight of 1910 over the Lloyd George budget. 'The English Conservatives do not preach resignation to the workers, but discontent. Whereas the Prussian Conservatives, for example, are in the habit of telling the working classes that nowhere in the world are they so well off as in Germany, the English Conservatives assure their constituents that nowhere in the world are the workers

* In Spain the official newspaper sometimes published the election results before they had taken place. Unlike the *Chicago Tribune*, which in 1948 announced a victory for Dewey, it got them right.[77]

† In the 'transformist' phase of Italian politics the franchise was, similarly, severely restricted.

worse off than in England.'[79] But only under a Liberal government of course.

It was Lowell's belief that if the two parties did not hold different views on the question of the day, public life would 'revolve about the personal ambitions and intrigues of leading politicians'.[80] In the continental systems that he had in mind, governments were not changed by general elections. In Italy, Spain and Portugal the government fixed the election instead of the elections fixing the government; in France the government did not fix the election, nor did the election fix the government—anyway for more than a few months. In these countries governments were changed by court and parliamentary intrigues and manoeuvres, not by the voters. Cavour, one of the classical exponents of the system, secured his majority by a *connubio* between right centre and left centre, and set the pattern of Italian politics until Mussolini. France achieved her centrism by shifting coalitions usually based upon that triumph of balance, the Radical party.

The normal *connubio* of the centre in England is quite different. It is tacit but not illicit. The continental system brought together politicians who fundamentally differed; the British system keeps apart politicians who fundamentally agree. But though sensible moderation keeps the leaders close to each other, competition for votes and office prevents collusion. There is always a residue of principle, policy and programme to separate the two sides and to edify the populace.

But that residue need not and should not be large. The competition for votes is enough to keep the party struggle honest.* The distortion of the perspective supplied by the possession of power is sufficient to make the government party hold a different view from the opposition. To the ideologue his party in opposition is like Dorian Gray: handsome, lean and innocent; but in power it grows like his picture: vicious, shop-soiled and corrupted. The discrepancy between Dorian Gray and the picture is by itself enough to stop the two parties becoming identical. Roebuck's description of the Whigs, 'When out of office they were demagogues, in power

---

* Will Rogers's description of the American election of 1928 was: 'Hoover wants all the drys and as many wets as possible. Smith wants all the wets and as many drys as he can get. Hoover says he will relieve the farmer, even if he has to call Congress; Smith says he will relieve the farmer even if he has to appoint a Commission. Hoover says the tariff will be kept up. Smith says the tariff will not be lowered. Hoover is strongly in favour of prosperity. Smith highly endorses prosperity. . . .'[81] British parties have not yet reached that stage.

they become exclusive oligarchs,'[82] can be applied more widely. The demagoguery of opposition and the exclusiveness of power suffice to keep the parties separate.

The centre rules but it does not always win. In order to stay mainly moderate, a government is often driven to make concessions to its more extreme supporters on a particular issue. So many aspects of the Wilson government's economic policy were deeply repugnant to its most enthusiastic supporters that steel renationalisation was an essential layer of sugaring for the pill, even though it was supported by only one quarter of the electorate. The entire Conservative and Liberal parties and a majority of Labour supporters were opposed to it, but Labour's ancestral gods had to be offered their propitiatory sacrifice so that the government might secure absolution from the rest of its traditional worship.

Keeping in the centre is far from a law of nature. 'The frightened, the defeated, the coward, and the knave,' General Eisenhower said in 1949, 'run to the flanks, straggling out of the battle under the cover of slogans, false formulas, and appeals to passion—a welcome sight to an alert enemy.'[83] And a disastrous sight for a wise leader. Some of those on the flanks, Mr. Enoch Powell and Mr. Michael Foot for instance, come into none of Eisenhower's categories, and they are powerful intellectual stimulants. But the fact remains that both party leaderships have to wage a brave and skilful fight to remain in the centre of the field.

The perennial delusion of the extreme wing of the losing party is that the cause of its defeat was the voter's inability to distinguish the difference between the parties. Just why the widening of the gap between the parties should make it easier for the supporters of the majority to step over to the minority party has never been satisfactorily explained. The theory of the need to polarise the losers and the winners has therefore to be bolstered by the belief that the firm supporters of the losers were so antagonised by their party's too close resemblance to their opponents that they stayed away from the polls. Such non-voters do exist though they can hardly be common. To recoil with disgust from the allegedly inadequate difference between the parties into a position of total indifference and abstention is self-evidently absurd. The theory that there were millions of supporters of the losing party sulking in their suburbs who would consent to emerge only if their party was shown to be utterly dissimilar from its opponents was tested by the Republican Party in 1964, and conclusively disproved.

Governments, too, may seek to polarise the party conflict, The governing Social Democrats in Sweden and more recently in Norway, with doubtful success, used the pensions issue to differentiate themselves more clearly from their opponents. For a brief moment in 1966 it seemed that the Labour party intended to use the issue of the control of the economy to bring about a polarisation of parties in this country. Mr. Crossman told the probably startled Coventry Fabians that the Government's measures were not 'a last ditch defence of government policy, but a last minute dash for freedom, a breakthrough into . . . new experiments in co-operation between state planning and collective bargaining'.[84] But his colleagues thought consensus politics better suited to the economic crisis than conflict politics, and a hurried return was made to 'last ditch defences of government policy'.

Irrespective of the intentions of the parties and their year-to-year tactics, the lessening of class and other differences and the dying away of the echoes of old battles may sooner or later leave a void, which may then be filled by a revival of ideology.* If this happens, it will probably not lead to great ideological differences between the parties. Because the parties contain the same kinds of people, both and not just one of them will embrace with varying degrees of enthusiasm the new ideology. They will do so slowly, and the conflict will not be clear cut.

> But by degrees to fullness wrought,
> The strength of some diffusive thought
> Hath time and space to work and spread.[85]

The parties will remain Siamese, joined together invisibly, while divided visibly amongst themselves; or so, at least, it must be hoped.

This is not because ideas are not important; obviously they are. It is because they are too lethal to be used in inter-party warfare. Interests can much more easily be adjusted than ideas. An ideological struggle is the most ferocious and least easily compromised. After his retirement Baldwin reminded a Canadian audience, in G. M.

* The new ideology, however, may be hostile to both parties and to the whole apparatus of 'bourgeois democracy',

Young's words, that 'party is founded on mutual tolerance while rival ideologies aim each at the extirpation of the other.'[86] The churches are often blamed and sometimes blame themselves for being an obstacle to the spread of the gospel. The great blessing of political parties in a two-party system is that they are almost by their very nature constrained to be obstacles to the full implementation of their own orthodoxies. The cutting across of the principles of a party by its interests abates the party struggle. If a party sticks to its principles, it will stick to opposition. Bernard Shaw saw this aspect of British politics when he advised the intelligent woman not to 'rush to the conclusion that Socialism will be established by a Socialist party and opposed by an anti-Socialist party.'[87] And it is often easier for a party to carry out its opponent's policy than its own.

Both parties and nearly everybody else usually follow the ideas of a few key thinkers. Hence the ideological gap may widen but it is unlikely to become a gulf. Ideas should and do play upon both parties. They should not produce a struggle between them.

Dangers

The two party system, then, is likely to continue to hold the country together. Even more than parliament or the monarchy the parties serve to gain consent. They cut across virtually every social and political division. They give people a sense of 'togetherness' and 'belonging', they reconcile conflicting interests, they aggregate demands, and they lessen the unpopularity of government by seeming to change it, though in reality it remains much the same. Integration is the most important function of parties, and the main British parties brilliantly fulfil it.

All the same, the stability of the system and its centrism have their dangers. Fearful of giving their opponents an opening, the parties refuse to espouse causes that may turn out to be unpopular. Belloc thought that 'not one great national issue since the repeal of the Corn Laws' had received 'full and reasoned debate'[88] between the two parties. The requirement of 'full and reasoned debate' is a high one. Influenced by the same leading ideas, seeking to appeal to the same sort of people, responding to and attempting to influence the same public opinion, divided amongst themselves, parties normally seek to blur issues, not to define them. They are driven to such 'Irishisms' as Balfour's that protection was 'in harmony with the true spirit of free-trade.'[89]

The fault of the British party system is not that it divides the country too much. Admittedly party divisions sometimes make for weakness or paralysis. Lloyd George thought in 1910 that the party system made it impossible to do what was necessary. Perhaps the same was true of the 1930s. More often, though, the weakness or paralysis is not caused by a gulf between the parties. It is due to the parties being unable to perform unaided both their integrative and their decision-making functions. To win, they must seek to mirror in some degree the whole country; they must contain minorities of their opponents' majorities. They must be ecumenical. To preserve the unity that is imperative, differences have to be tolerated. The breadth of their support and their fear of alienating the narrow segment which makes the difference between victory and defeat inhibits them from risking offence. They may integrate opinion almost out of existence. By the time all the compromises have been made, ambiguity is rampant. Like the famous scene in *A Night at the Opera*, when the Marx Brothers tear off the bits of the contract they dislike, there may in the end be nothing left. Party unity may demand neutrality on an important issue. The party remains united; the country is left to look after itself.

The outcome is laudable moderation; it is also liable to be muddle and inertia. The parties do not stimulate, they paralyse, each other. In addition, the party conflict is often discounted. Differences within parties are news; differences between them are not. Hence the party battle fails to educate because it fails to interest.

The party battle does more to keep the country united than to ensure strong government. The squabbling of parties and their reluctance to say or do unpopular things is common to all free countries. In Britain, however, parties being more disciplined have taken over the system more completely than in other European countries or the United States. They have removed other institutions from the field and then have left it themselves.

Parliamentary committees have had no chance to mould opinion. The battles of Whitehall are fought in secret, and local government has usually been too weak even to be involved. If the parties cannot form opinion, and nobody else can, events will be the only shaper. The upshot is that a largely uninformed public—uninformed because a public opinion has not been crystallised by a grand party debate or by administrative controversy—looks to its leaders and its leaders look to the uninformed public, who are going to vote one set of them into power at the next election. The system is excellent for the securing of consent, so excellent indeed that sometimes it almost eliminates dissent. Its deficiencies lie in its inability to produce timely action. There is a shortage of friction and of publicity.

The danger of centrism and of the two party system as worked in Britain is immobilism. M. Pleven's coinage of the word to describe the technique of M. Queille is sufficient indication that immobilism is not a disease found only under a two party system. But with all its difficulties and failures, the Fourth Republic achieved a more active policy of economic reorganisation and a more realistic policy towards Europe than did Great Britain, which did not have to contend with either a strong Communist party on the left or a Gaullist or Poujadist movement on the right. Yet that was despite its party system not because of it; the French Civil Service bypassed the Chamber. Few would care to imitate the constitution of the Fourth Republic. French economic vitality was purchased at the price of political chaos and several devaluations.

The stability of the British party system is too valuable to be thrown away—even supposing that both parties or either of them would be prepared to sacrifice their privileged positions. When he dissolved the first Parliament of the Protectorate Oliver Cromwell told them: 'Yet I have another argument to the good people of this nation . . . whether they prefer the having of their will though it be their destruction, rather than comply with things of necessity.'[90] By forcing the roles of government and alternative government upon the two main parties, the two party system hinders them from preferring their own will and encourages them and the country to comply with things of necessity. The compliance is usually tardy, but that is only partly the fault of the party system. It is the job of the parties to provide coherence and consent, and they perform it well. The spur to action should come from elsewhere.

II

THE TORY PARTY

*The less ... man clogs the free play of his mind with political doctrine
and dogma, the better for his thinking.*   SIR LEWIS NAMIER[1]

*It is the duty of every Englishman and of every English party to accept a
political defeat cordially, and to lend their best endeavours to secure the
success, or to neutralise the evil, of the principles to which they have been
forced to succumb.*   LORD SALISBURY, 1867[2]

*The Duke talks to me of Conservative principles; but he does not inform
me what they are. I observe indeed a party in the state whose rule it is to
consent to no change, until it is clamorously called for, and then instantly to
yield; but those are concessionary, not conservative principles. This party
treats institutions as we do our pheasants, they preserve only to destroy them.*
    DISRAELI: *Coningsby*[3]

From 1886 to 1964 the Conservative party was the principal bene-
ficiary of the party system. The Tories, said Lloyd George,
'firmly believe that Providence has singled them out to govern this
land'.[4] Whether or not Providence has singled them out, the British
voter has certainly done so. Disraeli's 'leap in the dark' in 1867 was
a mightily profitable jump for his party. Since 1886 the Tories
have been the normal rulers of the country. They have been in the
eighteenth century sense the court party, and the Liberals and then
Labour the country party.

The Conservatives, Gladstone told his party in 1888, 'have
nearly the whole wealth of the country; they have the whole of the
men of social station in the country; they have a vast preponderance
of social strength.'[5] That lament was only just becoming true. 1886
saw a great ingathering of the rich into the Conservative party, a
further drawing together of what John Morley, referring to the big
industrialists' drift to Conservatism twenty years before, called 'the
old and the new feudalism'. And by the end of the nineteenth
century the Tory party for the first time in its history was the
natural choice of the wealthy man.[6]

It has remained the natural choice of the wealthy man, and it has retained its vast preponderance of social strength. Though most of the great interests in the country express no official electoral preference, their leaders are usually Conservative. The only great interest in avowed opposition to the party is the Trade Union movement.

That is not unexpected. The remarkable achievement of the Conservatives is that with the support of interests and elements usually thought to be widely unpopular they have so often gained electoral victory. No similar party in any other country has been so consistently successful.

In 1794, the Portland Whigs crossed the floor of the House and joined Pitt. This union between a faction of the Whigs and a government led by a man who never called himself a Tory is sometimes held to mark the birth of the modern Tory party; an unideological, almost casual, beginning which has been reflected in the party's subsequent history. The Tory party was essentially a coalition to defend property and order against the French Revolution and to defend Britain against Napoleon. Fox and his friends might welcome the French Revolution as a liberation:

> 'triumphant looks
> Were then the common language of all eyes:
> As if waked from sleep, the Nations hailed
> Their great expectancy.'[7]

The Tories were so alarmed that they started going regularly to church.

The July Revolution in France and Wellington's doctrinaire refusal to contemplate reform swept the Tories from power, and by 1833 they held only 150 seats, less than a quarter of the House of Commons. Peel's Tamworth Manifesto, his acceptance of the Reform Bill as 'a final and irrevocable settlement of a great constitutional question'[8] and his conduct in opposition set the pattern for the future performance of the Conservative party. To help the Whig government keep out of the clutches of the Radicals was the obvious tactic for the Tories. But it was not obvious to many of them, particularly in the House of Lords; and all the skill of Peel and the influence of Wellington were needed to keep them on the path of moderate opposition. This conception of moderate opposition has become traditional, despite the absence of its original cause—the existence of an extremist band of members on the other side of the government. It has however been joined by an older tradition, dating from Walpole, of all-out opposition to practically everything the government proposes. The combination has meant that the Tories in opposition have acted in appearance like Walpole by mounting a very strong attack against practically every action of the government, but in essentials like Peel by accepting what has been done and not seeking to undo it on returning to power. Only once, from 1906–14, has the Conservative party in opposition both in appearance and reality deserted that tradition.

The landed interest and the Anglican Church were the core of the Tory party led by Peel, but it also contained many men in the Pittite tradition: Peel himself, Gladstone, Graham, Aberdeen and many others, whose chief interest was politics and whose devotion to hunting and other country pursuits was as Laodicean as that of the (Whig) Duke of Omnium.* By means of such men Peel was able to form a government much abler and more competent than its Whig predecessors, but he wrecked the instrument he had fashioned when the Irish potato famine led him to repeal the Corn Laws. He did little to prepare his party for a measure which like Catholic Emancipation he had previously opposed and which offended his party's ideological susceptibilities and also its pockets. The resultant split left the Tories with its country gentlemen—and Disraeli. Then, if ever, the Tories were in J. S. Mill's often repeated insult 'the stupid party'. Except for three short periods of minority rule they were out of office from 1846 to 1874. They were the country party both in the sense of town and country, and in the sense of court and country. Their 'countryness' at least made them less ready than their opponents to accept as inevitable the appalling conditions in the factories. In one vote on Ashley's Ten Hours Bill, 81 Liberals voted against and 71 for, 73 Peelites out of 80 voted against, while 117 out of 168 Protectionists voted for it.[11]

Disraeli, like Bismarck in Germany, saw that a wider franchise might forge an electoral alliance between the urban masses and the landed classes, and his Reform Bill of 1867 enfranchised the urban artisan—the proletariat of his opponents. Disraeli had complained of Peel stealing the Whigs' clothes while they were bathing, and he

* Peel's father, according to his sons, 'always did consider a foxhunter an enemy to God and man'.[9] Bonar Law's inability to recognise a pheasant was therefore not contrary to all Tory traditions.[10]

was now doing the same, with the important difference, however, that his clothes lifting was done in the interests of his party and did not split it.

Peel favoured 'the correction of abuses',[12] but the presumption was against change and reform. Disraeli was far less suspicious of change. 'In a progressive country', he said, 'change is constant; and the great question is, not whether you should resist change which is inevitable but whether that change should be carried out in deference to the manners, the customs, the laws, and the traditions of people, or in deference to abstract principles and arbitrary and general doctrines.'[13] This was a repudiation of the view that it was the role of the party always to be conservative with a small 'c', to oppose change when possible and to delay it when it was not, irrespective of whether such conduct was not in the long run likely to produce more change not less. Disraeli was not content merely to terminate 'the monopoly of liberalism'[14] by enfranchising the urban artisans. His government's social legislation on such matters as trade unions and public health was far in advance of that of Gladstone's.

Unfortunately the impetus died with Disraeli. Lord Randolph Churchill tried to carry on the tradition, but his tactics were faulty, the old guard was strong, and his conception of Tory democracy lacked definition. Had it not been for Gladstone's miscalculation over Home Rule, the Tory party might have returned to the wilderness out of which Disraeli had led it. Instead, 'Home Rule' gave it new allies, a cause to defend, and, with one short interlude, twenty years in office. The Conservatives had to pay for the continued support of Chamberlain and the Liberal Unionists by enacting parts of the Radical programme. All the same, for the Tory party Chamberlain was a poor exchange for Lord Randolph Churchill, who resigned saying that he had failed to 'induce the Tories into the path of rational liberalism'.[15] With Churchill near the top, the party might have preserved the Disraelian tradition of the virtues of whole-hearted reform.

The accession of Chamberlain merely brought the application of his doctrine of 'ransom' within the Conservative party. Though they were often extensive, the reforms were grudging, and the party's attitude to change partially reverted to the pre-Disraelian conception of the rearguard action, a rearguard action admittedly with an occasional skirmishing counter-attack, but only in the context of a fighting retreat. As early as 1892 Chamberlain put old age pensions among the most important reforms, but the Salisbury and Balfour governments produced nothing but enquiries. It was left to the Liberals and Asquith to bring in the first Old Age Pensions Bill in 1908; Bismarck's Germany had had Old Age Pensions since 1889. Particularly towards the end of the period 1886–1914, the Conservatives came nearer than at any time in their history to resembling a continental party of the Right or the Republican party of America without Theodore Roosevelt; nearer to being dominated by a single interest, the rich, and to neglecting their wider responsibilities to the nation as a whole.

Salisbury himself was a subtle and civilised statesman, but his chief interest was foreign affairs to which as Prime Minister he devoted most of his time. He had resigned in 1867 in protest at Disraeli's Reform Bill, and although not opposed in principle to state action* he was possessed of a deep pessimism of the future, and of suspicion of either the need or the possibility of a programme of social reform. Speaking in the sixties about Conservative opposition to the abolition of church rates, he said that at least the Conservatives 'had obtained delay and delay was life. They had kept church rates alive for thirty years. ... At any rate with their present numbers they might keep tithes twenty years after that and endowments twenty years longer still. That brought them to fifty years and that period was something in the life of a nation.'[17] It certainly was. Fortunately, Chamberlain's influence prevented this outlook from taking fully practical form under Salisbury's premiership.

'My uncle is a Tory', said Balfour, 'and I am a Liberal,'[18] yet he bore a closer resemblance to Salisbury than to Lord Randolph Churchill. His government was not without legislative achievement and in defence and foreign affairs was relatively radical, but its appetite for social reform was small. For an issue to revive the party after the Boer war Chamberlain was driven not to urgent social measures but to tariff reform without any of the trimmings that would have made it palatable to the working class voter. Admittedly, tariff reform was intended to relieve unemployment and to provide money for further social advance. And Chamberlain was much more far sighted than his opponents in his assessment of the future of British industry. But tariff reform was also part of a grand scheme of Empire unity, which the Colonies did not want and which necessitated taxes on food. The scheme as a whole was therefore both impracticable and unpopular. Stripped of its imperial

---

* When accused in 1884 of turning Socialist, he remarked of *laissez faire* that 'there are no absolute truths or principles in politics'.[16]

grandeur it was fully viable and would have led to social reform; as presented, however, it merely succeeded in splitting the Conservatives into three, and the party remained divided on the issue until the 1930s. Unable to keep his followers together, Balfour clung to office until the Committee of Imperial Defence was fully established and then went down to disastrous defeat.

A Liberal M.P., Samuel Plimsoll, had said in 1875 that 'the interests of the working classes when at issue between themselves and the capitalists are safer with the Conservatives than the Liberals'.[19] Despite the fact that the Conservatives drew increased support from the urban masses, this became less true after Lord Randolph's resignation. 'The Labour interest,' Churchill wrote in the nineties, 'is now seeking to do itself what the landed interest and the manufacturing capitalist interest did for themselves when each in turn commanded the disposition of State policy. . . . It is our business as Tory politicians to uphold the Constitution . . . if it should unfortunately occur that the Constitutional party . . . are deaf to hear and slow to meet the demands of Labour . . . the result may be that the Labour interest may identify what it will take to be defects in the Constitutional party with the Constitution itself, and in a moment of indiscriminate impulse may use its power to sweep both away.'[20] Such wisdom was unusual. To Baldwin's regret, nothing was done to undo the Taff Vale judgment.

Labour's success in the election of 1906 was thought by Balfour to be 'the faint echo of the same movement which has produced massacres in St. Petersburg, riots in Vienna, and socialist processions in Berlin',[21] a remark comparable in folly with those of Laski and Cripps in the thirties about the dangers of counter-revolution in England. The same class-ridden blindness was evident in Conservative relish of the Osborne judgment in 1909, which, had it not been reversed, would have driven the Trade Unions out of politics and back to industrial action. So the credit for the adhesion of the Trade Unionists and the Socialists to the constitution in the first years of this century must go to the Liberals, Lloyd George above all, and of course to Labour itself, not to Lord Randolph's 'constitutional party', still less to the judges.

Indeed so far from bringing anybody else within the constitution, the Conservatives found it impossible to remain within it themselves. Damaging in office, the doctrine and mentality of retreat was, disastrous in opposition, leading all too logically to the taking up of a do or die position in the last ditch against the Lloyd George

Budget and the reform of the House of Lords. Balfour tried to restrain his followers, but the Lords were beyond restraint, at least by Balfour. The lessons taught by Peel followed those of Disraeli into oblivion. Opposition was fractious, inflamed, and, under Balfour's successor Bonar Law, unconstitutional. Justly could the Liberal leader Asquith claim 'we the progressive party find ourselves here today . . . occupying Conservative and constitutional ground. . . .'.[22] Having infringed the spirit of the constitution by opposing Lloyd George's budget in the House of Lords, the Tories condoned sedition and violence over Ulster's opposition to Home Rule. They became what Bright had accused them of being fifty years before, 'the turbulent party of this nation'.[23] From 1906-14 the Conservative party in opposition betrayed itself and came close to betraying its country.

Their offence was to some extent mitigated by the government's conduct of the issue. Lacking an overall majority, the Liberals blatantly bowed to blackmail by the Irish Nationalists. Whether or not Ulster was right to fight, the government was certainly wrong. The difficulty of deciding boundaries and territories in free countries is better appreciated now than it was then. Yet the obvious solution for the government, as both Churchill and Lloyd George realised, was to compromise over Ulster, and the obduracy of Bonar Law and the Unionists does not excuse Asquith's failure to do so, any more than the government's unjustifiable attitude to Ulster excuses the general extremism of the Conservative leaders.

After taking part in Asquith's coalition, the Conservatives were the preponderant part of Lloyd George's war and post-war coalition governments. In 1922 the backbenchers revolted, Lloyd George resigned, and Bonar Law formed his government of 'under-secretaries', most of the Conservative leaders electing to stay with Lloyd George outside. Bonar Law once said that before the war the 'only two things [he] really cared for' were Tariff Reform and Ulster, 'the rest was mainly a game'[24]—a startling confession if seriously meant. Certainly the condition of the people does not seem to have preoccupied him. Fortunately the attitude of his successor, Baldwin, towards Labour was similar to that of Lord Randolph Churchill. Baldwin's objective was to mitigate or avoid a class war in Britain. In this he was strikingly successful. He did not prevent his party passing the Trade Disputes Bill of 1927 after the General Strike, but he kept its revenge down to little more than the minimum. Though merciless to the Labour party electorally he was conciliatory to Labour politically. He treated its leaders with courtesy and its aspirations with respect. He once said that Socialism and *laissez-faire* are like the North and South Pole—they don't really exist.[25] And he acted accordingly.

The inter-war period saw considerable economic progress and much useful if unspectacular social legislation. The two large blots on the Conservative inter-war record are unemployment and foreign policy. But over unemployment they followed the orthodox economic ideas of the time, and nobody else did much better. The Labour party did not, nor did Roosevelt. The problem in America was admittedly worse than in England, but it was rearmament, not F.D.R.'s public works programme, which finally cured it. 'Taken as a whole, both in administration and legislation, these were four years of solid progress,' Mr. Macmillan wrote of 1931–5. 'Nevertheless . . . I found myself with many of my friends, increasingly convinced that more radical remedies were required for the basic weaknesses of our economic system.'[26] Radical remedies were not tried, but, whether because or in spite of the government's policies, Britain made a quicker recovery than her competitors, the nation's income rising by 20 per cent between 1932 and 1937. The government's foreign and defence policy is harder to excuse, though it was better than that of their opponents and their determination to avoid war at practically any price fitted the mood of most of the country.

With Sir Winston Churchill the party returned at last to the traditions of both Peel and Disraeli. The all-party wartime coalition under Churchill produced such outstanding social legislation as Mr. Butler's Education Act, and after the Labour landslide in 1945 the party set out to create itself anew. Macmillan thought four years later that defeat had saved the Tory party.[27] Butler refreshed the party's policy and Woolton repaired its organisation. Conservative opposition to the Labour government was ruthless but not reactionary. The Welfare State was accepted as final, and only two of Labour's nationalisation measures were marked for reversal. The Conservative party became once again a genuinely national party. In the four years of Churchill's post-war premiership, the country enjoyed the best government it has had since the war. Full employment was maintained, the party built 300,000 houses in a year as it had promised, building controls and rationing were abolished, Eden as Foreign Secretary played an important part in limiting war in the Far East. The Churchill government went out of its way to be conciliatory to the Trade Unions, the country was better off than ever before, and the party was not afraid of change and reform.

A disastrous interregnum followed in the middle fifties. Over Cyprus and Suez Sir Anthony Eden became the prisoner of his right wing, and for the first time since before the first world war the party was led from the right. Under Mr. Macmillan, despite some hesitation over Africa and the end of Empire the party resumed its centre course. But the attempt to redeem the great Conservative omission of the fifties and to enter Europe ended in rejection and failure.

The Conservative years of 1951 to 1964 saw a transformation of the country. The standard of living rose more than it had in the previous half century. Taxation was lowered, controls were eased, the social services were expanded, and the whole quality of the nation's life was heightened. Poverty was not eliminated, but prosperity was a fact. Any Tory who had in 1951 correctly prophesied the improvements that the next thirteen years were to bring would have been greeted with rank disbelief as a deluded or dishonest crank. In the sixties, however, the government became increasingly accident prone; it seemed, to adapt a phrase of Macmillan's, precarious but not brilliant. The financial crisis of 1961 appeared to justify Labour's charges of mismanagement. The slogan 'You've never had it so good' was derided, and Mr. Macmillan's exact words 'most of our people have never had it so good', together with his qualification 'we cannot forget that some of our people have not shared in this general prosperity',[28] were forgotten. There seemed to be paralysis in the government and malaise in the country. By unjustifiably hanging on to power until the last moment, the party staged an extraordinary recovery and nearly won its fourth election running. But 1964 turned out to be only the first instalment of defeat; the second followed in 1966. Far better for both the country and the Tory party had the 1964 election been held earlier in the year and the 1964–6 interregnum avoided.

Representation and Money

Aneurin Bevan thought a party which picked its M.P.s 'from unrepresentative types [was] in for trouble'.[29] If he was right, the Tory party should have been in trouble long before now. In the 1966 parliament, over 25 per cent of Conservative members went to Eton or Harrow, and 80 per cent to public schools.[30] Parliamentary candidates are genuinely chosen from the base; they are not imposed upon associations by Central Office.* A list of approved candidates is drawn up and provided by Central Office, but it is not necessary to be on that list to be adopted. Since the war only one candidate adopted by a local association has been vetoed by the party.

'Conservative candidates,' Professor Rose believes, 'have tended to be socially homogeneous, though not alike politically, because party workers show a consensus about who should be an M.P.'[32] The absence of the locality rule has also contributed. Constituencies do not correspond to communities; some, as Mr. Nigel Birch said, contrasting Stockton with Orpington, are 'real places', others are scarcely even geographical expressions. Their social composition is often entirely haphazard, and the social complexion of local associations in consequence fortuitous. Also because of boundary adjustments and redistributions, it is by no means permanent.

The financial abuses of the system of choosing candidates were dealt with after the war. Before it, some constituencies demanded as much as £3,000 a year from their candidate,[33] obviously making it impossible for any but a fractional minority to apply. Since the Maxwell Fyfe reforms, able but relatively poor contenders no longer have economic or other obstacles in their way.†

The Tories in Parliament are palpably not a microcosm of the party in the country, still less of the nation; nor for that matter is the parliamentary Labour party. There is no virtue in reproducing in parliament a small scale model of the people of this country. The most photographic or representative (in this sense) parliament in the world is the East German;[34] and the People's Chamber of East Germany is as powerless as the people themselves. In all free parliaments the middle class is over-represented at the expense of the working class. The peculiarity of the House of Commons is that it has relatively more upper class and more working class members than other assemblies.

Apart from choosing their candidates, Conservative associations, like the associations of the other parties, do not concern themselves overmuch with national politics. Their proclivities vary. Perhaps the commonest situation outside the largest towns is that which Professor Birch found in his study of politics in Glossop: 'The three

* As Vice-chairman of the party, Mr. Paul Bryan had 'some influence on the choice of persons to be interviewed . . . . But at that point one's influence ended.'[31]

† But in fact nearly all the vintage 1950 intake had been chosen before the new rules were promulgated.

parties . . . are essentially social organisations whose members turn
to political activities only when this is forced upon them by national
or local elections. . . .'35 But elections come round fast, and most of
the social events have as their object the raising of money for politics.
Emphasis upon social activities is most clearly marked among the
Conservatives. The Primrose League and the Tory workingmen's
clubs were useful social auxiliaries to the Conservative army.
James I and his Bishops favoured sports and other innocent pastimes
for the populace as a means of saving people from imbibing dangerous ideas by reading the Bible. Lord Woolton realised that people,
particularly the young, could be enlisted in the Conservative cause
and kept out of political mischief by enrolment in the party and
absorption in social activity. Enough politics are mixed with the
pleasure to produce opinion leaders and ensure enthusiasm at
elections. Over the years the Young Conservatives, the only nation
wide youth movement, has become increasingly and, in its higher
reaches almost entirely, political. But many Young Conservative
branches still provide a relaxed introduction to politics and like the
debutante season in London, only with far less expense and vulgarity,
a marriage market and a social exchange.

The Conservative rank and file are drawn from every sort and
section. The Tories get about one-third of the working class vote,
nearly three-fifths of the lower middle class and almost three-
quarters of the middle class vote.36 Roughly half their voting
strength comes from the working class and half from the middle
class. Thus while they seem in Parliament to be the most class-
ridden and least representative of parties, they are, from another
point of view, the widest based and most representative. This almost
exact division of support between the workers and the middle class
is a virtual guarantee of moderate social policies.

Coleridge thought 'the stock-jobbing and moneyed interest is so
strong in this country, that it has more than once prevailed in our
foreign councils over national honour and national justice. Canning
felt this very keenly, and said he was unable to contend against the
city train-bands.'37 The moneyed interest is likely to be weaker not
stronger if there are some rich men sitting on the Tory benches.
Although they will obviously be opposed to attacks on wealth in
general, they will not be at the service of a particular interest and
they should be able to stand up to social and financial pressures. As
Mayor Kelly of Chicago pointed out to a reforming mayor: 'If
you don't run the machine, the machine will run you.'38 The same

applies to politicians and the great business 'machine'. Another American once remarked that he had never met a politician who had bribed himself. And though bribery of M.P.s is not a danger, the presence in the Tory parliamentary party of those who are immune to business blandishments is no loss.

The connections of M.P.s with business interests have been the subject of much recent research and polemic. But it would be difficult to show that a particular business or industry represented in this way had fared any better than one not so represented. All Tory M.P.s favour a system of private enterprise diluted in greater or lesser degree by state control. And there is no reason to believe that businessmen in the parliamentary party are more free enterprise-minded than non-businessmen. The most prominent exponent of the virtues of the market, Mr. Enoch Powell, is not a businessman. Indeed businessmen are not usually averse to state interference as such. They cannot afford ideological purity.

The Conservative party has been given a lot of money by the business community. But it has not been wholly dependent on such donations. By making it impossible for local associations to be financed by rich M.P.s, the Maxwell Fyfe reforms forced the local parties to rely upon a large number of small contributions. For most of their history there has been something dubious about the party funds of both the Conservative and the Labour parties. The Tories refused to publish their accounts, fearing that the munificence of big business would cause misunderstanding were it to be known in detail. Labour has been ashamed not of the enthusiasm but the indifference of its supporters. Most of its money comes from the political levy, which is paid by every Trade Unionist who lacks the wish or the courage to 'contract out'.*

After the General Strike the Conservatives altered 'contracting out' to 'contracting in' and levy payers fell by 25 per cent.[39] Other things being equal, 'contracting in', as it is more genuinely voluntary, is a fairer arrangement than 'contracting out', and maybe some Tory reprisal for the strike was inevitable. But the party system cannot work unless the major parties have adequate supplies of money, and the 1927 Act broke what was in effect a tacit bargain between them: Conservative secrecy about where their money comes from in return for Labour obtaining cash from people who do not want to pay it.

* Under 'contracting out', a Trade Unionist subscribes to the Labour Party unless he expressly declines; under 'contracting in' he does not pay unless he expressly applies.

The Attlee Government restored 'contracting out'. Under 'contracting in', 55 per cent of Trade Unionists paid the levy; in 1964 under 'contracting out' 81 per cent paid it.[40] Then Labour in its turn broke the tacit party pact by compelling companies to reveal their political contributions. There is much to be said for openness in these matters. Yet publicity carries the danger of discrimination by Labour local authorities against companies which support the Conservative party. A future Tory government, in the unlikely event of its thinking such action expedient, would be entitled to retaliate by making the Trade Union levy only payable by those who wanted to pay it.

At all events business has never achieved the dominating position in the Tory party that it possesses in the American Republican party.[41] Its general irritation with the Conservative government by 1964 does not suggest that business felt the government had given it what it wanted. Whether Sir Frank Kearton, chairman of Courtaulds, was right or wrong in saying that 'the Socialists seemed to have a better appreciation of business matters than the previous government',[42] his words imply that the Conservative party and government were not subservient to the wishes and interests of the business community.

The Conservative leadership since the war has also failed to reflect a business dominance. Churchill was in no way connected with business. Sir Anthony Eden, similarly, was not in the city mould. Mr. Macmillan was indeed a publisher, but publishing, at least when Macmillan became Premier, was scarcely in the mainstream of business, industry or finance. Sir Alec Douglas-Home was as far away from the City of London as in this country it is possible to get. Mr. Heath has for two short periods worked in a merchant bank. But he is not by upbringing, occupation, or temperament, a businessman, and his most conspicuous legislative achievement, the ending of Resale Price Maintenance, could not be depicted as a response to business pressure.

In 1903 Winston Churchill maintained that if the Tories adopted a policy of protection 'the old Conservative Party . . . would disappear, and a new party would arise, rich, materialist, and secular, whose opinions would turn on tariffs, and who could cause the lobbies to be crowded with the touts of protected industries.'[43] The old Conservative party has not disappeared. In the twenties there were some Conservative M.P.s who were active only in the budget season[44] and attended only when their own affairs could be furthered. But the forty thieves, as they were called, are a thing of the past. The party of the concurrent majority has not become a slave to the interests that support it. Though not buttressed by ideology, it has been able to control those interests. Politics have remained superior to business, politicians superior to businessmen, and the party superior to pressure groups. The organisation of the party, the concentration of power in the leadership, its wide electoral support, its empirical approach, its will to power, have assured its primacy over those behind it.

The Leadership

The former magical process whereby the Conservatives evolved a leader or a Prime Minister without a contested election has been abandoned. In 1955 Sir Anthony Eden succeeded Churchill. Probably he had more support in the parliamentary party than Mr. Butler. Whether he had or not, he would still have become Premier. As Lord Chandos said: 'As half a dozen of the most powerful of us had unreservedly decided to back Anthony Eden for the succession, the ambitions of others appeared illusory, even ridiculous.'[45] After Eden resigned, Lords Salisbury and Kilmuir took a poll of the Cabinet as to whether the successor should be Macmillan or Butler.* Many backbenchers took steps to convey their views to the Whips, and probably most of them supported Macmillan. But the key factor in bringing him the Premiership was the overwhelming backing of the Cabinet.

In 1963 all backbenchers gave their preferences to the Chief Whip, or were asked by their Whips whom they would like, and who was their second or third choice. As in referenda, the power to ask the question and to frame it in various ways was important. And as usual in referenda, the askers seem to have got the answer they wanted. At the same time the Cabinet was polled by the Lord Chancellor*, the views of the peers were sought by the Lords Whip, and the preferences of the areas, the Young Conservatives, and the Women's National Advisory Committee were sought and noted. This information was conveyed by Mr. Macmillan, who had himself interviewed many Ministers and others in hospital, and the result was the evolution of the Earl of Home into Sir Alec Douglas-Home.

Perhaps the choice of Sir Alec was the best way of keeping most

* After the death of Henry Pelham, George II asked the Cabinet to suggest a First Lord of the Treasury. But the Lord Chancellor thought it unseemly to 'poll in Cabinet' for a Prime Minister.[46]

of the party united. Certainly the public row, the coincidence of
Mr. Macmillan's retirement with the party conference, and the
manoeuvring, the electioneering and the arguments, made the
Conservative party more interesting that it had been for years. But
those who liked the result did not like the row, and those who liked
the row did not like the result. The method of selection indeed had
been either too formal or not formal enough. There is much to be
said for totally informal soundings and weighings to ascertain the
man best able to hold the party together. But once it is claimed that
the views of everybody have been carefully invited and fairly
assessed, there is a strong case for conducting the process under
proper rules, which will preclude even the most disaffected from
alleging that the selection was rigged.

Sir Alec therefore set up an enquiry, and the Shadow Cabinet
produced a scheme of unnecessary complexity. The House of
Lords, the Women's Advisory, and the Young Conservatives have
been eliminated. Only M.P.s have a vote, but the procedure contains the extraordinary feature that the winner does not necessarily
win. There has to be a second and possibly third ballot if the leader
on the first does not get 15 per cent more of the votes than the
runner up. A winner of the first ballot with more than 50 per cent
of the votes might not get the job and might be displaced by one
who had not even stood on the first ballot. In practice if a candidate
does gain a majority his rivals are likely to withdraw and to make
the second ballot purely formal, as happened in 1965.

Election now taking place by a secret ballot, there is a process of
whiteballing rather than blackballing; a leader is chosen because
of the support he commands, not because of the lack of opposition
to him. 'Safe' men have lost their advantage.

Professor Mckenzie has argued that despite the apparently great
differences in structure between the Conservative and Labour
parties in reality the distribution of power within the two parties is
overwhelmingly similar; and he points to 'the striking fact that in
this century there have been fewer Labour leaders deposed than
there have been Conservative'.[47] Certainly the monolithic and
placid Conservative exterior often conceals bitter inner conflicts,
and unlike the Labour party the Conservatives have four or five
times in this century got rid of their leader. That, however, does
not prove Dr. Mckenzie's thesis. A leader or ruler, who is subject
to violent overthrow, may be a great deal more powerful until he
is overthrown than a leader or a ruler whose position is not in

similar jeopardy. Almost half the mediaeval kings of England were murdered, deposed, or had to contend with serious revolts at one time or another, yet they possessed far more power than, say, King Edward VII or George V, whose thrones were not at risk. Similarly the violent mortality rate among renaissance princes in Italy was high but their power was often complete. Frequent assassination is an indication of despotism not of its absence.

Every Conservative leader appointed in this century except Bonar Law has either been dismissed by his party or the House of Commons, or has been at some time under heavy pressure to leave.* Apart from Bonar Law and Churchill, only Baldwin's retirement was entirely voluntary, and in 1930–1 his position was in the greatest jeopardy. But for his famous attack on the press lords and Duff Cooper's victory in the St. George's bye-election he would have had to resign. Put like this, the position of Conservative leaders seems politically rather like that of Sheik of Abu Dhabi, only one of the last thirteen of whom has died a natural death. Considered individually, however, the Conservative leader's hold on power appears rather more secure.

There were strong reasons for the departure of Balfour and both the Chamberlains. Balfour had lost three elections and control of the party. Moreover he resigned, he was not overthrown. If he had chosen to fight, he would probably have carried the day. Austen Chamberlain seemed to be trying to merge the party with one of its opponents, to lead his troops into another camp. His followers not unnaturally objected to a project fundamentally in conflict with the history, traditions and objectives of the party, and fundamentally at variance with the customs and spirit of the British political system. A party exists to fight its opponents, not to join them, to gain power not to hand it over to others. Neville Chamberlain's appeasement policy had demonstrably failed and he was a plainly unsuitable war leader. Even then the vast majority of the party continued to support him: only thirty-three M.P.s voted against him and forty abstained.

The resignations of Eden and Macmillan were precipitated by ill health. Possibly Eden would anyway have had to go later; Macmillan would have led his party into the next election had it not been for his operation. Still if ill health was the immediate cause of both resignations, it would not by itself have been sufficient. Both

---

* Even Churchill was told by his Chief Whip in 1947 that a number of his senior colleagues felt he should retire. 'He reacted violently, banging the floor with his stick,'[48]

Prime Ministers were in trouble before their illnesses, and Mr. Macmillan only narrowly survived a serious revolt after the collapse of the Brussels negotiations. Yet their opponents could not have removed a fit Eden or Macmillan.

Sir Alec Douglas-Home, like Balfour, could, had he wished, have stayed on—for a time. But once he lost possession of Downing Street, his weakness on television outweighed the great personal affection he generated.

It is because so much is demanded of him, that a Tory leader is vulnerable. There is in the party a disposition to obey, a belief that the direction of policy and the party should be left to the leadership. All this amounts to a strong streak of Bonapartism or Gaullism. The leader is a mystical representative of the party, embodying in his person its tradition, faith, and ideals, and thus deserving of loyalty, support, and obedience. Yet should he fail to lay low the enemy, he is liable, like other sacred kings and fertility symbols, to find himself sacrificed in favour of a successor better fitted to bring deliverance and prosperity to the party.

Party Organisation and Party Conference

The Conservative party in parliament long preceded the party organisation outside, and its supremacy has never been in question. The National Union formed in 1867, while more than the equivalent of those bands of women and campfollowers which until recently were indispensable adjuncts to an army in the field, has never been more than the equally indispensable supply services without which a modern army would be unable either to move or to fight. It has rarely suffered from the illusion that it was in command of the army or that it was the elite force in the front line.

The position accorded to the leader rules out formal democracy. The National Union has, nevertheless, an elaborate structure of representative institutions. Attention is paid to what is said in them especially on pocket book and voting issues, but high policy is little affected and not often discussed. Prominent members of Parliament in disagreement with the party leadership on a major issue may take their fight to the National Union, as happened over Ireland in the twenties and India and rearmament in the thirties; but even if the leadership were defeated, it would not have to change its policy, so long as the bulk of the parliamentary party remained loyal. The representative institutions of the National Union enable it to preserve some limited local autonomy over its own affairs within a context of quiet Central Office supervision. They are not designed to give it control of the party as a whole.

The National Union is little more than an ammunition train, but it is an essential one. If it cannot control the party leaders, the party leaders could not operate without it. The constituency activists work not only through the National Union; more often they work directly upon the party's M.P.s. 'As long as the Conservative party continued to accept the [coalition]', Hoare wrote to *The Times* in 1922, 'the majority of the Conservative members of the House of Commons were prepared to support it. It is now certain that the rank and file ... have withdrawn this general acceptance.'[49] Shortly afterwards Conservative M.P.s did the same.

The Tory party is willing to be led, sometimes in strange directions and to strange places. But it is not blindfold and its patience and trust are not inexhaustible. Its veto is seldom used; the existence of that veto is nevertheless important. The party leader is not free to do what he likes. 'Toryism, or the policy of the Tories, being the proposed or practiced embodiment, as the case may be, of the national will and character', wrote Disraeli, 'it follows that Toryism must occasionally represent and reflect the passions and prejudices of the nation as well as its purer energies, and its more enlarged and philosophical views.'[50] The Bow Group can be only one facet of Toryism. The National Union is more representative with its generally right wing though not extremist attitudes, and the party leader cannot leave it behind. Lord Derby exaggerated when he said in 1912 'we can all of us split the party'.[51] Even in his day few people could, and the number is far fewer today. But the danger of a split is always there, and however anxious a Tory leader is to capture the centre he must be careful that in doing so he does not lose the solid right.

The party conference has had its importance both enhanced and diminished by television. The conference has now to cheer the faithful and to impress the infidel. Conservative conferences are carefully stage managed, and much of the proceedings are more of an exercise in revivalist enthusiasm than a serious discussion of issues and policy. Yet an excess of docility would on the television screen seem like spinelessness and sycophancy. Hence differences must not be totally muffled by meaningless resolutions and appeals not to weaken the hand of the leadership. Some genuine debate has to be allowed. On the other hand, everybody present realises that they are not, as it were, alone. No member of the conference wants to let down the party in front of the national audience. Everybody is on his best behaviour, naturally a great aid to the leadership.

Those who attend the conference are doubly unrepresentative. As well as the normal disparity between the party militant and the party voter, conference attenders are not mandated by their local associations but vote as they like. Hence they may not be even representative of the activists. Obviously it would be ridiculous for a body so composed to be able by its votes to bind anyone to anything, and conference votes do not in any way bind the party leaders. Yet because defeats for the leadership would look bad outside the party and might be depressing within it, considerable trouble is taken to avoid them. Probably, however, the effect of the party conference is exaggerated. The 1960 conference was dead; in the year following the party prospered. The 1961 conference at Brighton was considered to be particularly successful because of its endorsement of the government's policies on crime and on the Common Market. It was followed shortly afterwards by a series of crushing defeats in bye-elections.

If the National Union has not attained the 'complete discipline'[52] which Salisbury once urged upon a deputation from it, it has continued to provide the 'ardent partisans' without which it is impossible to fight an election. Conservative Central Office, the Civil Service of the party, has been an equally reliable instrument of the party leader, who appoints all its principal officers. Like other bureaucracies the party bureaucracy has increased its power at the expense of the elected element. Although there are a number of committees of the National Union which meet at Central Office and which advise the party on various matters, all these bodies are more consent-gaining than decision-taking institutions. Central Office in no way controls the elected leaders of the party in parliament—indeed it has remained firmly in their grip—but it largely controls the elected part of the party organisation.

Image and Style
In their most true blue moments Conservatives feel that it is contrary to the natural order of things for them to be out of power. Pointing to the solidarity and breadth of their electoral support, they see themselves as the only truly national party, and their opponents as well-meaning but heretical sectarians, always mistaking the part for the whole. In their view theirs is the only party consistently pursuing the national interest, undeluded by the claims

of doctrinal orthodoxy or outdated politica l dogma. In Tory eyes
the Liberal preoccupation with Home Rule and the avowed class
nature of the Labour party are equally schismatic. The preservation
of the national interests of the country is seen by the Tories to be
the particular care and skill of their party. They think it is the only
one able to run its own affairs efficiently and with dignity. And
pointing with scorn at the frequent factional squabbles of their
opponents, they believe that theirs is the only party to which the
government of the country can be safely entrusted.

Their opponents traverse all these claims. They see the Tories not
as a national party but as a narrow class party dedicated to the
preservation of inequality. They see the Tory party as fighting a
slow rearguard action in defence of the privileges of the ruling class.
Tory empiricism is dismissed as mere lack of principle or perhaps
as an inability to formulate and understand political doctrine. They
regard Tory zeal for reform as mere hypocrisy, and scoff that
Conservatives are in favour of every reform but the next one. So
far from the national interest and honour being safe in the hands
of the Conservatives, they allege that all the disasters and humilia-
tions the country has suffered—the Boer war, Munich, Suez—have
occurred under Conservative governments. They dismiss the power
structure of the Conservative party as a mere exercise in Fuehrer-
Prinzip. And looking at the public school bias in the parliamentary
party and the emphasis upon social activity in Conservative work in
the constituencies, they see the Conservative party at the national
and parliamentary level as the upper classes at work, and at the
constituency and local level as the middle and lower classes at play.*

The concentration of power in the leadership, the purposive
discipline of the rank and file, the feeling that quarrels should not
be pursued in public, usually enable the party to present to the
electorate a face of unity and order. In the guided democracy of
the Tory party there is more guidance than democracy. Conservatives
believe that when possible opinions should be weighed rather than

* 'A Tory,' said Hazlitt, 'is one who is governed by sense and habit alone. He
considers not what is possible but what is real; he gives might the preference over
right. . . . He has no principles himself, nor does he profess to have any, but will cut
your throat for differing with any of his bigoted dogmas, or for objecting to any act of
power that he supposes necessary to his interest. . . . He is not for empty speculations,
but for full pockets. . . .'53

votes counted, as in the old way of choosing the leader. The 1922 Committees and other party committees never vote; the sense of the meeting is conveyed to the party leaders, a practice which tends to heal not exacerbate divisions.

Disputes, too, are seldom embittered by ideological conflicts or accusations of heresy. All-out war is avoided, and the wide ranging coalition of interests, individuals and associations that makes up the party is enabled to maintain its unity and to stand together against its opponents. In 1922 most of the party's leaders were sundered from the party, but there were no *autos da fè*. They were not opposed by official party candidates, though some of them had to face Beaverbrook ones. They went into the wilderness but not into opposition, and the fissure was soon closed.

Not that the party is immune from heresy hunting. Some Conservative associations have a rabid zeal for orthodoxy, and their hand has been strengthened by the party's post-war financial reforms. Many others, while wishing their member to support the party, are reconciled to the view that it is a matter for him. And both the Whips and the leadership are remarkably tolerant. Tory M.P.s sometimes give up the whip; only two since 1914 have had it taken away*. After much criticism of the government's economic and foreign policies, Harold Macmillan even opposed his party's candidate, Quintin Hogg, at the Oxford bye-election in 1938 without losing the whip and without official rebuke. Until Munich, his rebellious activities did not lead to 'any sense of ill feeling . . . expressed by fellow members, by the Whips' office, or even, with few exceptions, by ministers themselves'.[54]

There is something of a 'lace-curtain' atmosphere in the party. Outward respectability must be maintained even if unmentionable vices are being stealthily practised inside. Yet outward decorum helps to produce inner decorum as well. The discipline and the manners spread inwards. This style of the Conservative party makes it a formidable electoral opponent. However much the voter dislikes the idea of being ordered about, he does not want this amiable anarchy to spread to the political parties. To his mind, parties if they are to govern the country successfully, should at least be able to govern themselves. In this respect the Conservative party with its internal good manners, its apparent inner peace, its leadership and its unity, usually cuts a better figure than Labour with its factional feuds, its boisterous quarrels, its ever-manoeuvring leader-

* Sir W. Wayland (for a time) and Captain Cunningham-Reid.

ship and its divided structure. Very occasionally, of course, when Labour is initially soothed by the possession of the sweets of office and the Conservatives are frustrated by their absence, the roles are reversed.

Principles

The Tory party has emotions but no doctrine. The idea of an apostolic succession of Conservative dogma from Bolingbroke to Chatham to Pitt, through Canning to Peel, and on to Disraeli and Salisbury, into the twentieth century with Balfour, continued in Bonar Law, Baldwin and Chamberlain, and culminating after the war in Churchill, Eden and Macmillan, is as mythical as Macaulay deemed the doctrine of apostolic succession in the Christian Church. It is mere ancestor-worship. Many Conservative leaders have not believed the same things themselves for any great length of time, let alone held the same views as their successors and predecessors. St. Vincent of Lérins's requirement of a doctrine that it should have been 'believed everywhere, always and by all' would be a far greater stumbling block for the Tory party than for the Roman Catholic Church. Nor would a transposition of Newman's doctrine of development bring continuity and consistency to the Tory deposit of faith. The Conservative party has maintained continuity and preserved its identity, but there has been no coherent ideological development.

For instance, the principles that the country's interests should not be lost sight of while factional squabbles take place within it, and that Britain should play a part in the world fully commensurate with her power seem today to be enshrined in the Tory ark and to be particularly associated with that arch imperialist Disraeli. Yet until about 100 years ago it was the Conservatives who traditionally favoured restraint abroad, Disraeli himself exclaiming in 1862 that '. . . to hold aloof from that turbulent diplomacy which only distracts the minds of a people from internal improvement . . . these were once the principles which regulated Tory statesmen. . . .'[55] Lord Randolph Churchill, who deplored Gladstone's imperialistic bombardment of Alexandria in 1882, was a Little Englander whose ideas on foreign policy accorded more with those of Fox than of Pitt.

Disraeli laid down Conservative principles in his speech at the Crystal Palace in 1872, Baldwin endorsed them in 1934, telling the party conference 'You cannot go wrong if you stick to them', and the Maxwell Fyfe Committee on party reorganisation said in 1948 that they were 'as valid today as when they were first propounded'. 'The Tory Party', said Disraeli, 'has three great objects . . . to maintain the institutions of the country . . . to uphold the Empire of England . . . and to elevate the condition of the people.'[56] The first and third, at least, of these principles are timeless, and their significance lies as much in what they are not as in what they are. Truth, as Baldwin might have said, is too many-sided to be expressed in simple confident statements. Few things concerning politics, government, and society, a Conservative believes, are as simple as they seem, and any statement of opinion, fact or belief will at best express part of the truth and often merely distort it. It will always be possible to imagine instances or circumstances which will seriously qualify if not contradict it.

> Reason, which fifty times for one does err.
> Reason, an *ignis fatuus* of the mind,
> Which leaves the light of Nature, sense, behind.[57]

If Conservatives do not go all the way with Rochester, they believe that Reason must be discliplined by the knowledge of its own inadequacy. Abstract propositions must be treated as at best mere approximations to the truth, liable to be discarded as soon as the conditions which produced their formulation have changed or passed away. This belief that there is more to politics than the maintenance over an extended period of a consistent set of doctrines is an intense irritation to all ideologues. Mr. Douglas Jay sternly admonished the Conservative party for never having 'stood consistently for any policy: neither for free trade against protection; nor *laissez-faire* against interference; nor collective security against pacifism; nor even private ownership against public ownership . . .'[58] Yet the attitude condemned by Mr. Jay is wholly sensible: when a country is stronger economically than other countries free trade is the right policy for it; when it is not stronger, protection may be the right policy. The battle lines between *laissez-faire* and state interference cannot be drawn for all time. Conservatives favour private ownership; they do not say that public ownership is wrong at all times and on all occasions. The scholastic conception of politics, the suggestion that it is the function of a political party to adopt a policy and to stick to it even when conditions change, is odious

D

to the Tory party. Principle and policy, the party believe, were made for party; not party for principle and policy.

The nearest thing the Tory party has to a doctrine is an anti-doctrine: they believe that all political theories are at best inadequate, at worst false. This, the party's great strength, is the only sensible basis for a Conservative party. Even in the static eighteenth century David Hume pointed out that 'all human institutions, and none more than government, are in continual fluctuation'.[59] In the infinitely more dynamic and fluctuating twentieth century it is futile to think that the only things which should not change are political institutions, political arrangements, and political ideas. Change cannot be prevented, but it can be guided. That is what sensible Conservatism tries to do. Reactionary Conservatism tries to prevent change or, failing that, tries to undo it. 'Rule and change nothing', said the will of the Emperor Francis I,[60] an attitude that leads to an explosion or to impotence, neither of which is conservative. As Canning warned, 'they who resist indiscriminately all improvements as innovations may find themselves compelled at last to submit to innovations although they are not improvements.'[61] Conservative principles and the Conservative party must change in line with everything else. In every age Conservatives have to do what Disraeli erroneously believed Bolingbroke to have done: 'eradicate from Toryism all those absurd and odious doctrines which Toryism had adventitiously adopted'.[62]

Scepticism and empiricism are the foundations of Conservatism: scepticism of all human ideas and all human endeavour, and the determination to look at things as they are. Of course the scepticism often hardens into orthodoxy. Principles and institutions are claimed to be immutable, part of the sacred inheritance in whose defence suicide would be preferable to ignoble surrender. This was a common attitude in 1911. And empiricism often degenerates into, so to speak, post-empiricism: looking at things as they were instead of as they are.

At its highest level the conflict between scepticism and orthodoxy might be dramatised as a conflict between the two greatest conservative philosophers, Hume and Burke. Hume, believing that 'all general maxims in politics ought to be established with great caution',[63] was sceptical about everything, in favour of moderation in all things, averse to last ditches, empirical without curb. Burke shared Hume's suspicion of general political truths and knew change to be inevitable. But his reverence for Britain, her history, her constitution, and his Whig overlords, sometimes on crucial issues ossified his prejudices into dogma and made the finished product of his thought inconsistent with its basic conceptions. Thus he defended the eighteenth century representative system in opposition to Pitt's attempts at reform, and insisted that peace never could and never should be made with the revolutionary government in France. Burke's occasional dogmatism was Whiggish, and there has often been a deal of Whiggery in the old guard's perennial attempts to prevent the Conservative party following the path of empiricism, a path which frequently leads disconcertingly close to the headquarters of the other side.

Hume, said Dr. Johnson, was 'a Tory by chance.'[64] Chance or no, Hume's Toryism is the dominant strand in British Conservatism. Yet the empiricism of the Conservative leaders has always drawn outraged protests from the less flexible and more 'highly-principled' members of the party. The noblest of the laments for lost Tory virtue was perhaps Ashley's denunciation of the first years of Peel's government: 'The disappointment is general; men looked for high sentiments and heard small opinions: for principles and were put off with expediency.' Ashley went on to attribute to Peel 'a mighty desire to reverse the rule of the apostle and be first peaceable and then pure',[65] a desire which would be a laudable ambition in any leader of the Conservative party or indeed of any other party. Salisbury said of Disraeli's 1867 Reform Bill that it was 'a political betrayal which has no parallel in our Parliamentary annals'.[66] 'I belong, I believe', said Carson, 'to what is called the Unionist party. Why it is called the Unionist party I fail to understand, unless it is to remind people in this country that it was the party that betrayed the Unionists.'[67] Such complaints that the party's principles have been abandoned by its leaders have down to the present day provided counterpoint to the empirical tune played by the Tory leadership.

The attitude of these post-empiricists is exemplified in a letter Hicks Beach wrote to Salisbury in 1886: 'I confess much doubt whether the country can be governed nowadays by persons holding opinions which you and I should call even moderately Conservative.'[68] Hicks Beach's attitude to Lord Randolph Churchill absolves him from being a fully representative old guardsman. But his assumption that Conservatism was something given from the past and should only under *force majeure* be influenced by the ideas and conditions of the present is typical of post-empiricism. The repudiation of such ideas and the acceptance, instead, of the belief, both that the Tory party must change in step with the country, and that the welfare of the party is more important than the preservation of some once cherished interests and attitudes, have distinguished the Conservative party from some other parties of the right. They are the foundation of its electoral success, and of the country's peaceful development. Carson's bitter gibe that he and Ulster and Ireland had been only puppets to 'get the Conservative party into power',[69] was in reality a compliment. The alternative, after all, to such behaviour by a party, is revolution or civil war. The Tory party has not been 'too fond of the right to pursue the expedient'. While it respects and reveres and relies upon the past, it is not wedded to the past, and it uses its sense of history to preserve not the past but the future.

If asked to state what it stands for, the answer of the Tory party is '*Si monumentum requiris, circumspice.*' It stands for the country at any given moment, for society as at present constituted, for all the various relationships and institutions, which make up the body politic, and for the religious, political, economic and social structure of the nation. To try to sum this up in neat doctrinal formulations would be an attempt to codify the mystery of life. Besides, the consistency of other parties is usually more one of name than reality, and ample casuistry is needed to conceal that their policies have fluctuated as much as those of the Conservatives. At rock bottom in the Conservative party, there is patriotism and fierce attachment to the institutions of the country, reliance on tradition and respect for continuity, belief in leadership and authority, belief in order and security, and distrust of puritanism, scepticism about politics, and hostility to abstractions. A certain pessimism because of his acceptance of the notion of original sin is also proper to a Conservative,* and above all, perhaps, a realisation of the intricacy and untidiness of things. In the Tory view, simplicity of doctrine and institutions, a dominant characteristic of the French Revolution, as Burke pointed out, is the path to tyranny. In consequence a Tory seeks a wide proliferation of relationships, associations, institutions and ideas as the strongest safeguard of freedom. Simplicity is the antithesis of Conservatism, complexity its foundation.

---

* Professor Rose has alleged that 'Conservatives appear to regard original sin as a sword with which to impale Socialists, rather than as a dilemma with Socialists impaled on one horn and Conservatives on the other.'[70] But a natural result of original sin is to believe opponents to be more at its mercy than allies.

Electoral Success

In the most highly industralised country in the world, the party which was created to further the interests of the industrial worker should on the face of it have been the normal governor. In fact, the Labour party has only three times in its life succeeded in winning a double figure majority in the House of Commons. The usual explanation of Conservative success is the 'deference voter'. Britain, the theory runs, is a country deeply imbued with aristocratic, not to say snobbish, feelings; hence large numbers of working class voters in deference to what they conceive to be social, educational or financial superiority, vote for the party which embodies aristocratic privilege and business success instead of for the party which protects and furthers their interests. But for workers to vote for a Conservative party is not an exclusively British aberration. In the United States, at least one in three of the lowest paid workers regularly vote Republican.[71] The French Socialist and Communist parties have been able to capture only 60 per cent of the industrial working class.[72] In Italy about 30 per cent of the poorer groups vote for the Christian Democrats or for parties further to the right.[73] In Germany, too, the Christian Democrats win a third of the working class vote.[74] There is, then, nothing peculiar about large numbers of voters in the lower income groups eschewing the Workers' or Socialist parties and plumping for the right. The only exceptional feature in Britain is that the right has usually been able to secure just that extra number of them that makes the difference between victory and defeat.

Besides, if the theory of the deference voter were true, Conservative working class voters would agree more with Labour policies than with Conservatives and be pulled to the Tory side by other considerations. In fact surveys have shown an exactly contrary state of affairs.[75] In the fifties Conservative voters agreed with more of their party's policies than did Labour voters, and more Labour voters than Conservative found themselves in agreement more with the opposing party than with their own. When the party was in power, Conservative policy was more popular than the Conservative party. So far from voters being seduced from their natural inclination to vote Labour by feelings of deference leading them to vote Conservative, the process was the other way: voters were weaned away from their own personal Conservative inclinations and ideas to vote Labour for reasons of class solidarity. There is in fact remarkably little difference between the attitude of Tory and Labour working class voters,[76] though the Tories tend to be rather better informed.[77]

The deference voter is merely a useful myth to conceal and excuse Labour's long electoral failure. The real reasons for the success of the Conservative party are more prosaic and obvious: the failings of its opponents, its unity, its other merits, and good luck. The Conservative party has sometimes gone into battle ill equipped for the modern world. But one side, after all, has got to win. Philip Guedalla once pointed out that in 1859 Napoleon III's army was perfectly attuned to fighting the last war—the wars of 1792 to 1815. But, he added, you couldn't beat the Austrians at that game; they went into battle all arrayed to fight the war before that. In an election as in war, it is difficult for both sides to lose. Yet, Labour's shortcomings are only part of the story.

In English politics the prizes go to the party that does not split. The Tories split over Catholic Emancipation in the eighteen-twenties and over the Corn Laws in 1846. The result was a long period of Liberal supremacy. They split again over Tariff Reform and the sequel was the Liberal victories of 1906 and 1910. Except on that issue, which did not cause a permanent division, the Conservatives have preserved their unity since 1867 and received occasional Liberal transfusions into their ranks. The Liberals have suffered major splits in 1886 and 1916 as well as several minor ones and have for the last half century been engaged in a losing fight with the Labour party. The Labour party started from nothing, had one major split in 1931 and throughout the fifties was in a condition of endemic fissure. In these circumstances Conservative dominance is understandable.

A split is usually only an outward and visible sign of an inner contradiction and deficiency. The Tories have remained in one piece because of the structure of their organisation, its centralisation and its flexibility, and because of their discipline and tolerance, which have generally enabled the party to be and to remain representative of the country.

The British Tory party has been the most successful right wing party in the world because it has not been right wing. The party has nearly always governed itself from the left and the country from the centre. It has therefore been able to enlist in its support the immense power of conservatism with a small c. 'All great peoples are conservative,' said Carlyle.[78] In fact, al peoples whether great or small are conservative. Man is a conservative animal. Woman is more so. The party that can appeal to people's basic love and trust of the familiar, and harness their fear of the strange and unknown, is likely to win. And paradoxically it is the parties of the left which have in the modern world usually ministered most effectively to this basic instinct. At the beginning of the Third Republic it was the left which was genuinely conservative, the right which wanted to reverse what had been done. And from 1875 to 1918 the right never won an election. The Radicals, the normal governing party of the Third Republic, were despite their name a profoundly conservative force. The Republican party in America has since 1932 been the normal minority party, because American voters for long believed that it did not properly accept the New Deal; so the Democrats were able to harness the forces of conservatism to their bandwagon. Similarly the Social Democratic parties of Scandinavia were so successful at donning the clothes of conservatism that they enjoyed prolonged periods of power. Up till now the Labour party has not been able to do the same.

By almost never being reactionary, but by being genuinely conservative, the Tories have avoided frightening the voters into believing that they would produce an upheaval if they were returned to power. Even when they were reactionary after the Liberal victory of 1906, they were careful to confine their efforts to such matters as did not closely affect the material interests of the workers, letting through the Trade Disputes Act and other measures.

Every time the Conservatives have fared badly in an election in this century in 1906, 1923, 1945 and 1966, they have either forfeited or lost the force of natural conservatism to the other side. They have not won all the other elections, but in their other defeats they have either been recovering from a previous disaster or as in 1964 done far better than could reasonably have been expected. 1906 was not a vote for radical reform. The Balfour government had offended natural conservatism by its Education Act and by the controversy over Tariff Reform. 'The demand was for a return to nineteenth century Gladstonianism, to the policies of Little England, to elected School Boards, and to Free Trade.'[79] In 1923 Baldwin without warning or preparation asked for a mandate to change the country's fiscal policy. No wonder Balfour talked about 'the unhappy folly of the late election'.[80] In 1945 Labour's emphasis on collectivism, planning, and social equality was nearer the wartime realities of full employment, austerity, and an uncompetitive and controlled economy, than were Conservative glorifications of

the ideal of free enterprise and the virtues of freedom and indivi-
dualism. Besides the Labour leaders had for five years been familiar
figures in the government. In 1966 the Conservatives fought the
election on policies to reform the Welfare State, reform the Trade
Unions, abolish agricultural subsidies, enforce far greater competition
in industry, and enter the Common Market. In 1966 as in some of
the other years they would almost certainly have lost anyway,
but a heavy emphasis on radical policies made their failure assured.
The creation of that kind of conflict is self-defeating.

The Tories will neglect their representative role at their peril.
It is no part of their function to put forward policies regardless of
their acceptability to the voters. That can be done well enough by
the Liberal party. More competition and efficiency are of course
essential. But a party which gets half its votes from the workers
and which believes in authority and security can not sensibly make
a religion out of the uncontrolled forces of the Market. The
devotees of that Supreme Being are a select band. Traditionally
the Conservatives have followed Bentham's maxim: 'So act that
people, as far as possible get what they want.'[81] Derided though
this can be, as the product of the Tories 'will to power',[82] it is a
proper and desirable way for a party to behave.

Because of its power structure, its unity and its discipline the
Tory party has generally been a good instrument of government.
'Post-empiricism' and the number of interests which support it
are a brake and have sometimes precluded much needed measures
of reform. But the nature of the party system and the attitude of the
electorate in any case limit the scope of drastic action open to a
political party. Parties can transmit radicalism, they can seldom
create it without going down to defeat. If the Tory party has rarely
been in front of the country, it has never for long been behind it.

The party which is in theory less addicted to change than its
opponents has been far better at changing itself than they have.
Tories have been prepared to sacrifice the alleged interests of
Conservatism to the real interests of the party. In so doing they
have acted not only to the party's advantage but to the advantage
of the country and in the spirit of the two-party system. For that
reason the Tory party can fairly claim to be a truly national party.

III

THE LABOUR PARTY

The aim of Socialism is to give greater freedom to the individual.
CLEMENT ATTLEE[1]

*I found myself . . . cheering the Red Flag in the midst of [Russian]
soldiers, not one of whom understood a word we were saying. However,
it was a great joy for me to feel myself in a Socialist country, even
though the masses were starving.*
GEORGE LANSBURY[2]

*The most conservative man in the world is the British trade unionist
when you want to change him. You can make a great speech to him on
unity, but when you have finished, he will say, 'What about
funeral benefits?'*
ERNEST BEVIN[3]

The Labour party was formed to secure working class representation in parliament. Yet it has never succeeded in gaining a
commanding predominance of the workers' vote. It has won
over sixty per cent of it, but under the normal laws of chance fifty
per cent would be expected to support the party. Had Labour
captured the class it avowedly exists to represent, it would have
been in permanent power like the Social Democrats in Sweden.
'If the wonderful unity in the strike', Ernest Bevin wrote in the
summer of 1926, 'would be shown in politics, Labour could solve
the mining and similar difficulties through the ballot box.'[4] The
party kept its vote remarkably steady between the wars and sharply
increased it afterwards, but it has never come anywhere near
transforming industrial into electoral unity.

Like the Republicans in America, the Labour party has been
identified with a single interest, and like them Labour for long
suffered from having virtually all its eggs in one basket. In the
fifties, Trade Unions were widely regarded not as stalwart defenders
of the downtrodden and the oppressed, but as over-mighty subjects
holding the rest of the country up to a yearly ransom. The unpopularity of the Unions and their reluctance to adjust themselves
to a new age rubbed off onto Labour.

93

In the sixties the Unions' unpopularity declined—perhaps because of the unpopularity of the government, perhaps because people thought the government should be blamed for not reforming them. At all events dislike of the Unions was not great enough to prevent Labour's victories in 1964 and 1966. Labour politicians have long had it in mind to loosen the Trade Union connection and to make their party more like the Democrats in America. Yet Labour's industrial strength ensures that the party, even when badly defeated electorally, can never be negligible. As George Buchanan said in parliament shortly before the formation of the first Labour government, 'this is not a Labour party. The Labour party are in the factories.'[5] Though the Trade Unions are sometimes Labour's albatross, they are its engine and its ballast as well.

In a predominantly two-party system the emergence of a third party depends less upon its own virtues than upon the deficiencies of the two parties in possession. Tradition, habit, inertia, money, the electoral system, all give the reigning parties an advantage over the newcomer, which, in the absence on their part of extreme political incompetence, should be decisive. In America there has been a succession of third parties, but only one, the Republican, succeeded in establishing itself as one of the two major parties. And the way of the Republican party was smoothed by the break up of one of the two major parties and by a serious split in the other one. In every other case the third party was not similarly favoured; it had to face two major parties and never succeeded in establishing itself.

In the 1890s there was more force behind the new Populist party in America than behind the formation of a new party in England. Yet by moving sharply to the left and nominating William Jennings Bryan for President, the Democrats swallowed the new party. In England the far weaker Labour infant survived. It was saved partly by its weakness: the other parties were not sufficiently alarmed to try very hard to kill it; and partly by the fear aroused in Britain by the attempts in the United States of militant employers' associations to use the law to emasculate trade unions. Industrial events in America thus helped to prevent an English repetition of American political events, the absorption of the third party. But chiefly the creation and survival of the Labour party was due to the inadequacy of the other two parties.

The Conservatives, as their growing success in urban and industrial constituencies proved, were by the end of the century at least as much the party of the urban workers as the Liberals – but not of the workers' leaders.* While most of the workers in the nineties were fervent imperialists, their leaders, for religious and social rather than political reasons, were practically all Liberals. Most of them were Noncomformists—Mawdsley who stood with Winston Churchill as a Tory candidate in 1899 came from Anglican Lancashire—and the strength of the Noncomformist tradition combined with an old fashioned belief in the virtues of *laissez-faire* was sufficient to keep them in the Liberal camp. Only a whole-hearted attack on the social problem by the Conservative party could have counteracted Nonconformity's pull to Liberalism. Possibly legislation reversing the Taff Vale decision would have stunted the Labour party shortly after its formation. But Balfour and his party were too languid and shortsighted to act, and in a debate in the House of Commons in 1902 only a few Conservatives voted for the law to be changed.

The Liberal party had been gravely weakened by the split in 1886. Ireland cost it one of its leading Radicals, Chamberlain, and the divorce courts removed the other one, Dilke. The Liberal party was maimed, and its mutilated remnants were afflicted by a neurotic obsession with Ireland. Chamberlain thought that Gladstone's diversion of Liberalism almost into a single Irish channel 'relegated to the dim and distant future any serious attempt to deal with the social problem'.[7]

Had Chamberlain and Dilke remained Liberal chiefs, they would surely have seen the urgency of nobbling the potential leaders of an independent workers' party by securing their adoption as Liberal candidates. As it was, Liberals in the constituencies refused to nominate working men for Parliament. Keir Hardie turned to Labour because the Liberals in Lanark rebuffed him at the bye-election in 1888. Ramsay Macdonald left the Liberals only after he had been rejected as a candidate by the Southampton Liberal Association in 1894 and a working man had been turned down at the Attercliffe bye-election in the same year. Arthur Henderson was similarly rejected as a Liberal candidate at Newcastle in 1895 after the executive had voted for his adoption by 84 to 3.[8] The Liberal Chief Whip wrote in 1888: 'I am strongly impressed with the

---

* In Bradford in 1892 a survey indicated 'that the Labour supporters were drawn in almost equal proportions from the Liberals and the Conservatives'.[6]

advantage of not only retaining but of increasing the numerical representation of labour in the House of Commons.'[9] But Liberals in the constituencies failed to see the advantage.

Apart from snobbery it was money that made Liberal associations so reluctant to support the candidatures of working men. Putting the expenses of returning officers on the rates and paying Members of Parliament would have done much to remove this difficulty. Both reforms were contained rather vaguely in the Newcastle Programme of 1891, but nothing was heard of them when the Liberals assumed office a year later. Chamberlain and Dilke could scarcely have allowed the party to be so heedless of its interests. Had men like Macdonald and Keir Hardie been accommodated by the Liberals there would probably have been no Labour party. Certainly there was little popular enthusiasm for it.

The decision in 1900 of the Trade Unions, by a narrow majority, to seek independent representation in parliament was naturally welcome to most Socialists, who played indeed an active part in its achievement. At the end of the 1880s there were about 2,000 active Socialists in the country.[10] When the Independent Labour Party was formed in 1893 the word socialist was kept out of its title to avoid scaring away the workers, most of whom still believed in capitalism. Even so, by 1900 the party boasted only 13,000 members, of whom only 4,000 were in branches active enough to be represented at their conference.[11] The Webbs and many of the Fabians deprecated the formation of a new party; less sophisticated Socialists doubted that Socialism would ever be achieved by working through the medium of those already in existence.

The Labour Representation Committee was scarcely more successful in its first electoral venture than the ILP had been five years before. Much more important than the victory or defeat of a few Labour candidates was the decision of the House of Lords in the Taff Vale case a year later, laying down that Trade Unions could be sued for the tortious acts of their members. The Taff Vale decision was the culmination of a series of Trade Union cases which had drastically curtailed what Trade Unions believed to be their rights and interpreted the law almost uniformly in a sense hostile to the interests of the unions.

Taff Vale convinced a number of unions which had been doubtful the year before of the necessity of political action. But the miners and the cotton spinners still held aloof, and the LRC's position would have been precarious but for the co-operation of the Liberal party. The Liberals, divided and demoralised, believed themselves in need of every possible assistance to have any chance of winning the next election. Accordingly Herbert Gladstone, the Liberal Chief Whip, secretly agreed with Ramsay Macdonald to give Labour a straight fight with the Conservatives in about thirty seats; in return Ramsay Macdonald was to try to prevent Labour candidates, who had no chance, from splitting the anti-Tory vote. The Labour party was founded upon the premise that the interests of Labour could not be secured through co-operation with the Liberals and that Lib-Labism was a snare and a delusion. Yet here was the new independent party duly coming to terms with the Liberals and co-operating with them in a way which differed from that favoured by the Lib-Lab members only in being on a far larger scale.

The electoral pact worked smoothly in 1906 and in both the elections in 1910. Nearly every Labour M.P. owed his seat to the absence of Liberal opposition. This determined their policitcal activities. Probably the great majority of Labour members had no desire to have it otherwise. They were anxious to prove themselves staid and respectable legislators of the traditional breed. Even Keir Hardie, whose disposition at Westminster in the nineties had been to shock, now took the view that Labour members must show themselves to be 'statesmen as well as agitators'.[12]

The Labour M.P.s made no attempt to emulate the social apartheid practised by Parnell, which had made the Irish party such an effective instrument of obstruction and pressure. 'We Labour men,' wrote Barnes, 'had harboured a spirit of aloofness which was soon dissipated in an atmosphere of geniality'.[13]

Labour persuasion induced the Liberal Prime Minister Cambell-Bannerman to throw over his own government's Trade Union bill and to bring in a new one in accordance with the demands of the Labour party. The 1906 Trade Disputes Act restored the position to that which had been generally thought to obtain before Taff Vale. Trade Unions were exempted from liability for tortious acts committed by their members and indeed in many ways were exempted from the law altogether. Thus just as the Unions were being brought into the constitution politically, they were being taken out of it legally. Elsewhere Labour pressure was less effective and Labour members were largely reduced to the status of loyal adjuncts of the Liberal army.

Naturally such docility was not to the taste of the Labour militants outside. Ben Tillett, the leader of the 1889 dock strike, described

Henderson, Snowden, and others in a pamphlet published in 1908 as 'sheer hypocrites', 'press flunkeys to Asquith', 'repaying with gross betrayal the class that willingly supports them'.[14] Disillusionment with the parliamentary Labour party and with parliament spread after the 1910 elections. The Liberals lost their majority over all other parties, and Labour was tied more closely to them than ever. The Osborne judgment by deciding that a compulsory Trade Union levy for parliamentary purposes was *ultra vires* had threatened to cripple the party financially. In fact it did not: the party's income was larger after the Osborne judgment than in the year before. Yet hindered in parliament by the Courts, the Trade Unions turned to industrial action. The judgment gave a spur to revolutionary agitation in England and a spate of strikes followed. No doubt the fall in real wages would in itself have produced industrial unrest. But the Osborne judgment gave the revolutionary trade unionists, the believers in direct industrial action, a useful stick with which to beat their trade union brethren who favoured electoral and parliamentary methods. The Trade Union Act of 1913 undid the Osborne Judgment and sent syndicalism back to the continent whence it had come.

At the outbreak of war Labour, like every other workers' party except those in Russia and Serbia, put patriotism before pacifism. Casting aside those doctrines of international brotherhood held by some of its members it loyally supported the war. A small minority clung to their pacificism; others like Ramsay Macdonald, though not pacifist, were opposed to the war, and Macdonald resigned his chairmanship of the parliamentary party. The war saw a great expansion of trade unionism, a recognition of the Labour party as a body entitled to participate fully in the highest affairs of state, and yet another serious split in the Liberal party. Labour which had gone into the war a small, eccentric and sectarian group, came out of it a national party. It also came out of it a Socialist party. In 1918 for the first time it inserted an avowed Socialist aim into its constitution.

In the 'coupon' election, Labour won only 58 seats but polled an impressive number of votes. The election of 1922 nearly trebled the party's M.P.s and brought militant socialist representation to the House, the first act of the militants being to help elect Ramsay Macdonald to the leadership over the head of Clynes. A year later Baldwin's decision to go to the country on the issue of protection made Macdonald Prime Minister. Granted that the British constitution works poorly when the government does not possess a majority in the House of Commons, the Labour government performed creditably, particularly in foreign affairs.

But to the party enthusiasts, who believed that through Socialism the party would transform society and the country, the maidenly inactivity of the first Labour government was a crushing disappointment. The party left the world at the end of its term of office much as it had been at the beginning; the golden age had been brought no nearer. The possibility that Utopias are not of this world was too dreadful to contemplate. Illusions had to be preserved, and the blame was laid on the Labour government's minority status and, in some quarters, on Macdonald himself.

By joining with the Conservatives to vote for an enquiry into the Campbell case, the Liberals turned Labour out of office and themselves out of effective opposition. The parliamentary Labour party's status as the official opposition and potential government was now beyond question; its status as the dominating force of the Labour movement was not. As had happened before and was to happen again when Labour's parliamentary forces were weak, the scene shifted away from Westminster. The parliamentary Labour party was dragged along in the coal dust of the miners, and Labour slowly drifted into the general strike. The parliamentary party played little part in it and had nothing to do with its ending.

In 1929 came Labour's worst misfortune. Despite the general strike, it emerged from the election with more seats than any other party, though with fewer votes than the Conservatives. In consequence it presided over the worst slump in British and world history. The Labour party existed to help the worker, whose chief grievance was chronic unemployment; yet Labour had made no plans whatever to deal with unemployment. Once in office it inevitably set up a committee; but its policy accorded with the strictest and most old-fashioned Treasury orthodoxy, and differed not at all from what the Conservative policy would have been.

To the next generation the 1931 crisis is barely credible, though it was evidently real enough to those taking part. Despite the vehement protests of the T.U.C. more than half the Cabinet were prepared to agree to the cuts in unemployment benefit and other government expenditure thought necessary for the raising of a loan in New York. The rest of the cabinet were prepared to agree to much but not to all that was demanded. Macdonald accordingly resigned and in response to appeals by the King and the other party

Universitas
BIBLIOTHECA
Ottaviensis

leaders took office again as leader of a 'National government' consisting of the Conservatives, most of the Liberals, and a small Labour rump of Snowden, Thomas and a few followers.

The thirties were Labour's most calamitous and discreditable decade. Granted that the party was unlucky, its retreat into sectarian extremism was surely excessive. Granted, too, that it had no responsibility for events from 1931 onwards, still its policies were divorced from reason and separated from reality. At no time did it measure up to its responsibilities as the alternative government.

Under the influence of Dalton the party gradually modified its attitude to defence and foreign affairs. But it continued until 1937 to vote against the defence estimates, and as late as April 1939 it opposed the introduction of a (very inadequate) system of conscription.

Labour refused to join a coalition at the beginning of the war, and after Chamberlain had suffered a moral defeat in the debate on the Norwegian campaign it again refused to serve under him. The party thus performed its best service to the state for many years in being instrumental in making Churchill Prime Minister. Labour served with distinction in the wartime coalition. The party leaders got used to office, and the voters to their being in office.

Apart from its unfortunate nationalisation adventures, the post war Labour government based, under Attlee, upon the formidable trio of Bevin, Morrison and Cripps, had valuable achievements, though, as Attlee later admitted, it tried to do too much. It carried out the policies decided upon by the wartime coalition, it enacted extensive welfare legislation, notably the National Health Service and the National Insurance Scheme, and it evacuated India and adopted a liberal colonial policy. Against this, its economic mismanagement was conspicuous. After the first two years or so Labour's much vaunted belief in planning did not translate itself into a planned economy, only a controlled one. There were controls without planning, probably the worst known combination. Rationing was maintained because the government did not know how to get rid of it, and because it felt that rationing in some way demonstrated planning.

By 1950 Labour had carried out the welfare legislation it had promised, and was bereft of both ideas and energy. It had little to offer except a catalogue of industries arbitrarily chosen for nationalisation. After electoral defeat, the defects of the party's constitution were laid bare by the Bevanite and nuclear disarmament quarrels. The loss of the 1955 election and the unprecedented increase in the government's majority did not bring Labour to its senses. The quarrels dragged on and Labour was so weak that contrary to Macmillan's expectation it was unable to remove the government after the Suez debacle. The Conservatives were allowed to recover and to increase their majority yet again in 1959. This defeat merely intensified the civil war in the party, and the leadership was humiliatingly beaten on unilateral nuclear disarmament at the 1960 conference.

In 1960 Labour looked as doomed and derelict as the Liberal party had seemed in 1901. Yet, like the Liberals sixty years before, Labour recovered to win the next election, and for similar reasons. Inspired by Mr. Gaitskell's courageous 'Fight, fight and fight again' speech at the 1960 conference, an organisation, 'Campaign for Democratic Socialism', was set up to persuade the Trade Unions and the constituency parties to reverse the party's commitment to unilateralism. C.D.S. was more successful with the big unions, four of which changed sides, than with the constituency parties which moved fractionally towards unilateralism. Still the reversal was accomplished, though the party remained divided. Unity was later achieved on the 'conservative' policy of opposing Britain's entry into Europe, just as Liberal unity had been achieved on the 'conservative' policy of defending an old-fashioned system of education. In his speech at the 1962 Conference of the party, Gaitskell spoke of a thousand years of history and brought the Conference to a fever of enthusiasm and unity against the possibility of Britain joining Europe. After all, such a thing might mean the end of the British Empire.

Meanwhile the opposition effectively attacked Conservative economic policy, Mr. Wilson denouncing 'masochistic and irrelevant cuts in our standard of living, harmful restrictions on our production and needless increases in our costs and price structure'.[15] Labour asserted its liberal credentials by vehemently opposing the government's proposals to curb immigration. Some of the party made clever, if disreputable, use of the Vassall and Profumo cases. The country was bored, if not worse, with the Conservatives. The slogan 'It's time for a change' had compelling appeal and evident cause. The prospect of office kept Labour united.

The Labour leadership might show a distressing inconsistency in its policy for science, but Mr. Wilson by promising to harness socialism to science and science to socialism managed to harness many of the younger voters to Labour. He gave the impression of understanding science, efficiency and the economy. Evidently he had the answer to the exasperations of stop-go. As Mr. Callaghan put it shortly after Labour's election victory, a 'credit squeeze, a pay pause and other measures led to the slowing down of British industry. On our first weekend . . . we determined that we would not tread that path again'.[16] Expectantly the country awaited the smack of firm government, the white heat of the scientific revolution, and a smoothly expanding economy.

Parliamentary Party and Candidates

In the House of Commons Labour presents a more variegated and representative appearance than the Conservatives. The Nuffield election studies classify the occupations of M.P.s under four headings: professions, business, miscellaneous, and workers. The miscellaneous consist of 'miscellaneous "white collar", private means, politicians, publicists, journalists, farmers, and housewives', and so are akin to the professions. Of the 258 Labour M.P.s elected in the 1959 parliament 38 per cent as against 46 per cent of the Tories came from the professions, 10 per cent as against 30 per cent from business, 17 per cent as against 23 per cent came under miscellaneous, while 35 per cent as against less than 1 per cent were workers.[17] There were 105 more Labour M.P.s in the 1966 than in the 1959 parliament: 6 more from business, 58 more from the professions, 22 more under miscellaneous and only 19 more workers. Thus the percentage of workers in the Labour parliamentary party declined from 35 to 30, and the combined percentage of professions and miscellaneous increased from 55 to 61. While the workers are only 30 per cent, the teaching profession has now gone up to 20 per cent, a balance between doing and teaching, which Bernard Shaw, at least, would have found disturbing.

Writing before the 1966 election Professor Ranney found that 'Labour candidates were no more representative of the general public or the working class occupationally than they were educationally . . . '[18] and concluded that 'in social status, personality, and outlook the parliamentary candidates of all three British parties, like their counterparts in other democracies, resemble each other more closely than they resemble their respective supporters'.[19] While Labour has increased its support outside the working class, the parliamentary Labour party has become less not more representative of its supporters.

In the country Labour is more narrowly based than the Conservatives. An overwhelming proportion of its voters come from the working class. In 1966, the swing to Labour among the middle class was not much less than among the very poor, greater than among the lower middle class, and considerably greater than among the skilled workers.[20] Even then, however, Labour did much less well with the middle class than the Conservatives did with the other three categories. Labour in 1966 gained only 15 per cent of the middle class and 30 per cent of the lower middle class vote.

Up to 1918 there were no individual members of the Labour party and not many local Labour parties, the I.L.P. filling the gap. The new party constitution produced constituency Labour parties all over the country, which cut down the influence and activity of the I.L.P. and gradually edged it out of business. Like the party constitution on the national level, the constitutions of the constituency parties are complex and cumbersome. Their chief peculiarity is that the party's individual members operate only at ward level; if a member wishes to operate in the rarefied atmosphere of the constituency level, he must get himself made a delegate of his ward or of one of the organisations which are affiliated to the local party. At the constituency level, therefore, the constituency party hardly exists; the parts, instead of making a whole, make a general Management Committee which administers the affairs of the constituency party.

Constituency Labour parties sometimes conjure up an image of earnest incendiary zealots fervently expounding the Marxist-Leninist scriptures or the new testament of Bevan, Foot and *Tribune*, and setting the world to rights regularly once a month. In fact the local Labour parties behave little differently from the Conservative local associations.*

Sometimes for financial reasons, but chiefly because of Labour's traditionally rigid discipline, Transport House has more influence upon the selection of candidates than does Tory Central Office, and it uses its power of veto much more frequently. Yet the constituency Labour parties are usually autonomous in their choice of candidates. When Morgan Phillips announced his intention of seeking a seat

* See also page 42.

in parliament and intimated shortly before the 1959 election that South West Derbyshire would be a convenient haven, the local Miners' Federation, in whose patronage the seat lay, engaged in feverish and successful manoeuvres to have Labour's General Secretary rejected by the constituency party.[21]

Trade Union sponsorship of candidates is in principle a reasonable practice. Many constituencies now, and many more in the past, could not finance an election out of their own resources. The Trade Unions supply most of the party's funds upon a national level; there is no reason why they should not supply funds at the constituency level as well. The Labour party was founded to secure representation of the workers in parliament. It would have been a curious way of achieving that object if its M.P.s had been all bright middle class intellectuals. Trade Union sponsorship has given the parliamentary Labour party its distinctive character: 'Unsponsored Labour candidates more closely resembled their Conservative opponents than their Union-sponsored Labour colleagues.'[22] But if the Unions now spurn workers as candidates in favour of school masters and professors, their borough mongering on a scale surpassing the eighteenth century Duke of Newcastle will have less obvious justification.

Daniel O'Connell scoffed at those who defended pocket boroughs with the argument that they provided able and impecunious young men with their only possible road into the House of Commons. 'Are there', he asked, 'no dull, drowsy, members ever returned for [pocket] boroughs? Members without talent to join in a debate but with sufficient perseverance to be able to attend at the division?'[23] The gibe was justified. Nevertheless Chatham, Pitt, Peel, Burke, Canning, Brougham, Macaulay and many others first made their way to parliament by means of a benevolent patron 'presenting' them to his borough. Trade Union patronage has not produced a comparable galaxy.

The original reason for Trade Union participation in parliament no longer applies. The T.U.C. does not have to catch the eye of Mr. Speaker in parliament in order to gain the ear of the government. Yet the Trade Unions have an obvious interest in influencing and, to as large an extent as possible, composing the parliamentary Labour party. They have extra-parliamentary means of influencing the leader of the party, but that will not be enough if the parliamentary party is in the hands of the wild men or their own nominees are indistinguishable from other Labour M.P.s.

Image and Style

Labour in its more apocalyptic moments regards itself as the salt of the earth. Dedicated to the puritan ideal of building the holy community on earth, it sees itself as pure and unpolluted by the sordid pursuit of individual gain, the only party selflessly seeking the well being of the whole country. At the same time, however, it believes this idealism to be tempered by the sturdy British virtues of common sense, pragmatism, and lack of logic; the party is socialist of course but not with any of that unyielding dogmatism so characteristic of those continental socialists. To Labour, Socialism is the path to the new and better life, and a belief in Socialist principles the infallible sign of virtue and intelligence, the sign of a man born again. Labour regards itself as the only democratic party in the country, the only party which preaches and practices equality, the true party of progress. Such virtues as the other parties possess, they owe to the influence of Labour; they have been shamed out of their previous jungle habits and tamed by the power of Labour's example.

Labour's opponents in their most partisan mood do not see the party as seeking to build a new and better world, but as attempting to return to an old and worse one, as peddling the wrong remedy for conditions that have long since passed away. They see the Labour party not as pioneers looking forward but as men firmly entrenched in positions adopted long ago, as old frontiersmen lamenting yet not fully comprehending that things are not what they used to be. So far from thinking the Labour party the salt of the earth, they see it as having a dangerous affinity to those who put their opponents into salt mines. Labour's latter day zeal for the Commonwealth after all its polemics against British imperialism they deride with the scorn Canning turned on those who, having always opposed Pitt during his life, then used his name to support their opposition to anything they disliked. 'Such perverse worship,' he said, 'is like the idolatry of barbarous nations, who can see the noonday splendour of the sun without emotions but who, when he is in eclipse, come forward with hymns and cymbals to adore him.'[24] The alleged democracy of the party is dismissed as an unfortunate mixture of irresponsible anarchy and Trade Union bossism.

The constitution of the party is largely responsible for Labour's characteristic style, which is noisy quarrelling. Not for Labour the

smooth ironing out of differences, the quiet give and take of private
argument, the self-sacrificing compromises for the common good,
the general air of harmony, efficiency, and unity. The frequency of
voting and the scattered citadels of power widen differences and
sharpen personal acrimonies. Still, the atmosphere of controversy
which the party commonly breathes is not fully explained by constitutional machinery. 'A Reformer', Hazlitt pointed out, ' is not a
gregarious animal,'[25] but members of the Labour party seem to
dislike and distrust each other rather more than is necessary. As
Citrine sarcastically remarked of 'certain people' in the Labour
movement: 'no other body can rival them in the comradely and
understanding way in which they engage in controversy and
indulge in loving criticism of one another'.[26] Though its Corsican
vendettas make Labour usually more interesting than the Conservatives, its style of conducting its own affairs does not add to its
electoral appeal. In government much of the discordance is drowned
by the heavy drum of governmental and Prime Ministerial rhetoric.
Even then the result is scarcely harmonious.

The Leadership

Labour is self-consciously democratic. When in opposition the
party leader is elected every year; so is the shadow cabinet and the
National Executive. The parliamentary party decides its policy by
majority vote at a weekly meeting, and the party conference indulges
in an annual orgy of resolutions and votes. The leaders do not submit
themselves for re-election when the party is in power but the
parliamentary Labour party at its meetings still puts resolutions to
the vote. In Professor McKenzie's view these democratic trappings
delude both Labour and its opponents: 'the Labour Party, almost
without realising it, came to accept a principle of party leadership
fundamentally similar in its essentials to that which operates in
the Conservative Party'.[27]

'The history of the working-class parties', Michels wrote in 1915,
'continually furnishes instances in which the leader has been in
flagrant contradiction with the fundamental principles of the movement'[28] without suffering dismissal. Three years before, Beatrice
Webb had expressed doubts as to how far Ramsay Macdonald was
in sympathy with the avowed aims of the Labour party, but Michels
can scarcely then have had Macdonald and the British Labour party
in mind. Yet Macdonald's career provided some *ex post facto*
evidence for Michels's dictum as well as for Dr. McKenzie's thesis.

Mrs. Beatrice Webb's doubts about Macdonald's Socialist orthodoxy became widespread in the 1920s, and Macdonald himself did little to allay them. He explained in 1924 that the party could not fulfil their Socialist pledges because 'it would be cutting green corn'. Even if he was Premier for 50 years, 'the pledges I have given you from my heart would still be unfulfilled not because I fainted or failed but because the corn was still green'.[29] Presumably, the divergence between Macdonald and the ostensible objectives of his party was due to his intelligent understanding of political realities not shared by many of his followers. Yet from his election as leader in 1922 until the break up of the party in 1931 Macdonald's position remained virtually unchallenged.

Ramsay Macdonald's long supremacy is the strongest piece of evidence for the view that the Labour leader is in almost as strong a position as the Tory leader, and that the parliamentary Labour party has to defer to the party outside parliament no more than its chief opponents have to bow down to their external organisations. Certainly the Labour leader has for most of the party's history not been in danger of sudden displacement. But permanence does not necessarily equal power.

Undoubtedly constitutional forms rarely if ever reflect the reality of power; but seldom are they without influence upon it. And in fact, the apparent dispersal of power among the parliamentary party, the Trade Unions, the National Executive, and the party conference leads not only to confusion both inside and outside the party but also to some genuine diffusion of power.

The Labour leader has to contend with powerful pressure groups whose position is entrenched by the constitution of the party, a federal rather than a unitary constitution, powerful 'feudal' magnates, and an often intractable rank and file. A Tory leader has to face none of these difficulties. The Co-operative Party, one of Labour's constituent pressure groups, forced Labour to drop its proposal to nationalise Industrial Life Insurance and was instrumental in persuading the Attlee government to make an important concession on C licences when it nationalised transport. Otherwise the Co-op. has been without influence. Inertia is its dominant characteristic.

The Trade Unions, Labour's other main constituent pressure group, are a very different matter. A left wing party needs the Trade Unions for money and electoral helpers, and a leader of such a party always has to pay considerable attention to the wishes and views of the Union leaders.* But the Labour party, as Ernest Bevin once told the T.U.C., 'grew out of the bowels of the T.U.C'.[30] Hence the unions are not merely indispensable to it financially and electorally; they have a vital constitutional role as well. The Trade Unions wield five-sixths of the votes at the party conference and control the election of two-thirds of the National Executive. The Labour leader is therefore in a weaker position with the Trade Unions than is the Tory leader in his dealings with business. Industrialists can denounce a Conservative leader in their clubs or in public, and they can lobby Members of Parliament and cut off their subscriptions to party funds. But they have no votes to promise or withhold other than their own. The half dozen or so big Trade Union leaders deal in hundreds of thousands of votes at the conference. In addition, the candidatures of about one-third of the parliamentary party are sponsored by Trade Unions.

The balance of power has sometimes tilted away from the parliamentary party towards the industrial wing. When most of Labour's articulate parliamentarians were defeated in the election of 1918, leadership of the Labour movement was exercised from outside parliament for the next four years. Much the same thing happened in 1926 and in 1931 and later. By stiffening the minority in Macdonald's cabinet, pressure from the T.U.C. probably contributed to the break up of the second Labour government. After the smash, the T.U.C. was certainly in control. The attitude of the Labour movement to the crisis and to the new national government was decided by the T.U.C., not by the parliamentary party. Bevin used to refer to the Labour party as the 'other wing' of the Trade Union movement,[31] and in the thirties he and his confrères ruled the parliamentary Labour party rather as Britain then ruled Iraq and was soon to rule Egypt: though there was nominal dependence real power lay elsewhere. This arrangement was institutionalised in Egypt and Iraq by the requirement that their foreign policy should always be in accordance with that of Great Britain and enforced by the presence of a British ambassador backed up by armed forces; it was institutionalised in the Labour movement by the setting up of a National Council of Labour as the chief policy making body and enforced by the Trade Union block vote at the

---

* President Roosevelt's remark at the time of the 1944 Democratic Convention, 'clear it with Sidney'—Sidney being Mr. Sidney Hillman, the leader of the C.I.O.—signalised, at least in the eyes of Republicans, the undue influence of the Trade Unions in the counsels of the Democratic Party.

annual party conference. Usually, however, indirect rule by the Trade Unions is neither so conspicuous nor so dominating.

The Trade Unions have control over the election of the majority of the National Executive Committee, in which the direction of the Labour movement between conferences is formally vested. In the early days the N.E.C. was often a more powerful body than the parliamentary party, though there was much overlapping of membership. In the First War Labour both joined and left the coalition at the instance of the N.E.C.; the parliamentary party had voted against both actions. After the war and up to the 1950s, the N.E.C. was usually kept in step with the parliamentary party, though Laski when chairman in 1945 tried to lay down the capacity in which Attlee should attend the Potsdam conference.

But from 1952 to 1964 the constituency parties voted left wing members of the parliamentary party on to the National Executive. And the breakdown of the solid alliance between the parliamentary leaders and the Trade Union leaders after the death of Deakin was naturally reflected in the N.E.C. The parliamentary leadership had to work hard not merely to build a majority for the important debates at the annual conference but to maintain a majority at the regular meetings of the executive. On Clause 4 Gaitskell was defeated in the N.E.C. After the 1964 election the N.E.C. was downgraded by Mr. Wilson together with the rest of Transport House. Trade Union leaders dealt directly with ministers and not through the machinery of the party.

Before casting their votes at the party conference, most Trade Union leaders have to face the conferences of their own unions. Some of them have little to fear. When Arthur Deakin was General Secretary of the Transport and General Workers Union—a life appointment—the Union never deviated on political matters from its orthodox 'right wing' line of support of the parliamentary leadership. Under Mr. Frank Cousins it has been almost equally undeviating in its support of a 'left wing' line of opposition to the leader of the party. Even if a vote goes wrong, a Union may be able to have what the lawyers call a 'second bite at the cherry'. In 1959 the right wing N.U.G.M.W. voted for unilateral Nuclear Disarmament by 150 to 126. This decision caused consternation among the Union leadership and among the leaders of the parliamentary party. The conference was recalled shortly afterwards, and this time no mistake was made. Delegates duly voted to support multilateralism and the official policy of the party by what would in other circumstances have been the convincing majority of 194 to 31.[32]

The Amalgamated Engineering Union was once the possessor of the most unworkable constitution since that of the Polish Monarchy. Its General Secretary no longer has to face frequent contests for re-election but he is still confronted with a powerful executive over which he has little control. However, like other Union leaders he retains some freedom at the T.U.C. and the party conference to 'interpret' his Union's decisions in the light of subsequent events. The greatest procedural triumph of this kind was that achieved by Mr. Carron in 1960 who managed to cast his union's vote both for and against a defence resolution. A less refined but equally effective manoeuvre was executed by some unions at the T.U.C. conference in 1966. This was to break the union rules and vote the opposite way to that laid down at the Union Conference.[33]

Bernard Shaw pointed out that despite 'crude democratic precautions . . . in practice a Trade Union secretary is the nearest thing on earth to an irremovable autocrat'.[34] All the same the leader of the party cannot ignore the difficulties which a friendly union secretary may have in gaining his union's support for the leadership in general or for a particular policy; and he may be forced to modify his stand on various matters in order to help gain that support.

For the Annual Conference of the party, the device of the Trade Union block vote was invented to preserve the appearance while eliminating the dangers of democratic voting. This complacently assumed that the Trade Unions would cast their block vote in favour of the leadership and against the 'fanatics and cranks and extremists',[35] who, according to Sidney Webb, often dominated the constituency parties. Since the accession of Mr. Cousins the Trade Union vote has no longer been a dependable weapon of the leadership. In any case, despite Mr. Webb's language, the party conference seldom sees a gladiatorial contest between the Trade Unions and the constituency parties. Both elements are always divided, usually with the majority of Trade Union votes and a minority of the constituency parties supporting the leadership. At Scarborough in 1960, however, Mr. Gaitskell was probably supported by two-thirds of the constituency Labour parties. It was the opposition of four of the six big unions that brought about his defeat. Similarly the government's defeats in 1966 and 1967 were encompassed by the unions and not by the constituency parties.

There can be no certainty about the true constitution of the Labour party, or about the true status of the party conference. 'The constitution is what the Judges say it is',[36] and though the Labour party has fitted itself with almost every kind of constitutional form and organ, it has not yet provided itself with judges. Before the war Attlee wrote that '. . . the Labour party conference . . . issues instructions which must be carried out by . . . its representatives in Parliament',[37] and in an unguarded moment in 1949 he republished the comment. No constituency party militant, enraged by what he regards as the pusillanimity and treacherous retreat from Socialism of the parliamentary party, could wish for a more extreme statement of the doctrine that the parliamentary party exists to obey and enforce the decisions of the *apparat* outside parliament. Yet the behaviour of Attlee the Premier did not follow the precept of Attlee the author. The policy of the Labour government was made at Whitehall and Westminster, not at the various seaside resorts chosen for the Annual Conference of the party.

In practice the Conference has neither the exalted status ascribed to it by Lord Attlee nor the virtually ceremonial position to which it was relegated by Dr. McKenzie.[38] It cannot 'issue instructions' to the parliamentary party with much hope of success, since it has no way of seeing that its instructions are obeyed. The most it can do is to lay down general principles, whose particular application is left to the discretion of the parliamentary party. This was the view put forward by Mr. Bevan as Minister of Health in 1947 when he resisted a resolution that tied cottages should be abolished forthwith. In the event the Labour government did not abolish tied cottages forthwith or later. The defeats that the government suffered in 1966 and 1967 were similarly ignored.

But if conference is not the commander-in-chief envisaged by Lord Attlee in opposition, it has exercised considerable influence upon the fortunes of the Labour party. The parliamentary leadership has seldom been defeated at conference on an issue of the first importance, but only because the leadership has taken good care to modify its policies and conform to the wishes of those who have large quantities of votes upon their cards.* The influence of the coming conference is often unseen; it is nonetheless real. Occasionally it has been conspicuous. In the thirties the decisive battles

---

* Even when the leader is Prime Minister, such manoeuvring is necessary as Mr. Wilson showed in 1967.

in the Labour movement over collective security, the League of Nations, pacifism and rearmament, were fought out at the annual conferences. Both before deciding to join Churchill's war cabinet and before deciding to leave it, Attlee consulted the party conference. The 1944 conference, by accepting Ian Mikardo's amendment to a resolution by the executive which did not mention the matter, insisted that nationalisation be the chosen instrument of the party, a decision which altered the course of the future Labour government and shaped the pattern of British politics for the next twenty years. This was a vastly more important intervention than the Conservative 'auction' at the 1950 conference, which urged the building of 300,000 houses a year upon a future Conservative government.

Through most of the fifties and the early sixties Labour politics revolved around the attempt of the Left to overthrow the policies of the leadership, first on German rearmament and then on nuclear disarmament. In 1954 it narrowly failed owing to a very late lapse into orthodoxy by the faithful Woodworkers.* The efforts of the leadership to avoid defeat at conferences during the fifties indicated their belief that the consequences would be serious. Yet when the leadership finally did suffer defeat in 1960, Hugh Gaitskell fought, fought and fought again, and the parliamentary party refused to become unilateralist overnight. The road to Scarborough or to Brighton pier was not the road to Damascus or Canossa. Westminster reigned; the upstart Conference did not. The parliamentary party's refusal to abide by the majority decision of the conference supports Dr. McKenzie's opinion, yet its efforts to undo that decision do not. Had the leadership again been defeated on the nuclear issue in 1961, it would not a second time have been able to preserve its relative insouciance. Gaitskell himself realised that another defeat would probably be fatal.[40]

When the party is in opposition the struggle between the parliamentary party and the party conference is unresolved, rather like that between the Empire and the Papacy in the middle ages. High claims are made by both sides, but bloodshed is usually avoided by dexterous manoeuvrings and delicate formulae. The leaders are aware that the flouting of conference decisions is a luxury contrary to the democratic beliefs of many of the party, and one which if frequently indulged would tear the party apart. When the party is

* Arthur Deakin was the inquisitor who secured this important conversion. 'We've fixed it', he said.[39]

in power the leader, though he still makes bargains, does not need conference support. The Pope's supremacy over the Council is plain. But revolts by his followers can be an embarrassment, and a prolonged war between a Labour government and the party conference would damage both.

Much of Labour's democracy can be slighted. Even when it is not tempered by adroit procedural arrangements like the block vote at the party conference or the attendance of peers at meetings of the parliamentary party, it is often a sham. The only result of the 'democratic process' is that policy is influenced or decided by a slightly larger but no more representative oligarchy than the leadership of the parliamentary party. On political matters Trade Union bosses do not represent their members. The ordinary member of the Transport and General Workers Union may have agreed with the right wing line of Arthur Deakin or with the left wing line of Frank Cousins. He can scarcely have agreed with both. The party's reversal on 'the bomb' in 1961 was not caused by a rich upsurge of democratic enthusiasm. The manipulated did not turn on the manipulators. All that happened was that a different set of people get their hands onto some of the levers.

It is not all a sham of course. The rank and file have a disposition to disagree.* Having originated outside parliament, the party is less exclusively orientated towards Westminster than its rival. Having created the parliamentary party, the Labour party outside parliament feels that it has rights, to which the Conservative organisation would not lay claim.

But sham or not, the leadership is not greatly helped. For the most part, Labour is a parliamentary party like the other parties, but not exclusively so. The elaborate constitutional machinery of the party has its effect. It leads to some dispersal of power. The crucial point is not the security of tenure of the leader, but the amount of manoeuvring he has to perform, the number of volte-faces he has to execute, the extent of the concessions he has to offer, the trouble he has to take to pacify potentially dissident elements, before a policy can be formulated which is not in danger

---

* After being shouted down at a May Day Rally in Glasgow in 1962, Mr. Gaitskell said: 'I have always said that the one thing that prevented the Labour party getting into power and staying in power was our inherent tendency to argue.'

of repudiation by the party conference or by a significant section of the rank and file. And it is the Labour not the Conservative leader who is more wearisomely, constantly and dangerously engaged in these sometimes humiliating activities.

In the forties Bevin's ascendancy in both the industrial and the parliamentary wings of the movement, and his loyalty to Attlee, gave the party a stability, which did not long outlast his death. Without the magnetic field of Bevin to draw them to the leadership, the forces of the Labour movement were seen to be naturally centrifugal. Attlee narrowly avoided disaster by virtue of having been Prime Minister, by refusing to expose himself in the front line, and by the survival in power of T.U. leaders in the Bevinite mould like Lawther and Deakin. His successor, Gaitskell, had none of these defences. He had not been Prime Minister, he favoured a form of leadership in which the Labour party had not been schooled, and one by one the old Trade Union giants disappeared from the stage.

Except when he had already been committed, as he was by Bevin over German rearmament, or when the opportunities or necessities of occupation of 10 Downing Street made the advance guard a position of safety, Attlee did not expose himself in the van. This ensured his survival, but prevented the party's modernisation. Attlee in short preserved his place as leader by refusing to lead. When Gaitskell tried to lead, the party for long refused to follow. Though he persuaded the party to reverse itself on unilateralism, he could not persuade it to discard Clause 4.

It was Harold Wilson, his opponent in 1961, who benefited from Gaitskell's conception of leadership. Chosen leader when Labour's electoral prospects were good, Wilson suffered from none of the disruptive challenges that he and other dissidents had made against Gaitskell. On becoming Prime Minister he was able to scatter his potential opponents round Whitehall, and until Mr. Cousins's resignation from the government, was left with no serious opposition in the party or at conference. When Labour is in opposition, the leader of the party can approach the supremacy of the Tory leader only if he can rely on the support of the big Trade Unions, which, as Gaitskell found, is far from automatic. When the party is in government, the power of the Premier is sufficient to triumph over paper constitutions, but whether his course is rough or smooth depends upon whether the dominant Trade Union leader is a Cousins or a Bevin.

Socialism and Parliamentarianism

For seventy years or so there have been two main strands of Socialism: one, believing that for Socialists to compromise with capitalism and to abide by the rules of the parliamentary game is to pollute and embourgeois Socialism, and to turn an erstwhile Socialist party into a poor imitation of its reactionary opponents; the other believing that to hold aloof from parliamentarianism and collaboration with non-Socialist parties, and to attempt to usher in the millenium by strikes and violence is to condemn Socialism to futility and the workers to misery and worse. The first strand has been rare in England; instead of Socialism guiding the Trade Unions into revolutionary action as tended to happen on the continent, the Trade Unions sidetracked the Socialists away from Socialism.* Labour was thus revisionist before it was Socialist. It has been a Labour party rather than a Socialist party, interested in social reform rather than revolution, usually working through parliament and elections, not through strikes and force. Because of this it has fitted into the political system instead of seeking to destroy it.

Labour's general commitment to the parliamentary game has not excluded occasional indiscretion and flirtations with the other strand of Socialism. Before the First War a number of Trade Union leaders were contemptuous of the parliamentary Labour party and favoured industrial action. During the war, direct action was used against Ramsay Macdonald by Havelock Wilson's Seamen's Union which refused to carry him to a peace congress in Stockholm. The seamen told the Labour delegates: 'If you want to go to Stockholm to kiss your German brothers, you must swim there'.[42] After the war direct action, called by Barnes 'a euphonism for anarchy',[43] was used against a more orthodox target. Led by Bevin, the dockers threatened to refuse to load arms that were to be used against the Bolsheviks, and the government changed its policy. Lloyd George claimed this to be a coincidence, dictated by the course of events in Russia. The Trade Unions, he said, had been pushing against an open door.

In 1926 the Trade Unions found themselves pushing against a closed door, and their push was half-hearted. As Wheatley said later in the year, 'I cannot see how a general strike, constitutionally

---

* On such a classic ingredient of Socialism, though, as the class war, most early British Socialists did not need much sidetracking. In 1904 a German Marxist sneered that the doctrine of even the I.L.P. was mere 'Nonconformism sicklied o'er with the pale cast of Socialist thought.'[41]

conducted, can attain its object. To be successful it would require to be swift and complete and backed by unconstitutional action.'[44] Most of the Trade Union leaders in 1926 were the last people to attempt unconstitutional action. A body of men less fitted to lead a general strike than the British Labour leaders of 1926 would be hard to find. George IV would have been no more incongruous at Waterloo, had he really been there, than were men like J. H. Thomas and Arthur Pugh embarking upon a trial of strength with the legally elected British government. The leaders realised this themselves. They did what they could to prevent the strike taking place; and when they failed they ended it at the first opportunity, thus ensuring its futility.

After 1931, defeated electorally, soured parliamentarily, some of Labour's leaders retreated into unconstitutional modes of thought though not of action. Even before the election there had been threats of direct action by Tom Johnston and Fenner Brockway, while Aneurin Bevan warned the government not to believe that 'we are going to confine ourselves to sterile Parliamentary opposition . . .'.[45] Throughout the thirties Harold Laski indulged in almost incessant Marxist speculations as to whether or not British capitalists would passively accept the advent of Socialism. Invariably coming to the conclusion that they would not, he urged Labour to be prepared accordingly. On taking office, he wrote, the Labour party 'would have to suspend the classic formulae of normal opposition'.[46] Had he been taken seriously, and had there been any immediate prospect of a Labour victory, Laski might have helped to produce what he presumably wished to prevent: violence and the suspension of the democratic process. Cripps, then regarded by Dalton as 'a dangerous political lunatic',[47] was no less extreme. He thought it unlikely that a Socialist party would 'be able to maintain its position of control without adopting some exceptional means such as the prolongation of the life of Parliament for a further term without an election'.[48]

Surprisingly, Attlee, one of the few ex-ministers to survive 1931 and so deputy-leader of the parliamentary party, was to be found in this company. 'I associate myself with [Cripps's] conclusions',[49] he wrote. Attlee went on to give his vision of the British Socialist paradise: 'Thus I conceive the district commissioner as something more than a public servant. He is the local energiser and interpreter of the will of the government. He is not impartial. He is a Socialist, and therefore in touch with the Socialists in the region, who are his colleagues in his campaign. It may be said that this is rather like the

Russian plan of commissars and Communist party members. I am not afraid of the comparison!'[50] Evidently worried, however, that other people might be afraid of the comparison, Attlee added: 'It will be seen therefore that though I may seem to have strayed into autocracy to some extent in the period of transition, I return to the full exercise of democracy as soon as the Socialist State is in being.'[51] After the dictatorship of the proletariat would come the bright new dawn.

With wise men rushing in, there was nowhere fools could fear to tread. Luckily the Trade Union leaders were not fools. The class war was fought in books and on the platform, not by strikes and violence. To the perpetual disgust of extremists the weapon of the industrial strike for political purposes has lain unused since 1926. While in this Labour has shown its good sense, direct action is a sharp weapon on its reverse edge. If Socialists refuse to play the parliamentary game according to the rules, and rely on other methods, it is they and their supporters, more than their opponents, who suffer. The refusal of the Spanish Socialists to participate in a government after the victory of the Left in the 1936 election was the chief immediate cause of the Civil War. Italian democracy might have been saved had the Socialists accepted Giolitti's invitation before the first world war to join his government. And Mussolini was given his chance after the war by the Socialist policy of strikes and talk of violence. A general strike is practically an invitation to counter-revolution.

Not that in England a series of political strikes would have been likely to lead to fascism: they would have been too thinly supported. As Orwell discovered at the time,[52] there was never even in the period of greatest distress between the wars much if any revolutionary sentiment in England among the workers. The Right would not have been sufficiently frightened, as it was in some other countries, to emulate Socialist violence; it would have been content to cash the electoral dividends.

The solid good sense of the Unions and most of the parliamentary party kept Labour parliamentary and constitutional. Yet the effusions of Laski and Cripps were in one way less foolish than they seem today. There was a basic discrepancy between the party's chosen parliamentary method and its alleged aims of Socialism, a

E

discrepancy summed up by Cripps when he wrote, 'it is no good pretending that Socialism can ever be accomplished by our existing parliamentary methods'.[53] Labour was committed to parliamentary methods long before it became committed to Socialism. In the sense of nationalising the occasional industry and bringing in the occasional welfare measure, Socialism is fully compatible with parliamentarianism. But Socialism in the early years of the Labour party was thought to mean something very different. The early Socialists did not work merely for increased collectivism; they envisaged a society in which competition was replaced by co-operation.

Plainly Socialism, in this sense or in the full Clause 4 sense, was not attainable by parliamentary means, if indeed it was attainable by any earthly means whatever. The acceptance of parliament as the medium of change entailed the abandonment of the idea of transforming society. It meant the subordination of distant ends to immediate means, the submersion of a simple all-embracing ideal under a sea of ambitions, votes, tactics and interests. It meant gradualness and social engineering instead of revolution and Utopia. It meant the reform of capitalism, not its abolition. Socialist rhetoric could survive, but Parliamentarianism meant the abandonment of Socialism. Hence the succession of defectors from the French Socialist party to the parties of the centre and right. Hence, too, the moderation of the British Labour leaders. An I.L.P. pamphlet might complain in 1910 that the parliamentary leaders had 'reduced the whole movement to acute anaemia or rabid melancholy'.[54] But this was the inevitable consequence of revisionism, and of parliament taking the place of Socialism and revolution.

Paradoxically Labour became officially Socialist after being parliamentary. It made this counter revisionist move in 1918.

> Like an ill-judging beauty, his colours he spread,
> And besplastered with rouge his own natural red.[55]

Clause 4 of the new constitution stated that the object of the party was 'To secure for the producers by hand or by brain the full fruit of their industry, and the most equitable distribution thereof that may be possible, upon the common ownership of the means of production, and the best obtainable system of popular administration and control of each industry or service.' At the same time Labour's commitment to the use of parliamentary methods was not abandoned.

Laski and Cripps and their followers regarded Labour's adoption of Socialism as an all embracing commitment and programme taking precedence over the parliamentary commitment. That, too is how Professor Beer regards it. 'The commitment made by the party in 1918,' he writes, 'was not merely a commitment to a social ethic, a system of values. It was also the acceptance of a theory of society, a system of beliefs about how the main social forces actually operated and how they could be brought to operate differently.'[56] 'The inter-war Socialist critique of capitalism implied a quite specific and programmatic consequence: as private ownership of the means of production was the source of existing evils, so common ownership was the main structural reform on which the new co-operative and democratic order would be founded.'[57] The Socialist transformation of society did not take place because the Attlee government in its last years tried to control the economy indirectly. '. . . This approach to planning is quite compatible with private ownership, competition, and profit-seeking. . . . It makes public ownership superfluous and the whole Socialist conception of the co-operative economy sustained by the public service motive irrelevant.'[58] 'The principal cause',[59] (of what on this view of the Labour party must be regarded as an extraordinary aberration) was Trade Union resistance to the control of labour. 'Here was a union movement which for more than a generation had steadfastly supported the Socialist vision of a new order, where co-operation would supersede competition and the motive of public service that of profit and gain. When the opportunity for putting this purpose into practice was presented, they refused to adapt their behaviour to its requirements.'[60]

For want of a nail the shoe was lost . . . Great events often have small causes. But if the Socialist commitment and programme was half as firm as Professor Beer suggests, the Labour leaders were curiously forgetful of it at their 1944 conference when they moved a resolution on future policy which did not mention nationalisation;* and the Attlee government was surely frivolous in so lightly abandoning the commitment, however strong the opposition of the Unions. In fact the post-war Labour government at no time created any long-term planning machinery whatever.[61]

Of course the Unions did help to kill Socialism, but not in 1948. They killed it at birth. The means determine the end. The decision by the Socialists to seek Socialism through the creation of a non-

* See also page 52.

Socialist Trade Union party put Socialism, at least as it was understood at the turn of the century, out of the question. When the Labour party was formed, the Trade Unions were not Socialist. As Barnes, one of the Trade Union founders of the party, said shortly before its foundation: 'Perfectionist propaganda and bewildering programmes should be resolutely tabooed . . . He will best contribute to the awakening of labour who leaves his "isms" on the doorsteps when entering the pending conference.'[62] Most of the leaders were rather old-fashioned liberals, and the rank and file had scant knowledge of what socialism was. In order to transform the country from capitalism to socialism, Socialists had been driven to supporting the creation of a non-Socialist party whose strongest roots were firmly sunk in the capitalist system. The contradiction between Socialists working to abolish capitalism and Trade Unionists actively engaged in making it work vitiated the hopes of the early Socialists. From 1911, when they preferred Lloyd George's insurance scheme to the State scheme drawn up by Mrs. Webb, through 1948 to 1968 when many of them were outraged by the government's proposals to control prices and incomes, the Unions have naturally opposed Socialism whenever it conflicted with their own interests.

Professor Beer's explanation also makes nonsense of most of the inter-war history of the Labour party. True, extremism sprouted after the defeat of 1931. But 'Socialism' was not mentioned in the party's 1929 election programmes.[63] And if the party really was united on its commitment and its programme, the bitter feuds that constantly wracked it are hard to explain. When Professor Beer talks about 'all major elements, whether leaders or followers, whether Right or Left [being] so much in agreement, serious questions of power were not raised',[64] the period he has in mind is not immediately apparent.

The two short periods of Labour government also tell against such an interpretation. Notoriously, the government neither time had a majority in the House of Commons. But on the second occasion, at least, Labour was not held back by the Liberals. Lloyd George was anxious for the government to be more radical, not less. Yet the advances made towards the Socialist state were minimal, the most notable being Herbert Morrison's nationalisation of London Transport, a measure finally carried into law by the anti-Socialist National Government. And former Liberals like Haldane or Jowitt, who at short notice agreed to serve in Labour governments, or like Wedgwood and many other Liberal M.P.s joined the Labour party, can scarcely have been stricken overnight with the realisation of the need to transform society from competition to co-operation.

Wilson Harris once asked Macdonald 'how far one was committed to Socialism by joining the Labour party'. 'Well,' Macdonald answered, 'it's like this. You ask a man whether he's a Christian.' 'Yes,' he says, 'certainly I am.' 'You ask him whether he believes in the Sermon on the Mount.' 'Er, yes, yes, I do.' . . . 'Do you believe in living according to the Sermon on the Mount?', you go on. 'Ah, well,' he will tell you, 'this is a practical world, and you can't carry your ideals beyond a certain point.' 'That,' said Macdonald, 'is how it is with the Labour party and Socialism.'[65]

Joseph Clayton, a life-long Socialist, in his book 'The Rise and Decline of Socialism in Great Britain, 1884–1924', published in 1926, expressed the same idea with less satisfaction. 'Socialism,' he wrote, 'was a proposal to end this struggle of classes . . . by the reorganisation of the community on a co-operative basis.' And his book was the story of the efforts 'to get the idea of Socialism understood and accepted . . . of the gradual abandonment of the idea and the transformation of the doctrine of Socialism; of the discovery forty years later that only the name remained . . . that Socialism with its idea of a co-operative commonwealth was dead'.[66]

To maintain therefore that in the inter-war period Labour was Socialist rather than revisionist is to follow the rhetoric and ignore the events. The rhetoric was always present and still is. All the same, Labour remained revisionist after Clause 4 as before it, in practice preferring parliament to Socialism and behaving much like the other parties.

Plainly, however, for those who took Socialist rhetoric seriously there was a fundamental conflict between ends and means. In believing that Socialism as opposed to social reform could not be achieved by constitutional and parliamentary means, Lenin, Cripps and Laski were correct. Indeed the right wing leaders of the Labour party agreed with them, though they drew the opposite conclusion. The extreme left rejected parliamentarianism in favour of Socialism. The Labour leaders rejected Socialism in favour of parliamentarianism. 'In many instances,' Michels suggested, 'reformism is no more than the theoretical expression of the scepticism of the disillusioned, of the outwearied, of those who have lost their faith; it is the Socialism of non-Socialists with a Socialist past.'[67] Equally, however, revisionism is often the practical expression of experience of democratic politics. Faced with a direct conflict between means and ends, the Labour leaders had either to pursue a non-Socialist policy or to take to the streets. They chose to adopt the methods and the policies of their capitalist opponents, and in so doing preserved the British political system. They deserve every credit, but they had little choice.

For, not content with an unattainable end, Socialists had neglected to equip themselves with any means. 'I only make my plans', Ney told Murat shortly before Austerlitz, 'in the face of the enemy.' That was too soon for the Socialists. The only plans they had concerned the period after the enemy had been beaten. The creed of Socialism provided no guidance on how to deal with the capitalist system, only on what to do after it had disappeared, and not much even then. Socialists in the twenties were in the position of an undertaker without a corpse. Capitalism was much alive, though far from well. An ambulance was needed, not a hearse, and the last thing the Socialists had was an ambulance. When in 1931 Capitalism looked as though it really might be dying, the Labour government did not attempt to substitute Socialism. How could it? Although the failure of capitalism was what Labour had always predicted and was presumably just what it wanted, it ran away, and blamed its failure on the failure of capitalism. 'What,' Mosley gibed, 'would you think of a Salvation Army which took to its heels on the day of judgment?'[68] More fortunate than the Salvation Army in such circumstances, Labour lived to fight another day.

In all its fights both before and after 1931 Labour has been damaged by its theoretical attachment to Socialism, which has served to obscure its usual avoidance of Socialist practice. No doubt its new constitution ensured its independence of the Liberals and in the short term paid off electorally. But by the end of the war the Liberal party had almost certainly lost its power to contain or swallow Labour. Clearly Lloyd George thought Liberalism had no future and indeed said as much.[69]

A radical party, not explicitly Socialist, could still have garnered the deep fund of genuine idealism, which has always been part of the Labour movement, without debasing that idealism with millenial fantasy and without producing an irretrievable break with the declining Liberals. War-time conditions and the Bolshevik Revolution were a powerful temptation, and Socialism as an aspiration was a stirring battle cry. It allowed unlimited denunciation of everything the Socialists disliked, and it promised unlimited felicities in the glorious future, a combination of censuring sin and predicting Utopia, which gave unequalled scope to modern evangelism. But it was a luxury which Labour could not afford and which ensured that its immediate future would not be glorious.

In a continental multi-party system Labour would probably have become the dominant party in a series of coalitions. A solid block of minority opinion was all that a continental party could hope to command. From 1922 to 1935 Labour constantly got about 33 per cent of the vote, a good performance by European standards but not good enough for a British party which must spread its net wide and not rely on a single pressure group or block of votes.

Thus whether or not Labour's independence was good for Labour, it was certainly good for the Conservatives. Clause 4 put a Lib-Lab alliance out of the question and the Conservatives into almost permanent power. In Clause 4, Labour presented a clear target for its opponents. It is always easier for the Tory party to maintain its cohesion in defence of something, and the Labour party's blatant espousal of Socialism gave the Conservatives a whole series of entrenchments to defend, from the traditional life of England through savings to freedom itself.

Clause 4 was a defiance of people's natural conservatism, for which Labour paid dearly in votes. By saddling itself with an extremist constitution, Labour appealed strongly to the faithful but repelled the publicans and sinners, and its concentration upon its own faith instead of upon the country's works prevented it reaching power between the wars.

Whatever else commitment to Socialism did or did not do, it did not bring the Socialist millennium or even a substantial slice of Socialism one whit nearer. More than twenty years before the Labour party was founded and forty before it adopted Socialism, John Morley pointed out that although Socialism had been less talked about in Britain than anywhere else in Europe, 'its principles have been most extensively applied'.[70] That continued to be true. Britain had sur-tax before either France or the United States had income tax. 'The whole nation,' Sidney Webb rightly said in 1923, before there had been a Labour government, 'had been imbibing Socialism without realising it.'[71] Where he went wrong was to think that 'It was now time for the subconscious to rise into conscious-ness.'[72] Few people like to become conscious all at once, which was what the Labour party by its 1918 constitution demanded of Britain; they prefer the process to be gradual. A great deal of socialistic legislation has unquestionably been introduced in this country by non-socialist governments. But because the Labour party was for long more concerned with the medicine than with the patient, the patient preferred to take its socialist medicine unconsciously, as it were, from the rival anti-socialist doctor, and the Labour party had to be content with influence instead of power.

And very probably the presence of a Socialist party frightened off Tory governments from producing as much Socialist legislation as they would have done, had they been faced with a mere radical opposition. All in all the introduction of Labour's Socialist con-stitution, though it was the work of two Fabians, Henderson and Webb, was a remarkably un-Fabian action. Webb disastrously forgot the truth of his own maxim: 'the inevitability of gradualness'.

The attitude of mind exhibited in the making of the constitution, the attitude of 'I'd rather be right than President' has always been prominent in the party. In the fifties, as Mr. Anthony Crosland noted,[73] Labour was less ready than its continental opposite num-bers to adapt itself to the new social and economic situation. Mrs. Barbara Castle thought Labour lost in 1959, because 'our ethical reach was beyond the mental grasp of the average person'.[74] Having originally been one of the most empirical of workers' parties, it became one of the most doctrinaire. The most successful Socialist party in Europe, the Swedish Social Democrats, dropped national-isation on coming into power in the thirties. Labour similarly dropped the capital levy when it first became the governing party, but it clung to nationalisation and Gaitskell could not persuade it to divest itself of Clause 4.

Alongside this dogmatism and usually in control of it has been the attitude 'I'd rather be President than right', a point of view not surprisingly held most strongly by the leadership. For most of its life Labour has put forward moderate policies at elections, but their appeal has been marred by a background of ideological ex-tremism. Hence the party has, from time to time, to do or say silly things in order to satisfy its fundamentalists. Hence, too, the contrast between the conduct of the party in office and in opposition, and the rhetoric of many of its politicians and publicists.

Labour's insistence upon sticking to 'the carcase of dead policies' was fortified by long periods of opposition. The moment when a party becomes the government and at last has the chance to put its principles into action, provides it with the best opportunity of discarding them. Labour was long deprived of such an opportunity; after 1964 it made up for lost time. This was 1918 in reverse. Save for the occasional ill-judged act of nationalisation and much government meddling, Socialism and the rhetoric of a lifetime were abandoned. The party took it astonishingly well, and the shock of the jettisoning of Socialism may be less damaging than was its adoption. On the other hand the embracing of pragmatism may have been too sudden and too complete. Few Labour supporters in 1964 can have expected a Labour government to keep the H-bomb, drastically cut down immigration, accept the Treaty of Rome, deliberately create unemployment, and set in train the biggest deflation since the war.

In any case pragmatism was all the rage. But even in its pragmatism the Labour government was hag-ridden by Labour's past rhetoric. The left wing no longer repudiates parliamentarianism in favour of Socialism, and in issues involving freedom its record has often been better than that of Labour's right wing stalwarts. But while the focus of the argument has changed, the left is still committed to a world that does not exist. Before the war, the left failed to accept the internal realities of British politics; after the war it failed to accept international realities. Once again, this led to unresolved contradictions in the party and to political discomfiture. Policies acceptable to the ordinary party zealot were anathema to foreign bankers. Policies acceptable to the bankers had, before they were acceptable to the party, to be so modified as to make them ineffective. The modification in turn excited the distrust of the bankers.

The antagonism between Labour's theory of Socialism and its practice, as well as the practice of the world it lives in, makes the party a much less serviceable instrument of government than it should be. The party's constitution has also impeded it. Sometimes much has been achieved, but Labour's inability to deal with a system which it theoretically repudiates has led it to economic disaster.

Labour has taken a long time to come into its inheritance because it has always squandered it. By all the rules it should have been the normal majority party of this country. On March 31 1966, Labour seemed at last to have gained that position, and to have at least ten years of power ahead of it. The economic crisis less than four months later, culminating in devaluation of the pound, and accompanied by a series of bye-election disasters incomparably worse than those suffered by the Tories in 1962–3, called the whole future of the party into question. Yet the British system favours the party in possession, and Labour's retreat from Moscow and its several Leipzigs need not necessarily end in its Waterloo.

IV

THE LIBERALS AND THIRD PARTIES

*Liberalism is not . . . the shibboleth of a party, or . . . a doctrine, a
programme which, its main objectives having now been achieved, may be
dismissed as of small account. It is a spirit and a principle capable in
itself of growth and of ever fresh application.*

C. P. SCOTT[1]

*'Why three,' I asked, my mouth full of lutchanika; 'Your Majesty,' I
added. King Carol replied that two parties were apt to share the spoils
between themselves, and a third party was necessary to restore the balance.*

HAROLD NICOLSON[2]

*He [Ramsay Macdonald] reverted again and again to this dislike and
distrust of the Liberals. He could get on with the Tories. They differed at
times openly then forgot all about it and shook hands. They were gentlemen,
but the Liberals were cads.*

C. P. SCOTT's Diary, July 15 1924[3]

The F.A. Cup is invariably won by a club in the First or Second
Division. Yet year after year some four hundred clubs from the
Third and Fourth Divisions and from minor and amateur leagues all
enter the competition. Their objective is not the same as the serious
contenders. They are not hoping to win; they are only hoping to
do well, to beat one or more of the big teams and to earn the label
of 'giant-killers'. The Liberal party is like these minor clubs. It is
engaged in a quite different activity from the leading parties. It may
do a bit of giant-killing—win the odd seat or raise its percentage
vote. But the hope of winning the election and forming a government is well beyond its range. And even if it succeeds in its giant-
killing, its best issues if not its players are soon transferred. Speaking
in the House of Commons in 1924, Baldwin looked at the Labour
members and said: 'the future lies between honourable members
opposite and ourselves'.[4] He was right. Since 1924 the Liberal
party has been relegated to a position different in kind from that of
Labour and the Conservatives.

All third parties are subject to the logic of the two party system.

There is room for third parties on the intellectual and geographical extremities. Intellectual extremists cater for opinions which are rarely found within the Conservative or Labour parties. Parties which address their message to a peripheral region of the country are usually intellectual extremists, though geography may by itself give them sufficient cause for existence. The position is different for a party that claims to be neither regional nor extremist. The Labour and Conservative parties are wide overlapping coalitions. A broad arc stretches without a gap from the right wing of the Conservative party to the left wing of the Labour party. Along that arc, every conceivable kind and intensity of opinion is to be found. There is no segment of 'centre' opinion which is not catered for by one or both of the major parties. Sometimes the Liberals discern a wide divergence between the main parties. After the 1950 election the party said[5]: 'only Liberalism can solve the deadlock between the opposing Right and Left ideologies, which the election had thrown into such startling relief'*. At other times Liberals see the main parties as virtually identical. 'Which twin is the Tory?' they ask. These contradictory complaints are the result of Liberal desperation at their inability to break out of the grip of the two party system.

The Liberals have no chance of gaining power and carrying out their policies. Most voters who support them do so, therefore, for reasons different from those which lead voters to support one or other of the main parties. Some vote Liberal for ancestral reasons, and a few because of their fanatical devotion to some Liberal panacea like the taxing of site values or co-partnership in industry. But the majority vote Liberal because they cannot bring themselves to vote for either of the other main parties. They may just dislike them; they may find them too blatant in their vote-catching; they may feel they lack idealism; they may despise their attitude to foreign affairs; they may be honourable political dissenters; they may feel neglected by both parties; the party they usually support may have done something they resent; they may be fed up with party politics; most often they have become more sympathetic to the other main party than to the one they have previously supported but feel it would be disloyal to cross over, so they use the Liberal party as a convenient stepping place.

* The author of the Nuffield Study of that election found that 'the most striking feature' of the Conservative and Labour manifestoes was their 'overlap in substance, though not in form', adding that 'their differences were in fact often differences only in attitude and emphasis . . .'.[6]

As a result the Liberal vote is in continual flux. Like a wartime transit camp, there are roughly the same number of people in it at any one time, but except for the devoted permanent staff they are all on their way somewhere else. Only about 30 per cent of Liberal support is constant. This is not the fault of Liberals; it is the result of being a third party in a two party system. People are coming in at one gate and going out the other. They are voting less for the Liberals than protesting against the two main parties.

The Liberals represent no interest. Beveridge called it 'the outstanding merit of Liberalism as a political creed—that it stands for the general interest . . . '.[7] Lacking the support of any particular interest, the general interest is all they have left. A party that is merely the mouthpiece of one particular interest will not get far in present-day Britain; but it is at least better off than a party which is separated from all interests. 'Interests' may occasionally sully a party; their presence is a sure sign that the party is involved in the political process. The Liberals' 'purity' is merely a sign of their irrelevance. Nobody bothers to 'dirty' them. Were the Liberals to become of some account, they would soon find themselves involved with interests. Meanwhile they are reduced to rationalising their absence of support from any definable body or interest as virtuous self denial. Their mass protest vote becomes the representation of the general interest.

Because of the nature of the party's support, there is a chasm between the Liberal leaders and their followers. This is not the fault of the leaders. As most of the Liberal support has virtually nothing to do with the party but is merely a vote against the other parties, policy is largely irrelevant. The Liberal party is always, as it were, being married by its voters on the rebound and then almost immediately divorced. The Liberal leaders wisely ignore these scarcely flattering relationships and go their own way with policy, as though they had been married for their own *beaux yeux* and never subsequently deserted.

The 1964 election showed the dissociation of the Liberal leaders from Liberal voters in its clearest form. Shortly before it, Mr. Grimond launched a 'charter for new men'. 'We shall not get abundance in our generation', he said, 'unless the people who understand and lead the technological revolution—the New Men—are given their heads.'[8] The result of the election showed that 'the new men' who heeded this appeal were clustered in Orkney and Shetland, Cornwall and Devon, rural Wales, and the Highlands of Scotland. The Liberals won not a single industrial seat, nothing in the New Towns, and only one seat in the suburbs. Except for Orpington, the understanding and the leadership of the technological revolution were left to the backward areas of Cornwall, Wales and Scotland.* The only seats the party gained at that election were in the Scottish Highlands. Well might one of the victorious candidates exult: 'It is all Liberal country now from Mickle Flugga to Ballachulish.' That cry summarised the Liberal position. They are not a party of the centre; they are a party of the extremities.

There is an obvious tendency for third parties to be regional: unless their support is concentrated geographically, they cannot win many seats. And a feeling of neglect or deprivation is liable to be created by geographical remoteness from the centre and by national or regional patriotism. The Liberal party is primarily a party of the Celtic fringe; apart from the South West it holds only three English seats. Even in their heyday the Liberals were always strongest outside England. In 1880 they won 54 out of 60 seats in Scotland[9] and 28 out of 30 in Wales.[9a] It was the fringe which usually produced their majority. In both the elections in 1910, for instance, the Conservatives won more seats in England than the Liberals. Hence Asquith, after his defeat at Paisley in 1923, was being less than generous to one of his party's most faithful strongholds when he remarked that he'd 'sooner go to Hell than to Wales'.[10]

Even in the Celtic fringe, however, the Liberals face tough competition. While they have put forward sensible and moderate 'Home Rule' policies for Scotland and Wales, the nationalist parties outbid them by demanding full independence. Fostering the delusion that Wales and Scotland subsidise England instead of the other way round, Plaid Cymru and the S.N.P.‡ say they would be better off without their poor relation, England.

As well as the Scottish and Welsh National parties, there is also a growing Cornish Nationalist organisation. 'Home Rule for Cumberland'[11] however has not been demanded since 1955. The Nationalist vote, like the Liberal vote, is largely protest. Few of

---

* Admittedly the atomic reactor at Dounreay is near Caithness. But Caithness and Sutherland was the only Scottish seat the Liberals lost in 1966.

‡ These are the only other third parties considered here. The Communists have some industrial but no electoral significance. The Fascists and other groups have neither.

those who vote for Plaid Cymru or the Scottish Nationalists support the full aims of those parties, and many are likely to desert at the next general election. Yet the Nationalists are in a happier position than the Liberals. Their support is concentrated and they have a genuine issue.

While the Liberal base in their Celtic fastnesses is eroded by the Nationalists, the main parties if they have any sense should be assuaging Nationalist feelings by eroding the base of both the Liberals and their rivals. The strengthening of the regions against the centre is urgent particularly in Wales and Scotland. And if the Scots and the Welsh wish their councils to be called parliaments, why should they not be permitted such solace? As well as a sop to hurt pride, the reform might well lead to a recreation of Celtic vigour.*

Liberal difficulties are at their most acute during general elections. Voters are choosing a government, and a Liberal government is not within the range of possible choices. In one respect, however, the Liberal position at elections has improved. Before television, Liberals used to remain in the background during the campaign. Now although still out of the main contest, they gain more of the limelight than they do at any other time except during their party conference. As a result the Liberals manage to expand their support just at the moment when they should be most subject to the two party squeeze.[12] The growing electoral importance of television and the declining electoral importance of mass organisations are just about the only encouraging features in the future of the Liberal party.

All the same, election results make dismal reading for Liberals. In 1950 the party was reduced to advertising in the press for parliamentary candidates.[13] In 1955 it received only 6 per cent of the votes and only 1 per cent of the seats; 1959 saw an increase of votes. The Head of the Liberal Research Department[14] was able to report with some satisfaction that fewer candidates had come within the category of 'total rout'. The improvement meant that he was able to promote them from the category of 'total rout' to that of 'devastating defeat'. In 1964 the party won 3,000,000 votes and 12 seats; another improvement, but even after this 'success' and seven years of Liberal revival the party was still not back to its 1945 position. In 1966 the Liberal vote declined, though the party ended up with

* See also pages 333–6.

three more seats. No wonder the party favours electoral reform! The alternative vote would scarcely help it, but Proportional Representation might enable it, at least for a time, to break out of its dreary cycle of lost deposits and mini-representation.

Still more depressing, perhaps, than its own failure is its lack of influence upon the election as a whole. Except in safe Tory or Labour seats, the Liberal vote splits fairly evenly between the main parties. The presence of a Liberal candidate increases the turn-out; it does not affect the result. Outside the very few constituencies which they win, Liberal intervention rarely makes a difference of more than two or three seats.

Stultified at elections, the Liberal party is no less frustrated in the House of Commons. 'The great point I think we ought to aim at,' Newcastle wrote a little prematurely in 1719, 'is that there should be but two parties, that for and that against the government . . . .'[15] In a parliament based upon a conflict between the government and the opposition, the Liberals are left out in the cold. Their role is embarrassing as well as small. Whatever the question nominally before the House, an important ingredient in it for M.P.s in the big parties is: Do I support or oppose the government? Since their electoral support is always split between those who prefer the government to the opposition and those who prefer the opposition to the government, this is a tricky question for Liberal M.P.s to answer. Robert Frost once wrote.

'I'm a Liberal
I mean one so altruistically moral
I never take my own side in a quarrel.'

That, of course, is not the position of the Liberal party. Liberals want to take their own side in a quarrel. They can't because they have not got a side. They are on both sides and on neither.

The House of Commons is not an easy arena for the Liberals. Yet their failure is partly their own fault. Only on rare occasions, like the Commonwealth Immigrants Act of 1968, has the party managed to impress the House or the country. Parliamentary procedure offers many openings for determined minorities, and campaigns of such a kind are still extensively reported. The Liberals have been unable or unwilling to take them. Millionaires can afford to squander their resources, starving men cannot.

The parliamentary incompetence of the Liberals may be the cause of Liberal contempt for the House of Commons or it may be the effect. More probably the two things feed on each other. At all events the Liberals switched their attack on the political system from the electoral laws to the working of parliament. In one way, at least, the switch was wise. The intricacies of Proportional Representation are mysteries which most voters are not prepared to explore. Parliament is a much more promising target. Also, while the Liberal interest in altering Parliament is almost as great as their interest in altering the mode of elections, it is much less blatant.

The tentacles of the two party system are so deeply embedded in the whole system of government that independent third parties, which are by definition opposed to the system, bear a resemblance to parties in other countries that do not accept the regime. In that sense the Liberals are a genuinely radical party.

Perhaps misled by this, Liberal leaders often visualise a great left wing radical non-Socialist party, which would consist of the Liberals and much of the Labour party.* But the word radical carries little meaning when used in a general sense. Whatever else might be said about Mr. Callaghan's first Budget in 1965, it was undoubtedly radical. The Liberal party voted against it 97 times.

The Trade Unions are a favourite target for the Liberal Party's radicalism; they are a bastion of Labour's conservatism. A common liking for being radical, for going to the roots of the matter, even if it existed, would not be an adequate basis for marriage, unless the two prospective spouses were agreed on what they wanted to dig up. So long as Labour and the Liberals differ on what is weed and what is healthy plant, such agreement is impossible.

There are other impediments to the marriage. Either the Labour party is still Socialist or it is not. If it is, then the marriage is off. If it is no longer Socialist, then presumably Labour is already that left wing radical non-Socialist party that the Liberals are always talking about. The thing has happened. More important the Liberal leaders have practically no votes to deliver. Their party is almost equally divided. If they led the official Liberal party to a wedding with Labour, almost half the party would attend a rival and unofficial wedding with the Conservatives.

* Such a marriage by making the Liberals a pillar of the two party system would of course rob them of their radical nature.

On policy the Liberals have often been in advance of the other parties. The Yellow and other coloured books issued by Lloyd George in the late twenties were incomparably superior to anything that the other parties produced; and in the 1929 election the Liberals were the only party that had any plans to deal with unemployment. Their foreign policy in the thirties was less inspiring. Lord Samuel likened Churchill's advocacy of rearmament to 'a Malay running amok',[16] and in 1939 the Liberals opposed conscription.

In the fifties the party again became creative. Of course the dissociation between the Liberal leaders and Liberal voters gives the party considerable freedom in policy. The leaders have only to carry their militants with them. The wearisome, time consuming, but highly essential task of integrating opinion and conciliating interests is not for them. They have no interests to conciliate and are too small to need to integrate opinion. Still, credit should be given them. They were the first to take up regionalism. And though the 1959 Liberal Manifesto did not advocate entry into the Economic Community,* the Liberals were also first in the field on Europe.

There is a fatal contradiction in almost everything to do with the Liberal party. Its ostensible object is often the opposite of its real one. Up to 1964 because the Conservatives had been in power for thirteen years, the Liberals had to reserve most of their condemnations for the Conservative government. In fact their only hope of prosperity was that the Tories should win again. In that event, they believed, Labour would break up and the Liberals inherit its position.

Again the Liberals naturally want as many seats as possible in order to exert leverage in Parliament, and in 1964, they very nearly achieved the position of holding the balance of power. In theory this should have been the Liberal opportunity. In fact it was nearly disastrous. Mr. Grimond incurred considerable odium among his right wing supporters for allegedly keeping Labour in office. Yet he could not risk forcing an election with the likelihood of losing several seats. In the last three bye-elections before the 1966 general election, the Liberal vote almost disappeared. Even if all the people

* 'People Count' did not mention the Common Market. The word 'Europe' only appeared in a sentence about Britain 'leading a partnership in the Commonwealth, in Europe and through the United Nations'.

who voted Liberal in those three seats had voted in the same
constituency, the Liberals would still have been a bad third. Mr.
Grimond found he could have a little parliamentary power, or at
least the appearance of it; or he could have electoral popularity. He
could not have both. The only way the Liberals can win and hold
votes is by being a discontented and powerless minority. The only
point of a British party winning votes is to achieve power. But as
soon as the Liberal party came near even the shadow of power,
they lost votes.

Thus Liberal action is self defeating. This is not the fault of the
Liberals; it is inherent in the position of a third party lacking a
solid regional or social base in a two party system. The more the
Liberal party reveals and plays upon discontent, the quicker it
ensures that the main parties take steps to remove that discontent.
The better policies it produces, the sooner they are filched by their
opponents. The nearer it gets to a position of power in parliament,
the more unpopular it becomes. Perpetual suicide is a built-in
feature of the Liberal position. Excluded from the benefits of the
two party system, the Liberals help to regulate that system to their
own detriment. They produce ideas for the main parties, they
identify disaffection for them, they goad and stimulate them, they
enable disgruntled voters to move from one to the other in gradual
stages, they provide a haven for their misfits. While appearing to
throw grit into the two party works, the Liberals are in reality a
lubricant. They play Dr. Jekyll to their opponents and Mr. Hyde to
themselves. Their well-intentioned idealism is employed in the
service of the two party system, which they despise. They are even
more altrusic than they themselves suppose.

When the Prince Consort invited the leading members of Cambridge University to Buckingham Palace, he offered them claret or
sherry. The Master of Caius College replied, 'Port, if you please.'[17]
The Liberals are like that Master of Caius. When there are only
two choices, they demand a third. Then even purport to offer a
third. The offer, like the demand, is spurious.

V

GENERAL ELECTIONS

No doubt but ye are the People—your throne is above the King's.
Whoso speaks in your presence must say acceptable things.

RUDYARD KIPLING, 'The Islanders'

We cannot be guided by the mood of the masses: that is changeable and unaccountable.

LENIN[1]

These are trying moments & seems to me a defect in our much famed Constitution, to have to part with an admirable government like Ld Salisbury's for no question of any importance, or any particular reason, merely on account of the number of votes.

QUEEN VICTORIA[2]

Prime Ministers can come and go without an election. A vote in the House of Commons, Cabinet intrigues, or unrest on the government backbenches, can remove a Prime Minister and end or create a coalition. But nowadays only a general election can change both Prime Minister and governing party. Elections rule the political process but not the government's policy. They decide who rules; they do not rule themselves.

Notwithstanding the importance of elections, the power of the voters is closely controlled. The main parties regard an election not as an opportunity for reaching decisions on important issues but as an occasion for capturing the government. Aneurin Bevan might say in 1950 that he was not interested in the election of another Labour government. 'I am interested in the election of a government that will make Britain a Socialist country.'[3] And in most governments and oppositions, some ministers and leaders, for ideological or personal reasons, want to lose. They believe that their ideas or their careers will be better furthered by defeat than victory. But the vast majority are anxious to win and either keep or gain a job. Accordingly they safeguard themselves from the historians by mentioning the most important issues facing the country, and from the electorate by discussing them in such muted terms that they do not disturb the voters.

Only once in modern Britain has a government called an election to ask for a mandate for a new and contentious policy. Surprisingly, it was the Conservatives who made this mistake. Baldwin said in 1923 that he had come to the conclusion that protection was the only way to cure unemployment, but that he felt precluded by Bonar Law's pledge the year before from introducing it. He therefore asked the country for a new mandate. That may have been the real reason for the election. If so, it was not the only one. The Conservatives were divided, and there were rumours that Lloyd George was about to come out for protection. This would have sharpened the split and possibly led to the creation of a new party under Lloyd George. Baldwin therefore beat him to it by going to the country.

That very professional politician, Senator Boise Penrose of Pennsylvania, is said to have remarked:[4] 'If a real politician ever faces a choice between losing control of his party or losing a specific election, he never hesitates a moment. He'll throw away the election and keep the party.'* Baldwin, too, was shrewd enough to know which of the two things was more important. And if he was primarily concerned to dish Lloyd George and end the split in his party, he was successful. He reunited the Conservatives—and also his Liberal opponents. If, however, Baldwin was primarily concerned with the election and with protection, his decision was disastrous. He handed natural conservatism to his traditionally free-trading Liberal opponents, the only time they had or have possessed this advantage since 1910 and the only time since then that they have been even moderately successful. He threw away his ample majority, and protection was postponed until the world slump.

On either interpretation 1923 was unique. It was also a discouraging warning to any politician who felt tempted to ask the voters to give him authority to introduce a controversial new policy.

Baldwin and his successors learned the lesson. To seek authority from the electorate for a big new departure was to invite rejection. Mencken wrote of Hoover in 1928: 'His judgment of the American people was cynical but sound. Whenever he fed them, it was with the mush that is now their pet fodder. He let Al [Smith, his opponent] bombard them with ideas, confident that ideas would only

---

* Bonar Law made much the same point at the Carlton Club meeting in 1922: 'I confess frankly that in the immediate crisis in front of us I do personally attach more importance to keeping our party a united body than to winning the next election.'[5]

affright and anger them. . . . His victory was a triumph of technique, of sound political engineering.'[6] Such now is the electoral technique of governments in Britain and, if they are wise, of oppositions too. The only fear the parties can safely rouse is fear of their opponents' proposals. Large conceptions and new issues are perilous, and so too is the future. Cries, slogans, posters, abuse and the past are much more promising campaign material.*

Even if the clear presentation of the most important issues were a profitable form of electioneering, the parties would have difficulty in doing it. They are not equipped to take a clear and unequivocal stand on many major issues. They may be firm on the reintroduction or abolition of prescription charges, expense allowances and other trivia, but on most major issues they must be vague, in order not to offend their actual or potential supporters.

The parties want to get out their own vote without stirring up the other side, regarding political conversion as by then out of the question. Frequently they discuss quite different things. Eisenhower was not the only politician to think it a waste of time 'answering the other fellow'.[8] The rival campaigns proceed along parallel lines and seldom meet. It was one of the great virtues of the Kennedy-Nixon television confrontations in 1960, that however imperfect the actual form of the programme, the candidates were forced to talk about the same things. The debate forced the two to converge, while most of the pressures in a modern campaign act to keep them apart. The daily round of press conferences in Smith Square begun in 1959 do something to bring the rival armies into hearing distance of each other. But they are a poor substitute for a genuine party confrontation, and the party dialogue remains incoherent and often meaningless.

To be sure, the parties produce programmes with which they solicit the voters. And usually they do their best to carry them out. Broken promises are wasteful and may be embarrassing. But inevitably the parts of the programme the parties stress are those which they believe to be popular. The bribes are highlighted; the cost is ignored, or put in very small print. Both because large issues are liable to alienate voters and because the events of the next five years cannot even be approximately foreseen, the party programmes

---

* Governor Dewey sent Sherman Adams a memorandum (not his own) advising Eisenhower to campaign in 1956 against former President Truman instead of against his opponent Adlai Stevenson, 'scaring hell out of the voters about war, about income taxes, high prices and depression'.[7]

on key issues often bear little relation to subsequent events.

In 1931 the national government refrained from telling the country they would introduce Protection if they won, though it was no secret that they would do so. Instead a Doctor's mandate was asked for and granted. After the Foreign Secretary, Hoare, had made a striking speech at Geneva, extolling the virtues of collective security, the government fought the 1935 election on that policy, which it then appeared to abandon a few months later by the signing of the Hoare-Laval pact.* Public outcry caused the sacrifice of Hoare and the repudiation of the pact, but the foreign policy of the government after the election bore a much greater resemblance to its policy before the election than either did to its policy during it.

The Attlee government carried out the promises of 'Let us Face the Future' with an old-fashioned punctilio ,and some of their actions would have been more appropriate to events if they had not. None of the election campaigns in the 1950s had great relevance to the problems facing the country. In 1964 the Conservatives were able to claim that they had carried out 92 of the 93 proposals named in their manifesto of 1959. But neither their manifesto nor their campaign had given any inkling of their two biggest policy steps in the next parliament: the winds of change in Africa and the attempt to join the Common Market. The chief connection between the Labour electoral campaigns of 1964 and 1966 and the subsequent actions of Mr. Wilson's government was the connection of opposites.

The withholding of important issues from the voters and the reliance instead upon slogans and fear have a respectable ancestry. They are not the invention of modern public relations techniques. Gladstone told Chamberlain in 1885 that his 'aim was for the election only',[9] and he did not confide to the voters his conversion to Home Rule until after he had won. The Democratic Presidential candidate in 1840 was told not to say 'a single word about what he thinks now or will do hereafter'. The slogans 'Tippecanoe and Tyler too', and 'Harrison, two dollars a day, and roast beef'[10] brought the party a comfortable victory. One of the Liberals' most powerful weapons

* This somersault was less spectacular than the manoeuvre executed by the Mollet government after the election of 1956. Within a few days of taking office M. Mollet was pelted with tomatoes by the Algiers mob, a sort of post-hustings procedure which was remarkably effective. The socialists and radicals dropped the Algerian policy on which they had fought the election and reverted to the policy of their opponents which they had been denouncing.

in 1906 was a poster which 'displayed a hideous yellow face, just that and nothing more'. 'Chinese slavery' was the perfect slogan. 'The market place roared with delight, but whether that delight expressed hostility to Chinamen, or hostility to their practical enslavement no student of the general election has ever been able to determine.'[11]

But traditional though such practices undoubtedly are, they plainly make it impossible, for 'the whole people to do the job', which Mr. Michael Stewart believes to be theirs, 'of determining the main line of policy for the next few years'.[12] Far from the whole people deciding the main line of policy, election campaigns are often segregated from the conduct of government. So much so indeed that when Mr. Churchill introduced into the general election campaign of 1950 the question of Summit talks, he was considered by his opponents and some serious commentators to be cheating. Such an important issue, it was thought, was not suitable for discussion in front of electors. Well might Mr. Churchill exclaim in a broadcast: 'What a reflection it would be upon our national dignity and moral elevation, and indeed upon the whole status of British democracy, if at this time of choice, this turning point in world history, we found nothing to talk about but material issues and nice calculations about personal gain or loss.'[13] In fact even the material issues are blurred and the nice calculations are fudged.

This is not a purely British phenomenon. It was not a British politician, but a future American president, L. B. Johnson, who said in 1960, 'the country wants to be comfortable. It doesn't want to be stirred up. Have a revolution, all right, but don't say anything about it until you are entrenched in office.'[14] Yet the closed British system is much more in need of electoral fresh air than those of other countries. The way in which elections are fought in Britain makes them a brake, not an accelerator. Instead of the publicity of elections spreading to government, the privacy of government has infected elections. Hence elections are unable to provide the push that the British system needs. The government is more frightened of what the next election may decide than spurred on by what the last one did decide. Where decisions or the impetus towards decisions are needed, elections like other British institutions chiefly provide consent.

This should not be blamed on the parties or the politicians. It is a logical outcome of the rest of the system. And the voters appear not to resent their walk-on part in the proceedings.* 'At a general election,' said L. S. Amery,[15] 'the voter is not in a position to choose either the kind of representative of the kind of government he would like if he had a free choice . . . his function is the limited and essentially passive one of accepting one of two alternatives put before him.'

But the elector has given no sign that he objects to this state of affairs. He has shown no inclination to discriminate between different strands of opinion in the parties. Liberal and right wing Conservatives, Bevanites, and anti-Bevanites, Labour supporters of C.N.D. and supporters of N.A.T.O. have all fared equally badly or well at successive elections. This disregard of candidates' political views is of long standing. In double member constituencies in 1880 the two candidates from the same party ran very close together however divergent their political opinions.[16] The elector in a midland constituency who said in 1951, 'I would vote for a pig if the party put one up',[17] was extreme in his language but typical in his opinion and sound in his constitutional understanding.† He was aware that he was primarily choosing a government, not an individual M.P.

To say, therefore, that the voter cannot choose 'the kind of representation . . . he would like' may be misleading. It is like saying that a woman who was quite indifferent to clothes might, when offered a choice between Courrèges and Balmain, have preferred instead Hardy Amies or Mary Quant. Most of the electorate are too uninterested in politics to resent the restrictions on their choice. 'The man who puts politics first', Mr. Hogg has said, 'is not fit to be called a civilised being, let alone a Christian';[19] the overwhelming majority of voters qualify to be called civilised beings.

The voters are no more anxious to receive a course in political education than the parties are to provide one. In the 1945 election, when it was a complaint of the left that the government had rushed the election, the *Daily Mirror* published a cartoon by Zec of an earnest young soldier racking his brains as to how he should vote.

* Those who do resent their walk-on part are seldom enthusiastic supporters of free elections.

† In 1959 many people in Sao Paulo voted for a female rhinoceros and elected her to the city council. This was not a demonstration of party loyalty but a protest against conditions in the city.[18]

It had the caption 'Why don't they give me time to think?'—an engaging picture of a general election as a nation-wide political seminar, but pure fantasy even in 1945. Elections are merely an expression and intensification of what is going on all the time. Some minds may be a little less closed than usual, but if in the law courts 'the state of a man's mind is just as much a fact as the state of his digestion', in politics the state of a man's digestion is rather more of a fact than the state of his mind. Most digestions are either satisfied or unsatisfied and their minds accordingly made up before the campaign begins. People not normally interested in politics do not become expert judges of political form during the short electoral season, and people who are interested in politics are unlikely to be swayed from a lifetime of party loyalty and prejudice by closely reasoned argument.

Sixty years ago Graham Wallas warned against exaggerating the intellectuality of man, and recent studies of electoral behaviour have confirmed that voters like other people are not guided by rational thought. Observers have tended to be dismayed by these revelations; they should have been pleased. A reasonable person relates his behaviour to the object or the activity concerned. A man on a sinking ship would be highly unreasonable if instead of helping to pump the water out he indulged in abstruse calculations as to why, or how much, water in the ship made it sink. The voter has only one vote with which to answer any number of questions. Does he approve of what the government has done? Does he approve of its future programme? Does he approve of the behaviour of the opposition? Does he approve of its programme? Does he think Mr. B. would make a better Prime Minister than Mr. A.? Does he think a spell in opposition would hurt party A? Does he think a spell in office would hurt party B? These are only some of the questions to which the voter has to give a composite answer. He is in the position of a witness asked to answer yes or no, not merely to the question, have you stopped beating your wife?, but have you stopped beating your wife, your sons, your daughters, your mother, and your dog? The irrationality of the voters is thus perfectly in tune with the system they are asked to operate.

At each election, about one-fifth of the electorate act differently from the time before,* but the transfer between the main parties, to and from the Liberals, and to and from abstention largely cancel

* In 1966 this proportion seems to have been appreciably higher; voters are evidently becoming more volatile.

each other out. The floaters used to be considered the electoral élite, the Solomons whose judgment was based on knowledge and wisdom. That conception was part of the old intellectualist fallacy, and the floating voter has now been dethroned. He is usually no more knowledgeable than the committed partisans and rather less interested. Nor does he come from any one stratum of the population. His change of mind is more frequently the result of cross-pressures on him from his work, his family or his friends,[20] than of agonised doubt as to the virtues of N.A.T.O. or devaluation. Although he has lost his elevated position as a man of wide ranging intelligence and strong yet flexible opinions, he is still important as a measurement of the intensity of opinion. Loyal party stalwarts may not change sides, but by complaints against their own leaders or by the magnitude or absence of their enthusiasm for their cause they influence the floaters in one direction of another.

Yet political factors of some sort are still electorally important. Throughout the Tory post-war years social trends seemed to favour the Tory party, but these were not enough to win the Conservatives the 1964 election. Economic issues are paramount. A government's popular standing depends upon the state of the economy. To a large degree this is fitting. Voters are better judges of their own interests than they are of matters on which they are uninformed. Interest is a more reliable guide to action than uninstructed opinion. Yet the voter's economic judgment appears to be confined to the immediate present and to be cut off from the future and past. In any case particular political issues either before or during the campaign do not influence many votes.

This may seem a haphazard way of choosing a government. But the irrationality of the voter and of elections is carefully circumscribed. The two party system and the single majority vote give less discretion to the voter than any other electoral procedure. And the similarity between the parties further diminishes the risks. Mr. Molotov once said to Sir Anthony Eden, 'the trouble with free elections is that you can't be certain about the outcome'.[21] The British political process takes care of that. The voters are like an inexperienced pilot being given his turn at the controls: there is little danger of a crash because the automatic pilot, the parties, will prevent an accident. All the same, in putting forward similar programmes and imitating their opponents, the parties are flattering not each other but the voters. Yet their flattery results in the voter being left with the minimum of political power.

The Electoral System

In Britain the purpose of elections is to provide a government. To over-simplify a little, in a two party system the parties choose the representatives and the people choose the government; and in a multi-party system the people choose the representatives and the parties choose the government. Opponents of the two party system believe that it is more important that an election should produce a parliament, which in its party strengths is an exact reproduction of the electorate, than a government with a parliamentary majority. They are offended by the spectacle of many M.P.s being elected upon a minority vote and by the discrepancy between votes won and seats obtained; they feel that the two party system falsifies the nation's verdict by being unfair to small parties.

Proportional Representation works satisfactorily in Scandinavia and elsewhere because it is accepted. Yet the two party system seems to be the most successful form of free government, and P.R. does not encourage a two party system. Exact representation of his opinion is of no help to the voter unless his representative can exercise power. And in a multi-party system the representative can exercise power only if he compromises the opinions which he allegedly represents by forming a coalition with people who allegedly represent different opinions. In practice, therefore, the multi-party system leads to no purer a representation of opinion than a two party system, though it does give the voter a greater freedom of choice.

Besides, even if it be assumed that an exact representation of opinion is both possible and desirable, there is no obvious reason why the representation of public opinion as it was on the day of election should be allowed to hold sway during the next four years, while public opinion itself has altered. If the faithful reproduction of a country's opinion is required, a photograph is insufficient. A motion picture is needed. Elections should take place at least once a year if not more frequently. But advocates of P.R. seldom follow their own logic. They shrink from frequent elections. As long as they were given a photograph, they would not mind it fading.

Efforts to achieve exact representation are as out of date in politics as they are in art. Proportional Representation has no greater theoretical justification than does the British system. Electoral systems can only be judged by their results.

Many members sit in the House of Commons though only a minority of their constituents supported them. This would be

avoided by introduction of the alternative vote or the single transferable vote, but those devices achieve a majority only by treating
second, third, or fourth preferences as of equal weight with first
preferences. Besides there is no magic in a bare absolute majority.
A majority vote is a useful device for gaining consent for a decision.
What form this majority takes, whether it is absolute or not is
unimportant, so long as the voters accept the result.

An M.P. may at successive elections be supported by 37.7 per
cent, 49 per cent, and 54.3 per cent of the electorate. He feels no
differently whether he has a majority or a minority vote behind him.
He has no more reason to be uneasy at having achieved less than
50 per cent of the vote in his constituency than do British
governments at having received less than 50 per cent of the total
vote of the country.

As to the alleged unfairness of the system, nearly all electoral
laws, even those based on proportional representation, discriminate
against very small parties. The difference between the single majority
vote and other systems is that the small parties against which the
former discriminate are bigger than those which suffer under P.R.

The supporters of the smaller parties maintain that they are an
essential element in the national verdict and that this verdict is
distorted by the present system. Professor Ramsay Muir, concerned
by the decline of the Liberal party, wrote of the 1929 election that
a straightforward two party contest between the Conservatives and
the Socialists would 'have falsified the real verdict of the nation. . . .
A two-party system would have led, whatever the result of the
election, to a misrepresentation of the nation's judgment. It was
only the effective interposition of a third party which enabled the
nation not only to give a clear verdict, but to do what by a large
majority it wanted to do . . . '.[22] How Muir knew that the outcome
of the election was what the nation wanted is obscure. All he could
know was that 38 per cent of the voters wanted a Conservative
government to continue, 37 per cent wanted it replaced by a Labour
government, and 23 per cent either wanted a Liberal government
or wanted the Liberal party to hold the balance. While therefore a
majority of the nation voted against either a Conservative or a
Labour majority government (as indeed it usually does), there was
an even greater majority against what actually happened—a minority
Labour government sustained by intermittent Liberal support—
a state of affairs which at the very most only 23 per cent of the
nation had sought to achieve.

In 1929 there were three fairly strong parties in existence and to have prevented one of them taking part in the election would have been to distort the political life of the country; it does not follow that an electoral result which gives substantial electoral success to three parties is somehow a more 'real verdict' than an election which gives success to only two. Three parties and a minority government no more faithfully reproduce the nation's mind, whatever that may be, than a majority government and a predominantly two party parliament.

The nation is not something separate from the two main parties. It is neither the Liberal party nor some Hegelian spirit high above the struggle, giving its verdict and distributing its honours according to strict principles of desert and merit. One might as well say of a civil war that the nation had finally decided in favour of the winners. Elections, like civil wars, are struggles not only for power but of power. Nor is there any resemblance between the electorate and a jury, the voters being very properly concerned more with their own interests than with returning verdicts on other people.

The conception of the nation bringing in a verdict and the attribution to it of sophisticated political wishes is not confined to professors. After the 1950 election Mr. Morrison said that 'the British electorate has a habit of knowing what it wants . . . this time I think it wanted Labour back with a smaller majority . . . '.[23] The 9.1 per cent who voted Liberal may have wanted Labour back with a smaller majority, and so may the abstainers, though most of them probably had little idea what they wanted. But it is improbable that many of the 46.1 per cent who voted Labour wanted Labour back with a smaller majority or that any of the 43.5 per cent who voted Conservative wanted Labour back at all.

Except in 1964, electoral behaviour has been remarkably uniform in different parts of the country, and the monotony of the swing in all regions and all classes lends some support to the conception of the electorate as an entity. Yet to talk of the mind of the electorate as expressed by general elections is political idolatry. Many electors react in a similar way to the same stimulus, but they are still all different. The reality is the individual voter, who is flattered, cajoled, bribed, bamboozled, browbeaten, and wooed by the parties. The party which persuades most voters to support it usually wins; but the large minority which votes for it cannot be identified with the electorate to the exclusion of the only slightly smaller minority which supported the losers.

There is no verdict; neither is there a mandate. The doctrine of the mandate was much invoked after the 1945 election, but it is an absurdly legalistic conception. Nobody can know whether voters voted primarily against the parties' previous record or in favour of their future proposals. And even if the voters are assumed to have looked forward rather than backward, plainly not all of them knew about, let alone approved, all the planks in their party's platform.

During the controversy on Tariff Reform, Joseph Chamberlain said that the issues on which they intended to 'take the opinion of the country' were not those which their opponents expected.[24] But whatever the politicians and parties prescribe as the issues at the election, there is no way of persuading people to accept that prescription in preference to one of their own choosing. Asquith rightly pointed out to the King in 1913 that a general election then would not be fought on Home Rule but on the Marconi contract and a score of other issues.[25] In the American Presidential election of 1960, the candidates talked at length about Castro, the U-2 incident, housing, experience in government, unemployment; they scarcely mentioned the issue which probably affected the most votes—the fact that Kennedy was a Roman Catholic.* The ostensible issues do not determine elections, still less does the small print of the party programme. Roosevelt's National Chairman in 1932, Farley, summed up the separation between votes and issues when he told Moley, F.D.R.'s speechwriter: 'I'm interested in getting him votes—nothing else. Issues aren't my business. They're yours and his. You keep out of mine, and I'll keep out of yours.'[28] Clearly voters do not give a mandate, though politicians like to think they receive one.

Of course a verdict and a mandate could easily be obtained by means of the referendum. But most countries have carefully avoided such democratic devices. In practice they do not consider the people's opinion to be worth taking, believing that people are incapable of making an intelligent choice upon particular measures, and that the most that can be asked of them is to make a general

---

* Possibly as many as 40 per cent of the Roman Catholics who would otherwise have voted for the Republicans voted for Kennedy and 20 per cent of Protestants who would otherwise have voted Democratic voted for Nixon. It has been estimated that Kennedy gained 2,800,000 and lost 4,300,000 votes because of his religion. Yet owing to the distribution of the Catholic vote in key states the religious issue probably helped him.[26] In 1948, also, religious affiliation appeared 'to be a stronger influence upon vote than any other single factor'.[27]

decision between two or more teams of politicians every few years. This belief has been given some foundation by experience of referenda elsewhere. In Australia and Belgium voters have given one answer to the question and yet voted for the party that favoured the opposite answer. Certainly, too, considerable advantage stems from the power to frame the form of words submitted to the electorate. A competent draftsman should be able to get the answer he wants. Business associations in America use referenda to demonstrate the solidarity of the organisation when there is no danger of getting an inconvenient answer. After the war the National Association of Manufacturers asked some of its firms: 'Do you believe that price controls hamper the production of manufactured goods?'[29] There are few issues moreover in which one question provides a genuine choice for both sides, and 'yes' and 'no' carry equivalent value. To nearly every question, one side's proper response is 'yes, but' or 'no, unless', qualifications which a referendum usually renders impossible.

British political leaders have occasionally attempted to resolve their difficulties by advocating a referendum. In 1910 Asquith briefly toyed with the idea during the conflict between Lords and Commons. In the same year Balfour produced an ambiguous proposal for a referendum on food taxes, and twenty years later Baldwin fleetingly agreed to one on the same subject. Churchill thought a referendum might secure public approval for continuing the wartime coalition without dissolving parliament. In general however the parties have preferred 'responsible government' to the referendum and similar devices.

The party system binds the country together by blurring conflicts and issues. Direct democracy, if honestly used, bares issues instead of blurring them. In so doing it offers the prospect of useful public dispute. Yet, historically, referenda have more often been a barrier than a passport to radical reform. Lord Hugh Cecil indeed specifically advocated them as a means of dishing the radicals.[30] They have also provided golden opportunities for pressure groups in Switzerland as well as California.* While therefore they should not be identified with Nazi Germany as Attlee did in 1945,[31] their absence is no loss. Yet the parties' rejection of machinery which would provide verdicts and mandates galore highlights the hypocrisy of a claim that a verdict or a mandate is given by the present system.

* See also page 342

The Government's Advantage

The electoral system is thus paternalist. The parties give the voters what they want while making sure that they, not the voters, rule. Any disadvantages there may be in counting votes instead of weighing them are minimised, and the advantages are not lost. Only the voters, after all, know where the shoe pinches, and for politicians to have to lick the boots of the electors periodically is a salutary change from the rather purer lip service they usually pay to democracy. As Mr. Morrison put it in more elevated language: 'Friends, an election is good for the soul of political leaders.'[32] Elections then are certainly beneficial for politicians, and often also for the electorate. The ultimate decision lies with the voters. This controls the politicians. At the same time the scope of that ultimate decision is closely confined. Thus the voters, too, are controlled.

Elections still adequately perform their basic function of providing a government. They are the most widely accepted method of gaining consent from the governed. The legitimacy of the British government was not questioned even in 1951 when it secured less popular votes than its opponents. In the performance of their second function, however,—producing a change of government—elections have become less efficient.

Post-war experience has shown how difficult it is for an incumbent government in Britain to get beaten. Notwithstanding nationalisation, austerity and restrictions, rising prices and rising taxes caused by the war in Korea, together with ministerial sickness and fatigue, the Labour government of Mr. Attlee still managed to win more votes than the Conservatives in 1951. It was driven out of office only by the bias in the electoral system. In 1955 the voters were beginning to enjoy the consumer revolution, and the Labour party was at best in a state of armed truce with itself. Not surprisingly the electors accepted the Conservatives' invitation to 'invest in success'. In 1959 however the Conservative advantage was less clear cut. The government's record included two economic crises, the highest level of unemployment since the fuel crisis of 1947, and the Suez disaster. These might have been expected to give the pendulum a push. Instead, the rise in living standards produced an increased majority for Mr. Macmillan.

1964 did bring a change of government, but it confirmed the impression caused by 1959. Despite the wrecking of its paramount policy of joining Europe and a consequent impression of drifting, despite an intensely unpopular economic policy, and an unpre-

F

cedented massacre of the Cabinet, and despite the unity of the Labour party on a moderate policy, the Conservatives were only just beaten and Mr. Wilson entered Downing Street with an overall majoritv of five.

1966 confirmed the overwhelming advantage of the government in an election. Labour had a strong case in 1964 and gained a majority of five. It had a weaker case in 1966 and gained a majority of 97. The mere possession of power was enough to increase Labour's popularity.

Oppositions have no pendulum to rely on. They can only get back to power by getting back into step with changed circumstances and public opinion. A party that loses an election is like a passenger who arrives at a station when the last train has just left. If he wants to catch the train, it is no good standing on the platform hoping for another; he will have to move on to the next station by taxi or other means. This operation was successfully carried out with conspicuous success by the Conservatives between 1945 and 1951. The Labour party on the other hand was in the 1950s inclined to remain sulking on the platform saying that the train should not have left, that it had gone on the wrong route, and that it should come back for its passengers.

Yet the experience of other countries indicates that Labour's ineptitude in opposition was not the prime cause of its electoral failure. The Christian Democrats have been in power in Germany with or without allies since the inception of the Federal Republic. Sir Robert Menzies retired undefeated after being Australian Prime Minister for twelve years. Mr. Erlander has been Prime Minister of Sweden for more than twenty years.

> 'And once in twenty years, their scribes record
> By natural instinct they change their Lord.'[33]

Twentieth-century electorates, it seems, are becoming scarcely more fickle than Dryden's Israelites, and post-war democratic governments show signs of becoming almost as long-lived as the most senior of twentieth-century dictatorships.

Electoral democracies have always had longer-lived governments than parliamentary democracies. The French Third Republic had 110 Cabinets in its 70 years;[34] between President de Gaulle's departure for Colombey les Deux Eglises in 1946 and his return in 1958, France had 21 governments; under the Weimar Republic there was on average a ministry a year; between the unification of Italy and Mussolini's 'march' on Rome there were sixty-seven ministries;[35] in the ten years up to 1932 Sweden had nine governments. Many of these changes of course were shuffles, not redeals; various ministers played musical chairs. There was neither stability nor genuine change.

In the United States long stretches of rule by one party are not a new phenomenon. Only two American Presidents have been defeated in this century: Taft, in 1912, when his party was split and he had to run against T. Roosevelt as well as Wilson; and Hoover, in 1932, who had to run against the depression as well as F. D. Roosevelt.* Even when the President is not seeking re-election, the party in charge of the White House rarely goes down to defeat. Kennedy in 1960 was the only man in this century to defeat the party in possession of the White House without the aid of a war, a catastrophic split in the incumbent party, or an unprecedently severe depression.

In Britain, on the other hand, Prime Ministers have frequently been rejected by the voters or forced out of office before they could be defeated. Apart from Balfour who resigned before defeat, Baldwin, Macdonald, Churchill, Attlee, Douglas-Home, all had to leave 10 Downing Street, after losing an election. Up to 1945, of those who were not defeated but forced out by other means, only Asquith and Lloyd George enjoyed periods of office similar to those normally enjoyed by American Presidents. Yet the feat of the Conservatives in increasing their majority in both 1955 and 1959 suggests that, except when a government is outstandingly incompetent, this country may be changing to the American pattern, or back to the pattern of eighteenth or early nineteenth-century Britain when long-lived ministries were the rule not the exception. Shortly after the 1959 election Professor Samuel Beer[36] contemplated without deep misgiving about democracy a further long period of Conservative rule. The Conservatives were defeated at the next election, but his argument may have been right though its occasion was wrong. One party rule need not be disastrous. Yet a reasonable rotation of governments would surely be preferable to Walpolean stretches of power by either party. 'It is a necessary precaution in a free state to change the governors frequently,' said Hume.[37] Two hundred years later it may no longer be a necessary precaution; it remains a wise one.

* Truman in 1952 and Johnson in 1968 would probably have been defeated had they run.

Until recently a reasonable rate of change has been achieved in Britain and if one party rule materialises in the seventies the principal reason will be clear. In the power of dissolution the British government possesses an advantage shared by scarcely any free government outside the Commonwealth. In other countries elections are at fixed times, or the power of dissolution is hedged around by conventions or rules. In Norway elections are at fixed four-yearly intervals, and there is no power of dissolution. Under the Third Republic the President had the power to dissolve the Chamber, but after MacMahon's dissolution in 1877 the power was never again exercised. Under the Fourth Republic the Prime Minister was given a more restricted power, which also was only exercised once, by M. Edgar Faure in 1955. In Italy, there is a power but it has not been used for fear that it might help the extremist parties. The German Bundestag can only be dissolved if it fails to elect a Chancellor. In Sweden there is a power of dissolution, but elections have still to take place at the fixed and proper time: a dissolution produces an extra election; it is not a substitution for the ordinary one. And there has been no dissolution there since 1921.

There are now no such conventions in Britain. In the eighteenth century there was until 1784 a convention that parliament would not be dissolved before its seventh year. George III broke it in 1784 and in 1807. In the nineteenth century, elections before parliament had run near its full term were brought about by a government defeat in the House. Early dissolutions were not caused by a government with a majority attempting to dish its opponents.* Disraeli said in 1880 that to have dissolved in 1878 after his diplomatic triumph at the Congress of Berlin, 'would have been one of the most unconstitutional acts of the century'.[38]

Yet by 1900 the Duke of Devonshire could use a cricketing analogy in defence of the Khaki election. 'We all know very well,' he told a Yorkshire audience, 'that the captain of a cricketing eleven, when he wins the toss puts his own side in, or his adversaries, as he thinks most favourable to his prospect of winning.'[39] Certainly dissolution is too useful a weapon for governments to neglect. Those countries where its use has been circumscribed by

---

* Grey's government dissolved in 1832 to give the new electorate a chance to vote. The new electorate of 1867 and 1885 were given similar chances by the minority governments of Disraeli, after a defeat in the House, and of Salisbury after a delay caused by the need to complete the new registers.

conventions are also mostly those where a multi-party system or other factors prevent it from being effective.

The timing of the 1918 election, like the Khaki election, has often been criticised. Yet parliament had run for eight years, the parties were disorganised, and it was better that a new one should be elected before the peace negotiations. On Chamberlain's return from Munich Halifax strongly counselled against an election, and Churchill said that to hold an 'inverted Khaki election' when the government had 'a large working majority' would be 'an act of historic constitutional indecency'.[40] Still, it is hard to see why it should be more indecent to attempt to cash in on a diplomatic triumph or disaster than on a temporary economic upsurge. Political, diplomatic or jingoistic euphoria is scarcely more disturbing to the voters' judgment than economic or financial euphoria. And in fact the only thing likely to stop a Prime Minister holding an election at what seems to be a favourable moment is the danger of the gambit seeming too obvious: the voters may think the government is guilty of sharp practice. In other words the only restriction on a government holding an election at an apparently favourable moment is that the moment may not turn out to be favourable.

Now that parliament cannot normally dismiss the government, there is no need for the government to have the right to dismiss parliament and choose the date of every election. Governments do not wish to consult 'the people'. The theory of the mandate is untenable. Elections are not great national debates. But the threat of dissolution helps governments to discipline their followers,* while its exercise enables the government to steal a march on the opposition. The best solution, therefore, would be to add fixed date elections every four years, as in Sweden, to the present power to dissolve.

But these matters are not resolved by such considerations, and governments are not concerned to be fair. The power to hold an election at virtually any time gives a preponderant advantage to the governing party and one that no government is likely to renounce. In the past, British Prime Ministers had to rely on intuition to choose a favourable moment to dissolve. Now they can dispense with anything so unscientific. They know that economic conditions predominantly determine elections. Usually they are able to control these conditions. They know when the government is popular, and they have a good idea of how people intend to vote. With modern techniques of controlling the economy and testing public opinion,

* See pages 263-4.

a Prime Minister, unless his economic mismanagement has been so complete that his government is in trouble for the last two years of its term, should always be able to choose a moment to go to the country that makes his confirmation in office highly probable.

The government's proclivity to win elections increases the stagnation of the British political process. A change of party is the chief element of change and impetus in the system. Unless British voters are good butchers, continuity of the elected politicians is added to the continuity of the permanent politicians.

Universal Suffrage

The advent of democracy was feared by such men as J. S. Mill because they believed that under universal suffrage the majority would swamp everything else. 'My firm conviction,' warned Macaulay, 'is that in our country universal suffrage is incompatible ... with all forms of government...'.[41] Mill and those who thought like him assumed that the newly enfranchised masses, like the Victorian middle class and aristocracy, would take an 'enlightened' view of their economic self interest and come flooding into parliament with the intention of despoiling the bourgeoisie of all that made life worth living. In this belief they managed to combine vulgar Marxism with the crude doctrine of the classical economists: they saw the workers marching into battle as a united class, and they imagined this class to be solidly composed of mythical 'economic man'. Hence Mill's advocacy of Hare's elaborate system of proportional representation which he thought might save something from the democratic wreckage.

In the event the workers confounded Mill, Salisbury, and the other prophets of doom. Instead of being the Jacobin mountain that nineteenth century Liberals and Conservatives feared, universal suffrage turned out to be a mouse. Indeed Maine's opposite fear that democracy would be reactionary not revolutionary proved to be nearer the mark.

Mass electorates have rarely shown themselves well disposed to radical new departures. Universal suffrage has led to apathy, not to revolution or the rapine and plunder of the middle classes. It has been the great tranquilliser. In *The Mask of Anarchy*, Shelley urged the 'Men of England' to

> Rise like lions after slumber
> in unvanquishable number

Shake your chains to earth like dew
Which in sleep had fallen on you...
Ye are many...they are few.

Universal suffrage has preserved the sleep and provided new voluntary chains.

People were misled because they thought in terms of dubious entities like 'universal suffrage' and 'the masses'. The development of mass parties, which Mill did not foresee, carved up these cloudy entities into real and genuine bodies; but while the parties transferred universal suffrage from the Chamber of Horrors to the Parliamentary Chamber they often lost a majority on the way. Thus in France under the Third Republic there was rarely a majority in favour of anything at all; Italy suffered from the same difficulty in a less acute form. In the Third Republic there was almost always an electoral majority for the Left, which increasingly often became a governmental majority of the Right. The Left, for religious, constitutional, and ancestral reasons, could combine at an election; for economic and social reasons it could not remain combined for long afterwards. Thus an assembly would regularly begin by supporting a government of the Left and end by supporting a government of the Right.

In Britain the parliamentary majority remains the same between elections. Bewildering coalitions between erstwhile opponents, as in Germany, are generally avoided. Yet there is only a tenuous connection between the electoral and the governing majority. An election manifesto cannot dictate a government's activities during the ensuing five years. British governments pay great attention to public opinion, but often the immediate need is to placate the interests involved, not the whole electorate. Past and future electoral power is offset by the present power of pressure groups. Universal suffrage having been tamed by parties has been hobbled by pressure groups.

But general elections still dominate the political system. They decide which party is to form the government. Together with the party system they determine the place of the executive and of parliament. Their plebiscitary character together with restrictions on candidates' expenditure ensures that only the leaders have any influence in the campaign. An M.P.'s electoral impotence ties his future to that of the party. The government has increased its control over elections, but it has not freed itself from their sway. The return of the reigning government has been made more probable.

That is all. The government has not become stronger thereby. The caution and concealment necessary for the winning of elections affects a government's subsequent conduct. On big issues the electors provide no whip or spur; indeed the government's previous complacency or deceit provides another restraint.

Léon Blum[42] called universal suffrage 'our judge and master'.* In England at least, it can scarcely be a judge, since the arguments and issues are usually neither presented nor heeded; and if it is the master, it is the master of men not events. The electorate chooses the rulers but does not decide what they do. The struggle for power produces consent; it does not stimulate decisions.

---

* When M. Blum paid his tribute to universal suffrage in France, the country did not in fact possess it. Up to 1945 France only had manhood suffrage.

PART TWO

THE PROCESS OF GOVERNMENT

I

THE CIVIL SERVICE AND THE
PUBLIC ADMINISTRATION

The time is now come, in which every Englishman expects to be informed
of the national affairs; and in which he has a right to have that expectation
gratified. For, whatever may be urged by Ministers, or those whom vanity
or interest make the followers of ministers, concerning the necessity of
confidence in our governours, and the presumption of prying with profane
eyes into the recesses of policy, it is evident that this reverence can be
claimed only by counsels yet unexecuted, and projects suspended in
deliberation. But when a design has ended in miscarriage or success, when
every eye and every ear is witness to general discontent, or general
satisfaction, it is then a proper time to disentangle confusion and illustrate
obscurity; to shew by what causes every event was produced, and in what
effects it is likely to terminate . . .

DR. JOHNSON[1]

Hitler grinned. 'Do you know, Mr. Delmer,' he said, 'I have made a
great discovery. There is nothing to this business of governing! Nothing at
all. It is all done for you . . . You simply sign your name to what is put
before you, and that is that!'

SEFTON DELMER[2]

'You've just put a lot of extra work on us,' said Mark Levett.
'Apparently our two chiefs lunched together today and the question of
waste rubber was brought up. The Permanent Secretary isn't too pleased
with Sir John Bunting for more or less promising our comments on your
proposals within a week.' 'A week!' Jim Pettiward gasped. 'Did you say
a week? You know, these politicians have absolutely no conception of time.
We have the same trouble at the Home Office.'

COMPTON MACKENZIE: The Red Tapeworm

The Civil Service is unaffected by the struggle for power. The
party battle is limited not merely in intensity but in extent. The
public administration carries on regardless of the fluctuating fortunes of the parties. The winning party captures and retains the
commanding heights of Whitehall, but only the heights: it is kept

off the slopes and the foothills. Party takes over parliament but not the executive. No matter what excesses the party politicians commit on the hustings or elsewhere, the Civil Service is there to see that the Queen's government is carried on and continuity maintained.

The coachman was tipsy, the chariot drove home.[4]

The Civil Service has attained a position not unlike that of the Church in the Middle Ages. Its power has steadily grown and it has become virtually autonomous. Its house having been put in order, it has become its own master in it; its regulations and reorganisation are carried out not by act of parliament but by Treasury minutes and Orders-in-Council. Mediaeval bishoprics could only be filled after the King's *congé d'élire* had been received. 'If', Pope Clement VI said in 1345, 'the King of England were to petition for his ass to be made a Bishop, we could not say him nay. . . .' Similarly the approval of the Prime Minister and the departmental minister concerned is necessary for appointments to the highest grades of the Civil Service, and the chieftains of the Civil Service could not say 'nay' to the Prime Minister if he had a strong preference. In practice, however, the Premier or the departmental minister seldom objects to a recommendation.[5] The power of appointment therefore lies with the Head of the Civil Service, together with the Permanent Secretary of the department in which there is going to be a vacancy. Like the mediaeval Church, Civil Servants have a dual allegiance to their political masters and to the Civil Service, to Westminster and to Whitehall; unlike the Church the Service has never been faced with a statute of Mortmain to restrict its power. Just as the Church held a religious monopoly and had exclusive charge of the route to heaven, so the Civil Service holds a virtual monopoly of the power of advising ministers and has exclusive charge of administration.

Yet the autonomy of the Civil Service is recent. Its insulation from party politics is less than one hundred years old. Until the Order-in-Council of 1870, entry into government departments, like appointments to 'independent' boards today, was by political patronage. This was not a spoils system. Even in 1660 and in 1688 there was continuity in such Civil Service as there was; and in the later eighteenth century, even in the 1762 'massacre of the Pelhamite innocents', there was no ruthless purge in the revenue departments of those appointed by the previous administration. Walpole alone among English politicians in the eighteenth century had what later became characteristically American ideas of patronage. In general from 1660 onwards 'to the victors' did not 'belong the spoils', only the vacancies. Political patronage was combined with security of tenure, an enervating mixture.

'Those whom indolence of temperament or physical infirmities unfit for active exertions,' said the crucial Northcote-Trevelyan report of 1853, 'are placed in the Civil Service, where they may obtain an honourable livelihood with little labour, and with no risk.'[6] The report exaggerated; the *ancien régime* contained at least in its higher strata a number of outstanding officials. But the general level was mediocre. Gladstone said in 1866 that he was 'far from thinking very highly of our rank as a nation of administrators'.[7]

Trevelyan and Northcote advocated entry into the Civil Service by competitive examination not patronage, promotion by merit, and a division between 'intellectual and mechanical' work. Political patronage, however, was still generally considered an essential element in the constitution, and recruitment continued to be by nomination. A former Chief Whip, through whom requests for patronage from Members of Parliament were channelled, and who gave jobs to M.P.s' constituents and relations in return for the promise of the member's trusty vote, told Trevelyan that 'it will not do for the Whipper-in to have nothing but his Whip left.'*[8]

In fact, as Gladstone realised, the political importance of Civil Service patronage was enormously exaggerated. Ever since the beginning of the movement for economical reform in the 1780s, there had been a relentless enclosure movement upon the pastures available for the feeding of hungry beasts, and by the 1850s the government could feed only a small herd of cattle of rather poor quality. Nevertheless, the illusory political advantages of patronage were thought to outweigh its real and obvious administrative disadvantages, until the doubling of the electorate by the Reform Bill of 1867 made it clear to even the most orthodox constitutionalists that Civil Service patronage was no longer the regulator of the House of Commons. The Order-in-Council of 1870 made entry into every government department except the Foreign Office dependent upon passing an open competitive examination, and shortly afterwards the Civil Service was divided into two main categories, a higher class who would do brain work and a lower who would do mechanical work. The Civil Service was thus thrown open to all who were proficient in Latin and Greek.

---

* Trevelyan's priggish description of the procedure was: 'a functionary of high standing is attached to the Central Department of the government with the recognised official duty of corrupting Members of Parliament and constituencies'.[9]

The story of Civil Service reform illustrates the tenacity of obsolete constitutional dogmas. The doctrine of ministerial responsibility is the present-day equivalent of nineteenth century political patronage in the Civil Service. It also governs the relationship of Civil Servants to ministers and parliament, and indeed determines the whole working of the bureaucracy.

'The personal responsibility of each minister to Parliament for matters within his competence,' said Sir John Anderson, 'is a basic principle of the constitution—a principle as fundamental as the rule of law or the sovereignty of Parliament.'[10] If that were all the doctrine meant, there would be no need to worry. Unfortunately it means both more and less than Anderson's statement of it implies. According to this principle, ministers are solely responsible to parliament for all the acts and omissions of their departments. They are *in loco parentis* to their officials. They, and nobody else, may punish erring subordinates. Indeed the press or M.P.s must not even criticise individual Civil Servants since they cannot answer back. To criticise them, as Chadwick said, is 'like striking a woman'.[11]

British government is anthropomorphic. Everything is done by the minister and not by the ministry. The eight or ten thousand planning appeals each year are, theoretically, decided by the Minister of Housing and not by his ministry. Civil Servants advise the minister and they execute his decisions, but the decisions are his, not theirs.

As Sir James Grigg described the position of officials: 'We had to go hand in hand to the Secretary of State and convince him that it was the right thing to do. But once he had decided . . . to adopt our suggestions, they became his own and he assumed the entire responsibility for them *urbe et orbi*. . . . Those of us who had advised or pressed the decisions upon him hid ourselves behind the cloak of the unique but universal accountability of a Secretary of State.'[12] A Civil Servant needs a minister to give him identity. Without one, he is a mere shadow who must on no account aspire to substance. When the Treasury discovered that the departmental committee set up in 1941 under Beveridge's chairmanship to enquire into the problems of social security was going to deal with large scale questions of policy, its prudery was outraged. The officials would 'commit' their ministers, which was unthinkable. All eleven Civil Servants on the committee therefore resigned. Beveridge was left as the sole member, all the other erstwhile members becoming his advisers. By this brilliant stroke, constitutional decency was triumphantly preserved, and the Beveridge Report appeared with only one signature instead of twelve.[13]

No party could run the complicated modern state without the aid of the bureaucracy, and the anonymity of officials enables them to serve both parties without embarrassment. Ministerial responsibility gives the public and parliament somebody to shoot at; otherwise the public would have only a vast impersonal bureaucracy on which to vent its frustrations. A scapegoat to atone for all the burdens of modern government is still useful, even if according to civilised and sophisticated principles the goat is always allowed to escape. Moreover, ministerial responsibility does provide fairly effective control of the Civil Service. The British party system might seem to afford the Civil Service almost unlimited protection. The mistakes of the Civil Service are the mistakes of the government, and the government's parliamentary majority is not enthusiastic to have them paraded. The Civil Service is always on the side of the majority of the House of Commons, and the majority of the House is always on the side of the executive. Yet in practice there have been few abuses of bureaucratic power. The system of a minister, subject to the harassment by letter or question of his parliamentary colleagues about routine matters in lower levels of his department, successfully mitigates bureaucracy. Ministers tend to support their subordinates in public even when they are wrong; in private their attitude is less comforting. Parliamentary majorities prevent censure but they do not safeguard an official's future career. Contrary to appearances, then, this parliamentary control does work. ministerial responsibility not only gives protective colouring to the bureaucracy; it also does much to protect the public from officialdom.

These are formidable advantages. Probably indeed the doctrine of ministerial responsibility possesses every advantage except that it is not true. It is contrary to the administrative and the political realities.

In 1853 the Civil Service contained about 16,000 people; today there are about 450,000 non-industrial Civil Servants. As Home Secretary in 1822 Peel had 'a staff of fourteen clerks, a précis writer, a librarian, and various porters and domestic officials'.[14] The Foreign Office had a staff of twenty in 1821, forty in 1841.[15] Canning wrote or dictated almost every despatch, and personally controlled every aspect of foreign policy.[16] Departments were small enough to be run by ministers, and there was no question of policy being divorced from administration. The functions of the Civil Service were regulative. Even as late as 1914 the activities of government did not greatly impinge upon the lives of most of the population. Now they impinge at every point, and the tasks of the Civil Service are no longer merely advisory and regulative but also managerial and decisive.

Government and government departments have developed not unlike industry, where small-scale enterprises run by the owner manager with a few men working under his direct supervision have given way to large-scale impersonal organisations with a very different relationship to the boss. In industry there have been new theories and practices to cope with the new facts. In government, by contrast, the vast increase in the Civil Service and in the volume of its activities has taken place without any alteration in constitutional doctrine. Constitutionally we are still living in the age of Nassau Senior and Ricardo.

The growth of the idea of ministerial responsibility in the nineteenth century led to the decline of 'independent' boards: by 1900 there were only six boards which were more than nominally independent of ministers.[17] In this century the burgeoning activities of government have produced more public boards than new ministries. But while the earlier decline of independent boards followed the development of ministerial responsibility, the resurgence of boards had led to no decline of the doctrine. Ministers have continued to extol the importance of ministerial responsibility, while supporting the creation of boards which defy it.

In no other large-scale sphere of activity, nor in the government of any other country, is the attempt made to pretend that all the important decisions are taken by the man at the top of the organisation. Ministers moreover are usually less versed in the activities of their departments and have more outside distractions than the heads of other organisations. The pretence is therefore transparent. Lord Templewood wrote[18] of the exercise of the prerogative of mercy when the Home Secretary was away: 'When cases were referred to me at the time that I was Secretary of State for Air . . . I had in fact to accept the recommendation made to me by the Home Office . . . what was required of me was a signature without which an execution could not take place and I was in no position to refuse it.'

Even if the decision is, formally, always the minister's, and Civil Servants always take the precaution of getting him to sign on the dotted line, it does not mean that it was really his or that he had any genuine freedom of choice. He signs the cheques, but officials write them out. Referring this time to the prerogative of mercy, when he was Home Secretary, Templewood said:[19] 'More than once, I had two capital cases to decide at the same time. They were brought to me in the midst of a mass of cabinet and departmental work. There were dozens of other urgent questions that were claiming my attention. . . . My decision was bound to be based on the advice of others, though I would not say that my own views might not occasionally modify theirs.' This kind of decision-taking is inevitably common; and in departments such as the Treasury officials took important decisions on their own even before the war.[20] The far wider ramifications of the post-war welfare state make such decision-taking commonplace and unavoidable in most ministries.

Politically, as well as administratively, the theory is at variance with the practice. The modern doctrine emerged only after the Reform Bill. The King could no longer secure a parliamentary majority for his ministers, hence he could no longer dismiss them. Parliament could. Between 1783 and 1830 no government resigned because it was defeated in the Commons. Between 1832 and 1867 resignation or dissolution after defeats in the House was common, and ministers became responsible to parliament. Even in those days the resignation of individual ministers because of mistakes committed by themselves or their department was rare, but resignation of the entire government was not. Nowadays governments are not defeated in the House of Commons and do not resign. Even less than in the past, do ministers resign because of their mistakes or because of departmental blunders. A resignation in such circumstances entails admission of error, and under the conditions of modern party politics admission of error is a more serious matter than error itself. Ministers are made to resign only if it suits the Prime Minister that they should. Unless there is a need to assuage the inflamed populace, as when Hoare was dropped because of the uproar over the Hoare-Laval pact, or unless the actions of a department are contrary to some deeply felt belief of the majority party, 'forced' resignations do not occur.* Only nineteen senior ministers have resigned in deference to this convention in the past one hundred years, and only two since 1945.[21]

* The Ministry of Agriculture's behaviour over Crichel Down offended the Tory party, but Sir Thomas Dugdale's resignation was more an act of exceptional punctilio which he himself felt forced to make than the result of party pressure.

A minister is still answerable to parliament for the actions of his department. This is the valuable and genuine part of the doctrine. But parliamentarily that is all it now means or entails. The then Home Secretary, Sir David Maxwell Fyfe, laid down in 1954 that 'where an official makes a mistake or causes some delay, but not in an important issue of policy . . . the Minister acknowledges the mistake, and he accepts the responsibility, although he is not personally involved. He states that he will take corrective action in the Department'. In plain English, to accept the responsibility for something means to take the blame; but since on Sir David's hypothesis the minister announces that he is going to take corrective action 'in the department' there is a clear implication that he is not taking the blame but is blaming somebody else. 'The minister,' Sir David went on, 'is not bound to approve of action of which he did not know, or of which he disapproves. But of course he remains constitutionally responsible to Parliament for the fact that something has gone wrong, and he alone can tell Parliament what has occurred, and render an account of his stewardship.'[22] In this context the phrase 'constitutionally responsible to Parliament' evidently means that the minister is the man who tells parliament that he was not responsible for the mistake.*

Ministerial responsibility thus protects the Civil Service from parliament without endangering the minister. While ostensibly opening government to legislative examination, ministerial responsibility effectively prevents such examination. So far from being a sword in the hands of parliament it is a shield on the arm of the government. Parliament must be prevented from knowing anything of what went on in the ministry before or after the minister's decision was reached. If M.P.s pried into such matters, so runs the orthodoxy, they would disrupt the smooth working of the department, disturb the relations between the minister and his advisers, bring the Civil Service into politics, pollute the disinterested purity of the advice officials give to their minister, and blur the responsibility of ministers to parliament.

'The King can do no wrong' sounds like an assertion of Divine

---

* When questioned on the Marrinan case and telephone tapping in 1957, Mr. Butler pointed out that the action had been taken by his predecessor and added: 'Therefore the Hon. Member is not quite exact in attributing responsibility to me personally. As Secretary of State, however, I am defending the situation, and I am right to do so.' Mr. Butler went on to say that such a thing would not happen again. In this exposition there was no doubt about the meaning of 'responsibility', though the meaning of 'defending' was perhaps not altogether clear.

Right, a prosaic version of Charles I's Declaration that 'princes are not bound to give account of their actions but to God alone'[23]; and in the early seventeenth century it was such an assertion. Yet it soon came to mean the opposite, to be the trumpet call of the Whigs, not the Tories. 'If the King can do no wrong,' Defoe[24] pointed out, 'somebody did the late King a great deal of wrong.' Too much wrong, indeed, for even the most extreme Whigs to want to repeat. But if the King could do no wrong, the wrongs committed by his ministers must be contrary to his will and nature, and his ministers should be dismissed and punished for their wrongdoing. Hence a doctrine, which originally proclaimed the secular unaccountability of the executive, came to proclaim its accountability to an exceedingly secular parliament.

The doctrine of ministerial responsibility to parliament has gone through a contrary process. Beginning as an expression of the executive's accountability to parliament, it has come to be an excuse for avoiding such accountability. Originally the trumpet call of parliament, it has become the incantation of the executive. The irony of ministerial responsibility is that it no longer shields the Civil Service from blame and obloquy. The 'statesmen in disguise' that Sir James Stephen rightly thought would be the product of the Trevelyan-Northcote report are no longer in disguise. Indeed Civil Servants have almost displaced politicians as the primary target of abuse.

All the same, whatever the inconsistencies, the absurdities and the unreality of the doctrine, it still largely determines the operations of the Civil Service. Indeed its ultimate absurdity is that while it is used to exalt the executive and to free it from interference by parliament, it in fact hinders the executive and prevents it being properly effective.

Performance and Criticism

Governmental secrecy stops outsiders from knowing what has gone on in the departments and makes the apportionment of praise and blame between politicians and Civil Servants a hazardous business. The authors of the official war histories, however, were given free access to departmental files. Before the war, the shipping planners were busily contracting the programme of food imports, while the food planners were no less busily expanding it. Neither paid any attention to the other.[25] Despite Oliver Lyttelton's warnings to officials, Britain entered the war with dangerously inadequate stocks of copper and other metals.[26] In 1939–40 Britain imported in greater quantities than in peace time such inessentials as wines and spirits and Spanish onions. 'According to the tests of necessity that Britain adopted in a leaner time 2 or 3 million tons of shipping space might possibly have been saved by pruning away this miscellaneous luxuriance.'[27]

The Ministry of Supply continued to make general use of costed contracts, long after it was plain that the system was piling up an unmanageable volume of arrears of costing and its object, to gain a guide to current prices, was thus being defeated.[28] Departments waged private war against each other. The Air Ministry provisioning branches tried to prevent the Ministry of Aircraft Production from knowing about its stocks.[29] Departmental empire building and hoarding continued unabated. Just as the Home Office hung on to the factory inspectors for some twenty years after they should have been transferred to the Ministry of Labour, the Ministry of Supply was reluctant to see itself divested of any of its functions in favour of the newly set up Ministry of Production in 1942.[30] In carrying out its policy for the concentration of industry, the Board of Trade spent some time concentrating the production of pianos.[31] And as late as 1941 Army chaplains had to make a monthly return of all their communicants.[32]

Such engaging bureaucratic peccadilloes were not peculiar to Britain; almost exactly similar things were done by our allies and our enemies.* And they were offset by many administrative triumphs particularly at the centre in the Cabinet offices. In the result Britain was more highly mobilised for war than any other country.

There are no official histories of the post-war years, and the Civil Service's recent performance is harder to judge. But the Treasury's record since the war can hardly have been due solely to the eleven Chancellors of the Exchequer who have been at its head. In particular the advice it and the Bank of England gave over convertability in 1947 proved to be wildly impracticable, and probably the same would have been said about its advice on the same subject in 1952, had Sir Winston Churchill been as willing as Mr. Dalton to act on it. Some of the Foreign Office advice about the possibilities of the E.E.C. succeeding and of the chances of a Free Trade area

---

* In 1953 the incoming Republicans 'uncovered a $20,000 a year man and two secretaries who were engaged in developing spruce lumber for use in construction of World War I aircraft'.[33]

being accepted by France was certainly wrong, though if it had been right it probably would not have been followed.

Attendance at the hearings of the Estimates and the Public Accounts Committees or a reading of the evidence does not impel the belief that the self-contained Whitehall process is necessarily productive of coherent and intelligent decision making. Nor do the reports of, say, the Bank Rate Tribunal or the enquiry into D Notices suggest that behind the impressive façade of ministerial responsibility and Cabinet government, efficiency order and calm reign in Whitehall. Attempts to find the cause of all our ills in the incompetence of the Civil Service can be ignored; the extent of Whitehall's failure has been much exaggerated, yet plainly something is wrong.

A parliamentary committee said of the Civil Service in 1944: 'The faults most frequently enumerated are over-devotion to precedent; remoteness from the rest of the community, inaccessibility and faulty handling of the general public; lack of initiative and imagination; ineffective organisation and waste of manpower; procrastination and unwillingness to take responsibility or to give decisions.'[34] In constitutional theory Civil Servants do not have responsibility and the minister takes decisions, so their 'unwillingness to take responsibility or to give decisions' is not unexpected. And in view of the secrecy imposed upon them it is harsh to complain of their 'remoteness from the rest of the community'. Much the same is true of most other common criticisms of the Civil Service. Its class composition, Treasury control, its amateurism, its over-centralisation in London, its out of date structure and organisation, its monopoly, its excessive secrecy—in so far as these criticisms have substance, the root cause of the troubles stems from the system of ministerial responsibility and from the representative nature of the Civil Service.

Alleging that many families looked upon 'patronage as a holy thing not to be touched by profane hands', Bright quoted the Bigelow papers:

'It is something like a fulfilling the prophecies,
When all the first families have all the best offices.'[35]

And indeed the common opinion was that the replacement of patronage by competitive examination would lead to a lowering of the social status of the Civil Service. In fact, as Chadwick pointed out in 1854, most of the patronage was obtained 'by persons of the lower condition.'[36] Gladstone knew what he was doing. In 1854 he had written to Lord John Russell[37] '. . . I do not hesitate to say that one of the great recommendations in my eyes would be its tendency to strengthen and multiply the ties between the higher classes and the possession of administrative power.' And so it proved.

The education necessary for the examinations was a luxury only provided by the public schools and the older universities. Latin and Greek guarded entry into the administrative class of the Civil Service as effectively as the English language test guarded immigration into Australia. Nevertheless long before the Fulton report, changes in the social complexion of the universities and the filling of many places by promotion from the executive class had given the administrative class a fairly wide social base.

Like the British, the French Civil Service is more 'democratic' than before the war, but the middle and upper classes still supply a disproportionate number of students.[38] In Sweden the top social group comprises five per cent of the population and provides 52 per cent of all higher officials.[39] In America sons of businessmen are five times, and sons of professional men, four times, as numerous in the Civil Service as they are in the population as a whole.[40] Though representative of the nation in other ways, the British Civil Service is not fully representative socially, but in this it is not out of line with other countries.

A long standing order of the House of Commons dating back to 1713 provides that no proposal causing a charge on the public revenue may proceed unless recommended by the Crown. Since 1861 the estimates of each department have to be approved by the Treasury before they can be presented to parliament. No memorandum proposing additional expenditure can be circulated by a minister until the proposal has been discussed with the Treasury.[41] This means that cabinet discussions take place on the basis of agreed figures.

Penny-pinchers have not been glorified since the days of Gladstone, though they are probably necessary in every large organisation. But the Treasury's distinction has been its obsession with the saving of candle ends to the exclusion of more important matters. Salter discovered that if you saved the government hundreds of

pounds nobody noticed, if you spent 7s. 6d. without prior authority
you had infinite trouble.[42] Rarely has the Treasury taken a long
view. Consequently it nearly wrecked British aviation in the
twenties.[43] In 1939 after losing the relevant file for a few weeks, the
Treasury delayed its sanction for the manufacture of essential
artillery ammunition until a fortnight after the war had started.[44]
During the war Cherwell found that the Treasury took the trouble
to send two officials to Whitchurch to investigate the payment of
charwomen in an officers' mess, while it was blithely paying India
£25 million for petrol instead of the proper figure of £5 million.[45]

The Treasury's parsimoniousness and the orthodoxy of its
financial ideas brought its eclipse at the end of the phoney war.
Only by the devious route of Mr. Dalton's budget indiscretion did
the Treasury return to its former estate at the head of the nation's
economic affairs. Its years in the shadows did little to chasten it, and
increasing numbers of people came to share Tizard's scepticism
about the failure of detailed Treasury control over the departments,[46]
believing that it cost and lost more money than it saved. As the
Plowden Report cautiously put it: 'the tendency is for expenditure
decisions to be taken piecemeal'.[47]

That report has accelerated the tendency to give greater freedom
to the departments to work out their own budgets within a limit
set by the Treasury, and it has encouraged the Treasury to look
beyond the end of the next financial year. Despite Plowden, however,
the Treasury still seems unduly concerned with current saving:
irrespective of whether they will not lead to greater expenditure in
the not so long run. The aviation industry has suffered once again.[48]
And the Treasury continued to favour the renting and not the
purchase of diplomatic accommodation overseas, while rents and
prices have soared. A profitable investment has thus been foregone,
and the nation pays more and owns less than it should.[49]

The Treasury's control of jobs began much later. A Treasury
minute of 1921 laid down that Permanent Secretaries, their Deputies,
and the accounting officer of each department should be appointed
by the Prime Minister, on the advice of course of the Permanent
Secretary to the Treasury, who was at the same time named Head
of the Civil Service.* Before 1921 Permanent Secretaries were

---

* The Treasury claims that this title was given to the Permanent Secretary of the
Treasury as long ago as 1867 but that the relevant minute has been lost. As Namier
once said, documents like cats have nine lives; so the Treasury's inability to produce the
1867 minute casts some doubt upon its claim.

appointed by the minister of the department concerned. Under this system the 'unsafe' man was not at a disadvantage and the golden opinion of the Treasury was not a necessary passport for advancement, though even before the 1921 circular, the Treasury sometimes interfered. In 1918 Bonar Law as Chancellor of the Exchequer vetoed Clynes's appointment of Beveridge as Permanent Secretary of the Ministry of Food and insisted upon the appointment of the 'safe' Sir John Beale. Clynes weakly accepted Bonar Law's edict.[50]

After 1921 promotion to the highest offices was dependent upon the favour of the Treasury chieftains; and the move from a departmental to a unified service also reduced the level of specialisation and expertise at the top, by making it probable that a head of a department would not be promoted from within that department but would come from outside.* The qualities needed for success were changed. Edges had to be smoothed away; departmentalism was a vice; harmony had priority, there must be no disturbance in the Athenaeum; officials had to take a larger view, which more often than not meant the Treasury view. Top Civil Servants became organisation men. A Morant or a Stephen would have found themselves doing the Civil Servant equivalent of governing New South Wales.

The ideal Civil Servant painted by Civil Servants is indeed remarkably like 'the well rounded man',[51] the aspiration of all good American graduates anxious for a career in business. They have stressed that administration is an art and that the necessary qualifications of a Civil Servant are not expertise in any particular subject but the ability to find an acceptable solution and to put through public business.[52] Successful management of men is more important than what is actually done by means of the successful management. The fleet must be kept in being even if it is never going to fight an action.

Sir Edward Bridges, praising the practice of frequent changes of duties both within and between departments, contended that a man who had done a number of jobs could spot the most crucial points for judgment with even 'the most cursory knowledge of the subject'.[53] The Civil Service and the Foreign Office have sometimes seemed to regard cursory knowledge as a positive asset. One diplomat, having spent four years on blockade work, joined the section of the British delegation in Paris dealing with African questions. 'I had never had anything to do with Africa and my

* Sir David Milne, P.U.S. at the Scottish Office until 1959, was exceptional in spending his whole career in one department.

ignorance was complete.'[54] Some pre-Reformation priests, who were alleged to be illiterate, were defended on the grounds that they knew the offices by heart. They could say *hoc est corpus* at the right moment, and that was enough. An element of hocus-pocus may be detected in the reverence higher Civil Servants have expressed for the mysteries of the transaction of public business to the exclusion of detailed knowledge. At all events their hocus-pocus no longer protects them, and they have been intemperately denounced for their amateurism and lack of expertise.

Notwithstanding the dogma of a unified as opposed to a departmentalised service, specialisation has become a necessity. Many departments have to negotiate with their opposite numbers in other countries, whose officials are often highly expert, and also with non-governmental experts at home. And to hold their own, British Civil Servants have had to become more expert in their job. The era of the brilliant all round amateur was over before the Fulton report condemned the species. The admirable Crichton must abandon administration, at least until the next revulsion against the cult of the expert.

Though the Civil Service was never as inexpert as it made itself out to be, no doubt the cult of amateurism was overdone. Sir John Anderson was not specially interested in Home Office subjects,[55] a drawback it might be thought in a Permanent Secretary of that department. Yet the idea that training, specialisation and the rule of the expert, will point to an era of bureaucratic bliss seems far fetched. In any case, having previously represented the British cult of the non-expert, the Civil Service is now speedily adjusting itself to the new cult of the technocrat. When the country distrusted experts, the Civil Service followed suit. Now that the country wants experts, the Civil Service starts a training centre and proudly displays the number of economists in the Treasury.

Much the same applies to the over-centralisation of the Civil Service in London. Top Civil Servants have no doubt been addicted to the London air.* But centralisation used to be the rage. Civil Servants were following the fashion, just as they are now following the regionalist fashion.

In a free state the Civil Service cannot fairly be expected to have

---

* In 1852 Palmerston told his successor at the Foreign Office that he would be 'struck with a very curious circumstance—namely that no climate agrees with an English diplomatist excepting that of Paris, Florence, or Naples'.[56] The climate abroad has of course altered slightly in the last 100 years.

attitudes at loggerheads with those prevalent in the rest of the
country, even if with hindsight such attitudes seem desirable. The
Civil Service was for long representative of the country in sharing
the general distrust of bureaucratic power. If lately it has been more
often criticised for failing to make the most of its opportunities than
for attempting to over-extend its empire, that would not have been
so in the past.

In general many of the defects and the virtues of the Civil Service
stem from its representative nature. When everybody else is right,
it too is right, sometimes a little belatedly perhaps. When everybody
else is wrong, it too is wrong. It does not lead, neither does it
usurp. It is an admirable servant, it is no leader. It is only too happy
to follow the people's will, but only rarely does the people have a
will. The discipline of the Civil Service and its lack of expertise
except in administration, its 'organisation man' aspect, its mode of
work and its secrecy, all prevent it from being a danger to the
liberties of the subject. At the same time they hinder government
from leading the country.

'In your Committee's opinion,' the Select Committee on National
Expenditure said in 1942,[57] 'as far as the Treasury was concerned,
the period from 1919–39 was marked by an almost complete failure
to foster the systematic study of organisation as applied to government departments;' and 'as a result of 20 years' neglect, the outbreak
of war found the Treasury insufficiently equipped to deal with the
problems of administrative organisation which were forced upon it.'

Once again the complacency of the Civil Service between the
wars reflected that of the politicians and the country as a whole.
With less excuse the Treasury has been similarly remiss in the
post-war period, when there has been a widespread realisation of
the need for reform. The Treasury was late in understanding the
'managerial revolution' which was, or should have been, taking
place in the Civil Service. It gave no consideration to the possibility
of organising the Service into various cadres on the lines of the
French *corps*. It did not experiment with different forms of organisation, or with the creation of special task forces formed of an inter-
departmental group of officials acting not as a committee but as a
team. It has done nothing to foster the 'hiving-off' of functions from
the Civil Service to other bodies. It has been slow to adopt the
new techniques of cost effectiveness and elimination of waste.

It has not fostered the growth of an adequate audit service. There is no efficiency audit in this country, as exists in France, Germany, America and most other advanced countries. 'It is the duty of state audit to seek out the complex facts of modern administration and inform legislatures, the heads of the executive and even public opinion about them without favour, fear, or partiality.'[58] Nothing of the sort happens in Britain. The Treasury has given the state audit service a status lower than that in any other major country in the western world.[59] The executive has more control of state audit here than elsewhere, and Mr. Normanton's verdict is that 'there is very considerably . . . less public accountability in the UK than in France, the United States or Federal Germany'.*[60] Nor has the Treasury done anything to institute a system of administrative law and sensible internal controls such as other countries have possessed for years.

More serious, the Treasury has passively watched the Balkanisation of Whitehall and the consequent impenetrable growth of interdepartmental committees.† Increasing government activity in the life of the country has led to a convergence of government departments on an ever growing number of subjects. Policy and administration have changed from a single road to a Piccadilly Circus. Welensky had reason to complain that at one time five different departments were saying different things about Africa.[61] The more departments there are, the more interdepartmental committees there will be, and the more time will be wasted and less action taken.

The Treasury failed to reform the interdepartmental structure of Whitehall; it was similarly remiss over the structure within departments. In the formative period in the middle of the last century, departments were small enough and their work simple enough for a straightforward hierarchy to be the natural and obvious form of organisation. Despite the vastly increased size of departments, the growing differentiation of function, and the sheer volume of work, the Civil Service has clung to its hierarchies with fanaticism. Its bigotry has been fed and is to some extent excused by the system of ministerial responsibility. The logic of the doctrine leads to a pyramid of advisers with the minister relying upon the apex of the pyramid, the Permanent Secretary, for the distillation of advice.

* See also pages 289–90.
† But the Treasury cannot be blamed for Mr. Wilson's carving up of the economic sector into a series of kingdoms for his troublesome or submissive colleagues.

Ironically the organisation of government, on the lines of collegiate responsibility with offices in commission, which used to be common, and which now exists in the nationalised industries and public boards, would in many ways be more suitable than the present form of organisation which grew out of it. Before the reorganisation of 1963 the Service departments were all run by a Council: the Admiralty by the Lord Commissioners of the Admiralty, the successors of the Lord High Admiral, the War Office by the Army Council reorganised in accordance with the recommendations of the Esher Committee of 1904, and the Air Ministry by the Air Council.* The presence of a Council does not necessarily affect the power of the Minister. The Air Council had little power.[62] The Secretary of State for War was usually able to hold his own with the generals, whereas the First Lord of the Admiralty was as a rule outgunned by the admirals, Churchill being the most notable exception. But a Council downgrades the Permanent Secretary from his usual position of king of a department to one of at the most *primus inter pares*, a state of affairs much more suitable for the running of a large concern than the nineteenth century hierarchy still existing in the other departments.

During the war the three supply ministries, the Ministry of Aircraft Production, the Ministry of Production, and to a much lesser degree the Ministry of Supply, adopted a similar form of organisation, partly because of their close connections with the service ministries, partly because the normal Civil Service administrative hierarchical system would have broken down, and partly because of the arrival of able and dynamic ministers from outside the peacetime political world. Beaverbrook instituted a highly non-hierarchical régime at the Ministry of Aircraft Production, and at Mr. Lyttelton's insistence the new Permanent Secretary cut down the the hierarchical element in his scheme of organisation for the new Ministry of Production[63]. At both these ministries the Permanent Secretary occupied a position similar to the Permanent Secretary in the Service departments: he was just one of the Minister's chief advisers. After Beaverbrook had left it, the Ministry of Aircraft Production gradually reverted to a more orthodox pattern, and the importance of the Permanent Secretary increased. Nevertheless Beaverbrook, Lyttelton and Duncan at the Ministry of Supply and Woolton at the Ministry of Food, all of whom were notably success-

---

* 'The British soldier,' said Shaw in *The Devil's Disciple*, 'can stand up to anything except the British War Office.' But that was before the Esher reorganisation.

ful ministers, all found it necessary to break the normal Whitehall mould.* A recasting of that mould either by reorganising ministries into separate service divisions or by hiving off much of the work at present done by the departments to executive agencies would bring back the conciliar principle. Nearly every department would have a council with the minister as chairman.

In the Civil Service, as in most organisations, disagreement with the chiefs is no help to a career. Few officials maintain the attitude of President Coolidge: 'While I have differed with my subordinates, I have always supported loyally my superiors.'[64a] But an inflexible hierarchy stifles the initiative of those lower down and stifles with overwork those higher up. One recent Permanent Secretary to the Treasury issued a directive that nothing was to go to the Chancellor that had not been through him. Most Permanent Secretaries are less rigid and seigneurial in their attitude; even so the great majority of papers go to them before reaching the minister, though only a bad Permanent Secretary attempts to conceal from a minister that there are divergent views in the department.

The hierarchy intensifies the pressure on top Civil Servants. At present they have to concentrate upon the immediate and the urgent; looking ahead and planning become almost impossible. Only in a very limited sense can the permanent officials take a long view. The most they can hope for is not to be overborne by events; to anticipate them is out of the question.

A Permanent Secretary to the Treasury once said that if he was not fully occupied with papers and immediate problems, he would not think great thoughts but sit back and read Proust.[65] Similarly, when a Civil Servant complained to Balfour that they were drugged by papers and there was no time to think, he replied 'Yes, but if there were no papers, there would be nothing to think about.'[66]

Yet a more lateral organisation would ease the day to day pressures on Permanent Secretaries and give them and others the opportunity, which the present volume of paper denies them, of thinking ahead and making wise long term plans. Perhaps they would not take it. One hundred and thirty years ago Sir Henry Taylor wrote: 'it is one business to do what must be done, another to devise what ought to be done. It is in the spirit of the British government as hitherto existing to transact only the former business.'[67] That is still true, and

* Winston Churchill organised his Ministry of Munitions on similar lines in the first war.[64]

perhaps that spirit would survive the lifting of some of the burden of overwork. Even so a more lateral organisation would be far more suitable for the running of large scale enterprises which most ministries now are. Perversely the Treasury made itself more, not less, hierarchical in the middle fifties.

In the nineteenth century Britain led the way in the techniques of free parliamentary government. In the twentieth century she has fallen well behind in devising new techniques to cope with free administrative government, and the Treasury has done nothing to help her catch up.

This is very far from being all the fault of the Treasury. The politicians are just as guilty. There are, moreover, immense difficulties in altering the system. 'The patient obstructiveness of the body,' said Mill, is 'in the long run more than a match for the fitful energy of one man.'[68] And when the body consists of all Whitehall, its patient obstructiveness is more than a match for the energy of virtually everybody. Yet the executive has retained complete power over its own organisation, and cannot escape responsibility for the defects.

Though the results have been small, the reorganisation of the Treasury that took place after 1956 made it a more rational instrument of Civil Service control. The establishment side headed by one Permanent Secretary, the head of the Civil Service, and its financial and economic side headed by the other Permanent Secretary were separated. But this more rational division of function made it all the easier to separate the establishment side from the Treasury altogether. And no Chancellor was able to give much time to that side of the Treasury.

On balance, therefore, the setting up of a new Civil Service department under the control of the Prime Minister and another minister of cabinet rank as recommended by the Fulton Committee was probably right. But unless the Treasury's financial control is also substantially reformed and the Civil Service's traditional manner of operation considerably altered, the existence of two overseeing central departments in Whitehall may lead to worse confusion and stagnation.

Monopoly and Outsiders
'The King has his councillors, who are his associates,' wrote Bracton in the thirteenth century; 'he who has associates has a master.' Yet the English Kings showed considerable ingenuity

in escaping from imprisonment at the hands of their principal councillors. As the Royal advisers became institutionalised, bureaucratised, and less under the control of the King, they were pushed further away from his immediate circle and a more intimate adviser was inserted between them and the Sovereign. The Great Seal was succeeded by the Privy Seal, which was followed by the Griffin, the Secret and other seals. The King's successors have not shown comparable skill in evading the embrace of their advisers. Within fifty years of Gladstone's Order in Council of 1870, the Civil Service had achieved at least in peacetime a virtual monopoly over advising ministers, something to which Gladstone himself was opposed.[69] Up till 1914 it was still usual for ministers to appoint their private secretaries from outside the Civil Service; and though Churchill had his Marsh, Bonar Law his Fry, Simon his Evans, even that practice has, partly for financial reasons, almost died out.

Lord Esher complained in 1920 that the view that the Civil Service should never 'be reinforced from the outside is to adopt from the Jews their theory of the Levite caste. It is turning the public service into a priesthood and insisting upon the "laying on of hands" by the Commissioners. Ministers and ex-Ministers are afraid of the Civil Service'[70].

The only two men, Lloyd George and Churchill, who have ventured to defy the Levite caste and create a rival priesthood had reasons of war behind them. Lloyd George's disturbance of the hierarchy was the more radical of the two: his 'garden suburb' was larger, more interfering and more powerful than Churchill's 'Prof' and his section of statisticians. When Mr. Churchill returned to power in 1951, he brought Cherwell with him, but he made an honest man of him in Civil Service eyes by taking him into the Cabinet. While Churchill respected officials, Lloyd George thought that 'diplomats were invented simply to waste time';[71] and Beveridge could write in January 1917: '. . . for the moment not only the last government but the whole Civil Service is out of office . . .'[72]

Traditionally the Labour party has not shared Lloyd George's profound antipathy to the Civil Service. Despite belief in Labour circles[73] that this time he should have 'a sound Labour man as principal private secretary', and despite his own uncomplimentary remark the year before about Foreign Office officials, 'their winks and their smiles and their little nudges and their indefinite walkings-out',[74] Macdonald insisted upon taking over Baldwin's private secretary, Vansittart; and P. J. Grigg was private secretary to the

Chancellor of the Exchequer from 1921–30. Attlee likewise took over Churchill's secretary. But the long years of opposition after 1951 fed distrust of the Civil Service, and the conviction grew that Labour ministers should take with them to Whitehall advisers who shared their political views. Envious eyes were cast at Washington and Europe. Once the Civil Service was transfused with outsiders on the American model and Labour ministers equipped with ministerial *cabinets* on the continental model, their isolation and and alleged impotence would be ended, and Whitehall would hum with the disinterested efficiency and socialist enthusiasm of Transport House and the trade union bureaucracies.

The comparisons however were misleading. In France under the Third and Fourth Republics, governments were so short lived that French bureaucrats necessarily cultivated considerable independence of their nominal masters. Also French ministries are much larger and more decentralised than British departments and rarely have Permanent Secretaries or Parliamentary Under-Secretaries. In consequence large ministerial *cabinets* were necessary for any degree of ministerial control. But even in France the political element of these *cabinets* has been increasingly displaced by Civil Service specialists. In the decade 1945–55, two thirds of those appointed to ministerial *cabinets* came from the Civil Service.[75] In most other European countries ministers are surrounded by men of political views similar to their own, but those 'posts of confidence' are mostly occupied by Civil Servants. Hence continental experience provides no warrant for reintroducing political patronage into the Civil Service.

Mr. Wilson, a wartime Civil Servant, did not share the naïve ideas of some of his supporters. As President of the Board of Trade he had found that he 'did far better when I relied on loyal Civil Servants, who knew what I wanted, in my private office . . .'[76] A *cabinet* was liable to produce a false division between the politicians and the Civil Servants. And indeed both Hugh Gaitskell and Douglas Jay, successively used by Dalton as a sort of one man political *cabinet*, found the same.[77] In 1964, therefore, political *cabinets* were not introduced.

Mr. Wilson is surely right, though for a minister to appoint an additional private secretary from outside the Civil Service would not be objectionable. The existence of a political phalanx in his private office is unlikely to help a minister who is unable to run his department. The only difference would be that he was run by a

Svengali in his *cabinet* instead of by his departmental officials. If ministers feel isolated in their departments, they can place more reliance upon their under-secretaries. Churchill was exceptional in refusing for some weeks even to see Halifax, his new Under-Secretary at the Colonial Office,[78] but many ministers are loath to make proper use of the political assistance that is provided for them.*

A change in the status of their principal official secretary might also help them. Sir Warren Fisher, Head of the Civil Service between the wars, favoured the appointment of more senior Civil Servants as Private Secretaries to Ministers than had been the practice formerly (or is the practice today).[79] Vansittart after being Private Secretary to Baldwin and Macdonald became Head of the Foreign Office. Fisher's object, presumably, was to increase the stranglehold of the department over the minister. But the tables would be turned on the idea if a senior Civil Servant as Private Secretary could become, not a watch on the minister, as Fisher designed, but a watch on the ministry. The checking of advice from the department, what the Americans call 'second-guessing', could be done more authoritatively if the minister's private secretary were always of the seniority that Fisher favoured, and more effectively if the private office were larger than it usually is now.

Though political *cabinets* were eschewed, the Wilson government brought into Whitehall a large invasion of outsiders, an invasion which did much to dispel the impression that what was wrong with Whitehall was the Civil Service monopoly. Part of the trouble was that some notoriously bad appointments were made, and part that a high percentage of the new arrivals were placed in a new ministry, which was itself based on the dubious idea that the economic direction of the country should be divided between two departments.† At all events the Department of Economic Affairs was outgunned by the Treasury, and Mr. George Brown found that his 'irregulars' were no match for 'the professionals when it came to discussion and decision making'.[80]

Despite this dashing of fashionable hopes, interchange between Civil Servants and academics and businessmen is desirable. So is the occasional insertion of a key administrator or adviser into a depart-

* By his wholesale creation of junior ministers, Mr. Wilson has provided his leading ministers with so much political assistance that they are saddled with something in the nature of a ministerial *cabinet*—which in some cases may be of more assistnace to the Prime Minister than to themselves.

† A similar experiment had been tried in France after the war but the new ministry was soon degraded.

ment, as when Mr. Macmillan, having found in 1951 that the official in charge of housing was primarily concerned with other duties, brought in Sir Percy Mills. A minister, too, as Lloyd George averred, has the right to send for 'any person either inside or outside his office, whatever his rank, to seek enlightenment on any subject affecting his administration'.[81] But the wholesale flooding of Whitehall by political appointees of the party in power is quite another matter. The idea is based upon a misreading of American practice. In the U.S.A. all the top policy making posts in the departments are political and are filled by the President. Political penetration of the departments extends down to the top four levels, and government is fertilised by a periodical invasion of men of all ages from a variety of professions.* The political element is strengthened at the expense of the bureaucratic element, and vitality is often brought to U.S. government sometimes at the cost of smoothness and efficiency. According to Professor H. Finer, 'the activities of the political executives in the departments show that they are confused, never fully oriented, plunging into affairs they know too little about, more apt to obstruct than to facilitate, and obliged to appeal to career administrators for instruction. They soon quit to make room for others.'[83] If he is anywhere near right, no wonder the Hoover Commission recommended the creation of a Senior Civil Service of 1,500 to 3,000 career administrators.[84]

Disordered administration, when intentional, is not without advantages. Roosevelt is said to have avoided laying down clear-cut lines of authority in order to keep decisions in his hands. The resulting quarrels and confusion compelled the various antagonists to come to the White House for the imposition of terms of peace.[85] At the Ministry of Aircraft Production during the war Beaverbrook used much the same methods as Roosevelt with considerable success. He took with him to the Ministry a batch of trusted outsiders and a distrust of formal designations. 'The very essence of Lord Beaverbrook's administration was its lack of definition of function.'[86] The usual channels did not exist, spheres of authority were confused, and a great many aeroplanes were produced.

In peace time, however, such methods are scarcely feasible in Britain. There is all the difference between importing outsiders into

* The system has its perils, and fertilisation is not always the right word. At the outset of the Eisenhower administration, the State Department was landed with a McCarthyish security officer, Scott McLeod, because the former President of Quaker Oats, who had just become Under Secretary of State for Administration, happened to hear his name when he was idly chatting to a neighbour in Chicago.[82]

a structure designed to accommodate them in its upper reaches and seeking to fit them into a structure where all the places are already filled. Improvisation can lead to brilliant results, but where there is machinery in existence, improvisation is more likely to wreck it.

There is, furthermore, great doubt as to whether outsiders do serve to make the bureaucracy more amenable to control by its political masters. Roosevelt said of the U.S. Treasury: 'I find it almost impossible to get the action and results I want . . .', and complained that 'to change anything in the Na-a-vy is like punching a feather bed.'[87] The British Service is not immune to bureaucratic inertia, but it is obedient. The Spanish saying, 'we obey the order but we do not carry it out', is not one of its mottoes. After stating all its objections to a proposed course of action, it is prepared loyally to implement those proposals. Political appointees are unlikely to be so well disciplined. Cripps when Ambassador in Moscow disobeyed his instructions to warn Stalin of Hitler's projected invasion of Russia.[88] Not only are the political appointees likely to disobey orders, they tend also to make the permanent bureaucracy less obedient. The presence of outsiders in appreciable numbers is a violation of the implied contract, whereby the Civil Service carries out the instructions of any government in return for being allowed by that government to retain the best jobs. Violation is liable to be repaid by Civil Service attempts to frustrate or squeeze out the intruders by obstruction and by *couloir* manoeuvrings.

The division of function between politicians and Civil Servants has a higher justification than any implied contract between them. There is little overt separation of powers in Britain. Hence it is all the more important to preserve the degree of separation of function and personnel that remains. Bagehot's contention that the British system depends upon a fusion of powers is still an exaggeration, though less so than when he made it,[89] and any complete fusion would not produce good government. The danger is not of over-strong government or of dictatorship, but of a progressive abuse of government services by the party in power, as has already begun in the Wilson government's handling of its press and public relations. A separation of function between politicians and officials does much to prevent such abuse, and it should not be endangered or diminished by a politicising of the Civil Service.

Attlee termed the Civil Service's 'remarkable attribute of impartiality . . . one of the strongest bulwarks of democracy', adding that he was 'often at pains to point this out and did so at a conference of Asiatic Socialists in Rangoon'.[90] But valuable as the political impartiality of the Civil Service undoubtedly is, it is not a very 'remarkable' phenomenon. The parties are close enough together for the most tender conscience to be seldom bruised by serving either of them. Party politics are largely concerned with 'place', and Civil Servants already have the best places, a privilege which could not survive if the Civil Service became identified with one party. Abstention from party politics is as much the condition of the Civil Service's survival as it is of the monarchy's. All the same, Attlee was plainly right in saying that political impartiality is one of the strongest bulwarks of democracy, and it should not be jeopardised for party advantage.

A non-political Civil Service is also something of a barrier against pressure groups. British officialdom is usually averse to knocking the heads of pressure groups together. It prefers compromise and the agreed solution. But if it has for better or worse never emulated the robust attitude of some French civil servants, it has maintained its detachment and has never been colonised by pressure groups. A political Civil Service would invite infiltration by the groups.

A final reason for not reintroducing political patronage into the Civil Service is that there is a widening field in the nationalised industries and the public domain outside the Civil Service where patronage already reigns. These political pastures should be enclosed not extended. Government by patronage takes a different form from that prevalent in the days of Trevelyan and Northcote, but it is no less objectionable. If it is not possible, in Trevelyan's infelicitous phrase, 'to knock the brains out of patronage',[91] it is plainly possible to avoid a converse process at least in the Civil Service. Friction in government is to be welcomed, but it must be looked for between departments, in greater publicity, and in the moderating of the doctrine of ministerial responsibility, not between political appointees and Civil Servants within departments.

Secrecy
British government is secret government, tempered by government public relations officers and parliamentary questions and debate. Secrecy has not been carried to the lengths it was in Nazi Germany when after the purge of June 30 1934 the composition of the Reichstag was declared a State secret.[92] Nevertheless what Woodrow Wilson called 'the taint of privacy'[93] attaches to the whole business of British government. The Official Secrets Acts prevent those who

are or have been in government service writing about their experiences without permission. In practice this means that the lowly are silenced, and the mighty write their memoirs in several volumes. The Home Office threatened the retiring public hangman, Mr. Albert Pierrepoint, with prosecution under the Official Secrets Act if he persisted with the publication of his memoirs in the *Sunday Empire News*. However devoid of literary or other merit, and however distasteful the subject, Pierrepoint's disclosure of the last words of Ruth Ellis does not appear to be on a par with Fuchs's or Blake's disclosure of secrets to the Russians, which were the sort of offence the framers of the Acts had in mind, so they said, when they were debated in parliament. When it suits them, government departments treat everything a public servant learns in the course of his duty as an official secret.

The government displays the same mania for secrecy in the Law Courts. For years an English though not a Scottish judge had to accept a minister's certificate that the production of official documents would be against the public interest, even when it was perfectly plain that the public interest was being confused with official convenience and ministerial advantage. 'The rule means . . . that every litigant against a government department,' said Mr. Justice Devlin, '. . . is denied as a matter of course the elementary right of checking the evidence of government witnesses against the contemporary documents.'[94]

In a case in 1964 when the Court of Appeal held that the Courts had a residual power to override the executive's veto where Crown privilege was unreasonably claimed, the Attorney General said that all communications with or within the ministry should be privileged even though the disclosure of their contents would not in themselves be injurious to the public interest.[95] Only in 1968 did the House of Lords finally reverse itself on Crown privilege, and decide that the Court could order the production of documents when the interests of justice so required.[96]

The executive's ruthless if selective operation of the Official Secrets Acts and its doctrinaire refusal to produce in court totally innocuous documents are merely superficial manifestations of its passion for secret government. The entire operation of government is carried on in what Lord Snow has called 'the euphoria of secrecy'.[97] The euphoria does not lead to secretiveness only towards the public. During the war the Air Ministry and the Ministry of Aircraft Production were initially unwilling to share their secrets.[98]

Departments were no less reticent to our ally than to each other. 'In the past,'[99] said Keynes in the autumn of 1944, 'we have made a great mistake and handicapped our representatives in Washington by an economy of information. So-called "reasons of security" must be reckoned at least as one of the minor, if not sometimes a major inefficiency of the machine of war.' Similarly, Hankey told Asquith in the First World War that 'secrecy . . . has been carried to such lengths as to be positively injurious to the conduct of the war'.[100]

In peacetime the British government's stealth is chiefly directed against the people it is seeking to govern,* though often it results in the Civil Service not knowing what is going on. The public, that is to say everybody outside the government, is allowed to know nothing of the arguments and disputes that take place either within a department or between different departments before a decision is reached. It is merely presented with the decision; often even that is withheld from it. Whatever the reality, the government must present an unbroken front to the world. 'One ought not to have a situation,' the Treasury solicitor told the Franks Committee on Tribunals, 'in which the conflict of departmental policies is threshed out in public.'[105] There is but one government and the Civil Service is its prophet. James I would have thoroughly approved of the views of the Treasury solicitor. 'That which concerns the mystery of the King's power,' he told the Judges in 1616, 'is not lawful to be disputed; for that is to wade into the weakness of princes, and to take away the mystical reverence that belongs unto them that sit in the throne of God.'[106]

Secrecy, it may be said, ensures strong government and speedy decision; it brings dignity to government; inter-departmental feuds and private wars would not edify the public. If Civil Servants are to preserve their impartiality, they must be safeguarded from public and parliamentary criticism, and if the file curtain of Whitehall were once breached and the process of government exposed to the public gaze, they would lose that protection. There would be a

---

* This furtiveness is occasionally accompanied with remarkable indiscretion to foreign powers. Lord Derby, the Foreign Secretary, divulged the secrets of Disraeli's Eastern policy to the Russian ambassador.[101] Lord Tweedmouth, the First Lord of the Admiralty, 'communicated our naval estimates to the Kaiser before submitting them to Parliament'.[102] Neville Chamberlain submitted a speech he intended to make in Parliament for Mussolini's prior approval.[103] The government often seems more adept at concealing security matters from the British people than from their enemies. As was said of the first American Secretary for Foreign Affairs: 'His office was mysterious and secret to all those, who ought to have a perfect knowledge of all it contained—it was undoubtedly public to all those, to whom it ought to have been a profound secret.'[104]

blurring of responsibility, Civil Servants would be blamed as well as politicians and ministers, and it would be difficult if not impossible for them to change their allegiance when the parties succeeded each other in power.

On the other side it can be said that secrecy adds nothing to the quality or the speed of decision or advice. 'Men,' runs an Italian adage, 'have one mind in the market-place, another in the palace.' But the mind is not necessarily better in the palace than in the market-place, and anyway Whitehall has more in common nowadays with a market-place than a palace. To believe otherwise is to be guilty of the intellectualist fallacy, and to assume that secret decisions are reached as a result of intelligent and rational debate instead of by a process of convenient procrastination and compromise. Angling for votes, speaking to Buncombe, the pursuit of mass or local popularity are obvious pressures upon democratic politicians. The private pressures upon both them and Civil Servants are just as strong if less apparent.

The pressure may simply be digestive. The number of anti-aircraft guns decided on for Malta at a meeting of the Committee of Imperial Defence 'had been suggested out of the blue and had been agreed without inquiry as it had been nearly one o'clock and everybody had to go to lunch'.[107] Or it may be anxiety not to offend superiors. At a committee on the defence estimates in the thirties the three chiefs of staff insisted upon asking for only five extra air squadrons which they knew they would be given instead of for the twenty-five which were necessary.[108] Dislike of a rival, lack of time, ill health, desire to keep in with the Prime Minister or the Treasury, or the wish of a Prime Minister to keep the peace with his colleagues, which Kirkpatrick[109] thought to be Baldwin's sole concern when presiding over a Cabinet Committee on disarmament, are only some of the possible influences that may sully the intellectual purity of secret discussions and secret decisions.

Secrecy is as productive of idiocy as the soapbox. It can lead to governmental claustrophobia, in which the issues are decided for absurd reasons, and the world outside is forgotten. The ridiculous tangle of committees, sub-committees, contingent decisions, reversed decisions, muddle, inactivity and confusion, which was the administrative story of the controversy over the setting up of the Ministry of Supply,[110] would not have been possible had it taken place in public.

Secrecy is more likely to produce complacency and delay than speed. 'The Cabinet did not allow itself to be hurried,' wrote the official historians of pre-war rearmament, but [in 1932 it] 'appointed a Defence Requirements Committee with instructions to "prepare a programme for meeting our worst deficiencies". This body . . . submitted its first report in 1934. In July of the following year a broader and stronger body, the Defence Policy and Requirements Committee was set up. . . . The summer of 1935—or perhaps the following winter, when the new Committee produced its first comprehensive recommendations—marked the real opening of the rearmament period. What had happened during the previous three years was only an overture.'[111]

When secrecy does produce speed, it often does so ill-advisedly. The British declaration of 1939 guaranteeing the frontiers of Poland was a momentous action fraught with the gravest consequences. Such a revolution in the government's foreign policy surely deserved anxious consideration. It received nothing of the kind. The declaration 'was an improvisation. It was drafted on the afternoon of March 30 by the Prime Minister with the help of Lord Halifax and Sir Alexander Cadogan, in reply to a Parliamentary question due to be answered on the following day . . . the idea seems to have sprung fully grown from the Ministerial mind'.[112] Similarly Chamberlain's decision to double the territorial army was taken without consulting the Committee of Imperial Defence or even the War Office.[113] Even the advantages of secret diplomacy can be easily exaggerated. In the Middle East Britain's contradictory undertakings in the First World War plague us still, and the old diplomacy was capable of such aberrations as making in 1898 a secret agreement with Germany at the expense of Portugal, and a year later a secret agreement with Portugal at the expense of Germany.[114]

At the Stresa Conference between Britain, Italy, and France in April 1935, incredibly enough 'Abyssinia was only spoken of among the expert advisers'.[115] Hazlitt described what happened in Paris in 1814: 'So Lord Castlereagh, drawing on his gloves, hemmed once or twice, while the French minister carelessly took snuff: he then introduced the question ["the idle question of Africa"] with a smile, which was answered by a more gracious smile from M. Talleyrand; his lordship then bowed as if to bespeak attention; but the Prince of Benevente bowing still lower, prevented what he had to say; and the cries of Africa were lost amidst the nods and smiles and shrugs of these devil puppets.'[116] Macdonald's and Mussolini's encounter at Stresa was less elegant but equally ineffectual.

In negotiations between sovereign states secret diplomacy is necessary because publicity inclines each side to harden its position, and any agreement is usually better than none. This is not true of internal politics, when the alerting of public opinion may induce contending interests to soften their demands, and a bad agreement may be worse than none at all.

Royal Commissions do something to mitigate the evils of private government, though they are sometimes given such ludicrous terms of reference, that any serious results from them are impossible. The Royal Commission on capital punishment set up by Lord Attlee was not allowed to discuss whether or not capital punishment should be abolished. Other Royal Commissions report and nothing happens. Although they are occasionally more of a device for preventing action than securing it, Royal Commissions do secure some public discussion of issues.

On the other hand the vast growth in committees to advise ministers increases the secrecy of government. There are about 280 permanent committees[117] of this kind as well as temporary ones. From the Civil Service point of view these committees have the advantage of muzzling criticism. They also provide an excuse for using outside experts in the department itself but not as full members of it. Lord Woolton found membership of the Board of Trade Advisory Committee a frustrating experience.[118] Outside experts are safely kept in the kennel and do not have to be let into the house.

The real secrecy of British government is partly camouflaged by the mass of information and statistics fed out by government departments and by the activities of government public relations officers. But almost none of this material is news, at least in the Hearstian sense. As a result government publicity seldom generates public interest commensurate with the effort that is put into it.

Of course Civil Servants cannot be expected of their own accord to make their arguments and activities public. Left to themselves they will not abandon tea at the Athenaeum for a bun fight on television. Publicity would have to be forced on them; and that could only be done by making them appear before Parliamentary Committees. Only then would the façade of executive unity be cracked, and the underlying differences exposed. Naturally the entire decision-making process could not be made public even if that was desirable. Much must remain secret. The object of exposing government to the public is not to make ministers and officials live in a goldfish bowl or even to give the governed the illusion that they are fully informed, but to gain the interest of the public and to reveal the assumptions on which the government's policies are based.

Excessive secrecy like most of the defects of the Civil Service and some of its virtues is intimately bound up with the dogma of ministerial responsibility. A Civil Servant's advice is to his minister and to nobody else, and the minister and nobody else is responsible to parliament for what is done. Hence the advice the minister receives and all the internal workings of his department must not be disclosed; parliament must be content with what he chooses to reveal. Yet the dogma thwarts the executive as well as the House of Commons. Instead of openly being managers in their own right, Civil Servants are in status merely members of the ministerial harem. They have power without responsibility. 'The same absence of direct responsibility,' says Lord Bridges,[119] 'is perhaps also responsible for the Civil Servant's highly developed sense of caution. But it is both natural and right to take more care, when you are advising a minister who will carry the responsibility himself, than you would if any blame were to fall on your own shoulders.' Because of the dogma, Civil Servants' activity is circumscribed and their advice a state secret. The system indeed is so unworkable that large tracts of governmental activity have had to be excluded from it.

Outside the Ministries
The publc administration now includes many more 'independent' boards than ministries. The distinction is far from absolute. Some ministries have been called boards, and some boards such as the Board of Inland Revenue are staffed by Civil Servants and come under the Treasury or some other ministry. Most independent boards, moreover, are not called boards but commissions, authorities, or corporations. Under the apparent confusion, however, there is a genuine distinction between ministries which are graced by ministers and staffed by Civil Servants, and independent boards which are not graced by ministers and are not staffed by Civil Servants. Ministries moreover are headed by politicians; boards are usually headed by ex-politicians.

All countries try to take some public functions out of politics, and most try to save some functions from the full rigours of their bureaucracies. There is no one mould for every kind of governmental activity. Yet other countries have made some attempts to assimilate the various moulds to each other. Not so Britain. The less bureaucratic elements are joined to the Whitehall departments by backstairs influence and ministerial patronage. But the clear demonstration that the new activities and functions could not be performed by government departments has not been allowed either to affect the orthodox mould or to prod the executive into providing proper constitutional control over the new creations.

Once it was decided that ministerial responsibility and the normal Civil Service routine were unsuitable for the running of nationalised industries, believers in ministerial responsibility could draw one or more of three possible conclusions: that the normal process of parliamentary control and the normal Civil Service routine should be reformed, that industries should not be nationalised, or that other means of parliamentary control should be devised. None of these was drawn. Instead, parliamentary control and the Civil Service routine were left as they were, but the nationalised industries were absolved from them, and their day-to-day running was sheltered from parliamentary questioning and enquiry. Enormous powers of patronage were placed in the hands of the ministers concerned, and the industries were placed at the mercy of ministerial influence behind the scenes, inevitably beyond the reach of parliamentary control. Bevan had reason to complain that 'the Boards of the nationalised industries' were 'a constitutional outrage'. 'It is not proper,' he added in a phrase which would have given Walt Whitman some wry satisfaction, 'that a member of parliament should be expected to defer to a non-elected person.'[120]

In contrast, Herbert Morrison tirelessly expounded the doctrine of ministerial responsibility as cardinal to the constitution, and yet was instrumental in securing the proliferation of nationalised boards, 'a vital feature' of which, according to Professor Robson,[121] is the elimination of ministerial responsibility. Not content with that, Morrison then opposed the attempts of parliament to play any part in controlling the nationalised industries. He found the proposal to set up a select committee of the House of Commons to examine the reports and accounts of the nationalised industries 'terrifying'.[122] And the Labour party voted against the establishment of the committee. Conservative ministers were little better. They set up a committee whose terms of reference were so restricted as to be unworkable; and it was four and a half years after a committee had reported in favour of setting up a select committee on the nationalised industries that such a committee with feasible terms of reference came into being.

British nationalised industries are probably under less effective public control than those of any other country. Because they are publicly owned, they cannot be fully independent and are subjected to tacit ministerial pressure. Because of the organisation of the Civil Service, they could not be run without disaster by the Civil Service on Civil Service lines. And because of the employment of the doctrine of ministerial responsibility to keep the House of Commons at bay, proper parliamentary supervision, despite the Select Committee on Nationalised Industries, is difficult. So until the Civil Service is reformed, and ministerial responsibility demythlogised, the nationalised industries will remain a constitutional outrage.

Not only are the constitutional arrangements for them grossly inadequate, their staffing is also at fault. They, together with the other 'independent boards', provide a vast field of ministerial patronage. Not counting the 16,000 lay magistrates, there are about 30,000 posts in the public field now filled by ministerial favour.[121a] Many of these posts are unpaid, and some degee of patronage is unavoidable. But its extent is altogether too wide. If the Civil Service was organised more sensibly and became more managerial, then the nationalised industries would become more assimilated to it as they are in France, and a new movement, as in 1784, to diminish patronage could begin.

Reform
The theory of ministerial responsibility, except in its true meaning that ministers are answerable to parliament for their departments, is now as implausible as was Divine Right in the seventeenth century. For long it fulfilled the object of a myth: 'to explain the world, to make its phenomena intelligible'.[123] Now it merely explains the nineteenth century world, but it still holds sway. The British like to think of themselves as an empirical people; in this they are bigoted doctrinaries. It is high time that Whitehall forgot its doctrine and dealt with the facts.

The exact consequences of the abandonment of the myth are impossible to predict. Nothing occurs exactly as expected, and the consequences would depend on, amongst other things, the extent of the abandonment and of reform elsewhere in the system.

But presumably there would be more parliamentary committees, before which ministers and Civil Servants would appear.* Indeed the extension and aggrandisement of such committees is probably the

* See page 287.

only means of properly scotching the myth and substituting publicity for much of the secrecy. Accountable management, advocated in the Fulton report,[124] and 'the hiving-off' of functions to outside bodies should both assist the burial of total ministerial responsibility, and lead to an extension of parliamentary investigation and control. Ministries would still be run by ministers, who would still answer for them on the floor of the House of Commons. But access to the Civil Service would no longer be confined to ministers of the Crown. The Civil Service would be thrown up to the public, and the pathological secrecy of government reduced. High officials would be questioned at Westminster on the reasoning behind government policies. Others would be responsible for specific tasks. Civil Servants would be allowed out of the ministerial harem, and M.P.s given a sight of the mysteries and glories of the seraglio. The gap between Civil Servants and other public servants would be narrowed, and the volume of departmental work diminished by 'hiving-off'. Civil Servants would have three not two masters— parliament as well as Civil Service and minister.

This would produce public quarrels. Treasury predominance and the closed circle of Whitehall virtually immune from the depredations of the press or parliamentary committees create a corporate Civil Service spirit and a realisation that quarrels should not be pushed too far. Under the present set up, officials have an obvious incentive to reach agreement without the intervention of politicians. Departmental disagreements are straightened out over tea and biscuits in the Treasury or Pall Mall. Unseemly rows are prevented, and nothing approaching that state of near war between departments which sometimes breaks out in Washington[125] occurs in Whitehall. Decorous though this undoubtedly is, it has more to do with departmental and Civil Service convenience than good government. The resulting compromise often has little to do with the merits of the case; it merely papers over the cracks and produces the required minimum of agreement. As Churchill said in the war, 'I am definitely of opinion that it is more in the public interest that there should be sharp criticism and counter criticism between the two departments than that they should be handing each other out ceremonious bouquets.'[126] Brickbats are also part of the standard Whitehall equipment and many departmental disputes have to go to the cabinet, yet compromise and agreement is the ordinary outcome.

With a more open system, the quarrels would be fiercer and no longer fully concealed. Yet Civil Service discretion would die hard, and governments would remain not over-prone to frankness. Parliamentary committees would have to work hard to smell out the Whitehall skeletons.

A former head of the Foreign Office, Lord Strang, has argued that 'the Minister's task is difficult and delicate enough without the dissemination of possibly divergent opinions from within his own house'.[127] In fact the dissemination of divergent views from within his own house is as likely to strengthen the minister as to weaken him. The divergence would at least as often be between him and the cabinet as between him and his officials. In the months between succeeding Eden at the Foreign Office and the outbreak of war, Halifax, at the urgings of his Foreign Office officials, was occasionally inclined to take a rather firmer line towards Hitler than were the Prime Minister and his other colleagues. Halifax's hand could hardly have been weakened had the Foreign Office been able to disseminate the departmental view. But in any case the convenience of ministers is not the chief object of government or of the constitution, and the unfortunate consequences of secrecy and the stifling of informed debate were well illustrated by the experiences of the thirties.

Britain's weak foreign policy and her failure to rearm adequately was and is blamed on the people's failure to understand the country's danger and the consequent need to rearm.[128] Why did the people not recognise the need? Because they were not properly told of the need. Why not? Because they might not have believed what they were told and voted for the Labour party. 'And then,' as Baldwin told Vansittart, you would 'have the Socialists, who give you no rearmament at all, instead of me who give you not enough!'[129] The government blamed public opinion for being foolish and uninstructed, while it took care not to instruct it.

What happened in the thirties, happened again in the fifties. The difference was that in the thirties Britain ignored the successes and strength of her enemies, and in the fifties she ignored the successes and strength of her allies. The progressive unification of Europe and the formation of the Common Market took place while Britain sat back in smug isolation, dreaming about the Empire and a special relationship with America, which did not exist. Admittedly even the most perceptive government circles were slow to understand the significance for this country of the European movement; as usual the Civil Service was representative of public opinion. But had officials been compelled to appear in public at Westminster, and the Foreign Office differences with the Treasury, which on this question was for long obscurantist, been fully revealed before Parliament, Britain's application for entry into the Common Market could hardly have occurred so late.

Indeed if the views of Foreign Office officials had been properly aired, Britain's European policy might have been on the right lines from the end of the war onwards. As Ambassador in Paris, Duff Cooper found Bevin and the Foreign Office 'in favour of the Western bloc, of customs union with France, common currency, etc. . . . but the officials of the Treasury and the Board of Trade—pig-headed as ever—won't hear of it'.[130] Many years passed before the basic truth of Britain's position sunk into the secret recesses of those departments. Publicity and fresh air might have done the job a lot quicker.

Disagreements between departments, it may be said, would destroy the doctrine of collective cabinet responsibility, and the revelation of divided counsels would fatally weaken the government. But the doctrine of collective responsibility merely says that all ministers are responsible for all Cabinet decisions and cannot pick and choose between those they like and dislike. It does not say that all officials of every department must always be in agreement. Manifestly they are not, and a revelation of some of these disagreements would not infringe Cabinet responsibility. There is admittedly a deep desire for unanimity. This used to be true of the House of Commons. Abandoned there, without damage, the same would be true of the bureaucracy. 'The empty pleasure of having one opinion'[131] would be seen to be what it is. The concealment of the process which leads to decisions and the security blackout on any inter- or intra-departmental disagreements, quarrels, or bargains, possibly conduces to the dignity of government, but also to the ignorance of M.P.s and the public, and it consequently damages the decision-making process.

The usual arguments against the publication of departmental advice, the same fears that the heavens would fall if light were let into government were heard at the Franks Committee about the proposal that the reports of inspectors at public enquiries should be published.[132] What, it was asked in hushed tones, if the minister differed from the conclusions of his inspector? But for the change recommended by that committee and finally adopted by the government, the public would never have known that the report of the inspector at the Stansted enquiry was explicitly at variance with the minister's decision, and opposition to an obvious piece of governmental idiocy would have been deprived of a valuable weapon. The publication of the inspector's report of the Stansted enquiry has surely removed all doubts about the value of the reform. The same would be true of other views within the department. They are unlikely to be released, however, without a struggle.

For secrecy is the means by which the executive exercises a monopoly of government, and naturally the beneficiaries of the monopoly like other monopolists want to preserve it. But this monopoly like many others is plainly contrary to the public interest —and also to the interests of the government. In the degree to which it is taken in Britain it has no rational or practical justification. Criticism and publicity produce efficiency and vitality; during the war Britain was more efficiently mobilised for total war than was totalitarian Germany.

Of course not all the results of diminishing what Boswell contemptuously termed 'the mysterious secrecy of office'[133] would be happy. Priorities would occasionally be decided according to the public relations and parliamentary skills of individual Civil Servants, and there would be some apparent loss of administrative coherence. Yet only those who believe that victory in the present Whitehall obstacle race is always deserved, and is not achieved by bumping and boring and other tricks of the bureaucratic trade, will think that a more open government would substitute political demagogery and administrative anarchy for intelligent and consistent decision-making. Mr. Christopher Mayhew has described the irrationality of the present process. After earnest discussion the government decided both to cut back defence expenditure and to preserve our world role.[134] The trouble with these decisions was that they were totally incompatible with each other.

At present, moreover, nobody outside the governmental machine can know anything about the calibre of individual Civil Servants. Some Civil Servants have a record, which few politicians could match, of being wrong on all major issues, yet none is ever sacked, and there is no opportunity to judge them by results. Even their names are scarcely known. Were this immunity from the normal penalties of failure partially removed, there would be some opportunity to judge the performance of Civil Servants, and it is unlikely that the performance itself would deteriorate. Plainly the opposition would make what capital it could out of disagreements within Whitehall. That would be balanced by the enhanced realism with which issues were discussed and by the greater public interest in what was going on.

The Civil Service already needs more legal control, and the abolition of total ministerial responsibility would sharpen that need. Having made the law for so long, the executive must now be made subject to it.*

Of course if the myth were abandoned and the doctrine or ministerial responsibility confined to that part of it which is in accordance with reality—ministers are answerable to parliament for the action and inaction of the department—none of these things might follow. British constitutional conservatism is notorious and British government might easily go on largely unchanged. Almost certainly however some improvement in efficiency would have been achieved.

Power

Harcourt's often quoted dictum, 'The minister exists to tell the Civil Servant what the public will not stand,' though endorsed by Attlee[135] not long ago, is seriously misleading in every respect. It conveys a picture of ruthlessly efficient Civil Servants dominated by a single-minded desire to control and reform every aspect of the country's life, and only restrained from driving the outraged public to violent revolution by a set of wonderfully human and worldly wise politicians in mystical touch with the popular mood.

In fact British officials have never been those paragons of bureaucratic zeal, energy and initiative envisaged by Laski and the Webbs. The characteristic attitude of the British Civil Service in contrast to the French is that of the referee, not the contestant, the representative rather than the ruler. Pressure groups have little to fear; still less has the public.

Some Civil Servants indeed seem to believe that virtue lies in not taking an initiative. Confronted with pressure groups and the public, the concern of the administrator, according to Mr. Sisson, is not to make his opinion 'prevail, for he has no right to one', but to see that 'at the end he is still upright and the forces around him have achieved a momentary balance'.[136] Why the forces around him should be any less likely to achieve a balance or why the administrator should not be just as upright, if he has an opinion and seeks to make it prevail, is not clear; but Mr. Sisson gives a truer picture than does Harcourt's dictum.

In addition, Civil Servants are often in close touch with the public. The mass of correspondence which pours into ministries and the

* See page 378.

multitude of advisory committees give them quite as good an indication of where the shoe is pinching as politicians receive from their constituents. The Civil Service is representative though not elected. Remedial policies probably more often well up from the depths of departmental experience than emerge from the brains of ministers. And ministers, though they are elected, are often quite out of touch with both events and the public mood.

'The soul of our service,' wrote Vansittart, 'is the loyalty with which we execute ordained error.'[137] No Civil Servant can have done more to try to prevent the ordination of error. He used to give Mr. Churchill information about developments in Germany. Unfortunately 'Winston took to striding into my room at the Foreign Office and turned our connivance into an open secret.'[138] In the twenties Vansittart had gone even further. At the San Remo Conference in 1920 he advised the French and Italians to stand up to Lloyd George over the Turkish Treaty.[139] Once again he was right on the issue, and once again to no avail.

Over Germany and rearmament Vansittart was joined by the head of the Civil Service, Fisher, who, like him, destroyed much of his influence by being prematurely right. They failed for the reason which normally works in favour of the power of the Civil Service: the inertia of policy. Once a policy has been decided upon, or at any rate followed, it is difficult to change. There are always very good reasons against changing a policy. The present policy may have obvious disadvantages, but who can guess the consequences of altering it? The devil we know is better than the devil we don't. If we go on as we are, it will probably end in disaster. But a change now will produce immediate trouble. The day of judgment may be on us soon, but not until after we have changed our jobs and after the next election. Only when a policy is visibly in ruins is it altered; often not even then.

In the thirties settled habits of mind and the inertia of policy were against Vansittart and Fisher. It was they not the politicians who were trying to make changes. And what would they have done instead? Hoare once said that 'we always asked Van what we should do. He always disagreed with what we wanted to do, but never had a real alternative'.[140] Of course he did not. Once a man has trodden on a banana skin and begun to fall, it is too late for somebody else to suggest where he should put his next step. But somebody, in this case Vansittart, can at least point out that he is about to fall hard and humiliatingly upon his back. Short, however, of a radical change of policy, which he was incapable of securing, there was nothing 'constructive' that Vansittart could suggest. He could only draw attention to the disaster ahead. 'Constructive' criticism means that the critic accepts the premises of those he criticises; 'destructive' or 'negative' criticism means that he does not. The first therefore is popular with the powers that be, and the second is not. No wonder 'constructive' was a favourite word of Geoffrey Dawson's. Usually a Civil Servant cannot be largely 'negative' or 'destructive'. If he is, he merely annoys his minister. Vansittart accordingly was kicked upstairs to the meaningless position of Chief Diplomatic Adviser.

Political control over the Foreign Office is far from complete. No Foreign Secretary can keep abreast of more than a small minority of major issues at any one time. Very often the officials have exclusive knowledge of a question, which it is impossible for the minister to check, and until an Ambassador makes a crashing mistake his telegraphed advice is likely to be given great weight. For most of the time the Foreign Secretary does what he is advised. The Prime Minister however may take matters out of the hands of the Foreign Office, and rely, like Chamberlain, on such diplomatic aides as Sir Horace Wilson, formerly in the Ministry of Labour, or the Head of the Conservative Research Department. Obviously a man who is not prepared to listen to advice cannot be influenced by officials. When Chamberlain made his trip to Berchesgaden in 1938, he took with him no one from the Foreign Office, and so far is known not even a brief.[141] He took an adviser, Strang, to Munich, but ignored his advice.[142] The Foreign Office was similarly ignored over Suez.

Most people have strong views on foreign affairs, as on religion, whatever their knowledge of the subject. On economics people are not as a rule similarly opiniated. The equivalent in economics of a Neville Chamberlain in foreign policy is a single-taxer or a man with a system at Monte Carlo. Such a man is unlikely to get very close to Great George Street. Hence the Treasury has less to put up with than the Foreign Office; its activities are no more diverse but much more complicated and getting more so.

Over small things the Treasury sometimes loses. Against its advice Mr. Churchill introduced his unsuccessful betting tax; and Mr. Selwyn Lloyd preferred the advice of influential back-benchers to that of his officials in delaying the imposition of a tax on capital gains.

But in general the Treasury is such a complicated organisation and deals with such difficult subjects that a Chancellor is almost bound to be largely run by his Civil Servants. His private secretary said of Neville Chamberlain, Chancellor of the Exchequer in 1923: '. . . he readily mastered briefs on the most complicated subjects and could expound them cogently and persuasively'.[143] How different from the peacemaker of the thirties who expounded his own briefs! The Treasury has so many ramifications that virtually the only contact many high officials dealing with important matters have with the Chancellor is that he occasionally reads out parts of speeches they have written for him on their particular subjects. Balfour, when Lord President of the Council, visited the D.S.I.R., for which he was responsible. The Department was astonished to see him. None of his eight predecessors had ever put in an appearance. If the Chancellor were to begin interfering in many of the Treasury activities, officials would be equally, though less agreeably, surprised.

'The activities of a government department over any given period,' said Sir Frank Lee, a few years ago, 'are influenced, and indeed in all important matters determined by its political chiefs. The belief that these are as clay in the terrible hands of high officials is sheer legend.'[144] But without subscribing to the 'sheer legend', to believe that when ministers take important decisions, they are not profoundly influenced by Civil Servants is sheer counter legend. 'It is indeed on these broad issues of policy,' says Lord Bridges,[145] 'that it is the duty of a Civil Servant to give his minister the fullest benefit of the storehouse of departmental experience, and to let the waves of the practical philosophy wash against ideas put forward by his ministerial master.' Against these departmental waves, the ministerial master is often as effective as were the courtiers of Canute.

The distribution of power between officials and the minister varies according to the personalities involved, the duration of the minister's stay and other factors. No doubt most political chiefs are far from being mere clay, yet a certain malleability is a necessary condition of ministerial life, and high officials are skilled and experienced potters.

There is a story that Colonel Jack Seely when introducing the Army Estimates to parliament was reading them for the first time. If true, this does not suggest much political interference in the War

Office before the first war. Sir John Anderson was always a very strong Civil Servant. The government's masterly plans for dealing with the General Strike were his and not those of his political superior, Sir William Joynson-Hicks.

Mr. Enoch Powell has pointed out that the minister 'can only take personal control and initiative on very few fronts at once'.[146] The department has time, convenience and security of tenure on its side. With all the demands upon his time and energy additional to administering his department—receiving deputations, attending functions, making speeches, various parliamentary duties, the cabinet and cabinet committees—any minister must lean heavily upon his advisers. Ministers are expected by Civil Servants to adopt the view of the department, even if as the head of another department they have been holding the diametrically opposite view. In the Admiralty-Treasury battle before the First War such strong ministers as Churchill and McKenna changed sides when they changed offices.

Not many ministers are as frank as Carson who on arrival at the Admiralty said, 'I am very much at sea,'[147] and announced that he would carry out the policy of his department. Obviously the proportion varies, but as a rule probably only about one minister in three runs his department. This is not a matter of intelligence or of a departmental conspiracy. Some of the most intelligent politicians have notoriously failed to take a proper grip on their department, and many Civil Servants rather like being told what to do.

Civil Service influence reaches unexpected places. The quintessential Baldwin was often thought to be the lover of pigs and the English countryside, which he described in moving and 'characteristic' language to the delight of his hearers and the profit of his party. An eminent official tells us that 'some of the best things he did in this vein were entirely his own'.[148] Sir Herbert Brittain always used to include in the speeches he wrote for Sir Kingsley Wood, as Chancellor, at least one Biblical quotation. Wood, a former lay preacher, never rejected any of Brittain's selections.[149]

Sir James Grigg was an outstanding Civil Servant; otherwise Mr. Churchill would not have made him Secretary of State for War in 1942. Churchill himself was an even more outstanding and formidable minister. Yet Grigg records that as Churchill's Joint Private Secretary he was occasionally 'allowed to suppress his minutes. . . . Many of my recollections are of heated and even violent arguments with Winston'.[150]

Lord Montgomery exaggerated only a little when he said: 'Political leaders seldom act on their own judgment and make decisions. Their decisions are always based on what they are told by their advisers.'[151] The vast agglomeration of business, the usual involvement of several government departments, and negotiations with foreign powers or other authorities, explain the steadily augmenting power of officials. The growth of interdepartmental committees and consultation, the 'organisation man' aspect of the Civil Service, has produced a tendency for problems to get settled at an early stage and at a low level. Unless he is very quick off the mark, the minister finds that a question has been answered and his department committed before he properly realises that it has been posed. Yet the power of Whitehall and the supremacy of officials are often wildly exaggerated. Nobody could seriously maintain that in the twentieth century British governments have produced a series of tough and unpopular policies which they have bulldozed through the House of Commons in the face of intense parliamentary and public displeasure. Perhaps Hoare agreed to the Hoare-Laval pact at the eloquent persuasion of his Permanent Under-Secretary Vansittart. Immediately there was a wave of anger in the country and in the Commons. The policy was abandoned, and so was its author. Perhaps Churchill agreed to return to the Gold Standard under pressure from his Treasury Civil Servants and from Montagu Norman at the Bank of England. This action soon became a conspicuous item in the demonology of the Left. Not at the time. The policy was so little unpopular that the Labour party did not even vote against it in the House of Commons.

The Civil Service and the Government do not seek to impose unpopular policies upon the country; nor do officials balk the policies of ministers, though they are a useful barrier to folly. If politicians fail to carry out popular and enlightened policies, it is because they have no such policies to carry out, not because they are obstructed by their officials. Lloyd George may have been the only Chancellor who was able to make the Treasury do what it did not want to do. Yet what the Treasury wanted to do or did not want to do at any given moment was usually much the same as what parliament wanted or did not want done. Lloyd George at the Treasury and Churchill in other departments showed what determined ministers could do if they knew their objectives.

The second Labour government failed to deal with unemployment because the economic doctrines of its Chancellor, Snowden, were, like those of the Treasury, free trade and nineteenth century liberalism. Had Jimmy Thomas had any conception of what should have been done, there is no reason to doubt that it would have been carried out. Mosley's proposals were rejected by the cabinet and by the parliamentary party; they were not vetoed by the Civil Service. The Socialists and the Civil Servants were equally opposed to the new economic doctrines of Keynes contained in the Yellow Book and Lloyd George's election proposals.

The most extreme example of ministers arriving in office without knowing what to do was the Attlee government over Nationalisation. On Mr. Shinwell's admission this great panacea, whose virtues had for years been extolled on countless Labour platforms, had remained a panacea and nothing more. No thought had been given as to how it would be put into practice.

The Conservative government of 1951 entered office with strong European ideas. Almost immediately no trace could be found of them. They were not obliterated by Civil Service obstructionism. Most of the 'European' ministers lost interest, and the 'anti-European' Eden was allowed to have his way.[152]

Of course the departments are strong. Of course there is often bureaucratic inertia. Often Civil Servants have a problem for every solution. Occasionally they are well behind the times as was the Board of Trade between the wars. Normally, however, a department's prejudices are similar to those of parliament and the public.

The government's policy is usually much to the liking of the House of Commons or to the majority of it; so parliamentary control is in at least one vital respect highly effective. Some would say too effective. Politicians and Civil Servants are so preoccupied with seeing what the public will not stand that too much is allowed to fall. The present system produces policies that are safe, dated, competent, and usually in line with the prejudices of the majority party in parliament, as well as with those of many of the voters.

The charmed circle from which power is exercised is in England small. D. N. Chester has suggested that during the war effective power was in the hands of between twenty to fifty men;[153] and the number in peace is certainly no more, and more than half of them are Civil Servants. Lord Esher thought that 'when it comes to a change of government, believe me it is six of one and half-a-dozen of the other . . . all these people are really cyphers. Remember not more than a dozen people in England count for anything (a large estimate)'.[154] G. W. E. Russell is reputed to have talked as early as 1903 of 'the permanent Civil Service whose chiefs have been, at least since the days of Bagehot, recognised as the real rulers of the country.'[155]

Both Esher and Russell exaggerated. The Civil Service are not the real rulers of the country, as the events of the thirties all too clearly demonstrate. The politicians are in ultimate charge. In the labyrinths of Whitehall officials are powerful enough. They are the collective *eminence grise* of the nation, and an important element in the underground separation of powers. But while the executive's system of operation has kept out trespassers, like parliament and the courts, it has also imprisoned Whitehall itself. Clandestine government keeps the executive as well as the other powers in its place. Ministerial responsibility and secrecy stultify its upholders as much as its opponents. By refusing to share its constitutional power, the executive has limited its political power.

II

THE CABINET AND THE PRIME MINISTER

I . . . always had to move with and focus political and professional opinion.
WINSTON S. CHURCHILL on his wartime Premiership[1]

I do not know what things we might have done with the people and the House of Commons heartily on our side, had we been 8 instead of 14.
LORD BROUGHAM on the Reform Bill Cabinet[2]

I urged Lord Rosebery not to bring too many matters before the Cabinet. as nothing was decided there . . .
QUEEN VICTORIA[3]

In this cabinet there is no such thing as a policy.
G. B. SHAW, *The Apple Cart*

I quite like Prime Ministers.
PRINCESS LIEVEN to Metternich in 1820[4]

Party and the big departments, the two most powerful political forces in Britain, come together in the cabinet. They do not meet face to face, because the two forces are embodied in the same people. Orderic Vitalis describes a French mediaeval Bishop who, while observing the strictest celibacy as a bishop, was married in his capacity of baron. The two capacities of a cabinet minister, that of party leader and that of departmental minister, are less starkly opposed to each other, and both are essential for the maintenance of cabinet government.

The essence of cabinet government is a plural executive based upon a parliamentary majority, and its reigning principle is collective responsibility. According, however, to a widely held view, the aggrandisement of the Prime Minister has now gone so far that he has become an 'elected monarch',[5] whose position and power are those of a president, the executive in fact if not in name has become single not plural, and the principle of collective responsibility is no longer real. Mr. Mackintosh has stated that 'the country is governed by the Prime Minister . . . ',[6] and Mr. Crossman has said that 'collective cabinet responsibility . . . now means collective obedience by the whole administration . . . to the will of the man at the apex of power'.[7]

Caesarism, democratic or dictatorial, is everywhere in the ascendant, and Britain has not escaped it. The loyalties of a large organisation are more easily directed onto one man than onto a caucus. Television, public opinion polls, and the personality cult of the press, especially during elections, force attention on 'number one'. More than fifty years ago Curzon plaintively told Bonar Law that there was little point in his making speeches since only those of the party leaders were reported.[8] A mass electorate and mass parties are more impressed by 'one person doing interesting actions' than by 'many . . . doing uninteresting actions'.[9] Bagehot's distinction between a monarchy and a republic is still valid.

Important, however, as the Prime Minister undoubtedly is, his ascendancy does not imply Prime Ministerial government, still less that the Prime Minister, unlike Lloyd George, can now do what he wants. The writers of the Prime Ministerial school make the same mistake about the Premier as the Whig historians made about George III and the monarchy: they overrate his power today and underrate the power he had in the past.

The development of the office has not been all one way; the progress towards Caesarism has been uneven and its starting point is uncertain. Buckingham was accused by the Commons of having obtained a 'monopoly of counsels'.[10] Danby built a parliamentary majority and tied it to a programme.[11] Sunderland has been called 'the true architect of Cabinet government in England'.[12] Walpole is usually entitled the first Prime Minister, but he could not choose his colleagues and he could not have found or kept a parliamentary majority without the aid of the King. The younger Pitt chose his colleagues except Lord Chancellor Thurlow and made higher claims for his office then any nineteenth century premier, but he did not feel able to bring in measures of which George III disapproved. George IV offered Cabinet posts,[13] and as late as 1828 Wellington was not at first allowed to discuss Catholic Emancipation in his cabinet.[14] William IV claimed the right to veto Cabinet decisions.[15]

Until 1832 the King, not the Prime Minister, was the head of the government. In one sense therefore Grey and Melbourne were more powerful than their predecessors, yet Greville said that Melbourne's cabinet was 'a complete republic and Melbourne their ostensible head, has no overriding authority'.[16] On the other hand, a writer in the sixties thought that Liverpool was the last Prime Minister who could be said to have governed England.[17]

In some ways Peel was both the first and the last Prime Minister: the first in that the Monarch was no longer powerful, the last in that he was able to oversee his ministers and the whole administration as none of his successors was able to do*. Peel called himself 'the country's minister', an expression which would raise eyebrows today. 'I treat him,' said Cobden, 'as the Government, as he is in the habit of treating himself.'[19] During Gladstone's second administration *The Times* noted that it was only occasionally that the public was reminded that the Cabinet contained other members, besides the Prime Minister.[20] Shortly afterwards, Lord Randolph Churchill derided the suggestion that without him Lord Salisbury could not form a government with the remark that Salisbury could 'form a ministry if necessary with waiters from the Carlton Club'.[21] Yet with the exception of Lloyd George, no Premier between Salisbury and Churchill was remotely Caesarist, and at least two of them, Balfour and Macdonald, were not even the most powerful men in their own government.

Mr. Churchill himself believed that he 'had as much direct control over the conduct of the war as any public man had in any country at this time'.[22] This was not due to any vast accretion of power to the office of Prime Minister. By his embodiment of the national mood and through his own abilities Churchill achieved a personal position of pre-eminence. Had he been killed on one of his many journeys, or succumbed to one of his severe illnesses, none of his possible successors, Eden, Anderson or Attlee, would have enjoyed a position in any way comparable to his.

Both Attlee and Chandos have stressed that Churchill did not always get his way with the cabinet.[23] Eden and the war cabinet, for instance, successfully insisted upon a peaceful approach to Portugal over the occupation of the Azores.[24] But the war cabinet did not interfere in strategy, being content to leave such matters to the Prime Minister and the Chiefs of Staff, and occasionally even asking not to be informed of future operations. Beaverbrook would scarcely

---

* Similarly his contemporary in America, President Polk, wrote: 'I prefer to supervise the whole operations of the Government myself than entrust the public business to subordinates, and this makes my duties very great.'[18] So great, indeed, that they killed him.

have refused to attend cabinet meetings had he thought he was missing much.

Churchill's inability to give Beaverbrook the powers he believed necessary because of opposition by Bevin and Attlee shows the practical restrictions upon the power of the Prime Minister.[25] On the whole, however, the checks on Churchill came less from his cabinet colleagues than from the departments and elsewhere in the government machine. Churchill prodded, cajoled, goaded, upbraided and occasionally tormented the Chiefs of Staff. But if all his pressures failed to shift them, he accepted their view. 'Not once during the whole war,' according to Lord Ismay, 'did he overrule his military advisers on a purely military question.'[26] Mr. Churchill himself recorded his failure to induce the Admiralty to send an armoured brigade through the Mediterranean in 1940, and added: 'My relations with the Admiralty were too good to be imperilled by a formal appeal to the Cabinet against them.'[27]

Both the war cabinet and the Chiefs of Staff Committee were to Mr. Churchill, in his own description, 'friendly tribunals'.[28] But they were far from being mere registrars of his decisions. Mr. Churchill deferred to the military advice of the Chiefs of Staff, and on non-military matters he sometimes gave way to the war cabinet. In 1922 Lloyd George rejected recommendations from his cabinet, and was aggrieved that they should have ventured to make them. 'The strain of the conference,' he wrote from Geneva, 'is great enough without further complications of that sort.'[29] Churchill never adopted such a tone to his war cabinet during his many wartime journeys, though at the Casablanca Conference he ignored its wishes over Italy and unconditional surrender.[30]

If Lloyd George never attained in the first war the dominance of Churchill in the second, this was not due to any increase in the powers of a Prime Minister between the wars. Apart from Churchill's personal qualities, it was due to Churchill being the undisputed leader of the largest party in the House. After initial disarray in 1940 his party was united and preponderant; Lloyd George's was bitterly split and no bigger than its opponents. More important Churchill, unlike Lloyd George, had not to worry about political opposition from the King, the Generals, or Fleet Street.

Though no post-war Premier, not even Churchill himself, has approached his wartime dominance, the Prime Minister is today much more powerful than any of his colleagues. He nearly always has been. Hence his name. In the past the Prime Minister was often said to be *primus inter pares*, but in 1889 after using that expression John Morley added that the Premier 'occupies a position which, so long as it lasts, is one of exceptional and peculiar authority'.[31] And the phrase *primus inter pares* by itself is liable to be a contradiction in terms. Medieval Kings of England and France were often said to be merely *primus inter pares*. They seldom were. So it has usually been with Prime Ministers, even in the nineteenth century. Peel, Palmerston, Gladstone, Disraeli, all towered over their colleagues. The primacy has always been there, and it has remained. But so too, in some vestigial sense, was the equality, and that too has remained, though some ministers are less equal than others.

Cabinet ministers are in the position of being tenants of the Prime Minister with no security of tenure.* The power of appointment and dismissal confers an enormous preponderance of influence upon the Prime Minister in his daily dealings with his colleagues as well as in the general direction of government policy. In 1929 Ramsay Macdonald shared the job of cabinet-making with Clynes, Snowden, Thomas and Henderson. Sir Alec Douglas-Home had little choice in 1963 but to maintain virtually all the appointments of his predecessor. Usually, however, a Prime Minister has considerable latitude in his distribution of offices. A new Prime Minister like Attlee, whose position in his party was far from pre-eminent, was able to interchange two such powerful colleagues as Bevin and Dalton at the Foreign Office and the Treasury, although each would have preferred the other's office. Once the government is formed, a Prime Minister's freedom of appointment and dismissal is lessened, but he and his colleagues know that his resignation entails that of all his ministers.

Resignation and Dismissal

The resignation of an ordinary cabinet minister has been called a 'double-bladed dagger'.[33] It is now doubtfully double-edged. The only edge which is sharp is the one turned towards the resigner.

As soon as a Conservative minister resigns he is in immediate trouble with his party. He has committed the unpardonable sin of rocking the boat. The boat may have been about to sink with all hands, it may have been steering straight for the rocks, the Captain

---

* They are luckier in New Zealand. No Cabinet Minister has ever been dismissed there. 'It would conflict with strongly held New Zealand views on the security of job tenure.'[32] In Britain in the nineteenth century Cabinet Ministers enjoyed fair security. There had to be a positive reason for their dismissal.

may have been ill and incapable. Still in the party's eyes, it was the duty of the minister to remain on board and keep his mouth shut. Mutiny is unpardonable.

Having mutinied, the resigning minister customarily has his hands full, quelling a mutiny against himself in his constituency association,* and keeping within reasonable bounds the unpopularity he has acquired among his colleagues in parliament. Although his resignation has made plain his differences with the government, the former minister has to hold his peace and pretend that nothing has happened. He has to convey discreetly that his jump overboard in no way implies criticism of the Captain or the crew, merely that he preferred the water.

He has lost the use of party platforms and has cut himself off from the resources of the party organisation. And he will not dare to make things difficult for the Prime Minister in the Commons. After their resignation speeches, Mr. Eden and Lord Cranbourne did not campaign against the policy which had caused their resignations. Eden 'intends', wrote Harold Nicholson in his diary, 'to make a few big speeches on such general topics as Democracy and Young England . . . while avoiding current topics in Foreign Affairs . . .'[34] Duff Cooper resigned because he could not stomach Munich, yet he urged Walter Eliot not to do the same. 'It would be easier for me to go alone, as I had no wish to injure the government, which I should not do if my resignation were the only one.'[35] In other words, resignation is a personal testimony, an act of conscience, occasionally an act of ambition. It is not an attempt to change a policy; otherwise Duff Cooper's attitude would have been the same as that of Harold Macmillan who telegraphed: 'Earnestly hope more of your colleagues will follow your example.'[36] So long as a Prime Minister can find enough crew for his ship, which he almost invariably can, an occasional man overboard gives him scant cause for alarm.

Mr. Thorneycroft, who resigned from the Treasury together with his junior ministers in 1958, was in a stronger position than Eden and Cranborne. Chamberlain's foreign policy was heartily supported by the great bulk of the party rank and file; Thorneycroft's stand against increased government expenditure and the burden of inflation appealed to many Tory supporters. Yet after a good and courageous resignation speech, Mr. Thorneycroft's fight against inflation took the form of a long cruise to Australia and New Zealand.

* Eden, exceptionally, was given a unanimous vote of confidence by his constituency party at Leamington.

These men were brave enough to risk their careers by resigning. Yet none of them was able to continue opposition after he had resigned. The party and parliamentary pressures in favour of conforming with the prevailing policy of the party were too strong. They all, as it were, had resigned themselves to silence.

In this century a senior Tory politician rarely has an independent source of power outside parliament. He has no votes to deliver, no great interest in his pocket. Lord Derby is no longer King of Lancashire. Labour, for all its belief in democratic centralism and the sanctity of majority decisions, has not so levelled the ground around its leader. The party's extraordinary constitution preserves independent, if declining, sources of power. The influence of a Bevin or a Cousins may be unparliamentary but it is as real as was that of the Grenvilles or the Pelhams. Yet the evidence from the Bevan-Wilson resignations suggests that much the same is true of Labour governments. As Attlee sharply pointed out in the letter accepting his resignation, Bevan significantly widened the area of dispute between him and the cabinet; and his resignation speech contained no word of regret at parting from his former colleagues. But, while Labour remained in power, he did not pursue his campaign against the government. Nor, probably, did his resignation help him in his subsequent bid for the party leadership. His former 'disloyalty' was implacably held against him by key trade union magnates and by the party's solid parliamentary centre. Mr. Wilson's resignation is harder to assess. His subtle manoeuvrings in the fifties prevented his resignation retarding the smooth progress of his career. He was only narrowly elected party leader in 1963, but the hostility that he had by then gathered round him probably owed more to his behaviour over the nuclear issue, and to his standing against Gaitskell for the leadership in 1960, than to his departure from the government in 1951.

Mr. Mayhew was not a member of the Cabinet, but after his resignation he said 'all there was to say in one major statement, and then shut up . . .'[37] Mr. Cousins's resignation did not fall into the usual modern pattern. He immediately began campaigning on the issue on which he had resigned, and did not shirk all-out opposition to the government. But he was a reluctant parliamentarian in the first place; and his union, of which he remained General Secretary on unpaid leave throughout his period of office, was from the start against the government's incomes policy. Mr. Cousins's career, talents and loyalties all lay on the industrial side of the Labour movement. His original acceptance of office and his behaviour while he was a cabinet minister were more peculiar than his campaign against the government after his resignation. Mr. Cousins's opposition to his party leaders nevertheless emphasises the customary docility of ordinary politicians after they have made their resignation speeches.

Ministers know that resignation is a risky weapon and are reluctant to risk threatening it—in case it should go off by mistake. Since 1918, the only cabinet minister whose career was certainly advanced by resignation is Sir Anthony Eden. Hoare, whose resignation comes into a different category, wrote late in his life: 'It is a safe course in public life never to abdicate. Stick to the position.'[38] Ministers stick. They have always inclined to the attitude adopted by Loreburn in 1912: '. . . I certainly should have resigned over the German business had I not believed . . . that I should serve the country best by staying, and trying to get a sensible policy. . . .'[39] Sidney Smith put it rather differently. 'Ministers,' he said, 'have a great deal of patience but no resignation.'[40]

To this traditional patience has now been added the greatly augmented claims of party loyalty, and the increased preoccupation of ministers with their own departments. Thus to his subsequent regret Mr. Macmillan was too engrossed with the Ministry of Housing to press the European issue.[41] In 1956 Monckton agreed with Mr. Nutting. He advised him to resign, and would have liked to do the same himself. Yet he did not do so, not because of political ambition, but because he felt his departure might topple the government.[42] Ten years later Mr. Brown disagreed with the government's measures and resigned his post at the Department of Economic Affairs. He was eventually persuaded to withdraw his resignation and to support the measures he disapproved of, provided he could do so from the safe distance of the Foreign Office.

Resignations will still occur. But almost always they will be acts of desperation, a last stand when all else is lost, not the beginning of an offensive. They will be an action bringing honour to the men who perform it; seldom will they bring fear to the Prime Minister to whom they are submitted.

Resignation is necessarily a less powerful weapon in an electoral than a parliamentary democracy; and as the minister's weapon of resignation has been weakened, that of the Premier, dismissal, has been strengthened. Gladstone doubted if he had the right to demand the resignation of a cabinet minister. But the problem for Prime

Ministers in the last century was how to keep ministers in the cabinet; their problem nowadays is how to get them out of it. At least in the twentieth century a Prime Minister's right to re-shape his cabinet has never been in question.* The Macmillanite Massacre of the Innocents was remarkable only in that it was a far more drastic remodelling than any previously known. It came after eleven years of power and some heavy defeats in bye-elections had suggested that either a new cabinet or a new Prime Minister was needed. The victims had nothing in common except that none of them excited much enthusiasm among the voters. The purge does not show that a Prime Minister may with impunity dismiss one third of his cabinet who happen to disagree with him. But it demonstrated the Prime Minister's sway over both cabinet and party. No cabinet minister resigned in protest and nobody refused the offer of promotion. As Lord Beaverbrook wrote of 1916: 'The reality was that men would serve under any efficient Premier.'[44] Mr. Macmillan was a highly efficient Premier, and there was no shortage of men anxious to serve him.

All the same, Mr. Macmillan's cabinet executions did the executioner himself great harm. The parliamentary party was shaken and angry. The Prime Minister could not have loaded the tumbrils a second time. Another attempted massacre would have been his Thermidor.

Collective Responsibility

The concentration of ministers on their own departments, their reluctance to jeopardise party unity by resigning, and the Premier's ascendancy and enhanced powers of dismissal, have threatened, without ending, collective responsibility. The principle was slow to grow and slow to decline. Plainly there could be no collective responsibility until the collectivity was clearly defined. In the eighteenth century, cabinets rarely came or went in a body. Some ministers who still enjoyed the favour of the King stayed on, while others were replaced. In the middle of the eighteenth century cabinet ministers could speak and vote against government measures. The King could still consult the ministers individually and not merely collectively through the Prime Minister. As late as 1825 George IV wrote to Liverpool desiring 'distinctly to know from

* The Duke of Devonshire wrote in 1903 of the departure of Ritchie and Lord Balfour of Burleigh: 'I never heard anything more summary and decisive than the dismissal of the two ministers . . .'[43]

H

his Cabinet, individually (*seriatim,*) whether the great principles of policy established by his government in the years 1814, 1815 and 1818, are, or are not to be abandoned'.[45] On Canning's insistence the Cabinet sent a joint reply to the King, but Liverpool did not suggest that the King's request for individual replies was unconstitutional.[46]

Melbourne's celebrated remark to his colleagues that it did not matter what they decided as long as they all told the same story was an unequivocal assertion of the basic principle underlying cabinet government; and collective responsibility to parliament, like individual ministerial responsibility, was at its zenith in the era of parliamentary democracy. Although it has survived the transition to the electoral era better than its individual brother, all it now means is that each member of the cabinet must accept responsibility for everything that the government does, however strongly he may disapprove of it. His only alternative is to resign.

Hence cabinet secrecy is essential. If a cabinet minister has to take responsibility for a decision, he cannot be allowed to express public disagreement with it. Apart from considerations of security, the point of secrecy in any gathering is to prevent people competing for power or popularity outside the gathering by what they say or do inside it. Harcourt, when he was Chancellor of the Exchequer and leader of the House of Commons, once wrote that he was 'not a supporter of the present government'.[47] Such sentiments have to be expressed in private if at all. The spectacle of ministers currying favour in their own party by dissenting from unpopular decisions would be more than their colleagues could bear. Cabinet secrecy is an indispensable ingredient of collective responsibility, and collective responsibility is an indispensable condition of cabinet government.

Twice in this century the principle of collective responsibility came under far greater strain than it is today. After his resignation in 1922 Montagu protested against 'the total, complete, absolute disappearance of the doctrine of Cabinet responsibility ever since he [Lloyd George] formed his Government'.[48] Montagu exaggerated only a little. Lloyd George interfered in the affairs of other departments, particularly the Foreign Office. He provoked Curzon to the point of writing, though not actually sending, his famous protest about the existence of two Foreign Offices, one in Downing Street and one in Whitehall. The Prime Minister worked with a small and powerful inner cabinet, and, in moments of crisis as at Chanak, the cabinet was not fully consulted. At other times it was bye-passed. Yet if Lloyd George behaved in some ways like a dictator,[49] he was not one in cabinet, and ironically Montagu's own forced resignation was a vindication of the principle or collective responsibility. Indeed it was not the Lloyd George coalition but the Macdonald-Baldwin coalition ten years later which most conspicuously flouted the principle. In January 1932 Snowden, Samuel, Sinclair and Maclean resigned in protest against the imposition of a tariff. In order to keep them in the cabinet it was agreed that they be allowed to speak and vote against the government's proposals, an unfortunate expedient which did not survive the Ottawa agreement and has not bee repeated.

Governments are seldom defeated in the Commons, and the electorate has no means of forcing an election; so governments are only 'responsible' in the sense that they must answer in the House of Commons for their policies, and retain the support of their supporters in parliament. A disaster for the country or an obvious failure of a policy does not lead to a government's resignation or even necessarily to subsequent electoral defeat. On such occasions the only concession governments make to collective responsibility is to invoke individual ministerial responsibility. To avoid all being hanged together, the government is prepared to let one minister hang separately. Thus Hoare, although the cabinet had agreed to his proposals, was hanged for the Hoare-Laval pact. After devaluation, Mr. Callaghan's hanging took the humane form of being appointed Home Secretary.

The principle of collective responsibility was dented by Mr. Cousins's ostentatious dissent from the incomes policy of the government to which he belonged, though largely repaired by his eventual resignation. A publicly threatened resignation is an obvious way of avoiding real as opposed to nominal responsibility for an unpopular policy.

Luckily however the maintenance of collective responsibility and the plural executive does not depend upon the good sense and restraint of politicians. Cabinet government is inseparable from parliamentary government. Political power resides in the leaders of the party or parties which command a majority in the House of Commons. Strict party discipline enhances the position of the most important leader; it does not fundamentally alter the character of the system.

A British Prime Minister is elected in the same way as every other

M.P. He can be overthrown by revolt or intrigue in his parliamentary party. Almost invariably the revolts and the intrigues ignominiously fail, but no Prime Minister can ignore the possibility of them succeeding. He has to retain the allegiance of his party in the Commons, and his cabinet contains his rivals and potential successors.

An American President is not subject to these hazards. The essence of the presidential system in America and elsewhere is that the chief executive is elected separately from the other party leaders. His position is different in kind from the rest of his party colleagues and from those he calls to help him run the executive branch of the government. He is the single executive. The responsibility is his alone. Initially the American President behaved in cabinet like a Prime Minister. He was merely its most important member. Washington and Jefferson treated their votes as being equal in kind to those of everyone else. This equality did not last. 'I have accustomed myself to receive with respect the opinions of others,' said Jackson, 'but always take the responsibility of deciding for myself.'[50] Over the Emancipation Proclamation, Lincoln said to the Cabinet 'that I had resolved upon this step, and had not called them together to ask their advice . . .'[51] Such an attitude was not confined to strong Presidents. Coolidge maintained that 'there never ought to be and never were differences of opinion in my cabinet'.[52]

The American cabinet is composed of men, whom the President may not have previously met,* who may be quite unknown to each other, who do not necessarily belong to the same party, who may have little or no experience of politics. So haphazard is the process of selection that Woodrow Wilson's first choice for Secretary of War was a Quaker. Such a body is not fitted to make decisions. But it is useful for gaining the consent of regions, clients, the President's party and to some extent the opposition party. The President uses it also to gain the consent of its own members and of the bureaucracy to his decisions. According to Truman 'the Cabinet presents the principal medium through which the President controls his administration'.[54] He insisted that his cabinet officers kept him informed 'in order to make certain that they supported the policy once I had made a decision'.[55]

Under F. D. Roosevelt the Cabinet was so little regarded as a proper place for discussion and decision that cabinet officers who had something important to say waited until the meeting was over

---

* Eisenhower had never met his Secretary of the Treasury, Humphrey, or his Secretary of Labour, Durkin.[53]

and then said it to the President privately.[56] F.D.R. did not even inform his cabinet of his 'court-packing' plan. Under Truman, too, the important business and discussion often took place after the cabinet meeting. A cabinet might open with a discussion of the prevalence of foot and mouth disease in Mexican cattle.[57] Such trivialities would have been out of place when the meeting was over. 'After the Cabinet meeting . . . the President held Forrestal back to tell him what the decision was to be.'[58] The Eisenhower cabinet was used to see that all members of the team played as a team and in accordance with the directions of the coach. For the first time the cabinet had a secretariat, an agenda, and also prayers, but little was decided there.[59] Dillon thought meetings of the Eisenhower cabinet 'great fun if you didn't have anything to do'.[60] Kennedy considered 'general Cabinet meetings . . . a waste of time',[61] and Eisenhower's elaborate procedural façade was abandoned.

The American cabinet can advise and debate. But because it does not have responsibility, no amount of smoothing of the susceptibilities of cabinet ministers, no observance of formal courtesies, no cabinet secretariat, not even prayer, can turn it into a decision-making body. Truman apologised to the cabinet, after protests by Forrestal and Anderson, for having merely informed them that he was going to veto the Taft-Hartley Bill. But he never allowed himself to forget that 'I ran the executive branch of the government'.[62] A responsible and decision-taking cabinet is no more possible in the U.S. today than it was in seventeenth century England. The President is alone responsible.

In Britain the cabinet is still a responsible body and has only a nominal resemblance to its American namesake. Yet the election of the Prime Minister taking place no differently from that of other M.P.s is not an infallible safeguard of cabinet government. If the cabinet were merely an assembly of the leading men in the party, it would be easily controlled by the Prime Minister. The weakness of ex-ministers after their resignation is proof of that. But because the cabinet is not merely a collection of party leaders, but an assembly also of ministers with mighty departments at their back, it is not the Prime Minister's court. During the war Mr. Churchill urged the House not 'to underrate the power of these great Departments of State. I have served over twenty years in Cabinets, in peace and war, and I can assure the House that the power of these great Departments is in many cases irresistible because it is based on knowledge and on systematised and organised currents of opinion. You must have machinery which carries to the Cabinet with the least possible friction the consent and allegiance of these great Departments'.[63] It is these citadels of power in Whitehall which bar the way to a Prime Ministerial system. While the political landscape round the Prime Minister has been flattened by the disappearance of most other peaks of power, the Whitehall pyramids have maintained or increased their stature. A cabinet minister in his capacity of head of, say, the Treasury may be emboldened to oppose the Prime Minister in a manner that he might not dare in his capacity of party lieutenant. The departments give reality to the theory of collective responsibility and prevent the cabinet being the servant of the Prime Minister. As a result, it is not a yes-man's assembly. The no-man has not been eliminated.

At the same time, if the captains of these great citadels in Whitehall were not parliamentarians but recruits from industry and universities, without parliamentary backing or standing, collective responsibility would be threatened from the other side. The departments would not be able to uphold the principle on their own. In revolt against the cult of the amateur many people see the running of Whitehall by 'expert' businessmen and industrialists as the path to Britain's salvation, a belief which seems to be based upon an idealised view of the Kennedy experience. Senator Taft's scepticism about the phalanx of businessmen, joined by one plumber, in Eisenhower's cabinet, was better founded. 'You know,' he said, 'I'm not at all sure that all these businessmen are going to work out. I don't know of any reason why success in business should mean success in public service.'[64] Business being different from politics, the installation of businessmen in Whitehall would not signal the arrival of professionalism in government, merely of another form of amateurism. Lord Woolton was one of the few men who have been both successful in business and also masterly political operators. Sir Paul Chambers would no more be a professional as Minister of Housing than as head of the *Daily Mirror*. At all events, the take-over of Whitehall by outsiders, even if they were all put in the House of Lords, would for better or worse spell the end of cabinet government.

That end has not come yet. Mr. Crossman's suggestion that under Attlee our government became Prime Ministerial was not a complaint that was made at the time. Attlee's colleagues grumbled that he was not prepared to give a lead, that he was not sufficiently Prime Ministerial. He preferred to wait and see what the prevailing view was and then sum up in its favour; if there was no prevailing view, he set up a committee. Morrison, Dalton and Cripps were all exasperated by his refusal to commit himself to any definite view or course of action until he knew that it was likely to be accepted.

The experience of Lord Cherwell over the setting up of the Atomic Energy Authority in 1953 shows how far this country still is from the American system and how far the British cabinet is from being an honorific body. Cherwell had been one of Churchill's closest advisers for thirty years. If the government was Prime Ministerial, Cherwell, because of his relationship with Churchill, was more likely than almost any other minister to get his way in a Whitehall battle. Alternatively if he could not get his way through that relationship, he should not, on the Prime Ministerial theory, have been able to get it in any other way. Yet this is precisely what he did. The Prof's 'classical method of persuading Churchill to his way of thinking, the minute and the argument . . . '[65] did not work. Eventually, with deep reluctance he brought the matter before the cabinet and won his point. Cherwell, the Paymaster General and member of the cabinet had succeeded, where the Prof, intimate adviser to the Prime Minister, had failed.[66]

Mr. Macmillan's butchery in 1962 was a striking demonstration of Prime Ministerial power, but it did not exchange cabinet government for Prime Ministerial government any more than the assassination of a King changes a monarchy into a republic. Macmillan was less dominant in his new cabinet than in his old. Sir Alec Douglas-Home had no chance to practice Prime Ministerial government. During the first two years of his government, Mr. Wilson's political position was strong both in the country and in his party; accordingly it was also strong in the cabinet. But even in that period the government was not a one man band, though the Prime Minister tried to make it seem so. He beat the big drum of publicity, but he did not choose all the tunes. The Prime Minister led the cabinet: he did not supersede it.

After Mr. Wilson's position had everywhere crumbled, Mr. George Brown seemed in his resignation letter[67] to accuse him of Prime Ministerial government. Yet faced with an American request in the middle of the night to declare a bank holiday, probably every Prime Minister and Chancellor of the Exchequer in this century would have behaved in the same way as Mr. Wilson and Mr. Jenkins. True, Mr. Brown projected into the past his disquiet 'at the way this Government is run and the manner in which we reach our decisions'. But this was evidently a gallant attempt to find a rational basis for an ill-conceived resignation. Mr. Wilson's Caesarism, if it ever existed, had long since turned to clay.

In any case, for the chairman and leader to tower above his colleagues is not inconsistent with cabinet government. Any chairman should be more powerful than those over whom he presides. The ascendancy of the Prime Minister has not concentrated all decision-making in his hands. The collective executive is still a reality. 'It is the collective view,' Mr. Powell has said, 'which is at the back of the mind of the individual minister all the time.'[68] That is the meaning of cabinet government.

Political Forces

By enabling cabinet ministers to stand up to the Premier, departmental forces may have been decisive in preserving cabinet government. In virtually everything else to do with the cabinet, political forces have had their way.

Wordsworth wrote of 'the unhappy counsel of a few weak men'.[69] Yet most people have believed that the counsel will be less unhappy if the men are indeed few. The growth of cabinets has been a perennial complaint since the eighteenth century. Pitt's first cabinet had only five members. Within a few days it had increased to seven. By 1805 it had grown to fourteen. In the twentieth century peacetime cabinets have never been less than sixteen and never more than twenty-three. As the conspicuous summit of the ambitions of politicians, the cabinet has been subject to the usual inflationary pressures.* Macdonald hoped for a cabinet of fourteen; he got one of twenty.[70] Churchill's, Eden's and Macmillan's cabinets all grew during their life. Having condemned the Douglas-Home cabinet of twenty-three as 'excessive' and as reflecting 'the relative weakness of the Prime Minister',[71] Mr. Wilson formed a cabinet of precisely the same number. Political necessity has always prevailed over administrative requirements.

For the cabinet is not primarily an advisory or administrative body but a committee of the leading men of the party which commands a majority in the House of Commons, and it has to govern by holding that majority together. Clearly the majority's allegiance, which is far from automatic, can be more easily assured by a large cabinet, representative of all the strands of opinion in the party, than by a small one. So the size of the cabinet has been determined not by

* The Senate Foreign Relations Committee grew from thirteen members in 1947 to nineteen in 1965.

the demands of efficiency but by the state of the party, the political debts which have to be paid, and the claims of ambition and friendship.

Both George I and Walpole thought no good ever came of a large cabinet; only in a small cabinet was Walpole sure of a majority.[72] Nowadays the opposite is true. The Prime Minister prefers a large cabinet because the lesser ministers tend to take his side. This is not the outcome of any recent increase in the power of the Premier; Palmerston commented upon it in the cabinet of Melbourne. The underlings look to the top. Austen Chamberlain complained bitterly of Lloyd George having 'appealed to the votes of minor members of the cabinet to overrule the advice of two Secretaries of State in the common affairs of their two offices'.[73] The least important and least able ministers are to the Prime Minister

> '. . . an easy tool,
> Deferential, glad to be of use,
> Politic, cautious, and meticulous;
> Full of high sentence, but a bit obtuse.'[74]

A large cabinet helps the Prime Minister to control his senior colleagues. A small cabinet would help his senior colleagues to control him. For most men it is much easier to dominate a body of twenty than one of five. The presence in the cabinet of ministers who are less than equals ensures that the Prime Minister remains more than first amongst them.

Efficiency has had little to do with the evolution of the cabinet system. In the first part of the nineteenth century there was a regular cabinet dinner, members of the cabinet taking it in turn to be host. Lyndhurst thought 'we should have no Cabinets after dinner. We all drink too much wine, and are not civil to each other.'[75] In addition to incivility, cabinet dinners led to leakages by waiters of what had been said and to more than usual confusion as to what, if anything, had been decided.

Sleeping was common. Sidmouth was an habitual offender; and, according to Kinglake, at the crucial meeting to decide upon the invasion of the Crimea, 'all the members of the cabinet except a small minority were overcome with sleep'.[76] In the Balfour cabinet the Duke of Devonshire was often asleep. He was either asleep or not paying attention[77] when Chamberlain managed to secure from the cabinet a provisional agreement for preferential tariffs for corn imports from the Empire.

Up to 1916 there was no secretariat, agenda or proper record of decisions. No wonder Salisbury thought 'nothing was ever settled satisfactorily in the Cabinet'.[78] No wonder ministers often left the meeting with utterly different impressions of what had happened and what had been agreed. In an attempt to discover a cabinet decision the Ministry of Munitions asked three separate ministers and 'received three different answers: (1) that the Arbitration Tribunal was to hold wages; (2) that the Arbitration Tribunal was not to hold wages; (3) that the Cabinet had reached no decision at all. We chose the answer that seemed to us the most desirable in the national interest.'*[79] Even if the decision had been clear, ministers might forget about it. After the cabinet had decided on July 29 1914 to put the precautionary measures of the war book into operation, one minister forgot to inform his department until late in the evening.[80]

The Lord of Chaos himself could hardly have devised more suitable arrangements for the furtherance of his objectives. It is barely credible that such a state of affairs should have lasted until 1916, when Lloyd George brought to 10 Downing Street the system that had worked well in the Committee of Imperial Defence. Thenceforward the cabinet had a secretariat, an agenda, and minutes. Ministers knew what they were going to talk about and what they had decided. The presence of a secretary and the need to record conclusions led to more decisions. Departments no longer had to rely on the memory of their minister for the transmission of cabinet decisions.

Since 1916 the British cabinet system has had all the advantages that an intensely able Secretariat can bring to it. The Civil Service apparatus has been unrivalled. But that in itself is not enough to make the system efficient. A Rolls Royce engine fitted to a dog cart would not make an efficient vehicle. The 1916 Reform, the creation of a cabinet office, has not been matched elsewhere in the system. The dog cart is still with us.

* Such flexibility is not wholly a thing of the past. One post-war Minister of Defence was incapable of speaking adequately in cabinet, a deficiency which his subordinates made good by getting the Secretary to the cabinet to insert into the Minutes what he should have said.

Except on minor issues the cabinet does not usually vote. The sense of the meeting prevails. Decisions are in theory unanimous.* The cabinet is less like the Polish Diet where each member had a veto than a convoy with the P.M. as the officer commanding the escort. He does not always have to travel at the speed of the slowest ship. He can go on ahead of a slow ship or two, leaving them to limp unhappily along in the rear. But obviously the escort cannot go faster than the entire convoy.

This does not make for speed of decision or indeed for decision at all. The cabinet proceeds by consensus, committee and compromise. When there is disagreement, a committee is set up and a compromise is screwed together. If the disagreement is fundamental, the compromise usually takes the form of inaction. The procedure is heavily weighted in favour of the 'noes'. The 'No' lobby, as Iain Macleod has said, nearly always wins in cabinet.[81]

A procedure depending upon harmony favours those disposed to discord. A negative minority has far greater power than it would possess in a system depending upon votes and majorities. But proceeding by consensus is the necessary condition of a collective executive, and delays, indecisiveness and meaningless compromises are the inevitable result.

The Prime Minister and the cabinet secretariat can mitigate some of the evils. Virtual unanimity gives greater scope to the chairman than any system of voting. Only the most ingenious can do much with the counting of votes. But the weighing of voices, the assessment of the intensity of opinion, the estimation of unanimity— these occult imponderabilia give the chairman wide latitude. Not being susceptible to exact measurement, his interpretation of them is not easily challenged particularly in a gathering where he is accorded considerable deference.[82] The Prime Minister can blandly assume agreement where agreement does not exist. If a discussion has tailed off into an aimless ramble, and the Prime Minister has failed to sum up in a way that suggests a decision, the Secretary to the cabinet may be able to insert in the minutes the decision that should have been reached. Yet invention by the Prime Minister of an unanimity which did not exist or by the Secretary to the cabinet of a decision which was not made is not enough to bring speed and decisiveness to the cabinet.

* Not always even in theory. A minister may ask for his dissent to be recorded in the minutes, a fairly pompous proceeding since nobody will learn about his brave stand for thirty years.

Cabinet government fitted the time scale of the nineteenth century better than it does the twentieth. A hundred years ago departmental work was much less exacting for ministers. Government by discussion and unanimity was not out of tempo with the times. Delay was not usually disastrous. Today, there are a multitude of decisions to be taken quickly. Most ministers are overburdened with departmental work. Inevitably many grudge hours spent discussing matters that do not intimately concern them.*

Conciliar government has its disadvantages even where a speedy decision is not required. Lengthy and scrupulous cabinet discussions may produce a policy which all can support only because much of its content has been removed. After a sharp difference of opinion, the cabinet may produce an agreed line which is less satisfactory than either of the original views put forward.† Compromises which seemed convenient and clever at the time but prove disastrous later are a feature of any system of government. But conciliar government is particularly prone to this. A tribunal which decides according to the sense of the meeting and which mostly consists of men not outstandingly expert on the subject they are debating, has a natural tendency towards blurring the edges and often the meaning. Eden in cabinet found that discussions under Baldwin's chairmanship 'were often too inconclusive'.[84] A cabinet ruling may decide nothing; and a series of cabinet decisions may be inconsistent with each other and render the pursuit of any coherent policy impossible.

A collective executive does not easily lend itself to firm and clear policies. Indecisiveness is its chronic defect, postponement its chosen instrument. 'So far as the cabinet were concerned the matter slumbered for another six or seven weeks' was the characteristic comment of a cabinet minister in the thirties.[85] Not even the best machinery for the recording and communicating of decisions, and for the bringing of ministers to the brink of making a decision can actually push them over and force them to make one. Ironside's judgment on the Chamberlain cabinet could have been made on most cabinets. 'I noticed how relieved the Cabinet was at not being asked to make a decision. I am sure it will be a dreadful moment when they have to make a decision.'[86]

---

* Grey wrote his dispatches in cabinet. Eden often used to leave after Foreign Office business had been taken. Asquith used to compose obituaries of his colleagues.

† One of Eisenhower's cabinet officers thought that 'Putting a pet project on the cabinet agenda is a good way to get it nibbled to death by ducks.'[83]

Time spent on profitless argument means that there is less time for other matters. Indecisiveness therefore occassionally leads to spurts of decision. Items which would have excited debate and opposition if placed early on the agenda may slide through an exhausted and hungry cabinet without a murmur of dissent, when placed at the bottom.

The tyranny of the deadline, the demands of lunch, the pre-occupation of ministers with the affairs of their own departments, the reluctance of busy men to tackle difficult issues, the gamesmanship of clever ministers in getting their proposals through without discussion, the unwillingness to look ahead or meet trouble until it can no longer be avoided, all conspire to upset the priorities of cabinet government. The unimportant tends to drive out the important; or when the important is permitted full discussion, the decisions tend to be vague and contradictory.

Failure to have a proper system of priorities is not of course a defect peculiar to the British cabinet system or to cabinet government in general. Necessity, as Cromwell nearly said, knows no priority. Governments of whatever kind will always deal with the things that have to be dealt with at the time, even though these are of much less moment than other matters on which action is not yet necessary. 'When watched at close quarters,' wrote Namier, 'the actions of men are in no way correlated in weight and value to the results they produce. The same men have to decide things big and small, and their decisions are reached by the same processes and reactions.'[87] Under any system of government, leaders spend disproportionate time on trivia.

Dudley's complaint made in the 1820s that things of no real importance were discussed in cabinet[88] has usually had some substance to it. In 1914 the cabinet was too preoccupied with Ireland to give attention to the European crisis until shortly before war broke out. Later, the cabinet made no preparations to save Antwerp. Only Churchill foresaw the danger.[89] The Passfield White Paper on Palestine went through the 1929 Labour Government without discussion.[90] On the other hand, both before the 1939 war and during it, Mr. Eden was occasionally exasperated by the cabinet's interference with such matters as the drafting of telegrams. As he subsequently complained, 'every detail became a negotiation in the Cabinet before it could be a factor in our foreign policy'.[91]

The third time Eden was Foreign Secretary he suffered no such meddling. By then the cabinet had swung to the opposite extreme.

Eden was left a free hand in foreign affairs both by Churchill, who did not want to embarrass his successor, and by the rest of the cabinet who were chary of walking where the great man refused to tread.[92]

The cabinet does not usually see the Chancellor's Budget proposals till the day before they are presented to the House of Commons, though even on Budget eve it is possible for the cabinet to make some changes. After discussion in the cabinet on his first budget,[93] Dalton altered his proposals on income tax allowances.

Steel was exhaustively debated in Attlee's cabinet, yet Dalton regarded cheap money as a departmental question and indeed only once mentioned 'an impending cheap-money move' to the Prime Minister.[94] At the height of the Palestine crisis in 1947 the High Commissioner and the G.O.C. were summoned to London to attend a cabinet meeting. Palestine came fourth on the agenda, following arrangements for the Olympic Games and before amendments to the National Health Bill.[95]

Of course these vagaries were not solely due to the inability to distinguish the important from the trivial. They have often been due to the wish of the Prime Minister or other ministers to exclude the cabinet from particular issues. The corner-stone in Mr. Crossman's argument that under the Attlee administration we passed from cabinet to Prime Ministerial government was his suggestion that Mr. Attlee took the decision to manufacture a British atomic bomb 'without any prior discussion in the Cabinet . . . and he had not revealed it to any but a handful of trusted friends'.[96] This was not in fact true. Mr. Strauss who was then Minister of Supply has shown that the decision was taken at the Defence Sub-Committee of the cabinet and that the minutes of the meeting were circulated to members of the cabinet.[97] Mr. Strauss further pointed out that not only was the decision not concealed from the cabinet, it was not even concealed from the House of Commons. The decision was communicated to parliament by the Minister of Defence in answer to a 'planted' question on May 12 1948.

But even if Mr. Crossman's version of events had been accurate, it would have come nowhere near proving his case. Failure to inform the cabinet of important foreign policy matters has been common since the eighteenth century. In order to conceal the details of the negotiations between Britain and France in 1797 from the cabinet, Malmesbury went to the length of writing 'ostensible' despatches' which could be circulated, and another set 'which must . . . be entirely suppressed . . .'[98] and were seen only by Grenville and Pitt. Castlereagh's secret Treaty of January 3 1815, which formed a defensive alliance between Austria, France and Britain and which could have led to war with Prussia and Russia, was signed without the cabinet's knowledge and indeed contrary to its instructions at the time he signed it.[99]

Palmerston conducted foreign affairs for many years without showing an over-scrupulous regard for the susceptibilities of his cabinet colleagues. When he formed the quadruple alliance in 1834, the cabinet was carried 'by a *coup de main*, taking them by surprise and not leaving them time to make objections! It was a capital hit, and all my own doing'.[100] As Prime Minister thirty years later his attitude to the cabinet was equally cavalier. 'I felt so little satisfied with the decision of the Cabinet on Saturday,' he told Russell in 1864, 'that I determined to make a notch off my own bat.'[101] The cabinet did not run him out.

At least once during the First War, the cabinet was by-passed without the excuse of military necessity, lack of time, or need for secrecy. Cyprus was offered to Greece without the cabinet being informed far less consulted.[102] After the war Lloyd George took decisions on foreign affairs independently of his cabinet and Foreign Secretary.[103] But by far the most important instance of withholding information from the cabinet was Grey's decision to hold military conversations with France in 1906. The only ministers informed of this crucial step were Campbell Bannerman, Haldane and Ripon.[104] Grey waited six years before he told the remainder of his colleagues,[105] a far more blatant case of deception of the cabinet than Attlee's would have been—had it taken place. If disclosure and discussion in cabinet of all important issues is the test of cabinet government, then this country has almost never enjoyed cabinet government.

Inner Cabinet
'In most governments,' said Lloyd George, 'there are four or five outstanding figures, who by exceptional talent, experience and personality constitute the inner council which gives direction to the policy of a ministry.'[106] Yet the inner cabinet, if there is one, does not necessarily consist of the 'outstanding figures' in the governments. Its composition depends more upon the needs and whims of the Prime Minister than upon the commanding abilities and characters of the individuals concerned.

When late in 1919 peace eventually compelled a return to a large cabinet*, Lloyd George's inner body was composed of Horne, Geddes and Greenwood, an unremarkable trio who were displaced in 1921 by Churchill and Birkenhead.[107] Apart from Lloyd George himself, Churchill and Birkenhead were certainly the 'outstanding figures' in the government. But their talents did not take them into the inner cabinet before 1921, and it was the Prime Minster's need to obtain an Irish settlement and the impossibility of doing so, unless Birkenhead and Churchill were closely involved in the negotiations, that forced him to accept them as his chief counsellors and confidantes. This triumvirate which determined British policy in the Chanak crisis, (overruling in the process Curzon and the Foreign Office),[109] was imposed upon the Prime Minister by the nature of the Coalition. Exceptionally, Lloyd George chose his inner colleagues because they did not agree with him, not because they did.

Neville Chamberlain's inner cabinet was not primarily determined by the talents of its members. It was composed of senior colleagues, who shared his views on how to deal with the dictators. 'By the Government,' wrote Duff Cooper, in his diary on September 12 1938, 'now is meant the P.M., Simon, Halifax, and Sam Hoare.[110]' Two days later Hore-Belisha recorded that Chamberlain, Halifax, Simon and Hoare 'had decided that his plan Z [of going to see Hitler] should be put into operation at once. . . . Apparently the P.M. had not found it possible to consult us all'.[111] At that stage the Prime Minister could easily have consulted all his cabinet had he been so minded, and indeed throughout most of the crisis it was inclination not necessity that led Chamberlain to confine the cabinet to being little more than a register of the decisions of the inner group. Those outside 'the big Four' were left with the alternatives of acquiescence or resignation. All but Duff Cooper chose acquiescence.

Similarly in 1956 the cabinet, as Lord Butler has said, 'came very little into the Suez crisis until towards the end'.[112] A cabinet committee consisting of six members and the Prime Minister was set up on July 27.† This knew more of the sequence of events and of the Prime Minister's intentions than the full cabinet. But as well

* Earlier, when Lloyd George was reconstructing his government after the war, he thought of doing without a cabinet altogether.[108]

† In the same talk Lord Butler said: 'It was the Prime Minister who set up a Cabinet Committee . . . ; the Cabinet would probably not have agreed to set up such a Committee.'

as this inner cabinet there was evidently an even more intimate body.*

On any view Butler was an outstanding member of the Eden government, yet while a member of the inner cabinet, he was not a member of the inmost group. Nor was Monckton, who as Minister of Defence until the middle of October might have been thought to be closely involved in the projected military operations. In September, Monckton admitted to Lester Pearson that press reports that the cabinet was split with Butler and himself leading the opposition were 'embarrassingly accurate'.[114] There could be no such split in the directing group. Membership of that body was confined to the leading colleagues of the Prime Minister who favoured an attack on Egypt.

Some members of the full cabinet felt that they were being told too little of what was going on; and a fairly senior minister, who was in general sympathy with the Prime Minister's policy in so far as he knew what it was, was deputed to complain to Eden of the lack of information and to ask for a cabinet to be called. Owing to its conspiratorial character, the Suez policy was not one which could be readily confided to the cabinet, but that is more an argument against the policy than a defence of the manner in which it was carried out. At all events on October 24 and October 25 the cabinet gave its agreement to Eden's policy.[115] How far its implications and meaning were explained or understood is not clear. Certainly a number of ministers later felt they should have been told more.† In any case ministers outside the inner ring had no influence upon events until after the venture had begun.

This sort of inner cabinet is less of a threat to the full cabinet than it seems, simply because it often does not exist. And when it does exist, it is less a threat to the cabinet than to the country. Lloyd George's Turkish policy, Munich and Suez demonstrate its dangers. Unlike the full cabinet, an inner cabinet is usually an advisory body; or rather it is a counter advisory body. It provides a means for the Prime Minister to deprive himself of the advice he does not want to hear. Strong and differing colleagues are excluded

---

* Even now there is good ground to demur against using the term "inner cabinet" because it tends to endow that fleeting shadowy group with a too formal and well-nigh official character. Some expression like "inner ring" or "directing group" would seem preferable.'[113] Namier's warning is much to the point on Suez.

† Referring to the earlier attack on Egypt in 1882 John Bright wrote to Joe Chamberlain: 'You will remember that the only reason given in and to the Cabinet was that there was danger to English subjects, not that the forts were to be bombarded and war to be begun. I agree with you that the question was not sufficiently discussed. . . .'[11] Bright, however, resigned.

from his counsel. Though powerful Civil Servants such as Wilson*
in 1938 and Kirkpatrick in 1956 may play influential parts as
individuals, the Civil Service machine, too, is disconnected. Departmental advice is not properly available; or it is ignored, on the
plausible pretext that those who are proffering it are not fully
informed. There is a double imbalance. The Prime Minister encircles
himself with ministers who out of conviction agree with him or
out of sycophancy applaud him; and those ministers themselves
lack the proper weight of official advice which is usually open to
them. The results have not been happy.

Most Prime Ministers need more intimate consultations to help
them shoulder the burdens of their office than a meeting of the
cabinet or official meetings with colleagues can provide. Bonar Law
thought that 'all Prime Ministers suffer by suppression. Their
friends do not tell them the truth; they tell them what they want
to hear.'[117] Friends outside the government are less likely to be
guilty of suppression than intimates selected from inside it. But
such relationships are not always possible. Some Prime Ministers
do not have any friends. Their only possible confidantes are their
colleagues.

Both the second Macdonald† government and the Attlee government contained a 'Big Five', but neither Macdonald nor Attlee had
a definable inner cabinet in the sense of a body meeting regularly in
order to reach decisions on major policy. Macdonald was secretive
and distrustful. Some of his leading colleagues reciprocated his
distrust. Confidential discussion of major policy between the big
five was out of the question. They were the big five of the party,
not an inner cabinet.

Attlee, like Macdonald, did not relish long discussions with his
senior colleagues or, indeed, with anybody else. Once again there
was a big five in the government, but because of Attlee's reserve
and the antipathy between Bevin and Morrison, it remained just
that. They were demonstrably the most important and powerful
ministers in the government, and on the negotiations for the
American loan, on the economic position in 1947, and on a number
of other matters, they formed an inner group.[118] But their meetings
were spasmodic, and there was no lasting inner cabinet.

The unitary nature of the Tory party combined with the structure
of Conservative cabinets has since the war avoided a 'Big Five' on the

---

* Horace, not Harold, who did not become a Civil Servant until 1940.
† The first Macdonald government had a 'Big Six'.

Labour model. More co-ordinating has been done by the Prime Minister and less by his senior colleagues.

The inner cabinet has not become institutionalised for the same reasons that have led to the survival of a large cabinet. An unofficial inner cabinet enhances the power of a Prime Minister, while an official one would diminish it. Naturally, therefore, an official inner cabinet is only mooted when the Prime Minister is in trouble. In 1947 Attlee felt his position so threatened that he offered to set up such a body.[119] But Morrison's disinclination to kill Charles in order to make James King, and Bevin's loyalty to his chief saved Attlee; and nothing more was heard of an official inner cabinet.

Similarly, when Mr. Wilson's position was threatened in 1968, he announced the formation of a Parliamentary Committee consisting of senior ministers. Since its membership was defined, it excited the jealousy of those excluded. Also, apparently, the minority could appeal to the full cabinet. However, these severe disadvantages were probably immaterial, as the parliamentary committee was evidently more of an expedient to help the Prime Minister than an administrative innovation.

The term 'inner cabinet' has an additional meaning. Tom Jones thought that an inner cabinet merely means that 'a Prime Minister turns more easily and more reliably for advice to some ministers than to others, usually one by one and not collectively'.[120] In that sense there is always an inner cabinet. It does not have a fixed composition but varies slightly with the subject in hand. This is almost certainly a better system than an inner cabinet consisting of the same men. It keeps ministerial jealousy to the minimum, opens the Prime Minister to a wide area of advice, and makes the dispatch of cabinet business reasonably expeditious.

Most cabinets contain one or two ministers, a Crewe or a Bridgeman, whose character and judgment enjoy respect but whose ability and public following are not conspicuous. Both the qualities and defects of such men fit them to be advisers to the Premier. Their judgment is good and their political talents are not disturbing; he can consult them knowing they are not his rivals. Yet aside from these intimates, the ministers that a Prime Minister most frequently relies upon are the heads of the leading departments. The near disappearance of independent pockets of political power has made the office more important than the man.

On economic questions, Amery thought the Treasury and its mouthpiece, the Chancellor,[121] were more powerful than the rest of the cabinet or the parliamentary majority. It is probably the most powerful government department in the west,[122] and a number of other departments are virtually its satellites. The Ministry of Agriculture is responsible for the government's agricultural policy, but that policy depends upon the money the government is prepared to offer for the support of British agriculture, and the Treasury has far more to do with determining that sum than does the Ministry of Agriculture.

The Ministry of Social Security is similarly placed; so to a slightly lesser extent are the Ministry of Transport and the Ministry of Education. Strong ministers may be able to carry out the policies they favour. 'The capable minister gets the swag,' as Admiral Fisher put it.[123] But their decisive battle lies nearly always with the Treasury. Another department which has increased in power in Whitehall, if not abroad, is the Foreign Office. Many matters previously exclusively internal now affect it. Conversely since the war, it has often been defeated on external affairs by the Colonial Office and the Ministry of Defence, usually to the country's detriment.

The great departments have extended their influence, and those who head them are more powerful than their colleagues. But this is not a recent development. 'Those ministers who hold great responsible situations,' said Fox in 1782, 'should have more interest in the cabinet than those who attended merely to give counsel, but without holding responsible situations.'[124] The inner cabinet in the Jonesian sense necessarily consists of the holders of the most important offices and is not a threat to cabinet government. The great departments may be overmighty subjects; but they and the Prime Minister do not produce a cohesive inner body manipulating the cabinet at will. When the Prime Minister and the great departments are agreed, the cabinet has to follow suit. Often, however, the great departments are not in agreement either with each other or with the Prime Minister. The cabinet is the *tertius gaudens* of conflict between the Prime Minister and the departments.

Cabinet Committees

The departments, great and small, take more decisions on their own than they ever did before the war. The sheer number of decisions that have to be made means that many matters which previously would have been taken to the cabinet now never trouble it. And the cabinet has had to divide itself up into a maze of committees. Dating from the Reform Bill, cabinet committees in the nineteenth century were often set up to draft legislation, occasionally to anticipate and resolve difficulties. But not until the first World War did inter-departmental committees, both ministerial and official, come into existence in great numbers. Hankey estimated that by 1918 there were 165 of them.[125] In the second war *ad hoc* committees were used with great effect by Mr. Churchill to turn the heat on to any project that seemed to be flagging. Under the Attlee government the jungle of cabinet committees reached its most exotic. By 1952 there were 700 inter-departmental committees, over one hundred of which were technically cabinet committees.[126]

Sir Winston Churchill tried to defoliate the jungle by abolishing most of the committees of officials. The relief was only temporary. The luxuriant vegetation soon sprouted anew.

The profusion of cabinet committees is the product of the departmental structure. The more departments there are, the more committees there must be to co-ordinate their activities. The more the activities of government departments impinge upon the life of the citizen, the more do government departments also impinge upon each other. Almost every departmental action involves other departments. A minor proposal to move Coventry's market brought in five different ministers.[127] In 1967 expenditure of space activities was borne upon fourteen separate votes.[128] Unfortunately there is no direct relation between the number of co-ordinators and co-ordinating committees and the degree of co-ordination that is achieved. Or if there is a relationship it is in inverse proportion. As committees proliferate, conflict and confusion grow. The system of cabinet committees in Britain is not unlike the state of the War Office before the Esher reforms.

General de Lattre once satirised the British fondness for making war by committee. 'Any one Committee which succeeded in coming to a decision was obliged to refer that decision to another committee, whose duty it was, so it often seemed, to reverse it or annul it or at best to refer it to yet another committee. By this means nobody became too powerful, no envies or jealousies were generated. . . .'[129] Unfortunately this nightmare has even greater application to peacetime.

In the thirties the maze of committees slowed up rearmament.[130] In 1937 there were three organs of Cabinet concerned with defence policy—the Commitee of Imperial Defence, and its two sub-Committees—'all', in Hankey's words, 'more or less independent of one another, all dealing with defence questions without very definite lines of demarcation'.[131] In the Attlee government a committee under the Prime Minister dealing with international economic policy, a committee under the Lord President of the Council dealing with domestic economic policy, and the Chancellor of the Exchequer dealing with financial policy, inevitably produced confusion.

As governments grow in age, so does the habit of appointing a committee. Born of indecision, committees usually lead to more indecision. Talk becomes a substitute for decision, and action recedes further into the future. Even such old committee hands as Attlee[132] and Templewood[133] have admitted that committees often make decisions slower and more difficult to reach. The more outspoken Oliver Lyttelton told Dalton that he had never expected to join 'so many second-rate debating societies'.[134]

Work spent in committee is arduous, time consuming, and often frustrating. Tom Jones recorded that Baldwin 'was groaning under the weight of work—long Cabinet meetings, an Indian Committee daily for two hours run by Sam Hoare . . .'[135] In addition to all his duties as Home Secretary, at the beginning of the war, Templewood was committed to 'almost daily attendance at the Committee of Imperial Defence and the Foreign Policy Committee'.[136] 'This afternoon,' complained Dalton in 1946, 'I sat in one of those endless India Committees. The P.M. in the chair is obviously very tired. So are the number of other ministers. The result is that the conversation wanders round and round and nothing is focussed. There have been five or six of these meetings in the last few days, each lasting several hours . . .'[137] Attlee as Prime Minister was chairman of seven cabinet committees.[138] In 1960 the Lord Chancellor was a member of twenty-three committees and chairman of sixteen of them.[139]

The monkey puzzle of co-ordinating committees strains the powers and the temper of leading ministers. From overwork to ill health to bad personal relations is a likely sequence and one that kills co-ordination. The most efficient system of co-ordination will not avail if the chief co-ordinators are unable to work together.

The Prime Minister decides the composition of cabinet committees, and so can influence the likely outcome of their deliberations. On the other hand, much of their composition is determined according to the relevant departments, and he cannot be chairman of all of them, whereas he is always chairman of the cabinet. Attlee's power was not enhanced by the shoal of committees which grew under his administration. One of the causes of the attempted coup d'état in 1947 was that under him, as Cripps told Dalton, decisions were 'referred to further official committees. There was no drive at the centre. With Bevin in charge it would be quite different. He would send for individual ministers, and settle things there and then, and everyone would much prefer it so.'[140]

If a committee's recommendations do not carry great weight with the cabinet, cabinet proceedings will be intolerably protracted, as they were in the Asquith administration during the first war, when everything was thrashed out in the Dardanelles committee and again in the full cabinet. The more important a matter, the more important will be the ministers on the committee. And always sitting on it will be the ministers whose departments are most directly concerned, and who are believed to have special knowledge of the subject. For a cabinet to refuse to accept its proposals will normally be the overruling of the informed by the ignorant, the occupational disease of cabinet government.

Nevertheless the cabinet does occasionally overrule its committees. In 1947 the Labour Cabinet rejected all the principal proposals of its Economic Planning Committee, an exceptionally powerful body including Dalton, Morrison and Cripps. Dalton's anger at this action suggests its rarity.[141] Still, it happened.

As a rule, however, cabinet committees reach many decisions which are then in effect merely registered at meetings of the full cabinet. This does not mean that the power of the cabinet has declined. An institution is in operation even when it is not in plenary session. Those who favour the introduction of the committee system into the British House of Commons have as their object the aggrandisement of parliament, not its diminution.

No institution takes decisions solely in the prescribed form. Prudent men do not arrive at meetings without having prepared the ground. Presumably Cardinals lobby between ballots when they are locked in the Vatican to elect a Pope. And British Premiers and Ministers have not drawn up cherished schemes only to put them out of their minds until they are discussed in cabinet. When he was Chancellor of the Exchequer, Lloyd George went next door in Downing Street almost every morning to see Asquith before the cabinet.[142] Hoare lobbied the Treasury, the Board of Trade, and also Baldwin, who was not much interested, before putting his proposals for his Geneva speech to the cabinet.[143] It makes little difference whether these early moves take place unofficially or in recognised committees or in both.

Cabinet committees in themselves do not diminish the power of the cabinet. If there was a cabinet committee which engrossed the most important part of public business and whose decisions were never upset by its parent body, that committee would be taking over the traditional functions of the cabinet and would have displaced it as the inner committee of power. During the war the Lord President's Committee became, in Churchill's words, 'almost a parallel cabinet concerned with home affairs'.[144] But in peacetime no committee has yet come near to engrossing a preponderant part of the cabinet business.

Saturn killed his children. Committees kill their parent bodies. Yet the cabinet has survived. An institution is not obliged to work in full consistory. By breaking itself up into committees, the cabinet has preserved its power, not surrendered it.

Schemes for Reform

Cabinet committees lighten the burden on the cabinet but increase the burden on cabinet ministers. A large cabinet and a cluster of cabinet committees are the consequence of the doctrine of ministerial responsibility and of the interests of leading politicians, the Civil Service, and the Prime Minister. These forces have been forgotten or rationalised out of the way by the protagonists of the present organisation of the executive, such as Sir John Anderson and Mr. Morrison, who claim that it exists not because it is the result of outside forces but because it is efficient. This is mere administrative positivism: what is, is efficient.

Administrative positivism has been a far from universal creed. But, like the positivists, many of the advocates of cabinet and administrative reform have disregarded the forces which have fashioned the system into its present state. Schemes for reform can be broadly divided into two: the Amery scheme advocating a small cabinet of non-departmental ministers, and the Haldane scheme seeking salvation through a rationalisation of the departmental structure.

Amery's admiration for the efficiency of the Prussian general staff led him to advocate its importation not merely into the British army but into the organisation of the cabinet. On the face of it, a policy planning cabinet consisting of ministers not weighed down by departmental work and not encumbered with inter-departmental jealousies would be a considerable improvement. Certainly the virtues Amery discovered in such a cabinet are not found under the present dispensation. Difficulties have been dealt with as they arise; they have not been anticipated. British government has always relied on curative not preventive medicine.

Yet the perennial British suspicion of separating advisers from executives has more behind it than mere traditionalism. As Churchill said of a non-departmental war cabinet, 'A group of detached statesmen, however high their nominal authority . . . tend to become more and more theoretical supervisors and commentators, reading an immense amount of material every day, but doubtful how to use their knowedge without doing more harm than good.'[145] The supervisors tend to become detached from reality as well as power. Their theoretical proposals are not anchored to feasibility by the knowledge that it will be their task to execute them. Field Marshal Robertson is reputed to have told Lloyd George: 'I could give you a hundred plans for winning the war if I had not got the responsibility for carrying them out.'[146] Although the unexpected usually happens in war, the problems which have to be anticipated are not unlimited. Maps can be prepared of all the terrain that is likely or unlikely to be fought over.* The objective is usually clear. The problems of peace are far less tidy, manageable, or open to intelligent planning. The maps are sketchy, the objectives nebulous, the route rambling and unmarked. A system suitable for running a highly disciplined army is not necessarily right for running a country in peacetime where practically every man is his own army.

Whether or not the Amery scheme would work is largely academic, since it conflicts with both Prime Ministerial and parliamentary realities. Churchill disliked the idea of a 'disembodied brains trust'.[149] He 'preferred to deal with chiefs of organisations rather than counsellors',[150] and he has told of his difficulties with Sir Stafford Cripps, when Cripps's lack of departmental work led him to interfere with the running of the war. A small cabinet consisting of ministers engaged in 'exalted brooding over the work done by others'[151] could hardly fail to promote their power at the expense of that of the Prime Minister. When all are 'exalted brooders', as they would be in the Amery cabinet, one man's brooding is as exalted as another's. Churchill was clear that exalted brooders would inhibit him, and nearly all his ministers were properly burdened with departmental work. Peacetime Premiers are likely to take the same view as Churchill.

Like Amery, Haldane was not untouched by German influences. The Army Council asked him, when he was at the War Office, what sort of Army he had in mind. His answer was: 'a Hegelian Army'.[152]

---

* In the late 1920s Britain was preparing for war against Russia in Afghanistan.[147] In the thirties she was fully prepared to defend the Suez Canal against Japan.[148]

And as Chairman of the Committee set up in the first war to discover what sort of machinery of government was needed, his answer was a Hegelian government. Having found that there was 'much over-lapping and consequent obscurity and confusion in the functions of the Departments of executive government',[153] the Haldane Committee proposed to abolish the overlapping and obscurity by organising the government on a rational basis. The Committee recommended that functions should be assigned to government departments according to one overriding principle: class of ser-vice.[154] The Committee's allocation of functions would produce ten ministries or groups of ministers,[155] and in consequence a cabinet of about a dozen.

Beatrice Webb recorded in her diary that 'we sit twice a week over tea and muffins in Haldane's comfortable dining room dis-cussing the theory and practice of government. I try to make them face the newer problems of combining bureaucratic efficiency with democratic control; they are forever insisting that the working of parliament makes sensible, leave alone scientific administration, impracticable.'[156] Mrs. Webb had her way in the report; parliament has had its way ever since.

For British government is not Hegelian. What Mrs. Webb was told over tea and muffins was the simple truth. Government is not just a question of the rational distribution of functions. Adminis-tration cannot be divorced from politics and parliament; and the cabinet is more of a political than an administrative body. The Haldane Committee enumerated the main functions of the cabinet as (a) The final determination of the policy to be submitted to Parliament; (b) the supreme control of the national executive in accordance with the policy prescribed by Parliament; and (c) the continuous co-ordination and delimitation of the activities of the several Departments of State.[157] But the Committee did not mention the most important function of the cabinet, which is to govern the country by maintaining its majority in the House of Commons.[158] A super-efficient general staff is useless if its army will not fight; and a super-efficient cabinet system would be useless if the cabinet was not able to preserve the unity and strength of its parliamentary party.

The cabinet and Whitehall are not just pieces of administrative machinery. The shape of the government is determined more by the strength and conflicting personalities of the leading politicians than by the demands of rational administration. The creation of the

Department of Economic Affairs was decided upon in a taxi[159] in order to provide a billet for Mr. George Brown. And while the Service departments have been rationalised into the Ministry of Defence, economic departments have been created and dismembered for personal and political reasons.

Besides departments have a representative as well as administrative function. Pressure groups would scarcely be willing to forego representation in the government in order to satisfy the intellectual purity of Haldane and Mrs. Webb. Finally the Haldane scheme would almost certainly lead to some ministers being more overworked than they are at present. And in view of the present surpassing importance of finance, any rational grouping of ministers would give the Chancellor of the Exchequer a degree of power which even the most self-effacing Premier would find vexatious.

The Haldane Committee made the mistake of thinking with Hegel that 'the rational is the real'. It also ignored the realities of power in the governmental machine. Reforms of government are seldom brought about by the lucid presentation of logical arguments. The governmental machine works in the way it does because it happens to suit the interests of those who work it. All the same 'the real' needs to be mixed with 'the rational'. Though the full Haldane scheme is not practicable, some Hegelianism could with advantage be added to the present administrative positivism to produce a workable and more efficient system.

Grouping and amalgamation of departments could beget a smaller cabinet. But just as a cabinet of twenty-three is too big, so one of ten or twelve would probably be too small. The proper leadership of the parliamentary party and the representative functions of the cabinet require a larger body of, say, sixteen to eighteen. So in fact do the demands of good administration. The development of cabinet committees has removed the need to cut the cabinet down to the Haldane size. Present inefficiency is caused not by a large cabinet but by the multitude of departments.

Clemenceau once laid down that the larger a committee is, the less able it is to function properly.[160] But this was not true of Churchill's war cabinet. The widely held belief that only a small war cabinet could function properly led to its official membership being kept low. Yet for the proper transaction of business there had to be a larger gathering. As a result there were the 'constant attenders', men whose presence at the meeting was necessary for the taking of decisions, but who were precluded from official membership, because of the belief that decisions would not be taken if the official membership of the cabinet were extended. The smaller the war cabinet was kept the more consent it gained—and the fewer decisions it would have been able to take.

The same situation may well occur in peacetime. The popularity of small cabinets may drive a future Prime Minister to gain credit by forming a cabinet which is nominally small. Almost certainly however its meetings will be swollen by the 'constant attenders'. The eighteenth century position will then be reversed, and the real cabinet will be larger than the nominal one.

A better solution than a small cabinet would be a reduction in the number of departments. It is the profusion of departments which creates the need for co-ordination and cabinet committees; and so long as the number of departments remained the same, a small cabinet would not help efficiency. Indeed it would increase the problem of co-ordination. A shrinking of the departments, on the other hand, would reduce both the problem of co-ordination and cut down cabinet committees.

This administrative reform would be facilitated by parliamentary reform. Yet until recently the cabinet was no more anxious to reform parliament than parliament was to reform the cabinet—or for that matter itself. A fully fledged committee system in the Commons would probably weaken the magnetic attractions of ministerial office. Once M.P.s were satisfactorily occupied in committee work, and their ambitions for office had slackened, to, say, that of Swedish M.P.s, the number of ministers could be more easily cut* and the administration reorganised on more coherent lines.

A cabinet or sixteen or eighteen would be neither unwieldy nor unrealistically small. It would include enough important politicians to diminish the 'constant attenders', and be adequately representative of Whitehall, Westminster, and the country. By some such system collective responsibility would be preserved and co-ordination improved.

Together with this creeping Haldane-ism the power of the Prime Minister is likely to grow, though this would still not amount to

* Under the Fourth Republic the French government had about thirty or thirty-five members. Under the Fifth, it has had about twenty-five. The Wilson government has over one hundred.

Prime Ministerial government. The Cabinet Office provides something like a department for the Premier. If with the multiplication of governmental functions and the growth of the Civil Service, the Prime Minister had continued to sit in 10 Downing Street, as did Asquith, with a staff of precisely two secretaries, then he would have resembled less an Elected Monarch than a Constitutional Monarch, reigning but not ruling.

The cabinet office has not pushed the Prime Minister far ahead of the field; it has enabled him to keep up with it, to retain the place he formerly held. Without a cabinet office, a Prime Minister would be at the mercy of the departments. A cabinet office of reasonable size has restored the Prime Minister's relative position to not far below what it was in the time of Peel, even though he may possess nothing of Peel's transcendent ability.

Mr. Wilson has said that 'the Cabinet Secretariat is the private department of the Prime Minister. Each member of the cabinet office staff services and serves the whole cabinet, but they are also my own staff.'[161] The cabinet office is an organ of collective responsibility as well as of the Prime Minister. Only Lloyd George and Churchill have employed private armies of their own to control and check the departments. Cherwell and his statisticians enabled Churchill to challenge his ministers on such diverse matters as the number of man hours needed to build an aircraft,[162] or the desirability of diverting feeding stuffs from beef cattle to hens.[163] Morrison has described the feelings of ministers who saw the Prime Minister paying more attention to 'the Prof's' brief comments than to the departmental paper.[164]

Such a system would not be feasible in peacetime. A Prime Minister who wanted to challenge the details of other departments would at least need his own department. In most other countries the Prime Minister does have a department of his own. Crispi, when Prime Minister of Italy, ran three other major departments.[165] Under the Third Republic a French premier needed another ministry to survive.[166] Since 1934 the Prime Minister of France has had a large department of his own. A British Prime Minister has to contend neither with an independent-minded Civil Service nor with a multiparty cabinet, but on the recommendation of the Fulton Committee he has gained the Civil Service department. But probably the possession of this department will not enable the Prime Minister to check the other departments, though it may help him to enter projects when they are embryonic. When before the 1964 election

Mr. Wilson talked of strengthening the cabinet secretariat, the idea received the *imprimatur* of Lord Bridges, who thought a strengthened secretariat would be useful in keeping the Prime Minister up to date on work 'still in the germinating stage'.[167]

Yet there are dangers in the Prime Minister being involved too soon. President Kennedy used his White House staff to see that he entered the argument at an early point and to gain independent advice and information.[168] 'He was not interested in unanimous committee recommendations. . . . He relied instead on informal meetings and direct contacts.'[169] Such methods tend to keep much of the decision-making at the top, but by trying to decide too much the top man may get committed to a course long before the time is ripe for decision. He may become part of the bureaucratic machine instead of a check on it. This seems to have happened to Kennedy over the Bay of Pigs. Had the full scheme been put to him at a later stage, he would surely have dismissed it out of hand. As it was, he and his advisers came into the project early on and were never able to stand back and take a dispassionate look at it.[170]

Further, early involvement in some issues will involve non-involvement in others. Under Kennedy's active and centralised Presidency, the American State Department issued without the President's knowledge a statement which toppled the Canadian Government, and the Defence Department by its handling of Skybolt created a crisis with the British Government, again without the President being informed.[171] Evidently salvation does not lie in greatly increased concentration of executive power.

The defects of the excessively closed and centralised British system would not be removed by making it still more closed and centralised—the likely result of increased power for the Prime Minister without reform elsewhere. Indeed while to increase the internal efficiency of the executive would no doubt be beneficent, to concentrate on such reforms is to miss the essential point: that the secret executive's manner of operation is out of joint with electoral democracy. The prime need therefore is to bring the executive into a proper relationship with the real world outside Whitehall by lessening its centralisation and mitigating its secrecy.

The executive should be opened up, though not the cabinet itself. The revelations of cabinet quarrels in 1931 and Mr. Wilson's airing of his alleged differences with Mr. Brown over South African arms in 1967 conferred no credit on anybody. Cabinet deliberations should remain shrouded, but the pretence should be abandoned that the executive is a *deus ex machina* existing outside space and time and ordering the universe. It is in fact very much part of the political process and often ordered by it.

A change in the relationship between the executive and those it seeks to govern can probably be achieved only by parliamentary reform sufficient to enable the Commons to compel disclosure, or by a voluntary renunciation by the executive of its vows of silence. It is after all largely the identification of constitutional with political power, which persuades the executive to cling to the present situation. The executive has an apparent monopoly of the power of formal decision. Yet that monopoly confines the monopolists as well as those who are shut out. The executive's manner of making decisions, because it cannot gain the interest or attention of the public, restricts the number and the scope of those decisions. Hence by loosening its monopoly and sharing its knowledge and powers with others the executive would add to its power of decision. Constitutional power is not the same as political power.

And the gain in strength from such a change would not be offset by a loss in consistency. The fact that decisions are theoretically taken by the same body does not mean that they are coherent, consistent and sensible. Policy may be made by predominantly reasonable men doing their best in all the circumstances, but that does not make policy-making a rational process. Policy is not created like the world. It is always imposed upon or growing out of what has gone before. Digging into it resembles excavations in an old city: there are traces of many different epochs. A cabinet moreover does not have a mind. Its decisions are the products of a series of discussions in which those taking part do not necessarily maintain a coherent view throughout. They may from time to time be influenced by extraneous factors. They may in the intervals have met different people. They may just change their minds. The item's place in the agenda may have its effect. Public or party opinion may have shifted. Secrecy does not insulate the cabinet from pressure. The decisions are not taken once and for all, and they impinge on each other. Dalton talked of a speech of Attlee's having 'to be built up from a multitude of confused, ambiguous and imprecise cabinet decisions'.[172]

A cabinet's policies are likely to shift, its allegiances to be variable, its emphases to be unpredictable, its decisions to be internally inconsistent, its deliberations to be guided by the different interests of the departments and by the need to gain the consent of parliament and public. Very often its fastening to the departments keeps the options within the realm of the sensible and prevents the long term interests of the state being overborne by the short term interests of the party. At other times the disposition of the departments in the cabinet is no more representative than the pre-Reform Bill parliament of early nineteenth century England. Old Sarum is represented while Manchester is not. The growth of the departments, after all, has been just about as fortuitous as that of parliamentary representation in England.*

More open government and less centralised decision-making would not therefore substitute irrationality and chaos for reason and order, but would recognise reality and bring greater political vitality to government. If the central executive no longer took all the decisions, it would more often take the right ones.

In the meantime cabinet government will continue much as in the past. The idea that the Prime Minister can do more or less what he likes is sheer myth. Attlee in 1948 was overruled on such a key issue as a British commitment to send an army to the continent in the event of war.[173] Mr. Macmillan was thwarted more than once by his Chancellors of the Exchequer. The cabinet has not lost control of broad continuing issues of policy. Whether or not steel should be nationalised, and if so, how, continually came before the Attlee cabinet with varying results. The decision to seek entry into the European Economic Community would have been taken much earlier, had it lain with Mr. Macmillan alone. It was preceded by seemingly interminable cabinet discussions in which the doubts and objections of many ministers had to be slowly whittled down before the attempt could be made. The Prime Minister has checks on every side. He has to carry his cabinet, the big departments and the bulk of his party with him. These cover a wide spectrum of conflicting views and interests. The checks are internal but very real. No peacetime premier since Lloyd George has for long had anything approaching a free hand, and none has been safe from overthrow.

* This haphazard, departmentalised, and inconsistent form of decision making should not be contrasted with the delightful prospect of a single all-seeing mind taking all the decisions in the light of all possible factors, and observing all the possible priorities while taking stock of all the relevant political realities. If such a mind happened to exist in British politics, it would be unlikely to reside in 10 Downing Street.

III

THE HOUSE OF COMMONS

The Constitution of this country is declining so rapidly that the House of Commons has in great measure ceased and will shortly entirely cease to be a place of much importance . . .

CHARLES JAMES FOX, in 1801[1]

'Mr. Kennedy never tells one anything. I doubt whether Mr. Kennedy thinks that any woman knows the meaning of the British Constitution.'
'Do you know what it means, Violet?' asked Lady Laura.
'To be sure I do. It is liberty to growl about the iron fleet, or the ballot, or the taxes, or the peers, or the bishops—or anything else, except the House of Commons. That's the British Constitution.'

ANTHONY TROLLOPE: Phineas Finn

Why do country gentlemen wish to get into Parliament, but to be seen there? Why do overgrown merchants and rich nabobs wish to sit there, like so many overgrown schoolboys?

WILLIAM HAZLITT[2]

Whatever happened in the time of Phineas Finn, liberty to growl about the House of Commons is now very much part of the British Constitution, and growling about it has for long been a minor industry. The commonest complaint has traditionally been that the House has steadily lost power to the executive and has now become little more than a rubber stamp. Sometimes, indeed, parliament seems to have been declining over the centuries almost as constantly as in the eyes of old fashioned historians the middle class was rising.

Contrary to popular belief, parliament as an independent body rarely has been powerful. 'An independent House of Commons,' a politician wrote in 1784, 'is no part of the English constitution. . . . A numerous assembly uninfluenced is as much a creature of imagination, as a griffin or a dragon . . .'[3] The House of Commons came nearest to being independent between 1832 and 1867 when the Crown was receding from the forefront of politics and the party organisations had not taken its place. In the fifties and sixties there was more—cross voting than before or since, and between the first two Reform Bills the House drove ten governments to resignation or to a dissolution of parliament. In some ways the House was then more powerful than it had been since the interregnum and more so than at any time since. Yet far from welcoming the spectacle, many contemporaries found the antics of the House disturbing.[4] And even in that exceptional period when parliament most resembled the French Chamber under the Third Republic, the 'numerous assembly' was not 'uninfluenced' either by the cabinet or by party. The position of the Commons today is not at variance with its historic role. To believe otherwise is to believe in griffins and dragons. The wonder is not parliament's lack of influence over the government but the extent of it.

Much of the disdain for the House of Commons arises from what Professor Oakeshott has called 'the misunderstanding in which institutions and procedures appear as pieces of machinery designed to achieve a purpose settled in advance, instead of as manners of behaviour which are meaningless when separated from their context'.[5] The House of Commons is not a piece of machinery; it is a place which imposes certain 'manners of behaviour'. Maitland said that the parliament of 1305 was 'still rather an act than a body of persons'.[6] Now parliament is rather a place than a body of persons; and the habit of looking at it merely as a body leads to misconceptions of what it should be and what it should or could do.

The House of Commons is a highly complex institution, in which many interests clash. Little more than a class does it now operate as a body. Up to the seventeenth century the Commons could be regarded as a body: although there were alway divisions within it, its power could be considered in relation or in contrast to that of the King. By the eighteenth century, the Crown usually had sufficient influence over enough of its members to be able to control it; the task of opposing the Crown was undertaken not by the House as a whole but by a small part of it. To regard the House of Commons as 'one' or to consider its power in contrast to that of the King became increasingly unreal. In the nineteenth century, the development of party and the gradual disappearance of the Crown from politics ended any question of the House as a whole being in antithesis to the executive. The House was invariably split.

In appearance, an all-powerful executive dominates an impotent parliament. The government almost invariably gets its business through the Commons. It can maintain itself in the face of disaster or humiliation; it can survive with a majority of only three. But, in reality, Cabinet and Commons are not a dualism. The system of government is monistic not dualistic. There is a dualism of parties, not of institutions. Cabinet and Commons are indissolubly joined together, and should not be put asunder.

The government has stolen parliament's clothes, and has dressed up its supporters in them. While these are dressed in the clothes of parliamentary legislators, their hearts or anyway their votes belong to the executive.* The confrontation between the executive and parliament is thus a sham one. More than half the parliamentary army is a stage army, and the government always wins. Yet the cabinet is composed of parliamentarians, and M.P.s choose the party leaders. Thomas Cromwell told Henry VIII at the opening of parliament in 1539 that the King had 'never more tractable parlement'.[8] Provided the government has a majority, all parliaments are now tractable. But, so too are governments.

The cabinet is embedded in parliament and governs in and through parliament. The government wins every battle; parliament wins the war. Unfortunately much of the war takes place behind the lines where it cannot be observed. Hence it does not provide the fruitful public controversy that the British system needs.

There are three reasons for parliament's continued ability to impose manners of behaviour upon British politics. The powers of parliament are as great as ever they were. The Queen in parliament knows no superior and no impediment. No competing institution stands in the way. No basic or constitutional laws trammel her sovereignty. Secondly, British political leaders are parliamentarians. The road to Downing Street runs from the House of Commons, not from the battlefield, the City of London, or the film studios.† The third reason is the continuance of conventions and arrangements from the previous era of parliamentary democracy.

In the eighteenth century, governments did not resign when

* As early as 1797 John Cartwright wrote contemptuously of men 'skipping like harlequins, from the cabinet to the legislature, from the legislature to the cabinet; here in the shape of executive directors, there in the form of popular deputies. . . .'
† See pages 276-7.

defeated on legislation or taxation.* The younger Pitt thought it 'unfortunate' that he did not have the confidence of the Commons, but it was the King's confidence, not the House's, which mattered; and in a few months he suffered more than twenty defeats, including votes of censure, without resignation. Later, he told his opponents that they were wrong to think that they would get rid of him by defeating his bills.[9] As late as 1815 the Liverpool government was defeated on the income tax without resigning.[10]

But by the middle of the nineteenth century a defeat on a major question or a series of defeats caused a government to resign or dissolve parliament. The convention took time to grow. Macaulay denied in 1841 that 'it could be called a want of confidence, if the House withheld its assent from any new legislative measure or refused to sanction the alteration of an old law'.[11] Peel repudiated such old fashioned ideas. Six years earlier he had argued that nothing could 'justify the administration in persevering against a majority but a rational and well founded hope of acquiring additional support and converting a minority into a majority'.[12] His own experience at the election of 1835 showed that such a hope was no longer rational.

Theoretically a government which had lost the confidence of the House of Commons could be forced out of office by the Commons failing to pass the annual Mutiny Act or failing to vote supply. In fact the Mutiny Act was not passed for three years after 1698,[13] without the omission creating any discernible effect; and since 1688 the Commons had never failed to vote supply even to minority governments. It was the logic of the situation, not these probably illusory sanctions, that was decisive. Legislation was becoming an increasingly important function of government; without a majority laws could not be made. The Reform Bill had destroyed the Crown's already diminished power to secure a majority for the ministers of its choice. The 1835 election was the first since 1679 which returned a House of Commons unfavourable to government policies, though those of 1741 and 1830 came near to doing so. After 1832, Governments could no longer be confident that by holding on to office they would improve their position in the House at the next election. Hence defeat in the Commons led naturally to resignation or dissolution.

---

* A change of ministry because of a defeat in the Commons was as rare before 1832 as it has been since 1867. Between 1714 and 1832 only Walpole, North, Shelburne and Wellington resigned after such a defeat, and North's resignation was not immediate.

That logical sequence of events which was common between the first two Reform Bills and spasmodic during the following thirty years* produced a constitutional convention widely thought to be still operative today. Once it was apparent that governments were normally changed by the voters and only rarely by parliament, the Commons might have been allowed, except on genuine matters of 'confidence', to cause defeats of the government without fear of precipitating the government's resignation or its own dissolution. In the event the opposite happened. While Palmerston had accepted on average twelve defeats a session,[14] government defeats by the end of the century averaged one a session. 'Confidence' became tacitly involved in almost every vote.

The necessity of the era of parliamentary democracy has thus survived as a relic in the electoral era. How superficially convenient for the Prime Minister and the government! Their followers must always support them for fear of bringing down the ministry. Naturally party leaders do not overdo their veneration of the relic. Governments treat defeat in the House in the way that suits them best. When they do not possess a majority, they behave like Ramsay Macdonald in 1924 and do not regard every vote as a matter of confidence. Defeat is tolerated because the alternative is resignation or dissolution. By August 1924 the Macdonald government had been defeated ten times. When however the government does have a majority, the convention is brandished to prevent defeat or to undo it. The wartime coalition wielded the big stick of confidence to set aside a vote in favour of equal pay for teachers.

Thus in circumstances similar to those which produced the convention, an unstable or non-existent majority, the convention does not operate, but in circumstances quite different, a stable or disciplined majority, it is rigorously used. Though the leaders would ignore the mystical powers of the relic if it suited them to do so, no such defiance is permitted to their followers. The priests may know that the liquifying blood in the phial is not that of the Saint; such guilty knowledge must be withheld from the profane laity. The

* Since 1867 only three governments possessing a majority in the House of Commons have resigned or dissolved because of a defeat there: in 1885, 1886 and 1895. On the first and third occasions they need not have done so, but were anxious to leave office. The Rosebery government was not defeated because of a revolt of its supporters. It was defeated because many more Conservatives voted than the government whips expected, and because a number of Liberal M.P.s, including Lloyd George, were absent unpaired attending a function in Wales, while others were visiting the Asquiths in Cavendish Square.

assumption that a government would resign if defeated in a major vote ensures that it never is beaten. The convention binds the followers, but not the leaders. Without any of the elaborate provisions which make the passing of a vote of no confidence extraordinarily difficult in both the Federal Republic of Germany and the Fifth Republic of France, the government in Britain is never defeated and always receives the House's confidence.

Not surprisingly what Charles James Fox called 'the pernicious doctrine of confidence'[15] has been persistently denounced by those seeking more freedom for the private member and less dictatorship by the government. Though on the surface the idea has attractions, the would-be reformers ignore the paradox that by apparently subduing parliament the executive has preserved parliamentary government. Were it not for the relic, British political manners of behaviour might not have remained parliamentary. In Britain government is carried on by parliamentary forms with the government supreme. The likely alternative is not parliamentary forms with parliament supreme, but non-parliamentary forms with government supreme. The tradition that governments must win all major votes in the House of Commons forces them to explain their case in parliament, and to make concessions in advance to their supporters and their opponents.

Without the tradition, parliament might have become a legislature and played a larger part in making laws like the American Congress; but the focus of events would have shifted elsewhere. In 1885 Woodrow Wilson wrote a book called 'Congressional Government'. Nobody would say now that the United States had 'Congressional Government'. Britain does have parliamentary government. Arguably, of course, Britain also has cabinet government, or party government, or electoral government or Prime Ministerial government. But, undeniably, Britain has parliamentary government in the sense that Britain is governed through parliament and under its pervasive influence.

In consequence, unlike Congress whose proceedings are sparsely reported, the American press concentrating its attention upon the White House and the executive, the House of Commons has been preserved as a useful and important source of news. Stories by lobby correspondents are not often concerned with parliamentary debates, but they are the consequence of the preservation of 'parliamentary manners' in Britain. Without parliamentary debates, these stories would emanate solely from 10 Downing Street. Many of them are in the nature of political advertising: they are the results of off-the-record briefings by ministers or opposition leaders. Yet were Westminster to be regarded as no more than a sort of political advertising agency circulating copy about government and parliament, this would still be valuable to parliament and to the opposition.

Lobby correspondents often have no alternative but to print what they have been told; they have no opportunity of revising the authorised version. At other times they do more than provide the pulpit for the preacher; they themselves can give their assessment and their version of the facts.* Naturally the deeds of the government are usually more newsworthy than the words of the opposition. If they are not, if it is the opposition which is in the limelight, this is not necessarily to the opposition's advantage; it is usually the result of a row which may produce publicity for the opposition but seldom prestige and popularity. Yet Lobby correspondents are based at Westminster, mix with opposition leaders as well as ministers and backbenchers on both sides, and are not Downing Street correspondents perpetually clustered around the Prime Minister's public relations office.† All this helps to mitigate the effects of the government's command of the news.

The Opposition
The maintenance of parliamentary manners of behaviour in British politics and the habits of the previous era are a boon to those out of power; they place the opposition on a level of near equality with the government. The prime object of parliamentary opposition was, and is, to get rid of the government; yet the technique of it has scarcely altered since the days when governments were changed by parliament, not by the electorate. This is not quite so odd as it seems. In the eighteenth century oppositions were sometimes reluctant to force divisions for fear of revealing their weakness and

* British lobby correspondents have sometimes been accused of lacking the calibre and status of political journalists in the United States, and of not achieving the scoops that are frequent in Washington. Westminster journalists do not possess the standing of Washington columnists, because the press in America is more important than it is here. That is not the fault of 'The Lobby'. They do not bring off the coups that are fairly common in Washington because of the closed nature of the British system. It is easy to criticise the Lobby, if the political conditions under which they have to work are ignored.

† They do however meet his press officer twice a day.

dispiriting their supporters. As Pulteney put it: 'Dividing was not the way to multiply.'[16] Nowadays oppositions seldom have any hope of 'multiplying' their numbers in the House; they go on 'dividing' in the hope of multiplying their supporters in the country. Unfortunately the terms of trade have moved against the opposition in the country as well as in the Commons. Election results bear little relation to the government's performance; as with the Garter there is 'no damned merit' about them. So long as prosperity is rising, the power of dissolution, the Keynesian techniques of managing the economy, and accurate means of measuring public opinion, give the government of the day an enormous advantage.

Professor Crick has argued that we must 'reverse the classical constitutional theory . . . that the electorate influences a parliament which has the real power to control the government. The theory which now best fits the facts is that parliament influences the electorate which has the real power to control the government.' 'British government,' Dr. Crick believes, 'has become more and more a matter of a Prime Minister governing absolutely, only restrained (from doing too little as well as too much) by the knowledge that his party sometime must face a general election.' There is 'a continuous election campaign . . . beginning on the first day of each new parliament'. Plainly, if Dr. Crick were right in all this, his belief that British government is 'both superbly strong and somewhat insensitive'[17] would have solid foundation.

But in the last thirty years or so oppositions have not been outstandingly successful in winning over the electorate. Of the three changes of government caused by the voters since 1931, that of 1945 plainly owed nothing to opposition or to a continuous election campaign, since Labour had only been out of the coalition and in opposition for a few weeks; that of 1951 was achieved by a majority of 17; and that of 1964 by a majority of 5. The Conservative opposition of 1945–51 has been much praised for its toughness and ruthlessness, but its record was not quite the success story that is often imagined. It made important blunders such as seeming to oppose the National Health Service, and it did not gain a single seat in bye-elections. Even the harrying of Labour's small majority in 1950–1, sensationalised by Lord Boothby's speech on the subject, and often thought to have consisted of a lengthy campaign of late night attrition lasted effectively for only four sitting days.[18]

In any case parliamentary opposition is plainly not the prime cause of a change of government. Events are more important than speeches. Governments are held responsible for matters outside as well as within their control. They are sacrificed like ancient Kings, if they fail to produce the rain that brings forth fertility throughout the country. Increasingly, however, they are not sacrificed for failing to produce fertility; they are rewarded for having produced it.

'A distant prospect of public censure,' as Hamilton[19] pointed out, would in any case be 'a very feeble restraint on power...' And in modern Britain the prospect of censure is usually unlikely as well as distant. For a government of minimum competence acclaim is more probable than censure. So with the opposition normally at a disadvantage and the deterrent of the government election defeat declining in credibility, governments should indeed be strong and insensitive if elections are the only restraint upon them. On Dr. Crick's eschatological view, that government and politicians are always looking to the end of the current parliament, the strong British government should have been riding roughshod over an impotent Commons and a powerless opposition. This has not happened. More especially, on the Crick theory, a government with a big majority should be strong and decisive and free from trouble. With the partial exception of the Attlee government of 1945, governments with big majorities have been nothing of the sort. The government of 1918 was in difficulties shortly afterwards. The government of 1931 had the biggest majority since the Reform Bill; it was anything but strong. The Attlee administration ran out of steam after three years. The Conservative government of 1959 was in trouble in little over a year. The Labour government of 1966 was in trouble within three months. Government difficulties stem in varying degrees from the opposition and government backbenchers. But whatever the proportions and combinations, even a government with a big majority does not avoid parliamentary trouble. No government can rely on the unswerving support of parliament. The House of Commons is far from impotent.

Admittedly, parliament no longer has 'a procedure of opposition',[20] as it had from the seventeenth century until 1882. Speaker Shaw Lefevre calculated in 1848 that the question had to be put on a bill eighteen times.[21] This was substantially less than in the old Swedish Estates where bills might be discussed forty-two times,[22] but enough to allow considerable scope for obstruction and delay. In 1843 Palmerston complained that a few determined opponents might 'so obstruct the progress of a bill through Parliament, that a whole session may be scarcely long enough for carrying through

one measure'.²³ Just how much scope the rules of procedure allowed
was fully demonstrated by Parnell, and the demonstration was
convincing enough to ensure that the procedure was changed. The
devices for curtailing debate introduced by Gladstone's second
ministry cut down obstruction and altered the procedure of the
House from one of opposition to one of government. Balfour's
reforms completed the change and almost all the alterations in
procedure since then, including those introduced by the Wilson
administration, have favoured the government.

The opposition party has taken the place of an opposition procedure. Just as the experience of prisoners of war subjected to brain-
washing in solitary confinement has shown that a man's personality
and beliefs are shaped by his environment and his companions,
and that he becomes quite different without these shaping influences,
so is a government shaped by the existence of the opposition and
would be utterly different without it. Government policy is not
merely the outcome of its own deliberations but of the political
dialogue between itself and the opposition. A government's measures are a compromise between what it would like to do if the
opposition did not exist and the opposition's wishes. No government ignores the opposition; it only affects to do so.*

'The essence of opposition,' said Dr. Schumacher in the first
debate in the West German Parliament, 'is a permanent attempt to
force the government and its parties by concrete proposals tuned to
concrete situations to pursue the political line outlined by the
opposition.'²⁴ Except that if they are wise they seldom make concrete proposals, British oppositions are by Dr. Schumacher's standards remarkably successful.

In 1826 Tierney, the Whig leader, said that 'although the gentlemen opposite are in office, we are in power. The measures are ours
but all the emoluments are theirs'.²⁵ And similar boasts have frequently been made by oppositions. 'The Tories are in office, but
the Radicals in power,' said Joseph Chamberlain in his radical
heyday.²⁶ More recently, the post-war Labour government was
often said to be carrying out the foreign policy of Mr. Churchill as
outlined in his Fulton speech. In 1955 Mr. Atlee remarked with pride
that 'today even our opponents cannot put forward something
entirely contrary to Labour's view'.²⁷ The Wilson government's
policies on immigration, the Common Market, and the Bomb, bore

---

* And even when, as in 1968, it abuses the procedure of the Commons, it still makes
concessions on the substance of its bills.

a greater resemblance to Tory policies than to those of Labour when in opposition. The claim of the opposition that it is in some ways running the country is usually justified. It is the natural result of the two party system and the parliamentary dialogue.

Suez was one of the few occasions when a government has formulated its policy in complete disregard of its opponents. To take the country to war on a bogus pretext without consulting or gaining the support of the opposition was certainly high-handed. Yet if the beginning of Suez indicated the powerlessness of the opposition, the ending of it suggested the reverse. Lord Avon wrote that during the Suez crisis he had only the morning hours for 'the urgent affairs of the nation'.[28] For the rest of the day he was withstanding attacks on his policy from the Labour opposition in the House of Commons. American pressure and Russian threats chiefly brought Britain to agree to a cease-fire, but the incessant parliamentary rows and opposition, as well as behind-the-scenes Conservative disquiet, can hardly have failed to contribute. At all events the House of Commons showed itself to be a more powerful engine of opposition than would the American Congress in remotely comparable circumstances, as the war in Vietnam has demonstrated.[29] Incidents like Suez would be normal if the conventional theory were correct. In fact the end of Suez was more characteristic than the beginning of it.

'The real power' of changing the government has admittedly in great part passed from parliament to elections. The electorate has a sanction which it occasionally uses, while parliament has a sanction which it virtually never uses. Nevertheless the 'real power' of the voters through much of a government's term and over many issues is illusory. Of course both parties are concerned to win the next election. But it is not their sole objective, and however election-minded politicians may be, it is simply not possible to conduct a continuous election campaign for five years.* Frequently there is no way of knowing what the voters think of a particular matter at the time, let alone of what they may think of it four years later. Much important business has no electoral significance whatever. The immediate power of organised groups is often far more pressing than the future power of the voter. For much of the time the

* H. L. Mencken, however, would have agreed with Professor Crick. According to him, 'Mr. Harding was inaugurated at noon on March 4, 1921, and began to run for re-election not later than 12.30 p.m. of the same day. Coolidge at least let a week slip by before he spat upon his hands and got down to *Geschäft*. He is a very scrupulous fellow.'[30]

election is so far distant and the means of winning it so divorced from politicians' everyday operations that it does not supply a sufficient motive for their actions.

Besides, a parliament trying to influence the electorate at the next election is fully compatible with the electorate influencing parliament. The case for nationalising gas was stronger than that for nationalising some of the other industries, but the Conservatives were far more vehement in their denunciations of it than of any other nationalisation measure, because by that time they knew for certain how unpopular nationalisation was. In 1957 Labour dropped Suez as an issue because they felt it would lose them votes, though the issue evoked passionate hostility from many M.P.s. While trying to influence and educate the electorate, parliament is itself being continually influenced and educated by them.

Governments like individuals should 'remember [their] creator in the days of [their] youth', and notoriously they often try to carry out the least popular parts of their programme in their first two years, while retaining some of their most succulent bribes till just before the next election. Nevertheless their behaviour is not so very different in youth from age, as it would be if it was only 'the real power' of the voters that restrained them. Mr. Macmillan's government was relatively inactive for eighteen months after the 1959 election. Mr. Callaghan's first budget of 1966 came immediately after a general election; unpopular though it later became, for all its relevance to the economic situation a visitor from Mars would have assumed that it was the immediate prelude to an election campaign.

The idea that the Prime Minister and the government are restrained only by the fear that they may lose the next election arises from the military view of British politics, the view that sees two completely disciplined parties entirely obedient to their leaders facing each other in serried lines with the bigger army of the two always winning. In fact Prime Ministers and M.P.s are not merely concerned with winning in the division lobby or with winning the next election. They want other people to think well of them. They do not wish to be made fools of in public. This puts strong if not always successful limitations upon their activities. The government is also restrained by the strength of organised groups, by the need to keep its supporters together, by the divisions within it and by the confrontation between itself and the opposition.

Mr. Macmillan summed up the real position to Sir Roy Welensky in 1960.

'He began,' Welensky wrote, 'by begging me to believe that the United Kingdom government were not concerned with their own political position, since the general election had made them secure. He asserted, however, that for good or ill the Federation's future depended on the British government's ability to carry their own party fully with them in parliament and to persuade reasonable opinion that it was a good thing. He had always told me that it would be difficult, and the election of a lot of young members made it more so.'[31]

Ministers have continually to defend their actions before men on their side, who secretly would like to take their places, as well as before those on the other side who are openly trying to get rid of them.

For most of the time, the day to day influence of the House of Commons is more effective than the remote control of the electorate. Parliament's sanctions are rusty, but under the British system readily usable sanctions are not necessary for the exercise of influence. This is another way of saying that the distinction between power and influence is more apparent than real. Even those who theoretically have the power still have to persuade. The sovereign parliament cannot legislate without taking group interests into account. The Prime Minister often has to use influence rather than power. And those who theoretically do not have power, in the sense that they have no means of enforcing their wishes, have influence. In other words, in the British system at least, 'real power' is as illusory a conception as the philosophical conception of 'real' freedom.

British troubles in this century have not been due to governments doing too much or being too powerful. They have been due to governments doing too little or doing the wrong things, to their being unable to use the power they allegedly possess. This is not a sign of impotent opposition. In the prevention or remedying of individual injustice and in stopping a government pursuing its party advantage too nakedly at the expense of the rest of the community, oppositions have a good if not unblemished record. No doubt much of the credit is due to the press and public opinion and to organised groups; these would be far less effective without the parliamentary confrontation and without the existence of a strong opposition ready to take over the government. To try to measure the power of an opposition in isolation from all the other restraints upon a government is as absurd as trying to measure the strength of an arm that has been severed from a body. The parliamentary opposition is merely the most conspicuous of many curbs upon the government. If its successes cannot be divorced from these other restraints, nor can its power.

While therefore oppositions have become less likely and slower to be metamorphosed into governments, parliament's influence upon government has been maintained. This influence is not exercised by victories in the House or by compelling the government to withdraw a measure, though that does occasionally happen. It is a restraint before the fact, not after it. The opposition indeed is more successful in helping to restrain the government than in helping to remove it from office. The British system which is one of control of men, not of measures, now seems to produce more of a control of measures than a changeover of men.

Backbenchers

Under a two party system the House of Commons is not unlike the Austrian and Hungarian parliaments which met from 1867 in the same building but in separate rooms. At private party meetings things can be said and issues discussed in a way that would be impossible or at least acutely unpopular on the floor of the House.

In 1827 Palmerston wrote that 'the real opposition of the present day sit behind the Treasury bench'.[32] This reversal of the normal line of battle and the loosening of party loyalties were caused by Canning's succession to the Premiership and the resentment of the diehard Tories who sat behind him. The tightening of party ties since the Second Reform Bill has produced a similar result. The opposition are a strong general restraint upon the government; the government's supporters are another restraint, and often a stricter one.

Yet government backbenchers, like parliament itself, are not a body. They are an artificial entity. Usually many of them disagree with each other more strongly than they do with the government, which (provided the Prime Minister knows his job) invariably contains men of every shade of opinion and is broadly representative of the parliamentary party. Some government backbenchers constantly and intensely admire what the government is doing; others dislike it or the Prime Minister more than most members of the opposition. 'The mountain', the fierce radicals of the left or right, rarely agree with one another, let alone with their comrades in the centre. 'The marsh' are naturally less differentiated, but still comprise great difference of opinion, outlook and interest. They are always divided amongst themselves.

The usual estimate of backbenchers is that they are powerless and contemptible, careless of conscience and punctilious in discipline, hungry for patronage, bullied by the Whips and their local parties alike. Backbenchers have never had a good press. Coleridge thought the House of Commons was like Noah's Ark—a few men and many beasts.[33] Eighty years later Meredith described a backbencher of the 1870s; 'Although not a personage in the House of Commons, he was a vote; . . . His was the part of chorus, which he performed with a fairly close imitation of the original cries of periods before parliaments were instituted, thus representing a stage in the human development besides the borough of Bevisham.'[34] Early in this century the historian Lecky, who was M.P. for Dublin University, declared that the private member was 'being turned into a mere voting machine'.[35] And Kipling growled that 'Pagett, M.P., was a liar and a fluent liar therewith.'

'What is the use,' asked Churchill in 1939, 'of sending members to the House of Commons who say just the popular things of the moment and merely endeavour to give satisfaction to the government whips by . . . walking through the Lobbies oblivious of the criticisms they hear. People talk about our parliamentary institutions and parliamentary democracy, but if these are to survive it will not be because the constituencies return tame, docile, subservient Members, and try to stamp out every form of independent judgment.'[36]

The hostile witnesses make a formidable array, yet the criticisms cannot all be taken at face value. There is a natural temptation for men who have failed to win their party over to their view, or whose career in the House of Commons was less successful than their talents warranted, to attribute their failure to the timidity and ambition of their fellow members.

The House of Commons has always contained what Brougham called 'thick-and-thin men',[37] M.P.s who invariably support the government. A glance at the history of other countries soon establishes that such men have their uses. They ensure the stability of the system. Not 'the thick-and-thin men' alone but all the M.P.s of the winning party were elected to sustain a government. Owing their election entirely to their possession of the right party clothes and to their willingness to follow their party leader to Timbuctoo and back again if necessary—as it sometimes is—M.P.s of the governing party have no wish and are in no position to turn out the government which the electorate has chosen and which they have been returned to support.

There is a commonly held and engaging idea that M.P.s are kept cowed and obedient by the bludgeoning of the party whips. It conjures up an image of the distraught M.P. in a perpetual struggle with his conscience as to how he should vote on some deeply important ideological issue, and after his conscience has at last won the battle and he has decided to abstain or vote against his party, of the opportune arrival of a Whip who by threats of dire punishment or promises of glittering advancement defeats the M.P. and his conscience, and preserves his future and the party's unity.*

Certainly most M.P.s inform their Whip as a matter of courtesy when they feel they cannot support the party. Naturally the Whip then tries to persuade them to change their mind. As Mr. Heath, a former Chief Whip, has pointed out, it is odd that it should be thought legitimate for everybody to try to influence the M.P. except his party.[39] But the cohesion of the parliamentary parties has more fundamental causes.

The Whips do not have to worry about M.P.s being swayed by speeches. They rarely have been. Burke deployed his eloquence upon the voters of Bristol to demonstrate the absurdity of Members' votes being dictated by those who had not heard the arguments. But in private he agreed with Sheridan that votes were not changed by a speech in the House.[40] Traditionally M.P.s have behaved like Edwin Montagu, who agreed with everything Asquith said, 'and went dismally into the Division Lobby against him'.[41] Members may be convinced by the arguments put forward; they seldom vote for them. The change since the eighteenth century is that M.P.s often do not even vote for their own arguments. They speak on one question, the question ostensibly before the House, and usually vote on another one, whether they support or oppose the government. On amendment after amendment to the 1965 Finance Act Mr. Harold Lever made able speeches criticising the proposals of the Chancellor and supporting the modifications put forward by the opposition, but he always voted for the Chancellor and against

---

* Even in this fantasy, however, M.P.s do not measure up to the ideal of Reza Shah Pahlevi, who referring to the Iranian Mejliss told the British Minister in the thirties: 'Before they were all dressed differently and they all said different things. This time they were all dressed alike and they all said exactly the same thing. That's what a Parliament should be.'[38]

his own arguments, genially explaining that he did so in order to keep the government in office.*

This disciplined voting enrages many people and brings the House into some disrepute, even though displays of independence by M.P.s are more popular in theory than in practice. Yet a high degree of party voting is fully understandable. M.P.s have a predisposition to vote for their party, otherwise they would not be there. Dr. Johnson said that in his time he knew of no question other than America on which 'a man might not very well vote either upon one side or the other'.[43] Except for the demands of party, much the same is true today.† Deep questions of principle are seldom involved. Many votes are on amendments to bills, and the average M.P. who has not taken part in debates on the bill often has no idea what the vote is about or on which side he should vote. Party is his only mentor.

An M.P. does not have time to master the whole legislative programme, and he is grateful for guidance. Usually the Whip is more of a shepherd than a sheep dog. Far less 'guidance' is given to U.S. Congressmen by their Whips, and Congressmen so far from revelling in their freedom regret that they are sometimes insufficiently informed of the party line and complain that the party leaders sometimes fail to fight hard enough for their position.[45]

When an M.P. decides that he cannot support his party there is not much the Whips can do. They can if they wish have the whip withdrawn. But this is not an effective weapon as it merely lessens the influence the party has over the offender. And in the Tory party it is virtually never used. The Labour party and Whips are less tolerant. Under the Attlee government some members of the extreme left and one member of the right were deprived of the Whip and expelled from the Labour Party. None of them was readopted. Aneurin Bevan, incredibly enough, only narrowly escaped losing the Whip in 1955. Five members of the left were again deprived of

---

* Bentham[42] did not believe that a Member's vote should necessarily agree with his speech. 'If,' he wrote, 'after *speaking* in *support* of an arrangement which in the opinion of his constituents is contrary to their particular interest [an M.P.] gives his vote against that same arrangement—in such conduct there is not any real inconsistency. By his speech his duty to the public is fulfilled; by his vote, his duty to his constituents.' Nowadays an M.P. by his speech fulfils his duty to himself and by his vote his duty to his party. Since he owes his seat much more to the party than to himself, this is not an unreasonable division.

† Another Dr. Johnson, then Conservative M.P. for Carlisle, complained of party ideology being introduced into the question of whether the Salk vaccine should be used in 1957.[44]

the Whip for insubordination over defence in 1960. This turned out to be more a reward than a punishment; they were able to behave in the Commons as they wished. The embarrassment caused by this freeing of some of the more vocal Labour M.P.s presumably made the party managers reluctant to repeat the experiment. Yet expulsion from the party as opposed to losing the Whip remains a potent threat.

If the Tory party managers are more tolerant than their Labour opposite numbers, Tory local associations are rather less so. Save when specifically local issues are involved, constituency associations seldom relish their member not following the party line—especially when their party is the government. Most of their activities are devoted to returning their man to parliament and their party to government. In most places the two objectives are considered identical; hence a defecting member seems to be fighting himself and them. But the local activists rarely take repressive action against an erring member. Suez was the great exception for both Tories and Labour. Constituency parties did not confine their invigilatory activities to M.P.s who had refused to support their party in the lobbies. Even some M.P.s who had voted with their party but had ventured to express doubts or reservations were called upon to explain their tentative flirtations with heresy.[46] Except over Suez, however, and except in Northern Ireland where local associations are harder to please, the associations of both parties tolerate much and almost invariably readopt their members.

An M.P. has to be very incompetent, quite exceptionally brave, or extremely unlucky to be denied renomination. If he is rejected, his exit is more likely to be caused by scandal, drink, unusual indolence, or some other personal disability, than by political differences with his local party. Joseph Chamberlain recommended that a politician should first make his constituency secure, and F. E. Smith told Boothby that the first essential in politics was 'a territorial base',[47] advice which was well taken. In Britain most politicians have a base rather more secure than American Congressmen. Failure to support his party in Congressional votes rarely endangers a Congressman, who can be re-elected over the opposition of his local organisation. But whether he has toed the party line or 'voted his district', he is in some danger of being defeated in the primary and losing the party nomination.*

* But incumbency confers almost as big an advantage as in Britain. About 90 per cent of incumbent Senators and Congressmen win their primaries.[48]

An M.P.'s security of tenure is a compensation for party discipline, and like that discipline it is a powerful influence in favour of centrism and moderation. Not having to face a sort of primary election every four or five years, M.P.s are not driven to extremism and demagogic gestures in parliament or the country, in order to present some fledgling enthusiast back home edging them out of their nest. They have to pay respectful attention to the political views of their local party. But intra-party 'democracy' is kept at bay. An M.P. remains subject to the moderate party leadership and to his parliamentary colleagues rather than to the constituency militants. His political career depends upon his looking upwards and inwards rather than downwards and outwards. It is his reputation in parliament, not in the country, which determines his standing in the party. The skilled publicity seekers and the inveterate rebels get their publicity but at the cost of influence.

Dissolution and Patronage

Lord Attlee has said that for the maintenance of party discipline the power of dissolution is 'essential'.[49] But a Prime Minister stands to lose far more by its use than do his recalcitrant followers. Moreover the Prime Minister and the Whips can have no certainty that the rebels will not be readopted.* A dissolution might well weaken the party in power without purging the dissidents.

This of course applies only to a voluntary dissolution, one decided upon by the Prime Minister as a deliberate act of discipline. What Attlee presumably had in mind was that the Prime Minister's power of dissolution in practice prevented an involuntary dissolution, one forced, or thought to be forced, upon a Prime Minister by a defeat in the House of Commons upon a major issue. And that is true. M.P.s are impervious to the fear of bringing about a voluntary dissolution; they are afraid of bringing about an involuntary one by defeating the government they were elected to support, especially when they know that an election will result in a heavy defeat for their party. Thus no less than 77 of the Labour members who signed a motion asking for reconsideration of the government's decision on Stansted Airport meekly changed sides when the matter was shortly afterwards debated in the House and in effect voted against their own motion.

* In his notorious 'dog speech' Mr. Wilson threatened dogs who bit more than once with withdrawal of their licenses. This threat could be carried out before an ordinary election. But after a penal dissolution there would be no time for the de-licensing procedure.

After all, if an M.P. rebels and succeeds in defeating the government, who gains? If the government accepts the defeat, the rebels gain. But mesmerised by the relic they assume that the government will not accept the defeat and will dissolve. If the government does dissolve and wins the election, and the rebel is readopted and also wins, he has not gained. If the government wins but he is not readopted, he may congratulate himself on his integrity and will have time to reflect upon the American slogan that 'a statesman has to be re-elected'. He will anyway realise that neither he nor his views have gained. The third possibility is that the opposition will win the election. For him to welcome that possibility and to regard it as a gain, the issue on which he rebelled must be so important that he is prepared to change parties, or at any rate abandon his party. Fortunately such issues seldom arise.

In sum, an M.P. is as reluctant to bring about an involuntary dissolution by causing a defeat of the government, as the Prime Minister is to dissolve voluntarily in an attempt to discipline his backbenchers. As a result neither sort of dissolution occurs. When a government summons the

'........................ resolution
to damn the knaves by dissolution',[50]

the knaves it damns or seeks to damn are the opposition, not its own dissident supporters.

The Whips and the party managers posssess an ever increasing number of carrots as well as sticks. Many M.P.s have an avidity for office unknown in countries like Sweden or Germany. The most outspoken and inveterate rebels are often ready to forego their rebellion in return for the offer of place. But the expansion of jobs is self-defeating. The more posts are provided the more are wanted. Appetite increases with supply. 'The statesman of the present day,' said Lord Londonderry in 1837, 'seem not to know that a body acting together must have the rewards of ambition, patronage, and place always before their eyes and within their expectation and belief of grasping, as well as the fine expressions of love of their country and the patriotism which is a virtue.'[51] The party leaders of the present day have no chance of forgetting the lesson taught by Lord Londonderry. Their hopeful or disgruntled followers give them frequent reminders.

Junior and other ministers are often nominated by the Chief Whip, and any Chief Whip has a bias in favour of the safe and sound man. Neville Chamberlain recorded in 1936 that 'Margesson [the Chief Whip] pressed for Inskip as the safest man.'[52] Yet frequently rebellion has been the route to promotion. A Chief Whip sometimes acts on the principle that if disobedience cannot be punished, it is better rewarded. 'The glittering prizes' in politics have not gone to the patient toe-ers of the party line. Churchill, Eden, and Macmillan differed strongly from their party over appeasement. Douglas-Home was an opponent of Yalta. Only Heath of the recent party leaders has never had his differences with his party.*

Of Labour leaders, Macdonald differed from the majority of his party in opposing Britain's entry into the first war. Lansbury rebelled against the party even when he was leading it, and Wilson resigned over false teeth and spectacles in 1951. Gaitskell, like Heath, had little time in which to revolt, though he would have resigned had he not got his way in 1951. That leaves only Attlee, who again did not have much chance to rebel, for out of his thirty-three years in parliament, he was leader or deputy leader of the party for twenty-three of them.

> As persecution and promotion
> Do equally advance devotion[53]

But while the Prime Minister's powers of patronage are un-doubtedly influential, they do not account for the opposition also remaining remarkably monolithic in its parliamentary voting. In opposition a wide latitude of opinion, as Lord Randolph Churchill and L. S. Amery pointed out, is imperative. An opposition sacri-fices intellectual vitality if it maintains disciplined uniformity. Regrettably the voters seem to have come to expect unity and discipline from both the rival armies, and the opposition may suffer electoral damage if it disappoints their expectations. In any case, the unity of the opposition indicates that it is not the Prime Minister's power of patronage which produces cohesive voting in parliament.

That an M.P.'s loyalty to his party is not only caused by his fear

* He had a serious difference before he was an M.P. He supported the independent Mr. Lindsay against the Conservative Mr. Hogg at the Oxford bye-election in 1938.

of defeating the government, or by hope of office, is further shown by the cohesion of the parties when there is no question of patronage or of bringing down the government. In committee the government can be defeated without any drastic consequences, yet even in committee there is remarkably little cross-voting. Similarly, in the House of Lords, to which the government is not responsible, whose support is in no way necessary to it and where most peers are well beyond hope of preferment, the parties are almost as cohesive in their voting as they are in the Commons.

The strongest pressures in favour of perpetual conformity come in the Labour party from the party managers and in the Conservative party from the 'ardent partisans' in the constituencies. Patronage is important in both parties. But party loyalty and the framework of British politics in which two parties compete against each other for electoral support and possession of the government, strongly reinforced by the idea that the government will resign unless it wins every major vote, are more basic causes of disciplined voting. Even all this, however, would not be enough to maintain cohesion, if governments were not prepared to compromise with their supporters. M.P.s do not want to disagree with their government or party. Equally the party leaders do not want their followers to disagree with them. Governments are careful not to place too great reliance on backbench loyalty and restraint. They themselves handsomely reciprocate.

So far from being the scourge of the private member, the Whips are double agents. Unlike MI6, M.P.s are well aware whose side the double agents are ultimately on. But while the Whips aim to keep backbenchers in line with the front bench, they also act to keep front benchers in line with the backbench. As well as the purveyors of front bench orthodoxy to the laity, they are also the retailers of backbench heresy to the clergy. They are continually transmitting the opinions and the feelings of M.P.s to their leaders, and the state of that opinion is a constant preoccupation of the Prime Minister and the leader of the opposition. The Conservative Chief Whip throughout the 1959 parliament, Mr. Redmayne, saw the Prime Minister every day;[54] it was the parliamentary weather that they discussed. Governments are kept closely informed of backbench opinion, and their responsiveness to it is notably high.

Churchill's experience in the thirties at first sight seems to contradict this and to demonstrate the dominance of the government and the subservience of backbenchers. In fact, though, it demonstrates the identity of view between them, the government and public opinion. Churchill had trouble with his constituency, receiving a vote of confidence of only three to two,[55] and had there been an election instead of a war in 1939, he might not have been readopted. But in parliament and in the press he constantly stated his fears and made clear his differences with the government. Unfortunately, neither his listeners in parliament nor his readers were convinced. Mr. Macmillan accused Tory backbenchers of 'servility' to Chamberlain.[56] Harold Nicolson was nearer the mark when he complained of their ignorance of foreign affairs.[57] Admittedly any government has a crushing advantage over a leader on the backbenches, even one of the calibre of Churchill. Powerful forces of loyalty and orthodoxy coalesce round the leader of the party. Besides in those days Churchill's political history was not outstandingly reassuring to his fellow members; and his relentless campaign over India (a rebellion which does not suggest either undue conformity by Tory backbenchers or the invariable desirability of backbench revolts), and his stand on the abdication hindered his political present from removing doubts about his past. In any case, with Eden, Cranborne and Duff Cooper the only ministers prepared to resign in protest, the backbenchers can scarcely be blamed for supporting the government.

Yet had the views of Churchill and Macmillan been widely shared in the Tory party, nothing could have prevented their expression in private, if not in public, and a consequent change in government policy. After all when Hoare offended the backbenchers and the public, he was promptly sacrificed. When Chamberlain found that his stoicism at the fall of Prague was not shared by his party, he hurriedly changed course and made a strong speech at Birmingham. And when backbench opinion stiffened over the Anglo-Russian negotiations and during the days and hours leading to Britain's declaration of war, the government obediently followed suit.[58]

The 1930s do not show a powerful government arrogantly resisting backbench and popular pressure. They show a weak government in tune with popular and most backbench opinion, and because it was buttressed by that opinion, able to ignore the attacks of Churchill and his small band of supporters. The 1930s indicate that something is wrong with the British system. They do not demonstrate that the defect is the impotence or the docility of backbenchers.

Much the same applies to Labour backbenchers. The left has

always been particularly contemptuous of the parliamentary party's performance under the second Labour government. On the key issues of unemployment and the economy, Labour M.P.s unquestionably followed their leaders, though the leaders were clearly not solving the problem. Still if the leaders did not know what to do, nor did anybody else in the party. Or rather practically nobody else. Mosley did have some good ideas, but he was defeated at the party meeting by 97 to 13. And in the light of after events Labour backbenchers can hardly be condemned for refusing to trust him. The left ascribed their fellow backbenchers' support of the government to the power of patronage or to their ineptitude and inertia. To Jennie Lee the bulk of the backbenchers 'on every occasion . . . reacted like a load of damp cement'.[59] To Snowden, on the other hand, 'the great majority of the Labour members were always reasonable when a case was put fairly and squarely before them'.[60] Both verdicts were misleading. Between August 1929 and January 1931 as many as 119 Labour M.P.s, or about half the backbenchers, voted against the government.[61] A refusal to support Ministers is not necessarily unreasonable; nor is a refusal to support the left synonymous with docility.

Revolts

In the sixties there were substantial Tory revolts on Europe and on Resale Price Maintenance, and Labour ones on the Prices and Incomes policy and Defence. Many other potential revolts which are blazoned in the newspapers fizzle out. An issue which looked insistent when a lobby correspondent telephoned may seem less clear cut the next day. The opinion of constituents may be stronger than was envisaged; the appeal to party loyalty may prove more compelling than was anticipated; the other members of the projected rebellion may all find pressing reasons for holding their hands: the government will be endangered; now that the minister has explained his policy there is more to be said for it; party unity is vital in view of the approaching bye-election; the rebels have already won a moral victory by a concession from the minister so there is no point in continuing rebellion as far as the division lobby; on the day of the debate a business trip to Rome cannot possibly be postponed. Though the reasons for retreat are often good, some M.P.s would do well to heed Clarendon's description of Hampden: 'without question, when first he drew his sword, he threw away the scabbard'.[62] Some of them having threatened revolt hang tightly on to their scabbard, and at the first available opportunity sheath their sword with alacrity and relief.

But their pusillanimity often has good cause. In spite of failing in the division lobby, a rebellion frequently succeeds in other ways. It may well give a right or left incline to policy. After a large Labour revolt on conscription A. V. Alexander, according to Montgomery, 'got the wind up',[63] and the period of conscription was temporarily reduced from eighteen months to twelve. A former Postmaster General, Reginald Bevins, has said that for twenty or more backbenchers to vote against a bill means the resignation of the minister.[64] The very fact that defeat of the government is virtually unthinkable lends greater weight to even a small number of abstentions among its own supporters. The amount of backbench opposition a minister can survive depends upon his standing, the nature of the issue, the degree of cabinet involvement and backing, and the calibre of the rebels. Mr. Heath defeated one amendment to his R.P.M. Bill by only one vote, 28 Tory M.P.s having voted against him, but that did not bring about his resignation or stop him becoming leader of his party within eighteen months. But unless those rebelling are the perpetually disgruntled, or are discredited by the weakness of their case, a rebellion is unlikely to improve a minister's position. His reputation in the party is a vital element in his career, and the revolt will certainly make him wary in future. No minister wants to be unpopular on his party's backbenches. If he is, he may be sacrificed to them. Backbench criticism of Mr. Shinwell clinched his departure from the Ministry of Fuel.[65] Besides in their own assessment many ministers are Prime Ministerial timber, and they do not forget that M.P.s choose the party leader. Hence the extravagant pains they take over their parliamentary performances and their dealings with members—exertion that does not go unnoticed by their Civil Servants.[66]

The index of revolts and non-revolts is not a proper guide to the influence or function of backbenchers, any more than the number of general strikes is a good test of the vitality of a country's industrial system. If the government does what most of its backbenchers want it to do, to complain that they do not revolt against it more frequently and steadfastly is to demand a quite unreasonable degree of recalcitrance. The paucity and apparent failure of backbench revolts are due to the docility of governments as well as to the docility of backbenchers. Concord and peace may signify backbench influence, not dull obedience. Thus there was no backbench

Tory revolt when Archbishop Makarios was suddenly packed off to the Seychelles. Without some such action, indeed, there would have been a revolt. The Tory right had been rendered particularly restive by King Hussein's dismissal of General Glubb; the Eden government pacified its right wing by countering with the banishment of the Archbishop. Similarly there would have been a Tory revolt had the government gone through with its plans to supply bombs to the U.N. in Katanga, and a Labour revolt had the government supplied arms to South Africa. As Neville Chamberlain wrote in 1917, 'the cabinet is highly sensitive to Parly. opinion'.[67] Backbenchers are seldom united, least of all against the government. But when a general sentiment manifests itself amongst them, the party managers make the necessary policy adjustments to assuage it.

In the eighteenth century the ministry, broadly comprising ministers, their followers, and 'the King's friends' who were predominantly Civil Servants, governed with the support of the independent country gentlemen and was opposed by a variable and disunited minority. What happened in the whole House in the eighteenth century now happens on a small scale on the government side of it. The King's friends today are junior ministers, who are becoming almost as numerous as their eighteenth century predecessors, and rather more loyal.* The average backbenchers are the country gentlemen who have a disposition to loyalty but cannot always be taken for granted. A variable and disunited minority on the government backbenchers are the congenital rebels, 'the grumbletonians', as they were called, who, from time to time gain support from some of the normally loyal backbenchers. This transitory combination, like the rebellious country gentleman in 1782, does not want to overthrow the government; it wants to change its policy. It does not often completely succeed, but the government makes concessions to it, as well as to its more reliable supporters.

Influence

Only in the division lobby and to a lesser extent on the floor of the House are government supporters under restraint. Elsewhere

* In 1900 only thirty-three M.P.s were members of the government. In 1941 a Select Committee recommended that there should not be more than sixty ministers who were M.P.s, and Churchill, thought the number of ministers should be kept as low as possible.[68] The increase continued. After the Machinery of Government Act of 1965 there were over one hundred ministers, including peers, and in 1967 there were,

they have freedom to act and talk, coerce and cajole. Cavour thought the worst chamber better than the best ante-chamber. The distinction is no longer clear. The inevitable result of the transition from parliamentary to electoral democracy is the transfer of much of the decisive political conflict from the public floor of the House to the private room upstairs. Instead of a chamber the House often becomes a collection of ante-chambers. In a two-party system the smoke-filled room is a more suitable place for the exercise of influence than the public chamber.

Backbenchers are more effective when trying to persuade the government to do something, than when trying to stop it from continuing what it has started. Once a government embarks upon a policy, its prestige is involved and the forces of loyalty are roused. Trying to push the government into starting something does not have to contend with these powerful counter pressures.

The most conspicuous recent example of backbench influence was the introduction by a group of Tory M.P.s of commercial television into the government's programme. The party had not mentioned the subject at the previous election, and at the beginning of the group's campaign almost the entire cabinet favoured the continuance of the B.B.C.'s monopoly.

Under the post-war Conservative governments backbenchers seem to have been most influential in the early years, probably because the 1950 intake was exceptionally large and talented and because its key members were not absorbed on to the front benches in the opening years of Sir Winston Churchill's administration. It was backbench pressure that led to the denationalisation measures of those days.[69] Normally, a backbench success is not spectacular. Indeed the best backbench coups with ministers are like the perfect murder: nobody is aware of what has been done, not even the victim. After all, ministers and backbenchers do not, as such, have different views. Some ministers may take more of a 'national' view, and some M.P.s more of a party view. In practice such a distinction is less between ministers and M.P.s than between moderate ministers and M.P.s and extremist ministers and M.P.s.

Backbench committees originally created to solve the problem of the under-employment of M.P.s have become a common channel

including Parliamentary Private Secretaries but not counting the Second Church Commissioner, 114 M.P.s associated with the government. Benjamin Constant thought that ministers should never constitute more than 1 per cent of a chamber. That is plainly idyllic, but equally plainly 15 per cent of the House and about one third of the government side of it is an objectionably high proportion.

of backbench influence on ministers.* They are more important, naturally, when the party is in government and there is a bigger gap between leaders and rank and file. A minister, unless very powerful, is embarrassed if the relevant party committee is in opposition to him. In the 1945 government Dalton took great pains with the party's Finance group, though Bevin took none at all with the External Affairs group, in the belief perhaps that nothing would reconcile it to his policies. These committeees may be used by pressure groups or individuals to whip up opposition against government policy. According to Welensky,[71] Iain Macleod was angered by the Federation Government's shrewd use of the Conservative Commonwealth Affairs Committee to thwart his policy.

Ministers keep in touch with their committee and try to carry it and particularly its officers with them. Apart from any question of backbench pressure, a minister may be genuinely concerned and influenced by what he hears. Even when he is not convinced, he learns the strength and extent of opposition to his policy, and will probably change direction accordingly. A Whip is always present and he conveys the sense of the meeting to the Chief Whip.

As well as formal meetings and discussions in party committees, backbenchers are constantly seeking interviews with ministers and Whips. Leading members of the 1922 Committee and of the parliamentary Labour party are also frequently used as conveyors of opinion between backbenchers and their leaders.

If backbenchers are always divided, so usually is the government. Ministers and their juniors accept the collective decision of the cabinet, but acceptance need not entail enthusiasm or even conversion. Ministers who have seen their view rejected in cabinet, or their advice spurned by a colleague, are rarely dismayed by backbenchers staging a rebellion in defence of that view or on lines which

---

* The development of party committees damaged the interests of back benchers by denuding the chamber of M.P.s except during the front bench speeches. Winterton complained after the war that the chamber contained only a handful of M.P.s because young members thought they could 'best serve the interests of the party and advance the prospects of their own careers by becoming immersed in the affairs of the numerous committees and sub-committees of the party . . .'[70] That development has continued, and it has been speeded by the lack of star quality in the Commons. In 1935 a foreign affairs debate was opened by the Foreign Secretary, Hoare. He was followed by Samuel, Attlee, Churchill, Lloyd George, and Austen Chamberlain. If such a cast could be assembled today, M.P.s would forego their committees and stay in the chamber.

they have warned their colleagues was probable. Even ministers who were neutral in the discussions may not find the spectacle altogether displeasing. The minister himself may have been over-ruled in cabinet or cabinet committee, or may have acceded to the advice of his Civil Servants with the utmost reluctance, in which case he himself is not in sympathy with the position he is defending. According to Dalton, Mr. Strauss, as Minister of Supply, was not an enthusiastic supporter of his own Steel Bill.[72] Rarely is a split in the cabinet as open as it was over the supply of arms to South Africa, or a minister's support of angry M.P.s as blatant as Mr. Wilson's was in that affair. But rebellious backbenchers are seldom pushing at a closed door against the whole-hearted weight of the entire government. Without their knowledge Neville Chamberlain had in cabinet been strongly in favour of a clause in the Trade Disputes Bill of 1927 similar to one supported by Macmillan, Mond and Lloyd George on the floor of the House.[73]

The Chief Whip, aware of previous dissension at the top, will be anxious to assuage backbench resentment and opposition below. Thus while the Postmaster General was trying to steer his Tele-vision Bill, which was unpopular with his party, through the Commons in 1963, he was not merely contending with backbench pressure but with the Chief Whip and senior ministers as well. Mr. Butler wrote to him, the Chief Whip and the Leader of the House interviewed him. The Chief Whip told him it was a 'bloody awful Bill and nobody liked it'. He was 'not prepared to risk further government unpopularity by a hostile demonstration by our back-benchers in the House'.[74] Mr. Bevins claimed that 'Martin Redmayne and Iain Macleod who were sitting on my right on the Treasury bench were openly applauding'[75] the speeches critical of the Post-master General. Whatever happened on that occasion, ministers often relish and silently applaud backbench attacks on their colleagues.

There is therefore never a set piece battle between backbenchers and government. Even to say there is guerrilla warfare would be to overformalise the confrontation. As is usual at Westminster, the lines of difference are blurred and change with bewildering fre-quency. There is nearly always more of a civil war among the back-benchers and within the government than there is between the government and backbenchers.

The distinction between government and backbenchers is artificial. The backbenchers are an identifiable set of men, but are never united. The government is an identifiable body of office holders, which formally presents a united front to the country and its supporters, but except on the rarest occasions it too is never united. Hence such phrases as 'the government always wins against its backbenchers' are of limited use. The government always wins, but nearly always the dominant faction or line of thought within it is supported by the dominant faction among the backbenchers. When the government ignores the feelings of its supporters, it is usually on matters on which they do not feel strongly such as decimal currency, or on which it has the support of the opposition.

The fault of the system is not that backbenchers do not have influence—in groups they often have too much influence—but that their influence is usually exercised in private and usually 'before the fact'. Governments tailor their policies to suit the known predilections of their backbenchers. Because ministers and most backbenchers are concerned to present to the electorate the picture of a united party, there is too seldom a beneficial public row. The essence of parliament is, or should be, publicity. Backbenchers exerting influence in private are more party men than parliamentarians. Their activities do not help either to explain the operations of the secret executive to the public or to free the executive from its own bonds.

Backbenchers do not determine the policy of the government or of the opposition. Nor should they. Government by the secret monarchical executive is much to be preferred to government by secret parliamentary caucus. Governments have to pay attention to events, to the opposition, to other countries, to expert and public opinion as well as to their own supporters. Backbenchers are not captains of the party, or government, ship. But they man it, and they have influence over its speed and its ports of call. If they are not to be found on the bridge, they are active in the engine room and other parts of the boat.

In this century backbench revolts have not defeated a government. Yet backbenchers have been responsible for some changes of Prime Minister. The fall of Asquith was dependent upon the willingness of many Liberal M.P.s to desert Asquith and follow Lloyd George. Backbenchers brought down Lloyd George at the Carlton Club in 1922. They brought down Chamberlain in 1940, and twenty-seven abstentions on the absurdly trivial issue of the Profumo case nearly laid low Mr. Macmillan in 1963. There has been something of a reversion to the eighteenth century when

Prime Ministers resigned though they had not been beaten in the House. With murder ruled out, a wound cuts all the deeper and may force suicide. The position of Prime Minister is not precarious; but he is chosen by the parliamentary party and if he is going to be pushed out it is backbenchers who are likely to push him. In this century they have been at least as successful as cabinet cabals in toppling Prime Ministers. 'You have taught me to look for the sense of my subjects in another place than the House of Commons,' George III told Pitt.[73] Lloyd George likewise looked beyond parliament, and he paid for his contempt of the House. A wise Prime Minister looks to his political base, his backbenchers, and does not take their support for granted.

Parliamentary Control

If ministers are responsive to M.P.s and to parliament, so are Civil Servants. Lord Franks has testified to the reality of parliamentary control of the Civil Service even in wartime,[77] and Lord Strang has said that tension relaxes in the departments when parliament rises.[78] The value of parliamentary questions is sometimes derided on the grounds that the answerer can usually deceive the questioner if he wants to.* That is true, but usually he does not want to. Civil Servants, like most people, do not relish the unearthing of their mistakes, but they are not engaged in a perpetual conspiracy against the public. Parliamentary questions are a valuable contact between Whitehall and the people.

Much of question hour is devoted to the party struggle, and a more effective method of redressing individual grievances is M.P.'s letters to ministers. These bring home to those at the top of a department mistakes, anomalies, or injustice in their administration. The same thing happens with the nationalised industries. Implicit in such correspondence is the threat of eventual publicity by means of a parliamentary question, but as elsewhere in the British system the action itself is more important than the sanction behind it.

M.P.s have no power over local authorities. But their ability to raise constituency matters in parliament ensures that a sensible local authority pays attention to the views of an M.P. and does its best to answer his enquiries on behalf of constituents. An M.P. acts as a sort of ombudsman on behalf of his constituents with local

---

* The Parliamentary Commissioner should be able to discover irregularities as well as making them less likely.

government. He has no access to the files, but his intervention is often effective, and when the local authority is entirely in the right he can help to remove a sense of grievance. His position outside local government yet representing the locality enables him to perform one of his most important functions: to interpret the ways of local government to his constituents, and the wishes and needs of his constituents to local authorities.

Lately the scope of Private Members' legislation has substantially expanded. Much as in the early nineteenth century important issues like Catholic Emancipation were open questions on which even members of the government could vote on different sides, so today some of the most important social matters are left to free votes and the initiative of backbenchers. Capital punishment, divorce, abortion, homosexuality, Sunday observance affect in various ways large segments of the population more closely than many government measures, but since the parties are divided on them governmental legislation is difficult and private members get their chance. Of course they usually need departmental assistance over drafting; even A. P. Herbert needed government help over his Divorce Bill in 1937.[79] But that does not detract from the greatly increased importance of the private member in legislation.

The power of the House of Commons as a Trade Union has if anything increased. It still possesses a closed shop in the best government offices. It has allowed a rival Trade Union, the House of Lords, to function side by side with it, but except for the Foreign Office the members of its rival are not allowed the highest posts. Just as an ambitious lawyer cannot practice at the bar without joining one of the Inns of Court and passing his bar exam, so, normally, an aspiring politician will get nowhere until he has joined one of the parties and has served some time in the Commons. War brings exceptions. Lloyd George favoured businessmen without seats in the Commons for the new wartime ministries. With Maclay, the shipping controller, the experiment worked, but its failure with Chamberlain as director of National Service in 1917 prevented its repetition in the second war. Men like Bevin, Lyttelton and Grigg were given high ministerial office in Churchill's coalition government without serving any parliamentary apprenticeship, but they were soon found seats in the Commons. Trade Unions also provide exceptions. Mr. Wilson's need to neutralise Mr. Frank Cousins led him to give Mr. Cousins a cabinet post and find him a safe parliamentary seat.

The Commons has not extended its restrictive practices to cover the increasingly important quasi-political offices, such as the Prices and Incomes Board, though such posts are frequently given to former members. Equally the Commons has prevented any encroachments on its preserves which have been made bigger by the progressive Balkanisation of Whitehall. Parliament still has a monopoly of men if not of measures.

Procedure

'Mr. Wilkes,' says Boswell, 'observed how tenacious we are of forms in this country, and gave as an instance, the vote of the House of Commons for remitting money to pay the army in America in *Portugal pieces*, when, in reality, the remittance is not made in Portugal money, but in our own specie.'[80] *Portugal pieces* are still the coin of parliamentary procedure. Oppositions press votes as though they had some chance of winning. A leader of the House can tell the House of Commons that it is primarily a legislative body. A speaker can say he knows nothing of Whips.

The great majority of parliamentary debates admittedly decide nothing. Even when from 1964–6 the government had a majority in the House ranging from three to five, it was defeated in only two sittings, one of which was on a Friday. Only when Whips are taken off and a free vote is allowed is the result in doubt. On almost all other occasions everybody knows the result before the debate has begun. Nor does a debate in the House of Commons lead to a solution of a problem through discussion and a meeting of minds. Party has long barred such a meeting. In the nineties Salisbury lamented that discussion of a measure was 'for any effective or useful purpose . . . rapidly becoming an impossibility in the House of Commons'.[81]

Yet the Commons custom of perpetual debate is more rational than it seems. Most of the real debate has taken place long before the parliamentary discussion. But the long process of study and negotiation and reconciliation of interests, which goes on behind the scenes, would be much less painstaking and effective but for the awareness of all concerned that eventually there will be discussion in parliament. Parliamentary debates may be partly ritual, but without the ritual the reality would be very different. For debates are far from being mere ritual. They perform the valuable service of forcing the government to show at least some of its hand, driving it to take some sort of public position. The deadline in a fortnight

K

of a parliamentary debate, in which a minister is anxious not to look a fool, concentrates the mind of the executive and brings some sort of conclusion, if not order, into its secret bargains and deliberations. Since debates oblige the minister to put forward some sort of rational case, they are on the side of the rational forces in government. Ministers' speeches reveal to those in government what the government policy is. They enable interest groups to know where they stand: a statement in parliament dispels the fog of bureaucratic prevarication. And, not least, debates educate the government; they also educate the public.

The difficulty is that a good deal of time is spent on subjects which have no educative value, and on which the public could not conceivably want or need to be educated. And those subjects on which the public could and should be educated are often the ones which are seldom debated. These are issues on which the parties are divided, or on which they are frightened of offending public opinion. Only the grievances and issues that are going to help the party concerned are chosen as subjects for debate. Added to these restraints is the one that arises from a government's frequent appeals not to embarrass it in the course of negotiations.

> 'When a delicate transaction
> Called for unexampled care,'[82]

the one thing that would jeopardise success is always, apparently, a parliamentary debate. The opposition may be sceptical about the government's real motives, but the appeal for forbearance and statesmanship is difficult to reject.

More serious, for parliament, like the stage and unlike television or the cinema, an audience is an integral part of the drama. And the shift of power away from the division lobby and the absence of uncertainty about the outcome of a debate have robbed parliament of much of its interest and excitement. Yet there is still more drama in the House of Commons than in other assemblies, and despite its refusal to allow television into the chamber, parliament gets a better audience perhaps than it deserves.

As a by-product, debate enables backbenchers to demonstrate their fitness for office. Stocking the front bench with people who have spoken well from the backbenches has lost some of its original justification. In the days when the House was a troublesome and wilful body, ability to handle it was an obvious qualification for promotion to the Treasury Bench. Now that the chamber has been tamed by party and the rules of procedure, such ability is less necessary. And indeed some remarkably bad parliamentarians have reached high office and managed to prosper there*. Yet an important requirement of a leading politician is that he should be a good communicator, and if an M.P. is unable to communicate his thoughts effectively to his fellow Members in the House, he is unlikely to be heard loud and clear outside it. So in general the 'tongue-favoured men' advance, and 'no stammerer of a minute painfully delivered'[84] gets far. Thus debate does have a selective function. The standing of ministers in the House and in their party is still largely determined by their performances in parliament.

Voting is an indispensable adjunct to debate. There can be no guarantee that the few who speak are representative of the majority who have to listen; so, as Churchill insisted during the war, there must first be 'freedom of debate and secondly a clear honest blunt vote thereafter'.[85] Voting demonstrates that an identifiable body of people composed of identifiable individuals are supporting or opposing the government's policies. M.P.s may and do support a government's policy in the division lobby even though they disapprove of it. But they do not relish doing so, and they will try to get the policy changed. At the same time, probably the opposition is fiercely opposing what the government is doing and piling up votes against it. This pressure has effect. On a continuing issue over which there is great public disquiet, the government will not long remain badly out of step with public opinion. This does not always lead to wise government measures, but its ability to bend government to public opinion is scarcely something that can be held against a representative chamber.

The present procedure of parliament has considerable value in gaining consent. It gives a genuine demonstration that our system is in the last resort government by discussion in public and not government by coercion decided upon in private. Its defect is that the government is so successful in gaining the consent of those inside the House that it has been losing some of its ability to gain the consent of those outside it. If parliament in this country has lost prestige through being too predictable, in France under the Fourth Republic and in

* This would have pleased Sir Thomas More, who, when Speaker of the House, pointed out to Henry VIII that 'as much folly is uttered with painted, polished speech, so, many boisterous and rude in language, see deep indeed and are of sound judgment and prove the wiser counsellors'.[83]

many other countries between the wars it lost prestige through being unstable.

Ambivalence of Parliamentary Reform

Nevertheless much obloquy has been heaped on parliament, and its reform has been strongly urged on a variety of grounds, its low public prestige, its impotence, its inefficiency, the unemployment or under-employment of M.P.s, the need to shift back power from the permanent part of the government to the elected part, the need to control the executive, the need to protect the liberties of the subject, the need to pass more and better laws, the need to bring publicity to the operations of secret government, the need to bring a higher standard of people into the House of Commons, the need for wholetime legislators, the need to make individual backbenchers more important and powerful, the need to make the executive more efficient. Some of these objectives, to say nothing of the premises on which the criticisms are based, are mutually exclusive. The House of Commons has a multitude of functions which cut across one another, and it is composed of sets of members whose interest in the performance or non-performance of these functions is utterly different. The power of parliament is so many-sided that a straightforward increase of it would almost be impossible to achieve. An attempted increase in one direction would be almost bound to produce a diminution in another. Besides, if parliament were made more powerful, it would probably become less efficient. And when it becomes more efficient, it probably becomes less powerful. Thus almost all Mr. Crossman's reforms of procedure made it easier for the government to get its business through and harder for the opposition to oppose and obstruct.

> 'I like a parliamentary debate
> Particularly when 'tis not too late.'[86]

Mr. Crossman and his supporters conspicuously shared Byron's preference, and no doubt by crippling the opposition's power to keep the government up all night they in some ways made the House of Commons more efficient.* But the cutting down of the opposition's opportunities to make things uncomfortable for the government is a funny way of strengthening parliament. 'The

* On the other hand there has since 1964 been a steep increase in all-night sittings of Parliamentary Committees. These, of course, help the government.

history of liberty has largely been the history of observance of procedural safeguards,' wrote Justice Frankfurter,[87] echoing Sir Henry Maine, and the wholesale removal of such safeguards would have more to do with the manipulation of procedure for party advantage than with the reform of the House of Commons. On any view, the Crossman reforms demonstrate the ambivalence of parliamentary reform.

Again one of the proposals which received wide assent from the new Labour intake into the House in 1964 was for the introduction of proxy voting. Government by ambulance is certainly undignified, though no more undignified now than it has been in the past*. Yet the parliamentary history of the Weimar Republic and of the French Third and Fourth Republics does not supply the happiest of precedents for proxy voting. But whatever the merits of the proposed reform, it would have removed the distinction between a government with a large majority and one with a majority of two or three. The government would be safely insulated from accident, illness, and other hazards. Yet proxy voting was one of the most popular expedients of the much publicised parliamentary reformers.

Without reform, it is sometimes claimed, men of adequate talents will not seek to enter the House. Yet all the time the House has allegedly been declining, the quality of its membership has probably been rising. Not all would agree. Attlee, for one, thought the quality of members had deteriorated. Almost certainly, however, present quality is good enough for its purpose. Without accepting Shaw's defence of the party system, that it enabled twenty-five capable men to run the rest of the House which consisted of '590 idiots with just enough intelligence to walk into the lobby pointed out to them by the Whips and give their names at the door',[90] or Lord Butler's approval of Bagehot's remark that a certain element of stupidity was necessary for the smooth working of the House, a dazzling standard of intelligence in parliament would undoubtedly be dangerous. As Acton pointed out, an assembly of celebrities such as More and Bacon would produce 'an encyclopaedia of error'.[91] It would also be, in any sense of the word, unrepresentative. Meredith[92]

---

* In the debate on general warrants in 1764 Horace Walpole wrote that 'votes were brought down in flannels and blankets till the House looked like the pool of Bethesda'.[88] And Greville records that the Whigs in 1841 left 'no stone unturned to procure a majority' against a vote of no confidence moved by Peel. They produced a mad Lord, who 'was brought in a chair; they got him into the House and then wheeled him past the tellers'.[89] Even the mad were not enough to save them. Melbourne was beaten by 1.

thought it was 'more salutary, besides more diverting to have the fools of the kingdom represented than not'. They are.

Parliament no longer contains the sages that it had in the past. No Gibbon is there, but Gibbon in his seven years of membership was an entirely silent supporter of Lord North. No John Stuart Mill is there, but Mill made it a condition of going forward as a candidate for Westminster that he should not have to do any constituency work[93]—an odd stipulation for the theorist of representative assemblies.* There is no Acton, but Acton's influence on Gladstone depended not at all upon his membership of the House, and his period as an M.P. conferred no great benefit on either the House or himself.

So the apparent contrast between a House to which a Gibbon, a Mill, an Acton were proud to belong and a Bagehot was so anxious to belong that he gained the censure of a Royal Commission for making corrupt payments when candidate for Bridgwater,[94] and a House which a Keynes[95] declined to join is not in reality great.† The cause is the increased volume of constituency work and the difficulty of being a silent M.P. like Acton and Gibbon. No constituency, today, would for long tolerate a member who displayed the cavalier attitude to his correspondence of the young Lloyd George, whose locker was found to be full of unanswered and unopened letters.[97] As late as the 1920s Halifax used to hunt his hounds in Yorkshire three days a week, during the session.[98] But nowadays most constituencies like to think their member is active on their behalf. In any case, it is the work involved that keeps, say, leading businessmen out of the House of Commons. And since parliamentary reforms would add to the work, reform would not introduce more such people into the House but less.

Reform would be just as likely to narrow membership as to broaden it. It is improbable that there are a lot of bright young men saying to themselves 'I should very much like to go into parliament, but I shall not do so until parliament reforms its procedure.' M.P.s and potential M.P.s have not been deterred from trying to enter the House by the fear of being powerless as backbenchers. They are encouraged by the hope that they will soon be powerful front benchers. M.P.s have preferred to be future executives than present legislators.

---

* He was beaten at the next election.

† Bagehot's bribery was retrospective. He did not know that votes were being bought for him. But though he had begun his campaign with a speech extolling electoral purity, he later reimbursed the purchasers for the £800 they had spent.[96]

Performance and Reform

'Instead of the function of government, for which it is radically unfit, the proper office of a representative assembly,' thought J. S. Mill, 'is to watch and control the government: to throw the light of publicity on its acts: to compel a full exposition and justification of all of them which any one considers questionable; to censure them if found condemnable, and, if the men who compose the government abuse their trust, or fulfil it in a manner which conflicts with the deliberate sense of the nation, to expel them from office, and either expressly or virtually appoint their successors.'[99]

Representative assemblies have gone down in the world since Mill's day. In the twentieth century the complexity of government, the growth of bureaucracy, the internationalisation of politics and the speed of events have all militated against them. In the United States the executive has vastly increased its power over legislation and over every other field. In Holland the Chamber seldom exercises its right of initiative.[100] The French Fourth Republic was a parliamentary not an electoral democracy, and the Chamber had great powers. It could and frequently did upset governments, yet much executive action remained outside its purview. The first Monnet plan was not even submitted to either the Chamber or the Senate.[101] The House of Commons is not further from meeting Mill's requirements than its brothers in other countries.*

'To watch and control the government.' Suez is often cited as an example of the inadequacy of parliamentary control and as something that could have been prevented, had the Commons possessed proper procedures. But the comparable American disaster of the Bay of Pigs occurred despite all the Committees of Congress and all the powers vouchsafed to it by the American constitution. The House of Commons's control of finance is certainly tenuous, but again the same is true of other legislatures. The Swedish Riksdag has lost its supremacy over the budget,[102] and while the U.S. Congress retains greater financial powers than the Commons, the preparation and scrutiny of the American budget has lain since 1921 with the Presidency, and the control of the estimates has effectively passed to the executive.[103]

British governments seldom do anything outrageous. They are nearly always in harmony with the majority of their party in the House of Commons, and when they are not they are almost

---

* Brothers or sisters, not sons or daughters. The House of Commons is not the Mother of Parliaments. Bright said: 'England, Mother of Parliaments.'

invariably in harmony with a large minority of their party and with most of the opposition. Such a state of affairs is surely the chief objective of parliamentary control.

'To throw the light of publicity upon its acts.' British government is more secret than almost any other free government. The House of Commons usually provides debate upon the acts of government, but it is not good at securing publicity about the origin of those acts. Nor is it successful in obtaining publicity before the government acts.

'To compel a full exposition and justification of all of them which anyone considers questionable.' Though it is deficient in investigatory powers, the House of Commons is better at securing an exposition and justification of governmental acts than are most representative assemblies. The hearings before Senator Fulbright and the Foreign Relations Committee of the Senate on Vietnam excited much envious comment in this country. But useful as those hearings were, they were a revelation of the inadequacy of Congress as a debating forum. The war had been going on for years. Yet apart from giving a vague authorisation to President Johnson many months before, Congress provided no discussion of it, let alone control of the administration's conduct of operations. The House of Commons would never stand idly by, while the British government waged a major war.

'To censure them if found condemnable . . . to expel them from office, and either expressly or virtually appoint their successors.' The two party system makes this virtually impossible in Britain as well as probably undesirable. Even in a country like Holland where there is a multiparty system, a feeling has grown up that dismissal is properly the work of the electorate, not the Chamber. And the dismissal of individual ministers is rare in all countries. In Sweden, the last time a minister was obliged to resign because of a complaint by the Committee on the constitution was in 1929.[104] In Switzerland a minister is never dismissed, though if his re-election is unlikely he does not stand again. The American Congress is unable to get rid of ministers it dislikes. The virulent Congressional campaign against Mr. Acheson merely strengthened the resolve of President Truman to retain his embattled Secretary of State. The nearest Congress comes to dismissing a member of the executive is a refusal by the Senate to agree to his appointment, as when the Senate refused to confirm President Eisenhower's nomination of Admiral Strauss as Secretary of Commerce in 1959. Such a refusal is rare.

Despite the hostile criticism, therefore, the House of Commons compares well with other representative bodies. Many of its critics seem unaware of, say, the suffocating boredom of the German Bundestag, the parliamentary malaise in Holland, or widespread American concern about the functioning of Congress. Much of the critics' disillusionment with parliament in reality stems from Britain's fall in status since 1914, not from the shortcomings of parliament itself.

There remain, however, two strong reasons for reform as well as some obvious minor ones. The first one is similar to the most important argument for the great Reform Bill. As the young John Russell expressed it, 'the votes of the House of Commons no longer imply the general assent of the realm'.[105] The unreformed parliament was no longer sufficiently acceptable; therefore it had to be reformed.

Today public discontent with the House of Commons is nowhere near as deep or as wide as it was then. People have seldom felt driven into the streets or the squares to pursue their ends or ideals by direct action instead of by political action at Westminster. And that after all is the test. The antics of the Committee of 100 have inspired little imitation. There is, all the same, a strong feeling in some quarters that the House of Commons does not function as effectively as it should, and to the extent that the feeling is justified it should be removed by reform. Parliament should gain consent for the political system, not add to the clamour against it.

The second and most important reason for reform is that the House of Commons plays too small a part in reconciling or removing the great contradiction in the British system: electoral supremacy and a secret executive. In Britain the executive is not all-powerful or over-mighty. The present system has placed all too effective curbs upon it. And there has been less executive infringement of the liberty of the subject than in most other countries. But parliament's nineteenth century procedure is no longer adequate to explain the ways of the executive to the political nation, or to help the executive to act in accordance with the needs, as opposed to the wishes, of the voters.

The televising of parliament would do something to explain the executive to the country. On the other hand it might increase public disillusionment with parliament. That is a risk which must be run. A television Hansard would bring obvious difficulties. Television might alter the character of debate, though not necessarily for the worse. It might give a distorted picture, but a first hand pictorial account of proceedings, even though necessarily selective, should not produce any greater distortion than the necessarily selective and second hand account provided by the press.

No doubt the government would still have the advantage on television, but the opposition's handicap would be less. Instead of the opposition having to match its words against the deeds of the government, the government and opposition would appear on television in virtual parity. Even more important than the benefit conferred on the opposition, television of the House would hinder governments making important announcements away from the Commons and strengthen parliament's position as a source of news. Instead of threatening parliamentary manners of behaviour, the televising of the House would help to consolidate them.

For the benefit of television to be fully realised, parliamentary procedure would have to be made more flexible, so that government statements could be permitted later in the day as well as after questions. It was no credit to the rules of the Commons that Mr. Wilson had to wait until the end of a debate on the Highlands and Islands Development Bill at 11 p.m. before he could make a parliamentary statement on the abortive Commonwealth peace mission to Vietnam, by which time of course he had already made the announcement on a television programme.

To reap the full harvest of television, the House of Commons should also do what it can to ensure the topicality of its debates. One of Mr. Crossman's procedural reforms which was undoubtedly beneficent to the House was the re-drawing of the Standing Order making it easier for the Speaker to consent to emergency debates. This has already done something to revive the chamber as a topical debating forum.

Theoretically, primary elections would increase public enthusiasm by giving large numbers of people the chance to participate in the selection of candidates and by making the behaviour of M.P.s less predictable.* But in the United States primaries have not fulfilled the hopes of the reformers of fifty years ago. And British voters have shown themselves uninterested in the personal political views of those who stand at elections.†[107] Election meetings are not well attended; primary meetings would be even less of a draw. Only if

---

* Primaries are not unknown in England: between 1867 and 1870 the Liberals held five trial ballots.[106] The expense of the proceedings and the corruption of the Liberal voters brought a quick end to the experiment.

† See also page 141.

candidates in primaries were allowed to advertise on television or in the press, which would be ruinously expensive and put a high premium on the support of pressure groups, or if they were already well known, would primary elections attract public interest. Television stars would be the ideal candidates. Mrs. Shirley Temple Black might have many British imitators. With or without advertising, the support of interest groups would be important.

Primaries might make M.P.s more independent of the party leadership as well as more local minded. But as party discipline is generally employed to maintain moderation, the diminished cohesion of the party would probably lead to more extremism. Admittedly the 7,000 members of Bournemouth East's Conservative Association,[108] who split almost evenly in the vote as to whether or not Mr. Nigel Nicolson should continue as their candidate, showed themselves to be more moderate than the executive of that association.[109] But they were voting two years after Suez by which time tempers had cooled, and Mr. Nicolson was helped by there being no other name on the ballot. Above all, Mr. Nicolson had rebelled on an issue when party discipline was exercised in favour of extremism. Were that frequently to happen, the case for primaries would be far stronger than it is. At present, however, party discipline and selection by local caucus produce moderation and consensus, while allowing members considerable latitude of opinion.*

Apart from the introduction of television, parliamentary reform must take the well-trodden path of the strengthening of the committee system. Nearly all legislatures use committees. They enable far more M.P.s to take part in proceedings than do debates in the chamber.† Committees infest every other sphere of government and are rife in most spheres of British life. To enjoy influence with the executive, M.P.s have to combine. An M.P. trying to deal with the executive by himself is like trying to stop a tank with a peashooter. The limitations of the chamber led to the creation of party committees in order to occupy M.P.s. Logically they should

---

* Selection of candidates at a large public meeting, which has taken place in some constituencies, has more in common with the present procedure than with primaries.

† In 1968 the government had so many committees of various kinds in operation that there were not enough M.P.s left for the chamber. A strengthening of the committee system should not be confused with a mere extension of it. Nor should the standing committees, which give detailed consideration to each bill and which have long been in existence, be considered part of any projected reform. These committees by removing business from the floor of the House help the executive; they do not produce more searching scrutiny of it. Unfortunately the Labour government's profligate use of such standing committees did something to discredit committees in general.

have led to the creation of parliamentary committees; the executive however preferred to follow its own logic.

Whitehall's conviction that anybody advocating parliamentary committees was seeking to combine all the worst features of the committees of the American Congress and the Parliamentary Committees of the French Fourth Republic was hysterical. Committees like those of the U.S. Congress have not been seriously envisaged. Quite apart from their unsuitability for a non-presidential system, modern legislation, like a modern army, needs a long 'tail', and that tail is in the possession of the executive, not parliament. Congress, itself, has nowadays more and more to rely on the executive for information and for drafting. Mr. Dean Acheson has said that the previous position has been reversed and that instead of Congress initiating legislation and the President either approving it or vetoing it, the President now initiates and frames legislation and Congress approves, amends, or vetoes it.[110] The Taft-Hartley law was one of the few major post-war pieces of law-making which was entirely Congress's own work. Congress still refuses its consent very much more often than does parliament, but it has lost its primacy in legislation.

Nor has anybody save F. W. Jowett ever suggested the municipalisation of parliament, and the running of government by a series of committees. The Jowett type committees would not in fact have their desired effect, since the government would still be able to use its majority to control the committees. Even under the Third Republic when during the Combes ministry there was for once a stable majority, the Committees of the Chamber were controlled by the Délégation des gauches.[111] The same would happen here.

In fact, however, owing to the strength of party and the conventions of British government, non-legislative investigatory committees are the only ones suitable for the House of Commons. Committees are a common device for shedding and spreading responsibility, but save under a minority government Commons committees would be under the sway of the government's majority. In consequence Woodrow Wilson's canon, 'Power and strict accountability for its use,'[112] would not be violated. Plainly such committees would not infringe ministerial responsibility in its legitimate meaning of policy being the responsibility of ministers and the government. With luck however they would in time destroy ministerial responsibility in its illegitimate sense: the mythology that all decisions are taken by the minister and Civil Servants are merely advisers.

The Committees the House has possessed for some time—the Public Accounts Committee, the Statutory Instruments Committee, the Estimates Committee, and the Committee on Nationalised Industries—are not supposed to intrude into 'policy'. They are supposed to keep to administration. But the distinction is bogus. A former chairman of the Public Accounts Committee, Mr. Osbert Peake, said in 1945: 'In theory we are not supposed to concern ourselves with policy, but policy and economy merge into each other with such subtle gradations that it is quite impossible to decide a clear-cut line between what is policy and what is not.'[113] Since then the committees, except for the one on Statutory Instruments, have made a gradual infiltration into the field of policy, though matters of acute political controversy are avoided so as to prevent committees splitting on party lines. Civil Servants appear before these committees, and ministerial responsibility is supposed to guide their answers. But the experience of the Committee on Nationalised Industries,[114] especially, has shown that Civil Servants in due time discard their non-identity as mere mouthpieces of the minister and express opinions of their own. And the more such committees there are, the more pronounced will this tendency become.

The Committee system would have been best extended by developing the Estimates Committee and enlarging its terms of reference to include the examination of how departments of state carry out their responsibilities. This was recommended by the Select Committee on Procedure,[115] and this would have made the co-ordination of Committees easier and their suppression more difficult. But the new Specialist Committees are still very welcome.

The existing Select Committees do much valuable work. They make useful reports, they make M.P.s better informed, and they provide employment for them.* But the point of the Committees is to improve the executive, not to improve parliament; and for them to have a significant effect in reforming the executive three things are necessary. The first is that they should not be diverted to peripheral subjects. The second is that they should have the backing of a comprehensive state audit system.† Such an audit would not be a matter of accountancy but a thorough going study of the efficiency of the executive branch. The state auditor should be 'an

* The reform of Parliament is sometimes said to necessitate full-time M.P.s. Rather it is the arrival of full-time M.P.s which has necessitated the reform of Parliament.

† The Prices and Incomes Board performs some of the functions of a state audit. But it is inadequately staffed, and it is the servant of the government not of Parliament.

impartial and studious general fact-finder about government'.[116]*
Once such a service is created and the present Comptroller and
Auditor General given duties and powers similar to those of his
equivalents in other countries, parliamentary committees will have
the expert assistance and backing they need to probe and scrutinise
the executive.

Probably the Comptroller and Auditor General should not be
explicitly attached to the legislature, as is the General Accounting
Office in the United States. In France and Germany the state audit
bodies are independent of both the executive and the legislature and
serve both of them.[117] All that matters is that he should be free from
Treasury muzzling, and that he should supply parliament and the
committees with a continuous stream of facts. Such a reform
would enormously add to the efficiency of the executive, and would
also do much to solve the problem of parliamentary control of the
nationalised industries.

Yet in itself such a reform would not be sufficient to redress the
imbalance between the secret executive and electoral democracy, or
to create the conflict that is necessary to catch the attention of the
public. The executive is locked in its own world of secrecy. To
enable the government properly to escape from its prison, parliament
like those who rescued Mr. C. Wilson from Birmingham gaol must
ultimately gain access to the prison, and overpower that guard and
gaoler, mythological Ministerial Responsibility. That is the third
requirement for a successful committee system. But it cannot be
achieved by immediate frontal assault. It must be done obliquely
and gradually.

Yet much can still be accomplished by the committees without
immediately toppling the idol of Ministerial Responsibility from
its altars in Whitehall and Westminster. Without offending the
priests of the cult, the committees can make the executive reveal its
assumptions, and by introducing publicity to places where before
there was only secrecy, they can enable the government to act more
intelligently and more intelligibly. Parliamentary debate is sufficient
for legislation but not for policy; for that, committees also are
needed. These committees will not be able to *decide*; but they should
be able to *discover*. However, the ultimate effects of reforms are
never certain.

Meanwhile the executive must be persuaded that secrecy does
not help it and that parliament could. The corollary of parliament

* See also page 175.

gaining access to Civil Servants is Civil Servants gaining access to parliament. Vansittart evidently thought he would have gained by the exchange.[118] L. S. Amery similarly thought that as a minister parliamentary committees would have helped him.[119] The executive should look upon committees as liberators, which will make their activities interesting. Unfortunately Whitehall has so fallen in love with its chains of secrecy that its steps towards freedom will be slow and hesitant, and probably Ministerial Responsibility in its extreme form will linger on.

There are of course dangers. The fear that committees would impair ministerial responsibility in its proper sense can be disregarded. The opposite danger that ministers would succeed in nobbling committees is more real. As Herbert Morrison pointed out, if the minister won over the opposition members of the committee, the opposition might later find itself hamstrung on the floor of the House.[120] Eden seems to have regretted that unlike America and France there was at Westminster no Foreign Affairs committee to which he could in secret make disclosures.[120a] If such a committee habitually met in secret it would be more useful to the Foreign Office than to parliament or the country. Foreign affairs and defence are doubtless exceptional, but parliamentary committees should be used to open up the executive, not to close parliament.

Even outside defence and foreign affairs, the attraction of being within the charmed circle of inside knowledge and confidentiality might be difficult to resist. In the first months of 1966, 35 per cent of the meetings of Congressional Committees were in secret.[121] An extension of secrecy from Whitehall to Westminster, instead of the reverse movement of publicity from Westminster to Whitehall, would defeat the whole object of parliamentary committees.

Much the greatest danger is that the committees will downgrade the debating chamber,* and in so doing blur the confrontation between government and opposition. Were that to happen, the House of Commons would become less of a parliament, more of a legislature, and would no longer be able to impose parliamentary manners of behaviour on British politics. Parliamentary reform would have ended in the exaltation of the executive.

In the United States, Congressional Committees have usurped the limelight from the floor of the House, and neither the Senate

* In 1968 Committees did damage, if not downgrade, the Chamber. But it was the venerable Standing legislative committees and the government's excessive use of them, which caused the trouble, not the new committees.

nor the House of Representatives is a debating forum. The June war in the Middle East was not debated, nor even, though America herself was involved in a war, was the President's State of the Union message debated in 1966. As Mr. Russell Baker wrote a few years ago, 'the great debate [on the U.N.] as any knowledgeable Senate watcher knew it would be, was clearly not a debate at all, but a procession of Senators talking to themselves. Nowadays when Senators want to talk to each other, they get together in a private room or pick up a telephone'.[122] British politicians, also, often seem to be talking to themselves but at least their political discussion is not entirely a soliloquy. In Congress the fragmentation of the legislature and the absence of debate make it impossible for the opposition to construct a coherent case and put it over to the public. In consequence the President, as Mr. Reston has pointed out, is able in foreign policy to obtain from Congress the legal authority for virtually what he wants, provided he chooses the right time to make the request.[123]

In Europe, too, there is generally more reliance upon committees and less upon a confrontation with the opposition. An accumulation of parties makes clear opposition difficult, and the committee system encourages co-operation. Attacks on a government in order to remove it, and collaboration with it in order to gain a share of power, go ill together. The dilemma tends to be dissolved in favour of collaboration. In Holland there is seldom an opposition ready to take over the government.[124] In Switzerland, also, opposition in parliament has been succeeded by co-operation.[125]

The politics of co-operation blurs responsibility, and conduces to a cosy complicity between the parties and to government by pressure group. The politics of opposition provides a better check on the politicians and on bureaucracy. It makes responsibility clear, and the alternation of different leaders preserves the health of the party system and helps to gain the consent of the voters. Even more important, a distinct opposition is a guarantee of the freedom of dissent. Naturally party can be as much overdone as co-operation, and in Britain it sometimes is. For every issue to be seen in party terms is damaging to party as well as demoralising to politicians.

But the extension of the committee system in Britain should not be at the expense of blurring the party confrontation. It would be folly to ruin party debate at the same time as creating administrative debate. The party battle should remain the main struggle in parliament; there should be added to it skirmishes between the executive and parliament. For these skirmishes to displace the party struggle as a main theatre of war at Westminster would hand a strategic advantage to the governing party. To cut down the party confrontation would exalt the government and diminish the opposition. Debate on the floor of the House is a struggle between near equals; any other procedure of investigating committee or questions is more a struggle between ruler and ruled. Debate on the floor of the House institutionalises the opposition; its criticisms excite some interest through being directed straight across the table at the Prime Minister or one of his leading colleagues. An opposition's supporters in the country can be encouraged only by conflict, not by the agreed recommendations, of a committee. Being clearly and invariably beaten in the division lobbies after debate is far more profitable to the opposition than would be the issuing of ineffectual challenges from afar or occasional success in a committee room. For an opposition there is no substitute for defeat. Committees must supplement not replace the party battle. Drama is essential.

The emphasis in Parliament on the confrontation between the parties is wise, though some find it offensive. Peel once said he never found 'any person denouncing these party animosities and conflicts, except mock philosophers, effeminate men, and sentimental women'.[126] His exceptions would have to be extended today. The Liberals find the confrontation between government and opposition irrelevant because it emphasises their own irrelevance. High minded people and newspapers are also apt to scorn the proceedings in the Commons. They find the spectacle of one party criticising the other distasteful and 'destructive'. The criticism that they direct at both parties is of course useful and 'constructive'.

Those who fail in parliament have an obvious tendency to criticise the Commons. Mr. Cousins, who did not number parliamentary talents among his abilities, thought parliament was 'a rather silly place'.[127] Leading statesmen, whose parties are in decline or whose personal fortunes are in eclipse, are tempted to blame the system, because under it power goes to the party leaders. The criticism of the Commons levelled by Churchill and Lloyd George in 1931 are often quoted. After he had been excluded from power for nine years, Lloyd George told the select committee on procedure that 'Parliament has really no control over the executive. It is pure fiction'.[128] But he did not feel the same when he was a minister. He told Hankey during the war that parliament 'is the only thing the government are afraid of'.[129] In the same way Churchill's far less hostile criticisms when he was out of power[130] should not be taken in isolation but in conjunction with the genuine respect he showed the House of Commons during the war and the eloquent tributes he paid it.[131]

Parliamentary control has been brushed aside as inadequate or non-existent because of the conception of 'political man'. 'Political man' responds only to the prospect of votes and is restrained only by the fear of losing them. He is always looking to the next election. Like Barrington Erle's ideal of a politician, he has no convictions,* he is not concerned with his reputation, he is impervious to rational persuasion. A creature possessing only political appetites, he reacts only to political pains and pleasures. And like economic man of the classical economists he never has existed and never will exist.

Once 'political man' is abandoned, the impotence of the Commons must be abandoned too, for the mouldering of parliamentary sanctions such as turning out a government or censuring a minister can then be seen not to be crucial. In politics as in modern war the more powerful the weapon the less likely it is to be used. Under a political system based on conventions, traditions and understandings, obsolete weapons are often as serviceable as real ones. Hostilities are formalised, and conflict minimised by prior adjustment.

The oft-presented picture of a commanding executive and a servile parliament is sheer illusion. The supremacy of the government in the Commons produces stability and coherence; it does not produce strong government. The trouble with parliament and the party system is that they work too well. The major parties are adept at reconciling conflicts and maintaining a united front against each other. This leads to dullness and to allegations of limitless obedience. Similarly the achievement of parliamentary control, because it is inconspicuous and does not entail defeats of the government, leads to disparagement of the House of Commons. The efficiency of the political process is its own undoing. The consequent predictability of the parliamentary battle impairs the prestige of the Commons and prevents it from engaging the public interest needed for decisive government. Maybe reform will enable it to do so.

---

* 'Convictions! There is nothing on earth that I am so much afraid of in a young Member of Parliament as convictions,' Barrington Erle told Phineas Finn. 'I've had to do with them all but a fellow with convictions is the worst of all.''

The House of Commons does not govern, could not govern, and is not intended to govern. But it controls government, it restrains government, it influences government, and if its leading members control the House, so does the House control those leading members. 'The centre of gravity of the State,' Lord John Russell once remarked, 'has been placed in the House of Commons.'[132] And there, despite all the changes of the last 150 years, it has remained.

IV

THE HOUSE OF LORDS

*Well, Mr. Speaker, if you have a motor car—and I believe some are still
allowed—you have to have a brake. There ought to be a brake. A brake, in
its essence, is one-sided; it prevents an accident through going too fast. It
was not intended to prevent accidents through going too slow. For that you
must look elsewhere, to another part of the vehicle . . .*
WINSTON CHURCHILL, Speech on the Second Reading
of the Parliament Bill, November 11 1947[1]

*These servants of the Crown in every part of the globe will not come here
in the first flush and bloom of their youth . . . What I fear is this, that
you will not strengthen the House of Lords as a legislative body, but that
you will turn it into a sort of legislative Bath or Cheltenham, or, perhaps,
if it is not disrespectful to say so, into a sort of legislative hydropathic
establishment, where these noble persons will take more care of their
constitutions than of the constitution of this House.*
LORD ROSEBERY in 1888[2]

When I want a peerage I will buy one, like an honest man.
LORD NORTHCLIFFE[3]

The House of Lords has had many distinctions: its curious composition, its long and almost uninterrupted history, its rudimentary
rules of procedure, its ability to function without a chairman wield-
ing disciplinary powers, its dependence upon the absenteeism of its
own members. It is unique, also, in the volume of colourful invective
and entertaining abuse which has been directed against it. No other
institution can so long have survived such an intensive onslaught of
denunciation and derision.

Tom Paine considered the idea of a hereditary legislature to be
as ridiculous as that of a hereditary mathematician or a hereditary
poet laureate.[4] Byron attacked from the inside. 'When a proposal is
made to emancipate or relieve,' he told their Lordships in his
maiden speech, 'you hesitate, you deliberate for years, you temporise
and tamper with the minds of men; but a deathbill must be passed
off hand, without a thought of the consequences.'[5] Another insider,

Ashley, remarked that peers had 'few sparks of generosity and no sentiment'.[6] In their different ways Swinburne and Morley said much the same thing.

> Where might is, the right is:
> Long purses make strong swords.
> Let weakness learn meekness:
>   God save the House of Lords,[7]

wrote Swinburne, while Morley declared that 'you might as well talk to the House of Lords about land as talk to a butcher about Lent'.[8] Labouchere, whose uncle Lord Taunton was sometimes confused with his father, was once congratulated on the admirable speech his father had just made in the House of Lords. 'The House of Lords?' Labouchere queried. 'Well, well, that is very satisfactory. Since his death the family have always been a little uneasy as to his whereabouts.'[9]

Churchill thought the House of Lords was 'a one-sided, hereditary, unprized, unrepresentative, irresponsible absentee'.[10] Even better philippics came from Joe Chamberlain and Lloyd George. 'I have no desire,' said Chamberlain in one of his more temperate utterances, 'to see a dull uniformity of social life. I am rather thankful than otherwise to gentlemen who will take the trouble to wear robes and coronets ... They are ancient monuments, and I should be sorry to deface them. But then, gentlemen, I don't believe that we can build upon these interesting ruins the foundations of our government. I cannot allow that these antiquities should control the destinies of a free empire.'[11]

Twenty-five years later Lloyd George talked in similar vein: '... when a Liberal government comes in you have these old Tories dug out of the cellars of the House of Lords ... stuff bottled in the Dark Ages ... not fit to drink, cobwebby, dusty, muddy, sour ...'[12] Speaking at Wolverhampton shortly afterwards he said: 'They have no qualifications—at least they *need* not have any. No testimonials are required. There are no credentials. They do not even need a medical certificate. They need not be sound either in body, or in mind. They only require a certificate of birth ... just to prove that they are the first of the litter. You would not choose a spaniel on these principles ...'[13]

Until the passing of the Parliament Act the anathemas issued against the House of Lords had much justification. In the late eighteenth and early nineteenth centuries the Lords could be depended upon to oppose every measure of amelioration or reform. In 1786 they rejected a bill substituting hanging for burning as a punishment for wives who murdered their husbands.[14] They obstructed the gradual abolition of the Slave Trade.[15] In three successive years they threw out bills to prevent boys being sent up chimneys.[16] They similarly thwarted attempts to disfranchise boroughs for corruption.[17] Six times in six years their Lordships refused to abolish the death penalty for stealing from shops goods worth five shillings.[18] And they found Catholic Emancipation almost as repugnant as relaxations of the Criminal Code.

Sidney Smith likened the attempt of the House of Lords to hold back Parliamentary Reform to Mrs. Partington trying to sweep back the Atlantic. But in lesser matters the Lords succeeded in sweeping back reform. They delayed the full removal of the civil disabilities of Jews for thirty years and the elimination of religious discrimination at Oxford and Cambridge for nearly forty.[19]

. In the middle of the century the tides of reform were so weak that Mrs. Partington was not called upon. But she was back with her broom in opposition to the abolition of the purchase of Army Commissions. 'The nation must buy back its own army from its own officers,'[19a] commented Gladstone sourly. Emboldened by its success in the 1890s in defeating Irish Home Rule and other Liberal legislation without disturbing public composure, the House of Lords embarked on an orgy of destruction of Liberal measures from 1906 culminating in its rejection of the Lloyd George budget. This ultimate debauchery, by precipitating the passage of the Parliament Act, brought to an end its career of dissipation. Henceforward the peers could block a non-money bill for only two years.

The House of Lords was not invariably wrong. Hankey even thought that by its rejection of the Declaration of London before the First War it justified its existence.[20] And the record of the Lords is in some respects no worse than that of the American Supreme Court. The Lords never did anything so rash as the Court's declaration in the Dred Scott case that the banning of slavery from the territories was unconstitutional. The House of Lords threw out the Lloyd George budget introducing super tax in 1909; the Supreme Court declared *income tax* unconstitutional in 1894. Justice Holmes might point out that the 14th Amendment had not enacted Mr. Herbert Spencer's 'Social Statics',[21] but over government interference with the railroads and the big corporations the majority of the Court, from the 1880s onwards behaved, as though it had. If the House of Lords refused to protect boy chimney sweeps in the early nineteenth century, the Supreme Court struck down governmental regulations of child labour in the early twentieth century. As late as 1923 the Court declared a minimum wage law for women unconstitutional, while in 1936 it ruled against New York State's regulation of the same matter.[21a]

The Supreme Court was less obstructive to the New Deal than the House of Lords was to the Liberal government of 1906 only because it was further from the scene of action. Only in 1935 did the first New Deal statute reach the court.[22] If Britain, as Joe Chamberlain once complained, was a peer ridden nation, America has often been judge ridden.* And if the Conservative party long controlled the House of Lords, the Republican party, as Roosevelt later remarked, was in 1929 in 'complete control of all branches of the Federal Government' including the Supreme Court.[24]

Some comfort may therefore be gained from America. All the same, the record of the House of Lords does not lend itself to whitewashing. The plain fact is that when the Lords differed from the Commons it was nearly always wrong. Throughout the nineteenth century a member of the Upper House might have echoed St. Peter's lament in Byron's Heaven:

> And seems the custom here to overthrow
> Whatever has been wisely done below.[25]

The modern history of the House of Lords begins with the Parliament Act. Since 1914 the House has been in purgatory or limbo. Although the preamble to the Parliament Act looked to the abolition of the hereditary principle, nothing was done for half a century. Between the wars the general Conservative dominance gave small temptation to the Lords to run amok once more. The House did defeat a government bill in 1928. It rejected the Rabbits Bill by 63 votes to 55.[26] On less contentious subjects it was quiescent.

Except partially on the nationalisation of steel, this restraint was maintained under the Attlee government. But the good behaviour of the Lords was, in Socialist eyes, not sufficient to cleanse it of previous sins or to atone for its hereditary composition, and the

---

* Chief Justice Taft wrote that a judge's robes should 'impress the judge himself with the constant consciousness that he is a high priest in the temple of justice and is surrounded with obligations of a sacred character that he cannot escape . . .'[23]

Parliament Act of 1948 reduced its powers of delay from two years to one. More palatable to the Lords than the stripping of its powers was the institution by the Conservatives of life peers in 1957. The change was partly illusory since there is little difference between a life peer and a first generation hereditary peer, but the dilution of the hereditary element enhanced the reputation of the Upper House. The Act allowing life peers into the Lords was followed, logically enough, by an Act allowing hereditary peers out of it. From 1963 the inheritance of a peerage was no longer a political life sentence.

Probably, however, the Upper House has gained more from the punishments of its opponents than from the rewards of its friends. The loss of its powers has strengthened it, just as the loss of the temporal power strengthened the Papacy. Not of course that the Lords now exercises spiritual power. But its influence is somewhat nebulous. The unpopularity of the Lords was usually far less than might have been expected. In much of its most reactionary behaviour it was not unrepresentative of a wide section of the country. Today at any rate its unpopularity has largely disappeared, and its prestige occasionally seems less tarnished than that of the Commons.

The clinging of nearly all Western democracies to two chamber government is largely superstitious. It is the number of parties not the number of chambers that influences the form of a country's government. In no country does the second chamber perform its allegedly classic function of imposing delay to enable the rash first chamber to have second thoughts, or to allow the voters to give their verdict on the question in dispute. Parties, the bureaucracy, pressure groups generally prevent a lower house passing hasty and rash legislation; at the same time the deification of the popular vote generally prevents a second chamber defeating or holding up such legislation when it is passed. Yet the idea of a second chamber has retained its popularity. Only Denmark, Norway, and New Zealand have dared to defy the superstition. Every state in America, save Nebraska, and every state in Australia, save Queensland, maintains the full panoply of a bicameral legislature. The number 2 seems to have acquired for legislatures the same mystical significance that the numbers 3 or 7 generally possessed in the ancient world.

Of course the interposition of delay is not the sole function of second chambers. They may also contribute to the smooth working of the political system; they may polish legislation and save the time of the Lower House, provide a link with the Judiciary and a platform for interest groups, be a useful forum of debate, and also furnish representation for local government or, in a federal system, for the states of the federation. The House of Lords to a varying degree performs all these functions except the last. Its chief use, however, has lain in the first.

In appearance the House is a tribute to gerontocracy, an acknowledgement of the value of age and experience. In fact the function of the House is to circumscribe gerontocracy in the British system. The Lords provides for tired statesmen and superannuated M.P.s a dignified and now remunerated refuge. Were it not for the Lords the Commons would be a much more ancient assembly. The loyalty of most constituency associations to the sitting member and the high proportion of safe seats cut down the political turnover of M.P.s. Without the Lords the totally obscure could, as now, be persuaded to retire, but the successful or the half-successful would refuse to deny their counsel to the nation. The House of Lords enables these patriotic anxieties to be gratified, while ensuring that the young and inexperienced get their chance in the Commons before they are too old to care.* Clearly the willingness of elected or previously elected legislators to proceed to 'another place' is dependent on the standing of that place. In consequence the prestige of the Lords has a bearing upon the proper working of the Commons.

The provision of decent indoor retirement and relief for elderly politicians is not the only way in which the House of Lords oils the political process. The second chamber qualifies men for ministerial office without forcing them to undergo the rigours of election or re-election. But except in wartime the Prime Minister chooses his ministers from the leaders of his party, who are predominantly in the House of Commons. And in war an electoral truce makes it easy for a Prime Minister to find seats in the Commons for the outsiders he wishes to bring into his government. Thus, despite the lack of enthusiasm of the chairman of the Conservative party, who talked about possibly getting him on to the short list for the Wrekin, Mr. Oliver Lyttelton was given Aldershot.[27] Similarly Mr. Ernest Bevin and Sir James Grigg were provided with parliamentary

---

* Of the 566 peers created between 1901 and 1957, 317 were former members of the House of Commons.

seats. When Lord Woolton was brought into his government by Neville Chamberlain, he was already a peer.

The House of Lords enables a peacetime Prime Minister to bring non-politicians into his cabinet like an American President. So far with trifling exceptions none has taken the opportunity. Apart from doubts as to the general suitability of businessmen for party politics, Prime Ministers are well aware that to raid big business or the universities and install the loot in the Lords and the Cabinet, thus depriving their followers in the Commons of the consolations of office would be tantamount to political suicide. Besides so long as power lies in the House of Commons, major figures brought into politics from other occupations prefer to sit there.

But the House of Lords provides a haven for electoral casualties. Many constituency parties do not relish the vanquished, however eminent, being foisted upon them, and the Leyton bye-election suggested that the reluctance of constituency parties to return generals to the field is shared by the voters.* Fortunately this ingratitude can be partly made good by the conferment of a peerage. The House of Lords thus does something to reduce the hazards of a political career and embalms without burying a number of useful politicians. By supplementing or contradicting the electoral process it adds a welcome element of flexibility to the political system.

By providing ministers the House of Lords, in theory at least, cuts down the number of M.P.s in the government and fosters the Commons's independence of the executive. In practice, however, the number of ministerial posts goes on increasing. The decisive factor in the increase is the desire of M.P.s for jobs, not the increase in the amount of work to be done. The House of Lords has therefore only a marginal effect on the number of ministerial offices filled by M.P.s.

The Lords has considerable legislative uses. So far from being a delaying chamber, it is a speeding up chamber. The shortage of time in the Commons prevents many bills being adequately discussed there. The most important bills are usually the most controversial. The opposition habitually tries to hold them up, and the government resorts to the guillotine. The more important the

---

* This is no new phenomenon. Three members of the government beaten in the 1922 election were all subsequently defeated in bye-elections in supposedly safe Conservative seats.[28]

measure, therefore, the less likely is it to be properly debated. Further the government may so arrange the guillotine time-table that the parts which would prove most awkward for it are never reached.[29] So the most controversial parts of the most controversial bills may not be debated in the Commons at all. Without the existence of the Lords, this situation would probably long since have been found intolerable even by the party in power. The Lords gives an opportunity for discussion, and the government has time for second thoughts and revision. The House of Lords can, as A. P. Herbert put it, correct grammar.[30] It can also make more important corrections, or rather the government can make the corrections in the House of Lords. Whether or not such a proceeding is preferable to a different procedure in the Commons is debatable; it is certainly preferable to no such proceedings at all.

The Lords provide a link with the judiciary, though it is doubtful if the association has benefited either of them. The Law Lords have traditionally been less unpopular than the Bishops, whom Bright once denounced as 'another kind of peer, that creature of—what shall I say—of monstrous, nay even of adulterous birth.'[31] But the judges have seldom shone as legislators, and their decision in the Taff Vale case probably redounded to the discredit of the political House of Lords.

'It is the duty of a judge of first instance to be quick, courteous, and wrong. This does not mean,' Lord Asquith of Bishopstone continued, 'that the Court of Appeal should be slow, rude, and right, for that would be to usurp the functions of the House of Lords.'[32] Yet whatever the manners or the speed of the Lords, its general rightness is open to considerable doubt. And in general the Law Lords have been more executive-minded than the bench as a whole.

Even before the advent of life peerages, the new peers created in this century represented every kind of industry, profession and trade.[33] The easy hours of the Lords and the absence of constituency obligations make infrequent attendance at Westminster quite feasible for the leading members of important interests, whereas only junior members of such interests can normally join the Commons. The House of Lords has been a gateway to the Corporative state, but so far the interests have declined to march through it.

The Lords provide another forum of debate, and any debate is welcome. But discussions there seldom excite much public attention.

A pronouncement by Lord Beeching, an outburst by Lord Montgomery, a readily misunderstood speech on homosexuality by the Archbishop of Canterbury may be widely reported. Yet most of the labours of the Lords might as well be carried on in secret session for all the public attention they receive.

The standard of Lords debates is often extolled, and certainly many well informed and considered addresses are delivered there. But the knowledge that normally nothing said there matters very much necessarily deadens the proceedings. When the Irish Treaty was debated in 1922 the presence of Carson and his duel with his former ally, Birkenhead, concentrated attention on the Lords, while Austen Chamberlain's statement in the Commons went largely unnoticed.[34] Such moments of glory in the life of the upper House are rare. Lords debates contain competent speeches, but they do not and indeed cannot add up to an exciting debate. The individual actors are good; there is no play.

Reform

Since the Parliament Act and particularly since 1945, the House of Lords has functioned rather well. Certainly it is no longer synonymous with reaction. Under the leadership of Birkenhead the peers in 1921 showed themselves to be far in advance of the Commons on divorce. And in 1966 the Lord Chancellor, Lord Gardiner, could say with much justification: 'I wrote to the Right Reverend Prelate, reminding him that this House is now the place for all social reform to be first discussed. . . .'[35]

But the liberalism of the present House has not been matched by strength. Two bills in recent years cried out for rejection and reconsideration. In the War Damage Bill the government was blatantly rigging the law in order to slide out of its obligations and to reverse what the Courts had decided. Moreover it was not a party issue. The opposition front bench in the Commons supported the bill, and the Conservative government had taken the same line as its Labour successors. Here was an almost perfect opportunity for peers to stand up for the rule of law. They did not take it.

Another measure no less deserving of rejection was the London Government Bill of 1967. Admittedly, this was a party issue. Admittedly, too, the bill applied to only part of the country, and rejection would have meant not merely delay but total defeat of the government's intentions. Nevertheless these intentions were eminently worthy of defeat. In a period of intense government unpopularity, the bill sought to put off for a year the elections in the London Boroughs, on the trumped up excuse that the electors would be muddled by having to vote for the Greater London Council and the London Boroughs at the same time. Remembering the vast array of public offices American voters manage to fill in the same elections, that point could not possibly be considered a valid reason for arbitrarily prolonging the elected life of largely Labour councils. The Bill was not a classic piece of gerrymandering, since it was gerrymandering by time not by space. But in these Keynesian days the date of an election may be every bit as crucial as the drawing of the electoral boundaries. If there is any matter over which the Upper House should exercise special vigilance, it is any attempt by the government and the Lower House to tamper with the electoral process. Yet, in the event, the House of Lords proved no better a defender of electoral purity than it had of the rule of law, and the bill was duly passed.

Admittedly the Lords did refuse a government order on Rhodesia in 1968. But ill-conceived though that action was, it had not the smallest effect on the country's policy, and it occurred at a time when the government was uniquely unpopular. Thus the Upper Chamber's farcical conduct did not demonstrate new found strength, only defective judgment.

Disraeli thought there was 'scarcely a less dignified entity than a patrician in a panic'.[36] Although the peers have preserved their dignity, they have been 'in a fright' since 1914. Knowing that the hereditary composition of the House is logically indefensible, they have not except in 1948–9 and in 1968 risked a head-on clash with a left wing government. In other words the hereditary principle, which had once made the House of Lords powerful by ensuring that it was composed of the richest landowners, has in modern times ensured its impotence.

Logically, therefore, the chief momentum for the abolition of the hereditary principle should have come from those Conservatives who believe in a strong second chamber, while Labour M.P.s who favour a weak one should have been last ditch defenders of the existing House. To the left, the absurdity of the House's membership should have been its highest recommendation. For one thing, the hereditary qualification has prevented the House using what powers it possesses. For another its hereditary membership prevented additional powers being conferred upon it. A House of Lords comprising only life peers may well attract greater powers and influence. The present liberalism of the House may turn out to be almost as fleeting as that of Pio Nono, and a defensible second chamber might be an effective barrier to reform. Logic, however, did not prevail.

A theoretical case can be made out for a strong second chamber. Governments occasionally do arbitrary and stupid things. They are sometimes in conflict with public opinion. They frequently do things unmentioned in, or contrary to, their election manifestos. Finally, since in Britain there is no distinction between constitutional and ordinary laws, a government could rig the constitution in its own favour without consulting the voters. For all these reasons, it could be argued, Britain needs an institution which can check governments when they are wrong, hold up dangerous legislation until the electors have had the chance to pronounce upon it, and protect the constitution from partisan violation.

Any governmental action of outstanding folly or arbitrariness, successfully forced through the Commons, produces anguished, appeals for the creation of such a body. The Labour government's conduct of its Prices and Incomes Bill in 1966 may be taken as a test case. The procedure of the Commons was shockingly abused. The most far reaching measure or control of the economy ever proposed in peacetime was in reality not given a second reading in the Commons. The committee stage was railroaded through up-stairs. A large minority of the cabinet was more than uneasy about the policy, twenty-five or thirty members of the parliamentary Labour party voted against the bill, and a far from negligible pro-portion of the remainder would have liked to do so. The opposition was sharply hostile to the measure.

Yet, however deplorable the government's behaviour, to say that rejection by the Lords would nevertheless have been desirable is either to go completely against the whole theory of responsible government, or to propose that the government should be respon-sible to the Upper as well as to the Lower House. According to the present theory the government is responsible to the House of Commons, and if it cannot persuade the Commons to accept the measures necessary to implement its policy it should resign or dissolve. At least since 1784 or 1806 when George III used defeats in the Lords as an excuse for dismissing ministries, British govern-ments have not been considered responsible to the House of Lords.

True the Lords has often thwarted British governments, but it has never rejected measures considered necessary to deal with a crisis. Even its rejection of Lloyd George's budget in 1909 did not come into that category. Similarly, rejection of such legislation as the War Damage or London Government bill would not have threatened government responsibility to the Commons, since those measures were plainly not an essential part of the government's policy.

A cabinet cannot be responsible to two chambers—unless they always agree in which case the second House is by definition not strong. And the ending of government by a cabinet responsible to the House of Commons would be a high and paradoxical price to pay for the creation of a strong Upper House. A strong second chamber able to deal with crisis situations is therefore out of the question.

But should there not be an institution not directly involved in the party struggle that can interpret public opinion and restrain a government which flies in the face of it? The trouble is that such an institution is always liable to confuse its opinion with that of the public, or to exert itself only when the two opinions coincide. Besides, there are occasions when the government is justified in defying public opinion. No more than an institution allegedly embodying the law, can an institution allegedly embodying public opinion supply an infallible guide to the problems of politics. In any case, the voicing of public opinion and attention to its wishes are in no danger of being neglected in the British system. The danger is the opposite one: that British governments seldom feel strong enough to fly in the face of public opinion. Public opinion is not under-represented in Britain.

Neither can substantial delaying powers for an Upper House be justified on the grounds that government should be prevented from passing unpopular legislation for which they have no mandate, until after a general election. The doctrine of the mandate has no rational basis. By voting for a party, the voter cannot be held to have endorsed every feature of that party's policy. Nor do most voters cast their votes as a result of consideration of particular items of policy. So to talk of holding up legislation until the people have had a chance to pronounce upon it is as senseless as to talk about a mandate.

If a party or a government went mad and tried to set up a dictatorship, a strong second chamber might have some value. Had the Crippsian view become dominant in the Labour Party in the thirties and had Labour won an election at that time, then the House of Lords would have been fully justified in throwing out its enabling act. The trouble is that an electorate foolish enough to adopt such ideas, would probably not have been greatly affected by an adverse vote in the House of Lords. A second chamber is not a bulwark against revolution. It would simply crumble. Political systems are not preserved by the existence of bulwarks against revolution. They are preserved by their ability to prevent revolutionary situations arising. In any case, any such reserve power should be in the hands of the monarch, who would exercise it only in the last resort.

The British system of government does not require another long-stop; it needs more bowlers and batsmen. Broadly-based parties, a strong civil service, entrenched government departments, a parliamentary atmosphere, an octopus of interest groups, a somnolent electorate—all these are usually adequate brakes on the government. What is needed is more power in the engine. Of course an even better brake would also be an asset, provided it was only used when the government was going too fast or recklessly. A second chamber which succeeded (as in 1968) in making the government have second thoughts on Stansted, and which rejected the War Damage and London Government bills, while not attempting to interfere with 'crisis situations' or with the operation of responsible government would be ideal. But such an institutional paragon is unknown, and would probably not be considered 'strong'.

The plea for a strong second chamber is based upon a fundamentally false diagnosis of what is wrong with British government. But even if that diagnosis were correct and the government were too strong and needed curbing, the proposed cure would not work. A second chamber cannot be used as a *deux ex machina* to correct all the other faults of the machine. If the first chamber is working badly, that is where reform is needed. If the forces producing the abuse in the first chamber are strong enough to prevent its remedy, they will be strong enough to prevent its attempted remedy by the backdoor of the second chamber. The alleged disease precludes its remedy. In Britain, happily, the disease is almost unknown.

If a second chamber cannot be the arbiter of the political process, it can be a useful adjunct to it. The present House of Lords is unquestionably useful, but undoubtedly in need of reform.

The best replacement for the present body would be one composed of representatives of the English regions and of Scotland, Wales and Northern Ireland. These representatives could be directly elected by the voters of the regions (though not at the same time as the House of Commons), or nominated as in West Germany by the regional governments. Such a house would normally be rather differently aligned from the Commons, and might produce some useful controversy. There would be considerable advantage in the struggles between the Whitehall and regional bureaucracies emerging into public view, as occasionally happens in the Bundesraat. As with the Parliament Act of 1911, reform of the House of Lords should be accompanied by a reduction in the life of a parliament—this time from five years to four. In these days, both governments and parliaments soon lose their freshness.

A regional House of Lords, though it would no longer aid the rejuvenation of the Commons, would be preferable either to a largely hereditary body or to a wholly nominated body with or without increased powers. Regrettably it is highly unlikely to materialise.

There is a widely held idea that an elected second chamber is not feasible, because it would vie with the House of Commons for supremacy. This is simply not true. Protagonists of second chambers cite the experience of other countries as an argument against a single chamber; but they totally ignore the experience of other countries when considering what form the second chamber should take. Only Canada has a wholly nominated second chamber, and the Canadian Senate has not been a successful body. In every other country the second chamber is elected, but at least where there is cabinet government it does not attempt to rival the other House. The reason is simple: a cabinet must be responsible to one House; it cannot be responsible to both, unless they are joined together. This principle has prevailed even in a federation such as Australia.

Because of the delusion that an elected Upper House is impossible, a proposal originally made by the Clerk of the House of Lords, Mr. Henry Burrows, holds the field. According to this scheme, the House would be a wholly nominated body. The government of the day would always have a reasonable majority over all opposition parties, but not a majority in the House as a whole. Its majority over the other parties would be smaller than the number of crossbenchers in the House. On a change of government the party composition

L

of the Lords would be adjusted by fresh creations on the recommendations of the incoming Prime Minister.

Such a proposal sounds well enough. At a time when neither politicians nor party stand high with the public, to exalt the non-political is popular and looks honest and enlightened. In practice, however, although life peers have been prepared to forget their creators, the new non-party peers in a more easily defensible chamber will probably have better memories. They will be only superficially non-party, being in reality for the most part sympathisers of the party leader who nominated them. To the traditional categories of peers will be added two new ones: Tory crossbenchers and Labour crossbenchers. When considering appointments to the bench, Theodore Roosevelt drew a distinction between 'the *nominal* politics of the man', which were irrelevant, and 'his real politics [which were] all-important'.[37] In so far as the new House of Lords acquires any influence, a potential peer's nominal non-politics will be of no account; his real politics will be vital and well known in advance.

It is just as well, indeed, that the non-party façade should be thoroughly fraudulent. A fairly random selection of elderly non-party individuals is not the most obvious repository of political power. There is no inherent virtue in being non-party or in refusing to take sides in public. Nor does such a refusal provide any guarantee of impartiality, as was clearly shown in the Army-McCarthy dispute in the United States. A counsel for the hearings had to be found, who had not expressed himself for or against the Senator. In fact, of course, silence was much more likely to denote support for McCarthy than opposition: those who were appalled by McCarthy felt compelled to speak out, those who approved of him could keep complacently silent. And in the event, the Committee's choice, Mr. Ray Jenkins, 'a veteran defender of moonshiners and husband-shooters in Tennessee',[38] turned out to be fully for McCarthy.

A reluctance to join the party battle may stem from a robust independence of mind or from a spiritual aversion from the degradations of party politics. Alternatively, it may stem from a wish to have the best of both worlds, from mere laziness, ignorance or lack of courage. The non-party and the non-political are not necessarily worse than those who are not afraid to take sides. They are certainly no better. And they cannot be plausibly regarded as a collective Cincinnatus ready to turn from other pursuits to be the saviours of their country.

Fortunately, the powers of the reformed House will still be severely limited. But freed from its hereditary albatross the House of Lords may gain undue influence. It may be used to give a spurious veneer of non-political approval to highly partisan acts of government. Should the reputation of politicians sink lower, and should the party and cabinet systems be further discredited, the reformed House might even facilitate the substitution of a Presidential system with most of the 'President's' officers and courtiers possessing seats in the Lords. But that is unlikely. Although a wholly nominated chamber will appreciably extend the Prime Minister's already excessive powers of patronage, the reform will probably not make a great deal of difference.

Congratulating the French Radical party on its success in avoiding single chamber government in the Fourth Republic, Edouard Herriot said: 'We have at least a chamber and a half.'[39] That is surely the right number, and in all probability the nominated House will not increase it. But what a lost opportunity, not to have set up an elected regionally based second chamber!

V

THE MONARCHY

On the whole, it is wise in human affairs and in the government of men, to separate pomp from power.

WINSTON CHURCHILL[1]

The time of a prince is the property of his people.

EDWARD GIBBON[2]

The Crown signifies a nominal office of a million sterling a year, the business of which consists in receiving the money.

TOM PAINE[3]

After the briefest conversation with the Kaiser, Oscar Browning is said to have murmured: 'Quite my favourite Emperor!' In those days Mr. Browning had several Emperors to choose from; now only the Negus and the Mikado are left. Together with the Emperors, the Kings have disappeared from most of the globe. None survives in Central Europe. Only the Kings of Jordan and Saudi Arabia, and the Shah of Persia remain in the Middle East.* In the countries on the Mediterranean only the King of Morocco, the Bey of Tunis, and the King of Libya still reign, and in the far east only the Kings of Thailand, Cambodia and Tonga. South America is kingless, and so is Africa south of the Sahara.

The Emperors of Japan and Abyssinia apart, three Kings in the Far East, three in the Middle East, and three on the shores of the Mediterranean, are all that remain of the monarchical principle outside Western Europe and the British Commonwealth. And most of these are less secure on their thrones than the Monarchs of Western Europe. Indeed a world in which every country outside Western Europe is a republic is not unlikely. In that case all the dictatorships would be republican, and all the monarchies free.

The United States and Switzerland, together with France, West Germany, Finland, and Italy, and temporarily, at least, India and a very few other countries would spoil the symmetry by being both republican and free. There has also been some co-existence between

* There are also sheikhs, sultans and emirs.

monarchs and modern dictators. King Victor Emmanuel perched on his throne throughout Mussolini's supremacy, and King Alfonso reigned throughout the dictatorship of Primo de Rivera; not surprisingly, neither king long survived his country's reversion to non-dictatorial rule. But notwithstanding these and other exceptions, the correlation between constitutional monarchy and free government is in the West remarkably high. Except in the United States, Switzerland and Uruguay, free government has flourished with any degree of stability only under Kings and Queens. Norway, Sweden, and Denmark, Belgium, Holland and Luxembourg, Britain, Canada, Australia and New Zealand have been and remain monarchies.

There is nothing puzzling about this. Increased understanding of the strength of emotional forces in politics, and of their rationality of leaders and led, has undermined the democratic theorising that led to the inevitable conclusion that republics are more democratic. Napoleon's contemptuous aside that it is with baubles that men are led has proved to be far nearer the mark than the abstract propositions of a Sieyès or a Robespierre. An hereditary king is a unique symbol of the history, continuity, permanence, and unity of a people. Popular craving for mystery, colour, and pageantry can be satisfied by royalty. The monarch is a person and a symbol. He makes power and the state both intelligible and mysterious. Presidents make them neither. Legitimacy, the acceptance by the governed of the political system, is far better aided by an ancient monarchy set above the political battle than by a transient President, who has gained his position through that battle. A monarch can also engage the affections and the loyalty of the armed forces more easily than can a President and so serve to avert military rule.* And the existence of a royal family on the throne makes almost impossible the emergence of a quasi royal family among the ranks of politicians. The monarchy saves us from 'dynastic' politics.

'Myth and ritual express the most deeply rooted hopes, fears and emotions of a community concerning the practical and urgent problems of daily life, physical and spiritual.'[4] Modern societies still need myth and ritual. A monarch and his family supply it; there is no magic about a mud-stained politician. No wonder constitutional monarchies have proved more lasting than free republics!

---

* The Republican U.S. has avoided military rule but not military Presidents. Yet General Eisenhower proved more successful at keeping America out of war than any civilian President since 1945.

James I talked of himself being married to his Kingdom: 'I am the husband and all the whole isle is my lawful wife,'[5] language typical of the seventeenth century. He and others could even talk of a village constable being the vice-gerent of God. Yet James's language is not incomparable with that of the leading modern theorist of the Monarchy, Mr. Dermot Morrah, who also sees a mystical union between the Queen and her subjects.

'. . . The importance of the Queen in the life of her many peoples,' writes Mr. Morrah, 'resides not at all in what she does, but entirely in what she is. She is the embodiment of their tradition and their future, the focus of their aspirations, the symbol of their unity, their universal representative.'[6] 'In its deeper meaning for the British peoples [the monarchy] is scarcely a system of government at all. It is their way of life.'[7] Again Elizabeth 'is Queen not because she governs England, but because England would not be itself without her'.[8]

Most devotees of the monarchy do not possess the eloquence of Mr. Morrah nor perhaps his intensity of devotion. It is always difficult to intellectualise emotions, and most people do not try to. But whether or not they would subscribe to Mr. Morrah's exposition of monarchy, the Queen evokes from most people a far greater measure of affection and respect than any other institution or public figure. Like the King in Shaw's *The Apple Cart*, if she stood in an election, 'there won't be any poll; it will be a walk-over'.[9]

What Disraeli 120 years ago called 'the old wholesome superstition',[10] that the monarch exercises power has not been dispelled.* A mass observation survey found indeed that two people in five agreed that 'the Queen should be able to change what parliament decided'.[12] Thirty per cent apparently thought that she had gone through a process of Divine selection.[13]

Both in this country and abroad the Royal family enjoy an intense and widespread, though diminished, popularity and in some quarters near reverence. No matter how this is explained or explained away, millions of people feel that the Queen and the Royal family in some way represent them as well as the State.

* Mr. Wilson's remark shortly after Rhodesia's U.D.I. at the Lord Mayor's Banquet in 1965 may have strengthened that superstition as well as himself. 'I do not need to tell an audience such as this at the heart of the Commonwealth that any instruction or command issued by Her Majesty's Ministers in the name of the Queen could not and would not in any circumstances be issued without the specific authority and approval of Her Majesty herself.'[11]

In a letter to *The Times*,[14] after she had been criticised for living in widowed seclusion, Queen Victoria explained that 'mere representation' was not her only task. She had 'other and higher duties', which she could not 'neglect without injury to the public service'. And until the death of Albert, the monarch retained considerable political importance. The Prince Consort, said Lord John Russell, 'was an informal but potent member of all cabinets'.[15] The order, method, and industry of the Palace under the aegis of Albert, together with the highly confused state of the parties and the usual absence of an obvious parliamentary majority, made the monarchy almost another Whitehall department overseeing the government, especially the Foreign Office.

Constitutional monarchy in its present form was not the intention of anybody, least of all Victoria or Albert. The Prince once assured Stockmar that 'constitutional monarchy marches unassailably on its beneficent course'.[16] But that marching monarchy was very different from today's model. Thus, according to Stockmar, the Sovereign should be 'a permanent premier, who takes rank above the temporary head of the cabinet'.[17] Stockmar was wrong even at the time, but in the fifties such a situation was not unthinkable.

The monarchy withdrew from party politics because it had no means of influencing elections, and its identification with any of the political groups would in consequence have been disastrous. But in putting the Crown above politics neither Albert nor Victoria had any intention of putting it out of politics. The cause of the transition from 'above' to 'out of' was the revival of a two-party system which left no scope for any presidential forming of coalitions. Victoria thought it was 'impossible to have a strong government'[18] without a two-party system; she did not see that it was impossible to have a strong monarchy *with* one.

The end of coalition politics and minority governments would, even without Albert's death, have eventually driven the monarchy out of Whitehall. Had he lived, the retreat would merely have been slower and punctuated with well conceived counter attacks and a good deal of strife. The widowed Victoria continued to devour the red boxes and write spirited letters of complaints to her ministers; Gladstone and Salisbury both complained that the Queen needed a deal of handling. But the second half of her reign saw the beginning of modern constitutional monarchy. She still interfered more than her twentieth century successors, sometimes unconstitutionally, but while she was occasionally a rock that had to be avoided, she was neither a road block nor a sign post. The prestige of the Victorian monarchy grew as its power declined.

Edward VII made many journeys abroad, both State and private,* and he played a useful part in paving the way for the *Entente Cordiale*. Yet Balfour did not think he had ever suggested anything of political importance.[20] Since Queen Victoria, monarchs have been important, politically, only during a crisis. Victoria was a useful conciliator between the Houses in 1869 over Irish Disestablishment and in 1884 over Reform and Redistribution, when Gladstone thanked her for her 'wise, gracious and steady exercise of influence' and referred to her 'skilled and experienced hands'.[21] Edward VII tried to prevent a clash between the Houses on the Lloyd George budget. Over Ireland in 1921, over anti-strike legislation in 1926, and in 1931 George V played a moderator's part. Though his conduct in 1931 came in for some ill-considered criticism at the time, he acted throughout the crisis in a wholly constitutional manner. There has been no opportunity for the Sovereign to exercise similar influence since 1931: there has been only one constitutional crisis and that concerned the monarchy.

The Crown has traditionally taken an especial interest in the armed forces. Edward VII's most useful service was in the further-ance of naval reform. Fisher insisted on being A.D.C. to the King, as well as First Sea Lord in order to have the right of access.[22] Edward's services to the army were less, though he deserves credit for the reform of the medical system,[23] and he gave strong if not unswerving support to Haldane. Haig took care to correspond regularly with George V and enjoyed the King's support throughout the war. When he was purging the generals, Hore-Belisha kept George VI closely informed.[24]

Important though it is, royal concern with military matters is not political influence. Yet still the monarchy regards itself as hav-ing 'higher and other duties' to perform than 'mere representation'. The red boxes still proceed to the Palace. On his accession George VI 'stood appalled at the volume and the nature of the business which emerged day by day from those leather-clad dispatch boxes which inexorably dry the lip of every British sovereign'.[25] The chief argu-ment for the Sovereign absorbing state papers in massive quantities is that in doing so he builds up an unrivalled experience of public affairs which may be of use to his ministers, a view which implies

---

* The distinction was a fine one. On his visit to Naples in 1903 he was incognito, though escorted by eight battleships, four cruisers and eight destroyers.[19]

that a constitutional monarch may not be very effective at the beginning of his reign. But there can be no certainty that constitutional crises will helpfully take place only after the monarch has gained experience; and indeed George V succeeded in the middle of the worst constitutional crisis since 1832. More important, the monarch's experience, or at least that part of it derived from intensive ploughing through state papers, may be of little advantage to his ministers. Queen Victoria had unrivalled experience of public affairs, but the greater her experience the more partisan and extremist she became. Gladstone and Salisbury must have envied Melbourne.

The existence of a person and an institution above and apart from the party struggle has obvious benefits. Whether or not Lloyd George was right in thinking there is no friendship at the top, the monarch provides a valuable and disinterested, as well as utterly discreet, confidant for a Prime Minister. George VI wrote in his diary that Churchill 'tells me, more than people imagine, of his future plans and ideas and only airs them when the time is ripe to his colleagues and the Chiefs of Staff'.[26] Such a relationship is probably not exceptional.

According to Bagehot, 'you cannot argue on your knees'.* Ministers now do not kneel in the Royal presence, nor as in Victoria's reign do they have to remain standing. While treating the monarch with great consideration and respect, they have no inhibitions about arguing. Yet leaving aside all considerations of mystique, the need or the wish to explain decisions and policies to a disinterested observer in the fullest privacy is likely to have influence upon those decisions and policies, especially when the observer has strong views or is able to produce considerations which have been ignored or overlooked. George VI 'was aware that in his talks with ministers he was not infrequently successful in presenting arguments which caused them to reconsider decisions at which they had already arrived . . .'[30]

To gain this influence a monarch need not possess particular prescience or ability, which according to Bagehot is in any case unlikely to be found in an hereditary sovereign. George VI like Attlee, Dalton and Chamberlain, and most of the Tory back-

* Not literally true. When James I lectured the judges on the Royal prerogative, Coke riposted from a kneeling position.[27] Brougham was alleged, probably wrongly, to have delivered the peroration of his speech on the Reform Bill on his knees,[28] and the American shyster lawyer, Howe, once delivered his entire closing speech in defence of a murderer on his knees.[29] However, Coke was shortly afterwards dismissed, the Lords rejected Brougham's views, and Howe's client lost the case and his life.

benchers, was blind enough to favour Halifax to succeed Chamberlain in 1940. The influence a monarch gains is derived not from any innate qualities but from his position.

Confidants are seldom purely passive; they customarily acquire influence. Ministers used to advise the King; now the King advises ministers. According to Templewood, George V's advice was of great value particularly to Macdonald.[31] Morrison found that George VI was no puppet,[32] though if ministers insist the Monarch must give way. The Sovereign's 'silent influence',[33] is not confined to ministers. Edward VII secured the postponement of Fisher's resignation from the Admiralty in 1909.[34] George V prevented Lord Burnham resigning from the Simon Commission.[35] Probably the present Queen had some influence on Sir Humphrey Gibbs continuing to be Governor of Rhodesia. No doubt much of the Sovereign's influence depends upon his being well informed, but how far the requirement of a sound knowledge of affairs depends upon unremitting drudgery among State papers rather than upon other means of information and briefing must remain doubtful. Edward VII's dislike of desk work may have had more behind it than indolence. He concentrated on colour and ceremony. His successors while not neglecting ceremony have reverted to the Albertian tradition of ploughing through the boxes.

Prerogatives

The formal powers of the monarchy have fallen into disuse. The Sovereign can only act on the advice of her ministers and always has to accept that advice. The Royal veto on legislation has not been exercised since Queen Anne. Even before its last exercise in 1707, it was sparingly used. William vetoed five bills, Charles II two. Charles had a better method of preventing legislation he opposed: twice he 'lost' bills which he disliked[36]. This was much less crude than a veto. The Hanoverians refrained from its use not because of any constitutional scruples but because it was not necessary. Down to the Reform Bill, no government could introduce a measure without the King's consent, and in the eighteenth century the House of Lords could usually be relied upon to kill any legislation the government disliked.[37]

Royal dismissal of a ministry has occurred much more recently than a Royal veto, but is no less obsolete. William IV's dismissal of Melbourne and appointment of Peel in 1834 were not unpopular. Peel gained 100 seats at the subsequent election. Yet the move failed.

The King had to take Melbourne back again, and no subsequent monarch has been unwise enough to ignore the precedent. Queen Victoria retained some control over the appointment of ministers, notably Dilke, but none over their dismissal. And while her successors may make suggestions over appointments, their suggestions have no sanction behind them other than good sense. Balfour ignored Edward VII's urgings not to send Arnold Forster to the War Office. George VI believed he was responsible for the Bevin-Dalton switch in 1945, though Attlee denied this.[38] The highest Civil Servants may, like Morrison, have favoured the change and Attlee himself had second thoughts, but the King's wishes appear to have had some influence.

The Sovereign retains some constitutional power over the appointment of a Prime Minister: when the office is vacant there is nobody whose constitutional advice he must follow. But since Queen Victoria's choice of Rosebery, her successors have acted in strict accordance with the advice they received from the retiring Premier or other party leaders. In 1923 the retiring Prime Minister Bonar Law declined to give advice, but Balfour and others recommended Baldwin. The previously informal processes of the Conservative party have occasionally involved the Sovereign in criticism. But both in 1957 and 1963 the advice the Queen received left her no alternative to acting as she did. In 1957 the Labour party decided that only the elected leader of the Parliamentary Labour party may accept the Premiership from the Queen. The Tories have not followed suit, but their new formal process of election seems likely in practice to lead to the same result. In both cases the Queen will wait for a party leader to be elected before making a summons to the Palace.

The power of dissolution has largely but not completely passed from the Monarch to the Prime Minister. King George V was opposed to an election being held immediately after the end of the war, but after his warning had been rejected he had to grant Lloyd George a dissolution. In 1950 the King's then private secretary, Sir Alan Lascelles, wrote a pseudonymous letter to The Times authoritatively setting out the position. 'No wise sovereign . . .' he wrote, 'would deny a dissolution to his Prime Minister unless he was satisfied that: (1) the existing parliament was still vital, viable, and capable of doing its job; (2) a general election would be detrimental to the national economy; (3) he could rely on finding another Prime Minister who could carry on his government for a reasonable period, with a working majority in the House of Commons.'[39]

These conditions mean that a Prime Minister of a minority government cannot rely upon obtaining a dissolution. In 1924 Ramsay Macdonald was reluctantly granted one, only after it had been ascertained that neither Baldwin nor Asquith was prepared to form a government.[40] If a dissolution were refused to a minority government, a dissolution would presumably also, until after a reasonable lapse of time, be refused to its successor. Otherwise the Crown would be criticised for having granted to one party or combination of parties what it had refused to another.

In the normal conditions of majority government, Sir Alan's letter suggests that a Prime Minister will always be granted a dissolution, unless there is a split in his party and another member of it is probably in a position to carry on the government with a working majority in the House of Commons. This happened in South Africa in 1939 when Sir Patrick Duncan refused a dissolution to General Herzog, and a member of the same party, General Smuts, who had opposed a dissolution was able to govern with the support of the majority of the House. In all other cases the refusal of a dissolution would soon put the Crown in the invidious position of having to grant to one side what it had shortly before refused to the other. Party discipline being what it is, no Prime Minister leading a minority party could hope to find a working majority in the House of Commons, and would have to ask for a dissolution or resign. Even if the minority Prime Minister was able to find a working majority, he would be receiving the support of M.P.s who had been elected to support the other side. In any case, therefore, another election would be desirable, and the dissolution more appropriately granted to the previous Prime Minister.

A refusal of a dissolution to a Prime Minister even when the governing party was split, would entail the danger of seeming to interfere in the internal affairs of the party, and no doubt the premier would normally be given the benefit of the doubt. But the granting of a dissolution to a Prime Minister who was clearly opposed by most of his own party as well as by the other parties would almost certainly be wrong, even if a general election would not 'be detrimental to the national economy'. Luckily such a situation is unlikely to arise. For the Prime Minister probably would not have the time or the power to replace the dissident candidates of his party with his own nominees. Hence a dissolution would avail him nothing, and resignation would be the more dignified and likely course.

Yet the Sovereign is the guardian of the constitution. The

Monarch is not bound to sign his own abdication or death warrant if bills to that effect are passed. He is not, in Stockmar's phrase, 'a mandarin figure, which has to nod its head in assent, or shake it in denial, as his Minister pleases'.[41] The prerogative has always contained an element of emergency power, and unquestionably some emergency power remains in the Sovereign personally as opposed to the Crown. If a Prime Minister who had been closely beaten at a general election refused to resign and demanded another dissolution, the Queen would rightly refuse his request and dismiss him. Any analogous attempt by a government to perpetuate itself in power by unconstitutional methods she would similarly frustrate. The monarchy remains 'constitutional' only so long as the government does. Further, or in the alternative, as the lawyers say, the monarchy is under a duty not to consent to something that is contrary to its whole reason for existence. Thus the Queen would not be obliged to take up the contemptible position of Victor Emmanuel while a British Mussolini subverted the constitution. As the representative of the British people and the guardian of legitimacy, the Sovereign would fail in his duty if he gave protective colouring to the establishment of a party dictatorship, and by his consent gave constitutional sanction to a quite illegitimate break in the continuity of British history.

But if these contingent and safeguarding powers still remain in the monarchy, they only come into operation on an occasion of the direst emergency. Only if the whole fabric of the constitution were threatened, would the Sovereign be right to intervene. Royal action would be necessary and defensible only if the party in power abandoned the British parliamentary tradition and opted for a dictatorship. That is why the various expedients urged on George V during the Home Rule crisis—the revival of the veto, the dismissal of the government and the appointment of a caretaker administration—were all rightly rejected.

The contingent powers of the Crown may only be used to prevent unconstitutional action and to preserve the constitution. Their use at any other time would be unconstitutional, and instead of the constitution being preserved the monarchy would be destroyed. In fact, their use at any time would almost certainly mean the end of the monarchy. A dictator would be unlikely to accept his dismissal from the Queen. It would be she who was dismissed, yet the unconstitutional nature of the régime would have been starkly revealed. The British throne has survived through its willingness to evacuate the last ditch. There is only one real last ditch for the monarchy: an indisputable threat to the constitution.

Whatever Queen Victoria thought, and despite those red boxes, 'mere representation' is now 'the highest' of the Monarch's duties. Mostly, the Queen does not do interesting things. Opening hospitals and schools and laying foundation stones are surely in themselves the least interesting functions imaginable. The Queen brings interest to them, not they to her. She goes on tour at home and abroad, but her foreign tours excite less interest than they did. George III never went abroad. Victorian England was sometimes like present day Washington. 'We are overrun with visiting royalties present and prospective,' wrote Greville in 1857. 'It is a new feature of the present day, the flitting about of royal personages.'[42] George V refused to flit about. His view was that 'state visits have ceased to be of any political importance. . . .'[43] At the present time, of course, visits by Presidents and Prime Ministers are of considerable political importance to those who take part in them. To be seen as either the guest or the host of a prominent foreign leader is likely to have gratifying electoral results. But the Queen does not have to worry about votes; and whether or not her state visits expand or contract, she is liable to find her role of roving ambassador increasingly superseded by Prime Ministers who have learned that votes in Bootle and Margate may be harvested on the Ganges, in the Kremlin, or even by a well-timed visit to Balmoral.

The Queen can successfully compete with the Prime Minister or anybody else on great family occasions. When the Queen's third baby was expected, the comings and goings of her midwife, Sister Rowe, excited more public interest than the return of the Prime Minister, Mr. Macmillan, from Africa. And in general the Queen and her family remain a subject of consuming, if declining, interest to millions of people both here and abroad. Lord Holland complained that the return of Queen Caroline to England excited more public interest than the death of Grattan. 'Such is the happy effect of that beautiful institution called Monarchy, and such the disposition of that enlightened nation called England. A man of consummate wisdom . . . dies in the morning and an ugly mad woman . . . lands in the afternoon—not ten people in the metropolis think twice of the first melancholy event, and the whole world from the Prime Minister to the scavenger in the streets are occupied and agitated at the second.'[44] Admirable Whiggish sentiments! But the likely alternative to public interest in the Royal family is an enhanced interest not in White Papers and the deliberations of statesmen, but in people and matters even less acceptable to Holland House than Queen Caroline.

Like any other representative the Queen is sometimes abused.* In the fifties some of the criticism fastened on to the Queen's liking for horse racing. Disraeli's Mr. Rigby expressed the opinion that 'as for loyalty, if the present King went regularly to Ascot races, he had no doubt all would go right'.[46] Edward VII thought much the same. He told his mother that it was better by his patronage 'to elevate' a national sport than 'to win the approval of Lord Shaftesbury and the Low Church party' by staying away.[47] His popularity suggests he was right, though Victoria remained unconvinced. In fact, considerable interest attaches to the Queen when she is 'off duty', attending race meetings or polo matches. She is more visible on such occasions to more people both on the spot and on television than when she is carrying out some municipal ceremony; and a person who occasionally enjoys herself in public is far more human and appealing than one who doesn't. Mr. Rigby was a better judge than the modern puritan. To symbolise personality at the heart of the state, the Queen must represent leisure as well as work.

As the representative of the people as well as the state, the Queen is in the difficulty that people do not want the Royal family to be an exact replica of their own families or lives, while at the same time they do not want it to be so utterly different as to lose all connection with them. 'Bicycle monarchies' are one answer to the problem, but they lose much in pageantry and spectacle. The Royal family's solution, intentional or otherwise, has been to be in material matters a Rolls Royce monarchy and in moral matters a bicycle one. 'Royalty and virtue,' in Lytton Strachey's phrase,[48] has been the formula. They live in fine materialistic state without vulgar ostentation, while seeking to embody in their private lives the worthiest domestic virtues.

Certainly no amount of bicycling in material matters would save the monarchy if the Sovereign led a Rolls Royce moral life. Edward VII's humorous custom of pouring wine and brandy down the neck of

---

* Mr. Art Buchwald once pointed out that 'a portion of the British popular press has been as rough on Britain's Royal family as any press in the world including the Russian press'.[45]

his friends[49] would at best today be considered intolerably wasteful, and some of his other habits not wholly endearing. The inflexible moral code and the solid bourgeois virtues of George V, George VI and the present Queen have defied the censure of even the most pharisaic of their subjects. As a result of their efforts the Royal family is pictured as the representative and ideal of British family life, and the abdication of Edward VIII and one or two minor scandals on the Royal fringes are shrugged off as trifling blemishes or as pieces of shade which heighten the light in the centre of the picture.

'A king,' wrote Selden,[50] 'is a thing men have made for their own sakes, for quietness' sake . . .', a remark that in the seventeenth century was if not seditious at least incautious.* But today the remark, if questionable on the origins of kingship, is in essence true, and is both the cause and the defence of the monarchy. The Queen and the Royal family give pleasure and satisfaction to millions of her subjects. That by itself would be enough. But they have a higher justification. Free government lasts better with a King than with a President.

---

* Selden's *Table Talk* was not published until long after his death.

PART THREE

THE CONTEXT OF POLITICS

I

LOCAL GOVERNMENT

I wish there was no such thing as local government.

LORD SALISBURY in 1886[1]

Everything is true about local government, and so nothing is true.

J. A. G. GRIFFITH[2]

The theory has been advanced that the Age of Frustration is also marked by an interest in local politics. It is now known, however, that men enter local politics solely as a result of being unhappily married.

C. NORTHCOTE PARKINSON[3]

In *Coningsby*, Disraeli envisaged 'a vast pile of municipal and local government'.[4] Like the rest of Coningsby's imaginings, it did not materialise. Instead of a vast pile, there has been only a sprawl. Local government has not been a palace or a pyramid, merely a suburb and never a modern one. At present, indeed, its eccentric layout, air of neglect and old world charm give pleasure to some of its inhabitants and to occasional antiquarians, but its muddle and resistance to change lead to its being increasingly ignored by the outside world, which thunders down the main road beyond. Naturally, there have been periodic reforms, but none of them has ever caught up with the present, let alone looked to the future. In local government the anomalous is the normal. The present and the future are anachronisms; only the past exists.

For most of the nineteenth century local government in Britain was more functional than territorial. Though the Municipal Corporations Act of 1835 brought representative government to the towns, elsewhere particular tasks were assigned to different *ad hoc* authorities. Local government became territorial in 1888 with the creation of elected county councils, and in 1894 district and parish councils followed. South of the Tees the boundaries of the counties were largely those already in existence in the time of Ethelred the Unready. The passage of a thousand years had apparently made them indelible. The more modern divisions that were inserted in the bill were no less unsuitable. The original intention was for the county

327

councils to be set over all other units of local government save the largest towns; in committee, however, all towns of over 50,000 inhabitants were excluded from the counties and made county boroughs. This separation of town from country, barely suitable for the age of the bicycle, has survived substantially unchanged into the age of the motor car and aeroplane.

Neville Chamberlain in his Local Government Act of 1929, which, according to Jennings,[5] was fully understood by only two men in the House of Commons (Chamberlain himself and Sidney Webb), produced substantial rationalisation and reform but left the division between town and country untouched. The Attlee government set up a Local Government Boundary Commission whose proposals were too radical for Aneurin Bevan, and the Commission was abolished. In 1958 the Conservatives set up another Commission. In the conurbations it had some freedom of action and made some improvements, though its reports were uneven. Elsewhere, however, the Commission could only consider boundaries and not functions, and its proposals were virtually valueless. All it could recommend was the juggling of boundaries between city and county, the unmaking of a county borough here, the amalgamation of an administrative county there.

The expansion of towns at the expense of their surrounding counties, encouraged by the 1958 act, was occasionally reminiscent of eighteenth century war and diplomacy. Like eighteenth century rulers, city leaders lived in peace with the rulers of the county until they were given an opportunity to add to their dominions by capturing a slice of county territory. Then like Frederick the Great seizing Silesia or Louis XV occupying Lorraine, they struck and captured a valuable piece of the county. All the time of course the city leaders disclaimed any intention of harming their county neighbours. Like Maria Theresa they cried—and they took. These wars of aggrandisement were as irrelevant to the real needs of the inhabitants of the threatened areas as the dynastic quarrels of two hundred years ago. They were also profoundly unpopular. And because of its restricted terms of reference, the Commission's proposals were usually irrelevant to the needs of the next decades. Uniquely, therefore, they contrived to offend against the past, the present, and the future. They threatened to destroy the identity of genuine communities. They trifled with the wishes of the people involved. And they were bound themselves to be overthrown in a short space of time.

This absurd rigmarole was thrust upon the Commission by the act which created it, and was not the fault of its members. The Commission was not empowered to revive local government. All it could do was to dissect the corpse and laboriously rearrange the limbs. The Labour government rightly wound up the Commission, but characteristically appointed another.

Following a Royal Commission appointed by the Conservatives, the London Government Act of 1963 half reformed the government of the capital, despite the strong opposition of a Labour party outraged by the threatened slaughter of one of its most revered and venerable cows, the London County Council.* With the abolition of the L.C.C. in favour of a Greater London Council comprising a larger area, the government of London became less archaic than local government in the rest of the country, but the area was still the wrong size and the fundamental manner of government was left unaltered.

Twenty years after the war local government outside London was almost the same as it had been in 1945. Indeed not only had it not changed for the better despite the overwhelming evidence that its structure was obsolete; in one important respect the situation had changed for the worse. During the war an intricate and, on the whole, efficient system of regional administration grew up. There was nothing elective about this regionalism. The regional commissioners were appointed by the Prime Minister, and the administrators were civil servants. Yet had the organisation survived, elective regional government might have been grafted on to it. Regrettably, however, the regional commissions were abolished, and the chance for reform was lost.

The characteristics of British local government are multiplicity, pauperism, amateurism, anonymity and impotence. In England and Wales, apart from Greater London, there are 58 counties and 82 county boroughs. France, a much larger country and with only a

* Labour's opposition had its more practical aspect. Whereas the old L.C.C. had a virtually permanent Labour majority, the new G.L.C. seemed likely to have a similarly permanent Conservative majority. However, the Tory government allowed some of the outlying Tory areas to contract out of the new body and thus succeeded in gerrymandering the boundaries against their own side. This remarkable altruism or negligence lessened Labour opposition to the measure and produced a Labour majority at the first election of the new body.

slightly smaller population, makes do with 90 departments. As well as the counties and the county boroughs there are 275 non county boroughs, 547 urban districts and 473 rural districts. There are therefore 1,412 housing authorities, 161 education authorities, 174 planning authorities, and 997 authorities responsible for highways. Plainly, this collection of petty principalities is no more likely to add up to efficient government than was the Holy Roman Empire. And it does not.

Unlike the Holy Roman Empire, however, the various princedoms are financially dependent upon the centre. This is a direct outcome of the fragmentation of local government. Practically no local taxation, other than rates, is feasible under the present system. Because of the division between town and country many people live and work in different places. This makes a local sales tax difficult, or impossible. And the proliferation of authorities rules out a local income tax. As a result, while local authorities in 1968 spent some £5,250 million, about a third of all public expenditure, more than half their income was made up of grants from the central government. This financial subjection to Whitehall in turn ensures that a local authority is seldom able to withstand the central government on an important issue.

The fragmentation of local government makes it vulnerable to more than financial control from Whitehall. The capacity of large authorities to run their own affairs is greater than that of smaller ones. But the survival of small units—Rutland has roughly one hundredth of the population of Lancashire—gives government departments the excuse to interfere in all authorities of every size. The classic technique of imperial government is: divide and rule. Whitehall has used the technique even more successfully at home. By keeping local government units small and fragmented, central government control is ensured.

The labyrinth has been manned by amateurs, an expensive luxury. Many unpaid councillors have neither the time nor the experience to run local government. Thus decisions are taken by the permanent officials. And as there is no paid political executive, committees are the natural form of organisation. Unpaid councillors cannot be expected to travel long distances to sit on numerous committees, and so local authority areas have been kept small. The price therefore of keeping professional politicians out of local government is the transfer of power to the permanent officials, the imposition of an inefficient committee system, and the maintenance of unworkably small areas.

Such a system cannot excite public interest. Many councillors are shadowy figures even to those who bother to vote in local elections. The anonymity is greatly aggravated by the committee system. Committees are intrinsically anonymous, and local government committees particularly so. They usually sit in private, and people cannot be expected to know who are the members of the various committees and sub-committees. Anonymity deadens public interest, and public boredom reinforces anonymity.

The impotence of local government necessarily follows from its other attributes. Fragmentation, part-time amateurism, lack of public interest, individual and collective anonymity and financial dependence—any one of them would probably be sufficient to emasculate local government. In combination they are invincible.

Yet against local government's obvious defects, must be set some merits. It is probably less corrupt than in most countries. It is also an impressive witness to the tradition of voluntary service. Thousands of people devote a great deal of unrewarded time to working for their local community. In 1886 Salisbury said that local government was 'a very good thing', because 'it gets rid of the harshness and unbending woodenness which is the character of all governments which are directed exclusively from the centre'.[6] Local government, if the voting figures are any guide, has conspicuously failed to engage the affections or the enthusiasm of those it exists to serve, but by remaining close to the grass roots and city pavements, it has done something to vary the 'unbending woodenness' of the central government and to make government in its lower regions less impersonal and remote.

Reform

Nevertheless local government is the sick man of England. The sickness is not specifically British; the epidemic is almost world wide. There are few countries whose system of local government is not markedly inferior to their central political system. Yet the illness in Britain has been obvious for years. Nearly a century and a half ago Bentham suggested that all the multiplex authorities should be reduced to the Poor Law Union and the County. He thought places like Liverpool and Manchester should absorb the surrounding countryside and become counties in themselves.[7] Bentham was writing before Manchester was represented in parliament, yet the dichotomy between town and country still exists. Lloyd George's proposals for a coalition in 1910 called for the

creation of adequate regional bodies.[8] Churchill told the Select
Committee on Procedure in 1931 that he favoured 'considerable
changes in the direction of devolution to local bodies much larger
in scale than any that exist, or almost any that exist, in the country
at the present time'.[9] Radical reform, therefore, would hardly be
rushing things.

The two fundamental needs for local government are larger
units and enhanced public interest. Larger units would make it
more efficient and also enable it to stand up to Whitehall. London
and to a lesser extent Birmingham have shown how a powerful city
can challenge the central government.

The boundaries of the present economic planning regions are not
ideal, but for England they provide the obvious basis for a system
of regional government. In its evidence to the Royal Commission
on Local Government, however, Whitehall favoured the creation
of thirty or forty 'city regions', though without producing a
serious argument against 'the heptarchy' or the present regions.[10]
Thirty or forty city regions represent the minimum decentralisation
that Whitehall thinks it can get away with, and the maximum that
will not threaten its dominance. Yet the expression 'city region'
is misleading. The country does not possess thirty to forty regions,
and these so called city regions would produce not regional
government but a glorified municipalisation with Whitehall remaining in full control. If England is to have genuine regional government, the number of regions should be about eight to twelve.

The need for enhanced public interest is manifest. In 1967 the
electoral turn-out was lower in Greater London than in Municipal
Boroughs and Urban Districts and not appreciably higher than in
County Boroughs or the Counties. The year before, as many as
one third of Londoners did not know what the initials G.L.C. stood
for, and even when told the meaning they failed to understand
what that local authority was. Only one in fifty could name one of
his representatives on the council.[11] Plainly a rationalisation of
boundaries and the creation of regional or semi-regional bodies are
not sufficient to arouse public interest. The undergrowth of committees, sub-committees, aldermen, indirect elections and all the
traditional mumbo-jumbo of local government cut it off from the
voters.

Evidently something more is necessary: nothing less indeed than
a fundamental change in the whole manner of local government.
Its present defects could be repaired by one simple revolution. In

place of amateurism, anonymity, indirect election of the mayor, the committee system and the rest of the ritual, should be substituted direct election by the voters of the chief executive. Such an innovation would not only rescue local government from decision making by unelected officials, from the inefficient committee system, and from obscurity and public indifference, but would also be far more suitable for the administration of larger units. There would of course be a council as well, but the executive responsibility would be in the hands of the directly elected governor or mayor.

An executive form of government instead of a legislative committee form is a necessity. In France the mayor, though indirectly elected, has real power; direct elections are not necessary there because polls in local elections are usually high. In America directly elected mayors with councils run about forty per cent of towns with over 10,000 people, and city managers run another forty per cent of them.[12] The likely alternative to an elective executive system in Britain is a non-elective executive system: city managers appointed to run cities. Genuine representative local government would surely be far preferable.

Direct elections would bring back public interest. Local government would be dramatised and first class candidates attracted. The electorate would tend to vote on local issues instead of, as now, on national ones. Moreover such a set-up would facilitate the imposition of genuine regional government. Directly elected governors could impose some degree of political identity on large areas. Beneath the region there would have to be another tier. This, too, should have directly elected and paid executives.

The principal objection to these proposals is that they would produce something quite different from what the country has had before. But for years the situation has cried out for an upheaval. 'Considering the circumstances in which the country finds itself,' a Spanish conservative once said, 'the most conservative thing is to be a revolutionary'.[13] The same is true of British local government. Only a revolution will preserve it.

At present, British government is out of balance. Because local government is too small, central government is too big. Because local authorities are so fractional and competitive, decisions have to be taken by the central government. As a result, the decisions are often wrong. Ministers and Civil Servants are overworked and under-informed. By making local government bigger and more powerful, the central government would be made less bloated and more fitted for its central tasks.

But the case for devolution and regionalism does not rest on mere grounds of inefficiency. People want a greater say in the running of their own affairs. They feel cut off from the South East and neglected by it. They want to decide matters for themselves in their own areas and not to have solutions handed down from above. This frustration is most conspicuous in the Celtic fringe but not confined to it.

Unfortunately the urge for decentralisation is confronted by the well known regional paradox: centralisation helps the poorer regions. Almost by definition the most discontented regions are the poorest. By imposing uniform standards of social and other services, the central government subsidises the outlying areas at the expense of the centre. Centralisation and unity permit the pursuit of a 'regional' policy producing some degree of uniformity in all parts of the country. Without that unity, uniformity of services would disappear. Hence independence for the poorer regions would widen the gap between them and South Eastern England.*

Though figures are hard to come by, Scotland and Wales seem manifestly poorer than the South East or than England as a whole. Full independence would therefore entail an appreciable fall in the standard of living and the social services of Scotland and Wales. The power of the purse, which the Scottish and Welsh Nationalists always demand, would probably mean a much smaller purse. The zealots of the S.N.P. and Plaid Cymru are prepared to face this, but if the economic consequences of independence were widely known, their less fervent supporters would not similarly put a seat at the U.N. before butter.

A federation would solve this difficulty while creating other ones. The participating states would not have the power of the purse, and the richer states could subsidise the poorer. Even in America, which tolerates a greater diversity in prosperity than would probably be acceptable in Britain, New York pays out $3 for every $1 of Federal aid it receives, while Arkansas receives $2.50 for every $1 it gives.[14] But if the centre is going to subsidise the nations and provinces on

---

* In Spain on the other hand the areas which claim independence, Catalonia and the Basque country, are demonstrably richer and more advanced than Castile and the rest of the country. Economically they would have little to lose from a slackening of ties with the centre.

the periphery, there are severe limits to the amount of independence which it would find tolerable. Besides the federal principle, defined by Professor Wheare as 'the method of dividing powers so that the general and regional governments are each within a sphere co-ordinate and independent',[15] is not easily workable, even when conditions are favourable; and neither the nature of the constitution nor the imbalance between the different countries makes Britain an ideal laboratory for a federal expreiment. Federalism is usually thought to necessitate a second chamber in which the constituent elements in the federation enjoy virtually equal representation, and for England to have the same representation as Wales or Northern Ireland would seem scarcely rational. Admittedly there is a greater disproportion between New York and Nevada, but such a discrepancy is more defensible in an assembly of fifty states than in one of four. Also a federal Britain would either require a separate English Parliament or produce complications about Celtic representation in the Lower House. Federalism may occasionally be necessary to achieve or preserve union. It should be used only as a last resort.

All this does not mean that considerable devolution to Scotland and Wales and to the English regions is not possible and desirable. Both Scotland and Wales want their own parliament. This is an entirely legitimate demand by proud and ancient countries, and there seems no earthly reason why it should be denied. Scottish and Welsh parliaments on the Northern Ireland model would be a proper concession to national self-respect and might well achieve a resurgence of national energy. As in England, the need is for larger units and increased public interest. The creation of parliaments would do much to meet both objectives.*

Scottish and Welsh parliaments would be good in themselves. Opponents of the idea should ponder the history of Irish Nationalism, and may then conclude that at its lowest this would be a sensible way of calming much of the nationalist agitation. Anybody who disdains nationalist movements as retrograde tribalism can preserve his lofty metropolitan superiority by adopting the attitude of Carlyle: 'Oh, if in National Palaver (as the Africans name it) such blessedness is verily found, what tyrant would deny it to Son of

* The Scots and the Welsh would decide their own form of local government, but presumably city regions or even smaller units would be convenient. A Scottish parliament could scarcely be imposed on top of, say, three large Scottish regions, nor a Welsh parliament on top of two Welsh ones. Conciliar congestion would be altogether excessive.

Adam! Nay, might not there be a Female Parliament too, with "screams from the opposition benches", and "the honourable member borne out in hysterics"? To a Children's Parliament would I gladly consent; or even lower if ye wished it.'[16] That would seem to let in the Scots and the Welsh.

Local Government and the Political System

Despite local selection of candidates and single member constituencies, parish pump politics have been largely avoided at Westminster. For this the rotten and pocket boroughs deserve most of the credit. In the fifteenth century residence in the constituency was enjoined by law but not strictly observed, and by the later Elizabethan years the law was flouted and the great majority of borough members were already country gentlemen.[17] In seventeenth century Reading it was thought that 'a stranger can be no friend to this town',[18] and many places selected local men. But a member could hardly busy himself with the interests of such a place as Old Sarum, let alone live there. It existed only at election time. The franchise of most other boroughs was so indefensible that a member was bound to claim like Burke that he was a Member of Parliament rather than a Member for his particular town. Even when it was possible, many M.P.s would not have been prepared to live in their constituencies. 'Though I have the honour to represent Bristol,' said Burke, 'I should not like to live there; I should be obliged to be so much upon my good behaviour.'[19] Hence there could be no locality rule as there has been in America, and, in one way or another, in Denmark and Sweden. And in Britain, unlike America and France, there have never been indirect elections to a second chamber, which help to bind local and central government together.

As a result local politics have remained more separate from national politics than in almost any other country. In the Belgian parliament of 1950 all but one of the representatives were engaged in local government.[20] In France prominent deputies have often been the mayors of the largest town in their constituencies. M. Herriot was Mayor of Lyons for fifty years, M. Mollet Mayor of Arras, M. Mendès-France Mayor of Louviers, M. Pflimlin Mayor of Strasbourg. In the French Assembly of 1958 there were 58 mayors.

Joseph Chamberlain made his name as Mayor of Birmingham and also did much to make the city. As he himself claimed, it was 'parked, paved, assized, marketed, gas-and-watered, and improved all as a result of three years' active work'.[21] His son Neville was also

Mayor of Birmingham, a post which Lloyd George thought suitably matched his talents. Attlee was Mayor of Stepney, Herbert Morrison was for many years boss of the L.C.C., and Henry Brooke was a prominent Tory who came up through local government. But the frequent divergence between constituency boundaries and those of local government bodies and the greater strength of party have discouraged most British M.P.s from digging themselves into their constituencies by becoming mayors or other functionaries. About forty-five per cent of Labour and about thirty-five per cent of Tory M.P.s have experience of local government, a difference accounted for by the much greater participation in local government of trade union M.P.s.[22] But once elected, most British politicians devote their entire attention to national politics. They do not neglect their constituency, but leave its government to others.

The divorce between national and local politics has prevented single member constituencies from becoming 'the stagnant pools' that Briand complained of in France.[23] Almost certainly local government reforms would not alter this situation. The units would be too big to prime many parish pumps. They would strengthen local politics without localising national politics. Yet plainly the whole political system would be affected.

If the present economic planning regions became political units, then on the 1964 election figures when the parties were nearly equal, four regions would be safely Labour; three, including by far the largest, the South East, would be safely Tory and one, the West Midlands, would be marginal. Probably, however, voters would soon start to behave differently in regional elections to national elections, as happens in Germany and indeed in the United States. If they did not behave differently, the prevailing pattern of one-party areas would produce a strong case for primary elections. But whatever their voting habits, powerful centres of political, as well as governmental, influence would be built up outside London. Just as government would be less dominated by Whitehall, so the parties would be less dominated by Smith Square. There would be fruitful interchange and conflict between national and regional politics. Politicians could move from one to the other and back again, and political leadership would not be solely situated in London. The diffusion of power would probably reduce the cohesiveness of the parliamentary parties enough to increase public interest in parliament, yet not enough to threaten the stability of government. A dispersal of the Civil Service would be no less valuable.

The reform of local government would thus bring great fringe benefits to the political system. But it is for its own sake that reform is imperative. Britain is one of the most centralised countries in the world, administratively, culturally, journalistically, politically. This over-metropolitanisation of British life produces resentment on the periphery and inefficiency in London. A sensible system of local government, by lessening the strain on the heart and clearing the congestion in the lungs, would improve the blood circulation in the body and enable the whole country to breathe more freely.

II

INTEREST GROUPS

An association for political, commercial, or manufacturing purposes, or even for those of science and literature, is a powerful and enlightened member of the community, which cannot be disposed of at pleasure or oppressed without remonstrance; and which, by defending its own rights against the encroachments of the government, saves the common liberties of the country.

ALEXIS DE TOCQUEVILLE[1]

If, then, the general will is to be truly expressed, it is essential that there be no subsidiary groups within the State, and that each citizen voice his own opinion and nothing but his own opinion.

J. J. ROUSSEAU[2]

The Russian system is not really a revolutionary departure from our own. We are governed more by trade unions, co-operative societies, professional associations of doctors and lawyers, the judicial bench, the committees of the Privy Council, the bureaucracy, and by Boards of all sorts than by the Houses of Parliament.

BERNARD SHAW[3]

Britain has always been a Rousseau-ist nightmare. Partial societies of every kind proliferate and prosper. Cricket clubs and dart teams, trade unions and business associations, local government bodies and propagandist committees, churches and philanthropic societies, national campaigns and women's institutes, councils of animal defenders and leagues against other people's pleasures decorate and diversify the social and political landscape. Many of these groups rarely have anything to do with politics. But if an organised group is taken to be one which tries to exert influence on the government without seeking to take over the government, then about half the people in this country belong to an organised group—many to more than one—and they are, knowingly or unknowingly, willingly or unwillingly, in some sense represented by it. Their participation in the political process is thus not confined to what Carlyle called the 'liberty to send your fifty-thousandth part of a new Tongue-fencer into National Debating Club'.[4]

Not long ago interest groups were ignored; now they are sometimes used to explain everything about the government of a country from its political structure to its constitutional traditions and ideals. According to one school, dating back to Bentley's 'Process of Government', the entire political system consists of the activity of interest groups. The failure of interest groups always to get their way is accounted for by the existence of 'potential' interest groups. These potential interest groups, which represent 'widely held but unorganised interests', bring counter pressure to bear both on actual interest groups and on the government, and their presence is the explanation of 'the rules of the game' and the constitutional conduct of government.[5]

Professor Popper once likened the conspiracy theory of society, the belief that 'sinister pressure groups . . . are to be blamed for having planned the great depression and all the evils from which we suffer', to Homer's conception that 'whatever happened on the plain before Troy was only a reflection of the various conspiracies on Olympus'.[6] By humanising, not deifying, 'the rules of the game', and bringing them to life as potential interest groups, the followers of Bentley have produced a counter to the conspiracy theory, and made the activities of pressure groups fully legitimate. This neo-animism is often illuminating. But it is more than a trifle metaphysical, and theories which explain everything also in a sense explain nothing. Group activity is part of the political process, not the whole explanation of it.

Certainly the activities of organised groups* loom large in the political system. As government has grown bigger, so have interest groups and secondary powers. The country has become 'urbanised' politically as well as geographically. Instead of the scattered clusters of individuals in a 'rural' society, great cities of individuals have been formed. Government spends much time in negotiating with or consulting interests. In addition to the political system consisting of the discussion of policies in parliament, there has grown up a 'diplomatic' system consisting of talks in Whitehall between the government and the ambassadors of groups. Although the government pays attention to the views of M.P.s, parliament is largely excluded from this diplomatic roundabout.

* There seems no reason why single organisations should be considered separately from groups. Single organisations have a job of their own to do and are not solely concerned with securing favourable decisions from government or helping their members, and they are often not subject to the same rules as groups. But an enormous corporation, nationalised or private, commonly acts in a similar way to a trade association. What De Tocqueville called 'secondary powers' are not necessarily groups.

All the same, groups conform to the political system more than they shape it. There is no inherent reason why organised groups and interests should largely by-pass Westminster and head for Whitehall. In America and in many countries on the continent the legislature as well as the executive is the target of interest groups. British pressure groups largely operate in and on Whitehall, because it is there and not in the Commons that the relevant decisions are made. But the groups have not downgraded parliament. The party and electoral systems have determined the place of both parliament and the groups, and if the scope of parliament is circumscribed so is that of the groups.

The political system prevents organised groups from electing Members of Parliament. Only the political parties can do that. With the Trade Unions and the Co-operative Party forming two of the three constituent elements of the Labour party, there can be no rigid differentiation of status between an interest group and a political party. But there is a differentiation of function. As the secretary of the T.U.C. Mr. Woodcock once put it, 'the Labour party's job is to get votes. Our job is to get wages'.[7] Many candidates are sponsored and in effect selected by Trade Unions or the Co-operative Party, but they stand as Labour candidates who happen to be members of Trade Unions or the Co-op; and if they are elected their allegiance is to the parliamentary Labour party, not to their union. Even when their sponsoring body is in direct conflict with the Labour leadership as was the Co-op over S.E.T., and the Transport and General Workers' Union over the Prices and Incomes Act, the 'loyal' course of a sponsored M.P. is to support the party and the 'rebellious' one to support the sponsor. The Unions and the Co-op may be borough-mongers, but they do not break the monopoly of the political parties in parliament.

Other groups are further removed from the electoral process. After the first war one ex-serviceman's organisation, the National Federation, put up several candidates but all of them failed. The only ex-serviceman's candidate successful in 1918 or at any other election was a crypto-Conservative.[8] The National Farmers' Union came out in 1917 for Proportional Representation, and in the election of 1918 it sponsored six 'agricultural' candidates, all of whom lost. In 1922 it elected four members,[9] but these, like the ex-serviceman's candidate and all the other members sponsored by the Union between the wars, were Conservatives. The N.F.U. has not used its political fund since 1945. The candidate of an organised group

M

will not be elected unless he carries the *imprimatur* of one of the major parties.

The restrictions on electoral expenditure and the illegality of buying time on television still further diminish the electoral importance of groups. They can give money to party headquarters, and small sums to individual candidates. But, with some obvious Trade Union exceptions, few if any M.P.s owe their election to the donations or support of interest groups. They owe it to their possession of the party label.

And general elections and by-elections form in Britain the whole of the electoral process. Additional democratic trimmings, on which pressure groups and P.R. men thrive in some other countries, are here unknown. In California a voter may have the opportunity to make a decision on anything up to twenty different questions at one election. These proposals are put forward as a rule by interest groups, and the voter is influenced not by party but by public relations firms.* The most famous of these, Whitaker and Baxter, had by 1956 been successful on behalf of their clients in 90 per cent of the seventy-five contests in which they had been engaged.[11] Over here, there being no referenda, no initiatives, no recalls, no primary elections, the electoral process is virtually closed to groups. This determines their relations with M.P.s, and prevents them from colonising the House of Commons.

Diligent researches are made into M.P.s' connections with outside interests. Their directorships are tabulated, their subsidies from Trade Unions listed, and their previous activities detailed. Trade Union sponsorship and the part time tradition of the House of Commons, which enables Members to retain outside jobs, keep the number of lawyers in parliament lower than in most representative assemblies. Consequently more M.P.s are connected in their extra-political life with interest groups than are, say, American congressmen, though the connection is less prevalent here than in countries like Finland, Holland or Switzerland, where interest groups are not similarly excluded from the electoral process.

* Sir Denis Brogan 'once weighed on the bathroom scales the literature issued to the voters to enable them to decide on propositions affecting the county of San Francisco and the state of California. This literature weighed nearly a pound, it was printed in small and bad type and would have involved several days' close study before any citizen could have rationally made up his mind as to what his duty was'.[10]

Interest groups have not colonised parliament, but M.P.s like everybody else carry their own colonies with them. 'I am glad to have found a superman,' Ernest Bevin once flayed Lord Devonport, 'who can abstract himself from his 280,000 shares in Kearley and Tonge and the Independent Tea Stores . . . who can abstract himself from any of these influences and look after the interests of the great public. . . .'[12] Few M.P.s are supermen, and they mainly eschew abstraction. But nearly all are politicians first and representatives of interest groups second. Those M.P.s who are there chiefly to further their own financial interests seldom gain political influence, and are of no political importance.

Interests directly represented by M.P.s do not seem to fare better than those which rely on indirect representation. The British Union for the Abolition of Vivisection once expressed regret that 'out of 630 M.P.s, not a single one can be elected solely to represent the interests of animals'.[13] Yet sometimes all 600 seem to have been elected solely to represent the interests of animals. The animal lobby is one of the most successful and certainly does not suffer from not having an animal to represent it in the House. Unions which make a practice of sponsoring M.P.s do not secure more governmental favours than Unions which spend their funds in other ways. The twenty-seven M.P.s sponsored by the Transport and General Workers' Union were no particular help to that Union's opposition to the government's statutory wage freeze. Big business does not appear to have been caused undue hardship through most business representation in the House coming from small businessmen.

Owing their allegiance and their seats to party, M.P.s can safely ignore the importunities of organised groups. They can conciliate them, express sympathy, or offer to put their case for them. They can try to enlist the support of others. But this sympathy can rarely be expressed in the lobbies. While the Co-operative movement fulminated against Mr. Callaghan's Selective Employment Tax, the eighteen Co-operative M.P.s dutifully voted for it. They formed a deputation or two in protest; their vote was not involved. Except in the rare free votes, an M.P.s vote is not up for auction. Even definite and explicit election pledges are of no avail against the Whips. At the 1945 election 199 Labour M.P.s gave pledges to the Friendly Societies.[14] All of them broke them. Organised groups know that M.P.s are incorruptible or, on a harsher view, have already been corrupted by their party.

But interest groups can influence governments by influencing backbenchers, who in turn bring pressure to bear on their front bench. Most groups, however, show themselves remarkably deficient in the arts of party persuasion. Although M.P.s are bombarded with literature and propaganda of all sorts, these are usually a waste of the organisation's time and money. Knowing that M.P.s are most easily influenced through their constituencies, many organisations, especially religious and animal ones, organise postal campaigns. Printed cards and *pro forma* letters instigated by such bodies as the Anti-Vivisection Society or the Union of Catholic Mothers flood into the House of Commons.

When the vote is free and a Member has no strong views, these campaigns may have some influence. A few years ago the motor cycle lobby evinced surprising political strength. Lancashire M.P.s may be affected by the reminder that the Roman Catholic vote in their constituencies is heavy. Other M.P.s may decide as a result of their post bag to stay away from a division they would not otherwise have missed. But to most M.P.s these synthetic postal campaigns are only an irritation. They know the implied threats of electoral retribution are fraudulent. Groups cannot deliver the votes of their members. The great majority of voters are not sufficiently dominated by their group allegiance to penalise an M.P. for defying the group, even if they remember the incident at the next election—which they rarely do.

The most effective way of bringing constituency pressure to bear on Members is an approach by a few influential constituents. But such activity when retailed to the annual gathering of the group would seem less imposing to the group's members than a postal campaign, and most groups seem to think impressing their membership more important than influencing parliament.

On current issues groups usually prefer to deal direct with the government. Instead of themselves being intermediaries, they regard backbench M.P.s as intermediaries and unwelcome intruders. Arthur Deakin told his Union not to think 'you are going to get an advantage by people asking questions in parliament affecting your collective agreements, conditions of employment and those things which are more properly dealt with by the Union on the industrial level . . .'[15] The B.M.A. also by-passes medical M.P.s. Similarly, Dr. McI. Johnson, himself a publisher, when trying to help the book trade over the Restrictive Practices Bill, found the matter had been agreed between the government and the publishers without his having been informed, far less consulted.[16]

Of course the relevant groups have been in touch with the Minister long before a bill reaches parliament. Lloyd George was the first minister openly to consult the interests when preparing a bill. 'We consulted,' he said, 'the whole shipping interest and got very admirable assistance from them as to what they would like to include in the Bill, and also as to the grievances which they desired to have remedied.'[17] Though Lloyd George later omitted to secure the assent of the doctors before introducing his National Insurance Bill,[18] his example of conciliating the interests involved has generally been followed by ministers of all parties. Indeed the chief legislative achievement of the first Labour government was a practical Housing Act worked out by the left winger Wheatley in conjunction with the building industry.

The consultation of groups in the drafting of bills is not enjoined by the constitution as it is in Switzerland, but it almost invariably takes place.* The budget is the great exception; which proves the benefit of the rule. The government would surely not have had to move 440 amendments to its own 1965 Finance Bill, had there been consultation with interests beforehand; and in the following year the barest minimum of conversation with outside interests would have removed many of the absurdities in the original proposals for Selective Employment Tax.

Aneurin Bevan, who as a backbencher had always been quick to denounce agreements reached between the government and outside interests behind the back of parliament, sought as a minister to preserve the distinction between consulting outside interests, which was legitimate, and negotiating with them, which was not.[20] But this is more a matter of protocol than a real distinction. The status and outcome of the talks depend more upon the character of the Minister, the involvement or non-involvement of the cabinet or a cabinet committee, and the calibre of the interested groups than upon the title of the exchanges between them.

However intensive consultations have been before publication of the bill, groups are almost certain to want further concessions from the government during the committee stage. Party cohesion being still strong in committee, though less so than on the floor of the House, the minister remains the primary target of the groups. He can in committee make concessions without much loss of face.

* Speaking of the Wireless Telegraphy Bill the Postmaster General said: 'I have discussed the matter with [the dealers] at great length. We have had their co-operation in drawing up the Bill and their assistance on a great many points.'[19]

Also, he is no longer hag-ridden by a cabinet committee and other departments. He is his own master, and the bill is at last his bill. But the minister is more likely to be accommodating if his back-benchers favour concessions; so groups are wise not to confine their blandishments to the minister. Even if groups have no hope of amendments being accepted, they like their case to be stated. It is useful for them to have the government's position clarified and put on the record. At the same time briefs from groups, as well as help in drafting amendments, are useful for the opposition and occasionally for government backbenchers.

Despite this co-operation in committee there are grounds for mutual contempt between M.P.s and organised groups. If an M.P.'s attitude to groups is determined by their electoral impotence and general political incompetence, the attitude of an organised group to M.P.s is determined by their discipline in the division lobby.

In any case most of what pressure groups want is to be found in Whitehall, not Westminster. Administrative, not political, decisions are what normally concern them, and these are made in the depart-ments, not in the House of Commons. Whitehall can give the groups what they want, and in return they help Whitehall to function. Many organised groups came into existence because of the steady advance throughout the twentieth century of the frontiers of government activity into every sphere of life. Formed as a weapon of offence or defence against government, they have now become a necessity to government: so much so that where a group does not exist, the government finds it necessary to invent one. And of course important centres of power like the B.B.C. and the nationalised industries have been created by the government.

Government needs groups, on account of the information they bring. Without them it would be legislating blindfold. Sir Frank Lee's remarks about the Board of Trade are true of other ministries. 'What we do, in greater or less degree, is to keep in close touch with the industries concerned, to get to know their problems, personali-ties, structure, likely developments [and], to constitute ourselves their main link with the government machine. . . .'[21] Much as an invading army depends upon the specialised knowledge of the terrain that only the local inhabitants possess, so Whitehall depends upon the information of organised groups for its forays into their sphere. Like an invading army, it would probably react strongly against those who thwarted it. But while it could at a pinch run an industry or two, it could scarcely run some of the professions. Even the most versatile Civil Servants could not become doctors overnight. Fortunately Britain, unlike Belgium or Greece, has not yet seen a doctors' strike.

To cut the lines of information and co-operation is an act of war, and no group would be so foolish to resort to it until Whitehall was plainly bent on aggression. When the Attlee government nationalised steel, the industry refused to co-operate. By that stage it had nothing to lose. In 1956 school teachers refused to collect National Savings from their charges as a protest against the government's Super-annuation Bill. The doctors made warlike threats in 1965 and 1966 but did not carry them through. These 'strikes' by groups are of course their ultimate sanction, but as with the rest of the British system sanctions are generally kept in the background. On the whole, groups treat Whitehall with elaborate courtesy and a punctilio reminiscent of pre-1914 Europe.

No Single Controlling Interest

To one important strand of European thought the very existence of 'secondary powers' is repugnant. Rousseau believed that any organisation that stood between man and the state confused and distorted the general will; and the *Loi le Chapelier* of 1791 prohibited such associations. Although Article 126 of the Soviet constitution gives a place to interest groups, the Communist party is the only significant political organisation in the U.S.S.R. other than the police and the army, and 'democracy within the party' does not extend to the formation of groups within it.[22] In practice, therefore, though not in form, Russia is faithful to the tradition of Rousseau.

Of course, if one interest or group predominates, and representative institutions are a charade, the Rousseau-ist view has substance. At the turn of the century California possessed an elaborate system of representative government, but the state was in practice run by the Southern Pacific Railway. In Britain there is no single controlling interest. Such great institutions as the churches or the armed forces are not overweeningly powerful. Britain is neither clerical nor militarist. The churches bring pressure to bear on such matters as church schools, a subject on which they usually get their way, and the Roman Catholics campaign on such matters as abortion, on which they are less successful. When more than one hundred Conservatives voted against the opening of the Festival of Britain fun fair on Sundays they were voting against Herbert Morrison, not for the Lord's Day Observance Society.

The churches are usually divided among themselves. Their followers are distributed among all parties, and are to be found on both sides of every issue. Hence they have little political power. The utterances of politically minded bishops and other clerics are enough to stifle any yearnings for theocracy; all too often they merit the retort of Baldwin, who asked how the Bishops 'would like it if I referred to the Iron and Steel Federation the revision of the Athanasian Creed'?[23]

During the Victory procession in London after the first World War, Marshal Foch expressed surprise that a policeman should lead all the armed forces. Sir Henry Wilson replied: 'There you have the British constitution in a nutshell—the subordination of the military power to the civil authority.'[24] That was true even in those days. The Curragh was not a mutiny, and although Lloyd George fretted at his inability to rid himself of Robertson and Haig, his weakness was due to the breakdown of the party system, to division in his cabinet, and to the political support the generals enjoyed in parliament and Buckingham Palace, not to the danger of military domination. In the second war, as Churchill afterwards wrote, relations between the Prime Minister and the generals 'were of a most friendly and intimate character. . . . How different from the rows of the "Frocks" and "Brass Hats" which characterised the last War'.[25] Under the post-war Labour government Montgomery got the better of Attlee once or twice, but he could 'recall only one case of real unanimous agreement in the Chiefs of Staff Committee', and that agreement came to nothing 'since my two colleagues declined to face the music on the day of battle'.[26] The politicians were in charge. The Wilson government may have been reluctant to overstrain the loyalty of the forces by invading Rhodesia, but there has never been any danger of a military take over or revolt, as has occurred in so many countries, or even of the 'military industrial complex' acquiring the 'unwarranted influence' that Eisenhower spoke of in his Farewell Address as President of the United States.[27]

Interests such as the city, the banks, what Disraeli called 'the money interest, the fungus spawn of public loans',[28] the landowners, the farmers, the professions are thought by those who dislike them to be too powerful. But only the most determined believers in the conspiracy theory of history can see any of them, or the Jews, the

Masons, the Pope, the homosexuals, or any other collectivity as the secret but real rulers of the country.* The only interests which could be seriously considered to come anywhere near to running the country are producer groups: the Trade Unions and Industry.

There are in Britain about 1,300 manufacturing associations and about 2,500 trade associations in all. Some companies are big enough not to have to join associations in order to promote their interests; they have sufficient access to Whitehall on their own. And there are nearly 600 Trade Unions, of which some 170 are affiliated to the T.U.C. Powerful in all industrialised free countries and in some dictatorships, industry and the Trade Unions are sometimes thought to be especially powerful in Britain. Professor Beer, for instance, has talked of 'the vast power of organised producers groups' in this country.[30]

The power of groups is no easier to measure than that of parliament or of other institutions. They never stand alone, and the conflict between them and other bodies is seldom clear cut. The B.B.C., the Musicians' Union and the big record companies all favoured a restrictive policy over Pirate radios and the future of local broadcasting, and this formidable array easily defeated the public, the great majority of whom wanted the Pirates to stay afloat and failing that favoured a commercial substitute.† Yet it was not a pure pressure group victory. The Postmaster General's policy was in line with the traditional monopolistic attitude of the Post Office and with the ideological prejudices of most Labour M.P.s.‡

Business may be considered the most important interest in the Conservative party. But it is not a single interest, even if agriculture is not counted as an industry. On all but the most general issues business opinion is divided, and there are divergent interests within business. The Conservative party does not appear to have been dominated by business between the wars. In the 1920s Baldwin's memory of his defeat on protection at the 1923 election, and the presence of the free trader Churchill at the Treasury, were enough to hold up the extension of tariffs despite the wishes of industry and

---

* Mr. Peter Shore, M.P., when P.P.S. to Mr. Wilson, wrote that 'the government had to sustain itself with a tiny majority against . . . a wholly alienated City—prepared to use its power over sterling to blackmail and veto government decisions that it disliked'.[29] Mr. Wilson later promoted Mr. Shore to head the Department of Economic Affairs.

† The N.O.P. found that 19 per cent were in favour of banning the Pirates and 69 per cent against.[31] A Gallup poll found 62 per cent in favour of local radio stations accepting advertising and 22 against.[32]

‡ Similarly the introduction of Commercial Television was not a pure pressure group victory. The breaking of the B.B.C.s monopoly was ideologically attractive to Tory M.P.s.

of much of the Tory party. Silk was protected but not steel. The denationalisation measures of the post-war Churchill government were spurred on by backbenchers, not by industry. The City's disillusionment with the government by 1964 reflected its inability to influence the Tory party. Central Office has obtained large sums of money from industry and the City, but it has not sold control of policy to the providers of party funds. Whatever else the Macmillan and Douglas-Home administrations might be called, they could not be termed businessmen's governments.

Nor have particular industries gained control. Ever since Gladstone erroneously attributed his defeat in 1874 to being 'borne down in a torrent of gin and beer',[33] the brewers have ranked high in left wing demonology as the controllers of the Tory party. The first Act passed by the post-war Churchill government was indeed one to establish privately owned public houses in new towns. No doubt the brewers had contributed to Tory funds in 1951, but so had most industries; and Tory Chancellors like Labour Chancellors continued to single out for special victimisation the drinkers of alcohol. Not even the most sensitive 'breathalyzer' could have detected the influence of the drink trade on Tory fiscal policy.

Agriculture is often thought to be near the heart of the Tory party, though it was a Tory government which refused to aid home agriculture against the American wheat invasion of the 1870s. Disraeli talked of the 'rusty phrases of mine forty years ago' and did nothing. He regarded the issue as settled.[34] Today the agricultural vote is small, but at least eighty Tory M.P.s in the 1959–64 parliament had some constituency or personal connection with, or interest in, agriculture. Except over a general political issue, like the Common Market, the N.F.U. could rely on the friendly support of these M.P.s. Yet the idea that increased agriculture production would save imports made little headway against the deep-seated belief of the Board of Trade that, only by importing food from abroad, could foreign countries be persuaded to accept our industrial exports.

The idea that the Tory party is dominated by industry descends to farce when the chief industrial group, the Confederation of British Industry, is considered. The C.B.I. which came into existence in August 1965 has in its membership 12,500 manufacturing firms, about 200 Trade Associations and Employer Associations, and some 200 Commercial Associations. 'A significant addition to the C.B.I.'s strength, and a notable departure from the character of its antecedents,' wrote its Director General, Mr. John Davies,[35] 'has been the enrolment of ten nationalised industries. They are not in full membership but are strongly represented on the appropriate industries. The contribution they can make to the C.B.I.'s deliberations is powerful and influential and enables the organisation to claim with every justification that it speaks for British industry.' Obviously the nationalised industries are 'a significant addition' to the C.B.I., and no doubt 'their contribution . . . is powerful and influential', but it is difficult to imagine Mr. George Woodcock hailing the addition of Sir Paul Chambers and I.C.I. to the T.U.C. as entitling 'the organisation to claim with every justification that it speaks for British Trade Unionism'.

'The C.B.I.'s character, and perhaps its main *raison d'être*,' says Mr. Davies,[36] 'is geared to a dialogue with government . . . But it must be emphasised that the C.B.I. is politically neutral. It cannot be otherwise if it is to enjoy official confidence and have influence on the shaping of national policy.' Political neutrality is made necessary by the presence of the nationalised industries, the existence of many Socialist employers, and the wish of many businessmen to keep out of politics. But it is plainly not a requirement for the enjoyment of 'official confidence', or for the possession of 'influence on the shaping of national policy', as the experience of the T.U.C. conclusively demonstrates. Indeed the political neutrality of the C.B.I. is one of the causes of its outstanding lack of influence on both the Labour government's policy and the Tory party.

Even without the nationalised industries the C.B.I. would be far too amorphous a body to exercise power, and with them it can be little more than a convenience to government and industry. Its membership is so diverse that the organisation's views are representative only in the most general sense. The C.B.I. may be a reluctant servant of Whitehall; it is undoubtedly a servant and is probably more useful to government than to industry. There are of course limits to its obedience and its servitude. They vary according to the political strength of the government; the C.B.I. is tougher when it believes the Conservatives will win the next election. But as a producer group the C.B.I. offers no kind of threat to the supremacy of government. And it does not dominate the Tory party or anything else.

The Trade Unions occupy a different position in the Labour party, being a constituent element of it, and from time to time the industrial side of the movement has been in control. But it has only been dominant when the party was in opposition, never when the party has been in government. The General Secretary of the T.U.C., Fred Bramley, maintained that during the first Labour government he did not have five minutes conversation with Ramsay Macdonald,[37] and Citrine told the Webbs that 'at least' the Conservatives 'consult us. You did not even do that'.[38] During the post-war Labour government, the T.U.C. was nearly always consulted, but Citrine echoed his predecessor in saying 'I never had a really intimate talk with Attlee when he was Prime Minister'.[39] The Unions are not overwhelmingly popular in the country at large, and a Labour government that stands up to them gains more in popular favour than it loses in Trade Union support.*

Though much more effective as a group than the C.B.I., the T.U.C. also suffers from the number and diversity of its constituent parts. With 170 Unions affiliated to it, the T.U.C. has not been able to approach the centralised power of its equivalent in Germany where there are only sixteen Unions, or in Sweden where there are twenty-two. The Trade Union movement has always been more prone to advocating the reform of other parts of society than to reforming itself. At the 1963 conference of the T.U.C. Mr. George Woodcock, introducing a debate on Trade Union structure, said he was making a progress report but it was not the sort of progress he would have wished. All that he could report was that the T.U.C. would discuss the matter with the Unions. This was the same decision as the T.U.C. had reached in 1927. Centralisation is being forced upon it, but the possibility of the T.U.C. dominating a Labour or any other government still seems remote. Only a catastrophic Labour defeat and the emergence of a Union leader of the calibre of Bevin could produce a reassertion of Trade Union supremacy over the parliamentary party, and even if that happened, the inferiority of the parliamentary wing would not outlive a Labour victory at the polls.

A Labour government is no more anxious to antagonise the T.U.C. than a Conservative government is to antagonise industry. It needs the Unions' financial support and their aid at elections, but it is not run by them. It knows that ordinary Trade Unionists, whatever the antics of the activists, in normal times feel greater loyalty to the Labour party than to their Unions, while Tory

* The Wilson's government's Prices and Incomes freeze was in fact even more popular with Trade Unionists than with the country as a whole.[40]

Trade Unionists are as opposed to the Union leadership as they are to a Labour government. Moreover, most Trade Union leaders are prepared to put up with much in order to avoid embarrassing 'their' government; indeed they might be able to do more for their members if they were not quite so closely entwined with the Labour party. Trade Union leaders may have their private armies and wage baronial wars against other interests and each other, but unlike the Wars of the Roses the central government is still in charge, as the government's imposition of statutory control of wages and prices clearly showed.

A governing party wins considerable electoral popularity by slapping down its allied interests. By showing they were not dominated by business, the post-war Tory governments were for long able to hold the centre. By ignoring the wishes of the Trade Unions in 1966 Mr. Wilson impressed many previously Conservative voters. Nor do groups manipulate either elections or parliament. These negatives scarcely add up to a 'vast' accretion of power in the hands of organised producer groups.

What are called consumer groups—old age pensioners or council house tenants, for instance—do not in this context present a problem. With the improvement of market research techniques the parties are bound to direct much of their appeal to clearly identifiable groups of voters. Such appeals may be irresponsible. That is not the fault of the consumer groups. Besides, if voters as individuals should so far as possible have their wishes granted, there seems no reason why a similar indulgence should not be granted to voters clustered in groups.

During the war the Foreign Office thought that the Zionist movement had an undue influence on U.S. foreign policy.[41] After the war the American Defence Secretary, James Forrestal, thought the same. 'I said I thought it was a most disastrous and regrettable fact that the foreign policy of this country was determined by the contributions, a particular bloc of special interests might make to the party funds.'[42] The smaller cost of elections, the greater strength of departmental policy making, and the collective responsibility of the cabinet make a similar development less likely over here.

Groups and the Public Interest
Rousseau's conception of the general will is a mystical distortion of a highly complex process. Yet it is possible to wonder if the hubbub of sectional interests does not drown the still small voice

of the public interest. Bentham would have thought the question a silly one; for him the sum of individual interests *was* the public interest.* Some believe with Gladstone that 'the influence of the public interest . . . is too weak'.[44] Others think that the public interest does not exist, and that anyway there is no means of discovering what it is. According to the Bentley school, the public interest is merely the outcome of the struggle between sectional interests. Certainly the public interest is frequently a nebulous conception. But inability to find something is not sufficient reason for declining to look for it—even though it is often not there. Besides, the true sectional interest of a group is sometimes no easier to discover than the public interest; yet nobody denies the existence of sectional interests. The crude antithesis between sectional interests and the public interest is indeed false; not however because the public interest does not exist, but because the public interest and sectional interests are not self contained. Each contains elements of the other.

Jay Gould may have said that he was for the Republicans in a Republican County, for the Democrats in a Democratic County, but everywhere for the Erie Railroad.[45] Such single-mindedness is seldom possible for a British group. Few people have such an absorption in a group that they have no loyalties to anything else. A Communist may be so fired by his vision of the class struggle that he has no loyalties save to his party, but even many Communists have to pay regard to the interests of their union. An anti-vivisectionist or an enemy of factory farming may be similarly dominated by a single loyalty, but such fanaticism is rare. Most people live in several different worlds: at home with their family, at work, at leisure, in a community, and in other spheres. A man's membership of a group does not dominate all his worlds. He may wear its livery, while his basic loyalties lie elsewhere.

If individuals are divided, so are groups. Some members are for the Conservatives, some for Labour, and some for neither. The group is usually divided into factions of some sort, even when party politics are not involved. These conflicting loyalties and attitudes within people and groups weaken sectional interests and usually compel some attention to the public interest by group leaders. W. H. Vanderbilt's attitude, 'The public be damned'[46], is never the avowed aim of groups, though it is often the result.

* 'The public interest which you personify,' he wrote, 'is only an abstract term: it represents only the mass of the interests of individuals. . . . Individual interests are the only real interests.'[43]

At all events the overlapping membership and loyalties of groups inhibit their exclusive pursuit of sectional interests.

J. S. Mill wrote of the still surviving habit of regarding government as representing an opposite interest to that of the public.[47] That has now been replaced by the scarcely less mistaken habit of regarding the government as representing the same interest as that of the public. Certainly the Civil Service and the government do not just represent another interest and another form of pressure. But as pressure groups are not single-minded pursuers of their own interest to the exclusion of the public interest, so Whitehall is not a single-minded guardian of the public interest to the exclusion of everything else. Whitehall has its own private interests: a varying compound of previous policy decisions, administrative convenience, bureaucratic prestige, departmental rivalries, personal loyalties, and inertia, ambition, and fear of public opinion. So although the groups have not colonised the government as they have in some countries, the confrontation between organised groups and Whitehall is not a clear cut struggle between selfish private interests and the disinterested upholders of the embattled public interest.

On the face of it Civil Servants, stern upholders of the national interest, uncontaminated by party doctrine, enabled by their own permanence to take a long term view, are well placed to withstand group pressures and defend the public interest. Yet one of the traditions of the British Civil Service is to accommodate itself to pressure. That, put crudely, is the burden of the doctrine, that administration is an art in itself; the job of the Civil Service is to find the highest common factor of agreement and then to label it the right solution. Of course Civil Servants have often to contend with pressures other than those of groups. If the issue is likely to become political, the views of the minister, of the cabinet and of backbenchers have to be considered. But usually the matter is too technical to concern politicians, and so the administrator can just administrate and the groups can be brought to a respectable and ingenious compromise. No doubt the peace terms of the various interests often represent the public interest. But if the government is a referee and not a player, governmental leadership is out of the question. Agreement is all; the quality of the agreement is secondary.

Beatrice Webb scoffed that Lloyd George in the First War handed each government department over to the relevant interest to run. 'In that way,' she wrote, 'our little Welsh Attorney thinks, you combine the least political opposition with the maximum of technical knowledge.'[48] Such 'syndicalism' was almost inevitable. The same thing happened in the second war though at Civil Service, not ministerial, level. Beaverbrook brought businessmen into the Ministry of Aircraft Production,[49] Woolton brought them into the Ministry of Food,[50] and they were prominent in many other departments. And the increased governmental control of the economy since the war has ensured the maintenance of the closest links between ministries and industries.

The line between administrators and businessmen, doctors or farmers is inevitably blurred. No longer do businessmen enter the government as ministers or Civil Servants to run their industry. But interest groups are in continuous consultation with Civil Servants. Representatives of groups sit on a forest of advisory committees. There were 278 permanent standing advisory committees in 1967,[51] and these form almost a supernumary Civil Service. But 'departments cannot be sure that the advice they get will be congenial. Committees therefore cannot be simply added to the Civil Service as part of Whitehall—they are agencies through which the community's influence can be exerted'.[52] However, these committees are often kept under close control. Woolton could not remember any occasion when he was a member of the Board of Trade Advisory Committee 'on which the initiative was allowed to rest with the consultative committee'.[53]

The existence of a group may make an advisory committee unnecessary: the group acts as the committee. The B.M.A. has been called 'a vital part of the departmental decision-making machinery'.[54]

The group wants benefits from its ministry, and the ministry cannot do its job without the co-operation of the group and others like it. The vast amount of delegated legislation is discussed and negotiated with the relevant groups. Without the groups the government would be a prodigiously larger bureaucracy even than it is. The full co-operation of a group helps Civil Servants with the Treasury and other bodies; the co-operation of a ministry helps a group with its own members. Civil Servants influence groups just as the groups influence departments. The government is advising industry, and industry is advising the government. Advice and decisions become intermingled. Nobody knows who is running whom, because nobody is in charge. Everybody is bargaining.

> Yet some might find it matter for Research,
> Whether the Church taught him, or he the Church.[55]

Mr. Duncan Sandys remarked, when he was Minister of Housing and Local Government, that the local authority 'Associations have now virtually become a part of the constitution of the country'.[56] He scarcely exaggerated. Well might the secretary of the Association of Municipal Corporations say in the same month in 1956: 'our relationship with government departments is so good that we do not take steps to amend Bills without informing the department concerned'.[57] The quasi-constitutional status of the local authority associations and their 'so good' relationship gave them a veto on reform. Here was a clear example of a private marriage which was contrary to the public interest.

The marriage between the Ministry of Agriculture and the N.F.U. has been less deleterious to the public. The chief sufferer has probably been the Union. The intimacy between Union and ministry emphasises the role of the N.F.U. as the representative of a sectional interest trying to gain satisfaction for its claims from the government. Very likely, the N.F.U. would have been better able to convert opinion to its view, that the national interest demanded a great expansion of British agriculture, had it kept itself more at a distance from the Ministry of Agriculture.

To some all this may be sinister. Yet such consultation and overlapping of governed and government is surely how free governments should operate. For power to be diffused among a variety of bodies and not monopolised by the government, is the mark of a free society. The alternative is authoritarianism. Those who favour the governed influencing the government should not change sides merely because the governed are gathered in groups. Functional representation supplements geographical representation. It has not usurped the place of parliament or the electorate.

No doubt the sum of special interests does not always add up to the public interest. But nobody has found any better method than this pluralism of securing the triumph of the public interest. Group activity helps to produce peaceful change, which is unquestionably in the public interest. In any case there is little question of the public interest being continually submerged by private sectional interests. With interest groups directing most of their energies towards Whitehall, not Westminster, blatant log-rolling is seldom feasible. Groups may often get their way, but mostly in small things, and their hand is kept out of the till. Interest groups may be barons; they are not robber barons. They are usually aware, sometimes uneasily, of the public interest. Often they are restrained by their own diverse membership and by the opposition of other groups.

On the other side Civil Servants seldom surrender unconditionally to the pressure of one group, though they are vulnerable to general agreement among groups. Often more than one ministry is involved, with the result that there is counter pressure from Whitehall behind the originating department. During the war Mr. Butler was able to carry on negotiations for his Education Act with the churches and other interests without interference from the cabinet.[58] In the negotiations with the doctors over the National Health Service, however, Aneurin Bevan was saddled with a Cabinet Social Services Committee.[59] This cut down his freedom of manoeuvre; but such committees also inhibit pressure groups as well as departmentalism. But whether or not a cabinet committee is involved, neither the minister nor the cabinet wishes to gain the reputation of being the plaything of pressure groups.

Representativeness

While welcoming the participation of the governed in the decisions of government, it may be objected that groups are not representative of their members. The existence or absence of elections does not solve the problem of representation. Indeed anybody who puts forward his candidacy for an office which takes up a great deal of time is almost by definition unrepresentative of those who elect him. The vast majority of doctors do not wish to have anything to do with the administration of their association, or even to attend regular conferences; very few enthusiasts for temperance reform wish to fight the cause to the exclusion of their other interests.

The zeal of the leaders contrasts with the apathy of the rest. This is notoriously true of trade unions. Trade unionists do not bother to take part in the election of their leaders. The Committee of the Seamen's Union which conducted the strike in 1966 had been elected by 5 per cent of the membership. Apathy reigns even in matters much more closely related to the interests of members than the leadership of the union. When Equity held a poll on the establishment of a pension scheme for all members, only 2,722 voted out of a membership of 13,000.[60]

For a group to function at all, the leadership must act in many situations when its followers would dumbly acquiesce, and it must hold views on subjects which its members have scarcely heard of. Inevitably there is a great gulf between the group's executive bureaucracy and the mass membership. In these circumstances the frequency of elections is a minor matter. The General Secretary of the T. & G.W.U. is elected for life, but this does not appear to make him more out of touch with the rank and file than his colleagues on the general council of the T.U.C.

When people join a group such as a trade union, they do not do so because they wish to run it. They join, as Professor Blondel has pointed out, as an insurance policy.[61] And so long as the group seems to be safeguarding their interests, they are happy. However much they offended the susceptibilities of the U.S. Justice Department, Dave Beck and Jimmy Hoffa preserved their popularity in the Teamsters' Union, and it was imprisonment not an outraged membership which removed them from union headquarters. The vote-rigging by the Communist leaders of the Electrical Trades Union to preserve their dominance testified to a lesser degree of popularity. But both cases demonstrated Trade Unionists' lack of concern about the running of their Union, provided the Union leadership takes care to promote their interests and to see that on bread and butter issues there is no divergence between top and bottom.

Indifference is not confined to Trade Unions. In 1959 the owners of periodicals and provincial newspapers took little part in the dispute with the printing unions. 'Looking around as the brandy passed,' wrote their President, Claud Morris, of the Newspaper Proprietors' Association of South Wales, 'I was astonished at the faith these stolid Welsh gentlemen put in their national wage negotiations, chiefly handled by printing employers who had little interest, I thought, in newspapers.'[62]

Most manufacturing and trading associations elect their officers at the annual general meeting. When the association is small, as with the Society of Snuff Grinders, Blenders and Purveyors, which has only twelve members, such a procedure is neutral. When it is large, the procedure tends to centralise control of the group in the hands of its bureaucracy. But though groups may have difficulty in deciding whether to give greater weight to numbers than to size of contributions, employers' associations do not present a great problem of representation. Trade associations are usually far smaller than trade unions, their membership is less apathetic, and their aims are normally confined to matters concerning their particular trade or industry.

The crucial difference between a trade union and an employers' association is that a trade union is vastly more powerful than any of its members, whereas an employers' association is nearly always much less powerful than some of its members. The principal men in the union are necessarily its leaders; the principal men in an industry are often not even members of their trade association. Neither Vauxhall nor Ford belong to the Society of Motor Manufacturers and Traders. Indeed if the leaders of a trade union are not representative in that they are of so much greater calibre than the members of their union, an employers' association is often not representative in that those who run it are of much smaller calibre than some of those they seek to represent. Trade associations sometimes seem to have been staffed in the way composite army units were formed during the war: each battalion took the opportunity to get rid of those it did not want.

In considering the representativeness of groups, the form of elections, the presence of 'a democratic mould' and abstruse theories of representation are all irrelevant.* Nobody can know whether the often militant local organisers of the N.U.A.W. or the moderate Union leaders are the more representative of the union rank and file.[63] A group should be taken to represent its members so long as it maintains its cohesion, and so long as its efforts and pronouncements bear some relation to the purposes of the group. The attitude of the National Farmers' Union to the Common Market has seemed to some observers unrepresentative of its members. Either that impression is inaccurate or it is irrelevant: only if the rank and file are sufficiently aroused by the divergence between their attitude and that of union headquarters to protest, is the existence of disagreement significant. Unrest in a group is hard to conceal, and when it manifests itself the leadership must alter policy to appease it or the unrest will remain as standing evidence that the leadership is not representative. The strongly hostile resolution on advertising passed by the 1961 Annual Conference of the National Association of Women's Clubs did not produce civil war among women's clubs, but neither did it raise a serious presumption that most of their members really were 'greatly concerned at . . . advertising's distortion of the economy of the state' or passionately felt that the government should 'disallow advertising costs as a legitimate claim in the assessment of business taxes'.[64] Similarly Trade Union resolutions

---

* Trade Unions have a large involuntary membership. A Gallup Poll in September 1966 found that 17 per cent of trade unionists would leave their union if they were free to do so. It is hard to see how in the classic sense of representation trade union leaders can be said to represent that 17 per cent.

on pay and hours may be presumed to be representative, unlike their resolutions on the more abstruse political questions.

To test the representativeness of a group's leadership on any given issue by its success in preserving the cohesion of its members and by the relevance of the issue in question to the proper activities of the group is pragmatic and also logical. After all it is partly because people participate in politics much less than classic democratic ideas demanded that pressure groups are necessary. And since lack of participation helps to produce pressure groups, it is futile to expect much participation in pressure groups themselves. Most groups are undoubtedly paternalist, but so too is the electoral system. And the products of the first may be scarcely less representative than the products of the second.

A Third Chamber?

Groups are representative, but they have not been institutionalised. 'The real units,' wrote L. S. Amery, 'the great collective elements of the national life, the industries that are its organs, are unrepresented except by accident or in the most one-sided fashion.'[65] An economic chamber or House of Industry has had such distinguished advocates as Churchill, Amery, and Macmillan,[66] while G. D. H. Cole and the Guild Socialists thought that functional representation was the only genuine form of representation,[67] geographical representation being always defective. The idea was discredited by the association of corporativism with fascism, but the success of the Economics and Social Council in France and of similar bodies in other countries has restored it to some favour. If the corporative state is with us anyway, arguably it should be institutionalised into a third chamber.

An economic chamber would not govern: its primary role would be consultative. Were it to hold important debates in which there were genuine and interesting clashes of opinion, they would be a useful source of public education. But in order to preserve their influence with the departments, speechmakers would hesitate to be outspoken. And if the chamber had no powers of decision, its debates would seldom catch the public ear. The real work of the chamber would be done off the floor, and the public would learn no more about the activities of interest groups than they do already. Governments would continue to deal with the large interests direct, often by-passing the chamber, and when they did consult the chamber or its committees the important consultations would still take place in private and not in public.

In a divided country like France, the Economic and Social Council has brought people together who without it would have remained suspicious, hostile and apart.[68] But in England the people who would be members of such a body often meet each other anyway. They do not need an industrial club.

The task of deciding upon the composition of the functional chamber would be hard, though not impossible. Would producers' groups be the only ones represented, or would opinion groups and other associations also be recognised? Should employers or trade unions have a majority? If neither, who is to hold the balance? Even if these questions could be answered, difficulties of representation within the various categories would remain.

An even more serious objection to a functional or economic chamber is that it would tend to ossify groups and interests in their present structure. 'I conceive,' said Canning in 1822, 'that to establish one uniform right would inevitably be to exclude some important interests from the advantage of being represented in the House.'[69] He thought the practical accommodation to changes was 'a much more important consideration than whether the component parts of the House might be arranged with neater symmetry or distributed in more scientific proportions.' Canning's argument was inapplicable to parliamentary reform because the unreformed House had lost public acceptance, but it is a valid defence of the present 'unreformed' state of interest groups and Whitehall. Groups can be more representative, because more flexible, if they are left without an arena and without institutional form.

Pressure groups do provide representation of 'the great collective elements of the national life' and themselves provide the equivalent of a House of Industry. So while a functional chamber would not herald the end of freedom and the arrival of fascism, the balance of advantage seems clearly against it. Almost certainly a 'cabinet' body, like the N.E.D.C. before it was absorbed into a ministry, would be more effective than a 'chamber' body on the French model.

Groups and the Political Process

Yet the present procedure possesses a formidable defect. It suffers from, and itself reinforces, the congenital defect of British government: excessive secrecy. The groups which negotiate in Whitehall and secure benefits for themselves do so in private. Pressure group politics in this country are usually closed politics. Excluded from the hustings and the division lobby, groups operate in the soundproof rooms of Whitehall. Their most public arena is not television or Fleet Street but the Athenaeum or the clubs of Pall Mall. This secrecy often aids the groups. Outsiders can rarely interfere until a decision has been made, and then it may be too late. When an expert advisory committee representative of all the relevant groups and interests is agreed, that is usually the end of the matter.

Helpful though it is to the groups, the secrecy is not their fault; they take the system as they find it. Whitehall and the Civil Service work in secret; the groups conform. Yet secrecy prevents the mobilisation of the generally inattentive public, and conduces to the maintenance of the *status quo*. Of course, part of the attentive public may be an 'opinion' group, which has been formed to press for some particular action. But even 'opinion'* groups often succumb to secrecy. They are drawn into the departments to give advice, and as soon as they achieve a consultative role with the ministry their teeth are drawn Fearful of jeopardising that position, they exercise their pressure in private instead of risking a public row. A government concession on one point is paid for by their silence on others.

It is partly due to secrecy that groups cannot compensate for the lack of conflict in the British system; it is also partly due to their inclinations. With the exception of the Trade Unions, most interest groups try to keep out of party politics, to disclaim alliance with any party. They prefer to talk to government in undertones, not to take part in undignified party battles. 'Consultation' with the ministry becomes almost an end in itself, and the departments take full advantage of this attitude. Occasionally groups notice what stooges they have become. Thus during the 1965 Finance Act the Life offices risked a quarrel and gained the headlines with an attack on the provisions on capital gains. Almost immediately the government moved amendments to improve the situation. More typically, the Fire offices kept on with the consultations and got nothing.

Groups are also fearful of backing the wrong horse. By keeping aloof they may be able to persuade both parties to support their objectives; failing that they can at least behave as though they have

---

* The Bentley school denies the distinction between interest groups and opinion groups, maintaining that 'the shared attitude . . . constitute the interests',[70] but except that they are associations and seek to influence government action, the Campaign for Nuclear Disarmament or the Howard League for Penal Reform have nothing in common with, say, the Institute of Bankers or the Amalgamated Society of Woodworkers. Their dissimilarities surely exceed their resemblances.

always backed the right one. Their ideal picture of the political process is more like the United Nations than the House of Commons. They see Britain as a miniature United Nations with all the various interests organised in delegations, in almost perpetual conclave with other delegations, and with the government not something different in kind but merely *primus inter pares* like the American delegation at Lake Success.

All the same, most of the producer groups have close relations of one sort or another with one of the major parties. For the time being, the nationalised industries remain in the orbit of the Labour party, and most private businesses, with obvious exceptions, are in the orbit of the Tory party. When the interest's party is the government, there is no problem. The interest remains the party's satellite body. When, however, the interest's party is in opposition, the path of the satellite is no longer regular. It must be a satellite of the governing party as well as of its own primary planet. Thus while the opposition party loses no opportunity to criticise the government, the interests clustered around it usually prefer appeasement or surrender. If they are attacked by the government, they generally fight back. But a Mister Cube is a rarity. For most of the time, though opposed to the government in general, the interest is hoping to avoid being singled out for punishment. It wants to keep on friendly terms with Whitehall. Such interests and groups are usually therefore a restraint on the opposition. This is particularly true of Conservative interests. The Trade Unions need mass support or the semblance of it, and so a display of political militancy is occasionally essential. But business groups have no mass audience requiring proofs of political orthodoxy; they can concentrate on persuading an allegedly Socialist government to help groups which allegedly favour free enterprise and oppose governmental interference.

Some opinion groups do increase conflict. The Campaign for Nuclear Disarmament had no relations to spoil with ministries or government. It had no objective other than neutralism and unilateral disarmament that could be put at risk by its tactics.

Less extreme opinion groups like the Comprehensive Schools Committee and the National Education Association also add to conflict. But opinion groups which have semi-permanent aims resemble most interest groups in their methods. The Howard League for Penal Reform had long favoured the abolition of capital punishment, but it had many other objectives as well. Hence it was not prepared to jeopardise achievement of its other aims by courting the hostility of the Home Office with an all-out public battle for the end of hanging.[71]

On the whole, therefore, instead of parliamentary parties moderating social and industrial conflict between social forces and secondary powers, organised groups moderate political conflict between the main parties. Were a party or an important section of it to espouse a rigid doctrine, then the cool worldly influence of its pressure groups would be highly beneficent, as for example was the influence of the T.U.C. on the Labour party in the 1930s. But with the parties increasingly eschewing doctrine, the system is bland enough without the groups making it more so.

The pressure group system clearly has much in common with Calhoun's ideal of rule by the concurrent majority. According to Calhoun, 'There are two different modes in which the sense of the community may be taken; one, simply by the right of suffrage, unaided; the other by the right through a proper organism. Each collects the sense of the majority. But one regards numbers only, and considers the whole community as a unit, having but one common interest throughout; and collects the sense of the greater number of the whole, as that of the community. The other, on the contrary, regards interests as well as numbers;—considering the community as made up of different and conflicting interests, as far as the action of the government is concerned; and takes the sense of each, through its majority or appropriate organ, and the united sense of all, as the sense of the entire community. The former of these I shall call the numerical, or absolute majority; and the latter, the concurrent or constitutional majority.'[72]

Of course all free countries are governed by a combination of both majorities. In Scandinavia the concurrent majority is probably more important than the numerical majority. Professor Hecksher has said of Sweden: 'It is regarded as more or less inevitable that groups of this type and other organisations should exercise a power almost equal to that of parliament and definitely superior to that of parliamentary parties.'[73] Decisions are made more through a process of bargaining between the government and the big interests than as a result of the electoral process. Elections decide who will make the decisions, and subsequent bargaining decides what those decisions are to be. Corporatism is also conspicuous in Germany.

In Britain the process has not gone so far, though the most vital issues are seldom decided or even much discussed at elections. The two party system and the existence of an opposition preserve a clearer distinction between parties and pressure groups, and enable an inquest to be held on the bargaining and to set limits upon it. Without a clear opposition the concurrent majority has an easier and smoother passage; the manoeuvring of the parties mirrors rather than controls the manoeuvring of pressure groups. With such an opposition some accountability of the government is achieved, some governmental and group activity is brought into the open, and the numerical majority while sometimes ignored is never forgotten.

Yet so far from there being an antithesis between the concurrent and the numerical majorities, or between pressure groups and political parties, the two are complementary. While groups narrow the range of choice of both the government and the electorate, they are, too, an aid and comfort to the elected government. For pressure groups have a reverse effect. Their authority over their members is invaluable. They bring the consent of their members to acts of government. And, besides, they often act as offshoots of the state and do the government's work for it.

Swarms of 'secondary powers' so far from being a barrier to free government are its essential pre-condition. The 'new feudalism' provides an important connection between the government and the governed between elections. Freedom of association is at least as important as freedom of speech. If organised groups did not exist, Rousseau's gibe that the British people were free only at election times would be a charitable judgment. Those fleeting moments of freedom would soon cease. Twentieth century experience has amply confirmed Acton's doctrine that liberty is possible only in societies where there are organisations in existence other than political.[74] Only totalitarians want to sweep away countervailing centres of power, and the continued existence of such centres is the best defence against totalitarianism.

Interest groups represent the enlightened self interest of the community. They are the heirs and successors of 'property', and the safeguards of what Burke meant by prescription. They are a defence against momentary bouts of hysteria and the depredations of government. They are the slayers of the dragon of the 'general will', that myth with which dictators and Utopian parties clothe themselves to conceal the imposition of their own particular will.

Like broad based parties, interest groups encourage rule by interest instead of by ideology. They stand for Burke against Rousseau.

Governments seldom ride roughshod over them. Industry and the Trade Unions are great estates of the realm, and today social restraints on government are at least as important as constitutional ones. The government that ignored the first would be acting as unconstitutionally as one that ignored the second. But pressure groups do not rule. As Keynes said, '. . . the power of vested interests is vastly exaggerated compared with the gradual encroachment of ideas . . . soon or late, it is ideas not vested interests which are dangerous for good or evil'.[75] Interest groups act as a breakwater of ideology and ideas, until these are generally accepted by the community, when they are accepted by the interests as well. Besides, if interests represent Burke, broadcasting represents Rousseau. Through television, Government and particularly the Prime Minister can reach the people direct without the mediating influence of parties, interests or parliament.

Britain may be more 'organised' than America, but 'feudal groups' have not reduced the central power to impotence. Groups reinforce the tendencies of British government to weakness not by any exercise of power, undue or otherwise, but by extending the field of governmental secrecy and by scarcely adding to the field of public controversy. The entry of so many of them into the magic circle of Whitehall diminishes the opportunity of fruitful conflict at Westminster. In this, they are abiding by the rules of the system, not creating new ones.

Within the political system, secondary powers remain secondary. Hazlitt defined a Jacobin as 'one who would have his single opinion govern the world and overturn everything in it'.[76] Groups are a barrier to Jacobinism; they are not a barrier to strong government.

III

LAW

What looks like a stone wall to a layman is a triumphal arch to a lawyer.

'MR. DOOLEY'[1]

In another case of abuse of a charity, the case was 'actually called on' in the Court of Chancery, December 21st, a year and a half ago. But the court made up its mind that it would not make up its mind. On the 9th of April, for which it was fixed, the court with its usual promptitude determined that it would not determine. On the 13th of May it came on, and the court pronounced on one point . . . but reserved judgment on the other points. To elucidate those points the court [Lord Chancellor Eldon] took home the papers and no more was heard of the case for many months . . . It was postponed to the 20th of January, on which day it was not judged. Two days afterwards the same occurrence took place. It was then decided that it should not be decided till another day, on which other day it was again decided that it should not be decided till another day. . . . It was appointed positively *for the 29th of February, there being but 28 days in that month. . . . On a subsequent day it was mentioned. This word 'mentioned' was a light and airy word in that House, but in the Court of Chancery it was attended with fees to the counsel, fees to the agents. . . . In short a 'mention' was not the most inexpensive and agreeable procedure that could befall a suitor. Some days after, the court acknowledged that it had mislaid the papers which, so many months before, it had taken home to peruse, and desired that a brief (attended with considerable expense) might be left with the court. On the 17th of March it was again called on, and at length it was—not decided, for decided it was not until the present moment—but it was referred to the Master. That meant that it was sent out of one expensive court into another expensive court. . . . The Court of Chancery might be excellent for many purposes, but to the suitors in it it was ruinous.*

HENRY BROUGHAM in the House of Commons, 1818[2]

In 1929 the Lord Chief Justice of England, Lord Hewart, launched a fierce attack on the 'pretensions and encroachments' of the executive. 'There is in existence,' he wrote, 'a persistent and well-contrived system, intended to produce, and in practice producing, a despotic power which at one and the same time places government departments above the sovereignty of Parliament and beyond the jurisdiction of the Courts.' In place of the rule of law there was 'the new despotism' and 'administrative lawlessness'.[3] Hewart's attack would have been better directed against his own profession than against the Civil Service. The state of affairs which he deplored was the outcome of judicial abdication and retreat, a retreat which continued until well after the Second World War. The Judges could not claim, in the common phrase of the last war, to have been moving to better positions; still less could they say with the American General whose division in the Korean War was swiftly retiring: 'Gentlemen, we are not retreating. We are merely attacking in another direction.'[4] For a long time, indeed, the Judges did not notice that they were moving at all. Yet the result of their retreat is that British administrative law lags far behind that of many other countries.*

In the seventeenth century the Judges, except during the Civil War and Interregnum, held office at the King's pleasure and broadly were subservient to the Stuarts. Charles II dismissed twelve Judges in twenty-five years and James II ten in four years.[6] It was not until the Act of Settlement laid down that Judges should hold office during good behaviour that the Judiciary's independence of the executive was firmly established. In the lengthy row between John Wilkes and the government, the Courts were unequivocally on the side of the liberty of the individual.† In the great case of *Entick v. Carrington*[7] in 1765, Lord Camden, L.C.J., finely said: 'And with respect to the argument of State necessity, or a distinction which has been aimed at between State offences and others, the common law does not understand that kind of reasoning, nor do our books take notice of any such distinctions.' And in general that attitude prevailed, until towards the end of the nineteenth century. In 1885 Dicey exulted that in Britain there was no *droit administratif*; unlike France the servants of the executive were subject to the same rules as everybody else.[8]

The attitude of the Courts to parliament was different. In the

---

* 'Administrative law,' Professor William A. Robson has suggested, 'should be regarded as the law relating to public administration, in the same way as commercial law consists of the law relating to commerce, or land law the law relating to land.'[5]

† When the messengers sent to arrest Wilkes were in difficulties, the Secretary of State, Halifax, who lived nearby, invited Wilkes to come and see him at his house. Wilkes at first declined on the ground that he had not been introduced.

seventeenth century the common lawyers were allied with the House of Commons against the Crown and the Prerogative Courts. Their concern was with private rights; the concern of the Prerogative Courts was with policy. 'The Star Chamber,' said Maitland, 'was useful;' but 'it was a court of politicians enforcing a policy, not a court of judges administering the law.'[9] The Common Law Courts, having achieved victory, had no wish to assume the attributes of the vanquished, especially since to do so would have brought them into conflict with their ally parliament. They had been on the side of parliamentary supremacy, and once that supremacy was achieved it was not for the Courts to dispute it. Yet while the Courts did not follow Coke[10] or Holt[11] in holding that they could declare an Act of Parliament void, they were a long way from their later attitude of reverential servility to statutes. In 1863 Byles, J., said, 'although there are no positive words in a statute requiring that the party shall be heard, yet the justice of the common law will supply the omission of the legislature'.[12]

Only at the onset of the collectivist era did the great judicial flight begin, the Courts leaving the field just when their presence was most necessary. The Judges were bewildered and frightened. 'Do not imagine,' Maitland told his students in 1888, 'that English law is exhausted by those departments of it that you can study here —the law of crimes, the law of property, torst and contracts, and that part of constitutional law which is concerned with king and parliament. . . . If you take up a modern volume of the reports of the Queen's Bench Division, you will find that about half the cases reported have to do with rules of administrative law.'[13] But in recognising all this, Maitland was far ahead of the Judges.

Formerly their principle had been to treat government servants like private people and to contain the argument of State necessity; hence there was virtually no public law in England. But now the problem had changed. In the collectivist era there was now an argument of State necessity. The government was necessarily invading the sphere of private rights Instead of merely treating the State the same as everybody else and legalising its incursions, (provided they seemed to be properly authorised by parliament), the Courts should have concentrated on seeing that the way the government interfered was in accordance with the principles of law. Their laudable determination not to put the government above the law needed to be supplemented by a determination to see that the government conformed to the standards of ordinary people.

Otherwise the contest between the State and the wronged individual was bound to be unequal.

Yet the Courts ignored the changed situation. The growth of the bureaucracy, the manner of delegated legislation, the changed relationship between the executive and parliament all passed them by. Led by Law Lords, many of whom had a political background, they still acted as though parliament legislated as it had done up to about 1860, and as though parliament stood in relation to the executive as it had in the eighteenth century. In consequence they conducted themselves to parliament and the executive with a legalistic formalism reminiscent of their behaviour in the middle ages, and a subservience reminiscent of their behaviour in the early seventeenth century.

Anxious not to offend the executive, the Courts got themselves so entangled in their own procedures, fictions and inhibitions that 'the rusty curb of old father antick the law'[14] has curbed only itself, not the executive. They have slavishly worshipped at the shrine of parliamentary sovereignty. Not for them the reasoning of French Jurists of the seventeenth and eighteenth centuries, who while asserting the sovereignty of the King maintained that in the event of the King wishing to issue bad edicts '. . . the sovereign courts owe it to their reputation to offer to the prince grave remonstrances and to try in every sort of way to turn him from his course'.[15]

British Judges did not even emulate the realism and logic of medieval theologians. Contemplating the omnipotence of God the schoolmen used to speculate whether God being almighty could act contrary to his own nature: whether for example he could sin or whether he could make a square circle. They decided that, since sin was a failure, God could not sin, and that the question whether God could make a square circle was a nonsense question, which could not be answered since it could not in reason be asked.[16] British Judges, with the exception of Lord Denning,* have made no such speculations and taken no such decisions about the omnipotence of parliament. They were too scared of becoming involved in political controversy. So however fictional the notion that parliament had decided something, or that it intended a particular result, the Courts have treated parliament as more omnipotent than

---

* 'It is often said,' Lord Denning once pointed out in a dissenting judgment in the Court of Appeal, 'that Parliament can do anything, but I do not know that even Parliament can so divest itself of its functions as to leave the making of such an important enactment to a government department without any consideration of it by Parliament itself.'[17] But such common sense and realism has been rare.

the schoolmen treated God. Unlike the French Conseil d'Etat they have time and again allowed their jurisdiction to be ousted.

The two World Wars profoundly influenced the Judiciary. So did the generally high standards of the Civil Service. Though inevitably there have been abuses, the bureaucracy has usually tried to be fair and is seldom intolerably overbearing. But even a law-abiding community needs enforceable rules, as the Judges in every other branch of the law have always recognised.

And when all is said, the renunciation by the Judges of their duty to foster administrative law not administrative arbitrariness was not in the nature of things. It was the result of the personalities involved. Had there been more Judges like Lord Atkin, Lord Wright, Lord Denning, Lord Reid, Lord Devlin, Lord Justice Salmon, and (the latter-day) Lord Radcliffe, and had there been fewer like Lord Simon, Lord Jowett, Lord Simonds and Lord Greene, this country would today enjoy effective Judicial supervision of administrative behaviour.

The crucial case in determining whether the Judges would in quasi-judicial matters impose proper procedures upon the executive was *Local Government Board v. Arlidge*[18] in 1915. Yet that case might easily have gone the other way. The Court of Appeal decided by a majority that for a party not to be allowed to see the Inspector's Report of a public inquiry was a denial of natural justice. There was no reason why the House of Lords should not have done the same. After all, Sir Henry Taylor, eighty years earlier, had laid down that when a minister was called upon to 'deliver a quasi-judicial decision' he should always give reasons.[19] And forty years after *Arlidge*'s case, the Franks Committee on Administrative Tribunals and Enquiries maintained that 'openness, fairness and impartiality' should mark these procedures.[20]

But the House of Lords knew none of these things. 'That the Judiciary', said Lord Shaw of Dunfermline, 'should presume to impose its own methods on administrative or executive officers is a usurpation.'[21] The House of Lords preferred abdication; and the reasoning of their Lordships set the judicial tone for the next forty years. The Board was represented in Parliament by its responsible head, and he was answerable to parliament. If the department could be compelled to disclose the views of the Inspector, 'a serious impediment might be placed upon that frankness which ought to obtain among a staff accustomed to elaborately detailed and often most delicate and difficult tasks. . . '.[22] In other words their Lordships thought the convenience and alleged efficiency of the system of secrecy in executive departments was of greater moment than the denial of justice to a private litigant. In the name of parliamentary supremacy and ministerial responsibility, the Courts declined to prescribe proper rules for fair dealing between the departments and private individuals. It was only forty years later, as a result of the Franks Report, that the Court of Appeal's decision was in effect restored and the publication of Inspectors' Reports enjoined by the government.*

Many other important cases might also have been decided differently. In many of them, dissenting judgments were delivered by Judges at least as eminent as those who decided in favour of the executive. In *R. V. Halliday*,[25] Lord Shaw of Dunfermline (on the right side this time) said: 'And what remains is the argument that Parliament, not expressly dealing with a matter pre-eminently demanding careful delimitation, must be held to have accomplished by implication this far-reaching subversion of our liberties. To this argument I am respectfully unable to accede. I do not think that the Defence of the Realm Acts can be submitted to such a violent and strained construction. . . .' Yet the majority held that such a far-reaching subversion had been accomplished.

In the House of Lords twenty-four years later Lord Atkin laid down that a public board was under a duty to act with reasonable diligence. The rest of the House disagreed, thus throwing away the opportunity to develop a duty of diligence, and supported a proposition, which in Atkin's words was 'opposed to public interests when there are so many public bodies exercising statutory powers and employing public money upon them'.[26] Yet French administrative law has imposed a duty of diligence, and there was no reason why the House of Lords should not have done the same.

Lord Atkin's dissenting judgment in *Liversidge v. Anderson*[27] is famous. He viewed 'with apprehension the attitude of judges who

* The Court in Arlidge's case was entirely political: Haldane was the Liberal Lord Chancellor; Parmoor had been a Unionist M.P. from 1895 until the previous year and had been considered by Balfour as a possible law officer;[23] Moulton had been a Liberal M.P. on and off from 1881 to 1906; and Shaw of Dunfermline was Lord Advocate in the Liberal government up to 1909. Similarly of the 'good' judges named on page 372, none, except Reid who was a Tory M.P. for four years, was a politician, and all of the 'bad' ones were except Greene—and even he drafted most of Lloyd George's National Insurance Act.[24] Admittedly Simonds's judicial attitude was formed long before he became a politician; also some 'political' Judges like Birkenhead were 'good'. All the same the record of the House of Lords in its legal capacity in this century provides a strong argument for the separation of powers.

N

on a mere question of construction when face to face with claims involving the liberty of the subject, show themselves more executive-minded than the executive. . . . In this case I have listened to arguments which might have been addressed acceptably to the Court of King's Bench in the time of Charles I.'* Yet his colleagues, as Lord Devlin later wrote, held that the words ' "if the Secretary of State has reasonable cause to believe" did not mean if he had in fact reasonable cause to believe, but if he thought he had'.[30] Not surprisingly, Lord Reid recently described *Liversidge v. Anderson* as 'a very peculiar decision'.[31]

This sorry judicial abdication endured for ten years or so after the war. To take only the worst cases, the Courts held in 1951 and 1953 that licensing authorities could revoke licenses without giving their holders a hearing, even though the livelihood of the licence holder was at stake.[32] As Professor Wade has pointed out, 'not only have these decisions put us behind other countries of the democratic world . . . they silently ignore the long-established common law presumption that the duty to hear both sides is a universal principle of justice which is to be implied into statutory powers'.[33] Then in *Smith v. East Elloe R.D.C.*[34] a majority of the House of Lords, Lord Reid and Lord Somervill sensibly dissenting, held that a compulsory purchase order could not be questioned in any legal proceedings, even where *mala fides* was alleged.

This judicial surrender cannot be easily excused on the grounds that it was based on a wise restraint and a general anxiety not to trespass beyond the proper functions of the courts by indulgence in judicial law-making. Although there has been less judicial legislation in this century than in the past, there has been a good deal. That Judges make law is, as Lord Radcliffe has said, a 'fairly obvious conclusion'.[35] The Courts have not hesitated to make law in such matters as importing civil liability for damage suffered through factory owners failing to comply with regulations for the safety of workmen. And nobody could accuse the House of Lords of judicial restraint in the *Ladies' Directory* case,[36] when it upheld the conviction

* The presiding Law Lord in the case, Lord Maugham, gave unwitting support to Atkin's remark about executive-minded judges, by writing to *The Times* saying that in his own judgment he had not been able 'to make any protest about what I took to be an offensive remark in relation to the Attorney General and his eminent junior'. Had he known what Lord Atkin was going to say, he would have intervened, to 'protect the Attorney General'.[28] Just why Maugham felt he should protect the Attorney General against a judge much more distinguished than himself was not made clear. According to his brother, Somerset, Lord Maugham 'was very unpopular in the House of Lords, because, as one member told me, he treated the Peers as hostile witnesses'.[29]

of the defendant, Shaw, for conspiring with prostitutes to corrupt public morals, an extraordinarily vague offence, which was thought not to have existed since the seventeenth century.

Lord Reid, who has been one of the judges most alive to the need to develop administrative law, was the sole dissentient in *Shaw*'s case, saying that 'where Parliament fears to tread it is not for the Courts to rush in'. In revealing contrast Lord Simonds was one of the most prominent exponents of judicious passivity in civil cases. 'Nor will I easily be led,' he said in 1962, 'by an undiscerning zeal for some abstract kind of justice to ignore our first duty which is to administer justice according to the law, the law which is established for us by Act of Parliament or the binding authority of precedent . . . [Reform] is the task not of the Courts of Law, but of Parliament.'[37] Yet in the *Ladies' Directory* case he said: 'In the sphere of criminal law I entertain no doubt that there remains in the Courts of Law a residual power to enforce the supreme and fundamental purpose of the law, to conserve not only the safety and order but also the moral welfare of the state; . . . the Law must be related to the changing standards of life. . . .' But evidently not administrative law.

'It is the judges,' said Bentham, 'that make the Common Law. Do you know how they make it? Just as a man makes law for his dog. When your dog does anything you want to break him of, you wait till he does it, and then you beat him for it. This is the way you make laws for your dog, and this is the way the judges make law for you and me.'[38] Regrettably the Law Lords have been more willing, as it were, to beat prostitutes than ministers or Civil Servants.

So little inevitable, indeed, was the Judges' capitulation to the executive that dating roughly from the Crichel Down scandal and the Franks Report, and particularly during the last few years, there has been a distinct improvement. The Judges have begun to wake up to their responsibilities. In such cases as *Ridge v. Baldwin*,[39] (when they asserted the right to a fair hearing), *Conway v. Rimmer*[40] (when they overruled their own decision on Crown Privilege in *Duncan v. Cammel Laird*) and *Padfield and others v. Ministry of Agriculture*[41] (when they ordered the minister to consider a complaint by milk producers), the long obeisance to the executive seems at last to have ended.

Yet the half century of judicial pusillanimity has made the present task of the Courts much more difficult than it need have been. They are now shackled by their past. As a result, as Lord Reid has said, 'we do not have a developed system of administrative law—perhaps because until recently we did not need it'.[42] And Lord Devlin has said that he believes it 'to be generally recognised that in many of his dealings with the executive the citizen cannot get justice by process of law. I am not saying that he cannot get justice but that he cannot get it by process of law'.[43]

The Courts in the licensing and other cases have even weakened the principles of natural justice: the right to a hearing, and freedom from bias or prejudice. The Judges in their contradictory rulings over the prerogative writs have imposed puzzling and unnecessary limitations on their capacity to supervise administrative action. As Professor de Smith has said, 'judicial review in England lacks breadth and depth. Review of determinations made by bodies that have been constituted as distinct statutory tribunals is generally adequate; but review of the validity of the acts and decisions of other administrative bodies tends to be perfunctory and ineffective.'[44] There is no general rule that reasons must be given for administrative action. All too often the Courts have accepted the assertion of the relevant authority that it was 'satisfied' instead of enquiring as to whether it had genuine cause for such satisfaction. Consequently there is no English equivalent of the American 'substantial evidence rule'.[45] Nor is there a requirement in English law that administrative action must be reasonable.[46]

In England, therefore, much administrative action is guarded from judicial scrutiny.[47] In France, on the other hand, as has become almost a commonplace since the publication in 1954 of Professor Hamson's famous book *Executive Discretion and Judicial Control* the Conseil d'Etat often provides effective protection for the citizen against administrative action, when in England there would be none.

In 1949 Mrs. Woollett was told her three acres of requisitioned land in Essex would shortly be released to her. Accordingly she bought a lot of equipment for it. Then the ministry told her they were not going to release it. Mrs. Woollett had no redress.[48]

When there were regulations which seemed to the judge 'to purport to lay down mutually binding terms of employment between the Crown and the employee, to which the assent of employees has to be obtained',[49] they turned out to be valueless to him.

Some citizens of Southend bought some land on the assurance of the Chief Engineer of the Borough. Later the Borough said the Engineer had been wrong and went back on the assurance. The people concerned suffered damage through being totally misled, but they had no redress.[50] In all these cases the French Conseil d'Etat would not have allowed itself to be similarly stultified. It would have seen that the aggrieved citizens were given justice.

Plainly therefore the English system needs amendment and improvement. The Parliamentary Commissioner set up in 1966 will be able to rectify some cases of maladministration and injustice. But large fields of administration, including the whole of local government, are excluded from his purview. In any case the Parliamentary Commissioner is at best a palliative. The need is not for more and better policemen; the need is for more and better law.

There are two main paths for reform. The first possibility is the creation over here of something akin to a Conseil d'Etat, the setting up of an executive system of justice, divorced from the ordinary courts, to supervise the executive. In the Middle Ages there was often a close connection between government departments and courts of law; the Exchequer, the Chancery, the Privy Seal and the Court of Requests, and also the Admiralty, all had their own courts. So there is a precedent of a sort for such a development. Nor need any Diceyan prudishness about the creation of *droit administratif* be a bar to such a creation. Yet the Conseil d'Etat itself has, in Professor Hamson's words, 'grown more than it has been made'.[51] An institution that in France has evolved over a long period of time is unlikely to lend itself to a successful transplant to England in its fully developed form. An English Conseil d'Etat would almost certainly turn out to be very different from its French prototype.

A more promising line of development is an extension and improvement of present British procedures. Even a few years ago such an idea would have seemed a vain hope. Lord Devlin could 'doubt if judges will now of their own motion contribute much more to the development of the law'.[52] But that conclusion now looks over-pessimistic.* In any case there is every reason why statute should give the judges a helping hand.

* Yet more than 80 per cent of the time of the Judges of the Queen's Bench Division is spent in hearing motor car and other accident cases, which could probably be dealt with more effectively by special tribunals. At the same time really important matters which concern the rights of the people of this country have been withdrawn from the courts and handed over to special tribunals and inquiries. Prior to their elevation to the bench, leading barristers appear at these hearings; it is only after they have become judges that they are condemned to spending most of their time on trivia. That the Judiciary should have complacently accepted this self-evidently absurd state of affairs does not encourage optimism about the future.

The prerogative orders, certiorari, mandamus, and prohibition, are organic in English law. The rules relating to them should be simplified, codified and enacted. The barnacles that have been attached to them by the Courts' restrictive interpretation should be removed. Thus strengthened, the prerogative orders would be a formidable hindrance to administrative injustice. The Habeas Corpus Act of 1679 is a precedent for such a statute. The same act could give statutory effect to Lord Denning's dictum[53] that 'if a substantial question exists which one person has a real interest to raise, and the other to oppose, then the Court has a discretion to resolve it by a declaration, which it will exercise if there is good reason for so doing'.*

At the same time an Administrative Division of the High Court should be set up. The Statute creating such a division should also lay down that anybody affected by an administrative decision would be entitled to know the reasons for it. He would then be able to challenge the decision if it was wrong in law, or was based on wrong facts, or was unreasonable.

Yet while Parliament should again come to the rescue of the judiciary as it did in 1958, the prime requirement is for the Judges to adopt a more robust and realistic attitude to the executive, and for them to accept proper responsibility for the state of the law and the consequences of their judgments. This is not because the executive is intent on subverting our liberties or rights; nor even because maladministration is rife. It has been estimated that proportionately to the number of decisions there is probably no more maladministration than there are miscarriages of justice.[54] And nobody wants the Judges to make a practice of substituting their judgment for those of ministers or of administrative tribunals. What is wanted is that the rules of fair play should be observed, not merely between individuals but between individuals and the government. The Judges have a duty to preserve the rule of law, and there can be no rule of law if the powers of the executive are exercised arbitrarily and are not subject to judicial review.

If Judges shrug off responsibility for the state of the law, not only does justice suffer but also the law itself. 'A litigant today,' wrote

* Recently the most useful judicial remedy in administrative law has been the declaration, which carries no sanction. In this, the law is not out of step with politics.

Lord Evershed, a former Master of the Rolls, 'whose action depends on delicate problems of the interpretation of English statutes . . . may find himself carried from one court to another in the toils of a controversy that has in it no question of principle, no savour of common sense, but only the intricacies of a battle of words to which the final solution may seem to him in the end to have been determined no more persuasively than by the toss of the coin.' And he added that he was 'alarmed lest the individual citizen come to regard the law as an unintelligible mystique. . . . If the enacted law came to be regarded as inviting the use of sufficient ingenuity to find a means of evading its terms, there could be no moral sanction behind it'.[55]

Politicians and Civil Servants must bear much of the blame, nevertheless Lord Evershed's words are a stinging criticism of the philosophy of law which has been dominant on the bench for most of this century. A pre-war Lord Chancellor summed up that philosophy when he complained that Lord Atkin was 'rather apt to take the opportunity of making the law as it ought to be, instead of administering it as it is'.[56]

No doubt the law as 'it ought to be' attitude, now effectively represented by Lord Denning, can be exaggerated, but the law 'as it is' attitude leads to utter sterility and the consequences outlined by Lord Evershed. Judges undertake an oath to do justice according to law, not, as it were, to do law according to law. Like everybody else they should pay attention to the consequence of their own actions. In other words they should try to do justice in the particular case before them and they should build up a coherent body of law. After all, even if the Judges claim merely to interpret the law, not to make it, an attitude which has been described as 'the law is the law is the law', they are still bound to make law. The choice is not between making and not making law, it is between making reasonable law and unreasonable law.

The Judges cannot abandon responsibility for the rule of law to parliament. No legislature can make laws for every conceivable eventuality. Besides the rule of law is something far more than the corpus of enacted law at any moment.* If parliament's job is to govern the country, it is the judges' job to see that government is

* *Pace.* Mr. Justice Donaldson, who though not deferential to the executive in the Enfield Schools case allowed himself to say: 'The duty of the courts . . . is to be vigilant to ensure that the government of this country . . . is conducted in accordance with the will of Parliament, that is to say, according to the rule of law.'[57]

carried on according to law. As Mr. Justice Byles suggested one hundred years ago, the justice of the common law must supply the omission of the legislature. Instead of restricting their jurisdiction, as they have tended to do,[58] the courts should extend it. The objective is not that judges rather than politicians or civil servants should decide policy. That would be disastrous. The job of the Courts is to decide questions of law and to enforce minimum procedural safeguards.[59]

For the Courts to carry out their proper duties is as much in the interest of the executive as in that of the public and of the Courts themselves. Public acceptance of the executive's policies would be enormously aided by a confidence that fair procedures were being followed. Even the most executive-minded Judges should therefore alter their ways, since for the Courts to do their proper job would in fact help the executive, while judicial abdication hinders it. Naturally the breakdown of total ministerial responsibility will facilitate a more active judicial role as well as making it even more necessary.

Much as President Kennedy's tenure in the White House produced admiration for American government, so the recent prestige of the U.S. Supreme Court has evoked some desire over here for a written constitution and full Judicial Review. Yet the fallibility of Judges is one of the strongest arguments against such an importation. The Supreme Court's record is far from unblemished;* and Judges, as Justice Frankfurter[60] has said, 'unconsciously are too apt to be moved by the deep undercurrents of public feeling'.† And leaving aside the question whether or not parliament can bind its successors, and

---

* See pages 298-9.

† This was amply demonstrated by the Hiss case. After the jury had disagreed at the first Hiss trial, the local hysterical anti-Hiss newspaper 'coverage' of the case, the attacks on the trial judge by Mr. Nixon and the press—Nixon said the judge's 'prejudice against the prosecution' had been 'obvious and apparent'—and the publicity thrust upon the pro-Hiss jurors, a second trial in New York could plainly not be fair. But that was where it took place, and the U.S. judges denied Hiss's appeal. Yet within a year the Supreme Court allowed an appeal in a non-political case Justice Jackson saying: 'If freedoms of the press are so absurd as to make fair trial in the locality impossible, the judicial process must be protected by removing the trial to a forum beyond its probable influence.'[61]

R. V. Joyce, the 'Lord Haw-Haw' case, showed that English Judges, also, are moved by public feeling.

plainly, if it cannot, a written constitution would be valueless since the 'constitutional' laws would be no more strongly entrenched than any other law, liberties are still more secure in Britain without a written constitution than they are in other countries. This country is not in danger of dictatorship. Arbitrariness not autocracy is the threat.

Only in the sphere of administrative law have the Judges 'slept on the watch'. Elsewhere they have zealously guarded the fundamental freedoms of the people; they certainly have not 'gone over to the enemy'. Lord Denning has written of 'the part that the Judges have played. Men who have come of the common people themselves, they have evolved principles of law which express the spirit of the people—the spirit of freedom: and, with the practical genius of the people they have built up a procedure which protects that freedom more securely than any other system of law that the world has ever seen'.[62]

As Professor Mitchell has said, 'it is of the nature of our constitution to live in danger'.[64] In that atmosphere of danger the constitution has survived, and has preserved individual liberties more successfully than constitutions elsewhere. A written constitution and the might of the Supreme Court did not prevent shocking treatment of the Japanese Americans in the last war.[63] No such excesses were permitted in this country. A fixed constitution provides only the illusion of safety.

IV

THE PRESS AND TELEVISION

What should we think of that philosopher, who, in writing at the present day, a treatise upon naval architecture and the theory of navigation, should omit wholly from his calculation that new and mighty power . . . which walks the water like a giant rejoicing in its course . . . the power of steam . . . ?
So, in political science, he who, speculating on the British Constitution, should content himself with marking the distribution of acknowledged technical powers between the House of Lords, the House of Commons and the Crown . . . and should think that he had thus described the British Constitution as it acts and as it is influenced in its action: but should omit from its enumeration that mighty power of public opinion, embodied in a free press, which pervades, and checks, and perhaps, in the last resort, nearly governs the whole. Such a man would surely give but an imperfect view of the government of England. . . .

GEORGE CANNING[1]

Let it be impressed upon your minds, let it be instilled into your children, that the liberty of the press is the palladium of all the civil, political and religious rights of an Englishman.

JUNIUS[2]

If there is ever to be an amelioration of the condition of mankind, philosophers, theologians, legislators, politicians and moralists will find that the regulation of the press is the most difficult, dangerous and important problem they have to resolve. Mankind can not now be governed without it, nor at present with it.

JOHN ADAMS[3]

The British political system throws a fence up round decision making, and the press is left outside, seeing little and late. If 'the press', as Delane's *Times* put it, 'lives by disclosures',[4] it is stifled in present-day Britain by the essentially unitary character of British government. Newspapers thrive on division. Divisions breed disclosure; unity prevents it. One Civil Service, one party, one ministry, these unities all merging into one greater unity, the government one and indivisible, effectively banish the press from its proper territory of disclosing the differences, arguments and quarrels that precede the formulation of government policy, and leave it to report only what it is allowed to know about the policy itself. Once a government has decided upon policy, the press is encouraged to advertise it. Little wonder that having been excluded from the hunt, the press sometimes shows little interest in the carcase that is contemptuously flung to it.

Under a constitution like the American, based upon division not unity, the press cannot be similarly excluded. The division between the executive and Congress, the absence of flummery about ministerial responsibility, the lack of disciplined parties controlled from the centre, the heterogeneous character of the cabinet, all ensure that the press is flooded with leaked information. American critics occasionally complain that their government is practising British type secrecy. It is a pale imitation, for at any given moment publicity is in the interest of too many people. Because the executive cannot rely on getting its programme through Congress, it cannot merely tell Congress what it wants. Congressional opinion has to be sounded, and individual Congressmen placated. Members of Congress have nothing to gain from sealing their lips. Useful publicity in his district is often more important to a Congressman than pleasing the executive by guarding its secrets.

The testimony of Civil Servants and top military brass before Congressional committees frequently brings into the open differences within executive departments. Differences between departments as well as within them are also revealed, and in the competition for Congress's attention and money, publicity is a principal weapon.

Disclosure then is the stuff of American politics, as secrecy is of British politics. It was not always so. In the middle of the nineteenth century the press played as prominent a part in Britain as it does in America today. The narrower basis of government made politicians apprehensive of the world outside their own small circle. The garrison felt beleaguered. The newspapers, it believed, kept it in touch with public opinion, although respect for public opinion did not necessarily entail a respect for the alleged purveyors of it. Canning, for instance, combined an acute sense of the importance of public opinion with a profound contempt for newspapers.[5] Yet the feelings of politicians about the press were unimportant. Newspapers considered themselves to be the organs of public opinion and were usually taken at their own valuation.

The structure of government necessarily enhanced the power of the press. It was indeed fairly similar to that existing in America at the present time. Centralised disciplined parties were not yet in existence, the government was not immune from defeat in the House of Commons, the Civil Service was departmental not unified, and the idea that officials were like a vast Moslem harem that should be veiled to everybody except their masters was unknown. Leading politicians wrote for the press anonymously or under pseudonyms, a practice which is both indicative of and conducive to private disclosures to newspapers. Neither Brougham nor Palmerston, the two most prolific politician-journalists, thought anything of denouncing cabinet policy in their articles.* The press was inextricably involved in politics. Not only did the press in the nineteenth century have access to the top politicians who were anxious to use it, it had easy access to Civil Servants as well. Two of the more prominent leader writers on *The Times*, Reeve and Lowe, were Civil Servants.

The press and parliament are frequently thought, not least by M.P.s and journalists, to be in competition with each other.† In fact they stand or fall together. The golden age of parliament was also the golden age of the press. A quasi-independent parliament drives the executive into the open, produces publicity and a powerful press. A dependent parliament cannot flush the executive out of its dark recesses, and produces secrecy and a weakened press.

It was the eclipse of party and the fluidity of politics that allowed both parliament and press their brief heyday in the sun. Well might Delane be suspicious of the revival of party feeling in the 1860s. Shifting coalitions and undisciplined groups, controlled by neither the cabinet nor the voters, produced a continual flow of disclosures which gave him and *The Times* their power and position. Mass disciplined parties are the great enemies of the press. By extending their organisation to embrace the whole country, they deprive the

---

* This habit survived fitfully into a later age. Gladstone, anonymously, and Bonar Law, pseudonymously, attacked their own government's policy in the press.[6] Nowadays a minister criticises government policy or his colleagues by means of an off-the-record briefing of selected journalists.

† This is a long-standing attitude. The *Spectator* wrote in 1834: 'The tone in which newspapers are usually mentioned in the House of Commons is absurd. Men who cannot breakfast without one, in the evening pretend to be hardly cognisant of such things. Men who in private life look to them almost for their sole stock of opinions, are found in public sneering at their contents.'[7] Admittedly, the convention that government announcements should first be made in the House of Commons handicaps the press.[8] But while the convention determines the way in which the government releases the news, it need not always determine the way in which the press gets the news.

press of its claim to be the only true representative of public opinion. And by gaining control of the legislature, they enable the real decision-making to be done in secret. The press is put in a double squeeze. Party comes in between it and the public, and party prevents it disclosing the processes of government. Hence the paradox that in Britain the beginning of the move towards democracy saw the beginning of the political decline of the institution seemingly best adapted to democracy, the press. And except during the First World War, the decline continued.

Six years after the second Reform Bill, a Treasury memorandum drew attention to recent cases 'in which information derived from official sources has been communicated without authority to the public press, apparently by members of the Civil Service. . . . My Lords are of opinion that such breaches of official confidence are offences of the very gravest character which a public officer can commit, and they will not hesitate, in any case where they themselves possess the power of dismissal to visit such an offence with this extreme penalty . . .'.[9] The Civil Service was thus placed out of bounds to the press, and the consequences of the prohibition have grown with the increasing size and importance of government departments.

The passing of the Official Secrets Acts gave an additional weapon to the government to use against the press. Stricter than in any other free country, they effectively prevent the giving of information to newspapers by active or retired Civil Servants unless the disclosures are in the interests of the government. The Official Secrets Acts are the sanction behind secret government; they did not create it. They are merely the logical extension of Mr. Gladstone's Treasury memorandum of 1873 and of 'ministerial responsibility' and a silent Civil Service. Nevertheless the docility of the press in the face of them is surprising. It has accepted its exclusion from the crucial governmental processes with scarcely a whimper. As facilities for the press have expanded, its ability to ferret out real news has contracted. Press Agents* have under various names spread through government, and press conferences and off the record briefings have grown in frequency. All these developments, however, have merely given the press more opportunity to publish what the government wants published, and less opportunity to publish what the government does not want published. In 1964 the process was taken to its logical conclusion by Mr. Wilson. He

* The term originated in the American circus.[10]

forbade a minister to talk to journalists unless he was chaperoned by his press officer, who then sent a report of the proceedings to the Paymaster General at 10 Downing Street.*

The legal system like the political system is inimical to the proper workings of the press. 'The British press,' said Mr. Cecil Harmsworth King in 1962,[11] 'is in fact censored. Not directly: not openly by decree. But by the arbitrary operation of a series of loosely drawn laws which make it hazardous in the extreme for newspapers to comment or even report on a number of issues of vital public importance.'

The restrictions Mr. King had in mind were the Official Secrets Acts, contempt of court, the libel laws, and the law of parliamentary privilege. The Official Secrets Acts have already been dealt with. The law of parliamentary privilege is anomalous but does not seriously hamper the press. Some element of sense was introduced into the law of contempt of court by the Administration of Justice Act, 1960, which gave in England (but not in Scotland) the right of appeal to those convicted of contempt.

Newspaper comment on the courts and on crime is strongly inhibited. The words 'sub judice' have become in England as magical and as effective, in the opposite sense, as the words 'Open Sesame' were to Aladdin. They have only to be used for mouths to be shut, pens to be stilled, and typewriters silenced. The use of them has spread far beyond the confines of the law courts to outside bodies whose machinery of reaching decisions bears no resemblance to a judicial process.

So far as possible, juries should be influenced in their decisions only by the evidence given in court. The two Hiss trials in New York are a standing warning against trial by newspaper and a monument to the importance of juries being protected from contact with the press both during and after a trial. But judges should not be similarly protected. For one thing they are quite capable of excluding matters that are not evidence from their consideration; for another judges are in fact strongly influenced by the climate of opinion at any given time and nothing is gained by pretending

* On February 1, 1643, a House of Commons resolution forbade M.P.s to speak to foreign ambassadors 'without the leave and the consent of the House'. But Parliament was then at war.

otherwise. The *sub judice* rules should apply only where a jury is involved.

Though the popular adage, 'the greater the truth, the greater the libel', is strictly speaking true only of criminal libel, it has considerable application to civil cases as well. 'Justification' is a complete defence to a civil libel action, but a likely result of relying upon that defence is to encourage the jury to use multiplication tables in assessing the damages. The hazards of the plea of justification are so well known that there is a common saying at the bar: 'Never plead fraud or justification.' The fact that a libel was true is likely merely to introduce another element of danger into the case.

Instead of pleading justification, a newspaper usually pays the litigant a large sum of money and makes a statement in open court apologising for what it had published, protesting that it never intended to reflect upon the plaintiff, that what it said was quite untrue etc., when usually it had meant precisely what it said and what it had said was true. More unblushing untruths are told in these farcical apology scenes than in ordinary criminal proceedings.

After all, a newspaper cannot win a libel action. It can either lose or not lose. And even if it does not lose, it will still be substantially out of pocket. Far easier, therefore, and cheaper to pay danegeld and settle.

The libel laws inhibit useful muckraking. The general belief that there is very little corruption in local government in England is perhaps partly due to the fear of libel preventing the press from exposing it. The exposure of fraud and other parasitical activities is similarly inhibited. The law of libel provides an excuse and a reason for the British press not to do its proper job of 'living by disclosures', of finding out the truth and fearlessly publishing it. Since the public punishes it with massive damages when it tries to tell the country what is going on, the press can plausibly think that everyone will be happier and richer if it relies upon public relations hand-outs, or concentrates its fire upon targets that are unlikely or unable to retaliate.

Yet the press has nobody to blame but itself for its unpopularity with the public. And it is probably right that the law of libel should be heavily weighted against it, though not so outrageously as at present.* Over the Profumo case and its aftermath, sections of both the serious and the popular press showed traces of a moral McCarthy-

* The defence of qualified privilege, as suggested by Lord Shawcross and Justice, should certainly be made available to newspapers.

ism, a desire to prise open the secrets of people's private lives, which is perhaps only kept in check by a libel law that allows people to vindicate in court reputations which they are neither entitled to nor in fact possess. Privacy is more important than perjury, and the preservation of people's private lives is a greater good than the observance of strict canons of justice.

As if a political and a legal system inimical to the press were not enough, the economic environment is also hostile. Though there has been a concentration of ownership and a shrinkage of newspapers in both America and France, British newspaper economics are a jungle unto themselves. 'There is no substitute for circulation,' said William Randolph Hearst.[12] In Britain there is no substitute for advertising. A paper like the *News Chronicle*, which by the standards of any other country had a mass circulation, was killed and since 1956, four Sunday newspapers have disappeared, while one new one has started. The Economist Intelligence Unit forecast the disappearance of three more dailies by 1970.

In 1967 the *Daily Mirror* and the *Daily Express* accounted for nearly three-fifths of the circulation of national morning newspapers in the country. The *Daily Mail* accounted for about 12 per cent, and when the stable companions of the *Mirror* and the *Mail*, the *Sun* and the *Sketch*, are added in, these three groups possessed 85 per cent of the total morning circulation of Britain. A similar concentration exists in the Sunday newspaper field.

This trend towards monopoly has caused general alarm, particularly since it is likely to quicken. Indirect subsidies, as in France, seem to be the best hope, though such a system gives the most help to the richest papers. On the other hand, Lord Thomson has frequently expressed the view that there are too many papers in Britain,* the Mirror group believes there are enough,[13] and, a disinterested expert, Sir Linton Andrews, has pointed out that more newspapers does not necessarily mean more accurate newspapers. Fleet Street, moreover, does not have the field to itself. There are still a lot of local newspapers, though many are in chains. Yet London dominates British newspapers in a way that Paris or New York does not. Only a small percentage of Paris newspapers go beyond the Paris area, and the circulation of local newspapers is

* Other people have expressed the view that there are too many owned by him.

considerably larger than that of the Paris press. In Britain that position is reversed, and future technical developments are likely to favour the metropolitan papers at the expense of the provincial dailies.[14]

The Press Barons

The rise of popular press barons and their attendant empires is not unlike the rise of political parties in a multi-party system. Each strikes, by design or mistake, some chord of popular feeling and rises to a crescendo of success. Sooner or later his paper becomes a little dated, and another strikes a newer and more resounding chord; and so on, with the creations of the earlier maestros usually remaining in existence though often modified in character. The rise and reign of Northcliffe did much to conceal the decline of the British press since the onset of the democratic era. During the First War his prominence seemed to presage not an old power in decay, but a new power rising in triumph. Yet the new dawn was false. The breakdown of party politics and the formation of a coalition, together with quarrels between the politicians and the generals, removed the barriers against the press which had been erected during the previous half century. The normal governmental unities were shattered. At times even cabinet security was 'appallingly bad'.[15] Party was less important than individuals, and the most important servants of the executive, the generals, were not prepared to observe Civil Service rules of secrecy and obedience. 'G.H.Q. could not capture the Passchendaele Ridge,' wrote Lloyd George, 'but it was determined to storm Fleet Street.'[16]

The press was operating in conditions akin to those of its heyday in the middle decades of the nineteenth century. It had two additional advantages. The country's peril kept both public and political opinion in an unusually excitable condition; and an unprecedented agglomeration of press power was in the hands of one man, the greatest newspaper genius of the century, Lord Northcliffe. No wonder that during and just after the war, the press was feared, courted, enlisted, decorated, used and hated with an intensity previously unknown. 'I am quite alive to the fact,' said Carson in 1918, 'that it is almost high treason to say a word against Lord Northcliffe. I know his power and that he does not hesitate to exercise it to try to drive anybody out of any office or a public position if they incur his royal displeasure.'[17] And on Northcliffe's death three years later, Lloyd George said that when he exercised his power, 'most politicians bowed their heads'.[18]

Though the press seemed to derive its power from the expansion of the popular newspapers brought about by the Northcliffe revolution, its power in fact derived from the breaching of executive secrecy and from the suspension of the two party system, and declined as soon as the political system returned to normal. Indeed even during its moments in the sun, Fleet Street was less powerful than it seemed. Churchill's earlier remark that 'boldly and earnestly occupied, the platform will always beat the press'[19] was still true. Lloyd George was able to defy Northcliffe and thrive.

Northcliffe was succeeded as ruler in pandemonium by Lords Beaverbrook and Rothermere. These two, not realising that the success of Northcliffe had been due to the special conditions of the war and the coalition, tried to carry on where he had left off. They seriously overestimated their power. Forgetting that in 1918 his brother had been rebuffed by Lloyd George in similar circumstances, Rothermere made what Baldwin called a 'preposterous and insolent demand' that he be told in advance the names of Baldwin's 'most prominent colleagues in the next ministry'.[20] Beaverbrook was scarcely less ambitious. 'It is my purpose,' he announced in 1931, 'to break up the Conservative party if the Conservative party doesn't adopt the policy [of Empire Free Trade].'[21] Beaverbrook was Rothermere's candidate for the Premiership, being designated in the *Daily Mail* as 'the man for the hour', a compliment which he matched, not by proposing Rothermere for No. 10, but by calling his fellow press baron 'the greatest trustee of public opinion that we have ever seen in the history of journalism'.[22] The press lords were able to capitalise on the disunity of the Conservative party when it was in opposition and to fan the right wing's discontent with Baldwin's leadership, but in a famous speech when he likened them in a phrase of Kipling's to harlots 'seeking power without responsibility', Baldwin turned and routed them. They continued to prosper but power eluded them.

The controllers of the *Daily Mirror* did not originally make themselves as conspicuous as Beaverbrook or Rothermere. Although Mr. King had earlier claimed that the *Mirror* is 'easily the most powerful paper in this country',[23] he did not behave like a typical press baron until Labour won power in 1964. His attempt to sack Mr. Wilson had the characteristic result of such interventions: it strengthened the premier's position. The only abnormal feature of the episode was that it led to Mr. King being sacked instead; unlike his predecessors, he owned only a few shares in his newspaper.

Rothermere foreswore control of the *Mirror* in 1931, and it was under H. G. Bartholomew in the thirties that the revolution which was to give the *Mirror* the highest circulation in the country took place. The Bartholomew revolution was the conscious application of advertising techniques to the production and sale of a daily paper, the techniques and some of the staff to carry it out both coming from J. Walter Thompson, the biggest advertising agency in Britain. Newspapers having done so much to sell branded goods, it was natural that sooner or later a newspaper should decide to sell itself in the same way.

Beaverbrook was a successful minister in Churchill's government, but the Second World War did not bring a second false dawn to Fleet Street. The B.B.C. provided an alternative source of news, and there was no Northcliffe, though Beaverbrook gave spasmodic indications of seeing himself in that role. The coalition government did not disarrange party to the extent its First War predecessor had done, and there was much less scope under Churchill's dominance for the intrigues of individual politicians. Finally, the relatively good relations between the politicians and the generals, and the close control over the latter maintained by Churchill, prevented the press from penetrating into the quarrels and differences of the government.

The *Mirror* achieved a remarkable ascendancy in the forces though not with the generals. It combined the highly valuable function of publicist and redresser of servicemen's grievances with a persistent and niggardly criticism of those in charge of the government, which, as Churchill pointed out in a letter to King, would be 'much the most effective way in which to conduct a Fifth Column movement at the present time. . . . A perfervid zeal for intensification of the war effort would be used as a cloak behind which to insult and discredit one minister after another'.[24] But despite Morrison's threat to ban the paper after its publication of an ambiguous but largely harmless cartoon, the *Mirror*'s patriotism was not in doubt.

The early Northcliffe told his staff to remember that their job was 'not to direct the ordinary man's opinion but to reflect it'.[25] Lord Beaverbrook never held that view. He ran his newspapers, he told the Royal Commission on the Press in 1948, 'purely for the purposes of making propaganda'. The *Daily Mirror* has combined the two attitudes. It claims to reflect the opinion of its readers but on occasion it crusades for a particular cause. Yet whatever the initial attitude of a proprietor or a group, whether it is the desire to reflect, the ambition to propagandise, or a combination of the two, the end product is much the same. The proprietor who begins by trying to reflect the public's opinion soon expresses his own, believing it to be that of the public. Northcliffe's early anxiety to be a mirror to the public developed into a series of frenzied personal campaigns during the First World War and its aftermath. The proprietor who initially expresses merely his own opinion, soon believes that to do so is enough to make the public follow it, and that his opinion is theirs. 'While it is clear', wrote Beaverbrook, 'that the *Daily Express* correctly interprets public opinion, it is true, no doubt, that it also does a great deal to form that opinion.'[26] The group which begins by claiming to mirror public opinion and also to crusade, ends up not knowing which role to perform at any given moment. The day after the British ultimatum to Egypt, the *Mirror* was not yet ready to crusade. Instead of a leading article it carried a picture of a dancer doing 'the dance of fire'. Subsequently the *Mirror* opposed Eden and Suez, presumably in its role of crusader, but when circulation dropped it abandoned the crusade presumably in its role of the reflector of public opinion. The voice of the people, not its own voice, it decided, was the voice of God.

C. P. Scott thought 'the voice of the press must not be a megaphone';[27] but if you are addressing the whole nation you have to shout pretty loud. Much as Walpole found that the best way of breaking down barriers in diverse company was to talk smut, sensationalism and triviality are the only way for newspapers to catch everybody's attention. National popular newspapers are ruled by what Mr. Liebling called the 'classic trichotomy—blood, money and the female organ of sex—that made good papyrus copy in Cleopatra's time'.[28] Though because of Beaverbrook's manse background the *Express* has tended to play down sex, the *Mirror* has been in constant search of what Goldsmith called 'a neck and a breast that might rival Monroe's'.[29]

Mr. Cecil King has frequently criticised American newspapers, stigmatising them as 'unreadable and shabby products'.[30] His contempt is reciprocated. A columnist of the New York Herald Tribune, Mr. Roscoe Drummond, described the British popular press as 'a sensational restless hodge-podge of trash and trivia'.[31] Critics at home have been scarcely more respectful.

The Press and Opinion

Fleet Street's classic reply to criticism is that it is giving the people what they want.* 'Of course,' Mr. King has said, 'you have got to give the public what it wants, otherwise you go out of business . . . it is only the people who conduct newspapers and similar organisations who have any idea quite how indifferent, quite how stupid, quite how uninterested in education of any kind the great bulk of the British public are.'[32] Circulation figures suggest Fleet Street is much better informed about public taste than are its critics. Indeed popular newspapers, as Mr. King has claimed,[33] aim above, not below, public taste. There is no evidence that people 'really' want something other and better than what they buy. Most of the criticism directed at the popular press therefore is simply irrelevant.

Yet if the press knows and provides what the public wants, its opinions are not those of its readers. General Eisenhower once told Sherman Adams: 'If you want to find out how the people feel about things, read the papers, but not the New York or Washington papers.'[34] In England, Fleet Street's dominance makes all the leading British newspapers the equivalent of 'New York or Washington papers'. Owing to the smallness of the country and the concentration of the newspaper industry in London, there are too few newspapers chasing too many readers. Making every allowance for the homogeneity of Britain, for the printing of Northern and Scottish editions, and for the catering for different tastes within a group, the overwhelming preponderance of national newspapers in three sets of hands is of itself enough to make the popular press a deceptive index of opinion.

The considerable difference between public opinion and mere published opinion has often been demonstrated. Mr. Hugh Cudlipp, one of the three principal architects of the *Mirror* group's phenomenal success, while freely conceding the difference, has laid it down that 'No newspaper can succeed without men in charge who *instinctively* know what is right, who can assess the temper of public opinion without moving from their desks. Fleet Street calls it *FLAIR*'.[35] Yet, as Mr. Cudlipp himself admits, over the Abdication

* In his play 'What the Public Wants', Arnold Bennett made two comments on this claim. In answer to the remark of the press baron Sir Charles Worgan, 'But I've always maintained the right of the public to have what they want, and my right to give them what they want,' Emily says: 'Sell—not give.' Earlier after a similar claim by the press baron, his brother Francis exclaims: 'I'll only say this Charlie: if that's what the public wants—how clever you were to find it out! I should never have thought of it!'

the *Mirror* 'miscalculated public opinion'.[36] Arthur Christiansen, probably the most successful editor of a popular newspaper this century, recorded that when Lord Beaverbrook conducted a poll among his senior executives on the result of the 1945 election only one of them 'thought the Tories were out'.[37] This story is an interesting commentary upon a claim similar to Cudlipp's made by Beaverbrook himself many years earlier: 'They cannot believe that the press knows more of what the nation wants than the politicians do, until they are taught by the adverse results of the polls.'[38] More recently the *Daily Express* was the only London daily to support President Kennedy over Cuba, yet a poll taken before Mr. Krushchev's decision to withdraw his rockets showed fifty-six per cent of people supporting American policy.[39]

Over the Vassall affair the press drastically miscalculated public opinion on an issue very close to home: the public's attitude to newspapers and journalists. Fleet Street treated the summoning of journalists before the Radcliffe Tribunal as might a member of the Fronde a summons to appear before Mazarin—except of course that the journalists did turn up. All set to lead the legions of the righteous against the imprisonment of journalists for refusing to reveal their sources, the tribunes suddenly discovered that the people were reluctant to follow them. They found their readers notably unconcerned about the fate of the two journalists and highly sceptical about the quality of the sources used by the press, a scepticism which the Radcliffe report revealed to be not misplaced. Whatever the reason, Fleet Street discovered that the popular newspapers, however large their sale, were distinctly unpopular. Shortly afterwards, much of the press dealt with the Profumo affair with a mixture of salacity and sanctimoniousness, long familiar to readers of the less reputable Sunday papers.[40] Yet anyone who did not try 'to assess the temper of public opinion without moving from their desks' could have told it that its fairly nauseous attitude to the affair was far from being shared by its readers, who consistently displayed a degree of charity quite alien to the pharisees of Fleet Street and Printing House Square.

Mr. Cudlipp has claimed that 'the *Mirror* became an immense permanent Gallup poll survey of changing mass opinion. Whatever nonsense might be purveyed by politicians in Westminster, the staff of that newspaper were guided by the mood of the public and by their own faith'.[41] This touching confidence in the natural goodness and representative character of newspapers was once reposed in parliaments and legislatures. Unfortunately the same pressures that cause politicians in Westminster to talk nonsense cause the *Mirror* and other papers, despite all the resources and facilities at their disposal, to talk nonsense too. Their own views and interests—circulation, profits, personal ambition, and political advantage—see to that, and prevent popular newspapers from being trustworthy guides to the views of their readers.

Sometimes newspapers are unreliable guides because of what may be called a failure of method. 'I was regarded as having my finger on the nation's pulse,' wrote Christiansen,[42] 'and when I reported that the people were on Baldwin's side [over the abdication] there was not only dismay but signs of sour disbelief. In vain I quoted, as typical of provincial Englishwomen, the view of my mother. . . .'*

Sometimes papers are untrustworthy guides to the state of public opinion because they are trying to shape it or because for the purposes of circulation they are deliberately opposing it. 'The art of editorship', said Christiansen, 'is to know when to play tough news big and when to go for glamour—in other words not to interpret but to combat the public mood; cheer them up when they are depressed; depress them when they are cocky; mould them—and carry them along in what you are doing.'[44] The most notorious example of this conception of journalism was the coining and the plugging of the slogan 'there will be no war', which the *Daily Express* continued to run until August 1939.

Mr. Christiansen used to adjure his staff to 'Remember the People in the Back Streets of Derby',[45] or alternatively, 'The man on the Rhyl promenade'.† However laudable may be the objective of intelligibility to every reader, the techniques of the popular press are partly self-defeating. The stridency, the one-sidedness, the over-simplification, above all the brevity, which are necessary to secure the attention of a mass audience, prevent it from having much influence upon them. But public affairs are treated much more

* Baldwin's view of the method used by M.P.s to assess public opinion, when they return to their constituencies for the week-end, was rather similar: 'I suppose they talk to the station master.'[43]

† Before the war an American news agency used to tell its reporters that they were writing international politics for the Kansas City milkmen, and that if the Kansas City milkmen could not understand it, the despatch was badly written. 'Once in a while when I had taken too many at the bar, I'd think of the Kansas City milkman going his early morning rounds reading a newspaper and mumbling to himself: "What lousy copy. I can't understand it. The guy who wrote it must be a bum reporter".'[46]

seriously than they used to be. According to Mr. Sefton Delmer, when the mistress of a spy excited the interest of the press in the thirties, the order went out: 'Forget Hitler, find Marie Louise.'[47] That would not be typical today.

Yet many readers do not notice what the politics of their newspapers are: one in three of *Mirror* readers did not know which political party it supports.[48] When the Liberal *News Chronicle* bought up the Tory *Daily Despatch*, the *Daily Despatch* audience placidly transferred itself to the *News Chronicle*. When the reverse process occurred and the Tory *Daily Mail* absorbed the Liberal *News Chronicle*, few *News Chronicle* readers showed any immediate signs of objecting to their new political diet.[49]

At the end of 1964, admittedly when Labour was 12 per cent ahead of the Conservatives, a National Opinion poll[50] showed that the *Express* and *Sketch* had more Labour and Liberal readers than Conservative ones, 22 per cent of the *Mirror*'s readers were Conservatives, and when the parties are more evenly balanced that figure presumably rises towards 30 per cent. The Conservative readers of the *Mirror*, and the Labour readers of the *Sketch* and the *Express* can scarcely have been drawn to the paper of their choice by its politics, nor evidently were they influenced politically by what they read.

The *Mirror* was strongly in favour of the abolition of capital punishment, and the *Express* was strongly in favour of its retention. Yet exactly the same percentage of the readers of both papers were found by Mass Observation to be in favour of a trial suspension, while 1 per cent more of the *Mirror*'s readers were opposed to it.[51] On the other hand the *Express*'s campaign against the Common Market probably did have some influence.[52] In general the influence of popular newspapers varies inversely with their readers' knowledge of the subject.

A few years ago Lord Eccles told a German audience not to worry about the extreme anti-Germanism of a section of the British press because people in England only bought a paper 'to see what had won the 2.30'. With characteristic lack of humour about itself Fleet Street reacted with fury. But what Lord Eccles said was largely right. A great many people very properly do buy a paper for that or a related reason. The main function of popular newspapers is to entertain mass audiences.[53] Their secondary function is to please their advertisers. They perform both of them with great skill.

Sir William Haley believes that because 'the climate of a nation's opinions is more important than the opinions themselves . . . the mass circulation newspapers which help to set the national temper have as vital a role to play as those more serious journals which address themselves, relatively speaking, to the seminal few and to problem by problem. . . . A nation that is led to believe that in every activity from sport . . . to business and politics, favour, self-interest, and cupidity rule the roost will not long acquiesce in its leaders acting even in particular cases in a disinterested and far-seeing manner. It is a grave mistake, therefore, it seems to me, to discount and cease to care about the standards and philosophy of the popular press. . . . I believe that the climate of opinion is, in the long run, largely in its hands'.[54] All this sounds plausible enough. What could be more natural than that the climate of opinion should be determined by the daily reading matter of millions? What more likely than that their manners, morals, opinions and prejudices should be shaped by what is so skilfully and forcefully placed before them every day?

The only trouble is that it has not happened. Maybe when Sir William says 'in the long run', he means a very long run indeed. But in a run of fifty years the evidence is against him. Homo Beaverbrookensis, the man whose outlook has been dilineated by reading the *Daily Express*, is a rare species. So is Homo KingCudlippensis. However often they may be 'shown the most familiar aspects of life as mean, material or trivial',[54] people still contrive to see them through their own eyes. However frequently the nation 'is led to believe that in every activity . . . favour, self-interest, and cupidity rule the roost', it steadfastly refuses to accept it. Even if a very much less jaundiced view than Sir William's is taken of the popular press, there is small sign of Fleet Street shaping the general climate of opinion or the behaviour of its readers. The popular press's healthy glorification of material things has not turned a puritanical, moral and spiritual people into a nation of 'materialistic idolaters'. Fleet Street has merely given genuine expression to the natural desire of people to make life easier and more pleasant for themselves and their children.

In newspaper reading, as in other things, there appear to be two nations. Newspapers are divided between the heavies and the populars, with the centre being gradually squeezed out. But in fact there is no segregation, the readerships overlap: about a third of the readers of *The Times* also read the *Express*.

The Alsop brothers have complained that 'British serious newspapers are too often pretentious shams, with very little behind their fine impressive literate façades'.[55] Being fervent believers in on-the-spot reporting, they took particular exception to *The Times* having reported the Korean war, after its correspondent there had been killed, from New York and the war in Indo-China from Paris.* Certainly by the best American standards British news coverage is poor. But the serious British newspapers are greatly superior to their American opposite numbers in their style of writing, wit, and presentation; and as a combination they cannot be matched by any other country.

The serious papers, it is sometimes thought, eschew propaganda and present a judicious appraisal of the national scene, while the mass circulation papers are chiefly interested in propaganda. This distinction is invalid. Beaverbrook once said that 'the popular press is as nothing in the way of propaganda, when compared with the unpopular newspapers'.[56] Admittedly he was writing of a time when *The Times* under Geoffrey Dawson was closely involved in the government's appeasement policy. Nevertheless the difference in attitude of the heavies and the populars to news and opinion is one more of tone than substance. Indeed the popular press is often more concerned to find out what actually happened than its more sober counterparts, which occasionally seem to think that they know it all already and need not waste time discovering it. As a result the populars sometimes contain more news than the heavies.

Another myth is that the popular press reflects opinion, the serious press tries to mould it. But, as has been seen, the popular press often does not reflect public opinion. It reflects the opinions and prejudices of its controllers. And while the serious press probably does mould opinion it reflects almost as much as it guides. Hankey thought *The Times* 'always reflects British public opinion fairly accurately'.[57] That would be exaggeration today, yet the serious press as a whole is usually fairly well in step with its readers.

Hazlitt called *The Times* 'the greatest engine of temporary opinion in the world . . . it bears down upon a question', he wrote, 'like a first-rate man of war, with streamers flying and all hands on deck; but if the first broadside does not answer, turns round upon it, like a triremed galley, firing off a few paltry squibs to cover its retreat'.[58] The attitude of *The Times* to public opinion has usually been consistent. 'Manifestly', writes the official history of the paper, 'in so far as public opinion changes as a result of new information or

---

* In Evelyn Waugh's *Scoop*, 'Hitchcock reported the whole Abyssinian campaign from Asmara and gave us some of the most colourful eye-witness stuff we ever printed'.

other cause, and public men shift their ground, the political situation must be regarded as altered—in greater or less degree.'[59] *The Times*'s view of politics has traditionally been Hegelian. The right side is the winning side, and that is the one to support. It seems, however, that Hegel's ascendancy is now reaching its end; and in one important respect *The Times* has moved nearer to Marx, evidently believing that its business is not just to interpret the world but to change it.*

Northcliffe did not originally have strong political opinions. 'What are the views', asked Massingham in *The Nation*, 'of the Harmsworth journal? It has no views and all views, it can be Liberal and Conservative . . .'[61] The same could be said of Thomson newspapers. Lord Thomson, like Mr. Newhouse in America, has built up a newspaper empire purely as a business venture. He leaves his newspapers to express the opinions of their editors, or the opinions which they expressed under their previous ownership, or those which are likely to lead to the largest circulation.

The *Telegraph*, the *Observer* and the *Guardian* all have strong editorial views, but a certain decentralisation of opinion is taking place in the serious press quite aside from the non-interference of Lord Thomson. The rolling acres of the serious Sunday papers do not lend themselves to uniformity. More important, the object is to provide as much as possible for every sort of reader with most sorts of opinion. As some power has tended to spread from the editor to the business manager, it has shifted from both to writers and journalists. The editorial line becomes less rigid outside the leading articles. The business manager, if not the editor, feels like Mao Tse Tung: 'Let a hundred flowers contend. . . .' The more that individual writers are given their head, the more classes of readers can be brought into the net—and the more will liberal principles and advertisers be satisfied. All the serious papers have a mixed political readership. Even the *Daily* and *Sunday Telegraphs*, which have proportionately the highest Conservative readership, have 25 per cent of non-Tory readers. For the *Sunday Times* the figure is 35 per cent. On the other hand, the *Observer* and *Guardian* which are usually found on the left both have to contend with a readership that is respectively 30 and 42 per cent Conservative.[62] With readers of the heavies being more concerned with politics than those of most of the populars, the 'opposition' element in the readership

* Marx wrote: 'The philosophers have only interpreted the world in various ways; the point, however, is to change it.'[60]

should not be too sorely tried. Hence from all points of view consensus journalism is prudent.

At present readers of the serious papers are well served by three Sundays and three Dailies plus the *Financial Times*, the *Economist*, the *Spectator*, *New Statesman* and *Tribune*. Owing to their far smaller circulations the weeklies are not subject to the pressures of 'consensus journalism', but for the same reason they are not all free from financial pressures. And despite the steady rise in the circulation of the quality press, there is a disturbing possibility that one of the dailies and one of the Sundays will die.

Radio and Television

The number of newspapers has been reduced by market forces; the number of broadcasting authorities has been doubled by government action. The press's monopoly over the mass dissemination of news, comment and entertaintment was broken by the invention of radio and television; for thirty years the latter were allowed to be a monopoly of the B.B.C. Lord Reith, the Corporation's first Director General, believes that 'it was the brute force of monopoly that enabled the B.B.C. to become what it did; and to do what it did; that made it possible for a policy of moral responsibility to be followed'.[63] No doubt he is right. The monopolistic B.B.C. producing a picture of a country reeking of smugness and puritanical respectability was as unrepresentative of Britain as the competitive press. Taine found the Victorian Sunday 'like a cemetery'.[63a] He was spared subjection to the Reithian Sunday of the B.B.C.

The Corporation did not claim to be representative. Cultural dictatorship, not cultural democracy, was its policy. 'Few know what they want,' thundered Reith, 'and very few what they need.'[64] So they were not given what they wanted but what it was thought they ought to want. The result of this policy was first the creation of a national broadcasting service of which everybody could be proud, and secondly the capture by Radio Luxembourg and Radio Normandy, two commercial stations, of anything up to seven million listeners, who preferred entertainment to 'moral responsibility'.

The belief that Britain is a broadcasting island, that broadcast messages respect land frontiers, is one of the most remarkable examples of British self-deception. The B.B.C. has of course assiduously fed the delusion, fiercely defending its broadcasting frontiers both within and without the country. Following the failure of its diplomatic efforts to secure the ending of the commercial services from France and Luxembourg which were having the temerity to broadcast to this country, it asked the Post Office to jam them.[65] It led a strenuous rearguard action against the introduction of independent television in 1955, and was in the van of the attack on the pirate radio stations. The Corporation's interest in suppression is self-evident. Whenever its monopoly is breached, the inadequacies of its programmes are starkly revealed. Almost immediately commercial television began, the B.B.C. lost over half the national audience; and the success of the pirate radio stations revealed there was widespread dissatisfaction with the Corporation's sound programmes also.

A former Director General of the B.B.C., Sir Frederick Ogilvy, in a letter to *The Times* on June 26 1946, said: 'monopoly is inevitably a negation of freedom, no matter how efficiently it is run, or how wise and kindly the Board or Committee in charge of it. It denies freedom of choice to listeners.' Yet the proposal that 'the brute force of monopoly' should be overpowered, and people allowed to see what they wanted, stirred Bishops and distinguished lawyers as well as the B.B.C. and the Labour party to fierce opposition and moral outrage. It was as though a proposal had been made that atheism should be preached in church.*

But quite apart from the question of viewers' choice, it was constitutionally far better that the entire power of television should not be vested in Broadcasting House, and that government pressure should not be focused solely on the B.B.C. Reith's political ideas were not always clear. 'Assuming the B.B.C. is for the people,' he told Baldwin during the General Strike, 'and that the government is for the people, it follows that the B.B.C. must be for the government in this crisis too.'[67] The B.B.C. tended to genuflect to the government. As Sir Ian Fraser confessed in one of the debates on the introduction of commercial television, the Corporation allowed itself to be controlled by the government of the day: 'It was very wrong that the governors of that time—I was one of them—should have taken that view, but things looked so different afterwards.'[68]

* Reith's comment in the House of Lords a few years later was: '. . . somebody introduced Christianity into this country; somebody introduced the printing press; others the incalculable beneficence of medical and scientific discovery and applications. Somebody brought smallpox, the bubonic plague, the Black Death, greyhound racing and football pools. And commercial television was introduced by means conspiratorial and disreputable . . .'[69]

The introduction of a competing channel made it easier for unpopular opinions to be heard on the air, and also strengthened the backbone of the B.B.C. No more would a Winston Churchill be 'muzzled'[69] by the B.B.C., and reduced, as he was in 1929, to offering the Corporation £100 for the right to state his case on the air, and in the thirties to broadcasting on Radio Toulouse.[70] The arrival of I.T.V. emboldened the B.B.C. to take a firmer line with the government and the parties.

The Corporation, which in the week I.T.V. began was sending out such peak hour programmes as 'Disneyland, the Donald Duck Story', and 'Wilf and Mabel's Silver Wedding—Meet the Pickles and their friends', no longer had a captive audience and had to behave accordingly. The effect of competition upon its programmes was entirely beneficent, though in such matters as clinging to its hour of silence from 6 to 7 it showed that it was still prone, in Lord Hill's words, to 'a grandmotherly interference with people's freedom'.[71]

Subsequently, however, the B.B.C. decided to become up to date. Auntie was to be no more. Mutton was to be dressed as lamb. The Corporation was to be tough and uninhibited. Unfortunately, much as an aunt can only cease being an aunt by getting rid of her nieces and nephews, the B.B.C. could properly stop being Auntie only by ceasing to be a national institution financed out of public money. The B.B.C.'s privileges impose upon it certain obligations of respectability and restraint of behaviour. Once its standards are abandoned, so properly are its claims on the taxpayer. This the B.B.C. forgot.

As Mr. Val Gielgud wrote in 1965: 'the British Broadcasting Corporation as I knew it during 35 years, considered in terms of policies and personalities has largely ceased to exist. . . . And the worst of the mischief was the slur cast on the Corporation's professional integrity.'[72] Mr. Gielgud was referring to the B.B.C.'s satire programmes, on which Cassandra commented: 'cocking a snook at authority is a legitimate and highly necessary activity, but this embarrassing smug adolescent exhibitionism was in a very different category and to call it satire was an insult to every practitioner of that sharp and delicate art.'[73] Even Sir Hugh Greene, the Director General, noticed that something was wrong and conceded that 'one of the weaknesses of that programme in its closing stages was that it fell into abuse . . .'.[74] Yet, since similar programmes followed, it evidently did not occur to him that public ridicule of the recently dead and other boorishness, were not compatible with 'public service broadcasting'.* Nor were such stunts as the notorious interview with M. Bidault.

According to Sir Hugh Greene 'we have made it more possible to laugh at the established institutions including the monarchy, churches, parliament—all sorts of things—and so far from this being subversive, I think it has been very healthy'.[75] Notwithstanding its healthy attitude to other institutions, the B.B.C. is probably the most self-regarding institution in the world. In its yearly handbook it wrote: 'For B.B.C. television 1963 was a year of fruition and 1964 a year of fulfilment . . . a triumph of planning and organisation.' And during the last few years Greene, the Director General from 1960 to 1969, has said:

'We are, I would dare to claim, the most truly independent broadcasting organisation in the world.'[76]

'Power becomes dangerous if one thinks in terms of power and abuses it. We don't.'[77]

'One of the things the B.B.C. stands for is to see that the power of the medium shall always be kept within the limits of reason and justice.'[78]

'I'd say that the B.B.C. was the liveliest broadcasting organisation in the world.'[79]

'B.B.C. programmes are franker, closer to life, more critical, less inclined to cant and concealment than they have ever been. But this does not mean they are any less responsible, considerate, and humane or any more inclined to be unfair, partisan, or hostile to principle.'[80]

All this new-speak would have appealed to George Orwell whose Ministry of Truth in *1984* was based on the B.B.C.[81] When Manx Radio applied to the Performing Rights Tribunal for an extension of needle time, the B.B.C. opposed its application partly on the characteristic grounds that more popular music, in contrast to the balanced B.B.C. programmes, would tend to lower public taste. Not long afterwards, the B.B.C., in order to hang on to its monopoly, agreed to lower public taste by introducing an entirely unbalanced popular music programme.

The B.B.C. refuses to give the public what it wants, until somebody else does or wants to; and then the Corporation says, 'We are

* The meaning of this phrase, which is very dear to the B.B.C., is not at all clear. Sometimes, the unfriendly might think, it means private arrogance and public squalor. The Corporation seems to wish to convey by the phrase the idea that, because it is not subject to commercial considerations, it should and does maintain standards higher than any conceivable or actual rival.

a public service. If the public wants this rubbish, it is we who should give it to them.' And, holding their noses, they duly do so. While affecting to scorn viewing figures, the B.B.C. is a slave to them. Virtue is paraded but not practised; at the same time vice is not enjoyed.

> Unbridled yet unloving, loose but limp,
> Voluptuary, virgin, prude and pimp.[82]

Although the B.B.C., contrary to its own belief, is highly subject to human frailties, it had a good war record, and it still contains many people dedicated to the highest standards. The Corporation would never allow the head of the government or the head of state the sort of liberties French television has given to President de Gaulle and his government.*

The faults of the B.B.C. probably stem from its structure, and the absence of control over the permanent bureaucracy. 'The Chairman and Board are a humbug.' wrote Reith in 1927,[83] and at no time in the Corporation's history, at least until the appointment of Lord Hill, have the Governors possessed much power. It always seemed to Mr. Bevins, who was Postmaster General throughout the 1959 parliament, that the Governors 'were governed by the professionals', and that the professionals were 'not really responsible to anyone but themselves'.[84]

With the I.T.A., on the other hand, there is the opposite danger. The authority, which is set apart from the programme companies and, unlike the B.B.C. Governors, is not committed by what has already been done by those it controls, tends to interfere too much. But it is surely far better that the B.B.C. should become an I.T.A. without advertisements than that commercial T.V. should become a B.B.C. with them. Writing of the 'addiction to relaxation shared by the vast majority of the British public', Mr. Crossman has asserted 'the right to triviality . . . belonging to every viewer in a free society'.[85] If the independent channel does not give the viewer what he wants to see, it has no reason for existence. There is moreover no evidence that Commercial Television is providing programmes of a standard lower than people want. A former President of C.B.S. T.V. used to

---

* Yet, in 1965, 'the most truly independent broadcasting organisation in the world' caved in to pressure from 10 Downing Street, and unlike I.T.A. withdrew its invitation to Mr. Ian Smith to broadcast. The B.B.C. was once stigmatised by Cassandra as 'the quivering rampart'. The rampart still quivers.

refer to his audience 'as the soft underbelly of America'.[86] In this country the audience packs a punch; it can switch to two other channels or it can switch off altogether. The ideas, harboured by believers in cultural dictatorship that people 'really' want something better than they are given on T.V., and that somehow the programme companies fool them into thinking they want something they do not, are fallacious. If there were evidence that what the Companies are providing is unpopular, they would soon put out something different.

Power of the Press

Prince Albert once told Disraeli that the country 'was governed by newspapers'.[87] More recently Norman Angell thought that 'a few newspaper proprietors . . . come nearer, at just those junctures which are crucial, really to governing England . . . than Commons or Cabinet, Church or Trade Unions'.[88] Even if radio or television are added to newspapers, that is plainly not true today. The press can govern neither the opinion of its readers nor the actions of government.

There is a distinction, of course, between the power that is wielded by the controllers of the mass media and the power that can be exercised through them by the government or other bodies. If the government controlled the press, or if the mass media were unassailably controlled by a very small and united body of people, the distinction would practically disappear. The controllers would then have a veto on the power that was exercised through the media. But though the circle of controllers has been tightly contracted in Britain, they are not in unassailable control. They are in control during good behaviour. In certain circumstances the B.B.C. and I.T.A. would be vulnerable because they are public bodies. The press would also be vulnerable, because as the *Guardian* put it, 'the press does not stand high in public estimation at the moment largely because it is regarded as both irresponsible and self-satisfied'.[89]

Nor are they united. On only the rarest occasions can all the controllers of communications act in concert. The conflicting interests of a free press and a controlled television, the differing political views of the press publishers and financial competition usually keep the controllers divided. Maybe the danger of unity grows greater as numbers dwindle. But as newspapers grow fewer, they, like political parties, are driven to widen their appeal. While they still express strong opinions, they must be careful not to scare away

o

readers or advertisers. The possession of a readership of conflicting views limits a newspaper's freedom of action. Consensus journalism has its own imperatives.

Finally there is the countervailing power of those who work for the press and television. Nearly eighty per cent of American newspapers which expressed a preference gave Mr. Nixon their support in 1960,[90] yet he ascribed his defeat by President Kennedy to the hostility of the reporters covering the election; as Mr. Liebling put it, he 'charged that reporters were telling the truth behind their bosses' back'. Although Mr. Liebling thought that 'this was so inherently improbable that nobody took him seriously',[91] Kennedy's press secretary also thought that Kennedy '—on balance—got the best of the coverage'.[92] In Britain the strength of this countervailing power varies. Since journalists and producers lean more to the left than the right, it is greater in right wing papers than in left wing ones or the B.B.C. But the inhibition is always there. None of the owners or controllers now possesses a completely obedient and pliable instrument.

To Northcliffe, the *Daily Mail* was 'the greatest whispering gallery in the nation'. At present, television and wireless are greater whispering galleries than any newspaper. But the B.B.C. and the I.T.A. are not allowed to have an editorial view and are supposed to be impartial.* Hence the whispers are not, or at least are not supposed to be, those of the television controllers; they merely transmit and magnify them.

In Britain, therefore, there are more than enough checks and balances to prevent the power *of* the press and of television being the same as the much greater power wielded *through* the press and television. Northcliffe told his staff that 'the power of suppress' was greater than 'the power of the press'.[94] Nobody now has the power of suppress, and the political power of the press is surprisingly small.

Its electoral power has been shown often enough to be nil. Mr.

* Towards the end of the 1966 election Mr. Wilson had a row with the B.B.C. This may have been designed to throw off the scent those who believed that the B.B.C. had for some time tended to favour Labour or it may have been due, as the Nuffield Study suggested, to Wilson's fear of producers substituting 'their' election for the 'real' one.[93] Part of the B.B.C.'s megalomania is a strong belief in the divine right of its own interpretations. It believes that the issues between the parties can be explained, clarified and interpreted—impartially, of course—by itself. This is a similar fallacy to that which holds that political issues can be decided by Judges. While television should not during elections be the mere tool of the parties, Mr. Wilson had cause to dispute the view that the B.B.C. either is or should be an impartial referee of the party battle.

Douglas Jay claimed in 1962[95] that since the rise of the Labour party there had been perhaps only two fair elections: 1929 when the Beaverbrook and Rothermere papers were feuding with Baldwin, and 1945 when the press was almost equally divided between the two main parties. This ascription of electoral power to the press leaves unexplained the election of 1906 when there was an overwhelming Liberal victory, although the great majority of newspapers supported the Conservatives. Furthermore, President Roosevelt was regularly elected over the opposition of about three-quarters of the American press, and in the twenty-six campaigns in the hundred years before F.D.R.'s first victory, the winner had the backing of the majority of newspapers only fifteen times.[96] High claims have been made for the electoral power of the *Daily Mirror*.[97] These cannot be proved or disproved. Possibly the *Mirror*'s reversion to its more blatant advertising techniques in 1964 may have increased the Labour turn out, though as the Labour vote was the lowest since the war even that is doubtful. There is certainly no evidence that the *Mirror* succeeded in making political conversions.

In America, about 80 per cent of the papers are Republican, and they range, according to Mr. Liebling, from conservative to reactionary.[98] There, Adlai Stevenson's charge of 'a one party press' had substance.[99] The British press is far more balanced politically. Newspapers here seldom agree and usually cancel each other out. The effect of the Vassall tribunal, however, was to unite the overwhelming preponderance of the British press against the government. The campaign was impressive. 'When a great number of the organs of the press,' said De Tocqueville, 'adopt the same line of conduct their influence becomes irresistible,'[100] and it seemed as though he was going to be proved right. The Conservative party was discouraged, its supporters were divided and its opponents exultant. Nevertheless this massive onslaught by a virtually united press, not unaided from time to time by the actions of the government and the Conservative party, in the end had only limited effect.

Almost invariably, however, the press is divided. And then, so far from the press influencing the people, the people influence the press. Like the American Supreme Court, British newspapers 'follow the election returns'. Not merely in such obvious ways as the changes made in the *Mirror* after Labour's defeat in 1959 or the *Mirror*'s introduction of a Liberal column after Orpington,* but

---

* It seemed to get progressively smaller as the Liberal balloon steadily shrunk.

in the whole attitude of the press to politicians and the political scene. There is nothing like an election victory—even in local elections—for the obtaining of a favourable press.

Government and Press

Probably the mass media have more influence on governments than on the governed. The constant reiteration of the press leads a government to believe that what is being voiced really is public opinion. The serious press, the Sundays, the Dailies and the Weeklies, have sufficient space to analyse situations and policies in depth and to deploy serious arguments, and no doubt these discussions often influence either ministers and their advisers or those to whose opinions they pay attention. No doubt, too, some of their campaigns and those of the populars take effect. Hostile articles in the serious Sundays, particularly Mr. Rees Mogg's in the *Sunday Times*, appear to have influenced Sir Alec Douglas-Home's decision to resign as leader of the opposition. The press cannot do much with statesmen like Balfour or Attlee who scarcely read it or like Asquith who despised and ignored it.* But most politicians are surprisingly sensitive to criticism and surprisingly afraid of Fleet Street. Beaverbrook thought it was 'the men of the secondary rather than of the first rank in politics who are the most susceptible to criticism'.[101] That may be so, but even the first rank politicians are remarkably susceptible. In the Sudan Kitchener once told a band of journalists to, 'Get out of my way, you drunken swabs'.[102] No politician of any rank would display such an attitude today. Nearly all of them go to great lengths to avoid press criticism and to court press praise.

The press, said Croker, was 'never to be neglected with impunity',[103] and statesmen and governments act on his maxim. Lloyd George was sufficiently concerned by the power of the press to hand out an unprecedented bonanza of honours. Between July 1918 and July 1922 he created '49 Privy Councillors, Peers, Baronets, and Knights . . . all of whom are either proprietors, principal shareholders, editors, managing directors or chairmen of groups of newspapers . . . '.[104] Not since President Jackson gave federal jobs to fifty-seven journalists[105] had the qualities of newspapermen been so generously recognised. Even before the war, Lloyd George shocked one of his civil servants by his unending readiness to give interviews

---

* During the war Churchill devoted an hour a day to reading the newspapers. Chamberlain read nearly every newspaper every day. Mr. Wilson even reads them the night before.

to journalists, leaving his budget to his spare time.[106] During Suez Christiansen 'spent the afternoon of my fifty-second birthday in the Cabinet room alone with Mr. Eden while he explained the situation to me'.[107] Mr. Wilson takes more trouble over press relations than any politician since Lloyd George. When first he became Prime Minister, he met the parliamentary lobby three times a day.

How much difference all this makes, except in the very short term, is doubtful. Admittedly the Lobby often has no time to analyse what the government is doing and has no alternative but to retail what may be blatant party propaganda. But journalists are not gullible people, and the parliamentary lobby is an intelligent and well informed body of men. The assiduous wooing of them by Mr. Wilson and his entourage was effective for only a short time; after three years of Labour government, relations between the Prime Minister and political journalists had deteriorated to their lowest point in the political memory of a senior member of the lobby.[108] No amount of blandishment could reconcile the lobby to governmental deception and a diet of non-events.

So although the government usually influences the press more than the press influences the government, this is due not to its seduction of Fleet Street but to the workings of the political system. The British press is crippled by the limitations and lateness of its knowledge. It is weak because it has largely lost the power of disclosure. News is the decisive weapon in the encounter between government and press, and in Britain it is predominantly in the hands of the government. 'News,' said President Wilson, 'is the atmosphere of public affairs.'[109] In Britain the atmosphere is inevitably stuffy, a fact which is as damaging to the government as it is to the press.

The influence the *Observer* gained before the 1914 war through Fisher, the First Sea Lord, giving its editor J. L. Garvin the highest naval secrets, shows how much the press has lost by its exclusion from the executive's corridors of power.[110] Fisher's disclosures were admittedly an extreme case of public government, but they throw into relief the customary inability of the press to report the key struggles in the government machinery which precede the vital decisions. It is as though the eighteenth century press had been in fact, as well as in theory, utterly prevented from reporting the proceedings of parliament.

The alarm over the years caused by Mr. Chapman Pincher's uniquely successful disclosures in the *Daily Express*, and the extraordinary steps taken by the Wilson government to prevent their continuance, illustrate the decisive importance of the power of disclosure to the relationship between government and press. News, according to Hearst, is something which somebody wants suppressed —all the rest is advertising. Political news may be defined as what the government (or the opposition) does not want published, and political advertising as what it does want published. On that definition there is little political news published in Britain but a great deal of political advertising. Much of the political 'news' that is published is the result of briefings of the lobby by the Leader of the House, the Prime Minister and other ministers. Hence what has been called 'the ubiquitous it'.[111] 'It was learned', 'it was thought', 'it is known', by which is meant 'The Prime Minister or his press officer told us but we are not allowed to say so'. Obviously 'news' published in this form must usually be favourable to the government.

Not that such pseudo-events* are unique to England. They are common also in America. Senator McCarthy was a master, as in so much else concerning publicity, of the pseudo-event. He would procure publicity by calling a press conference to announce that he was going to call a press conference.[113] And President Eisenhower even had one of his cabinet meetings televised, a surely classic pseudo-event. But in England, because of government secrecy, the pseudo-event is the normal medium of political reporting and despite the efforts of the opposition it is almost wholly in the hands of the government.† Governmental secrecy and control of news force the press to adapt itself to the rules of statesmanship. Equality between cabinet ministers and journalists is lost. In America Joseph Alsop once terminated an interview with Lewis Strauss, then chairman of the Atomic Energy Commission, with the words: 'Admiral, you have just wasted half an hour of my time.'[114] Over here, where the channels of information are silted up by executive order backed by legal sanctions, such frankness would be improvident.

Mr. Reston of the *New York Times* believes 'that a newsman's duty is to dig out, expose and criticise the seeds of government policy before they become policy—so that there may be genuine public debate'.[115] No newsman can do that in England. He is not

* 'A pseudo-event is planted primarily (not always exclusively) for the immediate purpose of being reported or reproduced.'[112]

† Unless it is quarrelling or is otherwise in trouble, the Opposition only becomes news in the last few months before an election, though the leader of the Opposition like the leader of the House meets the lobby once a week.

allowed a sight of the seeds; he is only allowed to water the grown plant.

Since the war public access has been gained to many of the country's finest houses, but not to the Palace of Whitehall. Cabinet government based on disciplined parties, and ministerial responsibility based on a silent Civil Service, ward off the press until decisions have been taken. All too often the press becomes the public relations officer of the government. Influence is exercised through the press, not by it. Fleet Street sometimes complains of governmental control of parliament; it should pay more attention to governmental control of Fleet Street. Yet there is little it could do, even if it tried: the political system determines the working of the press, not the press the workings of the political system. The press cannot provide adequate public discussion if government prevents it.

Largely deprived of news as a weapon, the press can still fight with the weaker weapon of opinion. The press sets limits within which the government can and cannot act. With opinion, newspapers can sometimes influence the government and occasionally beat it. But the controversy created by the press is often too late. When the matter at issue is a *fait accompli*, there is nothing the press can do but complain. In Amery's words, quoting a Turkish proverb: 'The dogs bark, but the caravan passes on.'[116]

Yet though the political system keeps the press in a subordinate role, independent control of newspapers is vital. The Webbs thought it might 'be necessary to prohibit the publication of newspapers with the object of private profit . . . as positively dangerous to the community'.[117] More recently there have been occasional demands for public ownership of the press,[118] but they gain few adherents. The reluctance to interfere is based on a sound instinct. Public ownership of the press or a reintroduction of the B.B.C.'s monopoly would be pernicious. A modern version of the doctrine of the separation of powers is that the press should be under different control from the government. It still is, though only just. The danger is too little press power, not too much.

Britain is the most newspaper ridden country in the world, in the sense of newspaper consumption per head, but as Taper presciently remarked in *Coningsby*, 'the power of the press is gone by—they overdid it'.[119] Fleet Street is evidently resigned to its lot. 'Nowadays,' Mr. Macmillan pointed out in 1961,[120] 'when their shares are more widely held, most newspaper organisations are concerned not so much with power as with profit.' Dr. Johnson would have approved of the progression from Northcliffe through Beaverbrook to Lord Thomson. William Allen White wrote of an American press magnate who bought, killed and sold newspapers with an abandon which was then unusual: 'Frank Munsey contributed to the journalism of his day the talent of a meat packer, the morals of a money changer, and the manners of an undertaker. He and his kind have about succeeded in transforming a once noble profession into an eight per cent security.'[121] Lord Thomson is no Frank Munsey. By treating journalism purely as a business he has made the profession more, not less, secure. And so long as newspapers remain independent of the government and of each other, they fulfil much of their function and preserve the separation of powers.

V

PUBLIC OPINION

Public sentiment is everything. With public sentiment nothing can fail; without it nothing can succeed. He who moulds public sentiment goes deeper than he who enacts statutes or pronounces decisions. He makes statutes or decisions possible or impossible to execute.

ABRAHAM LINCOLN[1]

. . . Consider 'government by public opinion' as a formula . . . .It is an admirable formula: but it presupposes, not only that public opinion exists, but that on any particular question there is a public opinion ready to decide the issue. Indeed it presupposes that the supreme statesman in democratic government is public opinion. Many of the shortcomings of democratic government are due to the fact that public opinion is not necessarily a great statesman at all.

LORD GREY OF FALLODON[2]

That quaint conscience which was invented by English statesmen to keep themselves honest, and called by everybody public opinion, was overthrown as an idol. . . .

G. B. SHAW[3]

The expression public opinion has no fixed and definite meaning. The 'public' is a cloudy and variable entity, and 'opinion' has an almost equally indefinite significance. The government, the parties, pressure groups, the press, foreign governments, and other bodies influence or seek to influence the public, but the composition of that public continually changes. There are many publics. The public, in the sense of the people with a capital P, as Joe Chamberlain called it,[4] is not often involved. Sometimes, indeed, it seems to exist chiefly for the convenience of politicians and pollsters. Normally 'the public' means only a segment of the population. John Morley told Lord Esher that 'the great mass of the public' were not interested in the Education Bill of 1906 which was 'mainly fought by certain sects of Nonconformists'.[5] Depending upon the nature of the issue, the relevant public varies from an overwhelming majority of the country to a small informed minority. It may be a pressure group,

413

it may be the party activists, it may be a region, it may be the inner circle. The relevant public may have a very small p indeed.

The Protean nature of the public is shown by the following scales: about half the electorate willingly or unwillingly subscribe to a political party, about 1 in 10 of the electorate claim to be keenly interested in politics, and about 1 in 100 do unpaid work for the parties.[6]

The attentive political elite is about 1 in 7 of the electorate.[7] The remaining 6 out of 7 become concerned only if the issue is sufficiently dramatic to catch their attention or if their own personal interests are involved.

Opinions are often latent or non-latent; on many questions people do not have an opinion at all. They tell pollsters what they think. But in what sense they think it, and whether they would have thought it if they had not been asked is often doubtful. Raw opinion of this kind is like the spiritualist's ectoplasm. It needs the medium of the parties or gallup polls to make it exist or seem to exist. Until persuasion of one kind or another has been exerted, the result of a so-called public opinion poll—however painstaking—may be utterly misleading, and its publication a pseudo-event. The pollsters' impressive ability to predict the results of elections has attached prestige to their findings on matters of political opinion. But, in election campaigns polls are assessing people's intentions, not their opinions.[8] Intentions are more easily susceptible of measurement than opinions, and the polls' success with the first is far from implying their comparable success with the second.

The sheer fantasy which often informs people's answers is most clearly revealed when facts, not opinions, are involved. When the *Saturday Evening Post* made a survey to discover how many of its readers had been to the opera in 1956, the answer turned out to be 10,392,000 readers—'a figure at least four times as great as actual opera attendance in the United States during the year. . .'.[9] Obviously the unreliability of people's answers about their opinions cannot be so plainly demonstrated;[10] it can only be deduced from their factual ignorance and from the extraordinary fluctuations in polls of their so-called opinions.

The reality then behind the abstraction public opinion is a varying number of individual people, who have every kind of different opinion and hold them with varying degrees of intensity ranging from the passionate to the indifferent. The pollsters' attempt to aggregate all these varying opinions and non-opinions by arbitrarily giving the same value to each—a variation of the democratic principle to 'one man, one opinion'—giving exact percentages of what people allegedly think is often more gallant than useful. Hence when the expression public opinion is used, the epithet 'so-called' should often be understood to precede it.

The uncertainty that surrounds the 'public' and 'opinion' attaches to almost all matters relating to public opinion. Like the public, the parties are not fixed entities and overlap with both the public and the government. Communications between public opinion and government and other bodies run, like electricity, not on a straight line but on a circuit, though unlike electricity there is no clear distinction between the generator and the consumer. At different times the government or the parties influence the public, and the public influences the government and the parties, or each influences the others simultaneously. The current is alternating, not direct. The interaction of events, government and public opinion is circular; but the circuit is often broken.

Tenacity of Opinion
Fears have been expressed that modern techniques enable governments or other agencies to deceive and manipulate the public. But even in an age of instant communication and hidden persuaders, 'the engineering of consent'[11] still presents a formidable problem. In 1956 *Pravda* stated that, 'The Communist party has been and will be the only master of the minds and thoughts, the spokesman, leader and organiser of the people in their entire struggle for Communism'.[12] Yet with everything in its favour, the Russian Communist party has singularly failed to make itself 'the only master of the minds and thoughts' of the Russian people. After many years of anti-religious propaganda and persecution, millions of Russians decline to adopt the official atheism and cling to their religious faith.

Obviously nobody in Britain can mount such heavy artillery against 'the people' as can the Russian Communist party. The main parties direct much of their artillery against each other—thereby making the bombardment much lighter for the public. The healthy separation between the sacred and the secular, between church and state, between public and private life, and between the press and the government, all prevent the government, the parties, the churches, or anybody else making themselves 'the only masters of the minds and thoughts' of the British people.

Naturally the government, as Croker prophesied it would, does all it can to effect 'the regulation of public opinion'.[13] It has some control over the flow of news and influence on the news media. It makes energetic if not always successful use of these advantages. In 1953 one of President Eisenhower's aides said of his policies that 'we all suddenly realised we were busy manufacturing a product down here but nobody was selling it'.[14] Downing Street spares no effort to sell the product; only its existence is sometimes in doubt. 'Guidance' is given to lobby correspondents, diplomatic correspondents, defence correspondents, labour correspondents. Promises and pseudo-events are carefully timed. Juicy White Papers precede election campaigns. Bad news is buried under more news. The government announced the ending of TSR 2 on the day that Mr. Callaghan opened his spring budget.*

What the government does is news. The voters are constantly regaled with stories of the government's wise and energetic efforts to make life better. When Mr. Wilson strolls round to Lancaster House to prevent, in the nick of time, the breakdown of the Anglo-Irish negotiations, the press (and through it the public) are deprived of no colourful detail. In reporting the activities of British governments, the British press resembles the American press's treatment of McCarthyism. Much as American newspapers reported the Senator's allegations, because they were news, without also reporting that they were lies, which would have been bigger news, the British press often reports the propaganda of government without pointing out that it is propaganda. The behaviour of the American press stemmed from the cult of objectivity, that of the British from its inability to mention its source, which is usually a briefing from the Prime Minister's press officer.

In all ages some people have known how to create consent. On becoming party leader or on taking up an important post, a politician is given 'the build up' described by Professor Galbraith: 'He is a man transformed—indeed he is no longer a man but a superman. His eccentricities become the mark of a unique personality. His hobbies are the refreshment of an intense and active mind. His wife becomes a gracious, untiring, and selfless partner.'[15]

But politicians have long realised the importance of humanising themselves. 'We live in an age of advertisement. . . . The Prime

* Herr von Eckhardt, Dr. Adenauer's Chief Information Officer, maintained that on the approach of an election the Chancellor married him, but always divorced him afterwards. In Britain his married life would have been less unsettled.

Minister is the greatest living master of the art of personal political advertisement. Holloway, Colman, and Horniman are nothing compared with him.' That was not said of Mr. Wilson by a hostile Tory, but of Mr. Gladstone by Lord Randolph Churchill. 'For the purposes of recreation,' Lord Randolph went on, 'Mr. Gladstone has selected the felling of trees. . . . Every afternoon the whole world is invited to assist at the crashing fall of some beech or elm or oak. The forest laments, in order that Mr. Gladstone may perspire, and full accounts of these proceedings are forwarded by special correspondents to every daily paper every recurring morning.'[16]

Statesmen's recreations are today more leisurely; the forest is spared. Politicians make themselves interesting, human, and understandable by means of pigs and pipes, the wife driving the family car, hats, Trollope, HP sauce and other aids. The mass press and television may have enlarged the audience; they have not necessarily made it more responsive. For long Mr. Wilson's credibility gap was much smaller on television than at Westminster or in Whitehall. But then the great popular orators of the past also had far greater effect on a mass audience than they did in the House of Commons.

President Kennedy's performance in the television debates in 1960, particularly in the first one when he was aided by Mr. Nixon's disastrous make-up, helped to win him the election. And Mr. Wilson's television expertise and his successful purveying of 'the family doctor' image doubtless gained him votes in 1966.[17] But though television may tempt politicians, like Louis XIV,[18] to practise government by spectacle, they remember that the television public prefer sport or soap operas. Thus after becoming President, Kennedy was criticised not for making too many fireside chats on television but for making too few. The White House found that many of the public would not listen to a Presidential speech on legislation. Many of those who did listen would resent its replacement of their regular T.V. entertainment.[19] Within two and a half years of becoming Prime Minister Mr. Wilson had made more television appearances than the four Tory premiers had made in the previous thirteen years.[20] Yet even in his heyday Mr. Wilson knew that too many visits from the family doctor are unpopular; people prefer other television medicine.

Political advertising has not sold the product. After the Labour party had been advertising Mr. Wilson for a year, his standing with the voters was eight per cent lower than before the beginning of the campaign. After the Conservatives had spent nearly half a million pounds promoting Sir Alec Douglas-Home, he was ten per cent less popular than he had been before the money was spent.[21] The large sums spent by the steel companies seem to have been equally unproductive.[22] People remain almost as impervious to propaganda as to information. They just do not notice it.

Of course publicity makes a difference. Provided a party has a successful conference, its popularity immediately increases—for a time. The well publicised visits of the Prime Minister abroad, or the visits to London of distinguished foreign statesmen, also bring electoral dividends. But they have little lasting effect. People are influenced for a time by circuses; the influence of bread is more lasting.

Indeed, the government's influence on public opinion is derived less from the techniques of publicity and persuasion, than from the new techniques of economic management. Electorally, public opinion is largely determined by economic conditions; many voters see other issues through a pocket book darkly.*

The government's bombardment of the voters with the weapons of publicity, favourable news, and incessant ministerial exposure is so strenuous and prolonged that many people, like attacking generals in the First World War, believe that it is bound to hit its target and secure its objective. In fact the targets, also like those of the First World War, are often none the worse for the bombardment and carry on as though it had never taken place. People are not defenceless; they are not an amorphous mass but individuals with a series of interlocking relationships, associations, traditions and prejudices. Hence the pressure of government propaganda can be, and often is, withstood.

Party, which for most of the small political nation is the most important of those relationships, both reinforces and weakens government influence. Ostrogorski was shocked that 'left to their own inspiration, the [Liberal] associations for the most part did not know what line to take over Home Rule. They who were supposed to have the power of giving expression to public opinion and of pointing out the policy to be pursued by their rulers could do nothing but stammer'.[23] Yet 'as soon as the words of command had been issued from above, the local associations threw aside all their doubts and hesitation and plunged into the fray with their usual ardour'.[24]

The parties still command the obedience of the faithful. In September 1956 Conservatives were nearly evenly divided on the question

* See page 143.

of military action against Egypt, while Labour voters were 2 to 1 against. At the beginning of November after the military action had begun, Conservatives were 4 to 1 in favour, and Labour 4 to 1 against.[25] During the Macmillan government's attempt to join the Common Market, there was naturally much more Conservative than Labour support for the negotiations. When, however, Labour changed its policy, so did its supporters. Labour support for Mr. Wilson's attempt to join was greater than Conservative support.[26] Indeed though the Conservative leaders supported the government's policy, Conservative voters began to turn away from it— presumably because it was being carried out by a Labour government.[27]

Granted the impossibility of keeping up with every political issue, there is no need to share Ostrogorski's disdain for those who change their attitude in step with that of their party. Within limits that is a sensible way to behave. The nuances of policy are veiled, and only the broadest lines of the structure can be perceived. Issues are merged into one overriding question: support or oppose the government; and loyalty to party does the rest.

Yet people often have views considerably at variance with those of their party. Although one survey of working class attitudes found over half the respondents prepared to relinquish their views and adopt the position of their party,[28] voters do not necessarily change their opinions to bring them into line with their party's, nor do they change their party to bring their political allegiance into line with their views. By unconscious 'misperception', they distort the party view to what they would like it to be.[29] Often they are not aware of any divergence between their own views and those of their party.[30]

Politics come a long way down most people's list of priorities. A large part of the public do not understand what the parties are saying. When the term 'restrictive labour practices' was used in an election broadcast, about 50 per cent of a sample had no idea what the words meant.[31] Such conceptions as nationalisation and state control mean little to most voters.[32] Much of the time parties are just talking to themselves and occasionally to each other.

The parties contain within themselves the doubts and differences which are reflected in public opinion. They use public opinion as an excuse for inaction or the wrong action. Yet they themselves are the main pilots and channels of public opinion. When they say public opinion is against something they usually mean they themselves are against it. In moulding opinion, therefore, they are very far from being Michelangelos. They have neither mastery of their materials nor the will to dominate them. They themselves are part of the material on which they are working. Above all, votes not opinions are their currency; too clear and obtrusive a stand on a policy issue is liable to alienate the electors. In Disraeli's view party was 'organised opinion'. Today the organisation is there, but frequently the opinion is not.

The press has even less of a commanding position than the parties. As Mr. Cudlipp says: 'The assumption that newspapers form and control public opinion cannot be substantiated. . . . A newspaper may successfully accelerate but never reverse the popular attitude which commonsense has commended to the public.'[33] American experience is similar.[34] Television is so vivid a medium that it might be expected to have an overwhelming persuasive influence upon people's political ideas. Yet the study carried out at the 1959 election found its influence minimal.[35] Like the press, television tends to reinforce people's views; it does not change them. People pay remarkably little attention to what they disagree with; even if they initially take it in, they soon dismiss it from their minds. Alternatively they interpret it to bring it into line with their prejudices. Senator McCarthy's performance at the Army-McCarthy hearings which took place before a vast television audience is generally thought to have discredited him with the voters. No doubt it should have, but it did not. A Gallup poll showed that 38 per cent favoured him before the hearings and 36 per cent after them.[36] The audience enjoyed the drama and interpreted it in their own way. It did not influence them politically.

As a rule, opinion is remarkably tenacious and resistant to outside influence, even when conditions are ideal for propaganda and contrary opinions are forbidden. In Britain the forces that play upon public opinions are multifarious and antagonistic, and no one of them is able to control it. Nobody is the master of the minds of the British people. They decide for themselves.

Though people ultimately make up their own minds, or, which may be equally important, refuse to make them up, this is not an autonomous process. To say that the government and other forces have only limited effect is not to say that they either do, or should, have no effect at all. Hazlitt thought 'of public opinion as arising out of the impartial reason and enlightened intellect of the community'.[37] 'The *vox populi*,' he thought, 'is the *vox dei* only when it springs from the individual, unbiased feelings, and unfettered, independent opinion of the people.' To Hazlitt, public opinion, if it was not distorted by 'a mob of lords and gentlemen' and the corrupt organs of the press that 'exalt the war-whoop of the Stock-Exchange into the voices of undissembled patriotism',[38] would always point down the path to peace and general felicity.

The refutation of this noble savage view of public opinion can be found in the polls, which often reveal not natural goodness but blissful ignorance. Shortly before the 1959 election Dr. Mark Abrams found that twenty per cent could not name a single leading politician of any party.[39] In 1964 almost a quarter did not know the coal industry was nationalised.[40] As late as March 1966 100 out of 200 housewives interviewed had escaped learning who Mr. George Brown was.[41] After which it is perhaps surprising that in the fifties only about three times as many children in a secondary modern school had heard of Elvis Presley, as had heard of President Eisenhower.*[42]

The level of indifference or indecision is also high. The 'don't knows' are nearly always prominent. Throughout the Macmillan government's negotiations with Europe, about 30 per cent did not know whether or not they approved. The great majority of people can have no idea of how a crisis overseas should be resolved, unless they know something about the whereabouts of the place concerned and of its background.† Most voters can decide for themselves only after they have been subjected to stimuli from the government, the parties, the press, television and events. The view that people hold a sensible opinion until it is perverted by malignant propagandists is no less erroneous than the opposite view that the public are mere puppets manipulated by politicians and pressure groups.

Influence of Public Opinion
The 'don't knows' can be regarded as a depressing illustration of public ignorance and indifference, or as an encouraging demonstration of the public's partial immunity to government propaganda and

* There is nothing especially British about such ignorance. In 1964 28 per cent of Americans interviewed did not 'happen to know if there was any Communist government in China now'.[43] So much for the influence of the China Lobby.

† Sankey, Lord Chancellor in the second Labour government, adopted the sensible practice of taking a small atlas to cabinet meetings.[44]

of its sensible concentration upon its own affairs. The government's attitude to public opinion can similarly be interpreted as democratic acceptance of the popular will or as craven surrender to popular prejudice.

In the early nineteenth century public opinion was divorced from parliament; it worked on parliament but not through it. Opinion was organised by extra-parliamentary bodies, such as the People's Charter and the Anti-Corn Law League. Mild rioting provided a spur for the first two Reform Bills.

Public opinion was an outsider, an extra constitutional force, partly barred from parliament by the narrowness of the franchise. It was a *deus ex machina* whom statesmen knew how to treat. They made sacrifices to him from time to time, they treated him with outward deference and respect, they occasionally made him in their own image. Sometimes as over the Crimea they obeyed him, sometimes they used him as an excuse for action or inaction, but mostly they kept him at a safe distance and did not allow him to meddle in their more important affairs. He was allowed to operate only, as it were, on Sundays.

In the twentieth century public opinion, partly conquered by the parties and brought within the pale of the constitution, is no longer, to use the language of the Bishop of Woolwich, merely God 'out there',[45] but also God 'within us'. Like the God of South Bank religion, he has not lost all the attributes of divinity. But his workings have become more mysterious, and politicians and parties, like many Christian laymen, have become increasingly confused about his properties and the way to treat him.

God 'out there' is the mass opinion of the public in so far as it has no direct political expression except at elections. God 'within us' is public opinion as expressed by representative institutions; it is also the opinion of those in the inner circle of government and politics. There is only one God but he does not always say the same thing and he has at least three manifestations. Like the new theologians, we cannot pinpoint his exact whereabouts.

A better description for public opinion in the sense of 'out there' is sometimes public conscience or public sentiment. 'Other people's consciences are always odd,' Sir Kenneth Pickthorn once laid down, and the public conscience is no exception. It is a fairly blunt instrument, and an unpredictable one. It approved of Hitler occupying the Rhineland, it was outraged by the Hoare-Laval pact, it welcomed Munich. But it would not have tolerated another Munich a year later. It does not consider all the niceties of the situation or qualities of a man.* The public's broad view is not in itself much more likely to be wrong than the intricate calculations of experts and statesmen. Public opinion often shows a surer judgment than is exhibited by many of its would-be moulders. On Europe, for instance, the public was in the fifties far ahead of the politicians and the Civil Service.† But since public opinion, as Mr. Lippman has maintained, 'is primarily a moralised and codified version of the facts',[48] it is peculiarly dependent upon a reasonably accurate version of those facts being presented to it. The public supported the Anglo-French attack on Egypt in 1956 because it had been told and believed that the action was designed to stop the war. Had it been told the truth, its support would have been doubtful.

In appearance British government, except at election time, has largely freed itself from thraldom to public opinion 'out there'. There are few national campaigns. Few systematic courses of public education are put in hand to ease the passage of a controversial law. The country is governed by parliament, not by referenda. British politics are image politics, not issue politics. The government has to worry about its general popularity, not about its popularity on a particular issue. The appearance is strong government and a deferential populace. The reality is mutual deference. Even on particular issues the influence of public opinion 'out there' is much more real than it seems.‡ The government can never be sure that the issue in question will not disfigure its image.

This is necessarily difficult to document. The development of public opinion and its interaction with government is normally too complex a process for a simple causal relationship to be visible. Statesmen pretend to lead not to obey public opinion; they only blame the public when their policies lead to disaster. Public opinion is never a single agent. It always has allies, be they the opposition, informed opinion, the press, or government backbenchers. Yet in

* In July 1965 when Mr. Wilson was popular, the National Opinion poll found that 74 per cent thought he was sincere; his rating for being 'straightforward and plain-speaking' was 18 per cent higher than that of Sir Alec Douglas-Home.[46]

† Three months before the Treaty of Rome was signed the Gallup poll found 58 per cent saying they would approve of an attempt to join the Common Market.[47]

‡ Only when both parliamentary parties are broadly agreed is public opinion shut out. Even so, the only issue on which parliament has plainly defied the public is capital punishment. On other social issues, like abortion, the majority of the public has usually supported the parliamentary majority. On matters such as race parliament has avoided a direct confrontation with public opinion either by following it at a discreet distance or by judicious compromise.

the thirties the bowing of the government to public opinion over rearmament and Germany is well known. The same government also propitiated public sentiment by its approaches, unenthusiastic though they were, to Russia in 1939.[49] The respect the wartime coalition paid to opinion over such matters as rationing can be found in the war histories.[50] There was much truth in Beveridge's criticism in 1942 that on the home front the government 'in many ways has followed public opinion instead of leading it'.[51] The public conscience determined the government's attitude to Admiral Darlan after the Allied landing in North Africa.[52] After the war public opinion was remarkably slow to find political expression over immigration, presumably because the problem was only apparent in some quarters of the country. But eventually public opinion captured the Conservative party and after the 1964 election the Labour party.

The proof of the influence of public opinion lies in the failure of British governments to adopt unpopular policies so long as there is even an unlikely alternative. True all British governments since the war have adopted unpopular economic policies, but only when bankruptcy stared them in the face. They have moreover abandoned those policies under the pressure of unpopularity as soon as they could.

Obviously government does not always act in accordance with public opinion. It could not do so even if it wanted to. It does not always know what public opinion is. Frequently there is no such thing. Public opinion often favours contradictory objectives. Only as elections approach is a government thinking solely of the electorate. On becoming Prime Minister Sir Alec Douglas-Home told the Tory party that 'the fact that there is a general election ahead of us must never be out of our minds'.[53] But an election then seemed imminent. Nevertheless even between elections the influence of God 'out there' is felt. For most of the time both governments and oppositions are remarkably God-fearing people. Moreover mass opinion is never merely an outsider; it is deep within the political system and it is never alone.

Public sentiment is part of the political atmosphere. It cannot be excluded from Whitehall or Westminster. It is inhaled by politicians and Civil Servants and mingles with the various Whitehall opinions. More so than when Sir Henry Taylor wrote the words in 1836 has 'popular assent become an essential condition of the practicability of measures'.[54] Though the government may choose to ignore public sentiment, this is not necessarily a sign of strength. Frightened of public opinion and not knowing what they want to do, governments postpone a decision until events take it for them. The decision which is then forced on them (the choice of Stansted for the third London airport for example) may be unpopular, but it is usually weakness and indecision that cause the unpopularity, not firm government. Then if public reaction is even greater than expected, the decision is eventually reversed.

In any case, on important issues public sentiment is integral to the situation. If a government feels that it cannot carry public sentiment with it on a certain policy, it deceives the public or changes the policy. When Sir Gordon Richards was congratulated on having ridden a particularly strong finish, he used sometimes to reply: 'I couldn't have come without the horse.' Governments, too, cannot come without the horse, and they rarely try to.

The government is not one monolithic entity. A Prime Minister may conspire with the newspapers to defeat one of his government's bills as Lloyd George did over the Key Industries Bill.[55] A Prime Minister may suggest to a pressure group that they should attack the Colonial Secretary 'in such a way that he should be compelled to resign', as Ramsay Macdonald did to the Zionists.[56] These are extreme cases but governments are seldom united. There are always ministerial rivalries. There is almost always an element in the cabinet or the Civil Service that is opposed to the policy which is being pursued; and as the policy unfolds it will rely on, or seek to influence, public opinion for its purposes. During the outcry over the Hoare-Laval pact, some of the younger cabinet ministers were inciting *The Times* against Hoare.[57] Similarly there was an attempt to destroy Mr. George Brown, when he visited the U.N. after the Middle Eastern war in 1967. Public opinion has the entrée to Whitehall. It is always there.

The excessive metropolitanisation of British political and journalistic life produces a collectivity which may variously be described as 'inside opinion',* 'the establishment', 'the inner circle', or anything else. These collectivities are as much abstractions as public opinion, and their composition varies as much as the public itself. As Shaw pointed out, 'the quality and the mob . . . do not indicate two classes of entirely different persons. They are the same persons'.[59] Some are insiders on one matter, and outsiders on others. Yet with these reservations, it is no more misleading to talk about inside opinion than about public opinion.

* Keynes thought there were 'two opinions . . . the outside and the inside. . . '[58]

Due to this centralisation of opinion, issues which mostly affect only the provinces, like the distressed areas before the war or immigration after it, receive inadequate attention. And insider opinion is subject to bewildering changes. Not all insiders change their opinion of course. But intellectual and political fashions are clearly discernible. Thus in the early fifties a floating pound was a right wing recipe. Shortly afterwards it became a left wing recipe. Professor Devons has remarked that 'the speed at which [economics] fashion changes in current theory . . . is quite staggering'.[60] The play of fashion has also been seen over East of Suez, entry into Europe, Prime Ministerial government, the Middle East, and many other issues.[61] Inside opinion is better informed, but is no less fickle and often less reliable than outside opinion.

Governmental opinion is not necessarily the same as inside opinion. Salter noted that in its preparations for war the government of the day was far behind 'authoritative public opinion outside Whitehall'.[62] But the government and the attentive few interact on each other. And politicians are as subject to the general climate of opinion as anybody else. They are also normally dependent upon the ideas which were prevalent when they were about twenty. They cannot get away from either the present or the past. Public opinion like the Kingdom of Heaven is very much within them.

The point of representative institutions presumably is to keep the government in tune with public sentiment. And all the evidence is that in Britain they succeed in doing so. Politicians and governments do not for long pursue unpopular policies. When they do, they heavily disguise them. The need of the Conservative government to reveal only gradually the full implications of joining the Common Market slowed down the negotiations and helped to ensure their eventual failure. Lloyd George said that 'public opinion ultimately dominates the actions of government here to a degree incomprehensible'[63] to dictatorships. In reality, though seldom in appearance, this is so. Public opinion rules; it does not reign.

This of course is all very democratic. But what is needed is not mere public control of the government but some impulse to make the government act.

In the twentieth as in the eighteenth century public opinion is generally opposed to change. In the nineteenth century it tended to favour change. By no means always of course. Had the matter been left to public opinion, Roman Catholics would not have been emancipated in 1829, or so Gladstone believed. In general, however, opinion was mobilised *in favour of* something, like free trade or the abolition of the Corn Laws. Again, Civil Servants were sometimes a good deal more robust in their attitude to public opinion than they have been in the twentieth century. 'The law must be made to conform to public opinion,' said Chadwick, 'or the public opinion must by means of public instruction be made to conform to the law.'[64] Chadwick favoured the second alternative; his successors have favoured the first.

Dean Acheson has written that in the mouth of M. Robert Schuman, French 'public opinion' never seemed to want anything positive except financial support of French policies in Indo-China and North Africa. None of Schuman's inventiveness seemed directed towards ways of influencing public opinion directly'.[65] This abdication before public opinion has been just as conspicuous in Britain. British politicians, an official noted in the thirties, flattered opinion, they did not try hard to change it.[66] Nor did the serious papers. Before the first World War *The Times* did its best to bring home the German danger, irrespective of whether or not its policy was agreeable to public opinion.[67] Before the second War, *The Times* was content to follow public opinion, occasionally giving it a sharp nudge in the wrong direction. The historian of the B.B.C. admits that 'the B.B.C. was influenced on its political broadcasts policy not only by the parties but by the pressure of public opinions'.[68] With the Conservative government, *The Times*, and the B.B.C mesmerised by public opinion, the blind followed the blind.

Similarly in the last twenty years on the major issues of Britain's place in the world and the restoring of Britain's economy, British governments have failed to educate the public about what needed to be done. Foreign policy in the thirties and the fifties are only the most obvious examples of government being stultified by its inability to educate the opinion on which it depended.

Until governments have tried to make or change opinion they do not know what it really is. 'The process of discovering what may be called the will of the society is the process of making it.'[69] The ectoplasm can take many shapes, depending on the skill of the medium. Yet because the political system functions quite happily without the mobilisation of public opinion, little attempt is made

to educate it. As public opinion has been domesticated in this
century by being brought into the constitution, it has come to
dominate it—much as some old ladies are dominated by their
dogs.

G. M. Young thought that 'in 1922 and for many years afterwards,
it might be truly said that there was no public opinion, no common
settled attitude of mind: but in its place, an immense variety of sentiment, often quite uninformed, but not, for that, less passionately
entertained'.[70] After the First War convictions about Britain's place
in the world, her supremacy, her industrial leadership, that had
become fixed in the nineteenth century, were no longer self evident.
There was much room for uncertainty, and statesmen were not yet
accustomed to dealing with the problems of universal suffrage.
After the Second War there were even stronger reasons for confusion
and bewilderment. Yet the extra-constitutional status of public
opinion in the nineteenth century made it easier to identify; it did
not make it more genuine or even ensure its existence. The absence
of public opinion after 1922, if it was absent, was due to the failure
of the political system and hence of the parties to create or mould it.
The ectoplasm remained ectoplasm.

On straightforward party issues, the parties can lead opinion by
means of the clash between them. But most issues do not follow the
frontiers of party differences. And the primary objective of the
parties after all is to obtain people's votes, not to educate them; to
win the support of the old Adam, not to change him. To seek to
convert a man to a new view may only result in him being converted
to the other party. Caution is vital. The parties are better equipped
to integrate opinion than to lead it, and their success in preventing
anybody else giving such a lead largely accounts for the stagnation
of British opinion in this century. Having walled in the garden,
they are unable to cultivate it. Their fault, however, lies more in
the walling in than in the failure of cultivation.

As Professor W. J. M. Mackenzie has said, the parties are 'mediators between public opinion and public policy'.[71] And the Civil
Service also mediates between the various publics. There are too
many mediators and not enough leaders.

Parties and politicians have done nothing to alter the arrangements which have placed them in such a singularly ineffectual position. In Britain the parliamentary system makes the public dialogue
far more relevant and intelligible than in America. But it excites
insufficient public interest.

'Even in that certain hour before the fall
Unless men please they are not heard at all.'[72]

Too often the party dialogue in parliament does not please and is scarcely heard. In the result, as the means of manipulating opinion have grown, government's effective power over public opinion has declined.

The chief weakness of the British political system is that because British government works on a closed circuit it has insufficient means of reaching and persuading public opinion. Total ministerial responsibility prevents parliament from gaining access to the Civil Service, but it also cuts down the executive's effective access to the governed. Hence constitutional power is not translated into political power.

'John Bull, whose understanding is rather sluggish,' wrote Barnes, editor of *The Times* in the nineteenth century, 'requires a strong stimulus.'[73] For that understanding to be made less sluggish and public interest in government to be revived, additional stimuli must be injected. The only prescriptions which seem capable of providing it without undesirable complications are decentralisation of government by giving power to the regions, and, more important, the creation at the centre of administrative controversy by opening up the political system. By themselves, the party struggle and parliamentary debate are no longer a sufficient stimulus for John Bull.

So, while the British constitution may, as Churchill wrote, have 'grown up as the most thorough and practical mechanism yet devised in the modern world for bringing the force of public opinion to bear upon the conduct of our affairs',[74] it has so far failed to provide an adequate mechanism for ensuring that the force which is brought to bear upon the government is aware of what the country requires. Until that mechanism is fashioned, British government will continue to be strong in appearance and will remain weak in action.

REFERENCES

Page references are to the editions of works as listed in the Bibliography.

INTRODUCTION (*pages 1–19*)

1 Quoted in Agar, *The United States*, p. 239. **2** *Church and State*, pp. 90–1
3 *Democracy and the Organisation of Political Parties*, Vol. 2, pp. 718–9.
4 *War Memoirs*, Vol. 1, p. 632. **5** Riddell, *War Diary*, p. 317. **6** *Thoughts on
the Constitution*, pp. 18–19. **7** Bevan, *In Place of Fear*, p. 27. **8** *The French
Revolution*, Vol. 1, Bk. 3, Ch. 3. **9** *Democracy in America*, p. 80. **10** Quoted
in Thornton, *The Habit of Authority* p. 24. See also Crick, *The Reform of
Parliament*, p. 19. **11** Davis, *The Age of Grey and Peel*, p. 151. **12** *Vindication
of the English Constitution*, p. 39. **13** See Templewood, *Nine Troubled Years*
p. 125. **14** In *Defence of the American Constitution*, quoted by Max Beloff
in his Introduction to *The Federalist*, p. lxiii. **15** See Gash, *Politics in the
Age of Peel*, p. xiii. **16** Morgan, *Peace and War*, p. 130. **17** Rolo, *George
Canning*, p. 163. **18** Amery, op. cit., p. 21. **19** Beer, *Modern British Politics*,
pp. 94–8. **20** Ehrmann, *Democracy in a Changing Society*, pp. 85–6.
21 Carlyle, op. cit., Vol. 1, Bk. 2, Ch. 4. **22** Morley, *The Life of Richard
Cobden*, p. 130. **23** *Their Finest Hour*, p. 315. **24** Mack Smith, *Italy*, p. 435.
25 Address by General de Gaulle to Members of both Houses of
Parliament, April 7 1960. **26** *The English Constitution*, p. 4. **27** Millis, *The
Forrestal Diaries*, p. 36. **28** Schlesinger, *The Coming of the New Deal*,
pp. 201–2. **29** Grigg, *Prejudice and Judgment*, p. 94. **30** See Minney, *The
Private Papers of Hore-Belisha*, p. 186–8. **31** Taylor, *The Origins of the
Second World War*, p. 203. **32** Schlesinger, *A Thousand Days*, p. 593–4.
33 Owen, *Tempestuous Journey*, p. 533. **34** See Windlesham, *Communication
and Political Power*, pp. 28–9. **35** Samuel, *Memoirs*, p. 61. **36** *The Observer*,
September 26 1965. **37** Neale, *The Elizabethan House of Commons*,
pp. 397–8. **38** Hill, *The Century of Revolution 1603–1714*, p. 174. **39** Watson,
The Reign of George III 1760–1815, p. 64. **40** Critchley, *The Civil Service
Today*, p. 143. **41** Hill, *Lenin and the Russian Revolution*, p. 178. **42** Phrase
used by Joe Chamberlain in his Tariff Reform campaign, quoted in Amery,
My Political Life, Vol. 1, p. 275. **43** *Law and Public Opinion in England*,
p. 218. **44** Magnus, *Gladstone*, p. 161. **45** *Into Battle*, p. 71. **46** Hancock *and*
Gowing, *British War Economy*, pp. 62. **47** ibid., p. 59. **48** ibid., p. 95.
49 Baldwin, *My Father, the True Story*, p. 240. **50** *Old Men Forget*, p. 99.
51 Nicolson, *Lord Carnock*, p. 419. **52** Eden, *The Reckoning*, p. 9. **53** 'Ode
Inscribed to W. H. Channing.' **54** In *The History of England*, quoted in
Stewart, *The Moral and Political Philosophy of David Hume*, p. 234.
55 Quoted in Johnson, *Defence by Committee*, p. 11.

PART ONE: THE STRUGGLE FOR POWER

I   The Party System (*pages 23–62*)

1 'The Excursion,' Bk. 6, l. 457. 2 Quoted in Viereck, *Conservatism Revisited*, p. 98. 3 *Triumph and Tragedy*, p. 344. 4. Namier, *The Structure of Politics at the Accession of George III*, pp. 212–13. 5 Tarr, *The French Radical Party*, p. 2. 6 *Patriarcha*, pp. 57–8. 7 'Of the Parties of Great Britain,' *Philosophical Works*, Vol. 3, p. 73. 8 Petrie, *George Canning*, p. 238. 9 Aspinall, *Lord Brougham and the Whig Party*, p. 220. 10 Ostrogorski, *Democracy and the Organisation of Political Parties*, Vol. 1, pp. 21–2. 11 *Ralph the Heir*, Ch. 20. 12 Kennedy, *Salisbury 1830–1903*, p. 75. 13 Morley, *The Life of Gladstone*, Vol. 1, p. 1024. 14 Brogan, *The Development of Modern France*, pp. 130–1. 15 Morley, op. cit., Vol. 2, p. 369. 16 *Letters of Queen Victoria*, 2nd Series, Vol. 3, p. 569. 17 Brogan, op. cit., pp. 165, 434. 18 Butler, *The Electoral System in Britain since 1918*, p. 11. 19 Duverger, *Political Parties*, pp. 314–24. 20 Plumb, *Sir Robert Walpole*, Vol. 2, p. 310. 21 Raalte, *The Parliament of the Kingdom of the Netherlands*, pp. 23–4. 22 Michels, *Political Parties*, p. 154. 23 'Thoughts on the Cause of the Present Discontents.' *Works*, Vol. 2, p. 335. 24 'Reflections on the French Revolution.' *Works*, Vol. 5, p. 184. 25 Smellie, *A Hundred Years of British Government*, p. 53. 26 *Labour in the Affluent Society*, p. 6. 27 Disraeli, *Coningsby*, Bk. 2, Ch. 2. 28 Butler and King, *The British General Election of 1966*, p. 136. 29 Monypenny and Buckle, *Life of Disraeli*, Vol. 1, p. 1442. 30 ibid. 31 Craig, *A History of Red Tape*, p. 179. 32 Woolton, *Memoirs*, p. 351. 33 See Blondel, *Voters, Parties and Leaders*, p. 107. 34 Bealey and others, *Constituency Politics*, pp. 279, 285, 295. 35 Tarr, op. cit., p. 9. 36 Verney, *Parliamentary Reform in Sweden 1866–1921*, p. 198. 37 Carr, *The Bolshevik Revolution 1917–1923*, Vol. 1, p. 33. 38 Kennedy, op. cit., p. 349. 39 *Political Essays*, pp. xxxi–xxxii. 40 A. A. Milne, 'The King's Breakfast.' 41 Blake, *Disraeli*, p. 293. 42 Boardman, *The Glory of Parliament*, p. 48. 43 Templewood, *Nine Troubled Years*, p. 37. 44 In *My Life of Revolt*, quoted in Miliband, *Parliamentary Socialism*, p. 95. 45 Bealey and others, op. cit., p. 283. 46 Quoted in Gwyn, *Democracy and the Cost of Politics*, p. 144. 47 Williams, *Politics in Post-War France*, p. 50. 48 ibid., p. xxiv. 49 Stewart, *The Moral and Political Philosophy of David Hume*, p. 376. 50 Bealey and Pelling, *Labour and Politics 1900–1906*, p. 43. 51 *Chapters of Autobiography*, pp. 84–5. 52 Agar, *The United States*, p. 678. 53 Cecil, *Conservatism*, p. 192. 54 Ostrogorski, *Democracy and the Organisation of Political Parties*, p. 111. 55 Viereck, *Conservatism Revisited*, p. 114. 56 Cecil, op. cit., p. 246. 57 Rosebery in 1909, quoted in Asquith, *Fifty Years of Parliament*, Vol. 2, p. 83. 58 Dalton, *Call Back Yesterday*, p. 193. 59 Macleod, *Neville Chamberlain*, p. 162. 60 Morley, *The Life of Gladstone*, Vol. 1, p. 417. 61 'Of the Parties of Great Britain,' *Philosophical Works*, Vol. 3, p. 45. 62 *The Conservative Case*, p. 169. 63 In *The End of Laissez-*

Faire, quoted in Bullock *and* Shock, *The Liberal Tradition*, pp. 255.
64 See Miliband, *Parliamentary Socialism*, pp. 276–7. **65** Pelling, *A Short History of the Labour Party*, p. 96. **66** Hanson, *Parliament and Public Ownership*, p. 38. **67** On November 3, 1953, quoted in Kelf-Cohen, *Nationalisation in Britain*, p. 345. **68** *Daily Mirror*, August 6 1957.
69 Amery, *My Political Life*, Vol. 1, p. 234. **70** Gollin, *Proconsul in Politics*, p. 152. **71** Wright *and* Fayle, *A History of Lloyd's*, p. 80. **72** McDowell, *British Conservatism 1832–1914*, p. 84. **73** Wordsworth, 'The Prelude,' Bk. 3, l. 618. (1805 version) **74** Foot, *Aneurin Bevan*, p. 505. **75** Michener, *Report of the County Chairman*, p. 10. **76** Atkinson, *A History of Spain and Portugal*, pp. 312–3. **77** Brenan, *The Spanish Labyrinth*, p. 5. **78** Blake, *Disraeli*, pp. 428, 430. **79** *Political Parties*, p. 5. **80** *The Government of England*, Vol. 1, p. 329. **81** Quoted in Bendiner, *White House Fever*, pp. 112–13. **82** Bullock *and* Shock, *The Liberal Tradition*, p. xxx. **83** *Mandate for Change*, p. 36. **84** Speech to the Coventry Fabian Society, August 9 1966. **85** Tennyson, 'You ask me, why, tho' ill at ease'. **86** *Stanley Baldwin*, p. 247. **87** *The Intelligent Woman's Guide to Socialism and Capitalism*, p. 344. **88** Belloc *and* Chesterton, *The Party System*, pp. 155–6.
89 McDowell, *British Conservatism 1832–1914*, p. 172. **90** Carlyle, *Letters and Speeches of Oliver Cromwell*, Vol. 2, p. 425.

II The Tory Party (*pages 63–92*)

1 *Personalities and Powers*, p. 5. **2** Quoted in Kennedy, *Salisbury 1830–1903*, p. 60. **3** Disraeli, *Coningsby*, Bk. 3, Ch. 5. **4** Maccoby, *The Radical Tradition*, p. 223. **5** Bullock *and* Shock, *The Liberal Tradition*, p. xlvi. **6** W. L. Burn, 'English Conservatism,' *The Nineteenth Century and After*, February 1949, p. 69. **7** Wordsworth, 'The Prelude,' Bk. 6, l. 682. **8** White, *The Conservative Tradition*, pp. 157–8. **9** Quoted in Feiling, *The Second Tory Party 1714–1832*, p. 281. **10** Swinton, *Sixty Years of Power*, p. 60. **11** Halevy, *The Age of Peel and Cobden*, p. 119. **12** In the Tamworth Manifesto, quoted in White, op. cit., pp. 157–8. **13** Blake, *Disraeli*, p. 482. **14** Speech in 1867, quoted in White, op. cit., p. 171. **15** MacDowell, *British Conservatism 1832–1914*, p. 139. **16** Kennedy, op. cit., p. 147. **17** MacDowell, op. cit., p. 61. **18** Quoted in Young, *Balfour*, p. 196. **19** W. L. Burn, 'English Conservatism,' *The Nineteenth Century and After*, February 1949, p. 67. **20** Churchill, *Lord Randolph Churchill*, p. 799. **21** Dugdale, *Arthur James Balfour*, Vol. 1, pp. 438–9. **22** Bullock *and* Shock, op. cit., p. 201. **23** ibid, p. 153. **24** Blake, *The Unknown Prime Minister*, p. 433. **25** Young, *Stanley Baldwin*, p. 59. **26** *Winds of Change 1914–1939*, p. 309. **27** Sampson, *Macmillan*, p. 83. **28** Speech at Luton Hoo, July 20 1957. **29** *In Place of Fear*, p. 14. **30** Butler *and* King, *The British General Election of 1966*, p. 208. **31** *Daily Telegraph*, November 6 1965. **32** 'The Pathway to Power at Westminster,' *The Times*, December 6 1966. **33** Hogg, *The Purpose of*

Parliament, p. 38. **34** Heidenheimer, *The Governments of Germany*, pp. 186–7 **35** Birch, *Small Town Politics*, p. 92. **36** Butler *and* King, *The British General Election of 1964*, p. 296. **37** In *Table Talk*, quoted in Kirk, *The Conservative Mind*, p. 116. **38** Martin, *Adlai Stevenson*, p. 112. **39** Pelling, *A Short History of the Labour Party*, pp. 127–8. **40** Rose, *Influencing Voters*, pp. 250–1. **41** See White, *The Making of the President 1960*, pp. 72–4. **42** Speech to the American Chamber of Commerce, October 26 1966. **43** Quoted in Gollin, *Balfour's Burden*, p. 61. **44** Buchan, *Memory Hold the Door*, p. 239. **45** *The Memoirs*, p. 337. **46** Pares, *King George III and the Politicians*, p. 121. **47** McKenzie, *British Political Parties*, p. 365. **48** Stuart, *Within the Fringe*, p. 147. **49** Templewood, *Empire of the Air*, p. 22. **50** *Vindication of the English Constitution*, p. 193. **51** Churchill, *Lord Derby*, p. 166. **52** McKenzie, op. cit., p. 157. **53** *Political Essays*, pp. xxvi–xxvii. **54** *Winds of Change*, p. 323. **55** Monypenny *and* Buckle, *The Life of Benjamin Disraeli*, Vol. 2, p. 113. **56** McKenzie, op. cit., pp. 63, 144. **57** Rochester, 'A Satire against Mankind.' **58** *Socialism in the New Society*, p. 369. **59** 'Of the Coalition of Parties,' *Philosophical Works*, Vol. 3, p. 540. **60** Viereck, *Conservatism Revisited*, p. 110. **61** Feiling, *The Second Tory Party 1714–1832*, p. 329. **62** *Vindication of the English Constitution*, p. 188. **63** 'Of some Remarkable Customs,' *Philosophical Works*, Vol. 3, p. 411. **64** Boswell, *Life of Johnson*, p. 1215. **65** Davis, *The Age of Grey and Peel*, p. 298. **66** Blake, *Disraeli*, p. 473. **67** Hyde, *Carson*, p. 491. **68** Smellie, op. cit., p. 142. **69** Hyde, op. cit., p. 465. **70** 'Tensions in Conservative Philosophy,' *Political Quarterly*, Vol. 32. (1961), No. 3, p. 281. **71** Rossiter, *Parties and Politics in America*, pp. 93, 95. **72** Fauvet, *The Cockpit of France*, pp. 91–3. **73** Barnes, 'Italy', in Dahl, *Political Opposition in Western Democracies*, p. 318. **74** Heidenheimer, *The Governments of Germany*, p. 77. **75** Milne *and* Mackenzie, *Straight Fight*, p. 108, *Marginal Seat*, p. 119; Benney *and others*, *How People Vote*, pp. 143, 146; Butler *and* Rose, *The General Election of 1959*, p. 199. **76** See Nordlinger, *The Working Class Tories*, pp. 17, 65, 81, 84, 110, 231. **77** Rose, *Studies in British Politics*, pp. 26–7. **78** White, *The Conservative Tradition*, p. xviii. **79** Bealey *and* Pelling, *Labour and Politics 1900–1906*, p. 265. **80** Young, *Arthur James Balfour*, p. 433. **81** Quoted by Plamenatz in Ginsberg, *Law and Opinion in England in the Twentieth Century*, p. 34. **82** Beer, *Modern British Politics*, p. 299.

III   The Labour Party (*pages 93–126*)

1 In *The Labour Party in Perspective*, quoted in Pelling, *The Challenge of Socialism*, p. 266. **2** In *My Life*, quoted in Lyman, *The First Labour Government*, *1924*, p. 184. **3** Quoted in Bullock, *The Life and Times of Ernest Bevin*, Vol. 1, p. 383. **4** ibid., Vol. 1, p. 349. **5** Middlemas, *The Clydesiders*, p. 138. **6** Pelling, *The Origins of the Labour Party*, p. 107. **7** Quoted in Poirier, *The Advent of the Labour Party*, p. 11. **8** Hamilton, *Arthur*

Henderson, p. 30. **9** Pelling, op. cit., p. 59. **10** ibid., pp. 44–5. **11** Cole, *British Working Class Politics 1832–1914*, p. 151. **12** Miliband, *Parliamentary Socialism*, p. 28. **13** Barnes, *From Workshop to War Cabinet*, p. 72. **14** Quoted by McKenzie, *British Political Parties*, p. 396. **15** 645 H.C. Deb. 5s., c. 441. (July 26 1961.) **16** 701 H.C. Deb. 5s., c. 1,023. (November 11 1964.) **17** Butler *and* Rose, *The British General Election of 1959*, pp. 126–7; Butler *and* King, *The British General Election of 1966*, pp. 208–9. **18** Ranney, *Pathways to Parliament*, p. 204. **19** ibid., p. 279. **20** Butler *and* King, op. cit., p. 264. **21** See Paterson, *The Selectorate*, pp. 98–9. **22** Ranney, op. cit., p. 236. **23** Gash, *Politics in the Age of Peel*, p. 203. **24** Feiling, *The Second Tory Party 1714–1832*, p. 328. **25** *Political Essays*, p. xviii. **26** *Men and Work*, p. 314. **27** McKenzie, *British Political Parties*, p. 334. **28** Michels, *Political Parties*, pp. 85–6. **29** Quoted in Clayton, *The Rise and Decline of Socialism in Great Britain 1884–1924*, p. 213. **30** Shinwell, *Conflict without Malice*, p. 40. **31** Macdonald, *The State and the Trade Unions*, p. 115. **32** Harrison, *Trade Unions and the Labour Party since 1945*, p. 151. **33** *The Times*, September 8 1966. **34** *The Intelligent Woman's Guide to Socialism and Capitalism*, p. 451. **35** Quoted in McKenzie, op. cit., p. 505. **36** Chief Justice Hughes's remark about the U.S. Constitution, quoted in Schwartz, *American Constitutional Law*, pp. 129–30. **37** McKenzie, op. cit., p. 427. **38** McKenzie, op. cit., p. 488. **39** Hunter, *The Road to Brighton Pier*, pp. 80–1. **40** Rodgers, *Hugh Gaitskell 1906–1963*, p. 129. **41** Quoted in Poirier, op. cit., p. 226. **42** Quoted in Wootton, *The Politics of Influence*, p. 103. **43** Barnes, op. cit., p. 268. **44** Middlemas, op. cit., p. 206. **45** Bassett, *Nineteen Thirty-one: Political Crisis*, p. 233. **46** Bassett, *The Essentials of Parliamentary Democracy*, p. 153. **47** Dalton, *The Fateful Years*, p. 42. **48** Cripps *and others*, *Problems of a Socialist Government*, p. 39. **49** ibid., pp. 186–7. **50** ibid., pp. 204–5. **51** ibid., p. 208. **52** See Orwell, *The Road to Wigan Pier*, pp. 158–9, 208 and *passim*. **53** *News Chronicle*, June 22 1933, quoted in Bassett, *The Essentials of Parliamentary Democracy*, p. 203. **54** Quoted in Miliband, op. cit., p. 29. **55** Goldsmith, 'Retaliation'. **56** Beer, *Modern British Politics*, pp. 127–8. **57** ibid., p. 132. **58** ibid., pp. 199–200. **59** ibid., p. 200. **60** ibid., pp. 209–10. **61** Shonfield, *Modern Capitalism*, pp. 89–90. **62** Barnes, op. cit., p. 59. **63** Bullock, op cit., Vol. 1, p. 416. **64** Beer, op. cit., pp. 155–6. **65** Harris, *Life So Far*, p. 130. **66** Clayton, op. cit., pp. vii, viii. **67** Michels, op. cit., p. 212. **68** Foot, *Aneurin Bevan*, p. 138. **69** Wilson, *The Downfall of the Liberal Party 1914–1935*, p. 193. **70** Morley, *The Life of Richard Cobden*, p. 303. **71** Mowat, *Britain between the Wars 1918–1940*, p. 153. **72** ibid., p. 153. **73** 'On the Left Again,' *Encounter*, October 1960. **74** Quoted by Crosland, ibid.

IV   The Liberals and Third Parties (*pages 127–135*)

1 Quoted in *C. P. Scott 1846–1932: The Making of the Manchester Guardian*, pp. 206–7. **2** *Diaries and Letters 1930–1939*, p. 336. **3** Quoted in Wilson, *The Downfall of the Liberal Party 1914–1935*, p. 264. **4** Booth, *British Hustings 1924–1950*, p. 13. **5** Watkins, *The Liberal Dilemma*, p. 55. **6** Nicholas, *The British General Election of 1950*, p. 119. **7** Watkins, op. cit., p. 35. **8** Quoted in Rasmussen, *The Liberal Party*, p. 281. **9** Hanham, *Elections and Party Management*, p. 156. **9a** Vincent, *The Formation of the Liberal Party 1857–68*, p. 52. **10** Jenkins, *Asquith*, p. 505. **11** Thayer, *The British Political Fringe*, p. 177. **12** Pulzer, *Political Representation and Elections in Britain*, p. 82. **13** Rasmussen, op. cit., p. 16. **14** Quoted in Rasmussen, op. cit., p. 276. **15** Foord, *His Majesty's Opposition 1714–1830*, p. 65. **16** Boardman, *The Glory of Parliament*, p. 45. **17** Fulford, *The Prince Consort*, p. 197.

V   General Elections (*pages 136–156*)

1 Quoted in Carr, *The Bolshevik Revolution 1917–1923*, Vol. 1, p. 95. **2** Quoted in Longford, *Victoria R.I.*, p. 518. **3** Hunter, *The Road to Brighton Pier*, p. 22. **4** Michener, *Report of the County Chairman*, p. 45. **5** McKenzie, *British Political Parties*, p. 104. **6** Mencken, *A Carnival of Buncombe*, p. 210. **7** Adams, *First Hand Report*, p. 236. **8** Hughes, *The Ordeal of Power*, p. 26. **9** Chamberlain, *A Political Memoir*, p. 130. **10** Agar, *The United States*, p. 285. **11** Wells, *The New Machiavelli*, p. 278. **12** Stewart, *Modern Forms of Government*, p. 217. **13** Nicholas, *The British General Election of 1950*, p. 105. **14** Schlesinger, *A Thousand Days*, p. 18. **15** Amery, *Thoughts on the Constitution*, p. 16. **16** See Jennings, *Appeal to the People*, pp. 258–9. **17** Butler, *The British General Election of 1951*, p. 173. **18** Rossiter, *Parties and Politics in America*, p. 185. **19** Hogg, *The Conservative Case*, p. 13. **20** See Berelson *and others*, *Voting*, pp. 130–1, 148, 283–4. **21** Desmond Donnelly in the *Daily Herald*, March 16 1961. **22** *How Britain is Governed*, p. 151. **23** Quoted in Butler, *The Electoral System in Great Britain since 1918*, p. 207. **24** Quoted in Emden, *The People and the Constitution*, p. 223. **25** Jenkins, *Asquith*, p. 547. **26** See Pool *and others*, *Candidates, Issues and Strategies*, pp. 115–17. **27** Berelson *and others*, op. cit., p. 65. **28** Schlesinger, *The Crisis of the Old Order 1919–1933*, p. 427. **29** Truman, *The Governmental Process*, p. 198. **30** Cecil, *Conservatism*, p. 238. **31** McCallum *and* Readman, *The British General Election of 1945*, pp. xiii, 15. **32** Nicholas, op. cit., p. 133. **33** Dryden, 'Absalom and Achitophel.' **34** Campbell, *French Electoral Systems*, p. 28. **35** Mack Smith, *Italy*, p. 202. **36** 'One Party Rule in Britain?' *Political Quarterly*, April-June, 1961. **37** 'That Politics may be Reduced to a Science,' *Philosophical Works*, Vol. 3, p. 19. **38** Quoted in Carter, *The Office* *of Prime Minister*, p. 292. **39** Holland, *The Life of Spencer Compton, Eighth Duke of Devonshire*, Vol. 2, p. 278. **40** Speech, October 5 1938, *Into Battle*, p. 51. **41** Kirk, *The Conservative Mind*, p. 171. **42** Brogan, *The Development of Modern France*, p. 709.

PART TWO: THE PROCESS OF GOVERNMENT

I   The Civil Service and the Public Administration (*pages 159–204*)

1 Quoted in Boswell, *Life of Johnson*, p. 220. **2** *Trail Sinister*, p. 181.
3 *The Red Tapeworm*. **4** Goldsmith, 'Retaliation'. **5** See Morrison,
Government and Parliament, p. 327. **6** Reprinted as Appendix B of The
Civil Service Report of the Committee 1966–8. Chairman: Lord Fulton.
(Cmnd. 3638), Vol. 1, p. 108. **7** Kingsley, *Representative Bureaucracy*, p. 19.
8 E. Hughes, 'Sir Charles Trevelyan and Civil Service Reform 1853–55,'
English Historical Review, Vol. 64, p. 67. **9** ibid., p. 69. **10** *The Machinery of
Government*, pp. 3–4. **11** Finer, *The Life and Times of Sir Edwin Chadwick*,
p. 143. **12** *Prejudice and Judgment*, p. 351. **13** Beveridge, *Power and Influence*,
pp. 298–9. **14** Gash, *Mr. Secretary Peel*, p. 297. **15** Craig, *A History of Red
Tape*, p. 72. **16** Rolo, *George Canning*, p. 258. **17** F. M. G. Willson,
'Members and Boards,' *Public Administration*, Spring 1955, p. 48. **18** *The
Shadow of the Gallows*, pp. 58–9. **19** ibid., p. 59. **20** See for example Willson,
Administrators in Action, pp. 197–276. **21** S. E. Finer, 'The Individual
Responsibility of Ministers,' *Public Administration*, Winter 1956,
pp. 383–6. **22** 530 H.C., Deb. 5s., c. 1,286. **23** Gardiner, *Constitutional
Documents of the Puritan Revolution 1625–1660*, p. 83. **24** Hill, *The Century of
Revolution 1603–1714*, p. 238. **25** Hancock, *and* Gowing, *British War
Economy*, pp. 125–6. **26** Chandos, *Memoirs*, pp. 150–5. **27** Hancock *and*
Gowing, op. cit., p. 133. **28** Ashworth, *Contracts and Finance*, pp. 76, 232.
29 Devons, *Planning in Practice*, p. 144. **30** Hurstfield, *The Control of Raw
Materials*, p. 418. **31** Hancock *and* Gowing, op. cit., p. 323. **32** Mallalieu,
Passed to You Please, p. 50. **33** Gray, *Eighteen Years under Glass*, pp. 271–2.
34 Report of the Committee on the Training of Civil Servants, May 1944
(Cmd. 6525), quoted in Strauss, *The Ruling Servants*, p. 43. **35** Bullock *and*
Shock, *The Liberal Tradition*, p. 141. **36** Greaves, *The Civil Servant in the
Changing State*, pp. 31–2. **37** Morley, *The Life of Gladstone*, Vol. 2, p. 807.
38 Ridley *and* Blondel, *Public Administration in France*, p. 38. **39** Chapman,
The Profession of Government, p. 315. **40** Warner *and others*, *The American
Federal Executive*, pp. 12, 17. **41** Bridges, *The Treasury*, pp. 34–6. **42** Salter,
Memoirs of a Public Servant, p. 41. **43** See Templewood, *Empire of the Air*,
p. 92. **44** Macleod *and* Kelly, *The Ironside Diaries 1937–1940*, p. 129.
45 Birkenhead, *The Prof. in Two Worlds*, pp. 347–8. **46** Tizard, *A
Scientist in and out of the Civil Service*, p. 10. **47** Cmd. 1432 (1961), p. 5.
48 Hastings, *The Murder of TSR-2*, pp. 105, 148. **49** Fourteenth Report
from the Estimates Committee (Session 1966–7), pp. xix–xxiii.

P

50 Beveridge, *Power and Influence*, p. 144. **51** Whyte, *The Organisation Man*, p. 129. **52** See Dale, *The Higher Civil Service*, p. 220; Sisson, *The Spirit of British Administration*, p. 123; Strang, *Home and Abroad*, pp. 58–9. **53** Bridges, *Portrait of a Profession*, pp. 22–3. **54** Knatchbull-Hugessen, *Diplomat in Peace and War*, p. 21. **55** Wheeler-Bennett, *John Anderson*, p. 85. **56** Woodward, *The Age of Reform 1815–1870*, p. 251. **57** Sixteenth Report (1941–2), quoted in Campbell, *The Civil Service in Britain*, p. 69. **58** Normanton, *The Accountability and Audit of Governments*, p. 123. **59** ibid., p. 272. **60** ibid., p. 410. **61** Welensky, *4,000 Days*, p. 111. **62** See Templewood, *The Empire of the Air*, pp. 178–9. **63** Scott *and* Hughes, *The Administration of War Production*, pp. 294–5, 438. **64** *The World Crisis 1911–1918* (lv. edition), pp. 813–14. **64a** Brogan, American Themes, p. 108. **65** Private conversation with the author. **66** Knatchbull-Hugessen, op. cit., p. 28. **67** *The Statesman*, p. 79. **68** *On Representative Government*, p. 235. **69** E. Hughes, 'Civil Service Reform 1853–55', *History* (New Series), Vol. 27 (1942), No. 105, p. 52. **70** Esher, *Journals and Letters*, Vol. 4, p. 258. **71** Nicolson, *Curzon: The Last Phase*, p. 60. **72** Beveridge, *Power and Influence*, p. 142. **73** Allen, *Trade Unions and the Government*, p. 256; Dalton, *Call Back Yesterday*, p. 207; Vansittart, *The Mist Procession*, p. 376. **74** Taylor, *The Trouble Makers*, p. 97. **75** Ridley *and* Blondel, op. cit., p. 66. **76** *Whitehall and Beyond*, pp. 17–18. **77** See Rodgers, *Hugh Gaitskell 1906–1963*, p. 87. **78** Halifax, *Fulness of Days*, p. 95. **79** Grigg, *Prejudice and Judgment*, pp. 52–3. **80** In the *Sunday Times*, March 31 1968; see also Dudley Seers in Thomas, *Crisis in the Civil Service*, pp. 97, 98, 108. **81** *War Memoirs*, p. 696. **82** Hughes, *The Ordeal of Power*, pp. 84–5. **83** Finer, *The Presidency: Crisis and Regeneration*, p. 256. **84** ibid., p. 252. **85** See Schlesinger, *The Coming of the New Deal*, pp. 506, 511. **86** Scott *and* Hughes, op. cit., pp. 294–6, 389. **87** Neustadt, *Presidential Power*, p. 42. **88** Woodward, *British Foreign Policy in the Second World War*, pp. 148–9. **89** Vile, *Constitutionalism and the Separation of Powers*, pp. 224–8. **90** Robson, *The Civil Service in Britain and France*, p. 16. **91** Campbell, op. cit., p. 40. **92** Kirkpatrick, *The Inner Circle*, p. 58. **93** *Congressional Government*, p. 22. **94** Ellis v. Ellis, 1953, 2 All E. R., p. 135. **95** Re. Grosvenor Hotel. *The Times* Law Report, July 30 1964. **96** Conway v. Rimmer and another. *The Times* Law Report, February 28 1968. **97** *Science and Government*, pp. 39, 72. **98** Devons, op. cit, p. 184. **99** Hancock *and* Gowing, op. cit., p. 528. **100** Hankey, *The Supreme Command 1914–1918*, Vol. 1, p. 326. **101** Blake, *Disraeli*, p. 623. **102** Hardinge, *Old Diplomacy*, p. 150. **103** Churchill, *The Gathering Storm*, p. 267. **104** DeConde, *The American Secretary of State*, p. 7. **105** Committee on Administrative Tribunals and Enquiries, Minutes of Evidence (1956), column 273. **106** Prothero, *Statutes and Constitutional Documents 1558–1625*, p. 399. **107** Kelly, *The Ruling Few*, pp. 262–3. **108** Vansittart, *The Mist Procession*, p. 443. **109** Kirkpatrick, op. cit., pp. 38–9. **110** See Scott *and* Hughes, op. cit., p. 70. **111** Hancock *and* Gowing, op. cit., p. 63.

112 Strang, op. cit., p. 161. **113** Ismay, *Memoirs*, p. 93. **114** See Kennedy, *Salisbury 1830–1903*, pp. 317–19. **115** Sir Maurice Peterson, quoted in Vansittart, op. cit., p. 521. **116** *Political Essays*, p. 73. **117** 746 H.C., Deb. 5s. written answer 47. (May 2 1967.) **118** *Memoirs*, pp. 115–16. **119** *Portrait of a Profession*, p. 30. **120** Bevan, *In Place of Fear*, p. 98. **121** Robson, *Nationalised Industry and Public Ownership*, p. 60. **121a** P.E.P., *Government by Appointment;* and see List of Members of Public Boards as at November 1 1967. Cmnd. 3,493; and Appendix *i* to Report of Select Committee on Nationalised Industries, H.C. 298 of 1967–8. **122** Robson, op. cit., p. 186. **123** Professor Grimal's definition in *Larousse World Mythology*, quoted in *The Times Literary Supplement*, August 31 1967. **124** Cmnd. 3638 (1967), paragraphs 145–162. **125** See Acheson, *Sketches from Life*, p. 155. **126** Quoted in Young, *Churchill and Beaverbrook*, p. 175. **127** Strang, op. cit., p. 304. **128** Strang, op. cit., p. 153. **129** Vansittart, op. cit., p. 444. **130** Cooper, *Old Men Forget*, pp. 376, 378. **131** A Swedish politician, quoted in Verney, *Parliamentary Reform in Sweden 1866–1921*, p. 117. **132** See for example the Committee on Administrative Tribunals, Minutes of Evidence (1956), columns 265–74, 1146–56, and Appendix I, pp. 170–1. **133** Boswell, *Life of Johnson*, p. 212. **134** Mayhew, *Britain's Role Tomorrow*, pp. 131–2. **135** Robson, *The Civil Service in Britain and France*, p. 19. **136** Sisson, *The Spirit of British Administration*, p. 23. **137** Vansittart, op. cit., p. 313. **138** ibid., p. 497. **139** ibid., p. 247. **140** Private conversation with the author. **141** Taylor, *The Origins of the Second World War*, p. 174. **142** See Strang, op. cit., p. 147. **143** Grigg, op. cit., p. 119. **144** Lee, *The Board of Trade*, p. 6. **145** Bridges, op. cit., p. 19. **146** Powell, *A New Look at Medicine and Politics*, p. 6. **147** Hyde, *Carson*, p. 415. **148** Grigg, op. cit., p. 107. **149** *The Times* Obituary, September 8 1961. **150** Grigg, op. cit., p. 176. **151** 232 H.L., Deb. c.535. (June 20 1961.) **152** See Kilmuir, *Political Adventure*, pp. 187–9, 193; Macmillan, *Winds of Change*, p. 23. **153** Quoted in Beer, *Treasury Control*, p. 105–6. **154** Beloff, *New Dimensions in Foreign Policy*, p. 186. **155** Campion *and others*, *British Government since 1918*, p. 59.

II   The Cabinet and the Prime Minister (*pages 205–244*)

1 *The Grand Alliance*, p. 309. **2** Quoted in Southgate, *The Passing of the Whigs 1832–1886*, p. 53. **3** *The Letters of Queen Victoria. Third Series*. Vol. 1, p. 48. **4** Quoted in Namier, *Avenues of History*, p. 142. **5** See Benemy, *The Elected Monarch*. **6** Mackintosh, *The British Cabinet*, p. 451. **7** In his Introduction to Bagehot, *The English Constitution* (1963), p. 53. **8** Blake, *The Unknown Prime Minister*, pp. 166–7. **9** Bagehot, *The English Constitution* (1949), p. 35. **10** Tanner, *English Constitutional Conflicts of the Seventeenth Century*, p. 66. **11** ibid., p. 236. **12** Plumb, *The Growth of Political Stability in England 1675–1725*, p. 103. **13** Namier, op. cit.,

pp. 140–1. **14** Aspinall, *The Cabinet Council 1783–1835*, p. 239. **15** ibid.
p. 247. **16** August 24 1840, *The Greville Memoirs*. **17** Jennings, *The Appeal to the People*, p. 122. **18** Fenno, *The President's Cabinet*, p. 217. **19** Morley, *The Life of Richard Cobden*, p. 261. **20** Magnus, *Gladstone*, p. 299.
21 Churchill, *Lord Randolph Churchill*, p. 337. **22** *Their Finest Hour*, p. 485.
23 Williams, *A Prime Minister Remembers*, p. 45; Chandos, *Memoirs*, pp. 290–1. **24** Woodward, *British Foreign Policy in the Second World War*, pp. 379–81. **25** Young, *Churchill and Beaverbrook*, pp. 215, 224, 229.
26 Ismay, *Memoirs*, pp. 164–5; Montgomery, *Memoirs*, p. 536. **27** *Their Finest Hour*, p. 397. **28** ibid., p. 342. **29** Beaverbrook, *Men and Power 1917–1918*, p. 339. **30** Taylor, *English History 1914–1945*, p. 576. **31** *The Lfe of Walpole*, p. 157. **32** Milne, *Political Parties in New Zealand*, p. 156.
33 Nicolson, *Curzon: The Last Phase*, p. 23. **34** Nicolson, *Diaries and Letters 1930–1939*, p. 334. **35** *Old Men Forget*, p. 242. **36** Macmillan, *Winds of Change*, p. 568. **37** Mayhew, *Britain's Role Tomorrow*, p. 151.
38 Templewood, *Ambassador on Special Mission*, p. 282. **39** Heuston, *Lives of the Lord Chancellors 1885–1940*, p. 168. **40** Longford, *Victoria R.I.*, p. 157. **41** Macmillan, op. cit., pp. 23–4. **42** See Nutting, *No End of a Lesson*, p. 106–7. **43** Gollin, *Balfour's Burden*, p. 132. **44** *Politicians and the War*, p. 384. **45** Quoted in Rolo, *George Canning*, p. 124. **46** Pares, *King George III and the Politicians*, pp. 157–8. **47** Jenkins, *Asquith*, p. 83.
48 Mackintosh, op. cit., p. 363. **49** Blake, op. cit., p. 476. **50** Quoted by President Kennedy in his Foreword to Sorensen, *Decision-Making in the White House*, p. xiii. **51** Randall, *Lincoln the President*, Vol. 2, p. 155.
52 Fenno, *The President's Cabinet*, p. iii. **53** Eisenhower, *Mandate for Change*, pp. 124, 127–8. **54** Truman, *Year of Decisions*, p. 486. **55** ibid., p. 486. **56** Daniels, *The Man of Independence*, p. 259. **57** Millis, *The Forrestal Diaries*, p. 236. **58** ibid., p. 433. **59** Hughes, *The Ordeal of Power*, p. 134.
60 Schlesinger, *A Thousand Days*, p. 123. **61** Sorensen, *Kennedy*, p. 283.
62 Truman, *Years of Trial and Hope*, p. 207. **63** Speech on January 22 1941, quoted in *The Unrelenting Struggle*, p. 41. **64** Rovere, *Affairs of State: The Eisenhower Years*, p. 111. **65** Birkenhead, *The Prof. in Two Worlds*, p. 307. **66** ibid., pp. 307–11. **67** *The Times*, March 16 1968. **68** *Whitehall and Beyond*, p. 60. **69** 'The Prelude,' Bk. 10, l. 293. **70** Lyman, *The First Labour Government 1924*, p. 103. **71** *Whitehall and Beyond*, p. 26. **72** Plumb, *Sir Robert Walpole*, Vol. 2, p. 330. **73** Letter to Bonar Law, quoted in Beaverbrook, *Men and Power 1917–1918*, p. 398. **74** T. S. Eliot, 'The Love Story of J. Alfred Prufrock.' **75** Aspinall, *The Cabinet Council 1783–1835*, p. 186. **76** Kinglake, *The Invasion of the Crimea*, II, pp. 93–5, 520–1.
77 Amery, *My Political Life*, Vol. 1, p. 233. **78** Jennings, *Cabinet Government*, p. 217. **79** Beveridge, *Power and Influence*, p. 134. **80** Hankey, *The Supreme Command 1914–1918*, Vol. 1, p. 156. **81** Macleod, *Neville Chamberlain*, p. 91. **82** Mallaby, *From My Level*, p. 59. **83** Gray, *Eighteen Acres Under Glass*, p. 262. **84** Eden, *Facing the Dictators*, p. 479. **85** Zetland, *Essayez*, p. 211. **86** Macleod and Kelly, *The Ironside Diaries 1937–1940*,

p. 143. **87** Namier, *England in the Age of the American Revolution*, p. 148.
88 Aspinall, op. cit., p. 189. **89** Hankey, op. cit., Vol. 1, pp. 199–200.
90 Laski, *Reflections on the Constitution*, p. 122. **91** Eden, *The Reckoning*, p. 3.
92 Kilmuir, *Political Adventure*, p. 193. **93** Dalton, *High Tide and After*,
p. 25. **94** ibid., pp. 182–3. **95** Kimche, *Both Sides of the Hill*, p. 30.
96 Introduction to Bagehot, *The English Constitution* (1963), p. 55.
97 In letters to the *New Statesman*, May 10, May 24 and June 7 1963.
98 Aspinall, op. cit., pp.211–12. **99** Webster, *The Foreign Policy of Castlereagh
1812–1815*, pp. 370–1. **100** Guedalla, *Palmerston*, pp. 154–5. **101** ibid.,
p. 396. **102** Hankey, op. cit., p. 431. **103** See Nicolson, *Curzon : The Last
Phase*, p. 206; also Owen, *Tempestuous Journey*, p. 647. **104** Hankey,
op. cit., p. 62; Jenkins, *Asquith*, p. 242-3. **105** Hankey, op. cit., p. 63.
106 Lloyd George, *Memoirs*, pp. 621–2. **107** Beaverbrook, *The Decline
and Fall of Lloyd George*, pp. 101–3. **108** Chamberlain, *Down the Years*,
p. 139. **109** Blake, *The Unknown Prime Minister*, p. 446. **110** *Old Men
Forget*, p. 226. **111** Minney, *The Private Papers of Hore-Belisha*, p. 139.
112 *The Listener*, November 16 1965. **113** Namier, *Crossroads of Power*,
pp. 94–5. **114** Robertson, *Crisis*, p. 124. **115** Nutting, *No End of a Lesson*,
p. 104. **116** Chamberlain, *A Political Memoir*, p. 80. **117** Blake, op. cit.,
p. 439. **118** Dalton, op. cit., pp. 75, 268. **119** ibid., p. 245. **120** Jones,
A Diary with Letters 1931–1950, p. xxiv. **121** Amery, op. cit., Vol. 3, p. 50.
122 See Normanton, *The Accountability and Audit of Governments*, p. 371.
123 Gollin, *The Observer and J. L. Garvin 1908–1914*, p. 44. **124** Aspinall,
op. cit., p. 209. **125** Hankey, op. cit., p. 226. **126** Daalder, *Cabinet Reform
in Britain 1914–1963*, p. 245. **127** See Willson, *Administrators in Action*, pp.
21–130. **128** Thirteenth Report from the Estimates Committee (1966–7),
para 64. **129** Mallaby, op. cit., p. 183–4. **130** Johnson, *Defence in Committee*,
p. 225. **131** Ehrman, *Cabinet Government and War*, pp. 117–18. **132** Attlee,
As It Happened, p. 115. **133** Templewood, *Nine Troubled Years*. p. 330.
134 Dalton, *The Fateful Years*, p. 389. **135** Jones, op. cit., p. 69.
136 Templewood, op. cit., p. 421. **137** Dalton, *High Tide and After*, p. 172.
138 Brasher, *Studies in British Government*, pp. 23, 38. **139** Heuston, *Lives
of the Lord Chancellors 1885–1940*, p. xx. **140** Dalton, op. cit., pp. 243–4.
141 ibid., p. 195. **142** Lloyd George, op. cit., p. 446. **143** Templewood,
op. cit., pp. 165–7. **144** February 24 1942, *The End of the Beginning*, p. 66.
145 *The Gathering Storm*, p. 327. **146** Ismay, *Memoirs*, p. 165. **147** Cooper,
Old Men Forget, p. 194. **148** Kelly, *The Ruling Few*, p. 228. **149** *The Hinge
of Fate*, p. 499. **150** *The Gathering Storm*, p. 328. **151** ibid., p. 320.
152 Haldane, *An Autobiography*, p. 185. **153** Cmd. 9230 (1918, reprinted
1962), para. 4. **154** ibid, paras. 18–19. **155** ibid., para. 55. **156** Daalder,
op. cit., p. 274. **157** Cmd. 9230, para. 6 **158** See Willson, *Haldane and the
Machinery of Government*, p. 15. **159** George Brown in the *Sunday Times*,
March 28 1968. **160** Hankey, *The Supreme Control at the Paris Peace
Conference 1919*, p. 47. **161** *The Listener*, April 6 1967. **162** Scott and
Hughes, *The Administration of War Production*, p. 428. **163** Churchill,

The Hinge of Fate, p. 830. **164** Morrison, *An Autobiography*, pp. 192–3.
165 Mack Smith, *Italy*, p. 139. **166** Brogan, *The Development of Modern
France*, p. 537. **167** *Whitehall and Beyond*, pp. 68–9. **168** Sorenson, op. cit.,
pp. 258–9. **169** ibid., pp. 281–2. **170** ibid., pp. 301–6; Schlesinger, op. cit.,
p. 594. **171** See James Reston in the *New York Times*, February 8 1963.
172 Dalton, op. cit., p. 261. **173** Montgomery, *Memoirs*, pp. 500–2.

III   The House of Commons (*pages 245–295*)

1 Quoted in Foord, *His Majesty's Opposition 1714–1830*, p. 419. **2** *Political
Essays*, p. 275. **3** Soame Jenyns, quoted in Namier, *The Structure of Politics
at the Accession of George III*, p. 214. **4** Butt, *The Power of Parliament*,
pp. 69–78. **5** Oakeshott, *Rationalism in Politics*, p. 130. **6** Miller, *The
Origins of Parliament*, p. 6. **7** An Appeal on the Subject of the English
Constitution, quoted in Vile, *Constitutionalism and the Separation of Powers*,
p. 118. **8** Notestein, *The Winning of the Initiative by the House of Commons*,
p. 6. **9** Foord, op. cit., pp. 398, 431. **10** Halevy, *The Liberal Awakening
1815–1830*, pp. 7–8. **11** 58 Parlt. Deb. 3s. c. 881. p. 58. **12** Emden,
The People and the Constitution, pp. 156–7. **13** Hill, *The Century of Revolution
1603–1714*, p. 278. **14** Campion, *Parliament: a Survey*, p. 15. **15** Taylor, *The
Trouble Makers*, p. 26. **16** Foord, op. cit., p. 208. **17** Crick, *The Reform of
Parliament*, pp. 28, 25, 26, 43, 17. **18** Hoffman, *The Conservative Party in
Opposition 1945–1951*, p. 262. **19** (or Madison), *The Federalist*, number L,
p. 261. **20** Holdsworth, *A History of English Law*, Vol. 10, p. 536, quoted
by Foord, op. cit., p. 35. **21** Campion, op. cit., p. 143. **22** Verney,
Parliamentary Reform in Sweden 1866–1921, p. 23. **23** Asquith, *Fifty Years of
Parliament*, Vol. 1, p. 66. **24** Dahl, *Political Oppositions in Western
Democracies*, p. 242. **25** Foord, op. cit., p. 1. **26** Ostrogorski, *Democracy
and the Organisation of Political Parties*, Vol. 1, p. 285. **27** Butler, *The
British General Election of 1955*, p. 163. **28** Eden, *Full Circle 1951–1957*,
p. 549. **29** See Fulbright, *The Arrogance of Power*, pp. 50–2. **30** *A Carnival of
Buncombe*, pp. 65–6. **31** Welensky, *4000 Days*, p. 166. **32** New, *The Life of
Henry Brougham to 1830*, p. 268. **33** Entry for December, 1797, *The
Notebooks*, p. 322. **34** *Beauchamp's Career*, Ch. xliv. **35** Hyde, *Carson*, p. 185.
36 Brown, *Everybody's Guide to Parliament*, p. 110. **37** Southgate, *The
Passing of the Whigs 1832–1886*, p. 52. **38** Knatchbull-Hugessen, *Diplomat
in Peace and War*, p. 137. **39** Speech at Church House, Westminster,
March 16 1960. **40** Boswell, *Life of Johnson*, p. 902. **41** Letter to Lord
Reading, quoted in Beaverbrook, *The Decline and Fall of Lloyd George*,
p. 241. **42** *The Works*, Vol. 9, p. 161. **43** Boswell, op. cit., p. 880. **44** *A
Doctor in Parliament*, pp. 517–19. **45** Clapp, *The Congressman*, pp. 150, 152,
292. **46** Epstein, *British Politics in the Suez Crisis*, pp. 119–20, 197.
47 Boothby, *I Fight to Live*, p. 18. **48** Key, *Politics, Parties and Pressure
Groups*, pp. 441–2, 449–50. **49** Quoted in Wiseman, *Parliament and the*

Executive, p. 80. **50** Rochester, 'The Restoration, or The History of Insipids.'
51 Gash, *Politics in the Age of Peel*, p. 342. **52** Macleod, *Neville Chamberlain*,
p. 193. **53** Samuel Butler 'Hudibras'. **54** *The Listener*, December 19 1963.
55 Churchill, *The Gathering Storm*, pp. 258–9. **56** Nicolson, *Diaries and
Letters 1930–1939*, p. 397. **57** ibid., p. 392. **58** Woodward, *British Foreign
Policy in the Second World War*, p. 6; Taylor, *English History 1914–1945*,
pp. 450, 453. **59** Foot, *Aneurin Bevan*, p. 131. **60** ibid., p. 111. **61** Guttsman,
The British Political Elite, p. 265. **62** Clarendon, *The History of the
Rebellion*, 1826, Vol. 4, p. 94. **63** Montgomery, *Memoirs*, p. 477. **64** Bevins,
The Greasy Pole, p. 109. **65** Shinwell, *Conflict Without Malice*, p. 186.
66 Dale, *The Higher Civil Service*, pp. 114, 120. **67** Feiling, *Neville
Chamberlain*, p. 74. **68** *Onwards to Victory*, p. 56. **69** Enoch Powell in *The
Spectator*, March 6 1959. **70** *Orders of the Day*, pp. 317–18. **71** Welensky,
op. cit., p. 299. **72** Dalton, *High Tide and After*, p. 309. **73** Feiling, *Neville
Chamberlain*, p. 159; Macmillan, *Winds of Change*, pp. 228–9. **74** Bevins,
op. cit., p. 109. **75** ibid., p. 112. **76** Keir, *Constitutional History of Modern
Britain*, p. 340. **77** Franks, *The Experience of a University Teacher in the
Civil Service*, p. 13-14. **78** Strang, *The Diplomatic Career*, p. 15. **79** Herbert,
The Ayes Have It, p. 124. **80** Boswell, *Life of Johnson*, p. 1145. **81** Low,
The Governance of England, p. 76. **82** J. K. Stephen, 'A Political Allegory'.
83 Quoted in Laundy, *The Office of Speaker*, p. 156. **84** Wordsworth, 'The
Prelude,' Bk. 7, ll. 522, 530.   **85** *The End of the Beginning*, p. 13. **86** Byron,
'Beppo'. **87** Lewis, *Gideon's Trumpet*, p. 221. **88** Quoted in Namier,
Structure of Politics, p. 150. **89** *The Greville Memoirs*, June 6 1841.
90 *The Intelligent Woman's Guide to Socialism and Capitalism*, p. 350.
91 Bullock *and* Shock, *The Liberal Tradition*, p. 126. **92** *Beauchamp's
Career*, Ch. XVII. **93** Gwyn, *Democracy and the Cost of Politics*, p. 107.
94 O'Leary, *The Elimination of Corrupt Practices in British Elections
1868–1911*, pp. 53–5, 236–7. **95** Harrod, *The Life of John Maynard Keynes*,
pp. 488–9. **96** O'Leary, op. cit. **97** Owen, *Tempestuous Journey*, p. 70.
98 Halifax, *Fulness of Days*, p. 89. **99** Mill, *Representative Government*,
p. 226. **100** Raalte, *The Parliament of the Kingdom of the Netherlands*, p. 133.
101 Fauvet, *The Cockpit of France*, p. 34. **102** Håstad, *The Parliament of
Sweden*, p. 129. **103** Normanton, *The Accountability and Audit of
Governments*, p. 86; Finer, *The Presidency*, pp. 172, 243–6. **104** Håstad,
op. cit., pp. 133–4. **105** McCallum, *The Liberal Party from Earl Grey to
Asquith*, p. 23. **106** Hanham, *Elections and Party Management*, pp. 96–9.
107 Butler *and* King, *The British General Election of 1966*, p. 287.
108 Paterson, *The Selectorate*, p. 130. **109** See Nicolson, *People and Parliament*.
110 Acheson, *A Citizen looks at Congress*, pp. 26–7, 117. **111** Williams,
Politics in Post War France, pp. 159–60. **112** Wilson, *Congressional
Government*, p. 187. **113** Coombes, *The Member of Parliament and the
Administration*, p. 30. **114** ibid., *passim*. **115** Fourth Report from the
Select Committee on Procedure (1964–5), p. viii. **116** Normanton, op. cit.,
p. 123. **117** ibid., pp. 42, 375, 389. **118** Vansittart, *The Mist Procession*,

p. 399. **119** Amery, *Thoughts on the Constitution*, p. 54. **120** Morrison, *Government and Parliament*, p. 159. **121** Roscoe Drummond in *New York Herald Tribune*, June 27 1966. **122** *New York Times*, April 7 1962. **123** Reston, *The Artillery of the Press*, pp. 45–6, 103–4; *New York Times*, February 3 1966. **124** Raalte, op. cit., p. 193. **125** Hughes, *The Parliament of Switzerland*, p. 148. **126** 58 Parlt. Deb., 3s., c. 814. **127** *Daily Mail*, July 11 1966. **128** Jennings, *Parliament*, p. 131. **129** Hankey, *The Supreme Command 1914–1918*, Vol. 2, p. 555. **130** H.C. 161 of 1930–1, Minutes of Evidence taken before the Select Committee on Procedure on Public Business, pp. 138–53; Hughes, *Parliament and Mumbo-Jumbo*, pp. 142–52. **131** *Onwards to Victory*, pp. 250–1; *The Dawn of Liberation*, p. 256. **132** Quoted by Peel, 58 Parlt. Deb., 3s., c. 805.

IV   The House of Lords (*pages 296–311*)

1 *Europe Unite*, p. 201. **2** 328 H.L. Deb., 3s., c. 868. (July 10 1888). **3** Quoted in *History of The Times 1921–1948*, Vol. 2, p. 704. **4** Turberville, *The House of Lords in the Age of Reform 1784–1783*, p. 82. **5** On February 27 1812, in *Works* (1847), Vol. 2, p. 128. **6** Woodward, *The Age of Reform 1814–1870*, p. 153. **7** Swinburne, 'A Word for the Country.' **8** Mackintosh, *Echoes of Big Ben*, p. 54. **9** Pearson, *Labby*, p. 68. **10** Jenkins, *Mr. Balfour's Poodle*, p. 33. **11** Garvin, *The Life of Joseph Chamberlain*, Vol. 1, p. 468. **12** Gollin, *The Observer and J. L. Garvin*, p. 96. **13** Owen, *Tempestuous Journey*, p. 187. **14** Turberville, op. cit., p. 213. **15** Southgate, *The Passing of the Whigs 1832–1886*, p. 171. **16** Turberville, op. cit., p. 177. **17** O'Leary, *The Elimination of Corrupt Practices in British Elections 1868–1911*, pp. 13, 22. **18** Koestler, *Reflections on Hanging*, p. 30. **19** Turberville, op. cit., p. 344; Woodward, op. cit., p. 162. **19a** Kingsley, *Representative Bureaucracy*, p. 76. **20** Hankey, *The Supreme Command 1914–1918*, Vol. 1, p. 100. **21** Brogan, *Politics and Law in the United States*, pp. 88–9. **21a** Murphy *Congress and the Court*, pp. 49, 56. **22** Leuchtenberg, *Franklin D. Roosevelt and the New Deal 1932–1940*, p. 144. **23** Murphy, op. cit., p. 48. **24** Schlesinger, *The Politics of Upheaval*, p. 452. **25** Byron, 'The Vision of Judgement.' **26** Bromhead, *The House of Lords and Contemporary Politics*, p. 116. **27** Chandos, *The Memoirs*, pp. 195, 208. **28** Hemingford, *Backbencher and Chairman*, p. 90. **29** See Braithwaite, *Lloyd George's Ambulance Wagon*, pp. 219–20, 225–8. **30** Herbert, *The Point of Parliament*, p. 10. **31** Burn, *The Age of Equipoise*, p. 39. **32** R. A. Cline in *The Spectator*, October 13 1961. **33** Guttsman, *The British Political Elite*, pp. 122, 126. **34** Birkenhead *F.E.*, p. 389. **35** 278 H.L. Deb., c. 251. (November 23 1966). **36** *Coningsby*, Bk. 1, Ch. 3. **37** Quoted in Brogan op cit., p. 103. **38** Rovere, *Senator Joe McCarthy*, p. 166. **39** Tarr, *The French Radical Party*, p. 49.

V   The Monarchy (*pages 312–324*)

1 Quoted in Benemy, *The Queen Reigns: She Does Not Rule*, p. 173.
2 *The Decline and Fall of the Roman Empire* (Everyman edition), Vol. 3,
p. 100. **3** Quoted in Davis, *The Age of Grey and Peel*, p. 312. **4** James,
Myth and Ritual in the Ancient Near East, p. 305. **5** Speech at the opening
of Parliament, March 19 1604, quoted in Prothero, *Statutes and
Constitutional Documents 1558–1625*, p. 283. **6** Morrah, *The Work of the
Queen*, p. 33. **7** ibid., p. 37. **8** ibid., p. 38. **9** Act II. **10** *Sybil*, Bk. 1, Ch. 6.
11 *The Times*, November 16 1965. **12** Harris, *Long to Reign Over Us?*
pp. 75–6. **13** ibid., p. 43. **14** Strachey, *Queen Victoria*, pp. 187–8. **15** Fulford,
The Prince Consort, p. 276. **16** ibid., p. 165. **17** Strachey, op. cit., p. 148.
18 Longford, *Victoria R.I.*, p. 229. **19** Magnus, *King Edward VII*, p. 310.
20 Young, *Balfour*, p. 202. **21** Magnus, *Gladstone*, p. 319; Longford,
op. cit., p. 469. **22** Gollin, *The Observer and J. L. Garvin*, p. 35. **23** Magnus,
King Edward VII, p. 295. **24** Minney, *The Private Papers of Hore-Belisha*,
p. 74. **25** Wheeler-Bennett, *King George VI*, pp. 293–4. **26** ibid., p. 558.
27 Tanner, *English Constitutional Conflicts of the Seventeenth Century*, p. 40.
28 Turberville, *The House of Lords in the Age of Reform 1784–1837*, p. 272;
Aspinall, *Lord Brougham and the Whig Party*, p. 191. **29** Rovere, *Howe and
Hummel*, p. 164. **30** Wheeler-Bennett, op. cit., p. 653. **31** Templewood,
Nine Troubled Years, pp. 38–9. **32** Morrison, *An Autobiography*, p. 228.
33 Prince Albert's phrase, quoted in Fulford, op. cit., p. 240. **34** Magnus,
op. cit., pp. 372, 377. **35** Nicolson, *King George V*, p. 505. **36** Thomson,
A Constitutional History of England 1642–1801, p. 86. **37** Foord, *His
Majesty's Opposition 1714–1830*, pp. 185–6. **38** *The Observer*, August 23
1959, quoted in Dalton, *High Tide and After*, pp. 11–12. **39** Wheeler-
Bennett, op. cit., p. 775. **40** Nicolson, op. cit., p. 400. **41** Strachey, op. cit.,
p. 148. **42** Quoted in Fulford, op. cit., p. 238. **43** Quoted in Nicolson,
op. cit., p. 413. **44** Aspinall, op. cit., p. 111. **45** *New York Herald Tribune*,
January 20 1959. **46** *Coningsby*, Bk. 3, Ch. 2. **47** Magnus, op. cit., p. 93.
48 Strachey, op. cit., p. 116. **49** Sykes, *Four Studies in Loyalty*, pp. 27–9.
50 Prothero, op. cit., p. 412.

PART THREE: THE CONTEXT OF POLITICS

I   Local Government (*pages 327–338*)

1 Quoted in Churchill, *Lord Randolph Churchill*, pp. 603–4. **2** *Central
Departments and Local Authorities*, p. 17. **3** *Parkinson's Law*, p. 118.
4 Bk. 7, Ch. 2. **5** Jennings, *Parliament Must Be Reformed*, p. 43. **6** Kennedy
Salisbury 1830–1903, p. 175. **7** Finer, *The Life and Times of Sir Edwin
Chadwick*, p. 503. **8** Thomson, *David Lloyd George*, p. 194. **9** H.C. 161 of
1930–1. March 16Q 1513. **10** See for example the written evidence of the
Ministry of Housing and Local Government, 1967, Part II, para. 37.

11 Agenda of the Greater London Council, December 13 1966, p. 13.
12 Griffith, *The American System of Government*, pp. 144–5. **13** Brenan, *The Spanish Labyrinth*, p. 57. **14** Rockefeller, *The Future of Federalism*, p. 8.
15 Wheare, *Federal Government*, p. 10. **16** *The French Revolution*, Vol. 2, Bk. 1, Ch. 4. **17** Neale, *The Elizabethan House of Commons*, pp. 146–8.
18 Quoted in *Parliament through Seven Centuries*, p. 82. **19** Boswell, *Life of Johnson*, p. 1014. **20** W. J. M. Mackenzie, 'Local Government in Parliament,' *Public Administration*, Winter, 1954, p. 420. **21** Garvin, *The Life of Joseph Chamberlain*, Vol. 1, p. 202. **22** Ranney, *Pathways to Parliament*, pp. 197, 238. **23** Brogan, *The Development of Modern France*, p. 434.

II   Interest Groups (*pages 339–367*)

1 *Democracy in America*, p. 586. **2** *Social Contract*, p. 275. **3** *Everybody's Political What's What*, p. 35. **4** *French Revolution*, Vol. 2, Bk. 1, Ch. 4.
5 See for example Truman, *The Governmental Process*, pp. 51–2. **6** Popper, *Conjectures and Refutations*, p. 123. **7** Sampson, *The Anatomy of Britain*, p. 567. **8** Wootton, *The Politics of Influence*, pp. 138–9. **9** Self *and* Storing, *The State and the Farmer*, p. 43. **10** Brogan, *Citizenship Today*, p. 89.
11 Kelley, *Professional Public Relations and Political Power*, p. 43. **12** Bullock, *The Life and Times of Ernest Bevin*, Vol. 1, p. 124. **13** Potter, *Organised Groups in British National Politics*, p. 245. **14** Stewart, *British Pressure Groups*, pp. 111–13. **15** Harrison, *Trade Unions and the Labour Party since 1945*, p. 295. **16** Johnson, *A Doctor in Parliament*, pp. 81–2. **17** Thomson, *David Lloyd George*, p. 165. **18** ibid., p. 200. **19** 744 H.L. Deb., 5s., c. 433.
20 See Hill, *Both Sides of the Hill*, p. 87. **21** Lee, *The Board of Trade*, p. 26.
22 See Brogan *and* Verney, *Political Patterns in Today's World*, pp. 179–80.
23 Quoted in Raymond, *The Baldwin Age*, p. 158. **24** Quoted in Johnson, *Defence by Committee*, p. 3. **25** Montgomery, *Memoirs*, p. 409. **26** ibid., p. 489. **27** January 17 1961. **28** *Vindication of the English Constitution*, p. 180. **29** *Entitled to Know*, p. 150. **30** Beer, *Modern British Politics*, pp. 208–9. **31** *Evening News*, April 10 1967. **32** Gallup Political Index No. 81, p. 9. **33** Morley, *The Life of Gladstone*, Vol. 2, p. 103. **34** Blake, *Disraeli*, p. 698. **35** *The Steel Review*, January 1967, p. 7. **36** ibid., p. 7.
37 Allen, *Trade Unions and the Government*, p. 236. **38** Citrine, *Men and Work*, p. 270. **39** ibid., p. 368. **40** See Gallup Poll published in the *Daily Telegraph*, September 5 1966. **41** Woodward, *British Foreign Policy in the Second World War*, pp. 390–1. **42** December 3 1947, in Millis, *The Forrestal Diaries*, p. 332. **43** Bentham, *The Works*, Vol. 1, p. 321. **44** Vincent, *The Formation of the Liberal Party 1857–1868*, p. 217. **45** Brogan, *The American Political System*, p. 269. **46** Holbrook, *The Age of Moguls*, p. 95. **47** *On Liberty*, Ch. 1. **48** Guttsman, *The British Political Elite*, p. 213. **49** Scott *and* Hughes, *The Administration of War Production*, pp. 294–5. **50** Woolton,

The Memoirs, pp. 202–3. **51** 746 H.C. Deb., 5s., Written answers, p. 47. (May 2 1967.) **52** P.E.P., *Advisory Committees in British Government*, p. 107. **53** Woolton, op. cit., pp. 115–16. **54** Eckstein, *Pressure Group Politics*, p. 78. **55** Ronald Knox, 'Absolute and Abitofhell.' **56** Griffith, *Central Departments and Local Authorities*, p. 33. **57** Quoted in Potter, op. cit., p. 208. **58** Lord Butler on Cabinet Government, *The Listener*, November 16 1965. **59** Eckstein, op. cit., pp. 103–4. **60** *Equity Letter*, January 1967, p. 4. **61** *Voters, Parties and Leaders*, p. 174. **62** *I Bought a Newspaper*, p. 178. **63** See Self *and* Storing, op. cit., pp. 161–3. **64** Resolution, quoted in Birch, *The Advertising We Deserve?* p. 76. **65** Amery, *Thoughts on the Constitution*, pp. 64–5. **66** ibid., pp. 64–9; *Parliamentary Reform 1933–1960*, p. 32. **67** Glass, *The Responsible Society*, pp. 44–6. **68** Hayward, *Private Interests and Public Policy*, p. 52. **69** Rolo, *George Canning*, p. 164. **70** Truman, op. cit., pp. 33–4. **71** See Christoph, *Capital Punishment and British Politics*, pp. 28–9, 113. **72** Kirk, *The Conservative Mind*, p. 157. **73** Ehrmann, ed., *Interest Groups on Four Continents*, p. 170. **74** Lindsay, *The Essentials of Democracy*, p. 37. **75** Keynes, *The General Theory of Employment, Interest and Money*, pp. 383–4. **76** *Political Essays*, p. 82.

III   Law (*pages 368–381*)

1 Quoted in Nevins, *A Short History of the United States*, p. 305. **2** Quoted in New, *The Life of Henry Brougham to 1830*, pp. 216–17. **3** Hewart, *The New Despotism*, pp. v, 13–17. **4** Rees, *Korea: The Limited War*, p. 164. **5** Campion *and others*, *British Government since 1918*, p. 88. **6** Cecil, *Tipping the Scales*, p. 83. **7** Robertson, *Select Statutes, Cases and Documents*, pp. 458, 471. **8** Dicey, *The Law of the Constitution*. **9** Maitland, *The Constitutional History of England*, p. 263. **10** Jennings, *The Law and the Constitution*, pp. 323–4. **11** Devlin, *Samples of Lawmaking*, p. 110. **12** Cooper v. Wandsworth Board of Works [1863] 14 C.B. (n.s.), 194, quoted in Wade, *Towards Administrative Justice*, p. 63. **13** Maitland, op. cit., p. 505. **14** '*King Henry IV*,' Part I, Act I, Scene 2. **15** Le Bret's De La Souverainete du Roy, quoted in Jouvenel, *Sovereignty*, p. 206. **16** St. Thomas Aquinas, *Summa Theologica*, 1a XXV 3. **17** Earl Fitzwilliam's Wentworth Estates Co. Ltd. v. Minister of Town and Country Planning [1951] 2 K.B. 284. **18** See Allen, *Law and Orders*, pp. 243–4. **19** Taylor, *The Statesman*, p. 78. **20** Cmd. 218 (1957), para. 23. **21** L.R. (1915) A.C. 120 at 138. **22** ibid. **23** Heuston, *Lives of the Lord Chancellors 1885–1940*, p. 325. **24** Braithwaite, *Lloyd George's Ambulance Wagon*, pp. 129–31. **25** L.R. (1917) A.C. 260 at 278. **26** East Suffolk Catchment Board v. Kent [1941] A.C. 74. **27** [1942] A.C. 206 at 244. **28** Heuston, *Essays in Constitutional Law*, p. 175. **29** Heuston, *Lives of the Lord Chancellors 1885–1940*, p. 571. **30** Devlin, op. cit., p. 106. **31** Allen, op. cit., p. 256. **32** Nakkuda Ali v.

Jayaratne [1951] A.C. 66; R. v. Metropolitan Police Commissioner, ex-parte Parker [1953] I.W.L.R. 1150. **33** 'Law, Opinion and Administration,' *Law Quarterly Review*, Vol. 78, 1962, p. 198. **34** [1956] A.C. 736. **35** Radcliffe, *The Law and Its Compass*, p. 39. **36** Shaw v. D.P.P. [1961] 2 W.R.L. 897. **37** Scruttons Ltd. v. Midland Silicones Ltd. [1962] A.C. 446, quoted in R. B. Stevens, 'The Role of the Final Appeal Court in a Democracy: The House of Lords Today,' *Modern Law Review*, Vol. 28, 1965, No. 25, p. 520. **38** Quoted by Glanville Williams in *The Listener*, August 24 1961. **39** [1964] A.C. 40. **40** *The Times* Law Report, February 28 1968. **41** *The Times* Law Report, February 14 1968. **42** In Ridge v. Baldwin [1964], A.C. at 72. **43** Devlin, op. cit., p. 104. **44** De Smith, *Judicial Review of Administrative Action*, p. 17. **45** ibid., pp. 18–20. **46** ibid., p. 214. **47** ibid., p. 248. **48** Woollett v. Minister of Agriculture [1955] 1 Q.B. 103. **49** Riordan v. The War Office [1959] 3 All E.R. 552. **50** Southend-on-Sea Corporation v. Hodgson [1961] 2 All E.R. 46. **51** Hamson, *Executive Discretion and Judicial Control*, p. 54. **52** Devlin, op. cit., p. 23. **53** In Pyx Granite Co. v. Minister of Housing [1958] 1 Q.B. at 571, quoted in De Smith, op. cit., p. 375. **54** Wade, *Towards Administrative Justice*, p. 7. **55** Lord Evershed, 'The Judicial Process in Twentieth Century England,' *Columbia Law Review*, Vol. 61, 1961, pp. 764, 787. **56** Heuston, op. cit., p. 531. **57** *The Times* Law Report, September 16 1967. **58** Devlin, op. cit., p. 109. **59** See Kenneth Culp Davis, 'The Future of Judge-Made Public Law in England: a Problem of Practical Jurisprudence,' *Columbia Law Review*, Vol. 61, 1961, pp. 206–7. **60** Dennis v. United States, quoted in Acheson, *An American Vista*, p. 103. **61** See Jowitt, *The Strange Case of Alger Hiss*, pp. 144–6; Hiss, *In the Court of Public Opinion*, pp. 361–2; Cooke, *A Generation on Trial*, p. 283; Liebling, *The Press*, pp. 144–58. **62** Denning, *Freedom Under the Law*, p. 32. **63** See Rostow, *The Sovereign Prerogative*, pp. 193–267. **64** Stankiewicz *Crisis in British Government: The Need for Reform*, p. 20.

IV   The Press and Television (*pages 382–412*)

1 Quoted in Petrie, *George Canning*, pp. 223–4. **2** *Letters*, Dedication. **3** Quoted in Reston, *The Artillery of the Press*, p. 97. **4** From the famous article in *The Times* in 1852, quoted in *History of The Times 1841–1884*, p. 156. **5** Petrie, op. cit., pp. 224–5. **6** Taylor, *The Trouble Makers*, p. 74. **7** Beach Thomas, *The Story of the Spectator 1828–1928*, p. 45. **8** See David Wood, 'The Parliamentary Lobby,' *Political Quarterly*, Vol. 36, No. 3. pp. 315–16. **9** *History of The Times 1841–1884*, pp. 518–19. **10** Ross, *The Image Merchants*, p. 29. **11** Quoted in *The Press and the People 1962*. The Ninth Annual Report of the General Council of the Press. **12** Tebbel, *The Life and Good Times of William Randolph Hearst*, p. 79. **13** Cudlipp, *At Your Peril*, p. 355. **14** King, *The Future of the Press*, p. 115. **15** Jenkins,

Asquith, p. 418. **16** *War Memoirs*, p. 1318. **17** *History of The Times 1921–1948*, p. 1093. **18** ibid., p. 708. **19** Gollin, *The Observer and J. L. Garvin 1908–1914*, p. 94. **20** Young, *Stanley Baldwin*, p. 152. **21** Young, *Churchill and Beaverbrook*, p. 117. **22** Driberg, *Beaverbrook*, p. 204.
23 Cudlipp, op. cit., p. 23. **24** Edelman, *The Mirror*, p. 105. **25** Williams, *Dangerous Estate*, pp. 165–6. **26** Beaverbrook, *Politicians and the Press*, p. 55. **27** *C. P. Scott 1846–1932: The Making of the Manchester Guardian*, p. 169. **28** Liebling, *The Press*, p. 8. **29** Goldsmith, 'The Haunch of Venison! **30** For example, see *The Times*, April 22 1967. **31** Quoted in Thomas, *The Press and the People*, p. 7. **32** Williams, *Communications*, p. 97. **33** King, op. cit., pp. 73–4. **34** Adams, *First Hand Report*, p. 70.
35 Cudlipp, *Publish and Be Damned*, p. 75. **36** ibid., p. 101.
37 Christiansen, *Headlines All My Life*, p. 241. **38** Beaverbrook, op. cit., p. 94. **39** National Opinion Poll, published in the *Daily Mail*, October 26 1962. **40** See Sparrow, 'The Press, Politics and Private Life,' in *Controversial Essays*. **41** Cudlipp, op. cit., p. 236. **42** Christiansen, op. cit., pp. 135–6. **43** Young, *Stanley Baldwin*, p. 242. **44** Christiansen, op. cit., p. 90. **45** ibid., p. 2. **46** Packard, *The Kansas City Milkman*. **47** Delmer, *Trail Sinister*, pp. 204–5. **48** Cudlipp, op. cit., p. 123. **49** See Beavan, *The Press and the Public*, p. 11. **50** Published in *The Observer*, January 17 1965. **51** Christoph, *Capital Punishment and British Politics*, p. 121. **52** See Bealey *and others, Constituency Politics*, p. 281. **53** See Stephenson, *The Play Theory of Mass Communications*, p. 50, *passim*. **54** Haley, *The Formation of Public Opinion*, pp. 8–9. **55** Alsop, *The Reporter's Trade*, p. 11. **56** Wrench, *Geoffrey Dawson and Our Times*, p. 387. **57** Hankey, *The Supreme Command 1914–1918*, p. 152. **58** *History of The Times 1785–1841*, pp. 165–6. **59** ibid., p. 212. **60** Marx and Engels, *Selected Works*, Vol. 2, p. 361. **61** Gollin, op. cit., p. 4. **62** All these figures come from a National Opinion Poll survey, published in the *Sunday Times*, September 17 1967; Labour had a lead of 1 per cent. **63** Wilson, *Pressure Group*, p. 21.
63a Taine: Notes on England, 9, quoted in Arthur Bryant: English Saga, 137. **64** Briggs, *The Birth of Broadcasting*, p. 238. **65** See Briggs, *The Golden Age of Wireless*, p. 367. **66** 240 H.L. Deb., 5s. c. 224–5, (May 29 1962). **67** Quoted in Miliband, *Parliamentary Socialism*, p. 139; see also Briggs, *The Golden Age of Wireless*, p. 365. **68** Wilson, op. cit., p. 40. **69** Churchill's word, quoted in Briggs, op. cit., p. 145. **70** ibid., p. 364. **71** Hill, *Both Sides of the Hill*, p. 170. **72** *Years in a Mirror*, pp. 46–7. **73** *Daily Mirror*, March 31 1965. **74** *Sunday Times*, March 7 1965. **75** *The Listener*, November 16 1961. **76** ibid. **77** *The Observer*, March 24 1964. **78** ibid. **79** B.B.C. Record, Number 33. **80** *The Observer*, May 31 1965. **81** See Malcolm Muggeridge in the *New Statesman*, March 11 1966. **82** Raymond Asquith, 'In Praise of Young Girls.' **83** Briggs, op. cit., p. 427. **84** Bevins, *The Greasy Pole*, p. 117. **85** 'Thoughts of a Captive Viewer,' *Encounter*, August 1962. **86** Quoted by Murray Kempton in the *Spectator*, March 26 1965. **87** Monypenny *and* Buckle, *Disraeli*, Vol. 2,

p. 29. **88** Angel, *The Press and the Organisation of Society*, p. 10. **89** June 19 1963. **90** White, *The Making of the President 1960*, p. 336. **91** Liebling, op. cit., p. 11. **92** Salinger, *With Kennedy*, p. 46. **93** Butler *and* King, *The British General Election of 1966*, p. 147. **94** See Sir Linton Andrews's letter to *The Times*, July 10 1962. **95** Jay, *Socialism in the New Society*, p. 357. **96** Doob, *Public Opinion and Propaganda*, p. 436. **97** See Edelman, op. cit., pp. 152, 177–8, 197. **98** Liebling, op. cit., p. 33. **99** Stevenson, *Speeches*, pp. 85–7. **100** *Democracy in America*, p. 123. **101** *Politicians and the Press*, p. 110. **102** Magnus, *Kitchener*, p. 134. **103** Aspinall, *Politics and the Press 1780–1850*, p. 2. **104** The Duke of Northumberland, H.L., Deb., 5s., 51 c. 506 (July 17 1922). **105** Cater, *The Fourth Branch of Government*, p. 76. **106** Braithwaite, *Lloyd George's Ambulance Wagon*, p. 158. **107** Christiansen, op. cit., p. 283. **108** David Wood in *The Times*, September 11 1967. **109** Cater, op. cit., p. 32. **110** See Gollin, *The Observer and J. L. Garvin 1908–1914*. **111** Doob, op. cit., p. 271. **112** See Boorstin, *The Image*, p. 11–12. **113** Rovere, *Senator Joe McCarthy*, p. 132. **114** Alsop, op. cit., p. 13. **115** *Time Magazine*, February 15 1960. **116** Amery, *My Political Life*, Vol. 2, p. 329. **117** Birch, *Representative and Responsible Government*, p. 90. **118** Williams, *Communications*, pp. 121–30. **119** *Coningsby*, Bk. 2, Ch. 6. **120** 633 H.C. Deb., 5s., c. 782 (January 31 1961). **121** Quoted by Arnold Beichman in *Columbia University Forum*, Spring 1960, p. 10.

V Public Opinion (*pages 413–429*)

1 Quoted in Kelley, *Professional Public Relations and Political Power*, p. 45. **2** 'Some Thoughts on Public Life,' quoted in Lippman, *The Phantom Public*, p. **7**. **3** *The Intelligent Woman's Guide to Socialism and Capitalism*, p. 347. **4** Jennings, *The Growth of Parties*, p. 219. **5** Esher, *Journals and Letters*, Vol. 2, pp. 203–4. **6** See Birch, *Representative and Responsible Government*, p. 193. **7** Rose, *Influencing Voters*, p. 167. **8** See D. E. G. Plowman, 'Public Opinion and the Polls,' *British Journal of Sociology*, Vol. 13, 1962, p. 337. **9** Mayer, *Madison Avenue U.S.A.*, p. 202. **10** But see Doob, *Public Opinion and Propaganda*, pp. 145–50. **11** Edward Bernays's shorthand definition of the object of public relations, quoted in Ross, *The Image Merchants*, p. 15. **12** Siebert *and others*, *Four Theories of the Press*, p. 112. **13** Aspinall, *Politics and the Press 1750–1850*, p. 233. **14** Kelley, op. cit., p. 2. **15** *The Liberal Hour*, pp. 119–20. **16** Churchill, *Lord Randolph Churchill*, pp. 228–9. **17** See Butler *and* King, *The British General Election of 1966*, p. 136. **18** Clarke, *The Seventeenth Century*, p. 22. **19** Sorensen, *Kennedy*, pp. 329–30. **20** *Daily Express*, March 17 1967. **21** Rose, op. cit., p. 181. **22** ibid., pp. 183–4. **23** Ostrogorski, *Democracy and the Organisation of Political Parties*, Vol. 2, p. 289. **24** ibid., Vol. 2, p. 291. **25** Gallup polls, reproduced in Epstein, *British Politics in the Suez Crisis*, p. 142. **26** Gallup polls, published in *Daily Telegraph*, December 12 1966; in the *Sunday Telegraph*, April 30 1967. **27** Gallup poll, published in the *Daily Telegraph*, May 18 1967. **28** Nordlinger, *The Working Class Tories*, p. 92. **29** Berelson *and others*, *Voting*, pp. 218–22. **30** Benney *and others*, *How People Vote*, pp. 141–7; Milne *and* Mackenzie, *Marginal Seat*, pp. 117–21. **31** See Butler *and* King, op. cit., p. 189. **32** Rose, op. cit., p. 156. **33** Cudlipp, *Publish and Be Damned*, p. 225. **34** See for example Klapper, *The Effects of Mass Communication*. **35** Trenaman *and* McQuail, *Television and the Political Image*. **36** Stephenson, *The Play Theory of Mass Communication*, p. 170. **37** *Political Essays*, p. 318. **38** ibid., pp. 322–3. **39** Rose, *Studies in British Politics*, p. 135. **40** National Opinion poll, taken on behalf of Aims of Industry, reported in the *Sunday Times*, March 15 1964. **41** Mr. John Treasure, of J. Walter Thompson, reported in the *Daily Mirror*, March 19 1966. **42** Robson, *The Governors and the Governed*, p. 60. **43** *Time Magazine*, December 25 1964. **44** Heuston, *The Lives of the Lord Chancellors 1885–1940*, p. 527. **45** Robinson, *Honest to God*, p. 13. **46** National Opinion poll, Special Supplement, July 1965. **47** See the *Sunday Telegraph*, April 30 1967. **48** Lippman, *Public Opinion*, p. 125. **49** Taylor, *English History 1914–1945*, pp. 448–9. **50** See Hancock *and* Gowing, *British War Economy*, pp. 175–6. **51** Beveridge, *Power and Influence*, p. 289. **52** Strang, *The Diplomatic Career*, p. 138. **53** Speech on November 11 1963, at Church House Westminster. **54** *The Statesman*, p. 62. **55** See Beaverbrook, *The Decline and Fall of Lloyd George*, pp. 15–16, 260. **56** Weizmann, *The Impossible Takes Longer*, p. 113. **57** Jones, *A Diary with Letters*, p. 161; Macmillan, *Winds of Change*, p. 445. **58** Keynes, *A Revision of the Treaty*, p. 4. **59** *Everybody's Political What's What*, p. 30. **60** *Lloyd's Bank Review*, July 1965, p. 22. **61** See Windlesham, *Communication and Political Power*, Ch. 10. **62** Salter, *Memoirs of a Public Servant*, p. 354. **63** *War Memoirs*, Vol. 2, p. 1930. **64** Finer, *The Life and Times of Sir Edwin Chadwick*, p. 477. **65** *Sketches from Life*, p. 60. **66** Vansittart, *The Mist Procession*, p. 487. **67** See *History of The Times 1921–1948*, Vol. 2, pp. 817–8. **68** Briggs, *The Golden Age of Wireless*, p. 145. **69** Lindsay, *The Essentials of Democracy*, p. 40. **70** *Stanley Baldwin*, p. 367. **71** W. J. M. Mackenzie, 'Pressure Groups in British Government,' *British Journal of Sociology*, Vol. 6, No. 2, p. 138. **72** Kipling, 'The Fabulists.' **73** *History of The Times 1921–1948*, Vol. 2, p. 994. **74** *The World Crisis: V.S. The Aftermath*, p. 60.

ACKNOWLEDGEMENTS

I am grateful to the following authors, editors, agents and publishers for permission to quote from their books:

The Controller of H.M. Stationery Office:
Hamish Hamilton for *Sketches from Life* by Dean Acheson:
The Bodley Head for *The Reporters' Trade* by Joseph and Stuart Alsop;
Oxford University Press for *Thoughts on the Constitution* by L. S. Amery;
The Earl of Balfour and Cassell and Company for *Chapters of Autobiography* by Lord Balfour;
Herbert Jenkins for *From Workshop to War Cabinet* by George Barnes;
Macmillan & Company, London, for *Labour and Politics 1900–1906* by Frank Bealey and H. Pelling;
The Trustees of the Beaverbrook Foundation for *Men and Power, Politicians and the Press, Politicians and the War*, and *The Decline of Lloyd George* by Lord Beaverbrook;
Faber & Faber for *Modern British Politics* by Samuel H. Beer;
Mrs. Dorothy Cheston Bennett for *What the Public Wants* by Arnold Bennett;
MacGibbon and Kee for *In Place of Fear* by Aneurin Bevan;
Hodder & Stoughton and the Owner of the Copyright for *Power and Influence* by Lord Beveridge;
Hodder & Stoughton for *The Greasy Pole* by John Reginald Bevins;
William Collins, Sons & Company for *The Prof in Two Worlds* by The Earl of Birkenhead;
George Allen & Unwin for *Representative and Responsible Government* by A. H. Birch;
Lord Bridges for *Portrait of a Profession* by Sir Edward Bridges;
David Higham Associates for *Headlines All My Life* by Arthur Christiansen;
Cassell & Company for *The Second World War: Their Finest Hour, Triumph and Tragedy, Grand Alliance*, and *The Gathering Storm* by Sir Winston S. Churchill;
Hutchinson Publishing Group for *Autobiography* by Lord Citrine;
Faber & Faber for *Rise and Decline of Socialism in Great Britain* by Joseph Clayton;
Clarendon Press, Oxford, for *History of Rebellion* by Lord Clarendon;
Rupert Hart-Davies for *Old Men Forget* by Duff Cooper;
Weidenfeld and Nicolson for *The Reform of Parliament* by Bernard Crick;
Victor Gollancz for *Problems of Socialist Government* by Sir Stafford Cripps and others;
William Collins, Sons and Company for *Introduction to Bagehot's The English Constitution* by R. H. S. Crossman;

Mr. Hugh Cudlipp and Weidenfeld and Nicolson for *Publish and be Damned*, and *At Your Peril* by Hugh Cudlipp;

David Higham Associates for *High Tide and After* by Lord Dalton;

Martin Secker and Warburg for *Trail Sinister* by Sefton Delmer;

Cassell & Company for *The Reckoning, Facing the Dictators*, and *Full Circle* by Sir Anthony Eden;

Faber & Faber for 'The Love Song of J. Alfred Prufrock' from *Collected Poems* by T. S. Elliot 1909–62;

University of Chicago Press for *The Presidency, Crisis and Regeneration* by Herman Finer;

Cassell & Company and Laurence Pollinger for *The Forrestal Diaries*;

Hamish Hamilton for *The Liberal Hour* by Professor John K. Galbraith;

The Bodley Head for *Years in a Mirror* by Val Gielgud;

Macmillan & Company of Canada and London for *Twenty Acres Under Glass* by Robert Keith Gray;

Beaverbrook Newspapers for *Memoirs* by Lloyd George;

George Allen & Unwin for *Central Departments and Local Authorities* by J. G. Griffith;

The Executors of Sir James Grigg's Estate and Jonathan Cape for *Prejudice and Judgement* by Sir James Grigg;

Birkbeck College for the Haldane Memorial Lecture given in 1958 by Sir William Haley;

George Allen & Unwin for *The Supreme Command* by Lord Hankey;

William Kimber & Company for *Long to Reign Over Us* by Leonard M. Harris;

The Executors of the Wilson Harris Estate and Jonathan Cape for *Life So Far* by Wilson Harris;

Mr. Quintin Hogg and Penguin Books for *The Conservative Case* by Quintin Hogg;

William Heinemann for *Memoirs* by Lord Ismay;

Thames and Hudson for *Myth and Ritual in the Ancient and Near East* by E. O. James;

Oxford University Press for *Diary with Letters* by Thomas Jones;

Hollis & Carter for *The Ruling Few* by Sir David Kelly;

Macmillan & Company of London and Canada for *General Theory of Employment, Interest and Money* by John Maynard Keynes;

Mrs. George Bambridge and Methuen & Company for 'The Islanders' from *The Five Nations* by Rudyard Kipling;

Mrs. George Bambridge and Macmillan & Company for 'The Fabulists' from *The Diversity of Creatures* by Rudyard Kipling;

John Murray for *Diplomat in Peace and War* by Sir Hughe K. Knatchbull-Hugessen;

The Owner of the Copyright and Sheed & Ward for 'Absolute and Abitofhel' from *Essays in Satire* by Monsignor R. A. Knox;

Sir Frank Lee and Athlone Press for 'The Board of Trade' from the

Stamp Memorial Lecture given on November 11 1958 by Sir Frank Lee;
The Estate of A. J. Liebling and its agents, Laurence Pollinger and
James Brown Associates, Inc. for *The Press* by A. J. Liebling;
Clarendon Press, Oxford for *The Essentials of Democracy* by Lord
Lindsay;
Constable & Company for *Ironside Diaries* by Col. R. Macleod and
Denis Kelly (ed.);
William Heinemann for *British Political Parties* by R. T. McKenzie;
Sweet & Maxwell for *The British Cabinet* by J. P. Mackintosh;
Macmillan & Company of London and Canada for *Winds of Change
1914–1939* by Harold Macmillan;
Penguin Books and The Bodley Head for *Madison Avenue* by Martin
Mayer;
Mr. Christopher Mayhew and Hutchinson Publishing Group for
Britain's Role Tomorrow by Christopher Mayhew;
John Hopkins Press for *A Carnival of Bunconbe* by H. L. Mencken;
Dover Publications, Inc. for *Political Parties* by Robert Michels;
William Collins, Sons and Company for *Memoirs* by Montgomery of
Alamein;
William Kimber & Company for *The Work of the Queen* by Dermot
Morrah;
Arthur Barker for *I Bought a Newspaper* by Claud Morris;
Constable & Company for *How Britain is Governed* by Ramsay Muir;
Macmillan & Company of London and Canada for *England in the Age of
the American Revolution* by L. B. Namier;
Hamish Hamilton for *Personalities and Power* by L. B. Namier;
William Collins, Sons & Company for *Diaries and Letters 1931–39* by
Harold Nicolson;
Manchester University Press for *The Accountability and Audit of
Governments* by E. L. Normanton;
Methuen & Company for *Rationalism in Politics* by Michael Oakeshott;
Curtis Brown for *The Kansas City Milkman* (republished in 1959 as
Dateline: Paris; by Reynolds Packard;
John Murray for *Parkinson's Law* by C. Northcote Parkinson;
Routledge & Kegan Paul for *Conjectures and Refutations* by Sir Karl
Pepper;
Hogarth Press for *The Civil Service in Britain and France* by W. A. Robson;
Mr. Enoch Powell and Pitman Medical Publishing Company for *A New
Look at Medicine and Politics* by Enoch Powell;
Harcourt, Brace and World, Inc. for *Senator Joe McCarthy* by Richard
Rovere;
The Cresset Press for *Memoirs* by Lord Samuel;
Frederick Muller for *C. P. Scott 1846–1932 – The Making of the
Manchester Guardian*;
The Shaw Estate and the Society of Authors for *The Intelligent Woman's*

Guide to Socialism, and *Everybody's Political What's What* by Bernard Shaw;
MacGibbon & Kee for *Entitled to Know* by Peter Shore;
Faber & Faber for *The Spirit of English Administration* by C. H. Sisson;
Hodder & Stoughton for *Kennedy* by Theodore C. Sorensen;..
George Allen & Unwin for *Modern Forms of Government* by Michael Stewart;
The Bodley Head for *Within the Fringe* by James Stuart;
Andre Deutsch for *Home and Abroad* by Lord Strang;
Curtis Brown and Victor Gollancz for *The Shadow of the Gallows* by Lord Templewood;
William Collins, Sons and Company for *Ambassador on Special Mission* by Lord Templewood;
Hodder & Stoughton for *Memoirs* by Harry S. Truman;
Hutchinson Publishing Group for *The Mist Procession* by Lord Vansittart;
A. D. Peters & Company for *Scoop* by Evelyn Waugh;
William Collins, Sons and Company for *Four Thousand Days* by Sir Roy Welensky;
The Executors of H. G. Wells for *The New Machiavelli* by H. G. Wells;
Oxford University Press for *Federal Government* by Sir K. C. Wheare, published for the Royal Institute of International Affairs;
Macmillan & Company of London and Canada for *King George VI: His Life and Reign* by John W. Wheeler-Bennett;
A. D. Peters & Company for *Memoirs* by Earl Woolton;
Rupert Hart-Davies for *Stanley Baldwin* by G. M. Young;
John Murray for *Essayez* by Lord Zetland.

I am also grateful to The Gallup Poll, The National Opinion Poll and the Research Services Limited for permission to quote from their findings.

BIBLIOGRAPHY

The books listed below are, except where stated, published in Great Britain.

ABEL-SMITH, Brian *and* Stevens, Robert, *Lawyers and the Courts*. 1967.
ABRAMS, M., *and* Rose, R., *Must Labour Lose?* 1960.
ACHESON, Dean, *An American Vista*. 1956. *A Citizen Looks at Congress.* 1957. *Sketches from Life.* 1961.
ADAMS, Sherman, *First Hand Report*. 1962.
AGAR, Herbert, *The United States*. 1950.
ALDERMAN, R. K., *and* Cross, J. A., *The Tactics of Resignation*. 1967.
ALFORD, Robert R., *Party and Society*. 1964.
ALLEN, A. J., *The English Voter*. 1964.
ALLEN, C. K., *Law and Orders*. 3rd. ed. 1965. *Law in the Making.* 6th ed. 1958.
ALLEN, V. L., *Trade Unions and the Government*. 1960.
ALSOP, J., *and* Alsop, S., *The Reporter's Trade*. 1960.
AMERY, L. S., *My Political Life*. 3 Vol. 1933–55. *Thoughts on the Constitution.* 2nd ed. 1953.
ANDERSON, Sir John, *The Machinery of Government*. Romanes Lecture, 1946. *The Organisation of Economic Studies in Relation to the Problems of Government.* 1947.
ANDREWS, Sir Linton, *Problems of an Editor*. 1962.
ANGELL, Norman, *The Press and the Organisation of Society*. Rev. ed. 1933.
ANSTEY, Edgar, *Committees*. 1962.
ARNESON, B. A., *The Democratic Monarchies of Scandinavia*. 1949.
ASHWORTH, W., *Contracts and Finance*. 1953.
ASPINALL, A., *The Cabinet Council 1783–1835*. Raleigh Lecture. 1952. *Lord Brougham and the Whig Party.* 1927. *Politics and the Press 1780–1850.* 1949.
ASQUITH, Earl of, *Fifty Years of Parliament*. 2 Vols. 1926.
ATKINSON, W. C., *A History of Spain and Portugal*. 1960.
ATTLEE, C. R., *As it Happened*. 1954.

BAGEHOT, Walter, *The English Constitution*. World's Classics, 1949. *The English Constitution.* With an Introduction by R. H. S. Crossman. Fontana edition. 1963.
BAILEY, Sydney D., *British Parliamentary Democracy*. 1959.
BAILEY, Sydney D., *ed.*, *The Future of the House of Lords*. 1954.
BALDWIN., A. W., *My Father, the True Story*. 1956.
BALFOUR, Arthur James, *Chapters of Autobiography*. 1930.
BARNES, George, *From Workshop to War Cabinet*. 1924.
BASSETT, R., *The Essentials of Parliamentary Democracy*. 2nd ed. 1964. *Nineteen Thirty-one: Political Crisis.* 1958.
BEALEY, F., Blondel, J., *and* McCann, W. P., *Constituency Politics*. 1965.

BEALEY, F., *and* Pelling, H., *Labour and Politics 1900–1906.* 1958.

BEAVAN, John, *The Press and the Public.* Fabian Tract.

BEAVERBROOK, Lord, *The Abdication of King Edward VIII.* 1966. *The Decline and Fall of Lloyd George.* 1963. *Men and Power 1917–1918.* 1956. *Politicians and the Press.* [1926]. *Politicians and the War 1914–1916.* 1960,

BEER, S. H., *Modern British Politics.* 1965. *Treasury Control.* 2nd ed. 1957.

BEER, S. H., *and* Ulam, A. B., *eds.,* *Patterns of Government.* 2nd ed. New York. 1962.

BELLOC, Hilaire *and* Chesterton, C., *The Party System.* 1913.

BELOFF, Max, *The American Federal Government.* 1959. *Foreign Policy and the Democratic Process.* Baltimore, 1955. *New Dimensions in Foreign Policy.* 1961.

BENDINER, R., *White House Fever.* 1960.

BENEMY, F. W. G., *The Elected Monarch.* 1965. *The Queen Reigns: She Does Not Rule.* 1963.

BENNETT, Arnold, *The Strange Vanguard.* 1928. *What the Public Wants.* 1910.

BENNEY, Mark *and others,* *How People Vote.* 1956.

BENTHAM, Jeremy, *The Works.* 11 Vol. 1843.

BERELSON, B. R., *and others,* *Voting.* Chicago. 1954.

BERKELEY, Humphry, *The Power of the Prime Minister.* 1968.

BERLIN, Isaiah, *Mr. Churchill in 1940.* N.D.

BERRINGTON, Hugh, *How Nations are Governed.* 1964.

BEVAN, Aneurin, *In Place of Fear.* 1952.

BEVERIDGE, Lord, *Power and Influence.* 1953.

BEVINS, Reginald, *The Greasy Pole.* 1965.

BIRCH, A. H., *Representative and Responsible Government.* 1964. *Small Town Politics.* 1959.

BIRCH, Lionel, *The Advertising We Deserve?* 1962.

BIRCH, Nigel, *The Conservative Party.* 1949.

BIRKENHEAD, Earl of, *F.E.* 1959. *Halifax.* 1965. *The Prof. in Two Worlds.* 1961.

BLACK, Duncan, *The Theory of Committees and Elections.* 1958.

BLAKE, Robert, *Disraeli.* 1966. *The Unknown Prime Minister.* 1955.

BLOCK, G. D. M., *A Source Book of Conservatism.* 1964.

BLONDEL, J., *Voters, Parties and Leaders.* 1963.

BOARDMAN, Harry, *The Glory of Parliament.* 1960.

BONHAM, John, *The Middle Class Vote.* 1954.

BOORSTIN, D. J., *The Image.* 1961.

BOOTH, A. H., *British Hustings 1924–1950.* 1956.

BOOTHBY, Robert, *I Fight to Live.* 1947.

BOSWELL, James, *Life of Johnson.* 1952.

BOWLE, John, *Politics and Opinion in the Nineteenth Century.* 1954.

BRAITHWAITE, W. J., *Lloyd George's Ambulance Wagon.* 1957.

BRASHER, N. H., *Studies in British Government*. 1965.

BRIDGES, Sir Edward, *The Treasury*. 1964. *Treasury Control*. 1950. *Portrait of a Profession*. 1953.

BRIGGS, Asa, *The Birth of Broadcasting*. 1961. *The Golden Age of Wireless*. 1965.

BRENAN, Gerald, *The Spanish Labyrinth*. 2nd ed. 1950.

BRITTAIN, Sir Herbert, *The British Budgetary System*. 1959.

BRITTAN, Samuel, *The Treasury Under the Tories 1951–1964*. 1964.

BROGAN, D. W., *The American Political System*. 1943. *Citizenship Today*. North Carolina, 1960. *The Development of Modern France*. 1940. *The Free State*. 1945. *An Introduction to American Politics*. 1954. *Politics and Law in the United States*. 1941. *Roosevelt and the New Deal*. 1952. *American Themes*. 1948.

BROGAN, D. W., and Verney, D. V., *Political Patterns in Today's World*. 1963.

BROMHEAD, P. A., *The House of Lords and Contemporary Politics*. 1958.

BROWN, F. J., *The Sovereign People*. Melbourne, 1954.

BROWN, J. A. C., *Techniques of Persuasion*. 1963.

BROWN, W. J., *Everybody's Guide to Parliament*. 2nd ed. 1946.

BRYANT, Arthur, *English Saga*. 1940. *Triumph in the West*. 1959. *The Turn of the Tide*. 1957.

BRYCE, Lord, *Modern Democracies*. 2 Vol. 1921.

BUCHAN, John, *Memory Hold the Door*. 1940.

BULLOCK, Alan, *The Life and Times of Ernest Bevin*. Vol. 1: 1881–1940. 1960. Vol. 2: 1940–1945. 1967.

BULLOCK, Alan, and Shock, M., eds., *The Liberal Tradition*. 1956.

BURKE, Edmund, *Works*. 16 Vols. 1826.

BURN, W. L., *The Age of Equipoise*. 1964.

BUTLER, D. E., *The British General Election of 1951*. 1952. *The British General Election of 1955*. 1955. *Elections Abroad*. 1959. *The Electoral System in Great Britain since 1918*. 2nd ed. 1963.

BUTLER, D. E., and Freeman, J., *British Political Facts, 1900–1960*. 1963.

BUTLER, D. E., and King, Anthony, *The British General Election of 1964*. 1965. *The British General Election of 1966*. 1966.

BUTLER, D. E., and Rose, R. Richard, *The British General Election of 1959*. 1960.

BUTT, Ronald, *The Power of Parliament*. 1967.

CAMPBELL, G. A., *The Civil Service in Britain*. 1955.

CAMPBELL, Peter, *French Electoral Systems*. 1958.

CAMPION, Lord, and others, *British Government since 1918*. 1950. *Parliament: a Survey*. 1952.

CARLYLE, Thomas, *The French Revolution*. 3 Vols. 1837.

CARR, E. H., *The Bolshevik Revolution 1917–1923*. 3 Vols. 1950–3.

CARR, Raymond, *Spain 1808–1939*. 1966.

CARTER, B. E., *The Office of Prime Minister*, 1956.

CATER, D., *The Fourth Branch of Government*. Boston, 1959.

CECIL, Henry, *Tipping the Scales*. 1964.

CECIL, Lord Hugh, *Conservatism*. 1912.

CHAMBERLAIN, Sir Austen, *Down the Years*. 1935. *Politics from the Inside*. 1936.

CHAMBERLAIN, Joseph, *A Political Memoir*. 1953.

CHANDOS, Lord, *Memoirs*. 1962.

CHAPMAN, Brian, *British Government Observed*. 1963. *The Profession of Government*. 1959.

CHESTER, D. N., *and* Bowring, N., *Questions in Parliament*. 1962.

CHESTER, D. N., *and* Willson, F. M. G., *The Organisation of British Central Government 1914–1956*. 1957.

CHRISTIANSEN, Arthur, *Headlines All My Life*. 1961.

CHRISTOPH, James B., *Capital Punishment and British Politics*. 1962.

CHURCHILL, Randolph S., *Lord Derby*. 1959.

CHURCHILL, Winston S., *Closing the Ring*. 1952. *The Dawn of Liberation*. 1945. *The End of the Beginning*. 1943. *Europe Unite*. 1950. *The Gathering Storm*. 1948. *The Grand Alliance*. 1950. *The Hinge of Fate*. 1951. *Into Battle*. 1941. *Lord Randolph Churchill*. 1907. *Onwards to Victory*. 1944. *Secret Session Speeches*. 1946. *Their Finest Hour*. 1949. *Triumph and Tragedy*. 1954. *The Unrelenting Struggle*. 1942. *Victory*. 1946. *The World Crisis 1911–1918*. 5 Vols. 1923–9. 1 Vol. ed. 1964.

CITRINE, Lord, *Men and Work*. 1964. *Two Careers*. 1967.

CLAPP, Charles, *The Congressman*. Washington, D.C., 1963.

CLARKE, G. N., *The Seventeenth Century*. 2nd ed. 1947.

CLAYTON, Joseph, *The Rise and Decline of Socialism in Great Britain 1884–1924*. 1926.

COIT, M., *John C. Calhoun*. 1950.

COLE, G. D. H., *British Working Class Politics 1832–1914*. 1941.

COLE, Margaret, *The Story of Fabian Socialism*. 1961.

COLERIDGE, S. T., *Church and State*. 1839. *The Notebooks*. Edited by Kathleen Coburn. 1951.

COOKE, Alistair, *A Generation on Trial*. 1950.

COOMBES, David, *The Member of Parliament and the Administration*. 1966.

COOPER, Duff, *Old Men Forget*. 1953.

COOTE, Colin R., *Editorial*. 1965.

CRAIG, Sir John, *A History of Red Tape*. 1955.

CRAWFORD, Iain, *The Profumo Affair*. 1963.

CRICK, Bernard, *The Reform of Parliament*. 1964.

CRIPPS, Sir Stafford *and others*, *Problems of a Socialist Government*. 1933.

CRITCHLEY, J. A., *The Civil Service Today*. 1951.

CROMBIE, Sir James, *Her Majesty's Customs and Excise*. 1962.

CROSS, Colin, *The Liberals in Power 1905–1914*. 1963. *Philip Snowden*. 1966.

CROSSMAN, R. H. S., *Labour in the Affluent Society*. Fabian Tract. 1960.

CUDLIPP, Hugh, *At Your Peril*. 1962. *Publish and Be Damned*. 1953.
CUDLIPP, Hugh *and others*, *Only Connect*. 1968.

DAALDER, Hans, *Cabinet Reform in Britain 1914–1963*. 1964.
DAHL, Robert A., *ed.*, *Political Oppositions in Western Democracies*. New Haven, 1966. *Who Governs?* New Haven, 1961.
DALE, H. E., *The Higher Civil Service*. 1939.
DALTON, Hugh, *Call Back Yesterday*. 1953. *The Fateful Years*. 1957. *High Tide and After*. 1962.
DANIELS, Jonathan, *The Man of Independence*. 1951.
DAVENPORT, Nicholas, *The Split Society*. 1964.
DAVIS, H. W. C., *The Age of Grey and Peel*. 1929.
DeCONDE, Alexander, *The American Secretary of State*. 1963.
DELMER, Sefton, *Trail Sinister*. 1961.
DENNING, Alfred, *Freedom Under the Law*. 1949.
DE SMITH, S. A., *Judicial Review of Administrative Action*. 1959.
DEVLIN, Patrick, *Samples of Lawmaking*. 1962.
DEVONS, Ely, *Planning in Practice*. 1950.
DICEY, A. V., *Law and Public Opinion in England*. 2nd ed. 1962. *The Law of the Constitution*. 1885.
DILL, Marshall, *Germany*. Michigan, 1961.
DISRAELI, Benjamin, *Coningsby*. 1844. *Lord George Bentinck*. 1852. *Sybil*. 1845. *Vindication of the English Constitution*. 1835.
DONALDSON, F., *The Marconi Scandal*. 1962.
DONOVAN, R., *Eisenhower, the Inside Story*. 1958.
DOOB, L. W. L., *Public Opinion and Propaganda*. 2nd ed. Hamden, Conn., 1966.
DRIBERG, Tom, *Beaverbrook*. 1956.
DUGDALE, B. E. C., *Arthur James Balfour*. 2 Vols. 1936.
DUNNILL, Frank, *The Civil Service*. 1956.
DUVERGER, M. *The Idea of Politics*. 1966. *Political Parties*. 2nd ed. 1959.

ECKSTEIN, Harry, *Pressure Group Politics*. 1960.
EDELMAN, Maurice, *The Mirror*. 1966.
EDEN, Sir Anthony, *The Eden Memoirs:* Facing the Dictators, 1962. Full Circle. 1960. The Reckoning. 1965.
EDWARDS, J. L. J., *The Law Officers of the Crown*. 1964.
EHRMAN, John, *Cabinet Government and War*. 1958.
EHRMANN, H. W., *ed.*, *Democracy in a Changing Society*. 1965. *Interest Groups on Four Continents*. Pittsburgh, 1958.
EISENHOWER, Dwight D., *Mandate for Change*. 1965.
EMDEN, C. S., *The People and the Constitution*. 2nd ed. 1956.
ENSOR, R. C. R., *England 1870–1914*. 1936.
EPSTEIN, L. D., *British Politics in the Suez Crisis*. 1964.
ESHER, Viscount, *Journals and Letters*. 4 Vols. 1934–8.

EVANS, Rowland, *and* Novak, Robert, *Lyndon B. Johnson, The Exercise of Power.* 1967.

FABER, Richard, *Beaconsfield and Bolingbrooke.* 1961.
FAIRLIE, Henry, *The Life of Politics.* 1968.
FAUVET, Jacques, *The Cockpit of France.* 1960.
FEILING, Keith, *The Life of Neville Chamberlain.* 1946. *The Second Tory Party 1714–1832.* 1938.
FENNO, Richard, *The President's Cabinet.* Cambridge, Mass., 1959.
FILMER, Sir Robert, *Patriarcha.* Edited by Peter Laslett. 1949.
FINER, Herman, *The British Civil Servant.* 1937. *The Major Governments of Modern Europe.* 1960. *The Presidency: Crisis and Regeneration.* Chicago, 1960.
FINER, S. E., *Anonymous Empire.* 1958. *The Life and Times of Sir Edwin Chadwick.* 1952. *The Man on Horseback.* 1962.
FOORD, A. S., *His Majesty's Opposition 1714–1830.* 1964.
FOOT, Michael, *Aneurin Bevan.* Vol. 1: *1897–1945.* 1962.
FRANKS, Sir Oliver, *The Experience of a University Teacher in the Civil Service.* 1947. *Planning and Control in War and Peace.* 1947.
FULBRIGHT, J. W., *The Arrogance of Power.* 1967.
FULFORD, Roger, *Hanover to Windsor.* 1960. *The Prince Consort.* 1949.

GALBRAITH, J. K., *The Liberal Hour.* 1960.
GARDINER, S. R., ed., *The Constitutional Documents of the Puritan Revolution 1625–1660.* 3rd ed. 1947.
GARDNER, G., *and* Martin, A., eds., *Law Reform Now.* 1963.
GARVIN, J. L., *The Life of Joseph Chamberlain.* 4 Vols. 1932–4.
GASH, Norman, *Mr. Secretary Peel.* 1961. *Politics in the Age of Peel.* 1953. *Reaction and Reconstruction in British Politics 1832–1952.* 1965.
GENERAL Council of the Press, *The Press and the People.* 9th annual report, 1963.
GIELGUD, Val, *Years in a Mirror.* 1965.
GINSBERG, M., ed., *Law and Opinion in England in the Twentieth Century.* 1959.
GLADDEN, E. N., *Civil Service or Bureaucracy?* 1956.
GLASS, S. T., *The Responsible Society.* 1966.
GOLLIN, Alfred, *Balfour's Burden.* 1965. *The Observer and J. L. Garvin 1908–1914.* 1960. *Proconsul in Politics.* 1964.
GORDON, Strathearn, *Our Parliament.* 6th ed. 1964.
GRAUBARD, S. R., *Burke, Disraeli and Churchill.* Cambridge, Mass., 1961.
GRAY, R. K., *Eighteen Acres Under Glass.* 1962.
GREAVES, H. R. C., *The British Constitution.* 3rd ed. 1955. *The Civil Service in the Changing State.* 1947.
GREVILLE, Charles, *The Greville Memoirs.* 8 Vols. 1874–87.
GRIFFITH, E. S., *The American System of Government.* 1954.
GRIFFITH, J. A. G., *Central Departments and Local Authorities.* 1966.

GRIGG, P. J., *Prejudice and Judgment*. 1948.

GRIMOND, Jo, *The Liberal Challenge*. 1963. *The Liberal Future*. 1959.

GRISWOLD, E. N., *Law and Lawyers in the United States*. 1964.

GUEDALLA, Philip, *Palmerston*. 1926.

GUTTSMAN, W. L., *The British Political Elite*. 1963.

GWYN, W. B., *Democracy and the Cost of Politics*. 1962.

HALDANE, R. B., *An Autobiography*. 1929.

HALEVY, Elie, *A History of the English People in the Nineteenth Century*. 6 Vols. 1924–47.

HALEY, Sir William, *The Formation of Public Opinion*. Haldane Memorial Lecture. 1958.

HALIFAX, Earl of, *Fulness of Days*. 1957.

HALL, W. G., *The Labour Party*. 1949.

HAMILTON, M. A., *Arthur Henderson*. 1938.

HAMILTON, Alexander *and others, The Federalist*. Edited with an introduction and notes by Max Beloff. 1948.

HAMMOND, J. L., *and* M. Foot, R. D., *Gladstone and Liberalism*. 1952.

HANCOCK, W. K., *and* Gowing, M. M., *British War Economy*. 1949.

HANHAM, H. J., *Elections and Party Management*. 1959.

HANKEY, Lord, *Diplomacy by Conference*. 1946. *The Science and Art of Government*. Romanes Lecture. 1951. *The Supreme Command 1914–1918*. 2 Vols. 1961. *The Supreme Control at the Paris Peace Conference 1919*. 1963.

HANSON, A. H., *Parliament and Public Ownership*. 1961.

HANSON, A. H., *and* Wiseman, H. V., *Parliament at Work*. 1962.

HAMSON, C. J., *Executives Discretion and Judicial Control*. 1954.

HARDINGE, Lord, *Old Diplomacy*. 1947.

HARRIS, L. M., *Long to Reign Over Us?* 1966.

HARRIS, Wilson, *Life So Far*. 1954.

HARRISON, Martin, *Trade Unions and the Labour Party since 1945*. 1960.

HARRISON, Wilfrid, *The Government of Britain*. 5th ed. 1958.

HARROD, R. F., *The Life of John Maynard Keynes*. 1951.

HARVEY, C. P., *The Advocate's Devil*. 1958.

HARVEY, J., *and* Bather, L., *The British Constitution*. 1963.

HASTAD, Elis, *The Parliament of Sweden*. 1957.

HASTINGS, Stephen, *The Murder of TSR-2*. 1966.

HAYWARD, J. E. S., *Private Interests and Public Policy*. 1966.

HAZLITT, William, *Political Essays*. 1819.

HEIDENHEIMER, A. J., *The Governments of Germany*. 1965.

HEMINGFORD, Lord, *Backbencher and Chairman*. 1946.

HENDERSON, G. B., *Crimean War Diplomacy*. 1947.

HERBERT, A. P., *The Ayes Have it*. 1937. *Independent Member*. 1950. *The Point of Parliament*. 1946.

HEUSTON, R. F. V., *Essays in Constitutional Law*. 2nd ed. 1964. *Lives of the Lord Chancellors 1885–1940*. 1964.

HEWART, Lord, *The New Despotism*. 1929.

HILL, A., *and* Whichelow, A., *What's Wrong with Parliament?* 1964.

HILL, Christopher, *The Century of Revolution 1603–1714*. 1961. *Lenin and the Russian Revolution*. 1947.

HILL, Lord, *Both Sides of the Hill*. 1964.

HISS, Alger, *In the Court of Public Opinion*. 1957.

History of the Times: Vol. 1: 1785–1841. 1935. Vol. 2: 1841–1884. 1939. Vol. 3: 1884–1912. 1947. Vol. 4: 1912–1920. 1952. Vol. 5: 1921–1948. 2 Vols. 1952.

HODGKIN, Thomas, *African Political Parties*. 1961.

HOFFMAN, J. D., *The Conservative Party in Opposition 1945–1951*. 1964.

HOGG, Quintin, *The Conservative Case*. Rev. ed. 1959. *The Purpose of Parliament*. 1947. *Science and Politics*. 1963.

HOLBROOK, Stewart, *The Age of the Moguls*. 1954.

HOLLAND, B. H., *The Life of Spencer Compton, Eighth Duke of Devonshire*. 2 Vols. 1911.

HOLLIS, Christopher, *Along the Road to Frome*. 1958. *Can Parliament Survive?* 1949.

HOWARD, A., *and* West , R., *The Making of the Prime Minister*. 1965.

HUGHES, C. J., *The Parliament of Switzerland*. 1962.

HUGHES, Emmet J., *The Ordeal of Power*. 1963.

HUGHES, Emrys, *Parliament and Mumbo-jumbo*. 1966.

HUME, David, *The Philosophical Works*. 4 Vols. 1826.

HUNTER, Leslie, *The Road to Brighton Pier*. 1959.

HURSTFIELD, J., *The Control of Raw Materials*. 1953.

HURD, Douglas, *The Arrow War*. 1967.

HYDE, Montgomery, *Carson*. 1953.

INCE, Sir Godfrey, *The Ministry of Labour and National Service*. 1960.

ISMAY, Lord, *Memoirs*. 1960.

JACKSON, R. M., *The Machinery of Justice in England*. 4th ed. 1964.

JAMES, E. O., *Myth and Ritual in the Ancient Near East*. 1958.

JAMES, R. R., *An Introduction to the House of Commons*. 1961.

JAY, Douglas, *Socialism in the New Society*. 1962.

JENKINS, Roy, *Asquith*. 1964. *Mr. Balfour's Poodle*. 1954. *Pursuit of Progress*. 1953.

JENNINGS, Sir Ivor, *The British Constitution*. 3rd ed. 1950. *Cabinet Government*. 3rd ed. 1959. *The Law and the Constitution*. 5th ed. 1959. *Parliament*. 2nd ed. 1957. *Parliament Must be Reformed*. 1941. *Party Poliuics*. Vol. 1: Appeal to the People. 1960. Vol. 2: The Growth of Parties. 1961. Vol. 3: The Stuff of Politics. 1962.

JOHNSON, D. McI., *A Doctor in Parliament*. 1959.

JOHNSON, F. A., *Defence by Committee*. 1960.

JONES, Thomas, *A Diary with Letters 1931–1950*. 1954. *Lloyd George*. 1951.

JOUVENEL, Bertrand de, *Power*. 1948. *Sovereignty*. 1957.
JOWITT, Earl, *The Strange Case of Alger Hiss*. 1953.

KAUFMAN, Gerald, *ed.*, *The Left*. 1966.
KEETON, G. W., *The Passing of Parliament*. 1952. *Trial by Tribunal*. 1960.
KEITH, A. B., *The Constitution of England from Queen Victoria to George VI.*
  2 Vols. 1940.
KEIR, J. C., *Constitutional History of Modern Britain*. 3rd ed. 1946.
KELF-COHEN, R., *Nationalisation in Britain*. 2nd ed. 1961.
KELLEY, Stanley, *Professional Public Relations and Political Power*. Balti-
  more, 1956.
KELLY, Sir David, *The Ruling Few*. 1952.
KELSALL, R. R., *Higher Civil Servants in Britain*. 1955.
KEMP, Betty, *King and Commons 1660–1832*. 1957.
KENNEDY, A. L., *Salisbury 1830–1903*. 1953.
KERSELL, J. E., *Parliamentary Supervision of Delegated Legislation*. 1960.
KEY, V. O., *Politics, Parties and Pressure Groups*. 5th ed. New York, 1964.
  Public Opinions and American Democracy. New York, 1961.
KEYNES, J. M., *The General Theory of Employment, Interest and Money*. 1936.
  A Revision of the Treaty. 1922.
KILMUIR, Earl of, *Political Adventure*. 1964.
KIMCHE, J., *and* Kimche, D., *Both Sides of the Hill*. 1960.
KING, Cecil, *The Future of the Press*. 1967.
KINGSLEY, F. D., *Representative Bureaucracy*. Yellow Springs, Ohio, 1944.
KIRK, Russell, *The Conservative Mind*. 1954.
KIRKPATRICK, Sir Ivone, *The Inner Circle*. 1959.
KITZINGER, U. W., *German Electoral Politics*. 1960.
KLAPPER, J. T., *The Effects of Mass Communication*. New York, 1960.
KOESTLER, Arthur, *Reflections on Hanging*. 1956.
KNATCHBULL-HUGESSEN, Sir Hughe, *Diplomat in Peace and War*. 1949.

LAIRD, Dorothy, *How the Queen Reigns*. 1959.
LAKEMAN, Enid, *Voting in Democracies*. 1955.
LANDIS, J. M., *The Administrative Process*. New Haven, 1966.
LASKI, Harold J., *Parliamentary Government in England*. 1938. *Reflections on
  the Constitution*. 1951.
LAUNDY, Philip, *The Office of Speaker*. 1964.
LEE, Sir Frank, *The Board of Trade*. 1958.
LEONARD, R. L., *Guide to the General Election*. 1964.
LETWIN, S. R., *The Pursuit of Certainty*. 1965.
LEUCHTENBERG, W. E., *Franklin D. Roosevelt and the New Deal 1932–1940*.
  (1963).
LEWIS, Anthony, *Gideon's Trumpet*. 1966.
LIEBLING, A. J., *The Press*. New York, 1961.
LINDSAY, A. D., *The Essentials of Democracy*. 2nd ed. 1948.

LINDSAY, T. F., *Parliament from the Press Gallery*. 1967.

LIPPMAN, Walter, *The Phantom Public*. New York, 1925. *Public Opinion* 1922. *The Public Philosophy*. 1955

LIPSET, S. M., *Political Man*. 1960.

LLOYD GEORGE, David, *War Memoirs*. 2 Vols. 1938.

LONGFORD, Elizabeth, *Victoria R.I.* 1964.

LOW, Sydney, *The Governance of England*. 1904.

LOWELL, A. L., *The Government of England*. 2 Vols. 1908. *Public Opinion and Popular Government*. 1914.

LUBELL, Samuel, *The Future of American Politics*. 1952.

LYMAN, R. W., *The First Labour Government 1924*. 1957.

MCCALLUM, R. B., *The Liberal Party from Earl Grey to Asquith*. 1963.

MCCALLUM, R. B., *and* Readman, A., *The British General Election of 1945*. 1947.

MCCLOSKEY, R. G., *The American Supreme Court*. Chicago, 1960.

MACCOBY, S., *ed.*, *The Radical Tradition*. 1952.

MACCOLL, René, *Deadline and Dateline*. 1956.

MACDONALD, J. F., *The State and the Trade Unions*. 1960.

MCDOWELL, R. B., *British Conservatism 1832–1914*. 1952.

MACK SMITH, Denis, *Italy*. Michigan, 1959.

MACKENZIE, Kenneth, *The English Parliament*. 1950.

MCKENZIE, Robert, *British Political Parties*. 2nd ed. 1963.

MACKENZIE, W. J. M., *Free Elections*. 1958.

MACKENZIE, W. J. M., *and* Grove, J. W., *Central Administration in Britain*. 1957.

MACKENZIE, W. J. M., *and* Robinson, K. E., *Five Elections in Africa*. 1960.

MACKINTOSH, Sir Alexander, *Echoes of Big Ben*. N.D.

MACKINTOSH, John P., *The British Cabinet*. 1962.

MACLEOD, Iain, *Neville Chamberlain*. 1961.

MACLEOD, R., *and* Kelly, D., *eds.*, *The Ironside Diaries 1937–1940*. 1962.

MACMILLAN, Harold, *The Blast of War 1939–1945*. 1967. *Winds of Change 1914–1939*. 1966.

MACPHERSON, C. B., *The Real World of Democracy*. 1966.

MADARIAGA, Salvador de, *Spain*. 1942.

MAGNUS, Sir Philip, *Gladstone*. 1952. *King Edward VII*. 1964. *Kitchener*. 1958.

MAITLAND, F. W., *The Constitutional History of England*. 1908. *The Forms of Action at Common Law*. 1909.

MALLABY, George, *From My Level*. 1965.

MALLALIEU, J. P. W., *Passed to You Please*. 1942.

MANCHESTER, William, *The Sage of Baltimore*. 1952.

MARSHALL, G., *and* Moodie, G. C., *Some Problems of the Constitution*. 1959.

MARTIN, J. B., *Adlai Stevenson*. 1952.

MARTIN, Kingsley, *The Crown and the Establishment*. 1962.

MARX, Karl, *and* Engels, F., *Selected Works*. 2 Vols. Moscow, 1950.

MASON, A. T., *The Supreme Court from Taft to Warren*. New York, 1958.

MATHIOT, André, *The British Political System*. 1958.

MAYER, Martin, *Madison Avenue U.S.A.* 1958.

MAYHEW, Christopher, *Britain's Role Tomorrow*. 1967.

MENCKEN, H. L., *A Carnival of Buncombe*. Baltimore, 1956.

MENHENNET, D., *and* Palmer, J., *Parliament in Perspective*. 1967.

MICHELS, R. W. E., *Political Parties*. Dover ed. 1959.

MICHENER, J. A., *Report of the County Chairman*. 1961.

MIDDLEMAS, R. K., *The Clydesiders*. 1965.

MILIBAND, Ralph, *Parliamentary Socialism*. 1961.

MILL, John Stuart, *On Liberty*. 1859. *On Representative Government*. 1861.

MILLER, Edward, *The Origins of Parliament*. 1960.

MILLIS, W., *ed.*, *The Forrestal Diaries*. 1952.

MILNE, R. S., *Political Parties in New Zealand*. 1966.

MILNE, R. S., *and* Mackenzie, H. C., *Marginal Seat 1955*. 1958. *Straight Fight 1951*.

MINNEY, R. J., *The Private Papers of Hore-Belisha*. 1960.

MONCK, Bosworth, *How the Civil Service Works*. 1952.

MONTGOMERY, Lord, *Memoirs*. 1958.

MONYPENNY, W. F., *and* Buckle, G. E., *The Life of Benjamin Disraeli*. Rev. ed. 2 Vols. 1929.

MOODIE, G. C., *The Government of Great Britain*. 1964.

MORAN, Lord, *Churchill: The Struggle for Survival 1940–1965*. 1966.

MORGAN, Sir Frederick, *Peace and War*. 1961.

MORLEY, John, *The Life of Gladstone*. 2 Vols. 1905. *The Life of Richard Cobden*. 10th ed. 1903. *The Life of Walpole*. 1889.

MORRAH, Dermot, *The Work of the Queen*. 1958.

MORRIS, Claud, *I Bought a Newspaper*. 1963.

MORRIS, James, *The Outriders*. 1963.

MORRISON, Herbert, *An Autobiography*. 1960. *Government and Parliament*. 2nd ed. 1959.

MOWAT, C. L., *Britain between the Wars 1918–1940*. 1955.

MUIR, Ramsay, *How Britain is Governed*. 1930.

MURPHY, W. F., *Congress and the Court*. Chicago, 1962.

NAMIER, L. B., *Avenues of History*. 1952. *Crossroads of Power*. 1962. *England in the Age of the American Revolution*. 1930. *Personalities and Powers*. 1955. *The Structure of Politics at the Accession of George III*. 2nd ed. 1957.

NEALE, J. E., *The Elizabethan House of Commons*. 1949.

NEUSTADT, R., *Presidential Power*. New York, 1960.

NEVINS, Allen, *and* Commager, H. S., *A Short History of the United States*. New York, 1945.

NEW, Chester W., *The Life of Henry Brougham to 1830*. 1961.

NICHOLAS, H. G., *The British General Election of 1950*. 1951.

NICHOLSON, Max, *The System*. 1967.

NICOLSON, Harold, *Curzon: The Last Phase.* 1934. *Diaries and Letters: 1930–1939.* 1966. *Diaries and Letters 1939–1945.* 1967. *King George V.* 1952. *Lord Carnock.* 1930. *Monarchy.* 1962. *Peacemaking* 1919. 1944.

NICOLSON, Nigel, *People and Parliament.* 1958.

NORDLINGER, Eric A., *The Working Class Tories.* 1967.

NORMANTON, E. L., *The Accountability and Audit of Governments.* 1966.

NOTESTEIN, Wallace, *The Winning of the Initiative by the House of Commons.* Raleigh Lecture. 1924.

NUTTING, Anthony, *No End of a Lesson.* 1967.

OAKESHOTT, Michael, *Rationalism in Politics.* 1962.

OGG, David, *England in the Reigns of James II and William III.* 1955.

O'LEARY, Cornelius, *The Elimination of Corrupt Practices in British Elections 1868–1911.* 1962.

ORWELL, George, *The Road to Wigan Pier.* 1937. *Shooting an Elephant.* 1950.

OSTROGORSKI, M. Y., *Democracy and the Organisation of Political Parties.* 2 Vols. 1902.

OWEN, Frank, *Tempestuous Journey.* 1954.

PACKARD, Reynolds, *The Kansas City Milkman.* 1950.

PARES, Richard, *King George III and the Politicians.* 1953.

PARKINSON, C. Northcote, *Parkinson's Law.* 1958.

Parliament Through Seven Centuries. 1962. *Parliamentary Reform 1933–1960.* 1961. *Parliaments.* 2nd ed. 1966.

PATERSON, Peter, *The Selectorate.* 1967.

PATON, H. J., *The Claim of Scotland.* 1968.

PEARSON, Hesketh, *Labby.* 1936.

PEARSON, Lester B., *Diplomacy in the Nuclear Age.* 1959.

PELLING, H., *The Origins of the Labour Party.* 2nd ed. 1965. *A Short History of the Labour Party.* 1961.

PELLING, H., ed., *The Challenge of Socialism.* 1954.

PEP, *Advisory Committees in British Government.* 1960. *Government by Appointment.* 1960.

PETRIE, Charles, *George Canning.* 2nd ed. 1946.

PICKLES, Dorothy, *The Fifth French Republic.* 1960.

PINE, L. G., *Ramshackledom.* 1962.

PLUMB, J. H., *The Growth of Political Stability in England 1675–1725.* 1967. *Sir Robert Walpole.* 2 Vols. 1956–60.

POIRIER, P. P., *The Advent of the Labour Party.* 1958.

POOL, I. de S., *and others, Candidates, Issues and Strategies.* Cambridge, Mass., 1965.

POPPER, Karl R., *Conjectures and Refutations.* 1963. *The Open Society and Its Enemies.* 1945.

POTTER, Allen, *Organised Groups in British National Politics.* 1961.

POWELL, Enoch, *A New Look at Medicine and Politics.* 1966.

PROTHERO, G. W., ed., *Select Statutes and other Constitutional Documents 1558–1625*. 4th ed. 1913.

PULZER, Peter, *Political Representation and Elections in Britain*. 1967.

PUSEY, Merlo J., *Eisenhower the President*. New York, 1956.

RAALTE, Ernst von, *The Parliament of the Kingdom of the Netherlands*. 1959.

RADCLIFFE, Lord, *The Law and Its Compass*. 1961.

RANDALL, J. G., *Lincoln the President: Springfield to Gettysburg*. 2 Vols. [1945].

RANNEY, Austin, *Pathways to Parliament*. 1965.

RASMUSSEN, J. S., *The Liberal Party*. 1965.

RAYMOND, John, ed., *The Baldwin Age*. 1960.

REES, David B., *Korea: The Limited War*. 1964.

RESTON, James, *The Artillery of the Press*. New York, 1967.

RICHARDS, Peter G., *Honourable Member*. 1959. *Parliament and Foreign Affairs*. 1967. *Patronage in British Government*. 1963.

RIDDELL, Lord, *Intimate Diary of the Peace Conference and After*. 1933. *War Diary*. 1933.

RIDLEY, F., *and* Blondel, J., *Public Administration in France*. 1964.

ROBERTS, B. C., *Trade Unions in a Free Society*. 2nd ed. 1962.

ROBERTSON, Terence, *Crisis*. 1965.

ROBSON, R. J., *The Oxfordshire Election of 1754*. 1949.

ROBSON, W. A., *The British System of Government*. 1959. *The Civil Service in Britain and France*. 1956. *The Governors and the Governed*. 1946. *Local Government in Crisis*. 1966. *Nationalised Industry and Public Ownership*. 1960.

ROBSON, W. A., *and others*, *The British Civil Servant*. 1937.

ROCKEFELLER, Nelson A., *The Future of Federalism*. Cambridge, Mass., 1962.

RODGERS, W. T., ed., *Hugh Gaitskell 1906–1963*. 1964.

ROKKAN, Stein, *Readers, Viewers, Voters*. Guildhall Lecture. 1964.

ROLO, P. J. V., *George Canning*. 1965.

ROSE, Richard, *Influencing Voters*. 1967. *Politics in England*. 1965.

ROSE, Richard, ed., *Studies in British Politics*. 1966.

ROSS, Irwin, *The Image Merchants*. 1959.

ROSSITER, Clinton, *Parties and Politics in America*. Ithaca, N.Y., 1960.

ROSTOW, Eugene V., *The Sovereign Prerogative*. New Haven, 1962.

ROUSSEAU, J.-J., *Social Contract*. World's Classic edition.

ROVERE, Richard H., *Affairs of State: The Eisenhower Years*. New York 1956. *Howe and Hummel*. 1948. *Senator Joe McCarthy*. 1960.

RUNCIMAN, W. G., *Social Science and Political Theory*. 1963.

RYAN, A. P., *Lord Northcliffe*. 1953.

SALINGER, Pierre, *With Kennedy*. 1967.

SALTER, Lord, *Memoirs of a Public Servant*. 1961.

Q

SAMPSON, Anthony, *The Anatomy of Britain*. 1962. *Macmillan*. 1967.

SAMUEL, Viscount, *Memoirs*. 1945.

SCHLESINGER, Arthur M., *The Age of Roosevelt*. Vol. 1: The Crisis of the Old Order 1919–1933. 1957. Vol. 2: The Coming of the New Deal. 1960. Vol. 3: The Politics of Upheaval. 1961. *A Thousand Days*. 1965.

SCHUMPETER, Joseph A., *Capitalism, Socialism and Democracy*. 3rd ed. 1950.

SCHWARTZ, Bernard, *American Constitutional Law*. 1955. *An Introduction to American Administrative Law*. 2nd ed. 1962. *The Reins of Power*. 1964.

C. P. Scott 1846–1932: The Making of the Manchester Guardian. 1946.

SCOTT, J. D., *and* Hughes, R., *The Administration of War Production*. 1955.

SCOTT, Peter, *and* Storing, H., *The State and the Farmer*. 1962.

SHAW, G. B., *Everybody's Political What's What*. 1944. *The Intelligent Woman's Guide to Socialism and Capitalism*. 1928.

SHINWELL, Emmanuel, *Conflict Without Malice*. 1955.

SHONFIELD, Andrew, *British Economic Policy since the War*. 1958. *Modern Capitalism*. 1965.

SHORE, Peter, *Entitled to Know*. 1966.

SIEBERT, F. S., *and others*, *Four Theories of the Press*. Urbana, 1956.

SIMON, Viscount, *Retrospect*. 1952.

SISSON, C. H., *The Spirit of British Administration*. 1959.

SMELLIE, K. B., *A Hundred Years of British Government*. 2nd ed. 1950.

SMITH, T. E., *Elections in Developing Countries*. 1960.

SNOW, C. P., *Science and Government*. 1961.

SOMERVELL, D. C., *Stanley Baldwin*. 1953.

SORENSEN, Theodore C., *Decision-Making in the White House*. 1963. *Kennedy*. 1965.

SOUTHGATE, Donald, *The Passing of the Whigs 1832–1886*. 1962.

SPARROW, John, *Controversial Essays*. 1966.

STANKIEWICZ, W. J., *ed.*, *Crisis in British Government: The Need for Reform*. 1967.

STEPHENSON, William, *The Play Theory of Mass Communication*. Chicago, 1967.

STEVENSON, Adlai E., *Speeches*. 1953. *What I Think*. 1956.

STEWART, J. D., *British Pressure Groups*. 1958.

STEWART, John B., *The Moral and Political Philosophy of David Hume*. New York, 1963.

STEWART, Michael, *Modern Forms of Government*. 1959.

STRACHEY, Lytton, *Queen Victoria*. Collected edition. 1948.

STRANG, Lord, *The Diplomatic Career*. 1962. *Home and Abroad*. 1956.

STRAUSS, E., *The Ruling Servants*. 1961.

STRONG, L. F., *Modern Political Constitutions*. 6th ed. 1963.

STUART, James, *Within the Fringe*. 1967.

SWINTON, Earl, *Sixty Years of Power*. 1966.

SYKES, Christopher, *Four Studies in Loyalty*. 1946.

TANNER, J. R., *English Constitutional Conflicts of the Seventeenth Century 1603–1689.* 1928.

TARR, Francis de, *The French Radical Party.* 1961.

TAYLOR, A. J. P., *English History 1914–1945.* 1965. *The Origins of the Second World War.* 1961. *Politics in Wartime.* 1964. *The Trouble Makers.* 1957.

TAYLOR, Henry, *The Statesman.* 1957.

TEBBEL, John, *The Life and Good Times of William Randolph Hearst.* 1953.

TEMPLEWOOD, Lord, *Ambassador on Special Mission.* 1946. *Empire of the Air.* 1957. *Nine Troubled Years.* 1954. *The Shadow of the Gallows.* 1951.

THAYER, George, *The British Political Fringe.* 1965.

THOMAS, Harford, *The Press and the People.* 1962.

THOMAS, Hugh, *ed., Crisis in the Civil Service.* 1968. *The Establishment.* 1959.

THOMAS, Ivor Bulmer, *The Party System in Great Britain.* 1953.

THOMAS, W. Beach, *The Story of the Spectator 1828–1928.* 1928.

THOMSON, Malcolm, *David Lloyd George.* (1948).

THOMSON, Mark A., *A Constitutional History of England 1642–1801.* 1938.

THORNTON, A. P., *The Habit of Authority.* 1966.

TIZARD, Sir Henry, *A Scientist in and out of the Civil Service.* Haldane Memorial Lecture. 1955.

TOCQUEVILLE, Alexis de, *Democracy in America.* World's Classics edition.

TRENAMAN, J., *and* McQuail, D., *Television and Political Image.* 1961.

TREVOR-ROPER, Hugh, *Historical Essays.* 1957.

TRUMAN, David B., *The Congressional Party.* New York, 1959. *The Governmental Process.* New York. 1951.

TRUMAN, Harry S., *Year of Decisions 1945.* 1955. *Years of Trial and Hope 1946–1953.* 1956.

TURBERVILLE, A. S., *The House of Lords in the Age of Reform 1784–1837.* 1958.

UNESCO, *Decisions and Decision-Makers in the Modern State.* 1962.

UTLEY, T. E., *Occasion for Ombudsman.* 1961.

VANSITTART, Lord, *The Mist Procession.* 1958.

VERNEY, Douglas V., *The Analysis of Political Systems.* 1959. *Parliamentary Reform in Sweden 1866–1921.* 1957.

VERNON, R. V., *and* Mansergh, N., *eds., Advisory Bodies.* 1940.

VICTORIA, Queen, *The Letters.* Second Series. 3 Vols. 1926–8. *The Letters.* Third Series. 3 Vols. 1930–2.

VIERECK, Peter, *Conservatism Revisited.* 1950.

VILE, M. J. C., *Constitutionalism and the Separation of Powers.* 1967.

VINCENT, JOHN, *The Formation of the Liberal Party 1857–1868.* 1966.

WADE, H. W. R., *Towards Administrative Justice.* Michigan, 1963.

WALLAS, Graham, *Human Nature in Politics.* 1908.

WARNER, W. L., *and others, The American Federal Executive.* New Haven 1963.

472   BIBLIOGRAPHY

WATKINS, Alan, *The Liberal Dilemma*. 1966.

WATSON, J. Steven, *The Reign of George III 1760–1815*. 1960.

WEBSTER, C. K., *The Foreign Policy of Castlereagh*. Vol. 1: 1812–1815. 1931. Vol. 2: 1815–1822. 1934.

WELENSKY, Sir Roy, *4,000 Days*. 1964.

WEIZMANN, Vera, *The Impossible Takes Longer*. 1967.

WELLS, H. G., *The New Machiavelli*. 1911.

WHEARE, K. C., *The Civil Service in the Constitution*. 1954. *Federal Government*. 4th ed. 1965. *Government by Committee*. 1955. *Legislatures*. 1963. *Modern Constitutions*. 1951.

WHEELER-BENNETT, Sir John, *John Anderson, Viscount Waverley*. 1962. *King George VI*. 1958.

WHITE, R. J., ed., *The Conservative Tradition*. 1950.

WHITE, Theodore H., *The Making of the President 1960*. 1962. *The Making of the President 1964*, 1965.

Whitehall and Beyond. 1964.

WHYTE, W. H., *The Organisation Man*. 1957.

WILLIAMS, Francis, *Dangerous Estate*. 1957. *Press, Parliament and People*. 1946. *A Prime Minister Remembers*. 1961.

WILLIAMS, Philip, *The French Parliament 1958–1967*. 1968. *Politics in Post-war France*. 2nd ed. 1958.

WILLIAMS, Raymond, *Communications*. 1962.

WILLSON, F. M. G., *Administrators in Action*. 1961.

WILSON, Charles H., *Haldane and the Machinery of Government*. Haldane Memorial Lecture. 1956.

WILSON, H. H., *Pressure Group*. 1961.

WILSON, Norman, *The British System of Government*. 1963.

WILSON, Trevor, *The Downfall of the Liberal Party 1914–1935*. 1966.

WILSON, Woodrow, *Congressional Government*. Meridian edition. 1956.

WINDELSHAM, Lord, *Communication and Political Power*. 1966.

WINDSOR, Duke of, *A King's Story*. 1951.

WINTERTON, Earl, *Orders of the Day*. 1953. *Fifty Tumultuous Years*. 1955.

WISEMAN, H. W., *Parliament and the Executive*. 1966.

WOODWARD, Sir Llewellyn, *The Age of Reform 1815–1870*. 2nd ed. 1962. *British Foreign Policy in the Second World War*. 1962.

WOOLTON, Earl of, *Memoirs*. 1959.

WOOTTON, Graham, *The Politics of Influence*. 1963.

WRENCH, Sir John Evelyn, *Geoffrey Dawson and Our Times*. 1955.

WRIGHT, Charles and Fayle, C. E., *A History of Lloyd's*. 1928.

YOUNG, G. M., *Stanley Baldwin*. 1952.

YOUNG, George K., *Masters of Indecision*. 1962.

YOUNG, Kenneth, *Arthur James Balfour*. 1963. *Churchill and Beaverbrook*. 1966.

YOUNG, Roland, *The British Parliament*. 1962.

ZETLAND, Lord, *Essayez*. 1956.

INDEX

dissolution and patronage, 263–8
divisions in, 13, 14
guillotine and the Lords, 302–3
lobby correspondents, 250–1
needed reforms, 285–95
procedure, 277–80
restrictive practices, 277
revolts of members, 268–75
rules of procedure, 253, 254
televising of, 285–7
the Opposition, 251–8
value of debates, 277–80
House of Lords, 5, 19, 27, 29, 276, 296–311
abdication of judicial function, 372–3
and hereditary membership, 305–6
haven for electoral casualties, 302
introduction of life peers, 300
legislative duties, 302–3
loss of strength of, 304–5
modern liberalism, 304
opposition to reform, 298
powers of delay curbed, 300
proportional representation and, 32
proposals for reform, 309–11
reform, 69
standard of debates, 304
Tory dominance in, 299
tribute to value of age and experience, 301
voting in, 266
Howard League for Penal Reform, 363n, 364
Hume, David, 24, 47, 51, 86, 151
Humphrey, I., 216n
Hussein, King, 270

Ideology, political party, 59
Immigration, 254
Labour and, 101

Imperialism, 38
Independent Labour Party, 96, 103
Independent Television, 402
India, evacuation of, 100
India Committee, 234
Industrial life insurance, nationalisation, 107
Industry—
and nationalisation, 53
as interest group, 350
Inge, Dean, 28
Inner Cabinet, 227–32
composition, 229–30
official and unofficial, 231
Inskip, Sir T., 265
Inspectors' Reports, the law and publication of, 372–3
Ireland, 38, 88, 95
Irish Disestablishment, 316
Irish nationalism, 335
Irish party, 27
Irish Treaty debate, 304
Ismay, Lord, 208
Israeli-Arab War (1967), 292
Italy, 34, 38, 45, 55, 57
number of governments, 151
political system, 28
rise of fascism, 34
two-ballot system, 31
'transformismo' system, 46, 56
working class voters, 89

Jackson, Andrew, 216, 408
Jackson, Justice, 380n
James I, 73, 186, 314
James II, 369
Jay, Douglas, 85, 180, 407
Jefferson, Thomas, 216
Jenkins, Ray, 310
Jenkins, Roy, 219
Jenkins, Sir Ivor, 328
Johnson, Dr. McI., 261n, 344
Johnson, Dr. S., 49, 87, 159, 261, 411